The Quran

Translated by
Abdullah Yusuf Ali

Sultana Bookstore & More
A division of Sultana Publishing & Distributing House
1418 San Pablo Ave.
Berkeley, CA 94702
(510) 558-0120
(510) 559-3263 Fax
www.sultanabookstore.com

Sultana Bookstore & More
A division of Sultana Publishing & Distributing House
1418 San Pablo Ave.
Berkeley, CA 94702
Ph. : (510) 558-0120
Fax : (510) 559-3263
www.sultanabookstore.com

CONTENTS

Introduction   VII

1. The Opening (*Al-Fātihah*)   1
2. The Heifer (*Al-Baqarah*)   1
3. The Family of 'Imrān (*Āl 'Imrān*)   31
4. The Women (*An-Nisā'*)   49
5. The Table Spread (*Al-Mā'idah*)   67
6. The Cattle (*Al-An'ām*)   81
7. The Heights (*Al-A'rāf*)   97
8. The Spoils of War (*Al-Anfāl*)   115
9. The Repentance (*At-Tawbah*)   122
10. Jonah (*Yūnus*)   135
11. Hūd   144
12. Joseph (*Yūsuf*)   155
13. The Thunder (*Ar-Ra'd*)   165
14. Abraham (*Ibrāhīm*)   170
15. The Rocky Tract (*Al-Hijr*)   174
16. Bees (*An-Nahl*)   179
17. The Night Journey (*Al-Isrā'*)   189
18. The Cave (*Al-Kahf*)   198
19. Mary (*Maryam*)   207
20. Tā Hā   213
21. The Prophets (*Al-Anbiyā'*)   221
22. The Pilgrimage (*Al-Hajj*)   228
23. The Believers (*Al-Mu'minūn*)   235
24. Light (*An-Nur*)   241
25. The Criterion (*Al-Furqān*)   248
26. The Poets (*Ash-Shu'arā'*)   253
27. The Ants (*An-Naml*)   261
28. The Narrations (*Al-Qasas*)   267
29. The Spider (*Al-'Ankabūt*)   275
30. The Romans (*Ar-Rūm*)   281
31. Luqmān   285
32. The Prostration (*As-Sajdah*)   288
33. The Confederates (*Al-Ahzāb*)   290
34. Sheba (*Saba'*)   297
35. The Originator (*Fātir*)   302
36. Ya Sīn   306

37. Those Ranged in Ranks (*As-Sāffāt*) 311
38. Sād 316
39. The Crowds (*Az-Zumar*) 321
40. The Believer (*Al-Mu'min*) 328
41. Expounded (*Fuṣṣilat*) 335
42. Consultation (*Ash-Shūrā*) 339
43. The Gold Adornments (*Az-Zukhruf*) 344
44. The Smoke (*Ad-Dukhān*) 349
45. The Kneeling Down (*Al-Jāthiyah*) 351
46. Winding Sand-tracts (*Al-Aḥqāf*) 354
47. Muḥammad 358
48. The Victory (*Al-Fath*) 361
49. The Inner Apartments (*Al-Hujurāt*) 364
50. Qāf 366
51. The Winds That Scatter (*Adh-Dhāriyāt*) 368
52. The Mount (*At-Ṭūr*) 371
53. The Star (*An-Najm*) 373
54. The Moon (*Al-Qamar*) 375
55. The Most Gracious (*Ar-Rahmān*) 378
56. The Inevitable (*Al-Wāqi'ah*) 380
57. The Iron (*Al-Ḥadīd*) 383
58. The Pleading (*Al-Mujādalah*) 386
59. The Mustering(*Al-Hashr*) 389
60. The Examined One (*Al-Mumtaḥanah*) 391
61. The Ranks (*As-Saff*) 394
62. Friday (*Al-Jumu'ah*) 395
63. The Hypocrites (*Al-Munāfiqūn*) 396
64. The Mutual Loss and Gain (*At-Taghābun*) 397
65. Divorce (*At-Ṭalāq*) 399
66. Prohibition (*At-Tahrīm*) 401
67. The Dominion (*Al-Mulk*) 402
68. The Pen (*Al-Qalam*) 404
69. The Sure Reality (*Al-Ḥāqqah*) 406
70. The Ways of Ascent (*Al-Ma'ārij*) 408
71. Noah (*Nūḥ*) 410
72. The Spirits (*Al-Jinn*) 411
73. The Enfolded One (*Al-Muzzammil*) 413
74. The One Wrapped Up (*Al-Muddathihir*) 414
75. The Resurrection (*Al-Qiyāmah*) 416

76. Man (*Al-Insān*) 417
77. Those Sent Forth (*Al-Mursalāt*) 419
78. The Great News (*An-Naba'*) 420
79. Those Who Tear Out (*An-Nazi'āt*) 421
80. He Frowned (*'Abasa*) 423
81. The Folding Up (*At-Takwīr*) 424
82. The Cleaving Asunder (*Al-Infitār*) 425
83. The Dealers in Fraud (*Al-Mutaffifīn*) 425
84. The Rending Asunder (*Al-Inshiqāq*) 426
85. The Constellations (*Al-Burūj*) 427
86. The Night-Visitant (*At-Tāriq*) 428
87. The Most High (*Al-A'lā*) 429
88. The Overwhelming Event (*Al-Ghāshiyah*) 429
89. The Break of Day (*Al-Fajr*) 430
90. The City (*Al-Balad*) 431
91. The Sun (*Ash-Shams*) 432
92. The Night (*Al-Layl*) 432
93. The Glorious Morning Light (*Ad-Duhā*) 433
94. The Expansion of the Breast (*Ash-Sharh*) 433
95. The Fig (*At-Tin*) 434
96. The Clinging Clot (*Al-'Alaq*) 434
97. The Night of Power or Honour (*Al-Qadr*) 435
98. The Clear Evidence (*Al-Bayyinah*) 435
99. The Earthquake (*Az-Zalzalah*) 436
100. The Chargers (*Al-'Ādiyāt*) 436
101. The Great Calamity (*Al-Qāri'ah*) 436
102. The Piling Up (*At-Takāthur*) 437
103. The Time (*Al-'Asr*) 437
104. The Scandalmonger (*Al-Humazah*) 437
105. The Elephant (*Al-Fīl*) 438
106. The Quraysh (*Quraysh*) 438
107. The Neighbourly Assistance (*Al-Mā'ūn*) 438
108. Abundance (*Al-Kawthar*) 439
109. Those Who Reject Faith (*Al-Kāfirūn*) 439
110. The Help (*An-Nasr*) 439
111. The Plaited Rope (*Al-Masad*) 440
112. Purity of Faith (*Al-Ikhlās*) 440
113. The Daybreak (*Al-Falaq*) 440
114. The Mankind (*An-Nās*) 441
Index 442

Dear Reader,

This is a book of reverence! Great care of cleanliness and tremendous amount of respect is requested to honor this Holy Book while handling and reading.

Thank You!
Your Muslim Neighbor.

INTRODUCTION

PART I

At Mecca

MUHAMMAD, son of Abdullah, son of Abdul Muṭṭalib, of the tribe of Qureysh, was born at Mecca fifty-three years before the Hijrah. His father died before he was born, and he was protected first by his grandfather, Abdul Muṭṭalib, and, after his grandfather's death, by his uncle, Abû Tâlib. As a young boy he travelled with his uncle in the merchants' caravan to Syria, and some years afterwards made the same journey in the service of a wealthy widow named Khadîjah. So faithfully did he transact the widow's business, and so excellent was the report of his behaviour which she received from her old servant who had accompanied him, that she soon afterwards married her young agent; and the marriage proved a very happy one, though she was fifteen years older than he was. Throughout the twenty-six years of their life together he remained devoted to her; and after her death, when he took other wives he always mentioned her with the greatest love and reverence. This marriage gave him rank among the notables of Mecca, while his conduct earned for him the surname *Al-Amîn*, the "trustworthy."

The Meccans claimed descent from Abraham through Ishmael, and tradition stated that their temple, the Ka‘bah, had been built by Abraham for the worship of the One God. It was still called the House of Allah, but the chief objects of worship there were a number of idols which were called daughters of Allah and Intercessors. The few who felt disgust at this idolatry, which had prevailed for centuries, longed for the religion of Abraham and tried to find out what had been its teaching. Such seekers of the truth were known as Hunafa (sing. *Ḥanîf*), a word originally meaning "those who turn away" (from the existing idol-worship), but coming in the end to have the sense of "upright" or "by nature upright," because such persons held the way of truth to be right conduct. These Ḥunafa did not form a community. They were the agnostics of their day, each seeking truth by the light of his own inner consciousness. Muhammad son of Abdullah became one of these. It was his practice to retire with his family for a month of every year to a cave in the desert for meditation. His place of retreat was *Hirâ*, a desert hill not far from Mecca, and his chosen month was *Ramadân,* the month of heat.

The first revelation It was there one night toward the end of his quiet month that the first revelation came to him when he was forty years old. He was asleep or in a trance when he heard a voice say: "Read!" He said: "I cannot read." The voice again said: "Read!" He said: "I cannot read." A third time the voice, more terrible, commanded: "Read!" He said: "What can I read?" The voice said:

"Read: In the name of thy Lord Who createth.
"Createth man from a clot.
"Read: And it is thy Lord the Most Bountiful
"Who teacheth by the pen,
"Teacheth man that which he knew not."[1]

When he awoke the words remained "as if inscribed upon his heart." He went out of the cave on to the hillside and heard the same awe-inspiring voice say: "O Muhammad! Thou art Allah's messenger, and I am Gabriel." Then he raised his eyes and saw the

The vision of Mt. Hirâ angel, in the likeness of a man, standing in the sky above the horizon. And again the dreadful voice said: "O Muhammad! Thou art Allah's messenger, and I am Gabriel." Muhammad (God bless and keep him!) stood quite still, turning away his face from the brightness of the vision, but withersoever he might turn his face, there always stood the angel confronting him. He remained thus a long while till at length the angel vanished, when he returned in great distress of mind to his wife Khadijah. She did her best to reassure him, saying that his conduct had been such that Allah would not let a harmful spirit come to him and that it was her hope that he was to become the Proph-

[1] Sûr. XCVI, 1-5.

et of his people. On their return to Mecca she took him to her cousin Waraqa ibn Naufal, a very old man, "who knew the Scriptures of the Jews and Christians," who declared his belief that the heavenly messenger who came to Moses of old had come to Muhammad, and that he was chosen as the Prophet of his people.

To understand the reason of the Prophet's diffidence and his extreme distress of mind after the vision of Mt. Hirâ, it must be remembered that the *Hunafa*, of whom he had been one, sought true religion in the natural and regarded with distrust the intercourse with spirits of which men "avid of the Unseen,"[1] sorcerers and soothsayers and even poets, boasted in those days. Moreover, he was a man of humble and devout intelligence, a lover of quiet and solitude, and the very thought of being chosen out of all mankind to face mankind, alone, with such a Message, appalled him at the first. Recognition of the Divine nature of the call he had received involved a change in his whole mental outlook sufficiently disturbing to a sensitive and honest mind, and also the forsaking of his quiet, honoured way of life. The early biographers tell how his wife Khadîjah "tried the spirit" which came to him and proved it to be good, and how, with the continuance of the revelations and the conviction that they brought, he at length accepted the tremendous task imposed on him, becoming filled with an enthusiasm of obedience which justifies his proudest title of "The Slave of Allah." *His distress of mind*

The words which came to him when in a state of trance are held sacred by the Muslims and are never confounded with those which he uttered when no physical change was apparent in him. The former are the Sacred Book; the latter the *Hadîth* or *Sunnah* of the Prophet. And because the angel on Mt. Hirä bade him "Read!"---insisted on his "Reading"through he was illiterate---the Sacred Book is known as *Al-Qur'ân* "The Reading" the Reading of the man who knew not how to read. *The Koran or "Reading"*

---

[1] LXXXI, 24.

[2] Or "The Lecture," as it is here translated in passages where the term will hear translation, on the analogy of "Scripture," used for Sacred "writing"

For the first three years, or rather less, of his Mission, the Prophet Preached only to his family and his intimate friends, while the people of Mecca as a whole regarded him as one who had become a little mad. The first of all his converts was his wife Khadîjab, the second his first cousin Ali, whom he had adopted, the third his servant Zeyd, a former slave. His old friend abû Bakr also was among those early converts with some of his slaves and dependents.

First converts

At the end of the third year the Prophet received the command to "arise and warn," [1] whereupon he began to preach in public, pointing out the wretched folly of idolatry in face of the tremendous laws of day and night, of life and death, of growth and decay, which manifest the power of Allah and attest His sovereignty. It was then, when he began to speak against their gods, that Qureysh became actively hostile, persecuting his poorer disciples, mocking and insulting him. The one consideration which prevented them from killing him was fear of the blood-vengeance of the clan to which his family belonged. Strong in his inspiration, the Prophet went on warning, pleading, threatening, while Qureysh did all they could to ridicule his teaching, and deject his followers.

Beginning of persecution

The converts of the first four years were mostly humble folk unable to defend themselves against oppression. So cruel was the persecution they endured that the Prophet advised all who could possibly contrive to do so to emigrate to a Christian country, Abyssinia.[2] And still in spite of persecution and emigration the little company of Muslims grew in number. Qureysh were seriously alarmed. The idol-worship at the Ka'bah, the holy place to which all Arabia made pilgrimage, ranked for them, as guardians of the Ka'bah, as first among their vested interests. At the season of the pilgrimage they posted men on all the roads to warn the tribes against the madman who was preaching in their midst. They tried to bring the Prophet to a compromise, offering to accept his religion if he would so modify it as to make room for their gods as intercessors with Allah, offering to make him their king if he would give up attacking

The flight to Abyssinia

[1] LXXIV, 2.
[2] See XIX, introductory note.

idolatry; and, when their efforts at negotiation failed, they went to his uncle Abû Tâlib, offering to give him the best of their young men in place of Muhammad, to give him all that he desired, if only he would let them kill Muhammad and have done with him. Abû Tâlib refused. The exasperation of the idolaters was increased by the conversion of Omar,[1] one of their stalwarts. They grew more and more embittered, till things came to such a pass that they decided to ostracise the Prophet's whole clan, idolaters who protected him as well as Muslims who believed in him. Their chief men caused a document to be drawn up to the effect that none of them or those belonging to them would hold any intercourse with that clan or sell to them or buy from them. This they all signed, and it was deposited in the Ka'bah. Then, for three years, the Prophet was shut up with all his kinsfolk in their stronghold which was situated in one of the gorges which run down to Mecca. Only at the time of pilgrimage could he go out and preach, or did any of his kinsfolk dare to go into the city.

Conversion of Omar

The Sahîfah or deed of ostracism

At length some kinder hearts among Qureysh grew weary of the boycott of old friends and neighbours. They managed to have the document which had been placed in the Ka'bah brought out for reconsideration; when it was found that all the writing had been destroyed by white ants, except the words *Bismika Allâhumma* ("In thy name, O Allah") When the elders saw that marvel the ban was removed, and the Prophet was again free to go about the city. But meanwhile the opposition to his preaching had grown rigid. He had little success among the Meccans, and an attempt which he made to preach in the city of Tâ'îf was a failure. His Mission was a failure, judged by worldly standards, when, at the season of the yearly pilgrimage, he came upon a little group of men who heard him gladly.

Destruction of the Sahîfah

The men from Yathrib

They came from Yathrib, a city more than two hundred miles away, which has since become world-famous as *Al-Madînah*, "the City" *par excellence*. At Yathrib there were Jewish tribes with learned rabbis, who had often spoken to the pagans of a Prophet soon to come among the Arabs, with whom, when he came,

[1] See XX, Introductory note.

the Jews would destory the pagans as the tribes of
A'âd and Thamûd had been destroyed of old for their
idolatry. When the men from Yathrib saw Muhammad they recognised him as the Prophet whom the
Jewish rabbis had described to them. On their return
to Yathrib they told what they had seen and heard,
with the result that at the next season of pilgrimage a
deputation came from Yathrib purposely to meet the

First
pact of
Al-
Aqabah

Prophet. These swore allegiance to him in the first
pact of Al-'Aqabah, the oath they took being that
which was afterwards exacted from women converts,
with no mention of fighting. They then returned to
Yathrib with a Muslim teacher in their company, and
soon "there was not a house in Yathrib wherein there
was not mention of the mesenger of Allah."

Second
pact of
Al-
'Aqabah

In the following year, at the time of pilgrimage,
seventy-three Muslims from Yathrib came to Mecca
to vow allegiance to the Prophet, and invite him to
their city. Al Al-'Aqabah, by night, they swore to defend him as they would defend their own wives and
children. It was then that the Hijrah, the Flight to
Yathrib, was decided.

Soon the Muslims who were in a position to do so
began to sell their property and to leave Mecca un-
obtrusively. Qureysh had wind of what was going on.
They hated Muhammad in their midst, but dreaded
what he might become if he escaped from them. It
would be better, they considered, to destroy him now.
The death of Abû Tâlib had removed his chief pro-

Plot to
murder
the
Prophet

tector; but still they had to reckon with the vengeance
of his clan upon the clan of the murderer. They cast
lots and chose a slayer out of every clan. All these
were to attack the Prophet simultaneously and strike
together, as one man. Thus his blood would be on all
Qureysh. It was at this time (Ibn Khaldûn asserts,
and it is the only satisfactory explanation of what
happened afterwards) that the Prophet received the
first revelation ordering him to make war upon his
persecutors "until persecution is no more and religion
is for Allah only."[1]

The last of the able Muslims to remain in Mecca
were Abû Bakr, Ali and the Prophet himself. Abû
Bakr, a man of health, had bought two riding-

[1] VIII, 39.

camels and retained a guide in readiness for the Flight.
The Prophet only waited God's command. It came at
length. It was the night appointed for his murder. The
slayers were before his house. He gave his cloak to
Ali, bidding him lie down on the bed so that anyone
looking in might think Muhammad lay there. The
slayers were to strike him as he came out of the
house, whether in the night or early morning. He
knew they would not injure Ali. Then he left the
house and, it is said, a blindness fell upon the would-
be murderers so that he put dust on their heads as he
passed by-without their knowing it. He went to Abû
Bakr's house and called to him, and they two went
together to a cavern in the desert hills and hid there
till the hue and cry was past, Abû Bakr's son and
daughter and his herdsman bringing them food and
tidings after nightfall. Once a search-party came quite
near them in their hiding-place, and Abû Bakr was
afraid; but the Prophet said: "Fear not! Allah is with
us."[1] Then, when the coast was clear, Abû Bakr had
the riding-camels and the guide brought to the cave
one night, and they set out on the long ride to Yathrib.

THE HIJRAH (June 20th, 622 A.D.)

After travelling for many days by unfrequented
paths, the fugitives reached a suburb of Yathrib,
whither, for weeks past, the people of the city had
been going every morning, watching for the Prophet
till the heat drove them to shelter. The travellers arrived in the heat of the day, after the watchers had
retired. It was a Jew who called out to the Muslims in
derisive tones that he whom they expected had at last
arrived.

Such was the Hijrah, the Flight from Mecca to
Yathrib, which counts as the beginning of the Muslim
era. The thirteen years of humiliation, of persecution,
of seeming failure, of prophecy still unfulfilled, were
over. The ten years of success, the fullest that has
ever crowned one man's endeavour, had begun. The
Hijrah makes a clear division in the story of the
Prophet's Mission, which is evident in the Koran. Till
then he had been a preacher only. Thenceforth he was
the ruler of a State, at first a very small one, which
grew in ten years to the empire of Arabia. The kind
of guidance which he and his people needed after the

[1] IX, 40.

Hijrah was not the same as that which they had before needed. The Madînah sûrahs differ, therefore, from the Meccan sûrahs. The latter give guidance to the individual soul and to the Prophet as warner; the former give guidance to a growing social and political community and to the Prophet as example, lawgiver and reformer.

Classification of Meccan sûrahs

For classification the Meccan sûrahs are here subdivided into four groups: Very Early, Early, Middle and Late. Through the historical data and traditions are insufficient for a strict chronological grouping, the very early sûrahs are, roughly speaking, those revealed before the beginning of the persecution; the early sûrahs those revealed between the beginning of the persecution and the conversion of Omar; the middle sûrahs those revealed between the conversion of Omar and the destruction of the deed of ostracism; and the late sûrahs those revealed between the raising of the ban of ostracism and the Hijrah.

PART II

At Al-Madînah

IN THE first year of his reign at Yathrib the Prophet made a solemn treaty with the Jewish tribes, which secured to them equal rights of citizenship and full religious liberty in return for their support of the new State. But their idea of a Prophet was one who would give them dominion, not one who made the Jews who followed him brothers of every Arab who might happen to believe as they did. When they found that they could not use the Prophet for their own ends, they tried to shake his faith in his Mission and to seduce his followers; behaviour in which they were encouraged secretly by some professing Muslims who considered they had reason to resent the Prophet's coming, since it robbed them of their local influence. In the Madînah sûrahs there is frequent mention of these Jews and Hypocrites.

The Jews and Hypocrites

The Qiblah

Till then the *Qiblah* (the place toward which the Muslims turn their face in prayer) had been Jerusa-

:am. The Jews imagined that the choice implied a
lea ing toward Judaism and that the Prophet stood
in need of their instruction. He received command to
change the Qiblah[1] from Jerusalem to the Ka'bah at
Mecca. The whole first part of sûrah II relates to this
Jewish controversy.

The Prophet's first concern as ruler was to establish
public worship and lay down the constitution of the
State; but he did not forget that Qureysh had sworn
to make an end of his religion, nor that her had received command to fight against them till they ceased
from persecution. After he had been twelve months
in Yathrib several small expeditions went out, led   The firs
either by the Prophet himself or some other of the   expedi-
fugitives from Mecca, for the purpose of recon-   tions
noitring and of dissuading other tribes from siding
with Qureysh. These are generally represented as war-
like but, considering thier weakness and the fact that
they did not result in fighting, they can hardly have
been that, through it is certain that they went out
ready to resist attack. It is noteworthy that in those
expeditions only fugitives from Mecca were employed, never natives of Yathrib; the reason being (if
we accept Ibn Khaldûn's theory, and there is no other
explanation) that the command to wage war had been
revealed to the Prophet at Mecca after the Yathrib
men had sworn their oath of allegiance at Al-'Aqabah.
and in their absence. Their oath foresaw fighting in
mere defence, not fighting in the field Blood was shed
and booty taken in only one of those early expeditions, and then it was against the Prophet's orders.
One Purpose of those expeditions may have been to
accustom the Meccan Muslims to going out in war-
like trim. For thirteen years they had been strict paci-
fists, and it is clear, from several passages of the
Koran,[2] that many of them, including, it may be, the
Prophet himself, hated the idea of fighting even in
self-defence and had to be inured to it.

In the second year of the Hijrah the Meccan merchants' caravan was returning from Syria as usual by
a road which passed not far from Yathrib. As its
leader Abû Sufyân approached the territory of

[1] II, 144, 149, 150.
[2] *e.g,* II, 216.

Yathrib he heard of the Prophet's design to capture
the caravan. At once he sent a camel-rider on to
Mecca, who arrived in a worn-out state and shouted
frantically from the Valley to Qureysh to hasten to
the rescue unless they wished to lose both wealth and
honour. A force a thousand strong was soon on its
way to Yathrib; less, it would seem, with the hope of
saving the caravan than with the idea of punishing the
raiders, since the Prophet might have taken the caravan before the relief force started from Mecca. Did
the Prophet ever intend to raid the caravan? In Ibn
Hishâm, in the account of the Tabûk expedition, it is
stated that the Prophet on that one occasion did not
hide his real objective as had been his custom in other
campaigns. The caravan was the pretext in the campaign of Badr, the real objective was the Meccan
army. He had received command to fight his persecutors, and promise of victory; he was prepared to
venture against any odds, as was well seet at Badr.
But the Muslims, disinclined and ill-equipped for war,
would have despaired if they had known from the
first that they were to face a well-armed force three
times their number.

The army of Qureysh had advanced more than
half-way to Yathrib before the Prophet set out. All
three parties - the army of Qureysh, the Muslim army
and the caravan - were heading for the water of Badr
Abû Sufyân, the leader of the caravan, heard from
one of his scouts that the Muslims were near the
water, and turned back to the coast-plain. And the
Muslims met the army of Qureysh by the water of
Badr. Before the battle the Prophet was prepared still
further to increase the odds against him. He gave
leave to all the Ansâr (natives of Yathrib) to return
to their homes unreproached, since their oath did not
include the duty of fighting in the field; but the Ansâr
were only hurt by the suggestion that they could possibly desert him at a time of danger, The battle went
at first against the Muslims, but ended in a signal
victory for them. [1]

The victory of Badr gave the Prophet new prestige
among the Arab tribes; but thenceforth there was the
feud of blood between Qureysh and the Islamic State

[1] See also Sûr. VIII, introductory note.

in addition to the old religious hatred. Those passages of the Koran which refer to the battle of Badr give warning of much greater struggles yet to come.

In fact in the following year, an army of three thousand came from Mecca to destroy Yathrib. The Prophet's first idea was merely to defend the city, a plan of which Abdullah ibn Ubeyy, the leader of "the Hypocrites" (or lukewarm Muslims), strongly approved. But the men who had fought at Badr and believed that God would help them agianst any odds thought it a shame that they should linger behind walls. The Prophet, approving of their faith and zeal, gave way to them, and set out with an army of one thousand men toward Mt. Uhud, where the enemy were encamped. Abdullah ibn Ubeyy was much offended by the change of plan. He thought it unlikely that the Prophet really meant to give battle in conditions so adverse to the Muslims, and was unwilling to take part in a mere demonstration designed to flatter the fanatical extremists. So he withdrew with his men, a fourth of the army.

The battle on Mt. Uhud

Despite the heavy odds, the battle on Mt. Uhud would have been an even greater victory than that at Badr for the Muslims but for the disobedience of a band of fifty archers whom the Prophet set to guard a pass against the enemy cavalry, Seeing their comrades victorious, these men left their post, fearing to lose their share of the spoils. The cavalry of Qureysh rode through the gap and fell on the exultant Muslims. The Prophet himself was wounded and the cry arose that he was slain, till someone recognised him and shouted that he was still living, a shout to which the Muslims rallied. Gathering round the Prophet, they retreated, leaving many dead on the hillside.[1]

On the following day the Prophet again sallied forth with what remained of the army, that Qureysh might hear that he was in the field and so might perhaps be deterred from attacking the city. The stratagem succeeded, thanks to the behaviour of a friendly Bedawi, who met the Muslims and conversed with them and afterwards met the army of Qureysh. Questioned by Abû Sufyân, he said that Muhammad was in the field, stronger than ever, and thirsting for

[1] See also III, introductory note.

revenge for yesterday's affair. On that information, Abû Sufyân decided to return to Mecca.

The reverse which they had suffered on Mt. Uḥud lowered the prestige of the Muslims with the Arab tribes and also with the Jews of Yathrib. Tribes which had inclined toward the Muslims now inclined toward Qureysh. The Prophet's followers were attacked and murdered when they went abroad in little companies. Khubeyb, one of his envoys, was captured by a desert tribe and sold to Qureysh, who tortured him to death in Mecca publicly. And the Jews, despite their treaty, now hardly concealed their hostility. They even went so far in flattery of Qureysh as to declare the religion of the pagam Arabs superior to Al-Islâm.[1] The Prophet was obliged to take punitive action against some of them. The tribe of Banî Nadîr were besieged in their strong towers, subdued and forced to emigrate. The Hypocrites had sympathised with the Jews and secretly egged them on.[2]

In the fifth year of the Hijrah the idolaters made a great effort to destroy Al-Islâm in the War of the Clans or War of the Trench, as it is variously called; when Qureysh with all their clans and the great desert tribe of Ghatafân with all their clans, an army of ten thousand men rode against Al-Madînah (Yathrib). The Prophet (by the advice of Salman the Persian, it is said) caused a deep trench to be dug before the city, and himself led the work of digging it. The army of the clans was stopped by the trench, a novelty in Arab warfare. It seemed impassable for cavalry, which formed their strength. They camped in sight of it and daily showered their arrows on its defenders. While the Muslims were awaiting the assault, news came that Banî Qureyzah, a Jewish tribe of Yathrib which had till then been loyal, had gone over to the enemy. The case seemed desperate. But the delay caused by the trench had damped the ardour of the clans, and one who was secretly a Muslim managed to sow distrust between Qureysh and their Jewish allies, so that both hesitated to act. Then came a bitter wind from the sea, which blew for three days and nights so terribly that not a tent could be kept

Massacre of Muslims

Expulsion of Banî Nadîr

The War of the Trench

---

[1] IV, 51.
[2] LIX.

standing, not a fire lighted, not a pot boiled. The tribesmen were in utter misery. At length, one night the leader of Qureysh decided that the torment could be borne no longer and gave the order to retire.. [1] When Ghatafân awoke next morning they found Qureysh had gone and they too took up their baggage and retreared.

On the day of the return from the trench the Prophet ordered war on the treacheous Banî Qureyzah, who, conscious of their guilt, had already taken to their towers of refuge. After a siege of nearly a month they had to surrender unconditionally. They only begged that they might be judged by a member of the Arab tribes of which they were adherents. The Prophet granted their request. But the judge, upon whose favour they had counted, condemned their men to death, their women and children to slavery.

Punishment of Banî Qureyzah

Early in the sixth yeat of the Hijrah the Prophet led a campaign against the Banî'l-Mustaliq, a tribe who were preparing to attah the Muslims. It was during the return from that campaign that Ayeshas, his young wife, was left behind and brought back to camp by a young soldier an incident which give rise to the scandal denounced in sûrah XXIV. [2] It was on this campaign aslo that Abdullah ibnn Ubeyy, the "Hypocrite" chief, said: "When we return to the city the mightier will soon expel the wearker" [3] at sight of a quarrel between Muhâjirîn (immigrants from Mecca(and Ansâr (natives of Yatrib).

The slander against Ayeshah

In the same year the Prophet had a vision [4] in which he found himself entering the holy place at Mecca unopposed; therefore he determined to attempt the Pilgrimage. Besides a number of Muslims from Yathrib (which we shall henceforth call al-Madînah) he called upon the friendly Arabs, whose numbers had increased sinc the miraculous (as it was considered) discomfiture of the clans, to accompany him, but most of them did not respond.[5] Attired as pilgrims, and taking with them the customary offerings, a company of fourteen hundred men jour-

[1] See also XXXII, Introductory note.
[2] XXIV, 11 ff.
[3] LXIII, 8.
[4] XLVIII, 27.
[5] XLVIII, 11 ff.

neyed to Mecca. As they drew near the holy valley they were met by a friend from the city, wLo warned the Prophet that Qureysh had put on their leopard-skins (the badge of valour) and had sworn to prevent his entering the sanctuary; their cavalry was on the road before him. On that, the Prophet ordered a detour through mountain gorges and the Muslims were tired out when they came down at last into the valley of Mecca and encamped at a spot called Al-Ḥudeybiyah; from thence he tried to open negotiations with Qureysh, explaining that he came only as a pilgrim. The first messenger he sent towards the city was maltreated and his camel hamstrung. He returned without delivering his message. Qureysh on their side sent an envoy who was threatening in tone, and very arrogant. Another of their envoys was too familiar and had to be reminded sternly of the respect due to the Prophet. It was he who, on his return to the city, said: "I have seen Caesar and Chosroes in their pomp, but never have I seen a man honoured as Muhammad is honoured by his comrades."

Al-Ḥudey-biyah

The Prophet sought some messenger who would impose respect. Othmân was finallt chosen because of his kinship with the powerful Umayyad famly. While the Muslims were awaiting his return the news came that he had been murdered. It was then that the Prophet, sitting under a tree[1] in Al-Ḥudeybiyah, took an oath from all his comrades that they would stand or fall together. after a while, however, it became known that Othmân had not been murdered. A troop which came out from the city to molest the Muslims in their camp were captured before they could do any hurt[2] and brought before the Prophet, who forgave them on their promise to renounce hostility. Then proper envoys came from Qureysh. After some negotiation, the true of Al-Ḥudeybiyah was signed. For ten years there were to be no hostilities between the parties. The Prophet was to return to Al-Madînah without visiting the Ka'bah, but in the following year he might perform the pilgrimage with his comrades, Qureysh promising to evacuate Mecca for three days to allow of his doing so. Deserters

Truce of Al-Ḥudey-biyah

[1] XLVIII, 18.
[2] XLVIII, 24.

from Qureysh to the Muslims during the period of
the truce were to be returned; not so deserters from
the Muslims to Qureysh. Any tribe or clan who
wished to share in the treaty as allies of the Prophet
might do so, and any tribe or clan who wished to
share in the treaty as allies of Qureysh might do so.

There was dismay among the Muslims at these
terms. They asked one another: "Where is the victory
that we were promised?" It was during the return
journey from Al-Ḥudeybiyah that the sûrah entitled
"Victory"[1] was revealed. This truce proved, in fact,
to be the greatest victory that the Muslims had till
then achieved. War had been a barrier between them
and the idolaters, but now both parties met and talked
together, and the new religion spread more rapidly.
In the two years which elapsed between the signing
of the truce and the fall of Mecca the number of converts was greater than the total number of all previous converts. The Prophet travelled to Al-Ḥudey-
biyah with 1400 men. Two years later, when the
Meccans broke the truce, he marched against them
with an army of 10,000.

In the seventh year of the Hijrah the Prophet led
a campaign against Kheybar, the stronghold of the
Jewish tribes in North Arabia, which had become a
horners' nest of his enemies. The forts of Kheybar
were reduced one by one, and the Jews of Kheybar
became thenceforth tenants of the Muslims until the
expulsion of the Jews from Arabia in the Caliphate
of Omar. On the day when the last fort surrendered
Ja'far son of Abû Tâlib, the Prophet's first cousin,
arrived with all who remained of the Msulims who
had field to Abyssinia to escape from persecution in
the early days. They had been absent from Arabia
fifteen years. It was at Kheybar that a Jewess prepared for the Prophet poisoned meat, of which he
only tasted a morse! without swallowing it, then
warned his comrades that it was poisoned. One Muslim, who had already swallowed a mouthful, died
immediately, and the Prophet himself, from the mere
taste of it, derived the illness which eventually caused
his death. The woman who had cooked the meat was
brought before him. When she said that she had done

*The cam-
paign of
Kheybar*

---

[1] XLVIII.

it on account of the humiliation of her people, he forgave her.

Pilgrimage to Mecca

In the same year the Prophet's vision was fulfilled: he visited the holy place at Mecca unopposed. In accordance with the terms of the truce the idolaters evacuated the city, and from the surrounding heights watched the procedure of the Muslims. At the end of the stipulated three days the chiefs of Qureysh sent to remind the Prophet that the time was up. He then withdrew, and the idolaters reoccupied the city.

Mû'tah exprdition

In the eighth year of the Hijrah, hearing that the Byzantine emperor was gathering a force in Syria for the destruction of Al-Islâm, the Prophet sent three thousand men to Syria under the command of his freedman Zeyd. The campaign was unsuccessful except that it impressed the Syrians with a notion of the reckless valour of the Muslims. The three thousand did not hesitate to join battle with a hundred thousand. When all the three leaders appointed by the Prophet had been killed, the survivors obeyed Khâlid ibn al-Walîd, who, by his strategy and courage, managed to preserve a remnant and return with them to Al-Madîah.

Truce broken by Qureysh

In the same year Qureysh broke the truce by attacking a tribe that wasin alliance with the Prophet and massacring them even in the sanctuary at Mecca. Afterwards they were afraid because of what they had done. They sent Abû Sufyân to Al-Madînah to ask for the existing treaty to be renewed and its term prolonged. They hoped that he would arrive before the tidings of the massacre. But a messenger from the injured tribe had been before him, and his embassy was fruitless.

Conquest of Mecca

Then the Prophet summoned all the Muslims capsble of bearing arms and marched to Mecca. Qureysh were overawed. Their cavalry put up a show of defence before the town, but were routed without bloodshed; and the Prophet entered his native city as conqueror. The inhabitants expected vengeance for their past misdeeds. The Prophet proclaimed a general amnesty. Only a few known criminals were proscribed and most of those were in the end forgiven In their relief and surprise, the whole population of Mecca hastened to swear allegiance. The

Prophet caused all the idols which were in the sanctuary to be destroyed, saying: "Truth hath come; darkness bath vanished away;"[1] and the Muslim call to prayer was heard in Mecca.

In the same year there was an angry gathering of pagan tribes eager to regain the Ka'bah. The Prophet led twelve thousand men against them. At Ḥuneyn, in a deep ravine, his troops were ambushed by the enemy and almost put to flight. It was with difficulty that they were rallied to the Prophet and his bodyguard of faithful comrades who alone stood firm. But the victory, when it came, was complete and the booty enormous, for many of the hostile tribes had brought out with them everything that they possessed.

Battle of Huneyn

The tribe of Thaqîf were among the enemy at Ḥuneyn. After that victory their city of Ṭâ'îf was besieged by the Muslims, and finally reduced. Then the Prophet appointed a governor of Mecca, and himself returned to Al-Madînah to the boundless joy of the Ansâr, who had feared lest, now that he had regained his native city, he might forsake them and make Mecca the capital.

Conquest of Ṭâ'îf

In the ninth year of the Hijrah, hearing that an army was again being mustered in Syria, the Prophet called on all the Muslims to support him in a great campaign. The far distance, the hot season, the fact that it was harvest time and the prestige of the enemy caused many to excuse themselves and many more to stay behind without excuse. Those defaulters are denounced in the Koran.[2] But the campaign ended peacefully. The army advanced to Tabûk, on the confines of Syria, and these learnt that the enemy had not yet gathered.

The Tabûk expedition

Although Mecca had been conquered and its people were now Muslims, the official order of the pilgrimage had not been changed; the pagan Arabs performing it in their manner, and the Muslims in their manner. It was only after the pilgrims' caravan had left Al-Madînah in the ninth year of the Hijrah, when Al-Islâm was dominant in North Arabia, that the

[1] XVII, 81.
[2] IX, 38-99.

Declaration of Immunity

Declaration of Immunity,[1] as it is called, was revealed. The Prophet sent a copy of it by messenger to Abû Bakr, leader of the pilgrimage, with the instruction that Ali was to read it to the multitudes at Mecca. Its purport was that after that year Muslims only were to make the pilgrimage, exception being made for such of the idolaters as had a treaty with the Muslims and had never broken their treaty nor supported anyone against them. Such were to enjoy the privileges of their treaty for the term thereof, but when their treaty expired they would be as other idolaters. That proclamation marks the end of idol-worship in Arabia.

The Year of Deputations

The ninth year of the Hijrah is called the Year of Deputations, because from all parts of Arabia deputations came to Al-Madînah[2] to swear allegiance to the Prophet and to hear the Koran. The Prophet had become, in fact, the emperor of Arabia, but his way of life remained as simple as before.

The number of the campaigns which he led in person during the last ten years of his life is twenty-seven, in nine of which there was hard fighting. The number of the expeditions which he planned and sent out under other leaders is thirty-eight. He personally controlled every detail of organisation, judged every case and was accessible to every suppliant. In those ten years he destroyed idolatry in Arabia; raised woman from the status of a chattel to complete legal equality with man; effectually stopped the drunkenness and immorality which had till then disgraced the Arabs; made men in love with faith, sincerity and honest dealing; transformed tribes who had been for centuries content with ignorance into a people with the greatest thirst for knowledge; and for the first time in history made universal human brotherhood a fact and principle of common law. And this support and guide in all that work was the Koran.

The Farewell Pilgrimage

In the tenth year of the Hijrah he went to Mecca as a pilgrim for the last time-his "pilgrimage of farewell," it is called-when from Mt. 'Arafât he preached to an enormous throng of pilgrims. He reminded them of all the duties Al-Islâm enjoined upon

[1] IX, 1-12.
[2] XLIX.

them, and that they would one day have to meet their Lord, who would judge each one of them according to his work. At the end of the discourse, he asked; "Have I not conveyed the Message?" And from that great multitude of men who a few months or years before had all been conscienceless idolaters the shout went up: "O Allah! Yes!" The Prophet said: "O Allah! Be Thou witness!"

It was during that last pilgrimage that the sûrah entitled "Succour"¹ was revealed, which he received as an announcement of approaching death. Soon after his return to Al-Madînah he fell ill. The tidings of his illness caused dismay throughout Arabia and anguish to the folk of Al-Madînah, Mecca and Ṭâ'îf, the hometowns. At early dawn on the last day of his earthly life he came out from his room beside the mosque at Al-Madînah and joined the public prayer, which Abû Bakr had been leading since his illness. And there was great relief among the people, who supposed him well again. When, later in the day, the rumour grew that he was dead, Omar threatened those who spread the rumour with dire punishment, declaring it a crime to think that the Messenger of God could die. He was storming at the people in that strain when Abû Bakr came into the mosque and overheard him. Abû Bakr went to the chamber of his daughter Ayeshab, where the Prophet lay. Having ascertained the fact, and kissed the dead man's forehead, he went back into the mosque. The people were still listening to Omar, who was saying that the rumour was a wicked lie, that the Prophet who was all in all to them could not be dead. Abû Bakr went up to Omar and tried to stop him by a whispered word. Then, finding he would pay no heed, Abû Bakr called to the people, who, recognising his voice, left Omar and came crowding round him. He first gave praise to Allah, and then said; "O people! Lo! as for him who used to worship Muhammad, Muhammad is dead. But as for him who used to worship Allah, Allah is Alive and dieth not." He then recited the verse of the Koran:

"And Muhammad is but a messenger, messengers the like of whom have passed away before him. Will

Illness and death of the Prophet

¹ CX.

it be that, when he dieth or is slain, ye will turn back on your heels? He who turneth back doth no hurt to Allah, and Allah will reward the thankful." [1]

"And," says the narrator, and eye-witness, "it was as if the people had not known that such a verse had been revealed till Abû Bakr recited it." And another witness tells how Omar used to say: "Directly I heard Abû Bakr recite that verse my feet were cut from beneath me and I fell to the ground, for I knew that Allah's messenger was dead. May Allah bless and keep him!"

All the sûrahs of the Koran had been recorded in writing before the Prophet's death, and many Muslims had committed the whole Koran to memory. Bu the written sûrahs were dispersed among the people; and when, in a battle which took place during the Caliphate of Abû Bakr-that is to say, within two years of the Prophet's death-a large number of those who knew the whole Koran by heart were killed, a collection of the whole Koran was made and put in writing. In the Caliphate of Othmân, all existing copies of sûrahs were called in, and an authoritative version, based on Abû Bakr's collection and the testimony of those who had the whole Koran by heart, was compiled exactly in the present form and order, which is regarded as traditional and as the arrangement of the Prophet himself, the Caliph Othmân and his helpers being Comrades of the Prophet and the most devout students of the Revelation. The Koran has thus been very carefully preserved.

The arrangement is not easy to understand. Revelations of various dates and on different sunjects are to be found together in one sûrah; verses of Madînah revelation are found in Meccan sûranhs; some of the Madînah sûrahs, though of late revelation, are placed first and the very early Meccan sûrahs at the end. But the arrangement is not haphazard, as some have hastily supposed. Closer study will reveal a sequence and significance-as, for instance, with regard to the placing of the very early Meccan sûrahs at the end. The inspiration of the Prophet progressed from inmost things to outward things, whereas most people

[1] III, 144.

find their way through outward things to things within.

There is another peculiarity which is disconcerting in translation though it proceeds from one of the beauties of the original, and is unavoidable without abolishing the verse-division of great importance for reference. In the Arabic the verses are divided according to the rhythm of the language. When a certain sound which marks the rhythm recurs there is a strong pause and the verse ends naturally, although the sentence may go on to the next verse or to several subsequent verses. That is of the spirit of the Arabic language; but attempts to reproduce such rhythm in English have the opposite effect to that produced by the Arabic. Here only the division is preserved, the verses being divided as in the Koran, and numbered.

1. THE OPENING

1 In the name of Allah, Most Gracious, Most Merciful.

2 Praise be to Allah, the Cherisher and Sustainer of the Worlds;

3 Most Gracious, Most Merciful;

4 Master of the Day of Judgment.

5 You do we worship and Your aid we seek.

6 Show us the straight way,

7 The way of those on whom You have bestowed Your Grace, those whose (portion) is not wrath, and who go not astray.

2. THE HEIFER

In the name of Allah, Most Gracious, Most Merciful.

1 *Alif Lām Mīm*. 2 This is the Book; in it is guidance sure, without doubt, to those who fear Allah; 3 who believe in the Unseen, are steadfast in prayer, and spend out of what We have provided for them; 4 And who believe in the Revelation sent to you, and sent before your time, and (in their hearts) have the assurance of the Hereafter. 5 They are on (true) guidance, from their Lord, and it is these who will prosper.

6 As to those who reject Faith, it is the same to them whether you warn them or do not warn them; they will not believe. 7 Allah has set a seal on their hearts and on their hearing, and on their eyes is a veil; great is the penalty they (incur).

8 Of the people there are some who say: "We believe in Allah and the Last day;" but they do not (really) believe. 9 Fain would they deceive Allah and those who believe, but they only deceive themselves, and realize (it) not! 10 In their hearts is a disease; and Allah has increased their disease: and grievous is the penalty

they (incur), because they lied (to themselves). 11 When it is said to them: "Make not mischief on the earth," they say: "Why, we are only those who put things right!" 12 Of a surety, they are the ones who make mischief, but they realize (it) not. 13 When it is said to them: "Believe as the others believe:" they say: "Shall we believe as the fools believe?" — No, of a surety they are the fools, but they do not know. 14 When they meet those who believe, they say: "We believe;" but when they are alone with their evil ones, they say: "We are really with you; we (were) only jesting." 15 Allah will throw back their mockery on them, and give them rope in their trespasses; so they will wander like blind ones (hither and thither). 16 These are they who have bartered guidance for error: but their traffic is profitless, and they have lost true direction.

17 Their similitude is that of a man who kindled a fire; when it lighted all around him, Allah took away their light and left them in utter darkness. So they could not see. 18 Deaf, dumb, and blind, they will not return (to the path). 19 Or (another similitude) is that of a rain-laden cloud from the sky: in it are zones of darkness, and thunder and lightning: they press their fingers in their ears to keep out the stunning thunder-clap, the while they are in terror of death. But Allah is ever round the rejecters of Faith! 20 The lightning all but snatches away their sight; every time the light (helps) them, they walk therein, and when the darkness grows on them, they stand still. And if Allah willed, He could take away their faculty of hearing and seeing; for Allah has power over all things.

21 O you people! Worship your Guardian-Lord, who created you and those who came before you, that you may have the chance to become righteous; 22 Who has made the earth your couch, and the heavens your canopy; and sent down rain from the heavens; and brought forth therewith fruits for your sustenance ; then set not up rivals unto Allah when you know (the truth). 23 And if you are in doubt as to what We have revealed from time to time to Our servant, then produce a surah like thereunto; and call your witnesses or helpers (if there are any) besides Allah, if your (doubts) are true. 24 But if you cannot — and of a surety you

cannot — then fear the Fire whose fuel is Men and Stones — which is prepared for those who reject Faith. 25 But give glad tidings to those who believe and work righteousness, that their portion is Gardens, beneath which rivers flow. Every time they are fed with fruits therefrom, they say: "Why, this is what we were fed with before," for they are given things in similitude; and they have therein companions pure (and holy); and they abide therein (for ever).

26 Allah disdains not to use the similitude of things, lowest as well as highest. Those who believe know that it is truth from their Lord; but those who reject Faith say: "What means Allah by this similitude?" By it He causes many to stray, and many He leads into the right path; but He causes not to stray, except those who forsake (the path) — 27 Those who break Allah's Covenant after it is ratified, and who sunder what Allah has ordered to be joined, and do mischief on earth: these cause loss (only) to themselves. 28 How can you reject the faith in Allah? — seeing that you were without life, and He gave you life; then will He cause you to die, and will again bring you to life; and again to Him will you return. 29 It is He Who has created for you all things that are on earth; then He turned to the heaven and made them into seven firmaments; and of all things He has perfect knowledge.

30 Behold, your Lord said to the angels: "I will create a vicegerent on earth." They said: "Will You place therein one who will make mischief therein and shed blood? — while we do celebrate Your praises and glorify Your holy (name)?" He said: "I know what you know not." 31 And He taught Adam the names of all things; then He placed them before the angels, and said: "Tell Me the names of these if you are right." 32 They said: "Glory to You, of knowledge we have none, save what You have taught us: in truth it is You Who are perfect in knowledge and wisdom." 33 He said: "O Adam! Tell them their names." When he had told them, their names, Allah said: "Did I not tell you that I know the secrets of heaven and earth, and I know what you reveal and what you conceal?"

34 And behold, We said to the angels: "Bow down to Adam" and they bowed down: not so Iblīs: he refused and was haughty:

he was of those who reject Faith. 35 We said: "O Adam! dwell you and your wife in the Garden; and eat of the bountiful things therein as (where and when) you will; but approach not this tree, or you run into harm and transgression." 36 Then did Satan make them slip from the (Garden), and get them out of the state (of felicity) in which they had been. We said: "Get you down, all (you people), with enmity between yourselves. On earth will be your dwelling-place and your means of livelihood—for a time." 37 Then learnt Adam from his Lord words of inspiration, and his Lord turned towards him; for He is Oft-Returning, Most Merciful. 38 We said: "Get you down all from here; and if, as is sure, there comes to you guidance from Me, whosoever follows My guidance, on them shall be no fear, nor shall they grieve. 39 "But those who reject Faith and belie Our Signs, they shall be companions of the Fire; they shall abide therein."

40 O Children of Israel! call to mind the (special) favour which I bestowed upon you, and fulfil your Covenant with Me as I fulfil My Covenant with you, and fear none but Me. 41 And believe in what I reveal, confirming the revelation which is with you, and be not the first to reject faith therein, nor sell My Signs for a small price; and fear Me, and Me alone. 42 And cover not Truth with falsehood, nor conceal the Truth when you know (what it is). 43 And be steadfast in prayer; give Zakat (poor-due), and bow down your heads with those who bow down (in worship). 44 Do you enjoin right conduct on the people, and forget (to practise it) yourselves, and yet you study the Scripture? Will you not understand? 45 No, seek (Allah's) help with patient perseverance and prayer: it is indeed hard, except to those who are humble, 46 Who bear in mind the certainty that they are to meet their Lord, and that they are to return to Him.

47 O Children of Israel! call to mind the (special) favour which I bestowed upon you, and that I preferred you to all others (for My Message). 48 Then guard yourselves against a day when one soul shall not avail another, nor shall intercession be accepted for her, nor shall compensation be taken from her, nor shall anyone be helped (from outside). 49 And remember, We delivered you from the people of Pharaoh: they set you hard tasks and

chastisement, slaughtered your sons and let your women-folk live; therein was a tremendous trial from your Lord. 50 And remember We divided the Sea for you and saved you and drowned Pharaoh's people within your very sight. 51 And remember, We appointed forty nights for Moses, and in his absence you took the calf (for worship), and you did grievous wrong. 52 Even then We did forgive you; there was a chance for you to be grateful. 53 And remember We gave Moses the Scripture and the Criterion (between right and wrong): there was a chance for you to be guided aright. 54 And remember Moses said to his people: "O my people! You have indeed wronged yourselves by your worship of the calf: so turn (in repentance) to your Maker, and slay yourselves (the wrongdoers); that will be better for you in the sight of your Maker." Then He turned towards you (in forgiveness): for He is Oft-Returning, Most Merciful. 55 And remember you said: "O Moses! We shall never believe in you until we see Allah manifestly," but you were dazed with thunder and lightning even as you looked on. 56 Then We raised you up after your death: you had the chance to be grateful. 57 And We gave you the shade of clouds and sent down to you manna and quails, saying: "Eat of the good things We have provided for you:" (but they rebelled); to Us they did no harm, but they harmed their own souls.

58 And remember We said: "Enter this town, and eat of the plenty therein as you wish; but enter the gate with humility, in posture and in words, and We shall forgive you your faults and increase (the portion of) those who do good." 59 But the transgressors changed the word from that which had been given them; so We sent on the transgressors a plague from heaven, for that they infringed (Our command) repeatedly. 60 And remember Moses prayed for water for his people; We said: "Strike the rock with your staff." Then gushed forth therefrom twelve springs. Each group knew its own place for water. So eat and drink of the sustenance provided by Allah, and do no evil nor mischief on the (face of the) earth. 61 And remember you said: "O Moses! we cannot endure one kind of food (always); so beseech your Lord for us to produce for us of what the earth grows—its pot-herbs,

and cucumbers, its garlic, lentils, and onions." He said: "Will you exchange the better for the worse? Go you down to any town, and you shall find what you want!" They were covered with humiliation and misery; they drew on themselves the wrath of Allah. This because they went on rejecting the Signs of Allah and slaying His Messengers without just cause. This because they rebelled and went on transgressing.

62 Those who believe (in the Qur'an), and those who follow the Jewish (scriptures), and the Christians and the Sabians—any who believe in Allah and the Last Day, and work righteousness, shall have their reward with their Lord; on them shall be no fear, nor shall they grieve.

63 And remember We took your covenant and We raised above you (the towering height) of Mount (Sinai) (saying): "Hold firmly to what We have given you and bring (ever) to remembrance what is therein: perchance you may fear Allah." 64 But you turned back thereafter: had it not been for the Grace and Mercy of Allah to you, you had surely been among the lost. 65 And well you knew those amongst you who transgressed in the matter of the Sabbath: We said to them: "Be you apes, despised and rejected." 66 So We made it an example to their own time and to their posterity, and a lesson to those who fear Allah

67 And remember Moses said to his people: "Allah commands that you sacrifice a heifer." They said: "Do you make a laughing-stock of us?" He said: "Allah save me from being an ignorant (fool)!" 68 They said: "Beseech on our behalf your Lord to make plain to us what (heifer) it is!" He said: "He says: the heifer should be neither too old nor too young, but of middling age. Now do what you are commanded!" 69 They said: "Beseech on our behalf your Lord to make plain to us her colour." He said: "He says: a fawn-coloured heifer, pure and rich in tone, the admiration of beholders!" 70 They said: "Beseech on our behalf your Lord to make plain to us what she is: to us are all heifers alike. We wish indeed for guidance, if Allah wills." 71 He said: "He says: a heifer not trained to till the soil or water the fields; sound and without blemish." They said: "Now have you brought the truth." Then

they offered her in sacrifice, but not with good-will. 72 Remember you slew a man and fell into a dispute among yourselves as to the crime: but Allah was to bring forth what you did hide. 73 So We said: "Strike the (body) with a piece of the (heifer)." Thus Allah brings the dead to life and shows you His Signs: perchance you may understand.

74 Thenceforth were your hearts hardened: they became like a rock and even worse in hardness. For among rocks there are some from which rivers gush forth; others there are which, when split asunder, send forth water; and others which sink for fear of Allah. And Allah is not unmindful of what you do.

75 Can you (O you men of Faith) entertain the hope that they will believe in you? — seeing that a party of them heard the Word of Allah, and perverted it knowingly after they understood it. 76 Behold! when they meet the men of Faith, they say: "We believe:" but when they meet each other in private, they say: "Shall you tell them what Allah has revealed to you, that they may engage you in argument about it before your Lord?" — Do you not understand (their aim)? 77 Know they not that Allah knows what they conceal and what they reveal?

78 And there are among them illiterates, who know not the Book, but (see therein their own) desires, and they do nothing but conjecture. 79 Then woe to those who write the Book with their own hands, and then say: "This is from Allah," to traffic with it for a miserable price! Woe to them for what their hands do write, and for the gain they make thereby. 80 And they say: "The Fire shall not touch us but for a few numbered days." Say: "Have you taken a promise from Allah, for He never breaks His promise? Or is it that you say of Allah what you do not know?" 81 No, those who seek gain in Evil, and are girt round by their sins — they are companions of the Fire: therein shall they abide (for ever). 82 But those who have faith and work righteousness, they are inhabitants of the Garden: therein shall they abide (for ever).

83 And remember We took a Covenant from the Children of Israel (to this effect): worship none but Allah; treat with kindness your parents and kindred, and orphans and those in need; speak

fair to the people; be steadfast in prayer; and give zakat (poor-due), then did you turn back, except a few among you, and you backslide (even now).

84 And remember We took your Covenant (to this effect): shed no blood amongst you, nor turn out your own people from your homes: and this you solemnly ratified, and to this you can bear witness. 85 After this it is you, the same people, who slay among yourselves, and banish a party of you from their homes; assist (their enemies) against them, in guilt and rancour; and if they come to you as captives, you ransom them, though it was not lawful for you to banish them. Then is it only a part of the Book that you believe in, and do you reject the rest? But what is the reward for those among you who behave like this but disgrace in this life? — And on the Day of Judgment they shall be consigned to the most grievous penalty. For Allah is not unmindful of what you do. 86 These are the people who buy the life of this world at the price of the Hereafter: their chastisement shall not be lightened nor shall they be helped.

87 We gave Moses the Book and followed him up with a succession of Messengers; We gave Jesus the son of Mary clear (Signs) and strengthened him with the holy spirit. Is it that whenever there comes to you a Messenger with what you yourselves desire not, you are puffed up with pride? — Some you called impostors, and others you slay! 88 They say, "Our hearts are the wrappings (which preserve Allah's Word: we need no more)." No, Allah's curse is on them for their blasphemy: little is it they believe. 89 And when there comes to them a Book from Allah, confirming what is with them — although from of old they had prayed for victory against those without Faith — when there comes to them that which they (should) have recognized, they refuse to believe in it but the curse of Allah is on those without Faith. 90 Miserable is the price for which they have sold their souls, in that they deny (the revelation) which Allah has sent down, in insolent envy that Allah of His Grace should send it to any of His servants He pleases: thus have they drawn on themselves Wrath upon Wrath. And humiliating is the punishment of those who reject Faith.

91 When it is said to them, "Believe in what Allah has sent down," they say, "We believe in what was sent down to us:" yet they reject all besides, even if it be Truth confirming what is with them. Say: "Why then have you slain the Messengers of Allah in times gone by, if you did indeed believe?" 92 There came to you Moses with clear (Signs); yet you worshipped the Calf (even) after that, and you did behave wrongfully. 93 And remember We took your Covenant and We raised above you (the towering height) of Mount (Sinai): (saying): "Hold firmly to what We have given you, and hearken (to the Law):" they said: "We hear, and we disobey." And they had to drink into their hearts (of the taint) of the Calf because of their Faithlessness. Say: "Vile indeed are the behests of your Faith if you have any faith!" 94 Say: "If the last Home, with Allah, be for you specially, and not for anyone else, then seek you for death, if you are sincere." 95 But they will never seek for death, on account of the (sins) which their hands have sent on before them. And Allah is well-acquainted with the wrong-doers. 96 You will indeed find them, of all people, most greedy of life—even more than the idolators: each one of them wishes he could be given a life of a thousand years: but the grant of such life will not save him from (due) chastisement. For Allah sees well all that they do.

97 Say: Whoever is an enemy to Gabriel—for he brings down the (revelation) to your heart by Allah's will, a confirmation of what went before, and guidance and glad tidings for those who believe— 98 Whoever is an enemy to Allah and His angels and Messengers, to Gabriel and Michael—Lo! Allah is an enemy to those who reject Faith. 99 We have sent down to you Manifest Signs (āyāt); and none reject them but those who are perverse. 100 Is it not (the case) that every time they make a Covenant, some party among them throw it aside?—No, most of them are faithless. 101 And when there came to them a Messenger from Allah, confirming what was with them, a party of the People of the Book threw away the Book of Allah behind their backs, as if (it had been something) they did not know!

102 They followed what the Satans recited over Solomon's Kingdom. Solomon did not disbelieve, the Satans disbelieved,

teaching men magic, and such things as came down at Babylon to the angels Harut and Marut. But neither of these taught anyone (such things) without saying: "We are only for trial; so do not blaspheme." They learned from them the means to sow discord between man and wife. But they could not thus harm anyone except by Allah's permission. And they learned what harmed them, not what profited them. And they knew that the buyers of (magic) would have no share in the happiness of the Hereafter. And vile was the price for which they did sell their souls, if they but knew! 103 If they had kept their Faith and guarded themselves from evil, far better had been the reward from their Lord, if they but knew!

104 O you of Faith! Say not (to the Messenger) Ra'ina (words of ambiguous import), but say 'Unzurna' (words of respect) and hearken (to him): to those without Faith is a grievous punishment. 105 It is never the wish of those without Faith among the People of the Book, nor of the Pagans, that anything good should come down to you from your Lord. But Allah will choose for His special Mercy whom He will—for Allah is Lord of grace abounding. 106 None of Our revelations do We abrogate or cause to be forgotten, but We substitute something better or similar: know you not that Allah has power over all things? 107 Know you not that to Allah belongs the dominion of the heavens and the earth? And besides Him you have neither patron nor helper. 108 Would you question your Messenger as Moses was questioned of old? But whoever changes from Faith to Unbelief, has strayed without doubt from the even way.

109 Quite a number of the People of the Book wish they could turn you (people) back to infidelity after you have believed, from selfish envy, after the Truth has become manifest unto them: but forgive and overlook, till Allah accomplish His purpose; for Allah has power over all things. 110 And be steadfast in prayer and give zakat (poor-due): and whatever good you send forth for your souls before you, you shall find it with Allah: for Allah sees well all that you do. 111 And they say: "None shall enter Paradise unless he be a Jew or a Christian." Those are their (vain) desires. Say: "Produce your proof if you are truthful." 112 No—Whoever

submits his whole self to Allah and is a doer of good—he will get his reward with his Lord; on such shall be no fear, nor shall they grieve.

113 The Jews say: "The Christians have naught (to stand) upon; and the Christians say: "The Jews have naught (to stand) upon." Yet they (profess to) study the (same) Book. Like unto their word is what those say who know not; but Allah will judge between them in their quarrel on the Day of Judgment. 114 And who is more unjust than he who forbids that in places for the worship of Allah, Allah's name should be celebrated?—whose zeal is (in fact) to ruin them? It was not fitting that such should themselves enter them except in fear. For them there is nothing but disgrace in this world, and in the world to come, an exceeding torment. 115 To Allah belong the East and the West: wheresoever you turn, there is the Presence of Allah. For Allah is All-Pervading, All-Knowing. 116 They say: "Allah has begotten a son:" Glory be to Him—No, to Him belongs all that is in the heavens and on earth: everything renders worship to Him. 117 To Him is due the primal origin of the heavens and the earth: when He decrees a matter, He says to it: "Be," and it is.

118 Say those without knowledge: "Why speaks not Allah unto us? Or why comes not unto us a Sign?" So said the people before them words of similar import. Their hearts are alike. We have indeed made clear the Signs unto any people who hold firmly to Faith (in their hearts). 119 Surely, We have sent you in truth as a bearer of glad tidings and a warner: but of you no question shall be asked of the companions of the Blazing Fire. 120 Never will the Jews or the Christians be satisfied with you unless you follow their form of religion. Say: "The Guidance of Allah—that is the (only) Guidance." Were you to follow their desires after the knowledge which has reached you, then would you find neither Protector nor Helper against Allah. 121 Those to whom We have sent the Book study it as it should be studied: they are the ones that believe therein: those who reject faith therein—the loss is their own.

122 O Children of Israel! call to mind the special favour which I bestowed upon you, and that I preferred you to all others (for

My Message). 123 Then guard yourselves against a Day when one soul shall not avail another, nor shall compensation be accepted from her nor shall intercession profit her nor shall anyone be helped (from outside). 124 And remember that Abraham was tried by his Lord with certain Commands, which he fulfilled: he said: "I will make you an Imām (leader) to the people." He pleaded: "And also (Imāms) from my offspring!" He answered: "But My Promise is not within the reach of evil-doers."

125 Remember We made the House a place of assembly for men and a place of safety; and take you the Station of Abraham as a place of prayer; and We covenanted with Abraham and Ishmael, that they should sanctify My House for those who compass it round, or use it as a retreat, or bow, or prostrate themselves (therein in prayer). 126 And remember Abraham said: "My Lord, make this a City of Peace, and feed its people with fruits—such of them as believe in Allah and the Last Day." He said: "(Yes), and such as reject Faith—for a while will I grant them their pleasure, but will soon drive them to the torment of Fire—an evil destination (indeed)!"

127 And remember Abraham and Ishmael raised the foundations of the House (with this prayer): "Our Lord! Accept (this service) from us: for You are the All-Hearing, the All-Knowing. 128 "Our Lord! make of us Muslims, bowing to Your (Will), and of our progeny a people Muslim, bowing to Your (will); and show us our places for the celebration of (due) rites; and turn unto us (in Mercy); for You are the Oft-Returning, Most Merciful. 129 "Our Lord! send amongst them a Messenger of their own, who shall rehearse Your Signs to them and instruct them in Scripture and Wisdom, and sanctify them: for You are the Exalted in Might, the Wise."

130 And who turns away from the religion of Abraham but such as debase their souls with folly? Him We chose and rendered pure in this world: and he will be in the Hereafter in the ranks of the Righteous. 131 Behold! his Lord said to him: "Bow (your will to Me):" he said: "I bow (my will) to the Lord and Cherisher of the Universe." 132 And this was the legacy that Abraham left to his sons, and so did Jacob; "Oh my sons! Allah has chosen the

Faith for you; then die not except in the Faith of Islam." 133 Were
you witnesses when Death appeared before Jacob? Behold, he said
to his sons: "What will you worship after me?" They said: "We
shall worship your God and the God of your fathers—of
Abraham, Ishmael and Isaac—the One (True) God: to Him we
submit (in Islam)." 134 That was a People that has passed away.
They shall reap the fruit of what they did, and you of what you
do! You shall not be asked about what they did.

135 They say: "Become Jews or Christians if you would be
guided (to salvation)." Say you: "No! (I would rather) the
Religion of Abraham the True, and he joined not gods with
Allah." 136 Say you: "We believe in Allah, and the revelation
given to us, and to Abraham, Ishmael, Isaac, Jacob, and the Tribes,
and that given to Moses and Jesus, and that given to (all) Prophets
from their Lord: we make no difference between one and another
of them: and we submit to Allah." 137 So if they believe as you
believe, they are indeed on the right path; but if they turn back,
it is they who are in schism; but Allah will suffice you as against
them, and He is the All-Hearing, the All-Knowing. 138 (Our
religion is) the Baptism of Allah: and who can baptize better than
Allah? And it is He whom we worship. 139 Say: Will you dispute
with us about Allah, seeing that He is our Lord and your Lord;
that we are responsible for our doings and you for yours; and that
we are sincere (in our faith) in Him? 140 Or do you say that
Abraham, Ishmael, Isaac, Jacob and the Tribes were Jews or
Christians? Say: Do you know better than Allah? Ah! who is more
unjust than those who conceal the testimony they have from
Allah? But Allah is not unmindful of what you do! 141 That was
a people that has passed away. They shall reap the fruit of what
they did, and you of what you do! Of their merits there is no
question in your case:

142 The fools among the people will say: "What has turned them
from the *qiblah* (direction faced in prayer) to which they were
used?" Say: to Allah belong both East and West: He guides whom
He will to a Way that is straight. 143 Thus have We made you
a middle nation, that you might be witnesses to the people, and
the Messenger a witness to you; and We appointed the *qiblah* to

which you were used, only to test those who followed the Messenger from those who would turn on their heels (from the Faith). Indeed it was (a change) momentous, except to those guided by Allah. And never would Allah make your faith of no effect. For Allah is to all people most surely full of kindness, Most Merciful.

144 We see the turning of your face (for guidance) to the heavens: now shall We turn you to a *qiblah* that shall please you. Turn then your face in the direction of the sacred Mosque: wherever you are, turn your faces in that direction. The people of the Book know well that that is the truth from their Lord. Nor is Allah unmindful of what they do. 145 Even if you were to bring to the people of the Book all the Signs (together), they would not follow your *qiblah*; nor are you going to follow their *qiblah*; nor indeed will they follow each other's *qiblah*. If you, after the knowledge has reached you, were to follow their (vain) desires — then were you indeed (clearly) in the wrong. 146 The people of the Book know this as they know their own sons; but some of them conceal the truth which they themselves know. 147 The Truth is from your Lord; so be not at all in doubt.

148 To each is a goal to which Allah turns him; then strive together (as in a race) towards all that is good. Wheresoever you are, Allah will bring you together. For Allah has power over all things. 149 From whichever way you start forth, turn your face in the direction of the Sacred Mosque; that is indeed the truth from your Lord. And Allah is not unmindful of what you do. 150 So from whichever way you start forth, turn your face in the direction of the Sacred Mosque; and wheresoever you are, turn your face thither: that there be no ground of dispute against you among the people, except those of them that are bent on wickedness; so fear them not, but fear Me; and that I may complete My favours on you, and you may (consent to) be guided. 151 A similar (favour have you already received) in that We have sent among you a Messenger of your own, rehearsing to you Our Signs, and purifying you, and instructing you in Scripture and Wisdom, and in new Knowledge. 152 Then do you remember Me; I will remember you. Be grateful to Me, and reject not Faith.

153 O you who believe! seek help with patient Perseverance and Prayer: for Allah is with those who patiently persevere. 154 And say not of those who are slain in the way of Allah: "They are dead." No, they are living, though you perceive (it) not. 155 Be sure We shall test you with something of fear and hunger, some loss in goods or lives or the fruits (of your toil), but give glad tidings to those who patiently persevere— 156 Who say, when afflicted with calamity: "To Allah we belong, and to Him is our return:" — 157 They are those on whom (descend) blessings from Allah, and Mercy, and they are the ones that receive guidance.

158 Behold! Safa and Marwah are among the Symbols of Allah. So if those who visit the House in the Season or at other times, should compass them round, it is no sin in them. And if any one obeys his own impulse to good—be sure that Allah is He Who recognises and knows. 159 Those who conceal the clear (Signs) We have sent down, and the Guidance, after We have made it clear for the People in the Book—on them shall be Allah's curse, and the curse of those entitled to curse— 160 Except those who repent and make amends and openly declare (the Truth): to them I turn; for I am Oft-returning, Most Merciful. 161 Those who reject Faith, and die rejecting—on them is Allah's curse, and the curse of angels, and of all mankind. 162 They will abide therein: their penalty will not be lightened, nor will respite be their (lot).

163 And your God is One God: there is no god but He, Most Gracious, Most Merciful. 164 Behold! In the creation of the heavens and the earth; in the alternation of the night and the day; in the sailing of the ships across the ocean for the benefit of mankind; in the rain which Allah sends down from the skies, and the life which He gives therewith to an earth that is dead; in the beasts of all kinds that He scatters through the earth; in the change of the winds, and the clouds which they trail like their slaves between the sky and the earth—(here) indeed are Signs for a people that are wise.

165 Yet there are men who take (for worship) others besides Allah, as equal (with Allah): they love them as they should love Allah. But those of Faith are overflowing in their love for Allah. If only the unrighteous could see, behold, they would see the

Penalty: that to Allah belongs all power, and Allah will strongly enforce the Penalty. 166 Then would those who are followed clear themselves of those who follow (them): they would see the Punishment, and all relations between them would be cut off. 167 And those who followed would say: "If only we had one more chance, we would clear ourselves of them, as they have cleared themselves of us." Thus will Allah show them (the fruits of) their deeds as (nothing but) regrets. Nor will there be a way for them out of the Fire.

168 O you people! Eat of what is on earth, lawful and good; and do not follow the footsteps of Satan, for he is to you an avowed enemy. 169 For he commands you what is evil and shameful, and that you should say of Allah that of which you have no knowledge. 170 When it is said to them: "Follow what Allah has revealed:" they say: "No! we shall follow the ways of our fathers." What! even though their fathers were void of wisdom and guidance? 171 The parable of those who reject Faith is as if one were to shout like a goat-herd, to things that listen to nothing but calls and cries: deaf, dumb, and blind, they are void of wisdom.

172 O you who believe! Eat of the good things that We have provided for you, and be grateful to Allah, if it is Him you worship. 173 He has only forbidden you dead meat, and blood, and the flesh of swine, and that on which any other name has been invoked besides that of Allah. But if one is forced by necessity, without wilful disobedience, nor transgressing due limits—then is he guiltless. For Allah is Oft-forgiving, Most Merciful. 174 Those who conceal Allah's revelations in the Book, and purchase for them a miserable profit—they swallow into themselves naught but Fire; Allah will neither address them on the Day of Resurrection, nor purify them: grievous will be their Chastisement. 175 They are the ones who buy Error in place of Guidance and Torment in place of Forgiveness. Ah! what boldness (they show) for the Fire! 176 (Their doom is) because Allah sent down the Book in truth, but those who seek causes of dispute in the Book are in a schism far (from the purpose).

177 It is not righteousness that you turn your faces towards East

or West; but it is righteousness — To believe in Allah and the Last Day, and the Angels, and the Book, and the Messengers; to spend of your substance, out of love for Him, for your kin, for orphans, for the needy, for the wayfarer, for those who ask, and for the ransom of slaves; to be steadfast in prayer, and give zakat (poor-due), to fulfil the contracts which you have made; and to be firm and patient, in pain (or suffering) and adversity, and throughout all periods of panic. Such are the people of truth, the God-fearing.

178 O you who believe! The law of equality is prescribed to you in cases of murder: the free for the free, the slave for the slave, the woman for the woman. But if any remission is made by the brother of the slain, then grant any reasonable demand, and compensate him with handsome gratitude, this is a concession and a Mercy from your Lord. After this whoever exceeds the limits shall be in grave chastisement. 179 In the Law of Equality there is (saving of) Life to you, O you men of understanding; that you may restrain yourselves. 180 It is prescribed, when death approaches any of you, if he leave any goods, that he make a bequest to parents and next of kin, according to reasonable usage; this is due from the God-fearing. 181 If anyone changes the bequest after hearing it, the guilt shall be on those who make the change. For Allah hears and knows (all things). 182 But if anyone fears partiality or wrong-doing on the part of the testator, and makes peace between (the parties concerned), there is no wrong in him: for Allah is Oft-forgiving, Most Merciful.

183 O you who believe! Fasting is prescribed to you as it was prescribed to those before you, that you may (learn) self-restraint — 184 (Fasting) for a fixed number of days; but if any of you is ill, or on a journey, the prescribed number (should be made up) from days later. For those who can do it (with hardship), is a ransom, the feeding of one that is indigent. But he that will give more, of his own free will — it is better for him. And it is better for you that you fast, if you only knew. 185 Ramadan is the (month) in which was sent down the Qur'an, as a guide to mankind, also clear (Signs) for guidance and judgment (between right and wrong). So every one of you who is present (at his home) during that month should spend it in fasting, but if anyone is ill,

or on a journey, the prescribed period (should be made up) by days later. Allah intends every facility for you; He does not want to put you to difficulties. (He wants you) to complete the prescribed period, and to glorify Him in that He has guided you; and perchance you shall be grateful.

186 When My servants ask you concerning Me, I am indeed close (to them): I listen to the prayer of every suppliant when he calls on Me: let them also, with a will, listen to My call, and believe in Me: that they may walk in the right way. 187 Permitted to you, on the night of the fasts, is the approach to your wives. They are your garments and you are their garments. Allah knows what you used to do secretly among yourselves; but He turned to you and forgave you; so now associate with them, and seek what Allah has ordained for you, and eat and drink, until the white streak of dawn appear to you distinct from the blackness of night; then complete your fast till the night appears; but do not associate with your wives while you are in retreat in the mosques. Those are limits (set by) Allah: approach not near thereto. Thus does Allah make clear His Signs to men: that they may learn self-restraint. 188 And do not eat up your property among yourselves for vanities, nor use it as bait for the judges, with intent that you may eat up wrongfully and knowingly a little of (other) people's property.

189 They ask you concerning the New Moons. Say: They are but signs to mark fixed periods of time in (the affairs of) men, and for Pilgrimage. It is no virtue if you enter your houses from the back: it is virtue if you fear Allah. Enter houses through the proper doors: and fear Allah: that you may prosper. 190 Fight in the cause of Allah those who fight you, but do not transgress limits; for Allah loves not transgressors. 191 And slay them wherever you catch them, and turn them out from where they have turned you out; for tumult and oppression are worse than slaughter; but fight them not at the Sacred Mosque, unless they (first) fight you there; but if they fight you, slay them. Such is the reward of those who suppress faith. 192 But if they cease, Allah is Oft-forgiving, Most Merciful. 193 And fight them on until there is no more tumult and oppression, and there prevail justice and

faith in Allah; but if they cease, let there be no hostility except
to those who practise oppression.

194 The prohibited month for the prohibited month — and so for
all things prohibited — there is the law of equality. If then any one
transgresses the prohibition against you, transgress you likewise
against him. But fear Allah, and know that Allah is with those
who restrain themselves. 195 And spend of your substance in the
cause of Allah, and make not your own hands contribute to (your)
destruction; but do good; for Allah loves those who do good.

196 And complete the *hajj* or *'umrah* in the service of Allah.
But if you are prevented (from completing it), send an offering
for sacrifice, such as you may find, and do not shave your heads
until the offering reaches the place of sacrifice. And if any of you
is ill, or has an ailment in his scalp, (necessitating shaving), (he
should) in compensation either fast, or feed the poor, or offer
sacrifice; and when you are in peaceful conditions (again), if
anyone wishes to continue the *'umrah* on to the *hajj*, he must make
an offering, such as he can afford, but if he cannot afford it, he
should fast three days during the *hajj* and seven days on his return,
making ten days in all. This is for those whose household is not
in (the precincts of) the Sacred Mosque. And fear Allah, and know
that Allah is strict in punishment. 197 For *hajj* are the months well
known. If anyone undertakes that duty therein, let there be neither
obscenity, nor wickedness, nor wrangling in the *hajj*. And
whatever good you do, (be sure) Allah knows it. And take a
provision (with you) for the journey, but the best of provisions
is right conduct. So fear Me, O you that are wise.

198 It is no crime in you if you seek of the bounty of your Lord
(during pilgrimage). Then when you pour down from (Mount)
'Arafāt, celebrate the praises of Allah at the Sacred Monument,
and celebrate His praises as He has directed you, even though,
before this, you went astray. 199 Then pass on at a quick pace
from the place whence it is usual for the multitude so to do, and
ask for Allah's forgiveness. For Allah is Oft-forgiving, Most
Merciful. 200 So when you have accomplished your holy rites,
celebrate the praises of Allah, as you used to celebrate the praises

of your fathers—yes, with far more heart and soul. There are men who say: "Our Lord! Give us (Your bounties) in this world!" But they will have no portion in the Hereafter. 201 And there are men who say: "Our Lord! Give us good in this world and good in the Hereafter, and defend us from the torment of the Fire!" 202 To these will be allotted what they have earned; and Allah is quick in account. 203 Celebrate the praises of Allah during the Appointed Days. But if anyone hastens to leave in two days, there is no blame on him, and if anyone stays on, there is no blame on him, if his aim is to do right. Then fear Allah, and know that you will surely be gathered unto Him.

204 There is the type of man whose speech about this world's life may dazzle you, and he calls Allah to witness about what is in his heart; yet is he the most contentious of enemies. 205 When he turns his back, his aim everywhere is to spread mischief through the earth and destroy crops and cattle. But Allah loves not mischief 206 When it is said to him, "Fear Allah," he is led by arrogance to (more) crime. Enough for him is Hell—an evil bed indeed (to lie on)! 207 And there is the type of man who gives his life to earn the pleasure of Allah; and Allah is full of kindness to (His) devotees.

208 O you who believe! Enter into Islam whole-heartedly; and follow not the footsteps of Satan; for he is to you an avowed enemy. 209 If you backslide after the clear (Signs) have come to you, then know that Allah is Exalted in Power, Wise. 210 Will they wait until Allah comes to them in canopies of clouds, with angels (in His train) and the question is (thus) settled? But to Allah do all questions go back (for decision).

211 Ask the Children of Israel how many Clear (Signs) We have sent them. But if anyone, after Allah's favour has come to him, substitutes (something else), Allah is strict in punishment. 212 The life of this world is alluring to those who reject faith, and they scoff at those who believe. But the righteous will be above them on the Day of Resurrection; for Allah bestows His abundance without measure on whom He will.

213 Mankind was one single nation, and Allah sent Messengers

with glad tidings and warnings; and with them He sent the Book in truth, to judge between people in matters wherein they differed; but the People of the Book, after the Clear Signs came to them, did not differ among themselves, except through selfish contumacy. Allah by His Grace guided the believers to the Truth, concerning that wherein they differed. For Allah guides whom He will to a path that is straight.. 214 Or do you think that you shall enter the Garden (of Bliss) without such (trials) as came to those who passed away before you? They encountered suffering and adversity, and were so shaken in spirit that even the Messenger and those of faith who were with him cried: "When (will come) the help of Allah?" Ah! Surely, the help of Allah is (always) near!

215 They ask you what they should spend (in charity). Say: Whatever you spend that is good, is for parents and kindred and orphans and those in want and for wayfarers. And whatever you do that is good—Allah knows it well. 216 Fighting is prescribed for you, and you dislike it. But it is possible that you dislike a thing which is good for you, and that you love a thing which is bad for you. But Allah knows, and you know not.

217 They ask you concerning fighting in the Prohibited Month. Say: "Fighting therein is a grave (offence); but graver is it in the sight of Allah to prevent access to the path of Allah, to deny Him, to prevent access to the Sacred Mosque, and drive out its members." Tumult and oppression are worse than slaughter. Nor will they cease fighting you until they turn you back from your faith if they can. And if any of you turn back from their faith and die in unbelief, their works will bear no fruit in this life and in the Hereafter; they will be companions of the Fire and will abide therein. 218 Those who believed and those who suffered exile and fought (and strove and struggled) in the path of Allah— they have the hope of the Mercy of Allah: and Allah is Oft-forgiving, Most Merciful.

219 They ask you concerning wine and gambling. Say: "In them is great sin, and some benefit, for men; but the sin is greater than the benefit." They ask you how much they are to spend; say: "What is beyond your needs." Thus does Allah make clear to you His Signs: in order that you may consider— 220 (Their bearings) on

this life and the Hereafter. They ask you concerning orphans. Say: "The best thing to do is what is for their good; if you mix their affairs with yours, they are your brethren; but Allah knows the man who means mischief from the man who means good. And if Allah had wished, He could have put you into difficulties: He is indeed Exalted in Power, Wise."

221 Do not marry unbelieving women (idolators), until they believe: a slave woman who believes is better than an unbelieving woman, even though she is alluring to you. Nor marry (your girls) to unbelievers until they believe: a man slave who believes is better than an unbeliever, even though he appeals to you. Unbelievers do (but) beckon you to the Fire. But Allah beckons by His Grace to the Garden (of Bliss) and forgiveness, and makes His Signs clear to mankind: that they may receive admonition. 222 They ask you concerning women's courses. Say: They are a hurt and a pollution: so keep away from women in their courses, and do not approach them until they are clean. But when they have purified themselves, you may approach them in any manner, time, or place ordained for you by Allah. For Allah loves those who turn to Him constantly and He loves those who keep themselves pure and clean. 223 Your wives are as a tilth unto you; so approach your tilth when or how you will; but do some good act for your souls beforehand; and fear Allah. And know that you are to meet Him (in the Hereafter), and give (these) good tidings to those who believe.

224 And make not Allah's (name) an excuse in your oaths against doing good, or acting rightly, or making peace between persons; for Allah is One Who hears and knows all things. 225 Allah will not call you to account for thoughtlessness in your oaths, but for the intention in your hearts; and He is Oft-forgiving, Most Forbearing. 226 For those who take an oath for abstention from their wives, a waiting for four months is ordained; if then they return, Allah is Oft-forgiving, Most Merciful. 227 But if their intention is firm for divorce, Allah hears and knows all things. 228 Divorced women shall wait concerning themselves for three monthly periods. Nor is it lawful for them to hide what Allah has created in their wombs, if they have faith in Allah and the

Last Day. And their husbands have the better right to take them back in that period, if they wish for reconciliation. And women shall have rights similar to the rights against them, according to what is equitable; but men have a degree (of advantage) over them. And Allah is Exalted in Power, Wise.

229 Divorce is only permissible twice: after that, the parties should either hold together on equitable terms, or separate with kindness. It is not lawful for you, (men), to take back any of your gifts (from your wives), except when both parties fear that they would be unable to keep the limits ordained by Allah. If you (judges) do indeed fear that they would be unable to keep the limits ordained by Allah, there is no blame on either of them if she gives something for her freedom. These are the limits ordained by Allah; so do not transgress them if any do transgress the limits ordained by Allah, such persons wrong (themselves as well as others). 230 So if a husband divorces his wife (irrevocably), he cannot, after that, remarry her until after she has married another husband and he has divorced her. In that case, there is no blame on either of them if they reunite, provided they feel that they can keep the limits ordained by Allah. Such are the limits ordained by Allah, which He makes plain to those who know. 231 When you divorce women, and they (are about to) fulfil the term of their 'iddah[1], either retain them on equitable terms or set them free on equitable terms; but do not retain them to injure them, (or) to take undue advantage; if anyone does that, he wrongs his own soul. Do not treat Allah's Signs as a jest, but solemnly rehearse Allah's favours on you, and the fact that He sent down to you the Book and Wisdom, for your instruction. And fear Allah, and know that Allah is well acquainted with all things.

232 When you divorce women, and they fulfil the term of their ('iddah), do not prevent them from marrying their (former) husbands, if they mutually agree on equitable terms. This instruction is for all amongst you, who believe in Allah and the Last Day. That is (the course making for) most virtue and purity amongst you. And Allah knows, and you know not. 233 The

---

1. The prescribed period of waiting during which a woman may not remarry after being widowed or divorced.

mothers shall give suck to their offspring for two whole years, if the father desires to complete the term. But he shall bear the cost of their food and clothing on equitable terms. No soul shall have a burden laid on it greater than it can bear. No mother shall be treated unfairly on account of her child, nor father on account of his child. An heir shall be chargeable in the same way. If they both decide on weaning, by mutual consent, and after due consultation, there is no blame on them. If you decide on a foster-mother for your offspring, there is no blame on you, provided you pay her what you promised, on equitable terms. But fear Allah and know that Allah sees well what you do.

234 If any of you die and leave widows behind, they shall wait concerning themselves four months and ten days: when they have fulfilled their term, there is no blame on you if they dispose of themselves in a just and reasonable manner. And Allah is well acquainted with what you do. 235 There is no blame on you if you make an offer of betrothal or hold it in your hearts. Allah knows that you cherish them in your hearts: but do not make a secret contract with them except in terms honourable, nor resolve on the tie of marriage till the term prescribed is fulfilled. And know that Allah knows what is in your hearts, and take heed of Him; and know that Allah is Oft-forgiving, Most Forbearing. 236 There is no blame on you if you divorce women before consummation or the fixation of their dower; but bestow on them (a suitable gift), the wealthy according to his means, and the poor according to his means — a gift of a reasonable amount is due from those who wish to do the right thing. 237 And if you divorce them before consummation, but after the fixation of a dower for them, then the half of the dower (is due to them), unless they remit it or (the man's half) is remitted by him in whose hands is the marriage tie; and the remission (of the man's half) is the nearest to righteousness. And do not forget liberality between yourselves. For Allah sees well all that you do.

238 Guard strictly your (habit of) prayers, especially the Middle Prayer; and stand before Allah in a devout (frame of mind). 239 If you fear (an enemy), pray on foot, or riding, (as may be most convenient), but when you are in security, celebrate Allah's

praises in the manner He has taught you, which you knew not (before). 240 Those of you who die and leave widows should bequeath for their widows a year's provision and residence; but if they leave (the residence), there is no blame on you for what they do with themselves, provided it is reasonable. And Allah is Exalted in Power, Wise. 241 For divorced women provision (should be made) on a reasonable (scale). This is a duty on the righteous. 242 Thus does Allah make clear His Signs to you: in order that you may understand.

243 Did you not turn by vision to those who abandoned their homes, though they were thousands (in number), for fear of death? Allah said to them: "Die:" then He restored them to life. For Allah is full of bounty to mankind, but most of them are ungrateful. 244 Then fight in the cause of Allah, and know that Allah hears and knows all things. 245 Who is he that will loan to Allah a beautiful loan, which Allah will double unto his credit and multiply many times? It is Allah that gives (you) want or plenty, and to Him shall be your return.

246 Have you not turned your vision to the Chiefs of the Children of Israel after (the time of) Moses? They said to the Prophet (that was) among them: "Appoint for us a King, that we may fight in the cause of Allah." He said: "Is it not possible, if you were commanded to fight, that you might not fight?" They said: "How could we refuse to fight in the cause of Allah, seeing that we were turned out of our homes and our families?" But when they were commanded to fight, they turned back, except a small band among them. But Allah has full knowledge of those who do wrong. 247 Their Prophet said to them: "Allah has appointed Tālūt as king over you." They said: "How can he exercise authority over us when we are better fitted than he to exercise authority, and he is not even gifted, with wealth in abundance?" He said: "Allah has chosen him above you, and has gifted him abundantly with knowledge and bodily prowess : Allah grants His authority to whom He pleases. Allah cares for all, and He knows all things." 248 And (further) their Prophet said to them: "A Sign of his authority is that there shall come to you the Ark of the Covenant, with (an assurance) therein of security from your Lord, and the

relics left by the family of Moses and the family of Aaron, carried by angels. In this is a Symbol for you, if you indeed have faith."

249 When Tālūt set forth with the armies, he said: "Allah will test you at the stream: if any drinks of its water, he goes not with my army: only those who taste not of it go with me: a mere sip out of the hand is excused." But they all drank of it, except a few. When they crossed the river—he and the faithful ones with him—they said: "This day we cannot cope with Goliath and his forces." But those who were convinced that they must meet Allah, said: "How oft, by Allah's will, has a small force vanquished a big one? Allah is with those who steadfastly persevere." 250 When they advanced to meet Goliath and his forces, they prayed: "Our Lord! Pour out constancy on us and make our steps firm: help us against those that reject faith." 251 By Allah's will they routed them; and David slew Goliath; and Allah gave him power and wisdom and taught him whatever (else) He willed. And did not Allah check one set of people by means of another, the earth would indeed be full of mischief: but Allah is full of bounty to all the worlds.

252 These are the Signs of Allah: We rehearse them to you in truth: surely you are one of the Messengers. 253 Those Messengers We endowed with gifts, some above others: to some of them Allah spoke; others He raised to degrees (of honour); to Jesus the son of Mary We gave Clear (Signs), and strengthened him with the Holy Spirit. If Allah had so willed, succeeding generations would not have fought among each other, after Clear (Signs) had come to them, but they (chose) to wrangle, some believing and others rejecting. If Allah had so willed, they would not have fought each other; but Allah fulfils His plan.

254 O you who believe! Spend out of (the bounties) We have provided for you, before the Day comes when no bargaining (will avail), nor friendship nor intercession. Those who reject Faith—they are the wrong-doers. 255 Allah! There is no god but He—the Living, the Self-subsisting, Eternal. No slumber can seize Him nor sleep. His are all things in the heavens and on earth. Who is there can intercede in His presence except as He permits? He knows what (appears to His creatures as) Before or After or

Behind them. Nor shall they compass any of His knowledge except as He wills. His Throne does extend over the heavens and the earth, and He feels no fatigue in guarding and preserving them for He is the Most High, the Supreme (in glory). 256 Let there be no compulsion in religion: Truth stands out Clear from Error: whoever rejects evil and believes in Allah has grasped the most trustworthy hand-hold, that never breaks. And Allah hears and knows all things. 257 Allah is the Protector of those who have faith: from the depths of darkness He leads them forth into light. Of those who reject faith the patrons are the evil ones: from light they will lead them forth into the depths of darkness. They will be companions of the fire, to dwell therein (for ever).

258 Have you not turned your vision to one who disputed with Abraham about his Lord, because Allah had granted him power? Abraham said: "My Lord is He Who gives life and death." He said: "I give life and death." Said Abraham: "But it is Allah that causes the sun to rise from the East: do you then cause him to rise from the West." Thus was he confounded who (in arrogance) rejected faith. Nor does Allah give guidance to a people unjust.

259 Or (take) the similitude of one who passed by a hamlet , all in ruins to its roofs. He said: "Oh! how shall Allah bring it (ever) to life, after (this) its death?" But Allah caused him to die for a hundred years, then raised him up (again). He said: "How long did you tarry (thus)?" He said: "(Perhaps) a day or part of a day." He said: "No, you have tarried thus a hundred years; but look at your food and your drink; they show no signs of age; and look at your donkey: and that We may make of you a Sign unto the people, look further at the bones, how We bring them together and clothe them with flesh." When this was shown clearly to him, he said: "I know that Allah has power over all things." 260 Behold! Abraham said: "My Lord! Show me how You give life to the dead." He said: "Do you not then believe?" He said: "Yes! but to satisfy my own understanding." He said: "Take four birds; tame them to come to you; then cut them into pieces and a portion of them on every hill, and call to them: they will come to you (flying) with speed. Then know that Allah is Exalted in Power, Wise."

261 The parable of those who spend their substance in the way of Allah is that of a grain of corn: it grows seven ears, and each ear has a hundred grains. Allah gives manifold increase to whom He pleases: and Allah cares for all and He knows all things. 262 Those who spend their substance in the cause of Allah, and follow not up their gifts with reminders of their generosity or with injury—for them their reward is with their Lord: on them shall be no fear, nor shall they grieve. 263 Kind words and the covering of faults are better than charity followed by injury. Allah is Free of all wants, and He is Most Forbearing. 264 O you who believe! Cancel not your charity by reminders of your generosity or by injury—like those who spend their wealth to be seen of men, but believe neither in Allah nor in the Last Day. They are in parable like a hard, barren rock, on which is a little soil: on it falls heavy rain, which leaves it (just) a bare stone. They will be able to do nothing with what they have earned. And Allah guides not those who reject faith.

265 And the likeness of those who spend their wealth, seeking to please Allah and to strengthen their souls, is as a garden, high and fertile: heavy rain falls on it but makes it yield a double increase of harvest, and if it receives not heavy rain, light moisture suffices it. Allah sees well whatever you do. 266 Does any of you wish that he should have a garden with date-palms and vines and streams flowing underneath, and all kinds of fruit, while he is stricken with old age, and his children are not strong (enough to look after themselves)—that it should be caught in a whirlwind, with fire therein, and be burnt up? Thus does Allah make clear to you (His) Signs; that you may consider.

267 O you who believe! Give of the good things which you have (honourably) earned, and of the fruits of the earth which We have produced for you, and do not even aim at anything which is bad, in order that out of it you may give away something, when you yourselves would not receive it except with closed eyes. And know that Allah is Free of all wants, and Worthy of all praise. 268 The Satan threatens you with poverty and bids you to conduct unseemly. Allah promises you His forgiveness and bounties. And Allah cares for all and He knows all things. 269 He grants wisdom

to whom He pleases; and he to whom wisdom is granted receives indeed a benefit overflowing; but none will grasp the Message except men of understanding.

270.And whatever you spend in charity or devotion, be sure Allah knows it all. But the wrong-doers have no helpers. 271 If you disclose (acts of) charity, even so it is well, but if you conceal them, and make them reach those (really) in need, that is best for you: it will remove from you some of your (stains of) evil. And Allah is well acquainted with what you do. 272 It is not required of you (O Messenger), to set them on the right path, but Allah sets on the right path whom He pleases. Whatever of good you give benefits your own souls, and you shall only do so seeking the "Face" of Allah. Whatever good you give, shall be rendered back to you, and you shall not be dealt with unjustly. 273 (Charity is) for those in need, who, in Allah's cause are restricted (from travel), and cannot move about in the land, seeking (for trade or work): the ignorant man thinks, because of their modesty, that they are free from want. You shall know them by their (unfailing) mark: they beg not importunately from all and sundry. And whatever of good you give, be assured Allah knows it well. 274 Those who (in charity) spend of their goods by night and by day, in secret and in public, have their reward with their Lord: on them shall be no fear, nor shall they grieve.

275 Those who devour usury will not stand except as stands one whom Satan by his touch has driven to madness. That is because they say: "Trade is like usury," but Allah has permitted trade and forbidden usury. Those who after receiving direction from their Lord, desist, shall be pardoned for the past; their case is for Allah (to judge); but those who repeat (the offence) are Companions of the Fire: they will abide therein (for-ever). 276 Allah will deprive usury of all blessing, but will give increase for deeds of charity: for He loves not creatures ungrateful and wicked. 277 Those who believe, and do deeds of righteousness, and establish regular prayers and give zakat (poor-due), will have their reward with their Lord: on them shall be no fear, nor shall they grieve.

278 O you who believe! Fear Allah, and give up what remains of your demand for usury, if you are indeed believers. 279 If you do it not, take notice of war from Allah and His Messenger: but if you turn back, you shall have your capital sums: deal not unjustly, and you shall not be dealt with unjustly. 280 If the debtor is in a difficulty, grant him time till it is easy for him to repay. But if you remit it by way of charity, that is best for you if you only knew. 281 And fear the Day when you shall be brought back to Allah. Then shall every soul be paid what it earned, and none shall be dealt with unjustly.

282 O you who believe! When you deal with each other, in transactions involving future obligations in a fixed period of time, reduce them to writing. Let a scribe write down faithfully as between the parties: let not the scribe refuse to write: as Allah has taught him, so let him write. Let him who incurs the liability dictate, but let him fear his Lord Allah, and not diminish any of what he owes. If the party liable is mentally deficient, or weak, or unable himself to dictate, let his guardian dictate faithfully. And get two witnesses, out of your own men, and if there are not two men, then a man and two women, such as you choose, for witnesses, so that if one of them errs, the other can remind her. The witnesses should not refuse when they are called on (for evidence). Disdain not to reduce to writing (your contract) for a future period, whether it be small or big: it is juster in the sight of Allah, more suitable as evidence, and more convenient to prevent doubts among yourselves. But if it be a transaction which you carry out on the spot among yourselves, there is no blame on you if you reduce it not to writing. But take witnesses whenever you make a commercial contract; and let neither scribe nor witness suffer harm. If you do (such harm), it would be wickedness in you. So fear Allah; for it is Allah that teaches you. And Allah is well acquainted with all things. 283 If you are on a journey, and cannot find a scribe, a pledge with possession (may serve the purpose). And if one of you deposits a thing on trust with another, let the trustee (faithfully) discharge his trust, and let him fear Allah, his Lord. Conceal not evidence; for whoever conceals

it—his heart is tainted with sin. And Allah knows all that you do.

284 To Allah belongs all that is in the heavens and on earth. Whether you show what is in your minds or conceal it, Allah calls you to account for it. He forgives whom He pleases, and punishes whom He pleases. For Allah has power over all things. 285 The Messenger believes in what has been revealed to him from his Lord, as do the men of faith. Each one (of them) believes in Allah, His angels, His books, and His Messengers. "We make no distinction (they say) between one and another of His Messengers." And they say: "We hear, and we obey: (we seek) Your forgiveness, our Lord, and to You is the end of all journeys." 286 On no soul does Allah place a burden greater than it can bear. It gets every good that it earns, and it suffers every ill that it earns. (Pray:) "Our Lord! Condemn us not if we forget or fall into error; our Lord! Lay not on us a burden like that which You did lay on those before us; our Lord! Lay not on us a burden greater than we have strength to bear. Blot out our sins, and grant us forgiveness. Have mercy on us. You are our Protector; help us against those who stand against Faith."

3. THE FAMILY OF 'IMRĀN

In the name of Allah, Most Gracious, Most Merciful.

1 *Alif Lām Mīm.* 2 Allah! There is no god but He, the Living, the Self-Subsisting, Eternal. 3 It is He Who sent down to you (step by step), in truth, the Book, confirming what went before it; and He sent down the Torah (of Moses) and the Gospel (of Jesus) 4 Before this, as a guide to mankind, and He sent down the Criterion (of judgment between right and wrong). Then those who reject faith in the Signs of Allah will suffer the severest chastisement, and Allah is Exalted in Might, Lord of Retribution. 5 From Allah, surely nothing is hidden on earth or in the heavens.

6 He it is Who shapes you in the wombs as He pleases. There is no god but He, the Exalted in Might, the Wise.

7 He it is Who has sent down to you the Book: in it are verses basic or fundamental (of established meaning); they are the foundation of the Book: others are allegorical. But those in whose hearts is perversity follow the part thereof that is allegorical, seeking discord, and searching for its true meanings, but no one knows its true meanings except Allah. And those who are firmly grounded in knowledge say: "We believe in the Book; the whole of it is from our Lord:" and none will grasp the Message except men of understanding. 8 "Our Lord!" (they say), "Let not our hearts deviate now after You have guided us, but grant us mercy from Your own Presence; for You are the Grantor of bounties without measure. 9 "Our Lord! You are He that will gather mankind together against a Day about which there is no doubt; for Allah never fails in His promise."

10 Those who reject Faith—neither their possessions nor their (numerous) progeny will avail them at all against Allah: they are themselves but fuel for the Fire. 11 (Their plight will be) no better than that of the people of Pharaoh, and their predecessors: they denied Our Signs, and Allah called them to account for their sins. For Allah is strict in punishment. 12 Say to those who reject Faith: "Soon will you be vanquished and gathered together and driven into Hell—an evil bed indeed (to lie on)! 13 "There has already been for you a Sign in the two armies that met (in combat): one was fighting in the Cause of Allah, the other resisting Allah; these saw with their own eyes twice their number. But Allah does support with His aid whom He pleases. In this is a warning for such as have eyes to see."

14 Fair in the eyes of men is the love of things they covet: women and sons; heaped-up hoards of gold and silver; horses branded (for blood and excellence); and (wealth of) cattle and well-tilled land. Such are the possessions of this world's life; but in nearness to Allah is the best of the goals (to return to). 15 Say: Shall I give you glad tidings of things far better than those? For the righteous are Gardens in nearness to their Lord, with rivers

flowing beneath; therein is their eternal home; with spouses pure (and holy); and the good pleasure of Allah. For in Allah's sight are (all) His servants— 16 (Namely), those who say: "Our Lord! we have indeed believed: forgive us, then, our sins, and save us from the agony of the Fire;" 17 Those who show patience, firmness and self-control; who are true (in word and deed); who worship devoutly; who spend (in the way of Allah); and who pray for forgiveness in the early hours of the morning.

18 There is no god but He: thus testified Allah, His angels, and those endued with knowledge, standing firm in justice. There is no god but He, the Exalted in Power, the Wise. 19 The Religion before Allah is Islam (submission to His Will): nor did the People of the Book dissent therefrom except through envy of each other, after knowledge had come to them. But if any deny the Signs of Allah, Allah is swift in calling to account. 20 So if they dispute with you. say: "I have submitted my whole self to Allah and so have those who follow me." And say to the People of the Book and to those who are unlearned: "Do you (also) submit yourselves?" If they do, they are in right guidance, but if they turn back, your duty is to convey the Message; and in Allah's sight are (all) His servants. 21 As to those who deny the Signs of Allah and in defiance of right, slay the prophets, and slay those who teach just dealing with mankind, announce to them a grievous chastisement. 22 They are those whose works will bear no fruit in this world and in the Hereafter, nor will they have anyone to help.

23 Have you not turned your vision to those who have been given a portion of the Book? They are invited to the Book of Allah, to settle their dispute, but a party of them turn back and decline (the arbitration). 24 This because they say: "The Fire shall not touch us but for a few numbered days:" for their forgeries deceive them as to their own religion. 25 But how (will they fare) when We gather them together against a Day about which there is no doubt, and each soul will be paid out just what it has earned, without (favour or) injustice? 26 Say: "O Allah! Lord of Power (and Rule), You give Power to whom You please, and You strip off Power from whom You please: You endue with honour whom

You please, and You bring low whom You please: in Your hand is all Good. Surely, over all things You have power. 27 "You cause the Night to gain on the Day, and You cause the Day to gain on the Night; You bring the Living out of the Dead, and You bring the Dead out of the Living; and You give sustenance to whom You please, without measure."

28 Let not the Believers take for friends or helpers unbelievers rather than believers: if any do that, in nothing will there be help from Allah: except by way of precaution, that you may guard yourselves from them. But Allah cautions you (to remember) Himself; for the final goal is to Allah. 29 Say: "Whether you hide what is in your hearts or reveal it, Allah knows it all: He knows what is in the heavens, and what is on earth. And Allah has power over all things. 30 "On the Day when every soul will be confronted with all the good it has done, and all the evil it has done, it will wish there were a great distance between it and its evil. But Allah cautions you (to remember) Himself. And Allah is full of kindness to those that serve Him." 31 Say: "If you do love Allah, follow me: Allah will love you and forgive you your sins: for Allah is Oft-Forgiving, Most Merciful." 32 Say: "Obey Allah and His Messenger": but if they turn back, Allah loves not those who reject Faith.

33 Allah did choose Adam and Noah, the family of Abraham, and the family of 'Imran above all people— 34 Offspring, one of the other: and Allah hears and knows all things. 35 Behold! 'Imran's wife said: "O my Lord! I do dedicate unto You what is in my womb for Your special service: so accept this of me: for You hear and know all things." 36 When she was delivered, she said: "O my Lord! Behold! I am delivered of a female child!" And Allah knew best what she brought forth—"And nowise is the male like the female. I have named her Mary, and I commend her and her offspring to Your protection from Satan, the Rejected." 37 Right graciously did her Lord accept her: He made her grow in purity and beauty: to the care of Zakariyya was she assigned. Every time that he entered (her) chamber to see her, he found her supplied with sustenance. He said: "O Mary! Whence (comes) this to you?" She said: "From Allah: for Allah provides

sustenance to whom He pleases without measure."
38 There did Zakariyya pray to his Lord, saying: "O my Lord!
Grant unto me from You a progeny that is pure: for You are He
that hears prayer! 39 While he was standing in prayer in the
chamber, the angels called unto him: "Allah does give you glad
tidings of Yahya, confirming the truth of a Word from Allah,
and (be besides) noble, chaste, and a Prophet—of the (goodly)
company of the righteous." 40 He said: "O my Lord! How shall
I have a son, seeing I am very old, and my wife is barren?" "Thus,"
was the answer, "Does Allah accomplish what He wills." 41 He
said: "O my Lord! Give me a Sign!" "Your Sign," was the answer,
"Shall be that you shall speak to no man for three days but with
signals. Then celebrate the praises of your Lord again and again,
and glorify Him in the evening and in the morning." 42 Behold!
the angels said: "O Mary! Allah has chosen you and purified
you—chosen you above the women of all nations. 43 "O Mary!
worship your Lord devoutly: prostrate yourself, and bow down
(in prayer) with those who bow down." 44 This is part of the
tidings of the things unseen, which We reveal unto you (O
Messenger!) by inspiration: you were not with them when they
cast lots with arrows, as to which of them should be charged with
the care of Mary: nor were you with them when they disputed
(the point).

45 Behold! the angels said: "O Mary! Allah gives you glad
tidings of a Word from Him: his name will be Christ Jesus, the
son of Mary, held in honour in this world and the Hereafter and
of (the company of) those nearest to Allah; 46 "He shall speak
to the people in childhood and in maturity. And he shall be (of
the company) of the righteous." 47 She said: "O my Lord! How
shall I have a son when no man has touched me?" He said: "Even
so: Allah creates what He wills: when He has decreed a Plan, He
but says to it, 'Be,' and it is! 48 "And Allah will teach him the
Book and Wisdom, the Torah and the Gospel, 49 "And (appoint
him) a Messenger to the Children of Israel, (with this message):
"'I have come to you, with a Sign from your Lord, in that I make
for you out of clay, the figure of a bird, and breathe into it, and
it becomes a bird by Allah's leave: and I heal those born blind,

and the lepers, and I bring the dead, to life, by Allah's leave; and I declare to you what you eat, and what you store in your houses. Surely therein is a Sign for you if you did believe; 50 "'(I have come to you), to attest the Torah which was before me. And to make lawful to you part of what was (before) forbidden to you; I have come to you with a Sign from your Lord. So fear Allah, and obey me.'" 51 "'It is Allah Who is my Lord and your Lord; then worship Him. This is a Way that is straight.'"

52 When Jesus found unbelief on their part he said: "Who will be my helpers to (the work of) Allah?" Said the Disciples: "We are Allah's helpers: we believe in Allah, and do you bear witness that we are Muslims." 53 "Our Lord! we believe in what You have revealed, and we follow the Messenger; then write us down among those who bear witness." 54 And (the unbelievers) plotted and planned, and Allah too planned, and the best of planners is Allah. 55 Behold! Allah said: "O Jesus! I will take you and raise you to Myself and clear you (of the falsehoods) of those who blaspheme; I will make those who follow you superior to those who reject faith, to the Day of Resurrection: then shall you all return unto Me, and I will judge between you of the matters wherein you dispute. 56 "As to those who reject faith, I will punish them with severe chastisement in this world and in the Hereafter, nor will they have anyone to help. 57 "As to those who believe and work righteousness, Allah will pay them (in full) their reward; but Allah loves not those who do wrong. 58 "This is what we rehearse unto you of the Signs and the Message of Wisdom."

59 The similitude of Jesus before Allah is as that of Adam; He created him from dust, then said to him: "Be:" and he was. 60 The Truth (comes) from your Lord alone; so be not of those who doubt. 61 If any one disputes in this matter with you, now after (full) knowledge has come to you, say: "Come! let us gather together—our sons and your sons, our women and your women, ourselves and yourselves: then let us earnestly pray, and invoke the curse of Allah on those who lie!" 62 This is the true account: there is no god except Allah; and Allah—He is indeed the Exalted

in Power, the Wise. 63 But if they turn back, Allah has full knowledge of those who do mischief.

64 Say: "O People of the Book! come to common terms as between us and you: that we worship none but Allah; that we associate no partners with him; that we erect not, from among ourselves, lords and patrons other than Allah." If then they turn back, say you: "Bear witness that we (at least) are Muslims (bowing to Allah's Will)." 65 You People of the Book! Why dispute you about Abraham, when the Torah and the Gospel (Injil) were not revealed till after him? Have you no understanding? 66 Ah! You are those who fell to disputing (even) in matters of which you had some knowledge! But why dispute you in matters of which you have no knowledge? It is Allah Who knows, and you who know not! 67 Abraham was not a Jew nor yet a Christian; but he was true in Faith, and bowed his will to Allah's (which is Islam), and he joined not gods with Allah. 68 Without a doubt, among men, the nearest of kin to Abraham, are those who follow him, as are also this Messenger and those who believe: and Allah is the Protector of those who have faith. 69 It is the wish of a section of the People of the Book to lead you astray. But they shall lead astray (not you), but themselves, and they do not perceive! 70 You People of the Book! Why reject you the Signs of Allah, of which you are (yourselves) witnesses? 71 You People of the Book! Why do you clothe truth with falsehood, and conceal the Truth, while you have knowledge?

72 A section of the People of the Book say: "Believe in the morning what is revealed to the Believers, but reject it at the end of the day; perchance they may (themselves) turn back; 73 "And believe no one unless he follows your religion." Say: "True guidance is the Guidance of Allah: (fear you) lest a revelation be sent to someone (else) like unto that which was sent unto you? Or that those (receiving such revelation) should engage you in argument before your Lord?" Say: "All bounties are in the hand of Allah: He grants them to whom He pleases: and Allah cares for all, and He knows all things." 74 For His Mercy He specially chooses whom He pleases: for Allah is the Lord of bounties unbounded. 75 Among the People of the Book are some who,

if entrusted with a hoard of gold, will (readily) pay it back; others, who, if entrusted with a single silver coin, will not repay it unless you constantly stood demanding, because, they say, "there is no call on us (to keep faith) with these ignorant (Pagans)." But they tell a lie against Allah, and (well) they know it. 76 No — Those that honour their commitment and act aright — surely, Allah loves those who act aright.

77 As for those who sell the faith they owe to Allah and their own plighted word for a small price, they shall have no portion in the Hereafter: nor will Allah (deign to) speak to them or look at them on the Day of Judgment, nor will He cleanse them (of sin): they shall have a grievous Chastisement. 78 There is among them a section who distort the Book with their tongues: (as they read) you would think it is a part of the Book, but it is no part of the Book; and they say, "That is from Allah," but it is not from Allah: it is they who tell a lie against Allah, and (well) they know it! 79 It is not (possible) that a man, to whom is given the Book, and Wisdom, and the Prophetic Office, should say to people: "Be you my worshippers rather than Allah's:" on the contrary (he would say) "Be you worshippers of Him Who is truly the Cherisher of all: for you have taught the Book and you have studied it earnestly." 80 Nor would he instruct you to take angels and prophets for Lords and Patrons. What! would he bid you to unbelief after you have surrendered your will (to Allah in Islam)?

81 Behold! Allah took the Covenant of the Prophets, saying: "I give you a Book and Wisdom; then comes to you a Messenger, confirming what is with you; do you believe in him and render him help." Allah said: "Do you agree, and take this my Covenant as binding on you?" They said: "We agree." He said: "Then bear witness, and I am with you among the witnesses." 82 If any turn back after this, they are perverted transgressors. 83 Do they seek for other than the Religion of Allah? — while all creatures in the heavens and on earth have, willing or unwilling, bowed to His Will (accepted Islam), and to Him shall they all be brought back. 84 Say: "We believe in Allah, and in what has been revealed to us and what was revealed to Abraham, Ishmael, Isaac, Jacob, and the Tribes, and in (the Books) given to Moses, Jesus, and the

Prophets, from their Lord: we make no distinction between one
and another among them, and to Allah do we bow our will (in
Islam)." 85 If anyone desires a religion other than Islam
(submission to Allah), never will it be accepted of him; and in
the Hereafter he will be in the ranks of those who have lost (all
spiritual good). 86 How shall Allah guide those who reject faith
after they accepted it and bore witness that the Messenger was
true and that Clear Signs had come unto them? But Allah guides
not a people unjust. 87 Of such the reward is that on them (rests)
the curse of Allah, of His angels, and of all mankind;
88 In that will they dwell; nor will their punishment be lightened,
nor respite be their (lot)— 89 Except for those that repent (even)
after that, and make amends; for surely Allah is Oft-Forgiving,
Most Merciful. 90 But those who reject faith after they accepted
it, and then go on adding to their defiance of Faith—never will
their repentance be accepted; for they are those who have (of set
purpose) gone astray. 91 As to those who reject faith, and die
rejecting—never would be accepted from any such as much gold
as the earth contains, though they should offer it for ransom. For
such is (in store) a penalty grievous, and they will find no helpers.

92 By no means shall you attain righteousness unless you give
(freely) of that which you love; and whatever you give, of a truth
Allah knows it well. 93 All food was lawful to the Children of
Israel, except what Israel made unlawful for itself, before the
Torah was revealed. Say: "Bring you the Torah and study it, if
you be men of truth." 94 If any, after this, invent a lie and attribute
it to Allah, they are indeed unjust wrong-doers. 95 Say: "Allah
speaks the Truth: follow the religion of Abraham, the sane in
faith; he was not of the Pagans." 96 The first House (of worship)
appointed for men was that at Bakka: full of blessing and of
guidance for all kinds of beings: 97 In it are Signs Manifest; (for
example), the Station of Abraham; whoever enters it attains
security; pilgrimage thereto is a duty men owe to Allah—those
who can afford the journey; but if any deny faith, Allah stands
not in need of any of His creatures. 98 Say: "O People of the Book!
Why reject you the Signs of Allah, when Allah is Himself witness
to all you do?" 99 Say: "O you People of the Book! Why obstruct

you those who believe, from the Path of Allah, seeking to make it crooked, while you were yourselves witnesses (to Allah's Covenant)? But Allah is not unmindful of all that you do."

100 O you who believe! If you listen to a faction among the People of the Book, they would (indeed) render you apostates after you have believed! 101 And how would you deny Faith while unto you are rehearsed the Signs of Allah, and among you lives the Messenger? Whoever holds firmly to Allah will be shown a way that is straight. 102 O you who believe! Fear Allah as He should be feared, and die not except in a state — of Islam. 103 And hold fast, all together, by the Rope which Allah (stretches out for you), and be not divided among yourselves; and remember with gratitude Allah's favour on you; for you were enemies and He joined your hearts in love, so that by His Grace, you became brethren; and you were on the brink of the pit of Fire, and He saved you from it. Thus does Allah make His Signs clear to you: that you may be guided.

104 Let there arise out of you a band of people inviting to all that is good, enjoining what is right, and forbidding what is wrong: they are the ones to attain felicity. 105 Be not like those who are divided amongst themselves and fall into disputations after receiving Clear Signs: for them is a dreadful Chastisement, 106 On the Day when some faces will be (lit up with) white, and some faces will be (in the gloom of) black: to those whose faces will be black, (will be said): "Did you reject Faith after accepting it? Taste then the Chastisement for rejecting Faith." 107 But those whose faces will be (lit with) white — they will be in (the light of) Allah's Mercy: therein to dwell (forever). 108 These are the Signs of Allah: We rehearse them to you in Truth: and Allah means no injustice to any of His creatures. 109 To Allah belongs all that is in the heavens and on earth: To Him do all questions go back (for decision).

110 You are the best of peoples, evolved for mankind, enjoining what is right, forbidding what is wrong, and believing in Allah. If only the People of the Book had faith, it were best for them: among them are some who have faith, but most of them are perverted transgressors. 111 They will do you no harm, barring

a trifling annoyance; if they come out to fight you, they will show you their backs, and no help shall they get. 112 Shame is pitched over them (like a tent) wherever they are found, except when under a Covenant (of protection) from Allah and from men; they draw on themselves wrath from Allah, and pitched over them is (the tent of) destitution. This because they rejected the Signs of Allah, and slew the Prophets in defiance of right; this because they rebelled and transgressed beyond bounds.

113 Not all of them are alike: of the People of the Book are a portion that stand (for the right); they rehearse the Signs of Allah all night long, and they prostrate themselves in adoration. 114 They believe in Allah and the Last Day; they enjoin what is right, and forbid what is wrong; and they hasten (in emulation) in (all) good works: they are in the ranks of the righteous. 115 Of the good that they do, nothing will be rejected of them; for Allah knows well those that do right. 116 Those who reject Faith—neither their possessions nor their (numerous) progeny will avail them at all against Allah: they will be companions of the Fire—dwelling therein (forever). 117 What they spend in the life of this (material) world may be likened to a Wind which brings a nipping frost: it strikes and destroys the harvest of men who have wronged their own souls: it is not Allah that has wronged them, but they wrong themselves.

118 O you who believe! Take not into your intimacy those outside your ranks: they will not fail to corrupt you. They only desire your ruin: rank hatred has already appeared from their mouths: what their hearts conceal is far worse. We have made plain to you the Signs, if you have wisdom. 119 Ah! you are those who love them, but they love you not—though you believe in the whole of the Book, when they meet you, they say, "We believe:" but when they are alone, they bite off the very tips of their fingers at you in their rage. Say: "Perish in your rage; Allah knows well all the secrets of the heart." 120 If anything that is good befalls you, it grieves them; but if some misfortune overtakes you, they rejoice at it. But if you are patient and do right, not the least harm will their cunning do to you; for Allah compasses round about all that they do.

121 Remember that morning you did leave your household (early) to post the Faithful at their stations for battle: and Allah hears and knows all things: 122 Remember two of your parties meditated cowardice; but Allah was their protector, and in Allah should the Faithful (ever) put their trust. 123 Allah had helped you at Badr, when you were a humble little force; then fear Allah; thus may you show your gratitude. 124 Remember you said to the Faithful: "Is it not enough for you that Allah should help you with three thousand angels (specially) sent down? 125 "Yes — if you remain firm, and act aright, even if the enemy should rush here on you in hot haste, your Lord would help you with five thousand angels making a terrific onslaught." 126 Allah made it but a message of hope for you, and an assurance to your hearts: (in any case) there is no help except from Allah, the Exalted, the Wise: 127 That He might cut off a fringe of the Unbelievers or expose them to infamy, and they should then be turned back, frustrated of their purpose. 128 Not for you, (but for Allah), is the decision: whether He turn in mercy to them, or punish them; for they are indeed wrong-doers. 129 To Allah belongs all that is in the heavens and on earth. He forgives whom He pleases and punishes whom He pleases; but Allah is Oft-Forgiving, Most Merciful.

130 O you who believe! Devour not usury, doubled and multiplied; but fear Allah; that you may (really) prosper. 131 Fear the Fire, which is prepared for those who reject Faith: 132 And obey Allah and the Messenger; that you may obtain mercy. 133 Be quick in the race for forgiveness from your Lord, and for a Garden whose width is that (of the whole) of the heavens and of the earth, prepared for the righteous— 134 Those who spend (freely), whether in prosperity, or in adversity; who restrain anger, and pardon (all) men; for Allah loves those who do good; 135 And those who, having done something to be ashamed of, or wronged their own souls, earnestly bring Allah to mind, and ask for forgiveness for their sins—and who can forgive sins except Allah?—and are never obstinate in persisting knowingly in (the wrong) they have done. 136 For such the reward is forgiveness from their Lord, and Gardens with rivers flowing underneath—

an eternal dwelling: how excellent a recompense for those who work (and strive)! 137 Many were the Ways of Allah that have passed away before you: travel through the earth, and see what was the end of those who rejected Truth. 138 Here is a plain statement to men, a guidance and instruction to those who fear Allah!

139 So lose not heart, nor fall into despair: for you must gain mastery if you are true in Faith. 140 If a wound has touched you, be sure a similar wound has touched the others. Such days (of varying fortunes) We give to men and men by turns: that Allah may know those that believe, and that He may take to Himself from your ranks martyr-witnesses (to Truth). And Allah loves not those that do wrong. 141 Allah's object also is to purge those that are true in Faith and to deprive of blessing those that resist Faith. 142 Did you think that you would enter Heaven without Allah testing those of you who fought hard (in His Cause) and remained steadfast? 143 You did indeed wish for death before you encountered it: now you have seen it with your own eyes, (and you flinch!).

144 Muhammad is no more than a Messenger: many were the Messengers that passed away before him. If he died or were slain, would you then turn back on your heels? If any did turn back on his heels, not the least harm would he do to Allah; but Allah (on the other hand) would swiftly reward those who (served Him) with gratitude. 145 Nor can a soul die except by Allah's leave, the term being fixed as by writing. If any do desire a reward in this life, We shall give it to him; and if any do desire a reward in the Hereafter, We shall give it to him. And swiftly shall We reward those that (serve us with) gratitude. 146 How many of the Prophets fought (in Allah's way), and with them (fought) large bands of godly men? But they never lost heart if they met with disaster in Allah's way, nor did they weaken (in will) nor gave in. And Allah loves those who are firm and steadfast. 147 All that they said was: "Our Lord! Forgive us our sins and anything we may have done that transgressed our duty: establish our feet firmly, and help us against those that resist Faith." 148 And Allah

gave them a reward in this world, and the excellent reward of the Hereafter. For Allah loves those who do good.

149 O you who believe! If you obey the unbelievers, they will drive you back on your heels, and you will turn back (from Faith) to your own loss. 150 No, Allah is your Protector, and He is the best of helpers. 151 Soon shall We cast terror into the hearts of the unbelievers, for that they joined others with Allah, for which He had sent no authority: their abode will be the Fire: and evil is the home of the wrongdoers! 152 Allah did indeed fulfil His promise to you when you with His permission were about to annihilate your enemy—until you flinched and fell to disputing about the order, and disobeyed it after He brought you in sight (of the Booty) which you covet. Among you are some that hanker after this world and some that desire the Hereafter. Then did He divert you from your foes in order to test you. But He forgave you: for Allah is full of grace to those who believe. 153 Behold! you were climbing up the high ground, without even casting a side glance at any one, and the Messenger in your rear was calling you back. There did Allah give you one distress after another by way of requital, to teach you not to grieve for (the booty) that had escaped you and for (the ill) that had befallen you. For Allah is well aware of all that you do.

154 After (the excitement) of the distress, He sent down calm on a band of you overcome with slumber, while another band was stirred to anxiety by their own feelings, moved by wrong suspicions of Allah—suspicions due to Ignorance. They said: "Have we a hand in this affair?" Say you: "Indeed, this affair is wholly Allah's." They hide in their minds what they dare not reveal to you. They say (to themselves): "If we had had anything to do with this affair, we should not have been in the slaughter here." Say: "Even if you had remained in your homes, those for whom death was decreed would certainly have gone forth to the place of their death." But (all this was) that Allah might test what is in your breasts and purge what is in your hearts. For Allah knows well the secrets of your hearts. 155 Those of you who turned back on the day the two hosts met—it was Satan who caused them

to fail, because of some (evil) they had done. But Allah has blotted out (their fault): for Allah is Oft-Forgiving, Most Forbearing.

156 O you who believe! Be not like the unbelievers, who say of their brethren, when they are travelling through the earth or engaged in fighting: "If they had stayed with us, they would not have died, or been slain." This that Allah may make it a cause of sighs and regrets in their hearts. It is Allah that gives Life and Death, and Allah sees well all that you do. 157 And if you are slain, or die, in the way of Allah, forgiveness and mercy from Allah are far better than all they could amass. 158 And if you die, or are slain, lo! it is unto Allah that you are brought together. 159 It is part of the Mercy of Allah that you deal gently with them. Were you severe or harsh-hearted, they would have broken away from about you: so pass over (their faults), and ask for (Allah's) forgiveness for them; and consult them in affairs (of moment). Then, when you have taken a decision, put your trust in Allah. For Allah loves those who put their trust (in Him). 160 If Allah helps you, none can overcome you: if He forsakes you, who is there, after that, that can help you? In Allah, then, let Believers put their trust.

161 No prophet could (ever) be false to his trust. If any person is so false, He shall, on the Day of Judgment, restore what he misappropriated; then shall every soul receive its due — whatever it earned — and none shall be dealt with unjustly. 162 Is the man who follows the good pleasure of Allah like the man who draws on himself the wrath of Allah, and whose abode is in Hell? — A woeful refuge! 163 They are in varying grades in the sight of Allah, and Allah sees well all that they do. 164 Allah did confer a great favour on the believers when He sent among them a Messenger from among themselves, rehearsing unto them the Signs of Allah, purifying them, and instructing them in Scripture and Wisdom, while, before that, they had been in manifest error.

165 What! When a single disaster smites you, although you smote (your enemies) with one twice as great, do you say? — "Whence is this?" Say (to them): "It is from yourselves: for Allah has power over all things." 166 What you suffered on the day the two armies

met, was with the leave of Allah, in order that He might test the Believers— 167 And the Hypocrites also. These were told: "Come, fight in the way of Allah, or (at least) drive (the foe from your city)." They said: "Had we known how to fight, we should certainly have followed you." They were that day nearer to unbelief than to Faith, saying with their lips what was not in their hearts. But Allah has full knowledge of all they conceal. 168 (They are) the ones that say, (of their brethren slain), while they themselves sit (at ease): "If only they had listened to us, they would not have been slain." Say: "Avert death from your own selves, if you speak the truth."

169 Think not of those who are slain in Allah's way as dead. No, they live, finding their sustenance from their Lord; 170 They rejoice in the Bounty provided by Allah: and with regard to those left behind, who have not yet joined them (in their bliss), the (Martyrs) glory in the fact that on them is no fear, nor have they (cause to) grieve. 171 They glory in the Grace and the Bounty from Allah, and in the fact that Allah suffers not the reward of the Faithful to be lost (in the least). 172 Of those who answered the call of Allah and the Messenger, even after being wounded, those who do right and refrain from wrong have a great reward— 173 Those to whom men said, "A great army is gathering against you:" so fear them: but it (only) increased their Faith: they said: "For us Allah suffices, and He is the best Disposer of affairs." 174 And they returned with Grace and Bounty from Allah: no harm ever touched them: for they followed the good pleasure of Allah: and Allah is the Lord of bounties unbounded. 175 It is only Satan that suggests to you the fear of his votaries : be you not afraid of them, but fear Me, if you have Faith.

176 Let not those grieve you who rush headlong into unbelief: not the least harm will they do to Allah: Allah's Plan is that He will give them no portion in the Hereafter, but a severe punishment. 177 Those who purchase unbelief at the price of faith—not the least harm will they do to Allah, but they will have a grievous punishment. 178 Let not the unbelievers think that Our respite to them is good for themselves: We grant them respite that they may grow in their iniquity : but they will have a shameful

punishment. 179 Allah will not leave the believers in the state in which you are now, until He separates what is evil from what is good. Nor will He disclose to you the secrets of the Unseen. But He chooses of His Messengers (for the purpose) whom He pleases. So believe in Allah and His Messengers: and if you believe and do right, you have a reward without measure.

180 And let not those who covetously withhold of the gifts which Allah has given them of His Grace, think that it is good for them: no, it will be the worse for them: soon shall the things which they covetously withheld be tied to their necks like a twisted collar, on the Day of Judgment. To Allah belongs the heritage of the heavens and the earth; and Allah is well-acquainted with all that you do. 181 Allah has heard the taunt of those who say: "Truly, Allah is indigent and we are rich!" — We shall certainly record their word and (their act) of slaying the Prophets in defiance of right, and We shall say: "Taste you the Chastisement of the Scorching Fire! 182 "This is because of the (unrighteous deeds) which your hands sent on before you: for Allah never harms those who serve Him." 183 They (also) said: "Allah took our promise not to believe in a Messenger unless He showed us a sacrifice consumed by Fire (from heaven)." Say: "There came to you Messengers before me, with Clear Signs and even with what you ask for: why then did you slay them, if you speak the truth?" 184 Then if they reject you, so were rejected Messengers before you, who came with Clear Signs, and the Scriptures, and the Book of Enlightenment. 185 Every soul shall have a taste of death: and only on the Day of Judgment shall you be paid your full recompense. Only he who is saved far from the Fire and admitted to the Garden will have succeeded: for the life of this world is but goods and chattels of deception.

186 You shall certainly be tried and tested in your possessions and in your personal selves; and you shall certainly hear much that will grieve you, from those who received the Book before you and from those who worship many gods. But if you persevere patiently, and guard against evil — then that will be a determining factor in all affairs. 187 And remember Allah took a Covenant from the People of the Book, to make it known and clear to

mankind, and not to hide it; but they threw it away behind their backs, and purchased with it some miserable gain! And vile was the bargain they made! 188 Think not that those who exult in what they have brought about, and love to be praised for what they have not done — think not that they can escape the Chastisement. For them is a Chastisement grievous indeed. 189 To Allah belongs the dominion of the heavens and the earth; and Allah has power over all things.

190 Behold! in the creation of the heavens and the earth, and the alternation of Night and Day — there are indeed Signs for men of understanding — 191 Men who celebrate the praises of Allah, standing, sitting, and lying down on their sides, and contemplate the (wonders of) creation in the heavens and the earth, (with the thought): "Our Lord! not for nothing have You created (all) this! Glory to You! Give us salvation from the Torment of the Fire. 192 "Our Lord! any whom You do admit to the Fire, truly You cover with shame, and never will wrong-doers find any helpers! 193 "Our Lord! we have heard the call of one calling (us) to Faith, 'Believe you in the Lord,' and we have believed. Our Lord! Forgive us our sins, blot out from us our iniquities, and take to Thyself our souls in the company of the righteous. 194 "Our Lord! Grant us what You did promise unto us through Your Prophets, and save us from shame on the Day of Judgment: for You never break Your promise."

195 And their Lord has accepted of them, and answered them: "Never will I suffer to be lost the work of any of you, be he male or female: You are members, one of another: those who have left their homes, or been driven out therefrom, or suffered harm in My Cause, or fought and were slain— surely, I will blot out from them their iniquities, and admit them into Gardens with rivers flowing beneath; a reward from the Presence of Allah, and from His Presence is the best of rewards." 196 Let not the strutting about of the unbelievers through the land deceive you: 197 Little is it for enjoyment: their ultimate abode is Hell: what an evil bed (to lie on)! 198 On the other hand, for those who fear their Lord, are Gardens, with rivers flowing beneath; therein are they to dwell (for ever) — a gift from the Presence of Allah; and that which is

in the Presence of Allah is the best (bliss) for the righteous.
199 And there are, certainly, among the People of the Book, those
who believe in Allah, in the revelation to you, and in the revelation
to them, bowing in humility to Allah: they will not sell the Signs
of Allah for a miserable gain! For them is a reward with their
Lord, and Allah is swift in account. 200 O you who believe!
Persevere in patience and constancy; vie in such perseverance;
strengthen each other; and fear Allah; that you may prosper.

4. THE WOMEN

In the name of Allah, Most Gracious, Most Merciful.

1 O mankind! fear your Guardian-Lord, who created you from
a single Person, created, of like nature, his mate, and from them
twain scattered (like seeds) countless men and women; fear Allah,
through Whom You demand your mutual (rights), and (reverence)
the wombs (that bore you): for Allah ever watches over you.
2 To orphans restore their property (when they reach their age),
nor substitute (your) worthless things for (their) good ones; and
devour not their substance (by mixing it up) with your own. For
this is indeed a great sin. 3 If you fear that you shall not be able
to deal justly with the orphans, marry women of your choice, two
or three or four; but if you fear that you shall not be able to deal
justly (with them), then only one, or (a captive) that your right
hands possess. that will be more suitable, to prevent you from
doing injustice. 4 And give the women (on marriage) their dower
as a free gift; but if they, of their own good pleasure, remit any
part of it to you, take it and enjoy it with right good cheer.

5 To those weak of understanding make not over your property,
which Allah has made a means of support for you, but feed and
clothe them therewith, and speak to them words of kindness and
justice. 6 Make trial of orphans until they reach the age of
marriage; if then you find sound judgment in them, release their
property to them; but consume it not wastefully, nor in haste

against their growing up. If the guardian is affluent, let him claim no remuneration, but if he is poor, let him have for himself what is just and reasonable. When you release their property to them, take witnesses in their presence: but all-sufficient is Allah in taking account. 7 From what is left by parents and those nearest related there is a share for men and a share for women, whether the property be small or large — a determinate share. 8 But if at the time of division other relatives, or orphans, or poor, are present, feed them out of the (property), and speak to them words of kindness and justice. 9 Let those (disposing of an estate) have the same fear in their minds as they would have for their own if they had left a helpless family behind: let them fear Allah, and speak words of appropriate (comfort). 10 Those who unjustly eat up the property of orphans, eat up a Fire into their own bodies: They will soon be enduring a blazing Fire!

11 Allah (thus) directs you as regards your children's (inheritance): to the male, a portion equal to that of two females: if only daughters, two or more, their share is two-thirds of the inheritance; if only one, her share is a half. For parents, a sixth share of the inheritance to each, if the deceased left children; if no children, and the parents are the (only) heirs, the mother has a third; if the deceased left brothers (or sisters) the mother has a sixth. (The distribution in all cases is) after the payment of legacies and debts. You know not whether your parents or your children are nearest to you in benefit. These are settled portions ordained by Allah; and Allah is All-knowing, All-wise. 12 In what your wives leave, your share is a half, if they leave no child; but if they leave a child, you get a fourth; after payment of legacies and debts. In what you leave, their share is a fourth, if you leave no child; but if you leave a child, they get an eighth; after payment of legacies and debts. If the man or woman whose inheritance is in question, has left neither ascendants nor descendants, but has left a brother or a sister, each one of the two gets a sixth; but if more than two, they share in a third after payment of legacies and debts so that no loss is caused (to any one). Thus is it ordained by Allah; and Allah is All-knowing, most Forbearing. 13 Those are limits set by Allah: those who obey Allah and His Messenger

will be admitted to Gardens with rivers flowing beneath, to abide therein (forever); and that will be the supreme achievement. 14 But those who disobey Allah and His Messenger and transgress His limits will be admitted to a Fire, to abide therein: and they shall have a humiliating punishment.

15 If any of your women are guilty of lewdness , take the evidence of four (reliable) witnesses from amongst you against them; and if they testify, confine them to houses until death do claim them, or Allah ordain for them some (other) way. 16 If two men among you are guilty of lewdness, punish them both. If they repent and amend, leave them alone; for Allah is Oft-Returning, Most Merciful. 17 Allah accepts the repentance of those who do evil in ignorance and repent soon afterwards; to them will Allah turn in mercy: for Allah is full of knowledge and wisdom. 18 Of no effect is the repentance of those who continue to do evil, until Death faces one of them, and he says, "Now have I repented indeed;" Nor of those who die rejecting Faith: for them have We prepared a punishment most grievous.

19 O you who believe! You are forbidden to inherit women against their will. Nor should you treat them with harshness, that you may take away part of the dower you have given them— except where they have been guilty of open lewdness; on the contrary live with them on a footing of kindness and equity. If you take a dislike to them it may be that you dislike a thing, and Allah brings about through it a great deal of good. 20 But if you decide to take one wife in place of another, even if you had given the latter a whole treasure for dower, take not the least bit of it back: would you take it by slander and a manifest wrong? 21 And how could you take it when you have gone in unto each other, and they have taken from you a solemn covenant? 22 And marry not women whom your fathers married—except what is past: it was shameful and odious—an abominable custom indeed.

23 Prohibited to you (for marriage) are: your mothers, daughters, sisters; father's sisters, mother's sisters; brother's daughters, sister's daughters; foster-mothers (who gave you suck), foster-sisters; your wives' mothers; your step-daughters

under your guardianship, born of your wives to whom you have gone in—no prohibition if you have not gone in; (those who have been) wives of your sons proceeding from your loins; and two sisters in wedlock at one and the same time, except for what is past; for Allah is Oft-Forgiving, Most Merciful. 24 Also (prohibited are) women already married, except those whom your right hands possess: thus has Allah ordained (prohibitions) against you: except for these, all others are lawful, provided you seek (them in marriage) with gifts from your property—desiring chastity, not lust. Seeing that you derive benefit from them, give them their dowers (at least) as prescribed; but if, after a dower is prescribed, you agree mutually (to vary it), there is no blame on you, and Allah is All-knowing, All-wise. 25 If any of you have not the means wherewith to wed free believing women, they may wed believing girls from among those whom your right hands possess: and Allah has full knowledge about your Faith. You are one from another: wed them with the leave of their owners, and give them their dowers, according to what is reasonable: they should be chaste, not lustful, nor taking paramours : when they are taken in wedlock, if they fall into shame, their punishment is half that for free women. This (permission) is for those among you who fear sin; but it is better for you that you practise self-restraint. And Allah is Oft-Forgiving, Most Merciful.

26 Allah does wish to make clear to you and to show you the ordinances of those before you; and (He does wish to) turn to you (in Mercy): and Allah is All-knowing, All-wise. 27 Allah does wish to turn to you, but the wish of those who follow their lusts is that you should turn away (from Him)—far, far away. 28 Allah does wish to lighten your (difficulties): for man was created weak (in flesh).

29 O you who believe! Eat not up your property—among yourselves in vanities: but let there be amongst you traffic and trade by mutual good-will: nor kill (or destroy) yourselves: for surely Allah has been to you Most Merciful! 30 If any do that in rancour and injustice—soon shall We cast them into the Fire: and easy it is for Allah. 31 If you (but) eschew the most heinous of the things which you are forbidden to do, we shall expel out

of you all the evil in you, and admit you to a Gate of great honour. 32 And in no wise covet those things in which Allah has bestowed His gifts more freely on some of you than on others: to men is allotted what they earn, and to women what they earn: but ask Allah of His bounty. For Allah has full knowledge of all things. 33 To (benefit) everyone, we have appointed sharers and heirs to property left by parents and relatives. To those, also, to whom your right hand was pledged, give their due portion. For truly Allah is witness to all things.

34 Men are the protectors and maintainers of women, because Allah has given the one more (strength) than the other, and because they support them from their means. Therefore, the righteous women are devoutly obedient, and guard in (the husband's) absence what Allah would have them guard. As to those women on whose part you fear disloyalty and ill-conduct, admonish them (first), (next), refuse to share their beds, (and last) chastise them (lightly); but if they return to obedience, seek not against them means (of annoyance): for Allah is Most High, Great (above you all). 35 If you fear a breach between them twain, appoint (two) arbiters, one from his family, and the other from hers; if they wish for peace, Allah will cause their reconciliation: for Allah has full knowledge, and is acquainted with all things.

36 Serve Allah, and join not any partners with Him; and do good—to parents, kinsfolk, orphans, those in need, neighbours who are near, neighbours who are strangers, the Companion by your side, the wayfarer (you meet), and what your right hands possess: for Allah loves not the arrogant, the vainglorious; 37 (Nor) those who are niggardly or enjoin niggardliness on others, or hide the bounties which Allah has bestowed on them; for We have prepared, for those who resist Faith, a punishment that steeps them in contempt; 38 Nor those who spend of their substance, to be seen of men, but have no faith in Allah and the Last Day: if any take Satan for their intimate, what a dreadful intimate he is! 39 And what burden were it on them if they had faith in Allah and in the Last Day, and they spent out of what Allah has given them for sustenance? For Allah has full knowledge of them. 40 Allah is never unjust in the least degree:

if there is any good (done), He doubles it, and gives from His own presence a great reward.

41 How then if We brought from each People a witness, and We brought you as a witness against these people! 42 On that day those who reject Faith and disobey the Messenger will wish that the earth were made one with them: but never will they hide a single fact from Allah! 43 O you who believe! Approach not prayers with a mind befogged, until you can understand all that you say—nor in a state of ceremonial impurity (except when travelling on the road), until after washing your whole body. If you are ill, or on a journey, or one of you comes from offices of nature, or you have been in contact with women, and you find no water, then take for yourselves clean sand or earth, and rub therewith your faces and hands. For Allah does blot out sins and forgive again and again.

44 Have you not turned your vision to those who were given a portion of the Book? They traffic on error, and wish that you should lose the right path. 45 But Allah has full knowledge of your enemies: Allah is enough for a Protector, and Allah is enough for a Helper. 46 Of the Jews there are those who displace words from their (right) places, and say: "We hear and we disobey;" and "Hear what is not heard;" and "Rā'inā (words of ambiguous import);" with a twist of their tongues and a slander to Faith. If only they had said: "We hear and we obey;" and "Do hear;" and "Do look at us;" it would have been better for them, and more proper; but Allah has cursed them for their Unbelief; and but few of them will believe.

47 O you People of the Book! Believe in what We have (now) revealed, confirming what was (already) with you, before We change the face and fame of some (of you) beyond all recognition, and turn them hindwards, or curse them as We cursed the Sabbath-breakers, for the decision of Allah must be carried out. 48 Allah forgives not that partners should be set up with Him; but He forgives anything else, to whom he pleases; to set up partners with Allah is to devise a sin Most heinous indeed. 49 Have you not turned your vision to those who claim sanctity for themselves?

No—but Allah does sanctify whom He pleases. But never will they fail to receive justice in the least little thing. 50 Behold! how they invent a lie against Allah! But that by itself is a manifest sin!

51 Have you not turned your vision to those who were given a portion of the Book? They believe in Sorcery and Evil, and say to the Unbelievers that they are better guided in the (right) way than the Believers! 52 They are (men) whom Allah has cursed: and those whom Allah has cursed, you will find, have no one to help. 53 Have they a share in dominion or power? Behold, they give not a farthing to their fellow-men. 54 Or do they envy mankind for what Allah has given them of His bounty? But We had already given the people of Abraham the Book and Wisdom, and conferred upon them a great kingdom. 55 Some of them believed, and some of them averted their faces from him: and enough is Hell for a burning fire. 56 Those who reject our Signs, We shall soon cast into the Fire: as often as their skins are roasted through, we shall change them for fresh skins, that they may taste the chastisement: for Allah is exalted in Power, Wise. 57 But those who believe and do deeds of righteousness, We shall soon admit to Gardens, with rivers flowing beneath—their eternal home: Therein shall they have companions pure and holy: We shall admit them to shades, cool and ever deepening.

58 Allah does command you to render back your Trusts to those to whom they are due; and when you judge between man and man, to judge with justice: surely, how excellent is the teaching which He gives you! For Allah is He Who hears and sees all things. 59 O you who believe! Obey Allah, and obey the Messenger, and those charged with authority among you. If you differ in anything among yourselves, refer it to Allah and His Messenger, If you do believe in Allah and the Last Day: that is best, and most suitable for final determination. 60 Have you not turned your vision to those who declare that they believe in the revelations that have come to you and to those before you? Their (real) wish is to resort together for judgment (in their disputes) to Satan, though they were ordered to reject him. But Satan's wish is to lead them astray far away (from the Right). 61 When it is said to them: "Come

to what Allah has revealed, and to the Messenger:" You see the Hypocrites avert their faces from you in disgust. 62 How then, when they are seized by misfortune, because of the deeds which their hands have sent forth; then they come to you, swearing by Allah: "We meant no more than goodwill and conciliation!" 63 Those men — Allah knows what is in their hearts; so keep clear of them, but admonish them, and speak to them a word to reach their very souls.

64 We sent not a Messenger, but to be obeyed, in accordance with the Will of Allah. If they had only, when they were unjust to themselves, come unto you and asked Allah's forgiveness, and the Messenger had asked forgiveness for them, they would have found Allah indeed Oft-Returning, Most Merciful. 65 But no, by the Lord, they can have no (real) Faith, until they make you judge in all disputes between them, and find in their souls no resistance against your decisions, but accept them with the fullest conviction. 66 If We had ordered them to sacrifice their lives or to leave their homes, very few of them would have done it: but if they had done what they were (actually) told, it would have been best for them, and would have gone farthest to strengthen their (faith); 67 And We should then have given them from Our Presence a great reward; 68 And We should have shown them the Straight Way. 69 All who obey Allah and the Messenger are in the company of those on whom is the Grace of Allah — of the Prophets (who teach), the Sincere (lovers of Truth), the Witnesses (who testify), and the Righteous (who do good): ah! what a beautiful fellowship! 70 Such is the Bounty from Allah: and sufficient is it that Allah knows all.

71 O you who believe! Take your precautions, and either go forth in parties or go forth all together. 72 There are certainly among you men who would tarry behind: if a misfortune befalls you, they say: "Allah did favour us in that we were not present among them." 73 But if good fortune comes to you from Allah, they would be sure to say — as if there had never been ties of affection between you and them — "Oh! I wish I had been with them; a fine thing should I then have made of it!" 74 Let those fight in the cause of Allah who sell the life of this world for the

Hereafter. To him who fights in the cause of Allah — whether he is slain or gets victory — soon shall We give him a reward of great (value). 75 And why should you not fight in the cause of Allah and of those who, being weak, are ill-treated (and oppressed)? — men, women, and children, whose cry is: "Our Lord! Rescue us from this town, whose people are oppressors; and raise for us from You one who will protect; and raise for us from You one who will help!" 76 Those who believe fight in the cause of Allah, and those who reject Faith fight in the cause of Evil: so fight you against the friends of Satan: feeble indeed is the cunning of Satan.

77 Have you not turned your vision to those who were told to hold back their hands (from fight) but establish regular prayers and spend in regular charity? when (at length) the order for fighting was issued to them, behold! a section of them feared men as — or even more than — they should have feared Allah: they said: "Our Lord! Why have You ordered us to fight? Would You not grant us respite to our (natural) term, near (enough)?" Say: "Short is the enjoyment of this world: the Hereafter is the best for those who do right: never will you be dealt with unjustly in the very least! 78 "Wherever you are, death will find you out, even if you are in towers built up strong and high!" If some good befalls them, they say, "This is from Allah;" but if evil, they say, "This is from you" (O Prophet). Say: "All things are from Allah." But what has come to these people, that they fail to understand a single fact? 79 Whatever good, (O man!) happens to you, is from Allah; but whatever evil happens to you, is from your (own) soul. And We have sent you as a Messenger to (instruct) mankind. And enough is Allah for a witness.

80 He who obeys the Messenger, obeys Allah: but if any turn away, we have not sent you to watch over their (evil deeds). 81 They have "Obedience" on their lips; but when they leave you, a section of them meditate all night on things very different from what you tell them. But Allah records their nightly (plots): so keep clear of them, and put your trust in Allah, and enough is Allah as a disposer of affairs. 82 Do they not consider the Qur'ān (with care)? Had it been from other than Allah, they would surely have found therein much discrepancy. 83 When there comes to

them some matter touching (Public) safety or fear, they divulge it. If they had only referred it to the Messenger, or to those charged with authority among them, the proper investigators would have tested it from them (direct). Were it not for the Grace and Mercy of Allah unto you, all but a few of you would have fallen into the clutches of Satan.

84 Then fight in Allah's cause — you are held responsible only for yourself — and rouse the Believers. It may be that Allah will restrain the fury of the unbelievers; for Allah is the strongest in might and in punishment. 85 Whoever recommends and helps a good cause becomes a partner therein: and whoever recommends and helps an evil cause, shares in its burden: and Allah has power over all things. 86 When a (courteous) greeting is offered you, meet it with a greeting still more courteous, or (at least) of equal courtesy. Allah takes careful account of all things. 87 Allah! There is no god but He: of a surety He will gather you together against the Day of Judgment, about which there is no doubt. And whose word can be truer than Allah's?

88 Why should you be divided into two parties about the Hypocrites? Allah has upset them for their (evil) deeds. Would you guide those whom Allah has thrown out of the Way? For those whom Allah has thrown out of the Way, never shall you find the Way. 89 They but wish that you should reject Faith, as they do, and thus be on the same footing (as they): but take not friends from their ranks until they flee in the way of Allah (from what is forbidden). But if they turn renegades , seize them and slay them wherever you find them; and (in any case) take no friends or helpers from their ranks; 90 Except those who join a group between whom and you there is a treaty (of peace), or those who approach you with hearts restraining them from fighting you as well as fighting their own people. If Allah had pleased, He could have given them power over you, and they would have fought you: therefore, if they withdraw from you but fight you not, and (instead) send you (guarantees of) peace, then Allah has opened no way for you (to war against them). 91 Others you will find that wish to gain your confidence as well as that of their people: every time they are sent back to temptation, they succumb

thereto: if they withdraw not from you nor give you (guarantees) of peace besides restraining their hands, seize them and slay them wherever you get them: in their case we have provided you with a clear argument against them.

92 Never should a believer kill a Believer; but (if it so happens) by mistake, (compensation is due): if one (so) kills a believer, it is ordained that he should free a believing slave, and pay compensation to the deceased's family, unless they remit it freely. If the deceased belonged to a people at war with you, and he was a believer, the freeing of a believing slave (is enough). If he belonged to a people with whom you have treaty of mutual alliance, compensation should be paid to his family, and a believing slave be freed. For those who find this beyond their means, (is prescribed) a fast for two months running: by way of repentance to Allah: for Allah has all knowledge and all wisdom. 93 If a man kills a believer intentionally, his recompense is Hell, to abide therein (for ever): and the wrath and the curse of Allah are upon him, and a dreadful chastisement is prepared for him.

94 O you who believe! When you go abroad in the cause of Allah, investigate carefully, and say not to anyone who offers you a salutation: "You are none of a believer!"—coveting the perishable goods of this life: with Allah are profits and spoils abundant. Even thus were you yourselves before, till Allah conferred on you His favours: therefore carefully investigate. For Allah is well aware of all that you do. 95 Not equal are those believers who sit (at home) and receive no hurt, and those who strive in the cause of Allah with their goods and their persons. Allah has granted a grade higher to those who strive with their goods and persons than to those who sit (at home). Unto all (in Faith) has Allah promised good: but those who strive has He distinguished above those who sit (at home) by a special reward— 96 Ranks specially bestowed by Him, and Forgiveness and Mercy. For Allah is Oft-Forgiving, Most Merciful.

97 When angels take the souls of those who die in sin against their souls, they say: "In what (plight) were you?" They reply: "Weak and oppressed were we in the earth." They say. "Was not

the earth of Allah spacious enough for you to move yourselves away (from evil)?" Such men will find their abode in Hell— What an evil refuge!— 98 Except those who are (really) weak and oppressed—men, women, and children—who have no means in their power, nor (a guidepost) to direct their way. 99 For these, there is hope that Allah will forgive: for Allah does blot out (sins) and forgive again and again. 100 He who forsakes his home in the cause of Allah, finds in the earth many a refuge, wide and spacious: should he die as a refugee from home for Allah and His Messenger, his reward becomes due and sure with Allah: and Allah is Oft-Forgiving, Most Merciful.

101 When you travel through the earth, there is no blame on you if you shorten your prayers, for fear the unbelievers may attack you: for the unbelievers are unto you open enemies. 102 When you (O Messenger) are with them, and stand to lead them in prayer, let one party of them stand up (in prayer) with you, taking their arms with them: when they finish their prostrations, let them take their position in the rear. And let the other party come up which has not yet prayed—and let them pray with you, taking all precautions, and bearing arms: the unbelievers wish, if you were negligent of your arms and your baggage, to assault you in a single rush. But there is no blame on you if you put away your arms because of the inconvenience of rain or because you are ill; but take (every) precaution for yourselves. For the unbelievers Allah has prepared a humiliating punishment. 103 When you pass (congregational) prayers, celebrate Allah's praises, standing, sitting down, or lying down on your sides; but when you are free from danger, set up regular Prayers: for such prayers are enjoined on Believers at stated times. 104 And slacken not in following up the enemy: if you are suffering hardships, they are suffering similar hardships; but you have hope from Allah, while they have none. And Allah is full of knowledge and wisdom.

105 We have sent down to you the Book in truth, that you might judge between men, as guided by Allah: so be not (used) as an advocate by those who betray their trust; 106 But seek the forgiveness of Allah; for Allah is Oft-Forgiving, Most Merciful.

107 Contend not on behalf of such as betray their own souls; for Allah loves not one given to perfidy and crime. 108 They may hide (their crimes) from men, but they cannot hide (them) from Allah, while He is with them when they plot by night, in words that He cannot approve: and Allah does compass round all that they do.

109 Ah! These are the sort of men on whose behalf you may contend in this world; but who will contend with Allah on their behalf on the Day of Judgment, or who will carry their affairs through? 110 If any one does evil or wrongs his own soul, but afterwards seeks Allah's forgiveness, he will find Allah Oft-Forgiving, Most Merciful. 111 And if any one earns sin, he earns it against his own soul: for Allah is full of knowledge and wisdom. 112 But if any one earns a fault or a sin and throws it on to one that is innocent, he carries (on himself) (both) a falsehood and a flagrant sin. 113 But for the Grace of Allah to you and His Mercy, a party of them would certainly have plotted to lead you astray. But (in fact) they will only lead their own souls astray, and to you they can do no harm in the least. For Allah has sent down to you the Book and Wisdom and taught you what you knew not (before): and great is the Grace of Allah unto you.

114 In most of their secret talks there is no good: but if one exhorts to a deed of charity or justice or conciliation between men, (secrecy is permissible): to him who does this, seeking the good pleasure of Allah, We shall soon give a reward of the highest (value). 115 If anyone contends with the Messenger even after guidance has been plainly conveyed to him, and follows a path other than that becoming to men of Faith, We shall leave him in the path he has chosen, and land him in Hell—what an evil refuge!

116 Allah forgives not (the sin of) joining other gods with Him; but He forgives whom He pleases other sins than this: one who joins other gods with Allah, has strayed far, far away (from the Right). 117 (The Pagans), leaving Him, call but upon female deities: they call but upon Satan the persistent rebel! 118 Allah did curse him, but he said: "I will take of Your servants a portion

marked off; 119 "I will mislead them, and I will create in them false desires; I will order them to slit the ears of cattle, and to deface the (fair) nature created by Allah." Whoever, forsaking Allah, takes Satan for a friend, has of a surety suffered a loss that is manifest. 120 Satan makes them promises, and creates in them false desires; but Satan's promises are nothing but deception. 121 They (his dupes) will have their dwelling in Hell, and from it they will find no way of escape. 122 But those who believe and do deeds of righteousness -- we shall soon admit them to Gardens, with rivers flowing beneath -- to dwell therein for ever. Allah's promise is the truth, and whose word can be truer than Allah's?

123 Not your desires, nor those of the People of the Book (can prevail): whoever works evil, will be requited accordingly. Nor will he find, besides Allah, any protector or helper. 124 If any do deeds of righteousness -- be they male or female -- and have faith, they will enter Heaven, and not the least injustice will be done to them. 125 Who can be better in religion than one who submits his whole self to Allah, does good, and follows the way of Abraham the true in faith? For Allah did take Abraham for a friend. 126 But to Allah belong all things in the heavens and on earth: and He it is that encompasses all things.

127 They ask your instruction concerning the Women say: Allah does instruct you about them: and (remember) what has been rehearsed unto you in the Book, concerning the orphans of women to whom you give not the portions prescribed, and yet whom you desire to marry, as also concerning the children who are weak and oppressed: that you stand firm for justice to orphans. There is not a good deed which you do, but Allah is well-acquainted therewith. 128 If a wife fears cruelty or desertion on her husband's part, there is no blame on them if they arrange an amicable settlement between themselves; and such settlement is best; even though men's souls are swayed by greed. But if you do good and practise self-restraint, Allah is well-acquainted with all that you do. 129 You are never able to be fair and just as between women, even if it is your ardent desire: but turn not away (from a woman) altogether, so as to leave her (as it were) hanging (in the air). If you come to a friendly understanding, and practise self-

restraint, Allah is Oft-Forgiving, Most Merciful. 130 But if they disagree (and must part), Allah will provide abundance for all from His All-Reaching bounty: for Allah is He that cares for all and is Wise.

131 To Allah belong all things in the heavens and on earth. Surely, we have directed the People of the Book before you, and you (O Muslims) to fear Allah. But if you deny Him, beware! to Allah belong all things in the heavens and on earth, and Allah is free of all wants, worthy of all praise. 132 Yes, unto Allah belong all things in the heavens and on earth, and enough is Allah to carry through all affairs. 133 If it were His Will, He could destroy you, O mankind, and create another race; for He has power this to do. 134 If anyone desires a reward in this life, in Allah's (gift) is the reward (both) of this life and of the Hereafter: for Allah is He that hears and sees (all things).

135 O you who believe! Stand out firmly for justice, as witnesses to Allah, even as against yourselves, or your parents, or your kin, and whether it be (against) rich or poor: for Allah can best protect both. Follow not the lusts (of your hearts), lest you swerve, and if you distort (justice) or decline to do justice, surely, Allah is well-acquainted with all that you do.

136 O you who believe! Believe in Allah and His Messenger, and the scripture which He has sent to His Messenger and the scripture which He sent to those before (him). Any who denies Allah, His angels, His Books, His Messengers, and the Day of Judgment, has gone far, far astray. 137 Those who believe, then reject Faith, then believe (again) and (again) reject Faith, and go on increasing in Unbelief—Allah will not forgive them nor guide them on the Way. 138 To the Hypocrites give the glad tidings that there is for them (but) a grievous Torment— 139 Yes, to those who take for friends Unbelievers rather than Believers: is it honour they seek among them? No—all honour is with Allah.

140 Already has He sent you word in the Book, that when you hear the Signs of Allah held in defiance and ridicule, you are not to sit with them unless they turn to a different theme: if you did, you would be like them. For Allah will collect the Hypocrites

and those who defy Faith—all in Hell— 141 (These are) the ones who wait and watch about you: if you do gain a victory from Allah, they say: "Were we not with you?"—but if the unbelievers gain a success, they say (to them): "Did we not gain an advantage over you, and did we not guard you from the believers?" But Allah will judge between you on the Day of Judgment. And never will Allah grant to the unbelievers a way (to triumph) over the believers.

142 The hypocrites—they think they are overreaching Allah, but He will overreach them: when they stand up to prayer, they stand without earnestness, to be seen of men, but little do they hold Allah in remembrance. 143 (They are) distracted in mind even in the midst of it—being (sincerely) for neither one group nor for another. Whom Allah leaves straying—never will you find for him the Way. 144 O you who believe! Take not for friends unbelievers rather than believers: do you wish to offer Allah an open proof against yourselves? 145 The hypocrites will be in the lowest depths of the Fire: no helper will you find for them— 146 Except for those who repent, mend (their lives) hold fast to Allah, and purify their religion as in Allah's sight: if so they will be (numbered) with the believers. And soon will Allah grant to the believers a reward of immense value. 147 What can Allah gain by your punishment, if you are grateful and you believe? No, it is Allah that recognises (all good), and knows all things.

148 Allah loves not that evil should be noised abroad in public speech, except where injustice has been done; for Allah is He Who hears and knows all things. 149 Whether you publish a good deed or conceal it or cover evil with pardon, surely, Allah does blot out (sins) and has power (in the judgment of values). 150 Those who deny Allah and His Messengers, and (those who) wish to separate Allah from His Messengers, saying: "We believe in some but reject others:" And (those who) wish to take a course midway— 151 They are in truth (equally) unbelievers; and We have prepared for unbelievers a humiliating punishment. 152 To those who believe in Allah and His Messengers and make no distinction between any of the Messengers, We shall soon give their (due) rewards: for Allah is Oft-Forgiving, Most Merciful.

153 The people of the Book ask you to cause a book to descend to them from heaven: indeed they asked Moses for an even greater (miracle), for they said: "Show us Allah in public," but they were dazed for their presumption, with thunder and lightning. Yet they worshipped the calf even after Clear Signs had come to them; even so We forgave them; and gave Moses manifest proofs of authority. 154 And for their Covenant we raised over them (the towering height) Of Mount (Sinai); and (on another occasion) We said: "Enter the gate with humility;" and (once again) We commanded them: "Transgress not in the matter of the Sabbath." And We took from them a solemn Covenant.

155 (They have incurred divine displeasure): in that they broke their Covenant; that they rejected the Signs of Allah; that they slew the Messengers in defiance of right; that they said, "Our hearts are the wrappings (which preserve Allah's Word; we need no more)"—no, Allah has set the seal on their hearts for their blasphemy, and little is it they believe— 156 That they rejected Faith; that they uttered against Mary a grave false charge; 157 That they said (in boast), "We killed Christ Jesus the son of Mary, the Messenger of Allah"—but they killed him not, nor crucified him, but so it was made to appear to them, and those who differ therein are full of doubts, with no (certain) knowledge, but only conjecture to follow, for of a surety they killed him not— 158 No, Allah raised him up unto Himself; and Allah is Exalted in Power, Wise—

159 And there is none of the People of the Book but must believe in him before his death; and on the Day of Judgment he will be a witness against them— 160 For the iniquity of the Jews We made unlawful for them certain (foods) good and wholesome which had been lawful for them—in that they hindered many from Allah's Way— 161 That they took usury, though they were forbidden; and that they devoured men's substance wrongfully— We have prepared for those among them who reject Faith a grievous punishment. 162 But those among them who are well-grounded in knowledge, and the believers, believe in what has been revealed to you and what was revealed before you: and

(especially) those who establish regular prayer and practise regular charity and believe in Allah and in the Last Day: to them shall We soon give a great reward.

163 We have sent you inspiration, as We sent it to Noah and the Messengers after him: We sent inspiration to Abraham, Ishmael, Isaac, Jacob and the Tribes, to Jesus, Job, Jonah, Aaron, and Solomon, and to David We gave the Psalms. 164 Of some Messengers We have already told you the story; of others we have not—and to Moses Allah spoke direct— 165 Messengers who gave good news as well as warning, that mankind, after (the coming) of the Messengers, should have no plea against Allah: for Allah is Exalted in Power, Wise.

166 But Allah bears witness that what He has sent unto you He has sent from His (own) knowledge, and the angels bear witness: but enough is Allah for a witness. 167 Those who reject Faith and keep off (men) from the way of Allah, have surely strayed far, far away from the Path. 168 Those who reject Faith and do wrong—Allah will not forgive them nor guide them to any way— 169 Except the way of Hell, to dwell therein for ever. And this to Allah is easy. 170 O mankind! the Messenger has come to you in truth from Allah: believe in him: it is best for you. But if you reject Faith, to Allah belong all things in the heavens and on earth: and Allah is All-knowing, All-wise.

171 O People of the Book! Commit no excesses in your religion: nor say of Allah aught but the truth. Christ Jesus, the son of Mary, was (no more than) a Messenger of Allah, and His Word, which He bestowed on Mary, and a Spirit proceeding from Him: so believe in Allah and His Messengers. Say not "Trinity:" desist: it will be better for you: for Allah is One God: glory be to Him: (far Exalted is He) above having a son. To Him belong all things in the heavens and on earth. And enough is Allah as a Disposer of affairs. 172 Christ disdains not to serve and worship Allah, nor do the angels, those nearest (to Allah): those who disdain his worship and are arrogant—He will gather them all together unto Himself to (answer). 173 But to those who believe and do deeds of righteousness, He will give their (due) rewards—and more,

out of His bounty: but those who are disdainful and arrogant, He will punish with a grievous penalty; nor will they find, besides Allah, any to protect or help them.

174 O mankind! Surely, there has come to you a convincing proof from your Lord: for We have sent unto you a light (that is) manifest. 175 Then those who believe in Allah, and hold fast to Him—soon will He admit them to Mercy and Grace from Himself, and guide them to Himself by a straight Way. 176 They ask you for a legal decision. Say: Allah directs (thus) about those who leave no descendants or ascendants as heirs. If it is a man that dies, leaving a sister but no child, she shall have half the inheritance: if (such a deceased was) a woman, who left no child, her brother takes her inheritance: if there are two sisters, they shall have two-thirds of the inheritance (between them): if there are brothers and sisters, (they share), the male having twice the share of the female. Thus does Allah make clear to you (His law), lest you err. And Allah has knowledge of all things.

5. THE TABLE SPREAD

In the name of Allah, Most Gracious, Most Merciful.

1 O you who believe! Fulfil (all) obligations. Lawful unto you (for food) are all four-footed animals, with the exceptions named: but animals of the chase are forbidden while you are in the Sacred Precincts or in pilgrim garb: for Allah does command according to His Will and Plan. 2 O you who believe! Violate not the sanctity of the Symbols of Allah, nor of the Sacred Month, nor of the animals brought for sacrifice, nor the garlands that mark out such animals, nor the people resorting to the Sacred House, seeking of the bounty and good pleasure of their Lord. But when you are clear of the Sacred Precincts and of pilgrim garb, you may hunt and let not the hatred of some people in (once) shutting you out of the Sacred Mosque lead you to transgression (and hostility on

your part). Help you one another in righteousness and piety, but help you not one another in sin and rancour: fear Allah: for Allah is strict in punishment.

3 Forbidden to you (for food) are: dead meat, blood, the flesh of swine, and that on which has been invoked the name of other than Allah; that which has been killed by strangling, or by a violent blow, or by a headlong fall, or by being gored to death; that which has been (partly) eaten by a wild animal; unless you are able to slaughter it (in due form); that which is sacrificed on stone (altars); (forbidden) also is the division (of meat) by raffling with arrows: that is impiety. This day have those who reject faith given up all hope of your religion: yet fear them not but fear Me. This day have I perfected your religion for you, completed my favour upon you, and have chosen for you Islam as your religion. But if any is forced by hunger, with no inclination to transgression, Allah is indeed Oft-Forgiving, Most Merciful.

4 They ask you what is lawful to them (as food). Say: Lawful unto you are (all) things good and pure: and what you have taught your trained hunting animals (to catch) in the manner directed to you by Allah: eat what they catch for you, but pronounce the name of Allah over it: and fear Allah; for Allah is swift in taking account. 5 This day are (all) things good and pure made lawful unto you. The food of the People of the Book is lawful unto you and yours is lawful unto them. (Lawful unto you in marriage) are (not only) chaste women who are believers, but chaste women among the People of the Book, revealed before your time — when you give them their due dowers, and desire chastity, not lewdness, nor secret intrigues. If anyone rejects Faith, fruitless is his work, and in the Hereafter he will be in the ranks of those who have lost (all spiritual good).

6 O you who believe! When you prepare for prayer, wash your faces, and your hands (and arms) to the elbows; rub your heads (with water); and (wash) your feet to the ankles. If you are in a state of ceremonial impurity, bathe your whole body. But if you are ill, or on a journey, or one of you comes from offices of nature, or you have been in contact with women, and you find no water,

then take for yourselves clean sand or earth, and rub therewith your faces and hands, Allah does not wish to place you in a difficulty, but to make you clean, and to complete His favour to you, that you may be grateful.

7 And call in remembrance the favour of Allah unto you, and His Covenant, which He ratified with you, when you said: "We hear and we obey:" And fear Allah, for Allah knows well the secrets of your hearts. 8 O you who believe! Stand out firmly for Allah, as witnesses to fair dealing, and let not the hatred of others to you make you swerve to wrong and depart from justice. Be just: that is next to Piety: and fear Allah. For Allah is well-acquainted with all that you do. 9 To those who believe and do deeds of righteousness has Allah promised forgiveness and a great reward. 10 Those who reject faith and deny Our Signs will be Companions of Hell-fire. 11 O you who believe! Call in remembrance the favour of Allah unto you when certain men formed the design to stretch out their hands against you, but (Allah) held back their hands from you: so fear Allah. And on Allah let Believers put (all) their trust.

12 Allah did aforetime take a Covenant from the Children of Israel, and We appointed twelve captains among them. And Allah said: "I am with you: if you (but) establish regular Prayers, practise regular Charity, believe in My Messengers, honour and assist them, and loan to Allah a beautiful loan, surely, I will wipe out from you your evils, and admit you to Gardens with rivers flowing beneath; but if any of you, after this, resists faith, he has truly wandered from the path of rectitude." 13 But because of their breach of their Covenant, We cursed them, and made their hearts grow hard; they change the words from their (right) places and forget a good part of the Message that was sent them, nor will you cease to find them — barring a few — ever bent on (new) deceits: but forgive them, and overlook (their misdeeds): for Allah loves those who are kind.

14 From those, too, who call themselves Christians, We did take a Covenant, but they forgot a good part of the Message that was

sent them: so We estranged them, with enmity and hatred between the one and the other, to the Day of Judgment. And soon will Allah show them what it is they have done. 15 O People of the Book! There has come to you Our Messenger, revealing to you much that you used to hide in the Book, and passing over much (that is now unnecessary): there has come to you from Allah a (new) light and a perspicuous Book — 16 Wherewith Allah guides all who seek His good pleasure to ways of peace and safety, and leads them out of darkness, by His Will, into the light — guides them to a Path that is Straight. 17 In blasphemy indeed are those that say that Allah is Christ, the son of Mary. Say: "Who then has the least power against Allah, if His Will were to destroy Christ, the son of Mary, his mother, and all — everyone that is on the earth? For to Allah belongs the dominion of the heavens and the earth, and all that is between. He creates what He pleases. For Allah has power over all things."

18 (Both) the Jews and the Christians say: "We are sons of Allah, and His beloved." Say: "Why then does He punish you for your sins? No, you are but men — of the men He has created: He forgives whom He pleases, and He punishes whom He pleases: and to Allah belongs the dominion of the heavens and the earth, and all That is between: and unto Him is the final goal (of all)." 19 O People of the Book! Now has come to you, making (things) clear to you, Our Messenger, after the break in (the series of) our Messengers, lest you should say: "There came to us no bringer of glad tidings and no warner (from evil):" But now has come to you a bringer of glad tidings and a warner (from evil). And Allah has power over all things.

20 Remember Moses said to his people: "O my people! call in remembrance the favour of Allah to you, when He produced prophets among you, made you kings, and gave you what He had not given to any other among the peoples. 21 "O my people! Enter the holy land which Allah has assigned to you, and turn not back ignominiously, for then will you be overthrown, to your own ruin." 22 They said: "O Moses! In this land are a people of exceeding strength: never shall we enter it until they leave it: if (once) they leave, then shall we enter." 23 (But) among (their)

God-fearing men were two on whom Allah had bestowed His grace: they said: "Assault them at the (proper) Gate: when once you are in, victory will be yours; but on Allah put your trust if you have faith." 24 They said: "O Moses! While they remain there, never shall we be able to enter, to the end of time. Go you, and your Lord, and fight you two, while we sit here (and watch)."

25 He said: "O my Lord! I have power only over myself and my brother: so separate us from this rebellious people!" 26 Allah said: "Therefore will the land be out of their reach for forty years: in distraction will they wander through the land: but sorrow you not over these rebellious people."

27 Recite to them the truth of the story of the two sons of Adam. Behold! They each presented a sacrifice (to Allah): It was accepted from one, but not from the other. Said the latter: "Be sure I will slay you." "Surely," said the former, "Allah does accept of the sacrifice of those who are righteous. 28 "If you do stretch your hand against me, to slay me, it is not for me to stretch my hand against you to slay you: for I do fear Allah, the Cherisher of the Worlds. 29 "For me, I intend to let you draw on yourself my sin as well as yours, for you will be among the Companions of the Fire, and that is the reward of those who do wrong."

30 The (selfish) soul of the other led him to the murder of his brother: he murdered him, and became (himself) one of the lost ones. 31 Then Allah sent a raven, who scratched the ground, to show him how to hide the shame of his brother. "Woe is me!" said he; "Was I not even able to be as this raven, and to hide the shame of my brother?" Then he became full of regrets—

32 On that account: We ordained for the Children of Israel that if any one slew a person — unless it be for murder or for spreading mischief in the land — it would be as if He slew the whole people: and if any one saved a life, it would be as if he saved the life of the whole people. Then although there came to them Our Messengers with Clear Signs, yet, even after that, many of them continued to commit excesses in the land. 33 The punishment of those who wage war against Allah and His Messenger, and strive with might and main for mischief through the land is: execution,

or crucifixion, or the cutting off of hands and feet from opposite sides, or exile from the land: that is their disgrace in this world, and a heavy punishment is theirs in the Hereafter; 34 Except for those who repent before they fall into your power: in that case, know that Allah is Oft-Forgiving, Most Merciful.

35 O you who believe! Do your duty to Allah, seek the means of approach unto Him, and strive with might and main in His Cause: that you may prosper. 36 As to those who reject faith — if they had everything on earth, and twice repeated, to give as ransom for the penalty of the Day of Judgment, it would never be accepted of them, theirs would be a grievous Penalty. 37 Their wish will be to get out of the Fire, but never will they get out therefrom: their Penalty will be one that endures. 38 As to the thief, male or female, cut off his or her hands: a punishment by way of example, from Allah, for their crime: and Allah is Exalted in power. 39 But if the thief repents after his crime, and amends his conduct, Allah turns to him in forgiveness; for Allah is Oft-Forgiving, Most Merciful. 40 Know you not that to Allah (alone) belongs the dominion of the heavens and the earth? He punishes whom He pleases, and He forgives whom He pleases: and Allah has power over all things.

41 O Messenger! let not those grieve you, who race each other into Unbelief: (whether it be) among those who say, "We believe", with their lips, but whose hearts have no faith; or it be among the Jews — men who will listen to any lie — will listen even to others who have never so much as come to you. They change the words from their (right) times and places: they say, "If you are given this, take it, but if not, beware!" If anyone's trial is intended by Allah, you have no authority in the least for him against Allah. For such — it is not Allah's will to purify their hearts. For them there is disgrace in this world, and In the Hereafter a heavy punishment.

42 (They are fond of) listening to falsehood, of devouring anything forbidden. If they do come to you, either judge between them, or decline to interfere. If you decline, they cannot hurt you in the least. If you judge, judge in equity between them. For Allah

loves those who judge in equity. 43 But why do they come to you for decision, when they have (their own) law before them? — Therein is the (plain) command of Allah; yet even after that, they would turn away. For they are not (really) people of Faith.

44 It was We who revealed the Law (to Moses): therein was guidance and light. By its standard have been judged the Jews, by the Prophets who bowed (as in Islam) to Allah's Will, by the Rabbis and the Doctors of Law: for to them was entrusted the protection of Allah's Book, and they were witnesses thereto: therefore, fear not men, but fear Me, and do not barter away My Signs for a miserable price. If any do fail to judge by (the light of) what Allah has revealed, they are (no better than) Unbelievers. 45 We ordained therein for them: "life for life, eye for eye, nose for nose, ear for ear, tooth for tooth, and wounds equal for equal." But if any one remits the retaliation by way of charity, it is an act of atonement for himself. And if any fail to judge by (the light of) what Allah has revealed, they are (no better than) wrong-doers. 46 And in their footsteps We sent Jesus the son of Mary, confirming the Law that had come before him: We sent him the Gospel: therein was guidance and light, and confirmation of the Law that had come before him: a guidance and an admonition to those who fear Allah. 47 Let the People of the Gospel judge by what Allah has revealed therein. If any do fail to judge by (the light of) what Allah has revealed, they are (no better than) those who rebel.

48 To you We sent the Scripture in truth, confirming the scripture that came before it, and guarding it in safety: so judge between them by what Allah has revealed, and follow not their vain desires, diverging from the Truth that has come to you. To each among you have We prescribed a Law and an Open Way. If Allah had so willed, He would have made you a single people, but (His plan is) to test you in what He has given you: so strive as in a race in all virtues. The goal of you all is to Allah; it is He that will show you the truth of the matters in which you dispute.

49 And this (He commands): judge you between them by what Allah has revealed, and follow not their vain desires, but beware

of them lest they beguile you from any of that (teaching) which Allah has sent down to you. And if they turn away, be assured that for some of their crime it is Allah's purpose to punish them. And truly most men are rebellious. 50 Do they then seek after a judgment of (the Days of) Ignorance? But who, for a people whose faith is assured, can give better judgment than Allah?

51 O you who believe! Take not the Jews and the Christians for your friends and protectors: they are but friends and protectors to each other. And he amongst you that turns to them (for friendship) is of them. Surely, Allah guides not a people unjust. 52 Those in whose hearts is a disease— you see how eagerly they run about amongst them, saying: "We do fear lest a change of fortune bring us disaster." Ah! perhaps Allah will give (you) victory, or a decision according to His Will. Then will they repent of the thoughts which they secretly harboured in their hearts. 53 And those who believe will say: "Are these the men who swore their strongest oaths by Allah, that they were with you?" All that they do will be in vain, and they will fall into (nothing but) ruin.

54 O you who believe! If any from among you turn back from his Faith, soon will Allah produce a people whom He will love as they will love Him—lowly with the believers, mighty against the Rejecters, fighting in the Way of Allah, and never afraid of the reproaches of such as find fault. That is the Grace of Allah, which He will bestow on whom He pleases. And Allah encompasses all, and He knows all things. 55 Your (real) friends are (no less than) Allah, His Messenger, and the (Fellowship of) Believers— those who establish regular prayers and zakat (poor-due), and they bow down humbly (in worship). 56 As to those who turn (for friendship) to Allah, His Messenger, and the (Fellowship of) Believers— it is the Fellowship of Allah that must certainly triumph.

57 O you who believe! Take not for friends and protectors those who take your religion for a mockery or fun—whether among those who received the Scripture before you, or among those who reject Faith; but fear you Allah, if you have Faith (indeed). 58 When you proclaim your call to prayer they take it (but) as

mockery and fun; that is because they are a people without understanding. 59 Say: "O people of the Book! Do you disapprove of us for no other reason than that we believe in Allah, and the Revelation that has come to us and that which came before (us), and (perhaps) that most of you are rebellious and disobedient?" 60 Say: "Shall I point out to you something much worse than this, (as judged) by the treatment it received from Allah? Those who incurred the curse of Allah and His wrath, those of whom some he transformed into apes and swine, those who worshipped Evil — these are (many times) worse in rank, and far more astray from the even Path!"

61 When they come to you, they say: "We believe:" but, in fact, they enter with a mind against Faith, and they go out with the same. But Allah knows fully all that they hide. 62 Many of them you see, racing each other in sin and rancour, and their eating of things forbidden. Evil indeed are the things that they do. 63 Why do not the Rabbis and the doctors of law forbid them from their (habit of) uttering sinful words and eating things forbidden? Evil indeed are their works.

64 The Jews say: "Allah's hand is tied up." Be their hands tied up and be they accursed for the (blasphemy) they utter. No, both His hands are widely outstretched: He gives and spends (of His bounty) as He pleases. But the revelation that comes to you from Allah increases in most of them their obstinate rebellion and blasphemy. Amongst them we have placed enmity and hatred till the Day of Judgment. Every time they kindle the fire of strife, Allah does extinguish it; but they (ever) strive to do mischief on earth. And Allah loves not those who do mischief.

65 If only the People of the Book had believed and been righteous, we should indeed have blotted out their iniquities and admitted them to Gardens of Bliss. 66 If only they had stood fast by the Law, the Gospel, and all the revelation that was sent to them from their Lord, they would have enjoyed happiness from every side. There is from among them a party on the right course: but many of them follow a course that is evil.

67 O Messenger! proclaim the (Message) which has been sent

to you from your Lord. If you did not, you would not have fulfilled and proclaimed His Mission. And Allah will defend you from men (who mean mischief). For Allah guides not those who reject Faith.

68 Say: "O People of the Book! You have no ground to stand upon unless you stand fast by the Law, the Gospel, and all the Revelation that has come to you from your Lord." It is the Revelation that comes to you from your Lord, that increases in most of them their obstinate rebellion and blasphemy. But grieve you not over (these) people without Faith. 69 Those who believe (in the Qur'ān), those who follow the Jewish (scriptures), and the Sabians and the Christians — any who believe in Allah and the Last Day, and work righteousness — on them shall be no fear, nor shall they grieve.

70 We took the Covenant of the Children of Israel and sent them Messengers, every time there came to them a Messenger with what they themselves desired not — some (of these) they called impostors, and some they (go so far as to) slay. 71 They thought there would be no trial (or punishment); so they became blind and deaf; yet Allah (in mercy) turned to them; yet again many of them became blind and deaf. But Allah sees well all that they do.

72 They do blaspheme who say: "God is Christ the son of Mary." But said Christ: "O Children of Israel! Worship Allah, my Lord and your Lord." Whoever joins other gods with Allah — Allah will forbid him the Garden, and the Fire will be his abode. There will for the wrongdoers be no one to help. 73 They do blaspheme who say: Allah is one of three in a Trinity: for there is no god except One God. If they desist not from their word (of blasphemy), surely, a grievous penalty will befall the blasphemers among them. 74 Why turn they not to Allah, and seek His forgiveness? For Allah is Oft-Forgiving, Most Merciful. 75 Christ, the son of Mary, was no more than a Messenger; many were the Messengers that passed away before him. His mother was a woman of truth. They had both to eat their (daily) food. See how Allah does make His Signs clear to them; Yet see in what ways they are deluded

away from the truth! 76 Say: "Will you worship, besides Allah, something which has no power either to harm or benefit you? But Allah—He it is that hears and knows all things."

77 Say: "O people of the Book! Exceed not in your religion the bounds (of what is proper), trespassing beyond the truth, nor follow the vain desires of people who went wrong in times gone by—who misled many, and strayed (themselves) from the even Way.

78 Curses were pronounced on those among the Children of Israel who rejected Faith, by the tongue of David and of Jesus, the son of Mary: because they disobeyed and persisted in excesses. 79 Nor did they (usually) forbid one another the iniquities which they committed: evil indeed were the deeds which they did. 80 You see many of them turning in friendship to the unbelievers. Evil indeed are (the works) which their souls have sent forward before them (with the result), that Allah's wrath is on them, and in torment will they abide. 81 If only they had believed in Allah, in the Prophet, and in what has been revealed to him, never would they have taken them for friends and protectors, but most of them are rebellious wrongdoers.

82 Strongest among men in enmity to the believers will you find the Jews and pagans; and nearest among them in love to the believers will you find those who say, "We are Christians:" because amongst these are men devoted to learning and men who have renounced the world, and they are not arrogant. 83 And when they listen to the revelation received by the Messenger, you will see their eyes overflowing with tears, for they recognise the truth: they pray: "Our Lord! we believe: write us down among the witnesses. 84 "What cause can we have not to believe in Allah and the truth which has come to us, seeing that we long for our Lord to admit us to the company of the righteous?" 85 And for this their prayer has Allah rewarded them with Gardens, with rivers flowing underneath—their eternal home. Such is the recompense of those who do good. 86 But those who reject Faith and belie Our Signs—they shall be Companions of Hell-fire.

87 O you who believe! Make not unlawful the good things which

Allah has made lawful for you, but commit no excess: for Allah loves not those given to excess. 88 Eat of the things which Allah has provided for you, lawful and good; but fear Allah, in Whom you believe. 89 Allah will not call you to account for what is futile in your oaths, but He will call you to account for your deliberate oaths: for expiation, feed ten indigent persons, on a scale of the average for the food of your families; or clothe them; or give a slave his freedom. If that is beyond your means, fast for three days. That is the expiation for the oaths you have sworn. But keep to your oaths. Thus does Allah make clear to you His Signs, that you may be grateful.

90 O you who believe! Intoxicants and gambling, (dedication of) stones, and (divination by) arrows, are an abomination — of Satan's handiwork: eschew such (abomination), that you may prosper. 91 Satan's plan is (but) to excite enmity and hatred between you, with intoxicants and gambling, and hinder you from the remembrance of Allah, and from prayer: will you not then abstain? 92 Obey Allah, and obey the Messenger, and beware (of evil): if you do turn back, know you that it is our Messenger's duty to proclaim (the Message) in the clearest manner. 93 On those who believe and do deeds of righteousness there is no blame for what they ate (in the past), when they guard themselves from evil, and believe, and do deeds of righteousness — (or) again, guard themselves from evil and believe — (or) again, guard themselves from evil and do good. For Allah loves those who do good.

94 O you who believe! Allah does but make a trial of you in a little matter of game well within reach of your hands and your lances, that He may test who fears Him unseen: any who transgress thereafter, will have a grievous chastisement. 95 O you who believe! Kill not game while in the Sacred Precincts or in pilgrim garb. If any of you does so intentionally, the compensation is an offering, brought to the Ka'bah, of a domestic animal equivalent to the one he killed, as adjudged by two just men among you; or by way of atonement, the feeding of the indigent; or its equivalent in fasts: that he may taste of the penalty of his deed. Allah forgives what is past: for repetition Allah will exact from him the penalty. For Allah is Exalted, and Lord of Retribution.

96 Lawful to you is the pursuit of water-game and its use for food—for the benefit of yourselves and those who travel; but forbidden is the pursuit of land-game—as long as you are in the Sacred Precincts or in pilgrim garb. And fear Allah, to Whom you shall be gathered back. 97 Allah made the Ka'bah, the Sacred House, an asylum of security for men, as also the Sacred Months, the animals for offerings, and the garlands that mark them: that you may know that Allah has knowledge of what is in the heavens and on earth and that Allah is well-acquainted with all things. 98 Know you that Allah is strict in punishment and that Allah is Oft-Forgiving, Most Merciful. 99 The Messenger's duty is but to proclaim (the Message). But Allah knows all that you reveal and you conceal. 100 Say: "Not equal are things that are bad and things that are good, even though the abundance of the bad may dazzle you; so fear Allah, O you that understand; that (so) you may prosper."

101 O you who believe! Ask not questions about things which, if made plain to you, may cause you trouble. But if you ask about things when the Qur'ān is being revealed, they will be made plain to you. Allah will forgive those: for Allah is Oft-forgiving, Most Forbearing. 102 Some people before you did ask such questions, and on that account lost their faith. 103 It was not Allah who instituted (superstitions like those of) a slit-ear she camel, or a she-camel let loose for free pasture, or idol sacrifices for twin-births in animals, or stallion-camels freed from work: it is blasphemers who invent a lie against Allah; but most of them lack wisdom. 104 When it is said to them: "Come to what Allah has revealed; come to the Messenger:" they say: "Enough for us are the ways we found our fathers following." What! even though their fathers were void of knowledge and guidance? 105 O you who believe! Guard your own souls: if you follow (right) guidance, no hurt can come to you from those who stray. The goal of you all is to Allah: it is He that will show you the truth of all that you do.

106 O you who believe! When death approaches any of you, (take) witnesses among yourselves when making bequests—two just men of your own (brotherhood) or others from outside if you

are journeying through the earth, and the chance of death befalls you (thus). If you doubt (their truth), detain them both after prayer, and let them both swear by Allah: "We wish not in this for any worldly gain, even though the (beneficiary) be our near relation: we shall hide not the evidence before Allah: if we do, then behold! The sin be upon us!" 107 But if it gets known that these two were guilty of the sin (of perjury), let two others stand forth in their places — nearest in kin from among those who claim a lawful right: let them swear by Allah: "We affirm that our witness is truer than that of those two, and that we have not trespassed (beyond the truth): if we did, behold! the wrong be upon us!" 108 That is most suitable: that they may give the evidence in its true nature and shape, or else they would fear that other oaths would be taken after their oaths. But fear Allah, and listen (to His counsel): for Allah guides not a rebellious people.

109 One day will Allah gather the Messengers together, and ask: "What was the response you received (from men to your teaching)?" They will say: "We have no knowledge: it is You who know in full all that is hidden." 110 Then will Allah say: "O Jesus the son of Mary! Recount My favour to you and to your mother. Behold! I strengthened you with the holy spirit, so that you did speak to the people in childhood and in maturity. Behold! I taught you the Book and Wisdom, the Law and the Gospel. And behold! you make out of clay, the figure of a bird, by My leave, and you breathe into it and it becomes a bird by My leave, and you heal those born blind, and the lepers, by My leave. And behold! you bring forth the dead by My leave. And behold! I did restrain the Children of Israel from (violence to) you when you did show them the Clear Signs, and the unbelievers among them said: 'This is nothing but evident magic.'

111 "And behold! I inspired the Disciples to have faith in Me and My Messenger: they said, 'We have faith, and you bear witness that we bow to Allah as Muslims.'" 112 Behold! the Disciples said: "O Jesus the son of Mary! Can your Lord send down to us a Table set (with viands) from heaven?" Said Jesus: "Fear Allah, if you have faith." 113 They said: "We only wish to eat thereof and satisfy our hearts, and to know that you have

indeed told us the truth; and that we ourselves may be witnesses to the miracle." 114 Said Jesus the son of Mary: "O Allah our Lord! Send us from heaven a Table set (with viands), that there may be for us—for the first and the last of us—a solemn festival and a Sign from You; and provide for our sustenance, for You are the best sustainer (of our needs)." 115 Allah said: "I will send it down unto you: but if any of you after that resists faith, I will punish him with a penalty such as I have not inflicted on any one among all the peoples."

116 And behold! Allah will say: "O Jesus the son of Mary! Did you say unto men, 'Worship me and my mother as gods in derogation of Allah'?" He will say: "Glory to You! Never could I say what I had no right (to say). Had I said such a thing, You would indeed have known it. You know what is in my heart, though I know not what is in Yours. For You know in full all that is hidden. 117 "Never said I to them anything except what You did command me to say, to wit, 'Worship Allah, my Lord and your Lord;' and I was a witness over them while I dwelt amongst them; when you did take me up you were the Watcher over them, and You are a witness to all things. 118 "If You do punish them, they are Your servants: if You do forgive them, you are the Exalted in power, the Wise." 119 Allah will say: "This is a day on which the truthful will profit from their truth: theirs are Gardens, with rivers flowing beneath—their eternal home: Allah well-pleased with them, and they with Allah: that is the great success, (the fulfilment of all desires). 120 To Allah does belong the dominion of the heavens and the earth, and all that is therein, and it is He who has power over all things.

6. THE CATTLE

In the name of Allah, Most Gracious, Most Merciful.

1 Praise be to Allah, who created the heavens and the earth, and made the darkness and the light. Yet those who reject faith hold (others) as equal with their Guardian-Lord. 2 He it is Who created

you from clay, and then decreed a stated term (for you). And there is in His Presence another determined term; yet you doubt within yourselves! 3 And He is Allah in the heavens and on earth. He knows what you hide, and what you reveal, and He knows the (recompense) which you earn (by your deeds).

4 But never did a single one of the Signs of their Lord reach them, but they turned away therefrom. 5 And now they reject the truth when it reaches them: but soon shall they learn the reality of what they used to mock at. 6 Do they not see how many of those before them we did destroy?— generations We had established on the earth, in strength such as We have not given to you—for whom we poured out rain from the skies in abundance, and gave (fertile) streams flowing beneath their (feet): yet for their sins we destroyed them, and raised in their wake fresh generations (to succeed them).

7 If We had sent unto you a written (message) on parchment, so that they could touch it with their hands, the Unbelievers would have been sure to say: "This is nothing but obvious magic!" 8 They say: "Why is not an angel sent down to him?" If We did send down an angel, the matter would be settled at once, and no respite would be granted them. 9 If We had made it an angel, We should have sent him as a man, and We should certainly have caused them confusion in a matter which they have already covered with confusion. 10 Mocked were (many) messengers before you; but their scoffers were hemmed in by the thing that they mocked. 11 Say: "Travel through the earth and see what was the end of those who rejected Truth."

12 Say: "To whom belongs all that is in the heavens and on earth?" Say: "To Allah. He has inscribed for Himself (the rule of) Mercy. That He will gather you together for the Day of Judgment, there is no doubt whatever. It is they who have lost their own souls, that will not believe. 13 To him belongs all that dwells (or lurks) in the Night and the Day. For He is the One who hears and knows all things." 14 Say: "Shall I take for my protector any, other than Allah, The Maker of the heavens and the earth? And He it is that feeds but is not fed." Say: "No! but

I am commanded to be the first of those who bow to Allah (in Islam), and you be not of the company of those who join gods with Allah." 15 Say: "I would, if I disobeyed my Lord, indeed have fear of the Penalty of a Mighty Day. 16 "On that day, if the Penalty is averted from any, it is due to Allah's Mercy; and that would be (Salvation), the obvious fulfilment of all desire.

17 "If Allah touch you with affliction, none can remove it but He; if He touch you with happiness, He has power over all things. 18 "He is the Irresistible, (watching) from above over His worshippers; and He is the Wise, acquainted with all things." 19 Say: "What thing is most weighty in evidence?" Say: "Allah is witness between me and you. This Qur'ān has been revealed to me by inspiration, that I may warn you and all whom it reaches. Can you possibly bear witness that besides Allah there is another god?" Say: "No! I cannot bear witness!" Say: "But in truth He is the One God, and I truly am innocent of (your blasphemy of) joining others with Him."

20 Those to whom we have given the Book know this as they know their own sons. Those who have lost their own souls refuse therefore to believe. 21 Who does more wrong than he who invents a lie against Allah or rejects His Signs? But, surely, the wrongdoers never shall prosper. 22 One day shall We gather them all together: We shall say to those who ascribed partners (to Us): "Where are the partners whom you (invented and) talked about?" 23 There will then be (left) no subterfuge for them but to say: "By Allah our Lord, we were not those who joined gods with Allah." 24 Behold! how they lie against their own souls! But the (lie) which they invented will leave them in the lurch.

25 Of them there are some who (pretend to) listen to you; but We have thrown veils on their hearts, so they understand it not, and deafness in their ears; if they saw every one of the Signs, they would not believe in them; in so much that when they come to you, they (but) dispute with you; the Unbelievers say: "These are nothing but tales of the ancients." 26 Others they keep away from it, and themselves they keep away; but they only destroy their own souls, and they perceive it not. 27 If you could but see when

they are confronted with the Fire! They will say: "Would that we were but sent back! Then would we not reject the Signs of our Lord, but would be amongst those who believe!" 28 Yes, in their own (eyes) will become manifest what before they concealed. But if they were returned, they would certainly relapse to the things they were forbidden, for they are indeed liars.

29 And they (sometimes) say: "There is nothing except our life on this earth, and never shall we be raised up again." 30 If you could but see when they are confronted with their Lord! He will say: "Is not this the truth?" They will say: "Yes, by our Lord!" He will say: "Taste you then the Penalty, because you rejected Faith." 31 Lost indeed are they who treat it as a falsehood that they must meet Allah—until of a sudden the hour is on them, and they say: "Ah! woe upon us that we took no thought of it;" For they bear their burdens on their backs, and evil indeed are the burdens that they bear! 32 What is the life of this world but play and amusement? But best is the Home in the Hereafter, for those who are righteous. Will you not then understand?

33 We know indeed the grief which their words do cause you: it is not you they reject: it is the Signs of Allah, which the wicked condemn. 34 Rejected were the Messengers before you: with patience and constancy they bore their rejection and their wrongs, until Our aid did reach them: there is none that can alter the Words (and Decrees) of Allah. Already have you received some account of those Messengers. 35 If their spurning is hard on your mind, yet if you were able to seek a tunnel in the ground or a ladder to the skies and bring them a Sign—(what good?). If it were Allah's Will, He could gather them together unto true guidance: so be not you amongst those who are swayed by ignorance (and impatience)! 36 Those who listen (in truth), be sure, will accept: as to the dead, Allah will raise them up; then will they be turned unto Him.

37 They say: "Why is not a Sign sent down to him from his Lord?" say: "Allah has certainly power to send down a Sign: but most of them understand not." 38 There is not an animal (that lives) on the earth, nor a being that flies on its wings, but (forms

part of) communities like you. Nothing have we omitted from the Book, and they (all) shall be gathered to their Lord in the end. 39 Those who reject our Signs are deaf and dumb—in the midst of darkness profound: whom Allah wills, He leaves to wander: whom He wills, He places on the way that is straight.

40 Say: "Think you to yourselves, if there come upon you the wrath of Allah, or the Hour (that you dread), would you then call upon other than Allah?— (reply) if you are truthful! 41 "No— On Him would you call, and if it be His will, He would remove (the distress) which occasioned your call upon Him, and you would forget (the false gods) which you join with Him!"

42 Before you We sent (messengers) to many nations, and We afflicted the nations with suffering and adversity, that they might learn humility. 43 When the suffering reached them from Us, why then did they not learn humility? On the contrary their hearts became hardened, and Satan made their (sinful) acts seem alluring to them. 44 But when they forgot the warning they had received, we opened to them the gates of all (good) things, until, in the midst of their enjoyment of our gifts, of a sudden, We called them to account, when look! They were plunged in despair! 45 Of the wrong-doers the last remnant was cut off. Praise be to Allah, the Cherisher of the Worlds.

46 Say: "Do you think, if Allah took away your hearing and your sight, and sealed up your hearts, who—a god other than Allah— could restore them to you?" See how We explain the Signs by various (symbols); yet they turn aside. 47 Say: "Think you, if the punishment of Allah comes to you, whether suddenly or openly, will any be destroyed except those who do wrong? 48 We send the Messengers only to give good news and to warn: so those who believe and mend (their lives)—upon them shall be no fear, nor shall they grieve. 49 But those who reject our Signs—them shall punishment touch, for that they ceased not from transgressing." 50 Say: "I tell you not that with me are the Treasures of Allah, nor do I know what is hidden, nor do I tell you I am an angel: I but follow what is revealed to me." Say: "Can the blind be held equal to the seeing?" Will you then consider not?

51 Give this warning to those in whose (hearts) is the fear that they will be brought (to Judgment) before their Lord: except for Him they will have no protector nor intercessor: that they may guard (against evil). 52 Send not away those who call on their Lord morning and evening, seeking His Face. In nothing are you accountable for them, and in nothing are they accountable for you, that you should turn them away, and thus be (one) of the unjust. 53 Thus did We try some of them by comparison with others, that they should say: "Is it these then that Allah has favoured from amongst us?" Does not Allah know best those who are grateful?

54 When those come to you who believe in Our Signs, say: "Peace be on you: your Lord has inscribed for Himself (the rule of) Mercy: surely, if any of you did evil in ignorance, and thereafter repented, and amended (his conduct), lo! He is Oft-forgiving, Most Merciful. 55 Thus do We explain the Signs in detail: that the way of the sinners may be shown up.

56 Say: "I am forbidden to worship those—others than Allah—whom you call upon." Say: "I will not follow your vain desires: if I did, I would stray from the Path, and be not of the company of those who receive guidance." 57 Say: "For me, I (work) on a Clear Sign from my Lord, but you reject Him. What you would see hastened, is not in my power. The Command rests with none but Allah: He declares the Truth, and He is the best of judges." 58 Say: "If what you would see hastened were in my power, the matter would be settled at once between you and me. But Allah knows best those who do wrong." 59 With Him are the keys of the unseen, the treasures that none knows but He. He knows whatever there is on the earth and in the sea. Not a leaf does fall but with His knowledge: there is not a grain in the darkness (or depths) of the earth, nor anything fresh or dry (green or withered), but is (inscribed) in a Record clear (to those who can read).

60 It is He Who does take your souls by night, and has knowledge of all that you have done by day: by day does He raise you up again; that a term appointed be fulfilled; in the end unto Him will be your return; then will He show you the truth of all that you did. 61 He is the Irresistible, (watching) from above over His

servants, and He sets guardians over you. At length, when death approaches one of you, Our angels take his soul, and they never fail in their duty. 62 Then are men returned unto Allah, their True Protector, surely His is the Command and He is the Swiftest in taking account.

63 Say: "Who is it that delivers you from the dark recesses of land and sea, when you call upon Him in humility and silent terror: 'If He only delivers us from these (dangers), (we vow) we shall truly show our gratitude'?" 64 Say "It is Allah that delivers you from these and all (other) distresses: and yet you worship false gods!" 65 Say: "He has power to send calamities on you, from above and below, or to cover you with confusion in party strife, giving you a taste of mutual vengeance—each from the other." See how We explain the Signs by various (symbols); that they may understand. 66 But your people reject this, though it is the Truth. Say: "Not mine is the responsibility for arranging your affairs; 67 For every Message is a limit of time, and soon shall you know it."

68 When you see men engaged in vain discourse about Our Signs, turn away from them unless they turn to a different theme. If Satan ever makes you forget, then after recollection, sit not you in the company of those who do wrong. 69 On their account no responsibility falls on the righteous, but (their duty) is to remind them, that they may (learn to) fear Allah. 70 Leave alone those who take their religion to be mere play and amusement, and are deceived by the life of this world. But proclaim (to them) this (truth): that every soul delivers itself to ruin by its own acts: it will find for itself no protector or intercessor except Allah: if it offered every ransom, (or reparation), none will be accepted: such is (the end of) those who deliver themselves to ruin by their own acts: they will have for drink (only) boiling water, and for punishment, one most grievous: for they persisted in rejecting Allah.

71 Say: "Shall we indeed call on others besides Allah—things that can do us neither good nor harm—and turn on our heels after receiving guidance from Allah?—like one whom the Satans have

made into a fool, wandering bewildered through the earth, his friends calling 'Come to us,' (vainly) guiding him to the Path." Say: "Allah's guidance is the (only) guidance, and we have been directed to submit ourselves to the Lord of the worlds— 72 "To establish regular prayers and to fear Allah: for it is to Him that we shall be gathered together." 73 It is He Who created the heavens and the earth in true (proportions): the day He says, "Be," behold! it is. His Word is the Truth. His will be the dominion the day the trumpet will be blown. He knows the Unseen as well as that which is open. For He is the Wise, well acquainted (with all things). 74 Abraham said to his father Āzar: "Take you idols for gods? For I see you and your people in manifest error."

75 So also did We show Abraham the power and the laws of the heavens and the earth, that he might (with understanding) have certitude. 76 When the night covered him over, he saw a star: he said: "This is my Lord." But when it set, he said: "I love not those that set." 77 When he saw the moon rising in splendour, he said: "This is my Lord." But when the moon set, he said: "Unless my Lord guide me, I shall surely be among those who go astray." 78 When he saw the sun rising in splendour, he said: "This is my Lord; this is the greatest (of all)." But when the sun set, he said: "O my people! I am indeed free from your (guilt) of giving partners to Allah. 79 "For me, I have set my face, firmly and truly, towards Him Who created the heavens and the earth, and never shall I give partners to Allah." 80 His people disputed with him. He said: "(Come) you to dispute with me, about Allah, when He (Himself) has guided me? I fear not (the beings) you associate with Allah: unless my Lord wills, (nothing can happen). My Lord comprehends in His knowledge all things. Will you not (yourselves) be admonished?

81 "How should I fear (the beings) you associate with Allah, when you fear not to give partners to Allah without any warrant having been given to you? Which of (us) two parties has more right to security? (tell me) if you know. 82 "It is those who believe and confuse not their beliefs with wrong—that are (truly) in security, for they are on (right) guidance." 83 That was the reasoning about Us, which We gave to Abraham (to use) against

his people: We raise whom We will, degree after degree: for your Lord is full of wisdom and knowledge. 84 We gave him Isaac and Jacob: all (three) we guided: and before him, We guided Noah, and among his progeny, David, Solomon, Job, Joseph, Moses, and Aaron: thus do We reward those who do good.

85 And Zakariyyā and John, and Jesus and Elias: all in the ranks of the Righteous: 86 And Ishmael and Elisha, and Jonah, and Lūt: and to all We gave favour above the nations: 87 (To them) and to their fathers, and progeny and brethren: We chose them, and We guided them to a straight Way. 88 This is the Guidance of Allah: He gives that guidance to whom He pleases, of His worshippers. If they were to join other gods with Him, All that they did would be vain for them. 89 These were the men to whom We gave the Book, and Authority, and Prophethood: if these (their descendants) reject them, behold! We shall entrust their charge to a new People who reject them not. 90 Those were the (prophets) who received Allah's guidance: copy the guidance they received; say: "No reward for this do I ask of you: this is no less than a Message for the nations." 91 No just estimate of Allah do they make when they say: "nothing does Allah send down to man (by way of revelation):" say: "Who then sent down the Book which Moses brought? A light and guidance to man: but you make it into (separate) sheets for show, while you conceal much (of its contents): therein were you taught that which you knew not — neither you nor your fathers." say: "Allah (sent it down):" then leave them to plunge in vain discourse and trifling.

92 And this is a Book which We have sent down, bringing blessings, and confirming (the revelations) which came before it: that you may warn the Mother of Cities and all around her. Those who believe in the Hereafter believe in this (Book), and they are constant in guarding their Prayers. 93 Who can be more wicked than one who invents a lie against Allah, or says, "I have received inspiration," when he has received none, or (again) who says, "I can reveal the like of what Allah has revealed?" If you could but see how the wicked (do fare) in the flood of confusion at death! — the angels stretch forth their hands, (saying),"Yield up your souls: this day shall you receive your reward — a penalty of shame, for

that you used to tell lies against Allah, and scornfully to reject of His Signs!"

94 "And behold! you come to Us bare and alone as We created you for the first time: you have left behind you all (the favours) which we bestowed on you: we see not with you your intercessors whom you thought to be partners in your affairs: so now all relations between you have been cut off, and your (pet) fancies have left you in the lurch!" 95 It is Allah Who causes the seed grain and the date stone to split and sprout. He causes the living to issue from the dead, and He is the One to cause the dead to issue from the living. That is Allah: then how are you deluded away from the truth?

96 He it is that cleaves the day-break (from the dark): He makes the night for rest and tranquillity, and the sun and moon for the reckoning (of time): such is the judgment and ordering of (Him), the Exalted in Power, the Omniscient. 97 It is He Who makes the stars (as beacons) for you, that you may guide yourselves, with their help, through the dark spaces of land and sea: We detail Our Signs for people who know. 98 It is He Who has produced you from a single person: here is a place of sojourn and a place of departure: We detail Our Signs for people who understand.

99 It is He Who sends down rain from the skies: with it We produce vegetation of all kinds: from some We produce green (crops), out of which We produce grain, heaped up (at harvest); out of the date-palm and its sheaths (or spathes) (come) clusters of dates hanging low and near: and (then there are) gardens of grapes, and olives, and pomegranates, each similar (in kind) yet different (in variety): when they begin to bear fruit, feast your eyes with the fruit and the ripeness thereof. Behold! in these things there are Signs for people who believe. 100 Yet they make the Jinns equals with Allah, though Allah did create the Jinns; and they falsely, having no knowledge, attribute to Him sons and daughters. Praise and glory be to Him! (for He is) above what they attribute to Him!

101 To Him is due the primal origin of the heavens and the earth: How can He have a son when He has no consort? He created all

things, and He has full knowledge of all things. 102 That is Allah, your Lord! There is no god but He, the Creator of all things: then worship you Him: and He has power to dispose of all affairs. 103 No vision can grasp Him, but His grasp is over all vision: He is above all comprehension, yet is acquainted with all things. 104 "Now have come to you, from your Lord, proofs (to open your eyes): if any will see, it will be for (the good of) his own soul; if any will be blind, it will be to his own (harm): I am not (here) to watch over your doings." 105 Thus do We explain the Signs by various (symbols): that they may say, "You have learnt this (from somebody)," and that We may make the matter clear to those who know.

106 Follow what you are taught by inspiration from your Lord: there is no god but He: and turn aside from those who join gods with Allah. 107 If it had been Allah's Plan, they would not have taken false gods: but We made you not one to watch over their doings, nor are you set over them to dispose of their affairs. 108 Revile not you those whom they call upon besides Allah, lest they out of spite revile Allah in their ignorance. Thus have We made alluring to each people its own doings. In the end will they return to their Lord, and We shall then tell them the truth of all that they did. 109 They swear their strongest oaths by Allah, that if a (special) Sign came to them, by it they would believe. Say: "Certainly (All) Signs are in the power of Allah: but what will make you (Muslims) realise that (even) if (special) Signs came, they will not believe?"

110 We (too) shall turn to (confusion) their hearts and their eyes, even as they refused to believe in this in the first instance: We shall leave them in their trespasses, to wander in distraction. 111 Even if We did send unto them angels, and the dead did speak to them, and We gathered together all things before their very eyes, they are not the ones to believe, unless it is in Allah's Plan. But most of them ignore (the truth). 112 Likewise did We make for every Messenger an enemy—Satans among men and Jinns, inspiring each other with flowery discourses by way of deception. If your Lord had so planned, they would not have done it: so leave them and their inventions alone.

113 To such (deceit) let the hearts of those incline, who have no faith in the Hereafter: let them delight in it, and let them earn from it what they may. 114 Say: "Shall I seek for judge other than Allah?—when He it is who has sent to you the Book, explained in detail." They know full well, to whom We have given the Book, that it has been sent down from your Lord in truth. Never be then of those who doubt.

115 The Word of your Lord does find its fulfilment in truth and in justice: none can change His Words: for He is the One Who hears and knows all. 116 Were you to follow the common run of those on earth, they will lead you away from the Way of Allah. They follow nothing but conjecture: they do nothing but lie. 117 Your Lord knows best who strays from His Way: He knows best who they are that receive His guidance. 118 So eat of (meats) on which Allah's name has been pronounced, if you have faith in His Signs.

119 Why should you not eat of (meats) on which Allah's name has been pronounced, when He has explained to you in detail what is forbidden to you—except under compulsion of necessity? But many do mislead (men) by their appetites unchecked by knowledge. Your Lord knows best those who transgress. 120 Eschew all sin, open or secret: those who earn sin will get due recompense for their "earnings." 121 Eat not of (meats) on which Allah's name has not been pronounced: that would be impiety. But Satans ever inspire their friends to contend with you if you were to obey them, you would indeed be Pagans. 122 Can he who was dead, to whom We gave life, and a light whereby he can walk amongst men, be like him who is in the depths of darkness, from which he can never come out? Thus to those without Faith their own deeds seem pleasing.

123 Thus have We placed leaders in every town, its wicked men, to plot (and burrow) therein: but they only plot against their own souls, and they perceive it not. 124 When there comes to them a Sign (from Allah), they say: "We shall not believe until we receive one (exactly) like those received by Allah's Messengers." Allah knows best where (and how) to carry out His mission. Soon

will the wicked be overtaken by humiliation before Allah, and a severe punishment, for all their plots. 125 Those whom Allah (in His Plan) wills to guide — He opens their breast to Islam; those whom He wills to leave straying — He makes their breast close and constricted, as if they had to climb up to the skies: thus does Allah (heap) the penalty on those who refuse to believe.

126 This is the Way of your Lord, leading straight: We have detailed the Signs for those who receive admonition. 127 For them will be a Home of Peace in the presence of their Lord: He will be their Friend, because they practised (righteousness). 128 One day will He gather them all together, (and say): "O you assembly of Jinns! Much (toll) did you take of men." Their friends amongst men will say: "Our Lord! we profited from each other: but (alas!) we reached our term — which You did appoint for us." He will say: "The Fire be your dwelling-place: you will dwell therein for ever, except as Allah wills." For your Lord is full of wisdom and knowledge.

129 Thus do We make the wrongdoers turn to each other, because of what they earn. 130 "O you assembly of Jinns and men! Came there not unto you messengers from amongst you, setting forth unto you my Signs, and warning you of the meeting of this Day of yours?" They will say: "We bear witness against ourselves." It was the life of this world that deceived them. So against themselves will they bear witness that they rejected Faith. 131 (The prophets were sent) thus, for your Lord would not destroy for their wrongdoing men's habitations while their occupants were unwarned. 132 To all are degrees (or ranks) according to their deeds: for your Lord is not unmindful of anything that they do.

133 Your Lord is Self-sufficient, full of Mercy: if it were His Will, He could destroy you, and in your place appoint whom He will as your successors, even as He raised you up from the posterity of other people. 134 All that has been promised unto you will come to pass: nor can you frustrate it (in the least bit). 135 Say: "O my people! Do whatever you can: I will do (my part): soon will you know who it is whose end will be (best) in the Hereafter: certain it is that the wrongdoers will not prosper." 136 Out of what Allah

has produced in abundance in tilth and in cattle, they assigned
Him a share: they say, according to their fancies: "This is for
Allah, and this"—for our "partners"! But the share of their
"partners" reaches not Allah, while the share of Allah reaches their
"partners"! Evil (and unjust) is their assignment!

137 Even so, in the eyes of most of the Pagans, their "partners"
made alluring the slaughter of their children, in order to lead them
to their own destruction, and cause confusion in their religion.
If Allah had willed, they would not have done so: but leave alone
them and their inventions. 138 And they say that such and such
cattle and crops are taboo, and none should eat of them except
those whom—so they say—We wish; further, there are cattle
forbidden to yoke or burden, and cattle on which, (at slaughter),
the name of Allah is not pronounced—inventions against Allah's
name: soon will He requite them for their inventions.

139 They say: "What is in the wombs of such and such cattle
is specially reserved (for food) for our men, and forbidden to our
women; but if it is still-born, then all have share therein. For their
(false) attribution (of superstitions to Allah), He will soon punish
them: for He is full of wisdom and knowledge. 140 Lost are those
who slay their children, from folly, without knowledge, and
forbid food which Allah has provided for them, inventing (lies)
against Allah. They have indeed gone astray and heeded no
guidance. 141 It is He Who produces gardens, with trellises and
without, and dates, and tilth with produce of all kinds, and olives
and pomegranates, similar (in kind) and different (in variety): eat
of their fruit in their season, but render the dues that are proper
on the day that the harvest is gathered. But waste not by excess:
for Allah loves not the wasters.

142 Of the cattle are some for burden and some for meat: eat
what Allah has provided for you, and follow not the footsteps
of Satan: for he is to you an avowed enemy. 143 (Take) eight (head
of cattle) in (four) pairs: of sheep a pair, and of goats a pair; say,
has He forbidden the two males, or the two females, or (the young)
which the wombs of the two females enclose? Tell me with
knowledge if you are truthful.

144 Of camels a pair, and oxen a pair; say, has He forbidden the two males, or the two females, or (the young) which the wombs of the two females enclose? Were you present when Allah ordered you such a thing? But who does more wrong than one who invents a lie against Allah, to lead astray men without knowledge? For Allah guides not people who do wrong. 145 Say: "I find not in the Message received by me by inspiration any (meat) forbidden to be eaten by one who wishes to eat it, unless it be dead meat, or blood poured forth, or the flesh of swine — for it is an abomination — or, what is impious, (meat) on which a name has been invoked, other than Allah's." But (even so), if a person is forced by necessity, without wilful disobedience, nor transgressing due limits — your Lord is Oft-forgiving, Most Merciful. 146 For those who followed the Jewish Law, We forbade every (animal) with undivided hoof, and We forbade them the fat of the ox and the sheep, except what adheres to their backs or their entrails, or is mixed up with a bone: this in recompense for their wilful disobedience: for We are True (in Our ordinances).

147 If they accuse you of falsehood, say: "Your Lord is full of Mercy All-Embracing; but from people in guilt never will His wrath be turned back. 148 Those who give partners (to Allah) will say: "If Allah had wished, we should not have given partners to Him nor would our fathers; nor should we have had any taboos." So did their ancestors argue falsely, until they tasted of Our wrath. Say: "have you any (certain) knowledge? If so, produce it before us. You follow nothing but conjecture: you do nothing but lie."

149 Say: "With Allah is the argument that reaches home: if it had been His Will, He could indeed have guided you all." 150 Say: "Bring forward your witnesses to prove that Allah did forbid so and so." If they bring such witnesses, be not you amongst them: nor follow you the vain desires of such as treat our Signs as falsehoods, and such as believe not in the Hereafter: for they hold others as equal with their Guardian-Lord. 151 Say: "Come, I will rehearse what Allah has (really) prohibited you from:" join not anything as equal with Him; be good to your parents; kill not your childrer on a plea of want — We provide sustenance for you

and for them—come not near to shameful deeds, whether open or secret; take not life, which Allah has made sacred, except by way of justice and law: thus does He command you, that you may learn wisdom.

152 And come not near to the orphan's property, except to improve it, until he attain the age of full strength; give measure and weight with (full) justice—no burden do We place on any soul, but that which it can bear—whenever you speak, speak justly, even if a near relative is concerned; and fulfil the Covenant of Allah: thus does He command you, that you may remember.

153 Surely, this is My Way, leading straight: follow it: follow not (other) paths: they will scatter you about from His (great) Path: thus does He command you, that you may be righteous. 154 Moreover, We gave Moses the Book, completing (our favour) to those who would do right, and explaining all things in detail— and a guide and a mercy, that they might believe in the meeting with their Lord.

155 And this is a Book which We have revealed as a blessing: so follow it and be righteous, that you may receive mercy: 156 Lest you should say: "The Book was sent down to two Peoples before us, and for our part, we remained unacquainted with all that they learned by assiduous study;" 157 Or lest you should say: "If the Book had only been sent down to us, we should have followed its guidance better than they." Now then has come unto you a Clear (Sign) from your Lord—and a guide and a mercy: then who could do more wrong than one who rejects Allah's Signs, and turns away therefrom? In good time shall We requite those who turn away from Our Signs, with a dreadful penalty, for their turning away. 158 Are they waiting to see if the angels come to them, or your Lord (Himself), or certain of the Signs of your Lord! The day that certain of the Signs of your Lord do come, no good will it do to a soul to believe in them then if it believed not before nor earned righteousness through its Faith. Say: "Wait you: we too are waiting." 159 As for those who divide their religion and break up into sects, you have no part in them in the least: their affair is with Allah: he will in the end tell them the truth of all that they did.

160 He that does good shall have ten times as much to his credit: he that does evil shall only be recompensed according to his evil: no wrong shall be done to (any of) them. 161 Say: "Surely, my Lord has guided me to a Way that is straight — a religion of right — the Path (trod) by Abraham the true in Faith, and he (certainly) joined not gods with Allah."

162 Say: "Truly, my prayer and my service of sacrifice, my life and my death, are (all) for Allah, the Cherisher of the Worlds: 163 No partner has He: this am I commanded, and I am the first of those who bow to His Will. 164 Say: "Shall I seek for (my) Cherisher other than Allah, when He is the Cherisher of all things (that exist)? Every soul draws the meed of its acts on none but itself: no bearer of burdens can bear the burden of another. Your goal in the end is towards Allah: He will tell you the truth of the things wherein you disputed." 165 It is He Who has made you (His) agents, inheritors of the earth: He has raised you in ranks, some above others: that He may try you in the gifts He has given you: for your Lord is quick in punishment: yet He is indeed Oft-forgiving, Most Merciful."

7. THE HEIGHTS

In the name of Allah, Most Gracious, Most Merciful.

1 Alif, Lām, Mīm, Ṣād. 2 A Book revealed unto you — so let your heart be oppressed no more by any difficulty on that account — that with it you might warn (the erring) and teach the Believers. 3 Follow (O People!) the revelation given unto you from your Lord, and follow not, as friends or protectors, other than Him. Little it is you remember of admonition. 4 How many towns have We destroyed (for their sins)? Our punishment took them on a sudden by night or while they slept for their afternoon rest. 5 When (thus) Our punishment took them, no cry did they utter but this: "Indeed we did wrong." 6 Then shall we question those to whom Our Message was sent and those through whom

We sent it. 7 And, surely, We shall recount their whole story with knowledge, for We were never absent (at any time or place). 8 The balance that day will be true (to a nicety): those whose scale (of good) will be heavy, will prosper: 9 Those whose scale will be light, will find their souls in perdition, for that they wrongfully treated Our Signs.

10 It is We Who have placed you with authority on earth, and provided you therein with means for the fulfilment of your life: small are the thanks that you give! 11 It is We Who created you and gave you shape; then We bade the angels bow down to Adam, and they bowed down; not so Iblīs: he refused to be of those who bow down. 12 (Allah) said: "What prevented you from bowing down when I commanded you?" He said: "I am better than he: You did create me from fire, and him from clay." 13 (Allah) said: "Get you down from this: it is not for you to be arrogant here: get out, for you are of the meanest (of creatures)." 14 He said: "Give me respite till the day they are raised up." 15 (Allah) said: "Be you among those who have respite." 16 He said: "Because you have thrown me out of the Way, lo! I will lie in wait for them on Your Straight Way: 17 "Then will I assault them from front and rear, from their right and their left: nor will you find, in most of them, gratitude (for Your mercies)." 18 (Allah) said: "Get out from this, disgraced and expelled. If any of them follow you—hell will I fill with you all.

19 "O Adam! dwell you and your wife in the Garden, and enjoy (its good things) as you wish: but approach not this tree, or you run into harm and transgression." 20 Then began Satan to whisper suggestions to them, in order to reveal to them all their shame that was hidden from them (before): he said: "Your Lord only forbade you this tree, lest you should become angels or such beings as live forever." 21 And he swore to them both, that he was their sincere adviser.

22 So by deceit he brought about their fall: when they tasted of the tree, their shame became manifest to them, and they began to sew together the leaves of the Garden over their bodies. And their Lord called unto them: "Did I not forbid you that tree, and

tell you that Satan was an avowed enemy unto you?" 23 They said: "Our Lord! We have wronged our own souls: If You forgive us not and bestow not upon us Your Mercy, we shall certainly be lost." 24 (Allah) said: "Get you down. With enmity between yourselves. On earth will be your dwelling-place and your means of livelihood—for a time." 25 He said: "Therein shall you live, and therein shall you die; but from it shall you be taken out (at last)."

26 O you Children of Adam! We have bestowed raiment upon you to cover your shame, as well as to be an adornment to you. But the raiment of righteousness—that is the best. Such are among the Signs of Allah, that they may receive admonition! 27 O you Children of Adam! Let not Satan seduce you, in the same manner as he got your parents out of the Garden, stripping them of their raiment, to expose their shame: for he and his tribe watch you from a position where you cannot see them: We made the Satans friends (only) to those without Faith.

28 When they do anything that is shameful, they say: "We found our fathers doing so;" and "Allah commanded us thus:" Say: "No, Allah never commands what is shameful: do you say of Allah what you know not?" 29 Say: "My Lord has commanded justice; and that you set your whole selves (to Him) at every time and place of prayer, and call upon Him, making your devotion sincere as in His sight: such as He created you in the beginning, so shall you return." 30 Some He has guided: others have (by their choice) deserved the loss of their way; in that they took the Satan, in preference to Allah, for their friends and protectors, and think that they receive guidance.

31 O Children of Adam! Wear your beautiful apparel at every time and place of prayer: eat and drink: but waste not by excess, for Allah loves not the wasters. 32 Say: "Who has forbidden the beautiful (gifts) of Allah, which He has produced for His servants, and the things, clean and pure, (which He has provided) for sustenance?" Say: "They are, in the life of this world, for those who believe, (and) purely for them on the Day of Judgment. Thus do We explain the Signs in detail for those who understand." 33 Say: "The things that my Lord has indeed forbidden are:

shameful deeds, whether open or secret; sins and trespasses against truth or reason; assigning of partners to Allah, for which he has given no authority; and saying things about Allah of which you have no knowledge."

34 To every people is a term appointed: when their term is reached, not an hour can they cause delay, nor (an hour) can they advance (it in anticipation). 35 O you Children of Adam! Whenever there come to you Prophets from amongst you, rehearsing My Signs unto you—those who are righteous and mend (their lives)—on them shall be no fear nor shall they grieve. 36 But those who reject our Signs and treat them with arrogance—they are Companions of the Fire, to dwell therein (for ever). 37 Who is more unjust than one who invents a lie against Allah or rejects His Signs? For such, their portion appointed must reach them from the Book (of Decrees): until, when Our Messengers (of death) arrive and take their souls, they say: "Where are the things that you used to invoke besides Allah?" They will reply, "They have left us in the lurch," and they will bear witness against themselves, that they had rejected Allah.

38 He will say: "Enter you in the company of the Peoples who passed away before you—men and Jinns—into the Fire." Every time a new People enters, it curses its sister-People (that went before), until they follow each other, all into the Fire. Says the last about the first: "Our Lord! It is these that misled us: so give them a double penalty in the Fire." He will say: "Doubled for all": but this you do not understand. 39 Then the first will say to the last: "See then! No advantage have you over us; so taste you of the Penalty for all that you did!"

40 To those who reject our Signs and treat them with arrogance, no opening will there be of the gates of heaven, nor will they enter the Garden, until the camel can pass through the eye of the needle: such is Our reward for those in sin. 41 For them there is hell, as a couch (below) and folds and folds of covering above: such is Our requital of those who do wrong. 42 But those who believe and work righteousness—no burden do We place on any soul, but that which it can bear—they will be Companions of the Garden,

therein to dwell (forever). 43 And We shall remove from their hearts any lurking sense of injury—beneath them will be rivers flowing—and they shall say: "Praise be to Allah, who has guided us to this (felicity): never could we have found guidance, had it not been for the guidance of Allah. Indeed it was the truth, that the Prophets of our Lord brought unto us." And they shall hear the voice: "Behold! the Garden before you! You have been made its inheritors, for your deeds (of righteousness)."

44 The Companions of the Garden will call out to the Companions of the Fire: "We have indeed found the promises of our Lord to us true: Have you also found your Lord's promises true?"They shall say, "Yes," but a Crier shall proclaim between them: "The curse of Allah is on the wrongdoers— 45 "Those who would hinder (people) from the path of Allah and would seek in it something crooked: they were those who denied the Hereafter."

46 Between them shall be a veil, and on the Heights will be those who would know every one by his marks: they will call out to the dwellers of Paradise, "Peace on you." They will not have entered, but they will have hope (to enter it). 47 When their eyes shall be turned towards the Companions of the Fire, they will say: "Our Lord! send us not to the company of the wrong-doers." 48 Those men on the Heights will call to certain people whom they will know from their marks, saying: "Of what good to you were your hoards and your arrogant ways? 49 "See! are these not those whom you swore that Allah with His Mercy would never bless? Enter you the Garden: no fear shall be on you, nor shall you grieve."

50 The Companions of the Fire will call to the Companions of the Garden: "Pour down to us water or anything that Allah does provide for your sustenance." They will say: "Both these things has Allah forbidden to those who rejected Him— 51 "Such as took their religion to be mere amusement and play, and were deceived by the life of the world." That day shall We forget them as they forgot the meeting of this day of theirs, and as they were wont to reject Our Signs.

52 For We had certainly sent unto them a Book, based on

knowledge, which We explained in detail—a guide and a mercy to all who believe. 53 Do they just wait for the final fulfilment of the event? On the day the event is finally fulfilled, those who disregarded it before will say: "The Prophets of our Lord did indeed bring true (tidings). Have we no intercessors now to intercede on our behalf? Or could we be sent back? Then should we behave differently from our behaviour in the past." In fact, they will have lost their souls, and the things they invented will leave them in the lurch.

54 Your Guardian-Lord is Allah, Who created the heavens and the earth in six Days, then He settled Himself on the Throne (of authority): He draws the night as a veil over the day, each seeking the other in rapid succession: He created the sun, the moon, and the stars, (all) governed by laws under His Command. Is it not His to create and to govern? Blessed be Allah, the Cherisher and Sustainer of the Worlds! 55 Call on your Lord with humility and in private: for Allah loves not those who trespass beyond bounds. 56 Do no mischief on the earth, after it has been set in order, but call on Him with fear and longing (in your hearts): for the Mercy of Allah is (always) near to those who do good.

57 It is He Who sends the winds like heralds of glad tidings, going before His Mercy: when they have carried the heavy-laden clouds, We drive them to a land that is dead, make rain to descend thereon, and produce every kind of harvest therewith: thus shall We raise up the dead: perchance you may remember. 58 From the land that is clean and good, by the Will of its Cherisher, springs up produce, (rich) after its kind: but from the land that is bad, springs up nothing but that which is niggardly: thus do we explain the Signs by various (symbols) to those who are grateful.

59 We sent Noah to his people. He said: "O my people! Worship Allah! You have no other god but Him. I fear for you the Punishment of a dreadful Day! 60 The leaders of his people said: "Ah! we see you evidently wandering (in mind)." 61 He said: "O my people! No wandering is there in my (mind): on the contrary, I am a Messenger from the Lord and Cherisher of the Worlds! 62 "I but fulfil towards you the duties of my Lord's mission.

Sincere is my advice to you, and I know from Allah something that you know not. 63 "Do you wonder that there has come to you a message from your Lord, through a man of your own people, to warn you—so that you may fear Allah and haply receive His Mercy?" 64 But they rejected him, and We delivered him, and those with him, in the Ark: but We overwhelmed in the Flood those who rejected Our Signs. They were indeed a blind people!

65 To the 'Ād people, (We sent) Hūd, one of their (own) brethren. He said: "O my people! Worship Allah! You have no other god but Him will you not fear (Allah)?" 66 The leaders of the Unbelievers among his people said: "Ah! we see you are an imbecile!" and "We think you are a liar!" 67 He said: "O my people! I am no imbecile, but (I am) a prophet from the Lord and Cherisher of the Worlds! 68 "I but fulfil towards you the duties of my Lord's mission: I am to you a sincere and trustworthy adviser. 69 "Do you wonder that there has come to you a message from your Lord through a man of your own people, to warn you? Call in remembrance that He made you inheritors after the people of Noah, and gave you a stature tall among the nations. Call in remembrance the benefits (you have received) from Allah: that so you may prosper."

70 They said: "Have you come to us, that we may worship Allah alone, and give up the cult of our fathers? Bring us what you threaten us with, if so be that you tell the truth!" 71 He said: "Punishment and wrath have already come upon you from your Lord: you dispute with me over names which you have devised— you and your fathers—without authority from Allah? Then wait: I am amongst you, also waiting." 72 We saved him and those who adhered to him. By Our Mercy, and We cut off the roots of those who rejected Our Signs and did not believe.

73 To the Thamud people (We sent) Ṣāliḥ, one of their own brethren. He said: "O my people! Worship Allah: you have no other god but Him. Now has come unto you a Clear (Sign) from your Lord! This she-camel of Allah is a Sign unto you: so leave her to graze in Allah's earth, and let her come to no harm, or you shall be seized with a grievous punishment. 74 "And

remember how He made you inheritors after the 'Ād people and gave you habitations in the land: you build for yourselves palaces and castles in (open) plains, and carve out homes in the mountains; so bring to remembrance the benefits (you have received) from Allah, and refrain from evil and mischief on the earth."

75 The leaders of the arrogant party among his people said to those who were reckoned powerless—those among them who believed: "Know you indeed that Ṣāliḥ is a Prophet from his Lord?" They said: "We do indeed believe in the revelation which has been sent through him." 76 The arrogant party said: "For our part, we reject what you believe in." 77 Then they hamstrung the she-camel, and insolently defied the order of their Lord, saying: "O Ṣāliḥ! bring about your threats, if you are a prophet (of Allah)!" 78 So the earthquake took them unawares, and they lay prostrate in their homes in the morning! 79 So Ṣāliḥ left them saying: "O my people! I did indeed convey to you the message for which I was sent by my Lord: I gave you good counsel, but you love not good counsellors!"

80 We also (sent) Lūṭ. He said to his people: "Do you commit lewdness such as no people in creation (ever) committed before you? 81 "For you practise your lusts on men in preference to women: you are indeed a people transgressing beyond bounds." 82 And his people gave no answer but this: they said, "Drive them out of your city: these are indeed men who want to be clean and pure!" 83 But we saved him and his family, except his wife: she was of those who lagged behind. 84 And We rained down on them a shower (of brimstone): then see what was the end of those who indulged in sin and crime!

85 To the Madyan people We sent Shu'ayb, one of their own brethren: he said: "O my people! worship Allah; you have no other god but Him. Now has come unto you a Clear (Sign) from your Lord! Give just measure and weight, nor withhold from the people the things that are their due; and do no mischief on the earth after it has been set in order: that will be best for you, if you have Faith. 86 "And squat not on every road, breathing threats, hindering from the Path of Allah those who believe in Him, and

seeking in it something crooked; but remember how you were little, and He gave you increase. And hold in your mind's eye what was the end of those who did mischief. 87 "And if there is a party among you who believes in the Message with which I have been sent, and a party which does not believe, hold yourselves in patience until Allah does decide between us: for He is the best to decide.

88 The leaders, the arrogant party among his people, said: "O Shu'ayb! we shall certainly drive you out of our city—(you) and those who believe with you; or else you (you and they) shall have to return to our ways and religion." He said: "What! even though we do detest (them)? 89 "We should indeed forge a lie against Allah, if we returned to your ways after Allah has rescued us therefrom; nor could we by any manner of means return thereto, unless it be as in the will and plan of Allah, our Lord. Our Lord can reach out to the utmost recesses of things by His knowledge. In Allah is our trust. Our Lord! Decide You between us and our people in truth, for You are the best to decide." 90 The leaders, the Unbelievers among his people, said: "If you follow Shu'ayb, be sure then you are ruined!" 91 But the earthquake took them unawares, and they lay prostrate in their homes before the morning! 92 The men who rejected Shu'ayb became as if they had never been in the homes where they had flourished: the men who rejected Shu'ayb—It was they who were ruined! 93 So Shu'ayb left them, saying: "O my people! I did indeed convey to you the Messages for which I was sent by my Lord: I gave you good counsel, but how shall I lament over a people who refuse to believe?"

94 Whenever We sent a prophet to a town, We took up its people in suffering and adversity, in order that they might learn humility. 95 Then We changed their suffering into prosperity, until they grew and multiplied, and began to say: "Our fathers (too) were touched by suffering and affluence"... Behold! We called them to account of a sudden, while they realised not (their peril). 96 If the people of the towns had but believed and feared Allah, We should indeed have opened out to them (all kinds of) blessings from heaven and earth; but they rejected (the truth), and We

brought them to book for their misdeeds. 97 Did the people of the towns feel secure against the coming of Our wrath by night while they were asleep? 98 Or else did they feel secure against its coming in broad daylight while they played about (care-free)? 99 Did they then feel secure against the Plan of Allah?—But no one can feel secure from the Plan of Allah, except those (doomed) to ruin!

100 To those who inherit the earth in succession to its (previous) possessors, is it not a guiding, (lesson) that, if We so willed, We could punish them (too) for their sins, and seal up their hearts so that they could not hear? 101 Such were the towns whose story We (thus) relate to you: there came indeed to them their Prophets with clear (Signs): but they would not believe what they had rejected before. Thus does Allah seal up the hearts of those who reject Faith. 102 Most of them We found not men (true) to their covenant: but most of them We found rebellious and disobedient.

103 Then after them We sent Moses with Our Signs to Pharaoh and his chiefs, but they wrongfully rejected them: so see what was the end of those who made mischief. 104 Moses said: "O Pharaoh! I am a Messenger from the Lord of the Worlds— 105 One for whom it is right to say nothing but truth about Allah. Now have I come to you (people), from your Lord, with a clear (Sign): so let the Children of Israel depart along with me." 106 (Pharaoh) said: "If indeed You have come with a Sign, show it forth— if you tell the truth." 107 Then (Moses) threw his staff, and behold! It was a serpent, plain (for all to see)! 108 And he drew out his hand, and behold! It was white to all beholders! 109 Said the Chiefs of the people of Pharaoh: "This is indeed a sorcerer well-versed. 110 "His plan is to oust you from your land: then what is it you counsel?" 111 They said: "Keep him and his brother in suspense (for a while); and send to the cities men to collect— 112 And bring up to you all (our) sorcerers well-versed."

113 So there came the sorcerers to Pharaoh: they said, "Of course we shall have a (suitable) reward if we win!" 114 He said: "Yes, (and more)— for you shall in that case be (raised to posts) nearest (to my person)." 115 They said: "O Moses! Will you throw (first),

or shall we have the (first) throw?" 116 Said Moses: "Throw you (first)." So when they threw, they bewitched the eyes of the people, and struck terror into them: for they showed a great (feat of) magic. 117 We put it into Moses's mind by inspiration: "Throw (now) your staff": and behold! It swallows up straightaway all the falsehoods which they fake! 118 Thus truth was confirmed, and all that they did was made of no effect. 119 So the (great ones) were vanquished there and then, and were made to look small. 120 But the sorcerers fell down prostrate in adoration, 121 Saying: "We believe in the Lord of the Worlds, 122 "The Lord of Moses and Aaron."

123 Said Pharaoh: "Believe you in Him before I give you permission? Surely this is a trick which you have planned in the City to drive out its people: but soon shall you know (the consequences). 124 "Be sure I will cut off your hands and your feet on opposite sides, and I will cause you all to die on the cross." 125 They said: "For us, we are but sent back unto our Lord: 126 "But you do wreak your vengeance on us simply because we believed in the Signs of our Lord when they reached us! Our Lord! pour out on us patience and constancy, and take our souls unto You as Muslims (who bow to Your Will)!

127 Said the chiefs of Pharaoh's people: "Will you leave Moses and his people, to spread mischief in the land, and to abandon you and your gods?" He said: "Their male children will we slay; (only) their females will we save alive; and we have over them (power) irresistible." 128 Said Moses to his people: "Pray for help from Allah, and (wait) in patience and constancy: for the earth is Allah's, to give as a heritage to such of His servants as He pleases; and the end is (best) for the righteous." 129 They said: "We have had (nothing but) trouble, both before and after you came to us." He said: "It may be that your Lord will destroy your enemy and make you inheritors in the earth; so that he may try you by your deeds."

130 We punished the people of Pharaoh with years (of drought) and shortness of crops; that they might receive admonition. 131 But when good (times) came, they said, "This is due to us."

When gripped by calamity, they ascribed it to evil omens connected with Moses and those with him! Behold! In truth the omens of evil are theirs in Allah's sight, but most of them do not understand! 132 They said (to Moses): "Whatever be the Signs you bring, to work therewith your sorcery on us, we shall never believe in you."

133 So We sent (plagues) on them: wholesale death, locusts, lice, frogs, and blood: Signs openly self-explained: but they were steeped in arrogance—a people given to sin. 134 Every time the penalty fell on them, they said: "O Moses! On our behalf call on your Lord in virtue of His promise to you: if you will remove the Penalty from us, we shall truly believe in you, and we shall send away the Children of Israel with you." 135 But every time We removed the Penalty from them according to a fixed term which they had to fulfil—behold! they broke their word!

136 So We exacted retribution from them: We drowned them in the sea, because they rejected Our Signs and failed to take warning from them. 137 And We made a people, considered weak (and of no account), inheritors of lands in both East and West—lands whereon We sent down Our blessings. The fair promise of your Lord was fulfilled for the Children of Israel, because they had patience and constancy, and We levelled to the ground the great works and fine Buildings which Pharaoh and his people erected (with such pride).

138 We took the Children of Israel (with safety) across the sea. They came upon a people devoted entirely to some idols they had. They said: "O Moses! fashion for us a god like the gods they have." He said: "Surely you are a people without knowledge. 139 "As to these folk—the cult they are in is bound to destruction, and vain is the (worship) which they practise." 140 He said: "Shall I seek for you a god other than the (true) God, when it is He who has endowed you with gifts above the nations?" 141 And remember We rescued you from Pharaoh's people, who afflicted you with the worst of penalties, who slew your male children and saved alive your females: in that was a momentous trial from your Lord.

142 We appointed for Moses thirty nights, and completed (the

period) with ten (more): thus was completed the term (of communion) with his Lord, forty nights. And Moses had charged his brother Aaron (before he went up): "Act for me amongst my people: do right, and follow not the way of those who do mischief." 143 When Moses came to the place appointed by Us, and his Lord addressed him, he said: "O my Lord! show (Thyself) to me, that I may look upon You." Allah said: "By no means can you see Me (direct); but look upon the mount; if it abide in its place, then shall you see Me." When his Lord manifested His glory on the Mount, He made it as dust. And Moses fell down in a swoon. When he recovered his senses, he said: "Glory be to You! to You I turn in repentance, and I am the first to believe."

144 (Allah) said: "O Moses! I have chosen you above (other) men, by the mission I (have given you) and the words I (have spoken to you): take then the (revelation) which I give you, and be of those who give thanks." 145 And We ordained laws for him in the Tablets in all matters, both commanding and explaining all things, (and said): "Take and hold these with firmness, and enjoin your people to hold fast by the best in the precepts: soon shall I show you the homes of the wicked—(how they lie desolate)."

146 Those who behave arrogantly on the earth in defiance of right—them will I turn away from My Signs: even if they see all the Signs, they will not believe in them; and if they see the way of right conduct, they will not adopt it as the Way; but if they see the way of error, that is the Way they will adopt. For they have rejected our Signs, and failed to take warning from them. 147 Those who reject Our Signs and the Meeting in the Hereafter—vain are their deeds: can they expect to be rewarded except as they have wrought?

148 The people of Moses made, in his absence, out of their ornaments, the image of a calf, (for worship): it seemed to low: did they not see that it could neither speak to them, nor show them the Way? They took it for worship and they did wrong. 149 When they repented, and saw that they had erred, They said: "If our Lord have not mercy upon us and forgive us, we shall indeed be

among the losers." 150 When Moses came back to his people, angry and grieved, he said: "Evil it is that you have done in my place in my absence: did you make haste to bring on the judgment of your Lord?" He put down the Tablets, seized his brother by (the hair of) his head, and dragged him to him. Aaron said: "Son of my mother! the people did indeed reckon me as naught, and went near to slaying me! Make not the enemies rejoice over my misfortune, nor count you me amongst the people of sin." 151 Moses prayed: "O my Lord! Forgive me and my brother! Admit us to Your mercy! For You are the Most Merciful of those who show mercy!"

152 Those who took the calf (for worship) will indeed be overwhelmed with wrath from their Lord, and with shame in this life: thus do We recompense those who invent (falsehoods). 153 But those who do wrong but repent thereafter and (truly) believe—surely, your Lord is thereafter Oft-Forgiving, Most Merciful.

154 When the anger of Moses was appeased, he took up the Tablets: in the writing thereon was Guidance and Mercy for such as fear their Lord. 155 And Moses chose seventy of his people for Our place of meeting: when they were seized with violent quaking, he prayed: "O my Lord! If it had been Your will You could have destroyed, long before, both them and me: would You destroy us for the deeds of the foolish ones among us? This is no more than Your trial: by it You cause whom You will to stray, and You lead whom you will into the right path. You are our Protector: so forgive us and give us Your mercy; for You are the Best of those who forgive. 156 "And ordain for us that which is good, in this life and in the Hereafter: for we have turned to You." He said: "With My Punishment I visit whom I will; but My Mercy extends to all things. That (Mercy) I shall ordain for those who do right, and pay zakat (poor-due), and those who believe in Our Signs—

157 "Those who follow the Messenger, the unlettered Prophet, whom they find mentioned in their own (Scriptures)— in the Taurat and the Gospel —for he commands them what is just and

forbids them what is evil; he allows them as lawful what is good (and pure) and prohibits them from what is bad (and impure); he releases them from their heavy burdens and from the yokes that are upon them. So it is those who believe in him, honour him, help him, and follow the Light which is sent down with him—It is they who will prosper."

158 Say: "O men! I am sent unto you all, as the Messenger of Allah, to Whom belongs the dominion of the heavens and the earth: there is no god but He: it is He that gives both life and death. So believe in Allah and His Messenger, the unlettered Prophet, who believes in Allah and His Words: follow him so that you may be guided." 159 Of the people of Moses there is a section who guide and do justice in the light of truth.

160 We divided them into twelve Tribes or nations. We directed Moses by inspiration, when his (thirsty) people asked him for water: "Strike the rock with your staff": out of it there gushed forth twelve springs: each group knew its own place for water. We gave them the shade of clouds, and sent down to them manna and quails, (saying): "Eat of the good things We have provided for you": (But they rebelled); to Us they did no harm, but they harmed their own souls. 161 And remember it was said to them: "Dwell in this town and eat therein as you wish, but say forgive (us) and enter the gate in a posture of humility: We shall forgive you your faults; We shall increase (the portion of) those who do good." 162 But the transgressors among them changed the word from that which had been given them so We sent on them a plague from heaven. For they repeatedly transgressed.

163 Ask them concerning the town standing close by the sea. Behold! They transgressed in the matter of the Sabbath. For on the day of their Sabbath their fish did come to them, openly holding up their heads, but on the day they had no Sabbath, they came not: thus did We make a trial of them, for they were given to transgression. 164 When some of them said: "Why do you preach to a people whom Allah will destroy or visit with a terrible punishment?"— said the preachers: "To discharge our duty to your Lord, and perchance they may fear Him."

165 When they disregarded the warnings that had been given them, We rescued those who forbade evil; but We visited the wrongdoers with a grievous punishment, because they were given to transgression. 166 When in their insolence they transgressed (all) prohibitions, We said to them: "Be you apes, despised and rejected."

167 Behold! your Lord did declare that He would send against them, to the Day of Judgment, those who would afflict them with grievous chastisement. Your Lord is quick in retribution, but He is also Oft-forgiving, Most Merciful. 168 We broke them up into sections on this earth. There are among them some that are the righteous, and some that are the opposite. We have tried them with both prosperity and adversity: in order that they might turn (to Us).

169 After them succeeded an (evil) generation: they inherited the Book, but they chose (for themselves) the vanities of this world, saying (for excuse): "(Everything) will be forgiven us." (Even so), if similar vanities came their way, they would (again) seize them. Was not the Covenant of the Book taken from them, that they would not ascribe to Allah anything but the truth? And they study what is in the Book. But best for the righteous is the Home in the Hereafter. Will you not understand? 170 As to those who hold fast by the Book and establish regular Prayer—never shall We suffer the reward of the righteous to perish. 171 When We shook the Mount over them, as if it had been a canopy, and they thought it was going to fall on them (We said): "Hold firmly to what We have given you, and bring (ever) to remembrance what is therein; perchance you may fear Allah."

172 When your Lord drew forth from the Children of Adam— from their loins—their descendants, and made them testify concerning themselves, (saying): "Am I not your Lord (who cherishes and sustains you)?"— They said: "Yes! We do testify!" (This), lest you should say on the Day of Judgment: "Of this we were never mindful." 173 Or lest you should say: "Our fathers before us took false gods, but we are (their) descendants after them: will You then destroy us because of the deeds of men who

were wrong doers?" 174 Thus do We explain the Signs in detail; and perchance they may turn (unto Us).

175 Relate to them the story of the man to whom We sent Our Signs, but he passed them by: so Satan followed him up, and he went astray. 176 If it had been Our Will, We should have elevated him with Our Signs; but he inclined to the earth, and followed his own vain desires. His similitude is that of a dog: if you attack him, he lolls out his tongue, or if you leave him alone, he (still) lolls out his tongue. That is the similitude of those who reject Our Signs; so relate the story; perchance they may reflect. 177 Evil as an example are people who reject Our Signs and wrong their own souls. 178 Whom Allah does guide—he is on the right path: whom He rejects from His guidance—such are the persons who lose!

179 Many are the Jinns and men We have made for Hell: they have hearts wherewith they understand not, eyes wherewith they see not, and ears wherewith they hear not. They are like cattle—no more misguided: for they are heedless (of warning). 180 The most beautiful names belong to Allah: so call on him by them; but shun such men as distort His names: for what they do, they will soon be requited. 181 Of those We have created are people who direct (others) with truth. And dispense justice therewith. 182 Those who reject Our Signs, We will lead them step by step to ruin, in ways they perceive not; 183 Respite will I grant unto them: for My scheme is strong (and unfailing).

184 Do they not reflect? Their Companion is not seized with madness: he is but a perspicuous warner. 185 Do they see nothing in the government of the heavens and the earth and all that Allah has created? (Do they not see) that it may well be that their term is near drawing to an end? In what Message after this will they then believe? 186 To such as Allah rejects from His guidance, there can be no guide: He will leave them in their trespasses, wandering in distraction. 187 They ask you about the (final) Hour—when will be its appointed time? Say: "The knowledge thereof is with my Lord (alone): none but He can reveal as to when it will occur. Heavy were its burden through the heavens and the earth. Only,

all of a sudden will it come to you." They ask you as if you were eager in search thereof: say: "The knowledge thereof is with Allah (alone), but most men know not." 188 Say: "I have no power over any good or harm to myself except as Allah wills. If I had knowledge of the Unseen, I should have multiplied all good, and no evil should have touched me: I am but a warner, and a bringer of glad tidings to those who have faith."

189 It is He Who created you from a single person, and made his mate of like nature, in order that he might dwell with her (in love). When they are united, she bears a light burden and carries it about (unnoticed). When she grows heavy, they both pray to Allah their Lord, (saying): "If You give us a goodly child, we vow we shall (ever) be grateful." 190 But when He gives them a goodly child, they ascribe to others a share in the gift they have received: but Allah is exalted high above the partners they ascribe to Him. 191 Do they indeed ascribe to Him as partners things that can create nothing, but are themselves created? 192 No aid can they give them, nor can they aid themselves! 193 If you call them to guidance, they will not obey: for you it is the same whether you call them or you hold your peace! 194 Surely those whom you call upon besides Allah are servants like you: call upon them, and let them listen to your prayer, if you are (indeed) truthful!

195 Have they feet to walk with? Or hands to lay hold with? Or eyes to see with? Or ears to hear with? Say: "Call your 'god-partners,' scheme (your worst) against me, and give me no respite! 196 "For my Protector is Allah, who revealed the Book (from time to time), and He will befriend the righteous. 197 "But those you call upon besides Him, are unable to help you, and indeed to help themselves." 198 If you call them to guidance, they hear not. You will see them looking at you, but they see not.

199 Hold to forgiveness; command what is right; but turn away from the ignorant. 200 If a suggestion from Satan assail your (mind), seek refuge with Allah; for He hears and knows (all things). 201 Those who fear Allah, when a thought of evil from Satan assaults them, bring Allah to remembrance, when they see (aright)! 202 But their brethren (the evil ones) plunge them deeper into error, and never relax (their efforts).

203 If you do not bring them a Sign, they say: "Why have you not got it together?" Say: "I but follow what is revealed to me from my Lord: this is (nothing but) lights from your Lord, and Guidance, and Mercy, for any who have Faith." 204 When the Qur'ān is read, listen to it with attention, and hold your peace: that you may receive Mercy. 205 And you (O reader!) bring your Lord to remembrance in your (very) soul, with humility and in reverence, without loudness in words, in the mornings and evenings; and be not you of those who are unheedful. 206 Those who are near to your Lord, disdain not to worship Him: they celebrate His praises, and bow down before Him.

8. THE SPOILS OF WAR

In the name of Allah, Most Gracious, Most Merciful.

1 They ask you concerning (things taken as) spoils of war. Say: "(Such) spoils are at the disposal of Allah and the Messenger: so fear Allah, and keep straight the relations between yourselves: obey Allah and His Messenger, if you do believe." 2 For, Believers are those who, when Allah is mentioned, feel a tremor in their hearts, and when they hear His Revelations rehearsed, find their faith strengthened, and put (all) their trust in their Lord; 3 Who establish regular prayers and spend (freely) out of the gifts We have given them for sustenance: 4 Such in truth are the Believers: they have grades of dignity with their Lord, and forgiveness, and generous sustenance.

5 Just as your Lord ordered you out of your house in truth, even though a party among the Believers disliked it, 6 Disputing with you concerning the truth after it was made manifest, as if they were being driven to death and they (actually) saw it. 7 Behold! Allah promised you one of the two (enemy) parties, that it should be yours: you wished that the one unarmed should be yours, but Allah willed to justify the Truth according to His words and to cut off the roots of the Unbelievers— 8 That He might justify

Truth and prove Falsehood false, distasteful though it be to those in guilt.

9 Remember you implored the assistance of your Lord, and He answered you: "I will assist you with a thousand of the angels, ranks on ranks." 10 Allah made it but a message of hope, and an assurance to your hearts: (in any case) there is no help except from Allah: and Allah is Exalted in Power, wise. 11 Remember He covered you with a sort of drowsiness, to give you calm as from himself, and He caused rain to descend on you from heaven, to clean you therewith, to remove from you the stain of Satan, to strengthen your hearts, and to plant your feet firmly therewith. 12 Remember your Lord inspired the angels (with the message): "I am with you: give firmness to the Believers: I will instil terror into the hearts of the Unbelievers: smite you above their necks and smite all their finger-tips off them." 13 This because they contended against Allah and His Messenger: if any contend against Allah and His Messenger, Allah is strict in punishment. 14 Thus (will it be said): "Taste then of the (punishment): for those who reject, is the chastisement of the Fire."

15 O you who believe! When you meet the Unbelievers in hostile array, never turn your backs to them. 16 If any do turn his back to them on such a day—unless it be in a stratagem of war, or to retreat to a troop (of his own)—he draws on himself the wrath of Allah, and his abode is Hell—an evil refuge (indeed)!

17 It is not you who slew them; it was Allah: when you threw (a handful of dust), it was not your act, but Allah's: in order that He might confer on the Believers a gracious benefit from Himself: for Allah is He Who hears and knows (all things). 18 That, and also because Allah is He Who makes feeble the plans and stratagem of the Unbelievers. 19 (O Unbelievers!) if you prayed for victory and judgment, now has the judgment come to you: if you desist (from wrong), it will be best for you: if you return (to the attack), so shall We. Not of least good will your forces be to you even if they were multiplied: for surely Allah is with those who believe!

20 O you who believe! Obey Allah and His Messenger, and turn not away from him when you hear (him speak). 21 Nor be like

those who say, "We hear," but listen not: 22 For the worst of beasts in the sight of Allah are the deaf and the dumb—Those who understand not. 23 If Allah had found in them any good, He would indeed have made them listen: (as it is), if He had made them listen, they would but have turned back and declined (faith).

24 O you who believe! Give your response to Allah and His Messenger, when He calls you to that which will give you life; and know that Allah comes in between a man and his heart, and that it is He to Whom you shall (all) be gathered. 25 And fear tumult or oppression, which affects not in particular (only) those of you who do wrong: and know that Allah is strict in punishment.

26 Call to mind when you were a small (band), despised through the land, and afraid that men might despoil and kidnap you; but He provided a safe asylum for you, strengthened you with His aid, and gave you good things for sustenance: that you might be grateful. 27 O you who believe! Betray not the trust of Allah and the Messenger, nor misappropriate knowingly things entrusted to you. 28 And know you that your possessions and your progeny are but a trial; and that it is Allah with whom lies your highest reward.

29 O you who believe! If you fear Allah, He will grant you a Criterion (to judge between right and wrong), remove from you (all) evil (that may afflict) you, and forgive you: for Allah is the Lord of grace unbounded. 30 Remember how the Unbelievers plotted against you, to keep you in bonds, or slay you, or drive you out (of your home). They plot and plan, and Allah too plans; but the best of planners is Allah.

31 When Our Signs are rehearsed to them, they say: "We have heard this (before): if we wished, we could say (words) like these: these are nothing but tales of the ancients." 32 Remember how they said: "O Allah if this is indeed the Truth from You, rain down on us a shower of stones from the sky, or send us a grievous Chastisement." 33 But Allah was not going to send them a Chastisement while you were among them; nor was He going to send it while they could ask for pardon. 34 But what plea have they that Allah should not punish them, when they keep out (men)

from the Sacred Mosque — and they are not its guardians? No men can be its guardians except the righteous; but most of them do not understand. 35 Their prayer at the House (of Allah) is nothing but whistling and clapping of hands: (its only answer can be), "Taste you the Chastisement because you blasphemed."

36 The Unbelievers spend their wealth to hinder (men) from the path of Allah, and so will they continue to spend; but in the end they will have (only) regrets and sighs; at length they will be overcome: and the Unbelievers will be gathered together to Hell — 37 In order that Allah may separate the impure from the pure, put the impure, one on another, heap them together, and cast them into Hell. They will be the ones to have lost.

38 Say to the Unbelievers, if (now) they desist (from Unbelief), their past would be forgiven; but if they persist, the punishment of those before them is already (a matter of warning for them). 39 And fight with them on until there is no more persecution or oppression, and religion becomes Allah's in its entirety, but if they cease, surely Allah does see all that they do. 40 If they refuse, be sure that Allah is your Protector — the Best to protect and the Best to help.

41 And know that out of all the booty that you may acquire (in war), a fifth share is assigned to Allah — and to the Messenger, and to near relatives, orphans, the needy, and the wayfarer — If you do believe in Allah and in the revelation We sent down to Our Servant on the Day of Testing — the Day of the meeting of the two forces. For Allah has power over all things.

42 Remember you were on the hither side of the valley, and they on the farther side, and the caravan on lower ground than you. Even if you had made a mutual appointment to meet, you would certainly have failed in the appointment: but (thus you met), that Allah might accomplish a matter already enacted; that those who died might die after a clear Sign (had been given), and those who lived might live after a Clear Sign (had been given). And surely Allah is He Who hears and knows (all things). 43 Remember in your dream Allah showed them to you as few: if He had shown them to you as many, you would surely have been discouraged,

and you would surely have disputed in (your) decision; but Allah saved (you): for He knows well the (secrets) of (all) hearts. 44 And remember when you met, He showed them to you as few in your eyes, and He made you appear as contemptible in their eyes: that Allah might accomplish a matter already decided. For to Allah do all matters go back (for decision).

45 O you who believe! When you meet a force, be firm, and call Allah in remembrance much (and often); that you may succeed: 46 And obey Allah and His Messenger; and fall into no disputes, lest you lose heart and your power depart; and be patient and persevering: for Allah is with those who patiently persevere: 47 And be not like those who started from their homes insolently and to be seen of men, and to hinder (men) from the path of Allah: for Allah compasses round about all that they do.

48 Remember Satan made their (sinful) acts seem alluring to them, and said: "No one among men can overcome you this day, while I am near to you." But when the two forces came in sight of each other, he turned on his heels, and said: "I am clear of you; I see what you see not; I fear Allah: for Allah is strict in punishment." 49 The hypocrites say, and those in whose hearts is a disease: "These people—their religion has misled them." But if any trust in Allah, behold! Allah is Exalted in might, Wise.

50 If you could see, when the angels take the souls of the Unbelievers (at death), (how) they smite their faces and their backs, (saying): "Taste the chastisement of the blazing Fire— 51 "Because of (the deeds) which your (own) hands sent forth; for Allah is never unjust to His servants: 52 "(Deeds) after the manner of the People of Pharaoh and of those before them: they rejected the Signs of Allah, and Allah punished them for their crimes: for Allah is Strong, and Strict in punishment: 53 "Because Allah will never change the Grace which He has bestowed on a people until they change what is in their (own) souls: and, surely, Allah is He who hears and knows (all things)." 54 "The People of Pharaoh and those before them" treated as false the Signs of their Lord: so We destroyed them for their crimes, and We drowned the People of Pharaoh: for they were all oppressors and wrong-doers.

55 For the worst of beasts in the sight of Allah are those who reject Him: they will not believe. 56 They are those with whom you did make a covenant, but they break their covenant every time, and they have not the fear (of Allah). 57 If you gain the mastery over them in war, disperse, with them, those who follow them, that they may remember. 58 If you fear treachery from any group, throw back (their Covenant) to them, (so as to be) on equal terms: for Allah loves not the treacherous.

59 Let not the Unbelievers think that they have got away and get the better (of the godly): they will never frustrate (them). 60 Against them make ready your strength to the utmost of your power, including steeds of war, to strike terror into (the hearts of) the enemies, of Allah and your enemies, and others besides, whom you may not know, but whom Allah does know. Whatever you shall spend in the Cause of Allah, shall be repaid to you, and you shall not be treated unjustly. 61 But if the enemy incline towards peace, you (also) incline towards peace, and trust in Allah: for He is the One that hears and knows (all things). 62 Should they intend to deceive you — surely Allah suffices you: He it is that has strengthened you with His aid and with (the company of) the Believers; 63 And (moreover) He has put affection between their hearts: not if you had spent all that is in the earth, could you have produced that affection, but Allah has done it: for He is Exalted in might, Wise.

64 O Prophet! Sufficient for you is Allah — (for you) and for those who follow you among the Believers. 65 O Prophet! rouse the Believers to the fight. If there are twenty amongst you, patient and persevering, they will vanquish two hundred: if a hundred, they will vanquish a thousand of the Unbelievers: for these are a people without understanding. 66 For the present, Allah has lightened your (burden), for He knows that there is a weak spot in you: but (even so), if there are a hundred of you, patient and persevering, they will vanquish two hundred, and if a thousand, they will vanquish two thousand, with the leave of Allah: for Allah is with those who patiently persevere.

67 It is not fitting for a Prophet that he should have prisoners of war until he has thoroughly subdued the land. You look for the temporal goods of this world; but Allah looks to the Hereafter: and Allah is Exalted in might, Wise. 68 Had it not been for a previous ordainment from Allah, a severe penalty would have reached you for the (ransom) that you took. 69 But (now) enjoy what you took in war, lawful and good: but fear Allah: for Allah is Oft-forgiving, Most Merciful.

70 O Prophet! say to those who are captives in your hands: "If Allah finds any good in your hearts, He will give you something better than what has been taken from you, and He will forgive you: for Allah is Oft-forgiving, Most Merciful." 71 But if they have treacherous designs against you, (O Messenger!), they have already been in treason against Allah, and so has He given (you) power over them. And Allah is He Who has (full) knowledge and wisdom.

72 Those who believed, and emigrated, and fought for the Faith, with their property and their persons, in the cause of Allah, as well as those who gave (them) asylum and aid—these are (all) friends and protectors, one of another. As to those who believed but did not emigrate, you owe no duty of protection to them until they emigrate; but if they seek your aid in religion, it is your duty to help them, except against a people with whom you have a treaty of mutual alliance. And (remember) Allah sees all that you do. 73 The Unbelievers are protectors, one of another: unless you do this, (protect each other), there would be tumult and oppression on earth, and great mischief.

74 Those who believe, and emigrate, and fight for the Faith, in the cause of Allah as well as those who give (them) asylum and aid—these are (all) in very truth the Believers: for them is the forgiveness of sins and a provision most generous. 75 And those who accept Faith subsequently, and emigrate, and fight for the Faith in your company—they are of you. But kindred by blood have prior rights against each other in the Book of Allah. Surely Allah is well-acquainted with all things.

9. THE REPENTANCE

1 A (declaration) of immunity from Allah and His Messenger, to those of the Pagans with whom you have contracted mutual alliances— 2 Go you, then, for four months, backwards and forwards, (as you will), throughout the land, but know that you cannot frustrate Allah (by your falsehood) but that Allah will cover with shame those who reject Him. 3 And an announcement from Allah and His Messenger, to the people (assembled) on the day of the Great Pilgrimage—That Allah and His Messenger dissolve (treaty) obligations with the Pagans. If then, you repent, it were best for you; but if you turn away, know that you cannot frustrate Allah. And proclaim a grievous chastisement to those who reject Faith. 4 (But the treaties are) not dissolved with those Pagans with whom you have entered into alliance and who have not subsequently failed you, nor aided anyone against you. So fulfil your engagements with them to the end of their term: for Allah loves the righteous.

5 But when the forbidden months are past, then fight and slay the Pagans wherever you find them, and seize them, beleaguer them, and lie in wait for them in every stratagem (of war). But if they repent, and establish regular prayers and pay Zakat (poor-due), then open the way for them: for Allah is Oft-forgiving, Most Merciful. 6 If one amongst the Pagans ask you for asylum, grant it to him, so that he may hear the Word of Allah; and then escort him to where he can be secure. That is because they are men without knowledge.

7 How can there be a league, before Allah and His Messenger, with the Pagans, except those with whom you made a treaty near the Sacred Mosque? As long as these stand true to you, stand you true to them: for Allah does love the righteous. 8 How (can there be such a league), seeing that if they get an advantage over you, they respect not in you the ties either of kinship or of Covenant? With (fair words from) their mouths they entice you, but their hearts are averse from you; and most of them are rebellious and

wicked. 9 They have sold the Signs of Allah for a miserable price, and (many) have they hindered from His Way: evil indeed are the deeds they have done. 10 In a Believer they respect not the ties either of kinship or of covenant! It is they who have transgressed all bounds. 11 But (even so), if they repent, establish regular prayers, and pay zakat (poor-due) — they are your brethren in Faith: (thus) do We explain the Signs in detail, for those who understand.

12 But if they violate their oaths after their Covenant, and taunt you for your Faith — fight you the chiefs of Unfaith: for their oaths are nothing to them: that thus they may be restrained. 13 Will you not fight people who violated their oaths, plotted to expel the Messenger, and took the aggressive lead by being the first (to assault) you? Do you fear them? No, it is Allah Whom you should more justly fear, if you believe! 14 Fight them, and Allah will punish them by your hands, cover them with shame, help you (to victory) over them, heal the breasts of Believers, 15 And still the indignation of their hearts. For Allah will turn (in mercy) to whom He will; and Allah is All-Knowing, All-Wise.

16 Or do you think that you shall be abandoned, as though Allah did not know those among you who strive with might and main, and take none for friends and protectors except Allah, His Messenger, and the (community of) Believers? But Allah is well-acquainted with (all) that you do.

17 It is not for such as join gods with Allah, to visit or maintain the mosques of Allah while they witness against their own souls to infidelity. The works of such bear no fruit: in Fire shall they dwell. 18 The mosques of Allah shall be visited and maintained by such as believe in Allah and the Last Day, establish regular prayers, and pay zakat (poor-due), and fear none (at all) except Allah. It is they who are expected to be on true guidance. 19 Do you consider the giving of drink to pilgrims, or the maintenance of the Sacred Mosque, equal to (the pious service of) those who believe in Allah and the Last Day, and strive with might and main in the cause of Allah? They are not equal in the sight of Allah: and Allah guides not those who do wrong. 20 Those who believe,

and suffer exile and strive with might and main, in Allah's cause, with their goods and their persons, have the highest rank in the sight of Allah: they are the people who will achieve (salvation). 21 Their Lord does give them glad tidings of a Mercy from Himself, of His good pleasure, and of Gardens for them, wherein are delights that endure: 22 They will dwell therein for ever. Surely in Allah's presence is a reward, the greatest (of all).

23 O you who believe! take not for protectors your fathers and your brothers if they love infidelity above Faith. If any of you do so, they do wrong. 24 Say: If it be that your fathers, your sons, your brothers, your mates, or your kindred; the wealth that you have gained; the commerce in which you fear a decline: or the dwellings in which you delight—are dearer to you than Allah, or His Messenger, or the striving in His cause—then wait until Allah brings about his Decision: and Allah guides not the rebellious.

25 Assuredly Allah did help you in many battle-fields and on the day of Hunayn. Behold! your great numbers elated you, but they availed you naught: the land, for all that it is wide, did constrain you, and you turned back in retreat. 26 But Allah did pour His calm on the Messenger and on the Believers, and sent down forces which you did not see: He punished the Unbelievers; thus does He reward those without Faith. 27 Again will Allah, after this, turn (in mercy) to whom he will: for Allah is Oft-forgiving, Most Merciful. 28 O you who believe! Truly the Pagans are unclean; so let them not, after this year of theirs, approach the Sacred Mosque. And if you fear poverty, soon will Allah enrich you, if He wills, out of His bounty, for Allah is All-Knowing, All-Wise.

29 Fight those who believe not in Allah nor the Last Day, nor hold that forbidden which has been forbidden by Allah and His Messenger, nor acknowledge the religion of Truth, (even if they are) of the People of the Book, until they pay the *jizyah* (poll-tax) with willing submission, and feel themselves subdued. 30 The Jews call 'Uzayr a son of God, and the Christians call Christ the son of God. That is a saying from their mouth; (in this) they

but imitate what the Unbelievers of old used to say. Allah's curse be on them: how they are deluded away from the Truth! 31 They take their priests and their anchorites to be their lords in derogation of Allah, and (they take as their Lord) Christ the son of Mary; yet they were commanded to worship but One God. There is no god but He. Praise and glory to Him: (far is He) from having the partners they associate (with Him).

32 Fain would they extinguish Allah's Light with their mouths, but Allah will not allow but that His Light should be perfected, even though the Unbelievers may detest (it). 33 It is He Who has sent His Messenger with Guidance and the Religion of Truth, to proclaim it over all religions, even though the Pagans may detest (it).

34 O you who believe! There are indeed many among the priests and anchorites, who in falsehood devour the substance of men and hinder (them) from the Way of Allah. And there are those who bury gold and silver and spend it not in the Way of Allah: announce unto them a most grievous chastisement. 35 On the Day when heat will be produced out of that (wealth) in the fire of Hell, and with it will be branded their foreheads, their flanks, and their backs— "This is the (treasure) which you buried for yourselves: taste you, then, the (treasures) you buried!"

36 The number of months in the sight of Allah is twelve (in a year)—so ordained by Him the day He created the heavens and the earth; of them four are sacred: that is the straight usage. So wrong not yourselves therein, and fight the Pagans all together as they fight you all together. But know that Allah is with those who restrain themselves. 37 Surely, the transposing (of a prohibited month) is an addition to Unbelief: the Unbelievers are led to wrong thereby: for they make it lawful one year, and forbidden another year, in order to adjust the number of months forbidden by Allah and make such forbidden ones lawful. The evil of their course seems pleasing to them. But Allah guides not those who reject Faith.

38 O you who believe! what is the matter with you, that, when you are asked to go forth in the Cause of Allah, you cling heavily

to the earth? Do you prefer the life of this world to the Hereafter? But little is the comfort of this life, as compared with the Hereafter. 39 Unless you go forth, He will punish you with a grievous penalty, and put others in your place; but Him you would not harm in the least. For Allah has power over all things. 40 If you help not (your Leader), (it is no matter): for Allah did indeed help him, when the Unbelievers drove him out: he had no more than one companion; they two were in the Cave, and he said to his companion, "Have no fear, for Allah is with us": then Allah sent down His peace upon him, and strengthened him with forces which you saw not, and humbled to the depths the word of the Unbelievers. But the word of Allah is exalted to the heights: for Allah is Exalted in might, Wise.

41 Go you forth, (whether equipped) lightly or heavily, and strive and struggle, with your goods and your persons, in the Cause of Allah. That is best for you, if you (but) knew. 42 If there had been immediate gain (in sight), and the journey easy, they would (all) without doubt have followed you, but the distance was long, (and weighed) on them. They would indeed swear by Allah, "If we only could, We should certainly have come out with you." They would destroy their own souls; for Allah does know that they are certainly lying.

43 Allah may forgive you! Why did you grant them exemption until those who told the truth were seen by you in a clear light, and you had proved the liars? 44 Those who believe in Allah and the Last Day ask you for no exemption from striving with their goods and persons. And Allah knows well those who do their duty. 45 Only those ask you for exemption who believe not in Allah and the Last Day, and whose hearts are in doubt, so that they are tossed in their doubts here and there. 46 If they had intended to come out, they would certainly have made some preparation therefor; but Allah was averse to their being sent forth; so He made them lag behind, and they were told, "Sit you among those who sit (inactive)."

47 If they had come out with you, they would not have added to your (strength) but only (made for) disorder, hurrying to and

fro in your midst and sowing sedition among you, and there would have been some among you who would have listened to them. But Allah knows well those who do wrong. 48 Indeed they had plotted sedition before, and upset matters for you, until— The Truth arrived, and the Decree of Allah became manifest, much to their chagrin.

49 Among them is (many) a man who says: "Grant me exemption and draw me not into trial." Have they not fallen into trial already? And indeed Hell surrounds the Unbelievers (on all sides). 50 If good befalls you, it grieves them; but if a misfortune befalls you, they say, "We took indeed our precautions beforehand," and they turn away rejoicing. 51 Say: "Nothing will happen to us except what Allah has decreed for us: He is our Protector": and in Allah let the Believers put their trust. 52 Say: "Can you expect for us (any fate) other than one of two glorious things—(Martyrdom or victory)? But we can expect for you either that Allah will send His punishment from Himself, or by our hands. So wait (expectant); we too will wait with you."

53 Say: "Spend (for the Cause) willingly or unwillingly: not from you will it be accepted: for you are indeed a people rebellious and wicked." 54 The only reasons why their contributions are not accepted are: that they reject Allah and His Messenger; that they come to prayer without earnestness; and that they offer contributions unwillingly. 55 Let not their wealth nor their (following in) sons dazzle you: in reality Allah's Plan is to punish them with these things in this life, and that their souls may perish in their (very) denial of Allah. 56 They swear by Allah that they are indeed of you; but they are not of you: yet they are afraid (to appear in their true colours). 57 If they could find a place to flee to, or caves, or a place of concealment, they would turn straightaway thereto, with an obstinate rush.

58 And among them are men who slander you in the matter of (the distribution of) the alms: if they are given part thereof, they are pleased, but if not, behold! they are indignant! 59 If only they had been content with what Allah and His Prophet gave them, and had said, "Sufficient unto us is Allah! Allah and His

Messenger will soon give us of His bounty: to Allah do we turn our hopes!" (that would have been the right course). 60 Alms are for the poor and the needy; and those employed to administer the (funds); for those whose hearts have been (recently) reconciled (to Truth); for those in bondage and in debt; in the cause of Allah; and for the wayfarer: (thus is it) ordained by Allah, and Allah is full of knowledge and wisdom.

61 Among them are men who molest the Prophet and say, "He is (all) ear." Say, "He listens to what is best for you: he believes in Allah, has faith in the Believers, and is a Mercy to those of you who believe." But those who molest the Prophet will have a grievous penalty. 62 To you they swear by Allah. In order to please you: but it is more fitting that they should please Allah and His Messenger, if they are Believers. 63 Know they not that for those who oppose Allah and His Messenger, is the Fire of Hell?—wherein they shall dwell. That is the supreme disgrace.

64 The Hypocrites are afraid lest a sūrah should be sent down about them, showing them what is (really passing) in their hearts. Say: "Mock you! But surely Allah will bring to light all that you fear (should be revealed). 65 If you do question them, they declare (with emphasis): "We were only talking idly and in play." Say: "Was it at Allah, and His Signs, and His Messenger, that you were mocking?" 66 Make you no excuses: you have rejected Faith after you had accepted it. If We pardon some of you, We will punish others amongst you for that they are sinners.

67 The Hypocrites, men and women, (have an understanding) with each other: they enjoin evil, and forbid what is just, and are close with their hands. They have forgotten Allah; so He has forgotten them. Surely the Hypocrites are rebellious and perverse. 68 Allah has promised the Hypocrites men and women, and the rejecters, of Faith, the fire of Hell: therein shall they dwell: sufficient is it for them: for them is the curse of Allah, and an enduring punishment— 69 As in the case of those before you: they were mightier than you in power, and more flourishing in wealth and children. They had their enjoyment of their portion: and you have of yours, as did those before you; and you indulge in idle talk as they did. They!—Their works are fruitless in this

world and in the Hereafter, and they are the losers. 70 Has not the story reached them of those before them?—the People of Noah, and 'Ād, and Thamūd; the People of Abraham, the men of Midian, and the Cities overthrown. To them came their Messengers with Clear Signs. It is not Allah Who wrongs them, but they wrong their own souls.

71 The Believers, men and women, are protectors one of another: they enjoin what is just, and forbid what is evil: they observe regular prayers, pay Zakat (poor-due), and obey Allah and His Messenger. On them will Allah pour His mercy: for Allah is Exalted in power, Wise. 72 Allah has promised to Believers— men and women—Gardens under which rivers flow, to dwell therein, and beautiful mansions in Gardens of everlasting bliss. But the greatest bliss is the Good Pleasure of Allah: that is the supreme triumph.

73 O Prophet! strive hard against the Unbelievers and the Hypocrites, and be firm against them. Their abode is Hell—an evil refuge indeed. 74 They swear by Allah that they said nothing (evil), but indeed they uttered blasphemy, and they did it after accepting Islam; and they meditated a plot which they were unable to carry out: this revenge of theirs was (their) only return for the bounty with which Allah and His Messenger had enriched them! If they repent, it will be best for them; but if they turn back (to their evil ways), Allah will punish them with a grievous chastisement in this life and in the Hereafter: they shall have none on earth to protect or help them.

75 Amongst them are men who made a Covenant with Allah, that if He bestowed on them of His bounty, they would give (largely) in charity, and be truly among those who are righteous. 76 But when He did bestow of His bounty, they became covetous, and turned back (from their Covenant), averse (from its fulfilment). 77 So He has put as a consequence hypocrisy into their hearts, (to last) till the Day, whereon they shall meet Him: because they broke their Covenant with Allah, and because they lied (again and again). 78 Know they not that Allah does know their secret (thoughts) and their secret counsels, and that Allah knows well all things unseen? 79 Those who ridicule such of the

Believers as give themselves freely to (deeds of) charity, as well as such as can find nothing to give except the fruits of their labour—and throw ridicule on them—Allah will throw back their ridicule on them: and they shall have a grievous chastisement. 80 Whether you ask for their forgiveness, or not, (their sin is unforgivable). If you ask seventy times for their forgiveness, Allah will not forgive them: because they have rejected Allah and His Messenger: and Allah guides not those who are perversely rebellious.

81 Those who did not go forth (in the Tabūk expedition) rejoiced in their staying back behind the back of the Messenger of Allah: they hated to strive and fight, with their goods and their persons, in the Cause of Allah: they said, "Go not forth in the heat." Say, "The fire of Hell is fiercer in heat." If only they could understand! 82 Let them laugh a little: much will they weep: a recompense for the (evil) that they do. 83 If, then, Allah bring you back to any of them, and they ask your permission to come out (with you), say: "Never shall you come out with me, nor fight an enemy with me: for you preferred to sit inactive on the first occasion: then sit you (now) with those who lag behind." 84 Nor do you ever pray for any of them that dies, nor stand at his grave; for they rejected Allah and His Messenger, and died in a state of perverse rebellion.

85 Nor let their wealth and sons dazzle you: Allah's Plan is to punish them with these things in this world, and that their souls may depart while they are unbelievers. 86 When a sūrah comes down, enjoining them to believe in Allah and to strive and struggle along with His Messenger, those with wealth and influence among them ask you for exemption, and say: "Leave us (behind): we would be with those who sit (at home)." 87 They prefer to be with (the women), who remain behind (at home): their hearts are sealed and so they understand not. 88 But the Messenger, and those who believe with him, strove and struggle with their wealth and their persons: for them are (all) good things: and it is they for whom is success. 89 Allah has prepared for them gardens under which rivers flow, to dwell therein: that is the supreme felicity.

90 And there were, among the desert Arabs (also), men who made excuses and came to seek exemption; and those who were false to Allah and His Messenger (merely) sat behind. Soon will a grievous torment seize the Unbelievers among them. 91 There is no blame on those who are infirm, or ill, or who find no resources to spend (on the Cause), if they are sincere (in duty) to Allah and His Messenger: no ground (of complaint) can there be against such as do right: and Allah is Oft-forgiving, Most Merciful. 92 Nor (is there blame) on those who came to you to be provided with mounts, and when you said, "I can find no mounts for you," they turned back, their eyes streaming with tears of grief that they had no resources wherewith to provide the expenses. 93 The ground (of complaint) is only against such as claim exemption while they are rich. They prefer to stay with the (women) who remain behind: Allah has sealed their hearts; so they know not (what they miss).

94 They will present their excuses to you when you return to them. Say you: "Present no excuses: we shall not believe you: Allah has already informed us of the true state of matters concerning you: it is your actions that Allah and His Messenger will observe: in the end will you be brought back to Him who knows what is hidden and what is open: then will He show you the truth of all that you did." 95 They will swear to you by Allah, when you return to them, That you may leave them alone. So leave them alone: for they are an abomination, and Hell is their dwelling-place—a fitting recompense for the (evil) that they did. 96 They will swear unto you, that you may be pleased with them. But if you are pleased with them, Allah is not pleased with those who disobey.

97 The Arabs of the desert are the worst in Unbelief and hypocrisy, and most fitted to be in ignorance of the command which Allah has sent down to His Messenger: but Allah is All-Knowing, All-Wise. 98 Some of the desert Arabs look upon their payments as a fine, and watch for disasters for you: on them be the disaster of Evil: for Allah is He that hears and knows (all things). 99 But some of the desert Arabs believe in Allah and the Last Day, and look on their payments as pious gifts bringing them

nearer to Allah and obtaining the prayers of the Messenger. Yes, indeed they bring them nearer (to Him): soon will Allah admit them to His Mercy: for Allah is Oft-Forgiving, Most Merciful.

100 The vanguard (of Islam)—the first of those who forsook (their homes) and of those who gave them aid, and (also) those who follow them in (all) good deeds—well-pleased is Allah with them, as are they with Him: for them has He prepared gardens under which rivers flow, to dwell therein for ever: that is the supreme Triumph. 101 Certain of the desert Arabs round about you are Hypocrites, as well as (desert Arabs) among the Madīnah folk: they are obstinate in hypocrisy: you know them not: We know them: twice shall We punish them: and in addition shall they be sent to a grievous chastisement.

102 Others (there are who) have acknowledged their wrong-doings: they have mixed an act that was good with another that was evil. Perhaps Allah will turn unto them (in Mercy): for Allah is Oft-Forgiving, most Merciful. 103 Of their goods, take alms, so that you might purify and sanctify them; and pray on their behalf. Surely your prayers are a source of security for them: and Allah is One who hears and knows. 104 Know they not that Allah does accept repentance from his votaries and receives their gifts of charity, and that Allah is surely He, the Oft-Returning, Most Merciful? 105 And say: "Work (righteousness): soon will Allah observe your work, and His Messenger, and the Believers: soon will you be brought back to the Knower of what is hidden and what is open: then will He show you the truth of all that you did." 106 There are (yet) others, held in suspense for the command of Allah, whether He will punish them, or turn in mercy to them: and Allah is All-Knowing, Wise.

107 And there are those who put up a mosque by way of mischief and infidelity—to disunite the Believers— and in preparation for one who warred against Allah and His Messenger aforetime. They will indeed swear that their intention is nothing but good; but Allah does declare that they are certainly liars. 108 Never stand you forth therein. There is a mosque whose foundation was laid from the first day on piety; it is more worthy of the standing forth

(for prayer) therein. In it are men who love to be purified; and Allah loves those who make themselves pure. 109 Which then is best? — he that lays his foundation on piety to Allah and His Good Pleasure? — or he that lays his foundation on an undermined sand-cliff ready to crumble to pieces? And it does crumble to pieces with him, into the fire of Hell. And Allah guides not people that do wrong. 110 The foundation of those who so build is never free from suspicion and shakiness in their hearts, until their hearts are cut to pieces. And Allah is All-Knowing, Wise.

111 Allah has purchased of the Believers their persons and their goods; for theirs (in return) is the Garden (of Paradise): they fight in His Cause, and slay and are slain: a promise binding on Him in truth, through the Law, the Gospel, and the Qur'ān: and who is more faithful to his Covenant than Allah? Then rejoice in the bargain which you have concluded: that is the achievement supreme. 112 Those that turn (to Allah) in repentance; that serve Him, and praise Him; that wander in devotion to the Cause of Allah; that bow down and prostrate themselves in prayer; that enjoin good and forbid evil; and observe the limit set by Allah — (these do rejoice). So proclaim the glad tidings to the Believers.

113 It is not fitting, for the Prophet and those who believe, that they should pray for forgiveness for Pagans, even though they be of kin, after it is clear to them that they are companions of the Fire. 114 And Abraham prayed for his father's forgiveness only because of a promise he had made to him. But when it became clear to him that he was an enemy to Allah, he dissociated himself from him: for Abraham was most tender-hearted, forbearing. 115 And Allah will not mislead a people after He has guided them, until he makes clear to them what to fear (and avoid) — for Allah has knowledge of all things. 116 Unto Allah belongs the dominion of the heavens and the earth. He gives life and He takes it. Except for Him you have no protector nor helper.

117 Allah turned with favour to the Prophet, the Muhājirs (Migrants), and the Anṣār (Helpers) — who followed him in a time of distress, after that the hearts of a part of them had nearly swerved (from duty); but He turned to them (also): for He is unto

them Most Kind, Most Merciful. 118 (He turned in mercy also) to the three who were left behind; (they felt guilty) to such a degree that the earth seemed constrained to them, for all its spaciousness, and their (very) souls seemed straitened to them — and they perceived that there is no fleeing from Allah (and no refuge) but to Himself. Then He turned to them, that they might repent: for Allah is Oft-Returning, most Merciful.

119 O you who believe! Fear Allah and be with those who are true (in word and deed). 120 It was not fitting for the people of Madīnah and the Bedouin Arabs of the neighbourhood, to refuse to accompany Allah's Messenger, nor to prefer their own lives to his: because nothing could they suffer or do, but was reckoned to their credit as a deed of righteousness — whether they suffered thirst, or fatigue, or hunger, in the Cause of Allah, or trod paths to raise the ire of the Unbelievers, or inflicted any injury whatever on an enemy: for Allah suffers not the reward to be lost of those who do good — 121 Nor could they spend anything (for the Cause) — small or great — nor cut across a valley, but the deed is inscribed to their credit: that Allah may requite their deed with the best (possible reward).

122 Nor should the Believers all go forth together. If a group from every expedition remained behind, they could devote themselves to studies in religion, and admonish the people when they return to them — that thus they (may learn) to guard themselves (against evil).

123 O you who believe! Fight the Unbelievers who are around you, and let them find firmness in you: and know that Allah is with those who fear Him. 124 Whenever there comes down a sūrah, some of them say: "Which of you has had his faith increased by it?" Yes, those who believe — their faith is increased and they do rejoice. 125 But those in whose hearts is a disease — it will add doubt to their doubt, and they will die in a state of unbelief. 126 See they not that they are tried every year once or twice? Yet they turn not in repentance, and they take no heed. 127 Whenever there comes down a sūrah, they look at each other, (saying), "Does anyone see you?" Then they turn away: Allah has turned their hearts (from the light); for they are a people that understand not.

128 Now has come unto you a Messenger from amongst yourselves: it grieves him that you should perish: ardently anxious is he over you: to the Believers is he most kind and merciful. 129 But if they turn away, say: "Allah suffices me: there is no god but He: on Him is my trust — He the Lord of the Throne (of Glory) Supreme!"

10. JONAH

In the name of Allah, Most Gracious, Most Merciful.

1 *Alif Lām Rā* these are the Ayāt (Signs) of the Book of Wisdom. 2 Is it a matter of wonderment to men that We have sent our inspiration to a man from among themselves?— that he should warn mankind (of their danger), and give the good news to the Believers that they have before their Lord the lofty rank of Truth. (But) say the Unbelievers: "This is indeed an evident sorcerer!"

3 Surely your Lord is Allah, who created the heavens and the earth in six Days, and firmly established Himself on the Throne (of authority), regulating and governing all things. No intercessor (can plead with Him) except after His leave (has been obtained). This is Allah your Lord; Him therefore serve you: will you not receive admonition? 4 To Him will be your return — of all of you. The promise of Allah is true and sure. It is He who begins the process of Creation, and repeats it, that He may reward with justice those who believe and work righteousness; but those who reject Him will have draughts of boiling fluids, and a Torment grievous, because they did reject Him.

5 It is He who made the sun to be a shining glory and the moon to be a light (of beauty), and measured out stages for her; that you might know the number of years and the count (of time). Nowise did Allah create this but in truth and righteousness. (Thus) does He explain His Signs in detail, for those who understand. 6 Surely, in the alternation of the Night and the Day, and in all that Allah has created, in the heavens and the earth, are Signs for those who fear Him.

7 Those who rest not their hope on their meeting with Us, but are pleased and satisfied with the life of the Present, and those who heed not our Signs— 8 Their abode is the Fire, because of the (evil) they earned. 9 Those who believe, and work righteousness— their Lord will guide them because of their Faith: beneath them will flow rivers in Gardens of Bliss. 10 (This will be) their prayer therein: "Glory to You, O Allah!" and "Peace" will be their greeting therein! And the close of their prayer will be: "Praise be to Allah, the Cherisher and Sustainer of the Worlds!"

11 If Allah were to hasten for men the ill (they have earned) as they would happily hasten on the good— then would their respite be settled at once. But We leave those who rest not their hope on their meeting with Us, in their trespasses, wandering in distraction blindly. 12 When trouble touches a man, he cries unto Us (in all postures)— lying down on his side, or sitting, or standing. But when We have removed his trouble, he passes on his way as if he had never cried to Us for a trouble that touched him! Thus do the deeds of transgressors seem fair in their eyes!

13 Generations before you We destroyed when they did wrong: their Messengers came to them with Clear Signs, but they would not believe! Thus do We requite those who sin! 14 Then We made you heirs in the land after them, to see how you would behave!

15 But when Our Clear Signs are rehearsed unto them, those who rest not their hope on their meeting with Us, say: "Bring us a Qur'ān other than this, or change this." Say: "It is not for me, of my own accord, to change it: I follow nothing but what is revealed to me: if I were to disobey my Lord, I should myself fear the Penalty of a Great Day (to come)." 16 Say: "If Allah had so willed, I should not have rehearsed it to you, nor would He have made it known to you. A whole lifetime before this have I tarried amongst you: will you not then understand?" 17 Who does more wrong than such as forge a lie against Allah, or deny His Signs? But never will prosper those who sin.

18 They serve, besides Allah, things that hurt them not nor profit them, and they say: "These are our intercessors with Allah." Say:

"Do you indeed inform Allah of something He knows not, in the heavens or on earth?—Glory to Him! And far is He above the partners they ascribe (to Him)!" 19 Mankind was but one nation, but differed (later). Had it not been for a Word that went forth before from your Lord, their differences would have been settled between them.

20 They say: "Why is not a Sign sent down to him from his Lord?" Say: "The Unseen is only for Allah (to know). Then wait you: I too will wait with you." 21 When We make mankind taste of some mercy after adversity has touched them, behold! they take to plotting against Our Signs! Say: "Swifter to plan is Allah!" Surely, Our Messengers record all the plots that you make!

22 He it is Who enables you to traverse through land and sea; so that you even board ships—they sail with them with a favourable wind, and they rejoice thereat; then comes a stormy wind and the waves come to them from all sides, and they think they are being overwhelmed: they cry unto Allah, sincerely offering (their) duty unto Him, saying, "If you deliver us from this, we shall truly show our gratitude!" 23 But when He delivers them, behold! they transgress insolently through the earth in defiance of right! O mankind! your insolence is against your own souls—an enjoyment of the life of the Present: in the end, to Us is your return, and We shall show you the truth of all that you did.

24 The likeness of the life of the Present is as the rain which We send down from the skies: by its mingling arises the produce of the earth—which provides food for men and animals: (it grows) till the earth is clad with its golden ornaments and is decked out (in beauty): the people to whom it belongs think they have all powers of disposal over it: then reaches Our command by night or by day, and We make it like a harvest clean-mown, as if it had not flourished only the day before! Thus do We explain the Signs in detail for those who reflect.

25 But Allah does call to the Home of Peace: He does guide whom He pleases to a Way that is straight. 26 To those who do right is a goodly (reward)—Yes, more (than in measure)! No

darkness nor shame shall cover their faces! They are companions of the Garden; they will abide therein (for ever)! 27 But those who have earned evil will have a reward of like evil: ignominy will cover their (faces): no defender will they have from (the wrath of) Allah: their faces will be covered, as it were, with pieces from the depth of the darkness of Night: they are companions of the Fire: they will abide therein (for ever)!

28 One day shall We gather them all together. Then shall We say to those who joined gods (with Us): "To your place! you and those you joined as 'partners.'" We shall separate them, and their "partners" shall say: "It was not us that you worshipped! 29 "Enough is Allah for a witness between us and you: we certainly knew nothing of your worship of us!" 30 There will every soul see (the fruits of) the deeds it sent before: they will be brought back to Allah their rightful Lord, and their invented falsehoods will leave them in the lurch.

31 Say: "Who is it that sustains you (in life) from the sky and from the earth? Or who is it that has power over hearing and sight? And who is it that brings out the living from the dead and the dead from the living? And who is it that rules and regulates all affairs?" They will soon say, "Allah." Say, "Will you not then show piety (to Him)?" 32 Such is Allah, your real Cherisher and Sustainer: apart from Truth, what (remains) but error? How then are you turned away? 33 Thus is the Word of your Lord proved true against those who rebel: surely, they will not believe.

34 Say: "Of your 'partners,' can any originate creation and repeat it?" Say: "It is Allah Who originates creation and repeats it: then how are you deluded away (from the truth)?" 35 Say: "Of your 'partners' is there any that can give any guidance towards Truth?" Say: "It is Allah who gives guidance towards Truth. Is then He who gives guidance to Truth more worthy to be followed, or he who finds not guidance (himself) unless he is guided? What then is the matter with you? How do you judge?" 36 But most of them follow nothing but fancy: truly fancy can be of no avail against Truth. Surely, Allah is well aware of all that they do.

37 This Qur'ān is not such as can be produced by other than

Allah; on the contrary, it is a confirmation of (revelations) that went before it, and a fuller explanation of the Book—wherein there is no doubt—from the Lord of the Worlds. 38 Or do they say, "He forged it"? Say: "Bring then a sūrah like it, and call (to your aid) anyone you can, besides Allah, if it be that you speak the truth!" 39 No, they charge with falsehood him whose knowledge they cannot compass, even before the elucidation thereof has reached them: thus did those before them make charges of falsehood: but see what was the end of those who did wrong!

40 Of them there are some who believe therein, and some who do not: and your Lord knows best those who are out for mischief. 41 If they charge you with falsehood, say: "My work to me, and yours to you! You are free from responsibility for what I do, and I for what you do!" 42 Among them are some who (pretend to) listen to you: but can you make the deaf to hear—even though they are without understanding? 43 And among them are some who look at you: but can you guide the blind—even though they will not see? 44 Surely, Allah will not deal unjustly with man in anything: it is man that wrongs his own soul.

45 One day He will gather them together: (It will be) as if they had tarried but an hour of a day. They will recognise each other: assuredly those will be lost who denied the meeting with Allah and refused to receive true guidance. 46 Whether We show you (realised in your lifetime) some part of what We promise them—or We take your soul (to Our Mercy) (before that)—in any case, to Us is their return: ultimately Allah is witness, to all that they do. 47 To every people (was sent) a Messenger: when their Messenger comes (before them), the matter will be judged between them with justice, and they will not be wronged.

48 They say: "When will this promise come to pass—If you speak the truth?" 49 Say: "I have no power over any harm or good to myself except as Allah wills. To every People is a term appointed: when their term is reached, not an hour can they cause delay, nor (an hour) can they advance (it in anticipation)." 50 Say: "Do you see— if His punishment should come to you by

night or by day—what portion of it would the Sinners wish to hasten? 51 "Would you then believe in it at last, when it actually comes to pass? (It will then be said:) 'Ah! now? and you wanted (aforetime) to hasten it on!' 52 "At length will be said to the wrongdoers: 'Taste you the enduring punishment! You get but the recompense of what you earned!'"

53 They seek to be informed by you: "Is that true?" say: "Yes! by my Lord! It is the very truth! And you cannot frustrate it!" 54 Every soul that has sinned, if it possessed all that is on earth, would willingly give it in ransom: they would declare (their) repentance when they see the Penalty: but the judgment between them will be with justice, and no wrong will be done to them. 55 Is it not (the case) that to Allah belongs whatever is in the heavens and on earth? Is it not (the case) that Allah's promise is assuredly true? Yet most of them understand not. 56 It is He who gives life and who takes it, and to Him shall you all be brought back.

57 O mankind! there has come to you a direction from your Lord and a healing for the (diseases) in your hearts—and for those who believe, a Guidance and a Mercy. 58 Say: "In the Bounty of Allah, and in His Mercy—in that let them rejoice:" That is better than the (wealth) they hoard. 59 Say: "See you what things Allah has sent down to you for sustenance? Yet you hold forbidden some things thereof and (some things) lawful." Say: "Has Allah indeed permitted you, or do you invent (things) to attribute to Allah?" 60 And what think those who invent lies against Allah, of the Day of Judgment? Surely, Allah is full of Bounty to mankind, but most of them are ungrateful.

61 In whatever business you may be, and whatever portion you may be reciting from the Qur'ān—and whatever deed you (mankind) may be doing—we are witnesses thereof when you are deeply engrossed therein. Nor is hidden from your Lord (so much as) the weight of an atom on the earth or in heaven. And not the least and not the greatest of these things but are recorded in a clear Record. 62 Behold! surely on the friends of Allah there is no fear, nor shall they grieve; 63 Those who believe and (constantly) guard against evil— 64 For them are Glad Tidings, in the life

of the Present and in the Hereafter; no change can there be in the Words of Allah. This is indeed the supreme Felicity. 65 Let not their speech grieve you: for all power and honour belong to Allah: it is He Who hears and knows (all things).

66 Behold! surely to Allah belong all creatures, in the heavens and on earth. What do they follow who worship as His "partners" other than Allah? They follow nothing but fancy, and they do nothing but lie. 67 He it is that has made for you the Night that you may rest therein, and the Day to make things visible (to you). Surely in this are Signs for those who listen (to His Message).

68 They say: "Allah has begotten a son!"—Glory be to Him! He is Self-Sufficient! His are all things in the heavens and on earth! No warrant have you for this! Do you say about Allah what you know not? 69 Say: "Those who invent a lie against Allah will never prosper." 70 A little enjoyment in this world!—and then, to Us will be their return, then shall We make them taste the severest Torment for their blasphemies.

71 Relate to them the story of Noah. Behold! he said to his people: "O my People, if it be hard on your (mind) that I should stay (with you) and commemorate the Signs of Allah—yet I put my trust in Allah. Get you then an agreement about your plan and among your Partners, so your plan be not to you dark and dubious.[8] Then pass your sentence on me, and give me no respite. 72 "But if you turn back, (consider): no reward have I asked of you: my reward is only due from Allah, and I have been commanded to be of those who submit to Allah's Will (in Islam)." 73 They rejected him, but We delivered him, and those with him, in the Ark, and We made them inherit (the earth), while We overwhelmed in the Flood those who rejected Our Signs. Then see what was the end of those who were warned (but heeded not)!

74 Then after him We sent (many) Messengers to their Peoples: they brought them Clear Signs, but they would not believe what they had already rejected beforehand. Thus do We seal the hearts of the transgressors.

75 Then after them We sent Moses and Aaron to Pharaoh and his chiefs with Our Signs. But they were arrogant: they were a

people in sin. 76 When the Truth did come to them from Us, they said: "This is indeed evident sorcery!" 77 Said Moses: "Do you say (this) about the Truth when it has (actually) reached you? Is sorcery (like) this? But sorcerers will not prosper." 78 They said: "Have you come to us to turn us away from the ways we found our fathers following — in order that you and your brother may have greatness in the land? But we shall not believe in you!"

79 Said Pharaoh: "Bring me every sorcerer well-versed." 80 When the sorcerers came, Moses said to them: "Throw you what you (wish) to throw!" 81 When they had had their throw, Moses said: "What you have brought is sorcery: Allah will surely make it of no effect: for Allah prospers not the work of those who make mischief. 82 "And Allah by His Words does prove and establish His Truth, however much the Sinners may hate it!"

83 But none believed in Moses except some children of his People, because of the fear of Pharaoh and his chiefs, lest they should persecute them; and certainly Pharaoh was mighty on the earth and one who transgressed all bounds. 84 Moses said: "O my People! If you do (really) believe in Allah, then in Him put your trust if you submit (your will to His)." 85 They said: "In Allah do we put our trust. Our Lord! make us not a trial for those who practise oppression; 86 "And deliver us by Your Mercy from those who reject (You)."

87 We inspired Moses and his brother with this Message: "Provide dwellings for your People in Egypt, make your dwellings into places of worship, and establish regular prayers: and give Glad Tidings to those who believe!"

88 Moses prayed: "Our Lord! You have indeed bestowed on Pharaoh and his Chiefs splendour and wealth in the life of the Present, and so, our Lord, they mislead (men) from Your Path. Deface, our Lord, the features of their wealth, and send hardness to their hearts, so they will not believe until they see the grievous Penalty." 89 Allah said: "Accepted is your prayer (O Moses and Aaron)! So stand you straight, and follow not the path of those who know not."

90 We took the Children of Israel across the sea: Pharaoh and

his hosts followed them in insolence and spite. At length, when
overwhelmed with the flood, he said: "I believe that there is no
god except Him Whom the Children of Israel believe in: I am
of those who submit (to Allah in Islam)." 91 (It was said to him):
"Ah now!—But a little while before, you were in rebellion!—
and you did mischief (and violence)! 92 "This day shall We save
you in the body, that you may be a Sign to those who come after
you! But, surely, many among mankind are heedless of Our
Signs!"

93 We settled the Children of Israel in a beautiful dwelling-
place, and provided for them sustenance of the best: it was after
knowledge had been granted to them, that they fell into schisms.
Surely Allah will judge between them as to the schisms amongst
them, on the Day of Judgment.

94 If you are in doubt as to what We have revealed unto you,
then ask those who have been reading the Book from before you:
the Truth has indeed come to you from your Lord: so be in nowise
of those in doubt. 95 Nor be of those who reject the Signs of Allah,
or you shall be of those who perish.

96 Those against whom the Word of your Lord has been verified
would not believe— 97 Even if every Sign was brought unto
them—until they see (for themselves) the Penalty Grievous.
98 Why was there not a single township (among those we warned),
which believed—so its Faith should have profited it—except the
People of Jonah? When they believed, We removed from them
the Penalty of Ignominy in the life of the Present, and permitted
them to enjoy (their life) for a while.

99 If it had been your Lord's Will, they would all have
believed—all who are on earth! Will you then compel mankind,
against their will, to believe! 100 No soul can believe, except
by the Will of Allah, and He will place Doubt (or obscurity) on
those who will not understand.

101 Say: "Behold all that is in the heavens and on earth!" but
neither Signs nor Warners profit those who believe not. 102 Do
they then expect (anything) but (what happened in) the days of
the men who passed away before them? Say: "Wait you then: for

I, too, will wait with you." 103 In the end We deliver our Messengers and those who believe: thus is it fitting on Our part that We should deliver those who believe!

104 Say: "O you men! If you are in doubt as to my religion, (behold!) I worship not what you worship, other than Allah! But I worship Allah—who will take your souls (at death): I am commanded to be (in the ranks) of the Believers, 105 "And further (thus): 'set your face towards Religion with true piety, and never in anywise be of the unbelievers; 106 "'Nor call on any, other than Allah—such will neither profit you nor hurt you: if you do, behold! you shall certainly be of those who do wrong.'" 107 If Allah do touch you with hurt, there is none can remove it but He: if He do design some benefit for you, there is none can keep back His favour: He causes it to reach whomsoever of His servants He pleases. And He is the Oft-Forgiving, Most Merciful.

108 Say: "O you men! Now truth has reached you from your Lord! those who receive guidance, do so for the good of their own souls; those who stray, do so to their own loss: and I am not (set) over you to arrange your affairs." 109 Follow you the inspiration sent unto you, and be patient and constant, till Allah do decide: for He is the Best to decide.

11. HŪD

In the name of Allah, Most Gracious, Most Merciful.

1 *Alif Lām Rā.* (This is) a Book, with verses basic or fundamental (of established meaning), further explained in detail—from One Who is Wise and Well-Acquainted (with all things): 2 (It teaches) that you should worship none but Allah. (say): "Surely, I am (sent) to you from Him to warn and to bring glad tidings: 3 "(And to preach thus), 'Seek you the forgiveness of your Lord, and turn to Him in repentance; that He may grant you enjoyment, good (and true), for a term appointed, and bestow His abounding grace on all who abound in merit! But if you turn away, then I fear for you the Penalty of a Great Day: 4 "'To Allah is your return, and He has power over all things.'"

5 Behold! they fold up their hearts, that they may lie hid from Him! Ah! even when they cover themselves with their garments, He knows what they conceal, and what they reveal: for He knows well the (inmost secrets) of the hearts. 6 There is no moving creature on earth but its sustenance depends on Allah: He knows the time and place of its definite abode and its temporary deposit: all is in a clear Record.

7 He it is Who created the heavens and the earth in six Days — and His Throne was over the Waters — that He might try you, which of you is best in conduct. But if you were to say to them, "You shall indeed be raised up after death," the unbelievers would be sure to say, "This is nothing but obvious sorcery!" 8 If We delay the penalty for them for a definite term, they are sure to say, "what keeps it back?" Ah! On the day it (actually) reaches them, nothing will turn it away from them, and they will be completely encircled by that which they used to mock at!

9 If We give man a taste of Mercy from Ourselves, and then withdraw it from him, behold! he is in despair and (falls into) blasphemy. 10 But if We give him a taste of (Our) favours after adversity has touched him, he is sure to say, "All evil has departed from me." Behold! he falls into exultation and pride. 11 Not so do those who show patience and constancy, and work righteousness; for them is forgiveness (of sins) and a great reward.

12 Perchance you may (feel the inclination) to give up a part of what is revealed unto you, and your heart feels straitened lest they say, "Why is not a treasure sent down unto him, or why does not an angel come down with him?" But you are there only to warn! It is Allah that arranges all affairs! 13 Or they may say, "He forged it." Say, "Bring you then ten sūrahs forged, like unto it, and call (to your aid) whomsoever you can, other than Allah! — if you speak the truth! 14 "If then they (your false gods) answer not your (call), know you that this Revelation is sent down (replete) with the knowledge of Allah, and that there is no god but He! will you even then submit (to Islam)?"

15 Those who desire the life of the Present and its glitter — to them We shall pay (the price of) their deeds therein — without

diminution. 16 They are those for whom there is nothing in the Hereafter but the Fire: vain are the designs they frame therein, and of no effect are the deeds that they do!

17 Can they be (like) those who accept a Clear (Sign) from their Lord, and whom a witness from Himself does teach, as did the Book of Moses before it — a guide and a mercy? They believe therein; but those of the Sects that reject it — the Fire will be their promised meeting-place. Be not then in doubt thereon: for it is the Truth from your Lord: yet many among men do not believe!

18 Who does more wrong than those who invent a lie against Allah? They will be turned back to the presence of their Lord, and the witnesses will say, "These are the ones who lied against their Lord! Behold! the Curse of Allah is on those who do wrong! — 19 "Those who would hinder (men) from the path of Allah and would seek in it something crooked: these were they who denied the Hereafter!" 20 They will in no wise frustrate (His design) on earth, nor have they protectors besides Allah! Their penalty will be doubled! They lost the power to hear, and they did not see! 21 They are the ones who have lost their own souls: and the (fancies) they invented have left them in the lurch! 22 Without a doubt, these are the very ones who will lose most in the Hereafter!

23 But those who believe and work righteousness, and humble themselves before their Lord — they will be Companions of the Garden, to dwell therein for ever! 24 These two kinds (of men) may be compared to the blind and deaf, and those who can see and hear well. Are they equal when compared? Will you not then take heed?

25 We sent Noah to his People (with a mission): "I have come to you with a Clear Warning: 26 "That you serve none but Allah: surely, I do fear for you the Penalty of a Grievous Day." 27 But the Chiefs of the Unbelievers among his People said: "We see (in) you nothing but a man like ourselves: nor do we see that any follow you but the meanest among us, in judgment immature: nor do we see in you (all) any merit above us: in fact we think you are liars!"

28 He said: "O my People! See you if (it be that) I have a Clear Sign from my Lord, and that He has sent Mercy unto me from His own Presence, but that the Mercy has been obscured from your sight? Shall we compel you to accept it when you are averse to it? 29 "And O my People! I ask you for no wealth in return: my reward is from none but Allah: but I will not drive away (in contempt) those who believe: for, surely, they are to meet their Lord, and you I see are the ignorant ones! 30 "And O my people! Who would help me against Allah if I drove them away? Will you not then take heed? 31 "I tell you not that with me are the Treasures of Allah, nor do I know what is hidden, nor I claim to be an angel. Nor yet do I say, of those whom your eyes do despise that Allah will not grant them (all) that is good: Allah knows best what is in their souls: I should, if I did, indeed be a wrong-doer."

32 They said: "O Noah! You have disputed with us, and (much) have you prolonged the dispute with us: now bring upon us what you threaten us with, if you speak the truth!?" 33 He said: "Truly, Allah will bring it on you if He wills—and then, you will not be able to frustrate it! 34 "Of no good will be my counsel to you, much as I desire to give you (good) counsel, if it be that Allah wills to leave you astray: He is your Lord! And to Him will you return!"

35 Or do they say, "He has forged it?" Say: "If I had forged it, on me were my sin! And I am free of the sins of which you are guilty!"

36 It was revealed to Noah: "None of your People will believe except those who have believed already! So grieve no longer over their (evil) deeds. 37 "But construct an Ark under Our eyes and Our inspiration, and address Me no (further) on behalf of those who are in sin: for they are about to be overwhelmed (in the Flood)." 38 Forthwith he (starts) constructing the Ark: every time that the Chiefs of his People passed by him, they threw ridicule on him. He said: "If you ridicule us now, we (in our turn) can look down on you with ridicule likewise! 39 "But soon will you

know who it is on whom will descend a Penalty that will cover them with shame—on whom will be unloosed a Penalty lasting."

40 At length, behold! There came Our Command, and the fountains of the earth gushed forth! We said: "Embark therein, of each kind two, male and female, and your family—except those against whom the Word has already gone forth—and the Believers." But only a few believed with him. 41 So he said: "Embark you on the Ark, in the name of Allah, whether it move or be at rest! For my Lord is, be sure, Oft-Forgiving, Most Merciful!" 42 So the Ark floated with them on the waves (towering) like mountains, and Noah called out to his son, who had separated himself (from the rest): "O my son! embark with us, and be not with the Unbelievers!" 43 The son replied: "I will take myself atop some mountain: it will save me from the water." Noah said: "This day nothing can save, from the Command of Allah, any but those on whom He has mercy!"—and the waves came between them, and the son was among those overwhelmed in the Flood. 44 Then the word went forth: "O, earth! swallow up your water, and O sky! Withhold (your rain)!" And the water abated, and the matter was ended. The Ark rested on Mount Al-Jūdī, and the word went forth: "Away with those who do wrong!"

45 And Noah called upon his Lord, and said: "O my Lord! surely my son is of my family! And Your promise is true, and You are the Justest of Judges!" 46 He said: "O Noah! He is not of your family: for his conduct is unrighteous. So ask not of Me that of which you have no knowledge! I give you counsel, lest you act like the ignorant!" 47 Noah said: "O my Lord! I do seek refuge with You, lest I ask You for that of which I have no knowledge. And unless You forgive me and have Mercy on me, I should indeed be lost!"

48 The word came: "O Noah! Come down (from the Ark) with Peace from Us, and Blessing on you and on some of the Peoples (who will spring) from those with you: but (there will be other) Peoples to whom We shall grant their pleasures (for a time), but in the end will a grievous Penalty reach them from Us." 49 Such are some of the stories of the Unseen, which We have revealed

unto you: before this, neither you nor your People knew them. So persevere patiently: for the End is for those who are righteous.

50 To the 'Ād People (We sent) Hūd, one of their own brethren. He said: "O my people! Worship Allah! you have no other god but Him. (Your other gods) you do nothing but invent! 51 "O my people! I ask of you no reward for this (Message). My reward is from none but Him who created me: will you not then understand? 52 "And O my people! Ask forgiveness of your Lord, and turn to Him (in repentance): He will send you the clouds pouring abundant rain, and add strength to your strength: so do not turn back in sin!"

53 They said: "O Hūd! No Clear (Sign) have you brought us, and we are not the ones to desert our gods on your word! Nor shall we believe in you! 54 "We say nothing but that (perhaps) some of our gods may have seized you with imbecility." He said: "I call Allah to witness, and do you bear witness, that I am free from the sin of ascribing, to Him, 55 "Other gods as partners! So scheme (your worst) against me, all of you, and give me no respite. 56 "I put my trust in Allah, my Lord and your Lord! There is not a moving creature, but He has grasp of its fore-lock. Surely, it is my Lord that is on a straight Path.

57 "If you turn away—I (at least) have conveyed the Message with which I was sent to you. My Lord will make another People to succeed you, and you will not harm Him in the least. For my Lord has care and watch over all things." 58 So when Our decree issued, We saved Hūd and those who believed with him, by (special) Grace from Ourselves: We saved them from the Chastisement. 59 Such were the 'Ād People: they rejected the Signs of their Lord and Cherisher; disobeyed His Prophets; and followed the command of every powerful, obstinate transgressor. 60 And they were pursued by a Curse in this Life—and on the Day of Judgment. Ah! Behold! for the 'Ād rejected their Lord and Cherisher! Ah! Behold! Removed (from sight) were 'Ād the people of Hūd!

61 To the Thamūd People (We sent) Ṣāliḥ, one of their own brethren. He said: "O my people! Worship Allah: you have no

other god but Him. It is He Who has produced you from the earth
and settled you therein: then ask forgiveness of Him, and turn
to Him (in repentance): for my Lord is (always) near, ready to
answer." 62 They said: "O Ṣāliḥ! You have been of us!—A centre
of our hopes hitherto! do you (now) forbid us the worship of what
our fathers worshipped? But we are really in suspicious
(disquieting) doubt as to that to which you invite us." 63 He said:
"O my people! Do you see? if I have a Clear (Sign) from my
Lord and He has sent Mercy unto me from Himself—who then
can help me against Allah if I were to disobey Him? What then
would you add to my (portion) but perdition?

64 "And O my people! This she-camel of Allah is a symbol to
you: leave her to feed on Allah's (free) earth, and inflict no harm
on her, or a swift Punishment will seize you!" 65 But they did
hamstring her. So he said: "Enjoy yourselves in your homes for
three days: (Then will be your ruin): (behold) there a promise
not to be belied!" 66 When Our Decree issued, We saved Ṣāliḥ
and those who believed with him, by (special) Grace from
Ourselves—from the Ignominy of that day. For your Lord—He
is the Strong One, and Able to enforce His Will. 67 The (mighty)
Blast overtook the wrongdoers, and they lay prostrate in their
homes before the morning— 68 As if they had never dwelt and
flourished there. Ah! Behold! For the Thamūd rejected their Lord
and Cherisher! Ah! Behold! Removed (from sight) were the
Thamūd!

69 There came Our Messengers to Abraham with Glad Tidings.
They said, "Peace!" He answered, "Peace!" and hastened to
entertain them with a roasted calf. 70 But when he saw their hands
went not towards the (meal), he felt some mistrust of them, and
conceived a fear of them. They said: "Fear not: we have been
sent against the people of Lūṭ." 71 And his wife was standing
(there), and she laughed: and We gave her glad Tidings of Isaac,
and after him, of Jacob. 72 She said: "Alas for me! Shall I bear
a child, seeing I am an old woman, and my husband here is an
old man? That would indeed be a strange thing!" 73 They said:
"Do you wonder at Allah's decree? The grace of Allah and His

blessings on you, O you people of the house! For He is indeed worthy of all praise, full of all glory!"

74 When fear had passed from (the mind of) Abraham and the Glad Tidings had reached him, he began to plead with Us for Lūṭ's people. 75 For Abraham was, without doubt, forbearing (of faults), compassionate, and given to look to Allah. 76 O Abraham! Seek not this. The decree of your Lord has gone forth: for them there comes a Chastisement that cannot be turned back!

77 When Our Messengers came to Lūṭ, he was grieved on their account and felt himself powerless (to protect) them. He said: "This is a distressful day." 78 And his people came rushing towards him, and they had been long in the habit of practising abominations. He said: "O my people! Here are my daughters: they are purer for you (if you marry)! Now fear Allah, and cover me not with shame about my guests! Is there not among you a single right-minded man?" 79 They said: "Well do you know we have no need of your daughters: indeed you know quite well what we want!"

80 He said: "Would that I had power to suppress you or that I could betake myself to some powerful support." 81 (The Messengers) said: "O Lūṭ! We are Messengers from your Lord! By no means shall they reach you! Now travel with your family while yet a part of the night remains, and let not any of you look back: but your wife (will remain behind): to her will happen what happens to the people. Morning is their time appointed: is not the morning near?" 82 When Our decree issued, We turned (the cities) upside down, and rained down on them brimstones hard as baked clay, spread, layer on layer— 83 Marked as from your Lord: nor are they ever far from those who do wrong!

84 To the Madyan people (We sent) Shu'ayb, one of their own brethren: he said: "O my People! worship Allah: you have no other god but Him. And give not short measure or weight: I see you in prosperity, but I fear for you the Torment of a Day that will compass (you) all round. 85 "And O my people! give just measure and weight, nor withhold from the people the things that are their due: commit not evil in the land with intent to do

mischief. 86 "That which is left you by Allah is best for you, if you (but) believed! But I am not set over you to keep watch!"

87 They said: "O Shu'ayb! Does your (religion of) prayer command you that we leave off the worship which our fathers practised, or that we leave off doing what we like with our property? Truly, you are the one that forbears with faults and is right-minded!"

88 He said: "O my people! See you whether I have a Clear (Sign) from my Lord, and He has given me sustenance (pure and) good as from Himself? I wish not, in opposition to you, to do that which I forbid you to do. I only desire (your) betterment to the best of my power; and my success (in my task) can only come from Allah. In Him I trust, and unto Him I look. 89 "And O my people! Let not my dissent (from you) cause you to sin, lest you suffer a fate similar to that of the people of Noah or of Hūd or of Ṣāliḥ, nor are the people of Lot far off from you! 90 "But ask forgiveness of your Lord, and turn unto Him (in repentance): for my Lord is indeed full of mercy and loving-kindness."

91 They said: "O Shu'ayb! Much of what you say we do not understand! In fact, among us we see that you have no strength! Were it not for your family, we should certainly have stoned you! For you have among us no great position!" 92 He said: "O my people! Is then my family of more consideration with you than Allah? For you cast Him any behind your backs (with contempt). But, surely, my Lord encompasses on all sides all that you do! 93 "And O my people! Do whatever you can: I will do (my part): soon will you know who it is on whom descends the Penalty of ignominy; and who is a liar! And watch you! For I too am watching with you!"

94 When Our decree issued, We saved Shu'ayb and those who believed with him, by (special) Mercy from Ourselves: but the (mighty) Blast did seize the wrongdoers, and they lay prostrate in their homes by the morning— 95 As if they had never dwelt and flourished there! Ah! Behold! How the Madyan were removed (from sight) as were removed the Thamūd!

96 And We sent Moses, with Our Clear (Signs) and an authority

manifest, 97 Unto Pharaoh and his Chiefs: but they followed the command of Pharaoh and the command of Pharaoh was no right (guide). 98 He will go before his people on the Day of Judgment, and lead them into the Fire (as cattle are led to water): but woeful indeed will be the place to which they are led! 99 And they are followed by a curse in this (life) and on the Day of Judgment: and woeful is the gift which shall be given (unto them)!

100 These are some of the stories of communities which We relate to you: of them some are standing, and some have been mown down (by the sickle of time). 101 It was not We that wronged them: they wronged their own souls: the deities, other than Allah, whom they invoked, profited them not at all when there issued the decree of your Lord: nor did they add anything (to their lot) but perdition!

102 Such is the chastisement of your Lord when He chastises communities in the midst of their wrong: grievous, indeed, and severe is His chastisement. 103 In that is a Sign for those who fear the Penalty of the Hereafter: that is a Day on which mankind will be gathered together: that will be a Day of Testimony. 104 Nor shall We delay it but for a term appointed. 105 The day it arrives, no soul shall speak except by His leave: of those (gathered) some will be wretched and some will be blessed.

106 Those who are wretched shall be in the Fire: there will be for them therein (nothing but) the heaving of sighs and sobs. 107 They will dwell therein for all the time that the heavens and the earth endure, except as your Lord wills: for your Lord is the (sure) Accomplisher of what He plans. 108 And those who are blessed shall be in the Garden. They will dwell therein for all the time that the heavens and the earth endure, except as your Lord wills: a gift without break. 109 Be not then in doubt as to what these men worship. They worship nothing but what their fathers worshipped before (them): but, surely, We shall pay them back (in full) their portion without (the least) abatement.

110 We certainly gave the Book to Moses, but differences arose therein: had it not been that a Word had gone forth before from your Lord, the matter would have been decided between them,

but they are in suspicious doubt concerning it. 111 And, of a surety, to all will your Lord pay back (in full the recompense) of their deeds: for He knows well all that they do.

112 Therefore stand firm (in the straight path) as you are commanded — You and those who with you turn (to Allah); and transgress not (from the Path): for He sees well all that you do. 113 And incline not to those who do wrong, or the Fire will seize you; and you have no protectors other than Allah, nor shall you be helped. 114 And establish regular prayers at the two ends of the day and at the approaches of the night: for those things that are good remove those that are evil: be that the word of remembrance to those who remember (their Lord): 115 And be steadfast in patience; for, surely, Allah will not suffer the reward of the righteous to perish.

116 Why were there not, among the generations before you, persons possessed of balanced good sense, prohibiting (men) from mischief in the earth — except a few among them whom We saved (from harm)? But the wrong-doers pursued the enjoyment of the good things of life which were given them, and persisted in sin. 117 Nor would your Lord be the One to destroy communities for a single wrongdoing, if its members were likely to mend.

118 If your Lord had so willed, He could have made mankind one People: but they will not cease to dispute. 119 Except those on whom your Lord has bestowed His Mercy: and for this did He create them: and the Word of your Lord shall be fulfilled: "I will fill Hell with jinns and men all together."

120 All that We relate to you of the stories of the prophets — with it We make firm your heart: in them there comes to you the Truth, as well as an exhortation and a message of remembrance to those who believe. 121 Say to those who do not believe: "Do whatever you can: We shall do our part; 122 "And wait you! We too shall wait." 123 To Allah do belong the unseen (secrets) of the heavens and the earth, and to Him goes back every affair (for decision): then worship Him, and put your trust in Him: and your Lord is not unmindful of anything that you do.

12. JOSEPH

In the name of Allah, Most Gracious, Most Merciful.

1 *Alif Lām Rā'*. These are the Symbols (or Verses) of the Perspicuous Book. 2 We have sent it down as an Arabic Qur'ān, in order that you may learn wisdom. 3 We do relate to you the most beautiful of stories, in that We reveal to you this (portion of the) Qur'ān: before this, you too were among those who knew it not.

4 Behold! Joseph said to his father: "O my father! I did see eleven stars and the sun and the moon: I saw them prostrate themselves to me!" 5 Said (the father): "My (dear) little son! Relate not your dream to your brothers, lest they concoct a plot against you: for Satan is to man an avowed enemy! 6 "Thus will your Lord choose you and teach you the correct interpretation of events and perfect His favour to you and to the posterity of Jacob—even as He perfected it to your fathers Abraham and Isaac aforetime! For your Lord is full of knowledge and wisdom."

7 Surely, in Joseph and his brethren are Signs (or Symbols) for Seekers (after Truth). 8 They said: "Truly Joseph and his brother are loved more by our father than we: but we are a goodly body! Really our father is obviously wandering (in his mind)! 9 "Slay Joseph or cast him out to some (unknown) land, that so the favour of your father may be given to you alone: (there will be time enough) for you to be righteous after that!" 10 Said one of them: "Slay not Joseph, but if you must do something, throw him down to the bottom of the well: he will be picked up by some caravan of travellers."

11 They said: "O our father! Why do you not trust us with Joseph—seeing we are indeed his sincere well-wishers? 12 "Send him with us tomorrow to enjoy himself and play, and we shall take every care of him." 13 (Jacob) said: "Really it saddens me that you should take him away: I fear lest the wolf should devour him while you do not attend to him." 14 They said: "If the wolf

were to devour him while we are (so large) a party, then should we indeed (first) have perished ourselves!"

15 So they did take him away, and they all agreed to throw him down to the bottom of the well: and We put into his heart (this Message): "Of a surety you shall (one day) tell them the truth of this their affair while they know (you) not." 16 Then they came to their father in the early part of the night, weeping. 17 They said: "O our father! We went racing with one another, and left Joseph with our things; and the wolf devoured him... But you will never believe us even though we tell the truth." 18 They stained his shirt with false blood. He said: "No, but your minds have made up a tale (that may pass) with you, (for me) patience is most fitting: against that which you assert, it is Allah (alone) whose help can be sought"...

19 Then there came a caravan of travellers: they sent their water-carrier (for water), and he let down his bucket (into the well)...He said: "Ah there! Good news! Here is a (fine) young man!" So they concealed him as a treasure! But Allah knew well all that they did! 20 The (Brethren) sold him for a miserable price—for a few dirhams counted out: in such low estimation did they hold him!

21 The man in Egypt who bought him, said to his wife: "Make his stay (among us) honourable: maybe he will bring us much good, or we shall adopt him as a son." Thus did We establish Joseph in the land, that We might teach him the interpretation of events. And Allah has full power and control over His affairs; but most among mankind know it not. 22 When Joseph attained his full manhood, We gave him power and knowledge: thus do We reward those who do right.

23 But she in whose house he was, sought to seduce him from his (true) self: she fastened the doors, and said: "Now come, you (dear one)!" He said: "Allah forbid! Truly (your husband) is my lord! he made my stay agreeable! Truly to no good come those who do wrong!" 24 And (with passion) did she desire him, and he would have desired her, but that he saw the evidence of his Lord: thus (did We order) that We might turn away from him

(all) evil and shameful deeds: for he was one of Our servants, sincere and purified.

25 So they both raced each other to the door, and she tore his shirt from the back: they both found her lord near the door. She said: "What is the (fitting) punishment for one who formed an evil design against your wife, but prison or a grievous chastisement?" 26 He said: "It was she that sought to seduce me — from my (true) self." And one of her household saw (this) and bore witness, (thus) — "If it be that his shirt is rent from the front, then is her tale true, and he is a liar! 27 "But if it be that his shirt is torn from the back, then is she the liar, and he is telling the truth!" 28 So when he saw his shirt — that it was torn at the back — (Her husband) said: "Behold! It is a snare of you women! Truly, mighty is your snare! 29 "O Joseph, pass this over! (O wife), ask forgiveness for your sin, for truly you have been at fault!"

30 Ladies said in the City: "The wife of the (great) 'Azīz is seeking to seduce her slave from his (true) self: truly has he inspired her with violent love: we see she is evidently going astray." 31 When she heard of their malicious talk, she sent for them and prepared a banquet for them: she gave each of them a knife: and she said (to Joseph), "Come out before them." When they saw him, they did extol him, and (in their amazement) cut their hands: they said, "Allah preserve us! no mortal is this! this is none other than a noble angel!" 32 She said: "There before you is the man about whom you did blame me! I did seek to seduce him from his (true) self but he did firmly save himself guiltless!... And now, if he does not my bidding, he shall certainly be cast into prison, and (what is more) be of the company of the vilest!" 33 He said: "O my Lord! The prison is more welcome to me than that to which they invite me: unless You turn away their snare from me, I should (in my youthful folly) feel inclined towards them and join the ranks of the ignorant." 34 So his Lord hearkened to him (in his prayer), and turned away from him their snare: surely, He hears and knows (all things).

35 Then it occurred to the men, after they had seen the Signs, (that it was best) to imprison him for a time. 36 Now with him

there came into the prison two young men. Said one of them: "I see myself (in a dream) pressing wine." Said the other: "I see myself (in a dream) carrying bread on my head, and birds are eating thereof." "Tell us" (they said) "the truth and meaning thereof: for we see you are one that does good (to all)."

37 He said: "Before any food comes (in due course) to feed either of you, I will surely reveal to you the truth and meaning of this before it befall you: that is part of the (Duty) which my Lord has taught me. I have (I assure you) abandoned the ways of a people that believe not in Allah and that (even) deny the Hereafter. 38 "And I follow the ways of my fathers—Abraham, Isaac, and Jacob; and never could we attribute any partners whatever to Allah: that (comes) of the grace of Allah to us and to mankind: yet most men are not grateful. 39 "O my two companions of the prison! (I ask you): are many lords differing among themselves better, or Allah, the One, Supreme and Irresistible? 40 "If not Him, you worship nothing but names which you have named—you and your fathers—for which Allah has sent down no authority: the Command is for none but Allah: He has commanded that you worship none but Him: that is the right religion, but most men understand not...

41 "O my two companions of the prison! As to one of you, he will pour out the wine for his lord to drink: as for the other, he will hang from the cross, and the birds will eat from off his head. (So) has been decreed that matter whereof you two do enquire"... 42 And of the two, to that one whom he considered about to be saved, he said: "Mention me to your lord." But Satan made him forget to mention him to his lord: and (Joseph) lingered in prison a few (more) years.

43 The king (of Egypt) said: "I do see (in a dream) seven fat kine, whom seven lean ones devour—and seven green ears of corn, and seven (others) withered. O you chiefs! Expound to me my dream if it be that you can interpret dreams." 44 They said: "A confused medley of dreams: and we are not skilled in the interpretation of dreams." 45 But the man who had been released, one of the two (who had been in prison) and who now thought

of him after (so long) a space of time, Said: "I will tell you the truth of its interpretation: send you me (therefore)."

46 "O Joseph!" (he said) "O man of truth! Expound to us (the dream) of seven fat kine whom seven lean ones devour, and of seven green ears of corn and (seven) others withered: that I may return to the people, and that they may understand." 47 (Joseph) said: "For seven years shall you diligently sow as is your wont: and the harvests that you reap, you shall leave them in the ear — except a little, of which you shall eat. 48 "Then will come after that (period) seven dreadful (years), which will devour what you shall have laid by in advance for them — (all) except a little which you shall have (specially) guarded. 49 "Then will come after that (period) a year in which the people will have abundant water, and in which they will press (wine and oil)."

50 So the king said: "Bring him to me." But when the messenger came to him, (Joseph) said: "Go back to your lord, and ask him, 'What is the state of mind of the ladies who cut their hands'? For my Lord is certainly well aware of their snare." 51 (The king) said (to the ladies): "What was your affair when you did seek to seduce Joseph from his (true) self?" The ladies said: "Allah preserve us! no evil do We know against him!" Said the 'Azīz's wife: "Now is the truth manifest (to all): it was I who sought to seduce him from his (true) self: he is indeed of those who are (ever) true (and virtuous).

52 "This (say I), in order that he may know that I have never been false to him in his absence, and that Allah will never guide the snare of the false ones. 53 "Nor do I absolve my own self (of blame): the (human) soul is certainly prone to evil, unless my Lord do bestow His Mercy: but surely my Lord is Oft-Forgiving, Most Merciful."

54 So the king said: "Bring him to me; I will take him specially to serve about my own person." Therefore when he had spoken to him, he said: "Be assured this day, you are, before our own presence, with rank firmly established, and fidelity fully proved!" 55 (Joseph) said: "Set me over the store-houses of the land: I will indeed guard them, as one that knows (their importance)." 56 Thus

did We give established power to Joseph in the land, to take possession therein as, when, or where he pleased. We bestow of Our Mercy on whom We please, and We suffer not, to be lost, the reward of those who do good. 57 But surely the reward of the Hereafter is the best, for those who believe, and are constant in righteousness.

58 Then came Joseph's brethren: they entered his presence, and he knew them, but they knew him not. 59 And when he had furnished them forth with provisions (suitable) for them, he said: "Bring to me a brother you have, of the same father as yourselves, (but a different mother): see you not that I hand out full measure, and that I do provide the best hospitality? 60 "Now if you bring him not to me, you shall have no measure (of corn) from me, nor shall you (even) come near me." 61 They said: "We shall certainly seek to get our wish about him from his father: indeed we shall do it."

62 And (Joseph) told his servants to put their stock-in-trade (with which they had bartered) into their saddle-bags, so they should know it only when they returned to their people, in order that they might come back. 63 Now when they returned to their father, they said: "O our father! No more measure of grain shall we get (unless we take our brother): so send our brother with us, that we may get our measure; and we will indeed take every care of him." 64 He said: "Shall I trust you with him with any result other than when I trusted you with his brother aforetime? But Allah is the best to take care (of him), and He is the Most Merciful of those who show mercy!"

65 Then when they opened their baggage, they found their stock-in-trade had been returned to them. They said: "O our father! What (more) can we desire? This our stock-in-trade has been returned to us: so we shall get (more) food for our family; we shall take care of our brother; and add (at the same time) a full camel's load (of grain to our provisions). This is but a small quantity." 66 (Jacob) said: "Never will I send him with you until you swear a solemn oath to me, in Allah's name, that you will be sure to bring him back to me unless you are yourselves hemmed

in (and made powerless). And when they had sworn their solemn oath, he said: "Over all that we say, be Allah the Witness and Guardian!"

67 Further he said: "O my sons! enter not all by one gate: enter by different gates. Not that I can profit you at all against Allah (with my advice): none can command except Allah: in Him do I put my trust: and let all that trust put their trust in Him." 68 And when they entered in the manner their father had enjoined, it did not profit them in the least against (the Plan of) Allah: it was but a necessity of Jacob's soul, which he discharged. For he was, by Our instruction, full of knowledge (and experience): but most men know not.

69 Now when they came into Joseph's presence, he received his (full) brother to stay with him. He said (to him): "Behold! I am your (own) brother; so grieve not at any of their doings." 70 At length when he had furnished them forth with provisions (suitable) for them, he put the drinking cup into his brother's saddle-bag. Then shouted out a Crier: "O you (in) the Caravan! Behold! you are thieves, without doubt!" 71 They said, turning towards them: "What is it that you miss?" 72 They said: "We miss the great beaker of the king; for him who produces it, is (the reward of) a camel load; I will be bound by it." 73 (The brothers) said: "By Allah! Well you know that we came not to make mischief in the land, and we are no thieves!" 74 (The Egyptians) said: "What then shall be the penalty of this, if you are (proved) to have lied?" 75 They said: "The penalty should be that he in whose saddle-bag it is found, should be held (as bondman) to atone for the (crime). Thus it is We punish the wrong-doers!" 76 So he began (the search) with their baggage, before (he came to) the baggage of his brother: at length he brought it out of his brother's baggage. Thus did We plan for Joseph. He could not take his brother by the law of the king except that Allah willed it (so). We raise to degrees (of wisdom) whom We please: but over all endued with knowledge is One, the All-Knowing.

77 They said: "If he steals, there was a brother of his who did steal before (him)." But these things did Joseph keep locked in

his heart, revealing not the secrets to them. He (simply) said (to himself): "You are the worse situated; and Allah knows best the truth of what you assert!" 78 They said: "O exalted one! Behold! he has a father, aged and venerable, (who will grieve for him); so take one of us in his place; for we see that you are (gracious) in doing good." 79 He said: "Allah forbid that we take other than him with whom we found our property: indeed (if we did so), we should be acting wrongfully."

80 Now when they saw no hope of his (yielding), they held a conference in private. The leader among them said: "Know you not that your father did take an oath from you in Allah's name, and how, before this, you did fail in your duty with Joseph? Therefore will I not leave this land until my father permits me, or Allah commands me; and He is the best to command. 81 "Go you back to your father, and say, 'O our father! Behold! your son committed theft! We bear witness only to what we know, and we could not well guard against the unseen! 82 "'Ask at the town where we have been and the caravan in which we returned, and (you will find) we are indeed telling the truth.'"

83 Jacob said: "No, but you have yourselves contrived a story (good enough) for you. So patience is most fitting (for me). Maybe Allah will bring them (back) all to me (in the end). For He is indeed full of knowledge and wisdom." 84 And he turned away from them, and said: "How great is my grief for Joseph!" And his eyes became white with sorrow, and he fell into silent melancholy. 85 They said: "By Allah! (Never) will you cease to remember Joseph until you reach the last extremity of illness, or until you die!" 86 He said: "I only complain of my distraction and anguish to Allah, and I know from Allah that which you know not... 87 "O my sons! go and enquire about Joseph and his brother, and never give up hope of Allah's soothing Mercy: truly no one despairs of Allah's soothing Mercy, except those who have no faith."

88 Then, when they came (back) into (Joseph's) presence they said: "O exalted one! Distress has seized us and our family: we have (now) brought but scanty capital: so pay us full measure,

(we pray you), and treat it as charity to us: for Allah does reward the charitable." 89 He said: "Know you how you dealt with Joseph and his brother, not knowing (What you were doing)?" 90 They said: "Are you indeed Joseph?" He said, "I am Joseph, and this is my brother: Allah has indeed been gracious to us (all): behold, he that is righteous and patient—never will Allah suffer the reward to be lost, of those who do right."

91 They said: "By Allah! Indeed Allah has preferred you above us, and we certainly have been guilty of sin!" 92 He said: "This day let no reproach be (cast) on you: Allah will forgive you, and He is the Most Merciful of those who show mercy! 93 "Go with this my shirt, and cast it over the face of my father: he will come to see (clearly). Then come here to me together with all your family."

94 When the Caravan left (Egypt), their father said: "I do indeed scent the presence of Joseph: no, think me not a dotard." 95 They said: "By Allah! Truly you are in your old wandering mind." 96 Then when the bearer of the good news came, he cast (the shirt) over his face, and he forthwith regained clear sight. He said: "Did I not say to you, 'I know from Allah that which you know not?'" 97 They said: "O our father! Ask for us forgiveness for our sins, for we were truly at fault." 98 He said: "Soon will I ask my Lord for forgiveness for you: for He is indeed Oft-Forgiving, Most Merciful."

99 Then when they entered the presence of Joseph, he provided a home for his parents with himself, and said: "Enter you Egypt (all) in safety if it please Allah." 100 And he raised his parents high on the throne (of dignity), and they fell down in prostration, (all) before him. He said: "O my father! this is the fulfilment of my dream of old! Allah has made it come true! He was indeed good to me when He took me out of prison and brought you (all here) out of the desert, (even) after Satan had sown enmity between me and my brothers. Surely, my Lord understands best the mysteries of all that He plans to do. For, surely, He is full of knowledge and wisdom.

101 "O my Lord! You have indeed bestowed on me some power,

and taught me something of the interpretation of dreams and events—O You creator of the heavens and the earth! You are my Protector in this world and in the Hereafter. Take You my soul (at death) as one submitting to Your will (as a Muslim), and unite me with the righteous."

102 Such is one of the stories of what happened unseen, which We reveal by inspiration unto you; nor were you (present) with them when they concerted their plans together in the process of weaving their plots. 103 Yet no faith will the greater part of mankind have, however ardently you desire it. 104 And no reward do you ask of them for this: it is no less than a Message for all creatures.

105 And how many Signs in the heavens and the earth do they pass by? Yet they turn (their faces) away from them! 106 And most of them believe not in Allah without associating (others as partners) with Him! 107 Do they then feel secure from the coming against them of the covering veil of the wrath of Allah— or of the coming against them of the (final) Hour all of a sudden while they perceive not? 108 Say you: "This is my Way: I do invite unto Allah—on evidence clear as the seeing with one's eyes—I and whoever follows me. Glory to Allah! and never will I join gods with Allah!"

109 Nor did We send before you (as Messengers) any but men, whom We did inspire—(men) living in human habitations. Do they not travel through the earth, and see what was the end of those before them? But the home of the Hereafter is best, for those who do right. Will you not then understand? 110 (Respite will be granted) until, when the Messengers give up hope (of their people) and (come to) think that they were treated as liars, there reaches them Our help, and those whom We will are delivered into safety. But never will be warded off Our punishment from those who are in sin.

111 There is, in their stories, instruction for men endued with understanding. It is not a tale invented, but a confirmation of what went before it—a detailed exposition of all thing, and a Guide and a Mercy to any such as believe.

13. THE THUNDER

In the name of Allah, Most Gracious, Most Merciful.

1 *Alif Lām Mīm Rā'*. These are the Signs (or Verses) of the Book: that which has been revealed unto you from your Lord is the Truth; but most men believe not. 2 Allah is He Who raised the heavens without any pillars that you can see; is firmly established on the Throne (of Authority); He has subjected the sun and the moon (to His Law)! Each one runs (its course) for a term appointed. He does regulate all affairs, explaining the Signs in detail, that you may believe with certainty in the meeting with your Lord.

3 And it is He Who spread out the earth, and set thereon mountains standing firm and (flowing) rivers: and fruit of every kind He made in pairs, two and two: He draws the Night as a veil over the Day. Behold, surely in these things there are Signs for those who consider!

4 And in the earth are tracts (diverse though) neighbouring, and gardens of vines and fields sown with corn, and palm trees — growing out of single roots or otherwise: watered with the same water, yet some of them We make more excellent than others to eat. Behold, surely in these things there are signs for those who understand!

5 If you marvel (at their want of faith), strange is their saying: "When we are (actually) dust, shall we indeed then be in a creation renewed?" They are those who deny their Lord! They are those round whose necks will be yokes (of servitude): they will be companions of the Fire, to dwell therein (for ever)!

6 They ask you to hasten on the evil in preference to the good: yet have come to pass, before them, (many) exemplary punishments! But surely your Lord is full of forgiveness for mankind for their wrong-doing. And surely your Lord is (also) strict in punishment.

7 And the Unbelievers say: "Why is not a Sign sent down to

him from his Lord?" But you are truly a warner, and to every people a guide.

8 Allah does know what every female (womb) does bear, by how much the wombs fall short (of their time or number) or do exceed. Every single thing is before his sight, in (due) proportion. 9 He knows the Unseen and that which is open: He is the Great, the most High. 10 It is the same (to Him) whether any of you conceal his speech or declare it openly; whether he lie hid by night or walk forth freely by day.

11 For each (such person) there are (angels) in succession. In front and behind him: they guard him by command of Allah. Surely never will Allah change the condition of a people until they change it themselves (with their own souls). But when (once) Allah wills a people's punishment, there can be no turning it back, nor will they find, besides Him, any to protect.

12 It is He Who does show you the lightning, by way both of fear and of hope: it is He Who does raise up the clouds, heavy with (fertilising) rain! 13 No, thunder repeats His praises, and so do the angels, with awe: He flings the loud-voiced thunder-bolts, and therewith He strikes whomsoever He will. Yet these (are the men) who (dare to) dispute about Allah, with the strength of His power (supreme)!

14 For Him (alone) is prayer in Truth: any others that they call upon besides Him hear them no more than if they were to stretch forth their hands for water to reach their mouths but it reaches them not: for the prayer of those without Faith is nothing but (futile) wandering (in the mind).

15 Whatever beings there are in the heavens and the earth do prostrate themselves to Allah (acknowledging subjection)—with willingness or in spite of themselves: so do their shadows in the mornings and evenings. 16 Say: "Who is the Lord and Sustainer of the heavens and the earth?" Say: "(It is) Allah." Say: "Do you then take (for worship) protectors other than Him, such as have no power either for good or for harm to themselves?" Say: "Are the blind equal with those who see? Or the depths of darkness

equal with Light?" Or do they assign to Allah partners who have created (anything) as He has created, so that the creation seemed to them similar? Say: "Allah is the Creator of all things: He is the One, the Supreme and Irresistible."

17 He sends down water from the skies, and the channels flow, each according to its measure: but the torrent bears away the foam that mounts up to the surface. Even so, from that (ore) which they heat in the fire, to make ornaments or utensils therewith, there is a scum likewise. Thus does Allah (by parables) show forth Truth and falsehood. For the scum disappears like froth cast out; while that which is for the good of mankind remains on the earth. Thus does Allah set forth parables.

18 For those who respond to their Lord, are (all) food things. But those who respond not to Him—even if they had all that is in the heavens and on earth, and as much more, (in vain) would they offer it for ransom. For them will the reckoning be terrible: their abode will be Hell—what a bed of misery!

19 Is then one who does know that that which has been revealed unto you from your Lord is the Truth, like one who is blind? It is those who are endued with understanding that receive admonition—

20 Those who fulfil the Covenant of Allah and fail not in their plighted word; 21 Those who join together those things which Allah has commanded to be joined, hold their Lord in awe, and fear the terrible reckoning; 22 Those who patiently persevere, seeking the countenance of their Lord; establish regular prayers; spend, out of (the gifts) We have bestowed for their sustenance, secretly and openly; and turn off Evil with good: for such there is the final attainment of the (Eternal) Home— 23 Gardens of perpetual bliss: they shall enter there, as well as the righteous among their fathers, their spouses, and their offspring: and angels shall let them enter from every gate (with the salutation): 24 "Peace unto you for that you persevered in patience! Now how excellent is the final Home!"

25 But those who break the Covenant of Allah, after having

plighted their word thereto, and cut asunder those things which Allah has commanded to be joined, and work mischief in the land;—on them is the Curse; for them is the terrible Home! 26 Allah does enlarge, or grant by (strict) measure, the Sustenance (which He gives) to whomso He pleases. (The worldly) rejoice in the life of this world: but the life of this world is but little comfort compared to the Hereafter.

27 The Unbelievers say: "Why is not a Sign sent down to him from his Lord?" Say: "Truly Allah leaves, to stray, whom He will; but He guides to Himself those who turn to Him in penitence— 28 "Those who believe, and whose hearts find satisfaction in the remembrance of Allah: for without doubt in the remembrance of Allah do hearts find satisfaction. 29 "For those who believe and work righteousness, is (every) blessedness, and a beautiful place of (final) return."

30 Thus have We sent you amongst a People before whom (long since) have (other) Peoples (gone and) passed away; in order that you might rehearse unto them what We send down unto you by inspiration; yet do they reject (Him), the Most Gracious! Say: "He is my Lord! There is no god but He! In Him is my trust, and to Him do I turn!"

31 If there were a Qur'ān with which mountains were moved, or the earth were cloven asunder, or the dead were made to speak, (this would be the one!) but, truly, the Command is with Allah in all things! Do not the Believers know, that, had Allah (so) willed, He could have guided all mankind (to the Right)? But the Unbelievers—never will disaster cease to seize them for their (ill) deeds, or to settle close to their homes, until the promise of Allah come to pass, for, surely, Allah will not fail in His promise. 32 Mocked were (many) Prophets before you: but I granted respite to the Unbelievers, and finally I punished them: then how (terrible) was My requital!

33 Is then He Who stands over every soul (and knows) all that it does, (like any others)? And yet they ascribe partners to Allah. Say: "But name them! is it that you will inform Him of something He knows not on earth, or is it (just) a show of words?" No! to

those who believe not, their pretence seems pleasing, but they are kept back (thereby) from the Path. And those whom Allah leaves to stray, no one can guide. 34 For them is a Penalty in the life of this world, but harder, truly, is the Torment of the Hereafter: and defender have they none against Allah.

35 The parable of the Garden which the righteous are promised!—beneath it flow rivers: perpetual is the enjoyment thereof and the shade therein: such is the End of the Righteous; and the End of Unbelievers is the Fire.

36 Those to whom We have given the Book rejoice at what has been revealed unto you: but there are among the clans those who reject a part thereof. Say: "I am commanded to worship Allah, and not to join partners with Him. Unto Him do I call, and unto Him is my return." 37 Thus have We revealed it to be a judgment of authority in Arabic. Were you to follow their (vain) desires after the knowledge which has reached you, then would you find neither protector nor defender against Allah.

38 We did send Messengers before you, and appointed for them wives and children: and it was never the part of a Messenger to bring a Sign except as Allah permitted (or commanded). For each period is a Book (revealed). 39 Allah does blot out or confirm what He pleases: with Him is the Mother of the Book.

40 Whether We shall show you (within your life-time) part of what We promised them or take to ourselves your soul (before it is all accomplished)—your duty is to make (the Message) reach them: it is for Us to call them to account. 41 See they not that We gradually reduce the land (in their control) from its outlying borders? (Where) Allah commands, there is none to put back His command: and He is Swift in calling to account. 42 Those before them did (also) devise plots; but in all things the master planning is Allah's. He knows the doings of every soul: and soon will the Unbelievers know who gets home in the End.

43 The Unbelievers say: "No Messenger are you." Say: "Enough for a witness between me and you is Allah, and such as have knowledge of the Book."

14. ABRAHAM

In the name of Allah, Most Gracious, Most Merciful.

1 *Alif Lām Rā'*. A Book which We have revealed unto you, in order that you might lead mankind out of the depths of darkness into light—by the leave of their Lord—to the Way of (Him) the Exalted in Power, Worthy of all Praise!— 2 Of Allah, to Whom do belong all things in the heavens and on earth! But alas for the Unbelievers! For a terrible Penalty (their Unfaith will bring them)!— 3 Those who love the life of this world more than the Hereafter, who hinder (men) from the Path of Allah and seek therein something crooked: they are astray by a long distance.

4 We sent not a Messenger except (to teach) in the language of his (own) people, in order to make (things) clear to them. Now Allah leaves straying those whom He pleases and guides whom He pleases: and He is Exalted in Power, full of Wisdom.

5 We sent Moses with Our Signs (and the command). "Bring out Your people from the depths of darkness into light, and teach them to remember the Days of Allah." Surely, in this there are Signs for such as are firmly patient and constant—grateful and appreciative.

6 Remember! Moses said to his people: "Call to mind the favour of Allah to you when He delivered you from the people of Pharaoh: they set you hard tasks and punishments, slaughtered your sons, and let your daughters live: therein was a tremendous trial from your Lord." 7 And remember! your Lord caused to be declared (publicly): "If you are grateful, I will add more (favours) unto you; but if you show ingratitude, truly, My punishment is terrible indeed." 8 And Moses said: "If you show ingratitude, you and all on earth together—yet is Allah Free of all wants, worthy of all praise.

9 Has not the story reached you, (O people!), of those who (went) before you?—of the People of Noah, and 'Ād, and Thamūd?—and of those who (came) after them? None knows

them but Allah. To them came messengers with Clear (Signs); but they put their hands up to their mouths, and said: "We do deny (the mission) on which you have been sent, and we are really in suspicious (disquieting) doubt as to that to which you invite us."

10 Their Messengers said: "Is there a doubt about Allah, the Creator of the heavens and the earth? It is He who invites you, in order that He may forgive you your sins and give you respite for a term appointed!" They said: "Ah! you are no more than human, like ourselves! You wish to turn us away from the (gods) our fathers used to worship: then bring us some clear authority."

11 Their Messengers said to them: "True, we are human like yourselves, but Allah does grant His grace to such of His servants as He pleases. It is not for us to bring you an authority except as Allah permits. And in Allah let all men of faith put their trust. 12 "No reason have we why we should not put our trust in Allah. Indeed He has guided us to the Ways we (follow). We shall certainly bear with patience all the hurt you may cause us. For those who put their trust should put their trust in Allah."

13 And the Unbelievers said to their Messengers: "Be sure we shall drive you out of our land, or you shall return to our religion." But their Lord revealed (this Message) to them: "Surely, We shall cause the wrongdoers to perish! 14 "And, surely, We shall cause you to abide in the land, and succeed them. This for such as fear the Time when they shall stand before My tribunal — such as fear the Punishment denounced."

15 But they sought victory and decision (there and then), and frustration was the lot of every powerful obstinate transgressor. 16 In front of such a one is Hell, and he is given, for drink, boiling fetid water. 17 In gulps will he sip it, but never will he be near swallowing it down his throat: death will come to him from every quarter, yet will he not die: and in front of him will be a chastisement unrelenting.

18 The parable of those who reject their Lord is that their works are as ashes, on which the wind blows furiously on a tempestuous day: no power have they over anything that they have earned: that

is the straying far, far (from the goal). 19 See you not that Allah created the heavens and the earth in Truth? If He so will, He can remove you and put (in your place) a new Creation. 20 Nor is that for Allah any great matter.

21 They will all be marshalled before Allah together: then will the weak say to those who were arrogant, "For us, we but followed you; can you then avail us at all against the Wrath of Allah?" They will reply, "If we had received the guidance of Allah, we should have given it to you: to us it makes no difference (now) whether we rage, or bear (these torments) with patience: for ourselves there is no way of escape."

22 And Satan will say when the matter is decided: "It was Allah Who gave you a promise of Truth: I too promised, but I failed in my promise to you. I had no authority over you except to call you, but you listened to me: then reproach not me, but reproach your own souls. I cannot listen to your cries, nor can you listen to mine. I reject your former act in associating me with Allah. For wrongdoers there must be a grievous Penalty."

23 But those who believe and work righteousness will be admitted to Gardens beneath which rivers flow—to dwell therein for ever with the leave of their Lord. Their greeting therein will be: "Peace!"

24 See you not how Allah sets forth a parable?—A goodly Word like a goodly tree, whose root is firmly fixed, and its branches (reach) to the heavens— 25 It brings forth its fruit at all times, by the leave of its Lord. So Allah sets forth parables for men, in order that they may receive admonition. 26 And the parable of an evil Word is that of an evil tree: it is torn up by the root from the surface of the earth: it has no stability.

27 Allah will establish in strength those who believe, with the Word that stands firm, in this world and in the Hereafter; but Allah will leave, to stray, those who do wrong: Allah does what He wills.

28 Have you not turned your vision to those who have changed the favour of Allah. Into blasphemy and caused their people to descend to the House of Perdition?— 29 Into Hell? They will burn therein—an evil place to stay in! 30 And they set up (idols) as

equal to Allah, to mislead (Men) from the Path! Say: "Enjoy (your brief power)! But, surely, you are making straightway for Hell!"

31 Speak to my servants who have believed, that they may establish regular prayers, and spend (in charity) out of the Sustenance We have given them, secretly and openly, before the coming of a Day in which there will be neither mutual bargaining nor befriending.

32 It is Allah Who has created the heavens and the earth and sends down rain from the skies, and with it brings out fruits wherewith to feed you; it is He who has made the ships subject to you, that they may sail across the sea by His Command; and the rivers (also) has He made subject to you. 33 And He has made subject to you the sun and the moon, both diligently pursuing their courses; and the Night and the Day has He (also) made subject to you. 34 And He gives you of all that you ask for. But if you count the favours of Allah, never will you be able to number them. Surely, man is given up to injustice and ingratitude.

35 Remember Abraham said: "O my Lord! make this city one of peace and security: and preserve me and my progeny from worshipping idols. 36 "O my Lord! they have indeed led astray many among mankind; he then who follows my (ways) is of me, and he that disobeys me — but You are indeed Oft-Forgiving, most Merciful.

37 "O our Lord! I have made some of my offspring to dwell in a valley without cultivation, by Your Sacred House; in order, O our Lord, that they may establish regular Prayer: so fill the hearts of some among men with love towards them, and feed them with Fruits: so that they may give thanks.

38 "O our Lord! truly You know what we conceal and what we reveal: for nothing whatever is hidden from Allah, whether on earth or in heaven. 39 "Praise be to Allah, Who has granted unto me in old age Ishmael and Isaac: for truly my Lord is He, the Hearer of Prayer! 40 "O my Lord! make me one who establishes regular Prayer, and also (raise such) among my offspring O our Lord! And accept You my Prayer. 41 "O our Lord! cover (us) with Your Forgiveness — me, my parents, and (all) Believers, on the Day that the Reckoning will be established!"

42 Think not that Allah does not heed the deeds of those who do wrong. He but gives them respite against a Day when the eyes will fixedly stare in horror— 43 They running forward with necks outstretched, their heads uplifted, their gaze returning not towards them, and their hearts a (gaping) void!

44 So warn mankind of the Day when the Wrath will reach them: then will the wrongdoers say: "Our Lord! Respite us (if only) for a short term: we will answer Your Call, and follow the Messengers!" "What! were you not wont to swear aforetime that you should suffer no decline? 45 "And you dwelt in the dwellings of men who wronged their own souls; you were clearly shown how We dealt with them; and We put forth (many) Parables on your behalf!" 46 Mighty indeed were the plots which they made, but their plots were (well) within the sight of Allah, even though they were such as to shake the hills!

47 Never think that Allah would fail his Messengers in His promise: for Allah is Exalted in Power—the Lord of Retribution. 48 One day the Earth will be changed to a different Earth, and so will be the Heavens, and (men) will be marshalled forth, before Allah, the One, the Irresistible; 49 And you will see the Sinners that day bound together in fetters— 50 Their garments of liquid pitch, and their faces covered with Fire; 51 That Allah may requite each soul according to its deserts; and, surely, Allah is Swift in calling to account. 52 Here is a Message for mankind: let them take warning therefrom, and let them know that He is (no other than) One Allah: let men of understanding take heed.

15. THE ROCKY TRACT

In the name of Allah, Most Gracious, Most Merciful.

1 *Alif Lām Rā'*. These are the Āyāt of Revelation—of a Qur'ān that makes things clear. 2 Again and again will those who disbelieve, wish that they had bowed (to Allah's Will) in Islam. 3 Leave them alone, to enjoy (the good things of this life) and to please themselves: let (false) Hope amuse them: soon will

knowledge (undeceive them). 4 Never did We destroy a population that had not a term decreed and assigned beforehand. 5 Neither can a people anticipate its term, nor delay it.

6 They say: "O you to whom the Message is being revealed! Truly you are mad (or possessed)! 7 "Why bring you not angels to us if it be that you have the Truth?" 8 We send not the angels down except for just cause: if they came (to the ungodly), behold! no respite would they have!

9 We have, without doubt, sent down the Message; and We will assuredly guard it (from corruption).

10 We did send Messengers before you amongst the religious sects of old: 11 But never came a Messenger to them but they mocked him. 12 Even so do we let it creep into the hearts of the sinners— 13 That they should not believe in the (Message); but the ways of the ancients have passed away. 14 Even if We opened out to them a gate from heaven, and they were to continue (all day) ascending therein, 15 They would only say: "Our eyes have been intoxicated: no, we have been bewitched by sorcery."

16 It is We Who have set out the Zodiacal Signs in the heavens, and made them fair-seeming to (all) beholders; 17 And (moreover) We have guarded them from every accursed Satan; 18 But any that gains a hearing by stealth, is pursued by a flaming fire, bright (to see).

19 And the earth We have spread out (like a carpet); set thereon mountains firm and immovable; and produced therein all kinds of things in due balance. 20 And We have provided therein means of subsistence—for you and for those for whose sustenance you are not responsible.

21 And there is not a thing but its (sources and) treasures (inexhaustible) are with Us; but We only send down thereof in due and ascertainable measures. 22 And We send the fecundating winds, then cause the rain to descend from the sky, therewith providing you with water (in abundance), though you are not the guardians of its stores.

23 And surely, it is We Who give life, and Who give death: it

is We Who remain Inheritors (after all else passes away). 24 To Us are known those of you who hasten forward, and those who lag behind. 25 Assuredly it is your Lord who will gather them together: for He is Perfect in Wisdom and Knowledge.

26 We created man from sounding clay, from mud moulded into shape; 27 And the Jinn race, We had created before, from the fire of a scorching wind.

28 Behold! your Lord said to the angels: "I am about to create man, from sounding clay from mud moulded into shape; 29 "When I have fashioned him (in due proportion) and breathed into him of My spirit, fall you down in obeisance unto him." 30 So the angels prostrated themselves, all of them together: 31 Not so Iblīs: he refused to be among those who prostrated themselves. 32 (Allah) said: "O Iblīs! What is your reason for not being among those who prostrated themselves?" 33 (Iblīs) said: "I am not one to prostrate myself to man, whom You did create from sounding clay, from mud moulded into shape."

34 (Allah) said: "Then get you out from here; for you are rejected, accursed. 35 "And the Curse shall be on you till the Day of Judgment." 36 (Iblis) said: "O my Lord! Give me then respite till the Day the (dead) are raised." 37 (Allah) said: "Respite is granted you— 38 "Till the Day of the Time Appointed."

39 (Iblis) said: "O my Lord! Because You have put me in the wrong, I will make (wrong) fair-seeming to them on the earth, and I will put them all in the wrong— 40 "Except Your servants among them, sincere and purified (by Your grace)."

41 (Allah) said: "This (Way of My sincere servants) is indeed a Way that leads straight to Me. 42 "For over My servants no authority shall you have, except such as put themselves in the wrong and follow you." 43 And surely, Hell is the promised abode for them all! 44 To it are seven Gates: for each of those Gates is a (special) class (of sinners) assigned.

45 The righteous (will be) amid Gardens and fountains (of clear-flowing water). 46 (Their greeting will be): "Enter you here in Peace and Security." 47 And We shall remove from their hearts any lurking sense of injury: (they will be) brothers (joyfully)

facing each other on thrones (of dignity). 48 There no sense of fatigue shall touch them, nor shall they (ever) be asked to leave. 49 Tell My servants that I am indeed the Oft-Forgiving, most Merciful; 50 and that My Chastisement will be indeed the most grievous Chastisement.

51 Tell them about the guests of Abraham. 52 When they entered his presence and said, "Peace!" he said, "We feel afraid of you!" 53 They said: "Fear not! We give you glad tidings of a son endowed with wisdom." 54 He said: "Do you give me glad tidings that old age has seized me? Of what, then, is your good news?" 55 They said: "We give you glad tidings in truth: be not then in despair!" 56 He said: "And who despairs of the mercy of his Lord, but such as go astray?"

57 Abraham said: "What then is the business on which you (have come), O you Messengers (of Allah)?" 58 They said: "We have been sent to a people (deep) in sin, 59 "Excepting the adherents of Lūt: them we are certainly (charged) to save (from harm)—all— 60 "Except his wife, who, We have ascertained, will be among those who will lag behind."

61 At length when the Messengers arrived among the adherents of Lūt, 62 He said: "You appear to be uncommon folk." 63 They said: "Yes, we have come to you to accomplish that of which they doubt. 64 "We have brought to you that which is inevitably due, and assuredly we tell the truth. 65 "Then travel by night with your household, when a portion of the night (yet remains), and do you bring up the rear: let no one among you look back, but pass on whither you are ordered." 66 And We made known this decree to him, that the last remnants of those (sinners) should be cut off by the morning.

67 The inhabitants of the City came in (mad) joy (at news of the young men). 68 Lūt said: "These are my guests: disgrace me not: 69 "But fear Allah, and shame me not." 70 They said: "Did we not forbid you (to speak) for all and sundry?" 71 He said: "There are my daughters (to marry), if you must act (so)."

72 Surely, by your life (O Prophet), in their wild intoxication, they wander in distraction, hither and thither. 73 But the (mighty)

Blast overtook them before morning, 74 And We turned (the Cities) upside down, and rained down on them brimstones hard as baked clay. 75 Behold! in this are Signs for those who by tokens do understand. 76 And the (Cities were) right on the high-road. 77 Behold! in this is a Sign for those who believe!

78 And the People of the Wood were also wrong-doers; 79 So We exacted retribution from them. They were both on an open highway, plain to see. 80 The People of the Rocky Tract also rejected the Messengers: 81 We sent them Our Signs, but they persisted in turning away from them. 82 Out of the mountains did they hew (their) edifices, (feeling themselves) secure. 83 But the (mighty) Blast seized them of a morning, 84 And of no avail to them was all that they did (with such craft and care)!

85 We created not the heavens, the earth, and all between them, but for just ends. And the Hour is surely coming (when this will be manifest). So overlook (any human faults) with gracious forgiveness. 86 For surely it is your Lord who is the Master-Creator, knowing all things.

87 And We have bestowed upon you the Seven oft-repeated (Verses) and the Grand Qur'ān. 88 Strain not your eyes. (Wistfully) at what We have bestowed on certain classes of them, nor grieve over them: but lower your wing (in gentleness) to the Believers. 89 And say: "I am indeed he that warns openly and without ambiguity"— 90 (Of just such wrath) as We sent down on those who divided (Scripture into arbitrary parts)— 91 (So also on such) as have made the Qur'ān into shreds (as they please). 92 Therefore, by the Lord, We will, of a surety, call them to account, 93 For all their deeds.

94 Therefore expound openly what you are commanded, and turn away from those who join false gods with Allah. 95 For sufficient are We unto you against those who scoff— 96 Those who adopt, with Allah, another god: but soon will they come to know. 97 We do indeed know how your heart is distressed at what they say. 98 But celebrate the praises of your Lord, and be of those who prostrate themselves in adoration. 99 And serve your Lord until there come unto you the Hour that is Certain.

16. BEES

In the name of Allah, Most Gracious, Most Merciful.

1 (Inevitable) comes (to pass) the Command of Allah: seek you not then to hasten it: glory to Him, and far is He above having the partners they ascribe unto Him! 2 He does send down His angels with inspiration of His Command, to such of His servants as He pleases, (saying): "Warn (Man) that there is no god but I: so do your duty unto Me." 3 He has created the heavens and the earth for just ends: far is He above having the partners they ascribe to Him!

4 He has created man from a sperm-drop; and behold this same (man) becomes an open disputer! 5 And cattle He has created for you (men): from them you derive warmth, and numerous benefits, and of their (meat) you eat. 6 And you have a sense of pride and beauty in them as you drive them home in the evening, and as you lead them forth to pasture in the morning. 7 And they carry your heavy loads to lands that you could not (otherwise) reach except with souls distressed: for your Lord is indeed Most Kind, Most Merciful. 8 And (He has created) horses, mules, and donkeys, for you to ride and use for show; and He has created (other) things of which you have no knowledge.

9 And unto Allah leads straight the Way, but there are ways that turn aside: if Allah had willed, He could have guided all of you.

10 It is He Who sends down rain from the sky: from it you drink, and out of it (grows) the vegetation on which you feed your cattle. 11 With it He produces for you corn, olives, date-palms, grapes and every kind of fruit: surely in this is a Sign for those who give thought.

12 He has made subject to you the Night and the Day; the Sun and the Moon; and the Stars are in subjection by His Command: surely in this are Signs for men who are wise. 13 And the things on this earth which He has multiplied in varying colours (and qualities): surely in this is a Sign for men who celebrate the praises of Allah (in gratitude).

14 It is He Who has made the sea subject, that you may eat thereof flesh that is fresh and tender, and that you may extract therefrom ornaments to wear; and you see the ships therein that plough the waves, that you may seek (thus) of the bounty of Allah and that you may be grateful.

15 And He has set up on the earth mountains standing firm, lest it should shake with you; and rivers and roads; that you may guide yourselves; 16 And marks and sign-posts; and by the stars (Men) guide themselves.

17 Is then He Who creates like one that creates not? Will you not receive admonition? 18 If you would count up the favours of Allah, never would you be able to number them: for Allah is Oft-Forgiving, Most Merciful. 19 And Allah does know what you conceal, and what you reveal.

20 Those whom they invoke besides Allah create nothing and are themselves created. 21 (They are things) dead, lifeless: nor do they know when they will be raised up. 22 Your God is One God: as to those who believe not in the Hereafter, their hearts refuse to know, and they are arrogant. 23 Undoubtedly Allah does know what they conceal, and what they reveal: surely He loves not the arrogant.

24 When it is said to them, "What is it that your Lord has revealed?" they say, "Tales of the ancients!" 25 Let them bear, on the Day of Judgment, their own burdens in full, and also (something) of the burdens of those without knowledge, whom they misled. Alas, how grievous the burdens they will bear!

26 Those before them did also plot (against Allah's Way): but Allah took their structures from their foundations, and the roof fell down on them from above; and the Wrath seized them from directions they did not perceive. 27 Then, on the Day of Judgment, he will cover them with shame, and say: "Where are My 'partners' concerning whom you used to dispute (with the godly)?" Those endued with knowledge will say: "This Day, indeed, are the Unbelievers covered with Shame and Misery —

28 "(Namely) those whose lives the angels take in a state of wrong-doing to their own souls." Then would they offer

submission (with the pretence), "We did no evil (knowingly)." (The angels will reply), "No, but surely Allah knows all that you did; 29 "So enter the gates of Hell, to dwell therein. Thus evil indeed is the abode of the arrogant."

30 To the righteous (when) it is said, "What is it that your Lord has revealed?" they say, "All that is good." To those who do good, there is good in this world, and the Home of the Hereafter is even better and excellent indeed is the Home of the righteous — 31 Gardens of Eternity which they will enter: beneath them flow (pleasant) rivers: they will have therein all that they wish: thus does Allah reward the righteous — 32 (Namely) those whose lives the angels take in a state of purity, saying (to them), "Peace be on you; enter you the Garden, because of (the good) which you did (in the world)."

33 Do the (ungodly) wait until the angels come to them, or there comes the Command of your Lord (for their doom)? So did those who went before them. But Allah wronged them not: no, they wronged their own souls. 34 But the evil results of their deeds overtook them, and that very (Wrath) at which they had scoffed hemmed them in.

35 The worshippers of false gods say: "If Allah had so willed, we should not have worshipped any but Him — neither we nor our fathers — nor should we have prescribed prohibitions other than His." So did those who went before them. But what is the mission of Messengers but to preach the Clear Message?

36 For We assuredly sent amongst every People a Messenger, (with the Command), "Serve Allah, and eschew Evil": of the people were some whom th guided, and some on whom Error became inevitably (established). So travel through the earth, and see what was the end of those who denied (the Truth). 37 If you be anxious for their guidance, yet Allah guides not such as He leaves to stray, and there is none to help them.

38 They swear their strongest oaths by Allah, that Allah will not raise up those who die: no, but it is a promise (binding) on Him in truth: but most among mankind realise it not. 39 (They must be raised up), in order that He may manifest to them the truth

of that wherein they differ, and that the rejecters of Truth may realise that they had indeed (surrendered to) Falsehood. 40 For to anything which We have willed, We but say the Word, "Be," and it is.

41 To those who leave their homes in the cause of Allah, after suffering oppression—We will assuredly give a goodly home in this world; but truly the reward of the Hereafter will be greater. If they only realised (this)! 42 (They are) those who persevere in patience, and put their trust in their Lord.

43 And before you also the Messengers We sent were but men, to whom We granted inspiration: if you realise this not, ask of those who possess the Message. 44 (We sent them) with Clear Signs and Scriptures; and We have sent down unto you (also) the Message; that you may explain clearly to men what is sent for them, and that they may give thought.

45 Do then those who devise evil (plots) feel secure that Allah will not cause the earth to swallow them up, or that the Wrath will not seize them from directions they little perceive?— 46 Or that He may not call them to account in the midst of their goings here and there, without a chance of their frustrating Him?— 47 Or that He may not call them to account by a process of slow wastage—for your Lord is indeed full of kindness and mercy.

48 Do they not look at Allah's creation, (even) among (inanimate) things—How their (very) shadows turn round, from the right and the left, prostrating themselves to Allah, and that in the humblest manner? 49 And to Allah does obeisance all that is in the heavens and on earth, whether moving (living) creatures or the angels: for none are arrogant (before their Lord). 50 They all revere their Lord, high above them, and they do all that they are commanded.

51 Allah has said: "Take not (for worship) two gods: for He is just One God: then fear Me (and Me alone)." 52 To Him belongs whatever is in the heavens and on earth, and to Him is duty due always: then will you fear other than Allah?

53 And you have no good thing but is from Allah: and moreover,

when you are touched by distress, to Him you cry with groans; 54 Yet, when He removes the distress from you, behold! Some of you turn to other gods to join with their Lord— 55 (As if) to show their ingratitude for the favours We have bestowed on them! Then enjoy (your brief day): but soon will you know (your folly)! 56 And they (even) assign, to things they do not know, a portion out of that which We have bestowed for their sustenance! By Allah, you shall certainly be called to account for your false inventions.

57 And they assign daughters for Allah!—Glory be to Him!—and for themselves (sons—the issue) they desire! 58 When news is brought to one of them, of (the birth of) a female (child), his face darkens, and he is filled with inward grief! 59 With shame does he hide himself from his people, because of the bad news he has had! Shall he retain it on (sufferance and) contempt, or bury it in the dust? Ah! what an evil (choice) they decide on? 60 To those who believe not in the Hereafter, applies the similitude of evil: to Allah applies the highest similitude: for He is the Exalted in Power, full of Wisdom.

61 If Allah were to punish men for their wrong-doing, He would not leave, on the (earth), a single living creature: but He gives them respite for a stated Term: when their Term expires, they would not be able to delay (the punishment) for a single hour, just as they would not be able to anticipate it (for a single hour).

62 They attribute to Allah what they hate (for themselves), and their tongues assert the falsehood that all good things are for themselves: without doubt for them is the Fire, and they will be the first to be hastened on into it!

63 By Allah, We (also) sent (our Messengers) to Peoples before you; but Satan made, (to the wicked), their own acts seem alluring: he is also their patron today, but they shall have a most grievous penalty. 64 And We sent down the Book to you for the express purpose, that you should make clear to them those things in which they differ, and that it should be a guide and a mercy to those who believe.

65 And Allah sends down rain from the skies, and gives

therewith life to the earth after its death: surely in this is a Sign for those who listen.

66 And surely in cattle (too) will you find an instructive Sign. From what is within their bodies between excretions and blood, We produce, for your drink, milk, pure and agreeable to those who drink it. 67 And from the fruit of the date-palm and the vine, you get out wholesome drink and food: behold, in this also is a Sign for those who are wise.

68 And your Lord taught the Bee to build its cells in hills, on trees, and in (men's) habitations; 69 Then to eat of all the produce (of the earth), and find with skill the spacious paths of its Lord: there issues from within their bodies a drink of varying colours, wherein is healing for men: surely in this is a Sign for those who give thought.

70 It is Allah Who creates you and takes your souls at death; and of you there are some who are sent back to a feeble age, so that they know nothing after having known (much): for Allah is All-Knowing, All-Powerful.

71 Allah has bestowed His gifts of sustenance more freely on some of you than on others: those more favoured are not going to throw back their gifts to those whom their right hands possess, so as to be equal in that respect. Will they then deny the favours of Allah?

72 And Allah has made for you mates (and Companions) of your own nature, and made for you, out of them, sons and daughters and grandchildren, and provided for you sustenance of the best: will they then believe in vain things, and be ungrateful for Allah's favours?— 73 And worship others than Allah—such as have no power of providing them, for sustenance, with anything in heavens or earth, and cannot possibly have such power? 74 Invent not similitudes for Allah: for Allah knows, and you know not.

75 Allah sets forth the Parable (of two men: one) a slave under the dominion of another; he has no power of any sort; and (the other) a man on whom We have bestowed goodly favours from Ourselves, and he spends thereof (freely), privately and publicly:

are the two equal? (By no means;) praise be to Allah. But most of them understand not.

76 Allah sets forth (another) Parable of two men: one of them dumb, with no power of any sort; a wearisome burden is he to his master; whichever way he directs him, he brings no good: is such a man equal with one who commands justice, and is on a Straight Way?

77 To Allah belongs the Mystery of the heavens and the earth. And the Decision of the Hour (of Judgment) is as the twinkling of an eye, or even quicker: for Allah has power over all things.

78 It is He Who brought you forth from the wombs of your mothers when you knew nothing; and He gave you hearing and sight and intelligence and affections: that you may give thanks (to Allah).

79 Do they not look at the birds, held poised in the midst of (the air and) the sky? Nothing holds them up but (the power of) Allah. Surely in this are Signs for those who believe. 80 It is Allah Who made your habitations homes of rest and quiet for you; and made for you, out of the skins of animals, (tents for) dwellings, which you find so light (and handy) when you travel and when you stop (in your travels); and out of their wool, and their soft fibres (between wool and hair), and their hair, rich stuff and articles of convenience (to serve you) for a time.

81 It is Allah Who made out of the things He created, some things to give you shade; of the hills He made some for your shelter; He made you garments to protect you from heat, and coats of mail to protect you from your (mutual) violence. Thus does He complete His favours on you, that you may bow to His Will (in Islam).

82 But if they turn away, your duty is only to preach the Clear Message. 83 They recognise the favours of Allah; then they deny them; and most of them are (creatures) ungrateful.

84 One Day We shall raise from all Peoples a Witness: then will no excuse be accepted from Unbelievers, nor will they receive any favours. 85 When the wrong-doers (actually) see the Penalty,

then will it in no way be mitigated, nor will they then receive respite.

86 When those who gave partners to Allah will see their "partners," they will say: "Our Lord! These are our 'partners,' those whom we used to invoke besides You." But they will throw back their word at them (and say): "Indeed you are liars!" 87 That day shall they (openly) show (their) submission to Allah; and all their inventions shall leave them in the lurch. 88 Those who reject Allah and hinder (men) from the Path of Allah—for them will We add Penalty to Penalty; for that they used to spread mischief.

89 One day We shall raise from all Peoples a witness against them, from amongst themselves: and We shall bring you as a witness against these (your people): and We have sent down to you the Book explaining all things, a Guide, a Mercy, and Glad Tidings to Muslims.

90 Allah commands justice, the doing of good, and liberality to kith and kin, and He forbids all shameful deeds, and injustice and rebellion: He instructs you, that you may receive admonition.

91 Fulfil the Covenant of Allah when you have entered into it, and break not your oaths after you have confirmed them; indeed you have made Allah your surety; for Allah knows all that you do. 92 And be not like a woman who breaks into untwisted strands the yarn which she has spun, after it has become strong. Nor take your oaths to practise deception between yourselves, lest one party should be more numerous than another: for Allah will test you by this; and on the Day of Judgment He will certainly make clear to you (the truth of) that wherein you disagree.

93 If Allah so willed, He could make you all one People: but He leaves straying whom He pleases, and He guides whom He pleases: but you shall certainly be called to account for all your actions.

94 And take not your oaths, to practise deception between yourselves, with the result that someone's foot may slip after it was firmly planted, and you may have to taste the evil (consequences) of having hindered (men) from the Path of Allah,

and a mighty Wrath descend on you. 95 Nor sell the Covenant of Allah for a miserable price: for with Allah is (a prize) far better for you, if you only knew.

96 What is with you must vanish: what is with Allah will endure. And We will certainly bestow, on those who patiently persevere, their reward according to the best of their actions. 97 Whoever works righteousness, man or woman, and has Faith, surely, to him will We give a new Life, a life that is good and pure and We will bestow on such their reward according to the best of their actions.

98 When you read the Qur'ān, seek Allah's protection from Satan the Rejected One. 99 No authority has he over those who believe and put their trust in their Lord. 100 His authority is over those only, who take him as patron and who join partners with Allah.

101 When We substitute one revelation for another—and Allah knows best what He reveals (in stages)—they say, "You are but a forger": but most of them understand not. 102 Say, the Holy Spirit has brought the revelation from your Lord in Truth, in order to strengthen those who believe, and as a Guide and Glad Tidings to Muslims.

103 We know indeed that they say, "It is a man that teaches him." The tongue of him they wickedly point to is notably foreign, while this is Arabic, pure and clear. 104 Those who believe not in the Signs of Allah—Allah will not guide them, and theirs will be a grievous Penalty. 105 It is those who believe not in the Signs of Allah, that forge falsehood: it is they who lie!

106 Anyone who, after accepting faith in Allah, utters Unbelief—except under compulsion, his heart remaining firm in Faith—but such as open their breast to Unbelief—on them is Wrath from Allah, and theirs will be a dreadful chastisement. 107 This because they love the life of this world better than the Hereafter: and Allah will not guide those who reject Faith. 108 Those are they whose hearts, ears, and eyes Allah has sealed up, and they take no heed. 109 Without doubt, in the Hereafter they will perish.

110 But surely your Lord — to those who leave their homes after trials and persecutions — and who thereafter strive for the Faith and patiently persevere — your Lord, after all this, is Oft-Forgiving, Most Merciful. 111 One Day every soul will come up struggling for itself, and every soul will be recompensed (fully) for all its actions, and none will be unjustly dealt with.

112 Allah sets forth a Parable: a city enjoying security and peace, abundantly supplied with sustenance from every place: yet was ungrateful for the favours of Allah: so Allah made it taste of hunger and terror (in extremes) (closing in on it) like a garment (from every side), because of the (evil) which (its people) wrought. 113 And there came to them a Messenger from among themselves, but they falsely rejected him; so the Wrath seized them even in the midst of their iniquities.

114 So eat of the sustenance which Allah has provided for you, lawful and good; and be grateful for the favours of Allah, if it is He whom you serve. 115 He has only forbidden you dead meat, and blood, and the flesh of swine, and any (food) over which the name of other than Allah has been invoked. But if one is forced by necessity, without wilful disobedience, nor transgressing due limits — then Allah is Oft-Forgiving, most Merciful.

116 But say not — for any false thing that your tongues may put forth — "This is lawful, and this is forbidden," so as to ascribe false things to Allah. For those who ascribe false things to Allah, will never prosper. 117 (In such falsehood) is but a paltry profit; but they will have a most grievous Penalty.

118 To the Jews We prohibited such things as We have mentioned to you before: We did them no wrong, but they were used to doing wrong to themselves.

119 But surely your Lord — to those who do wrong in ignorance, but who thereafter repent and make amends — your Lord, after all this, is Oft-Forgiving, Most Merciful.

120 Abraham was indeed a model, devoutly obedient to Allah, (and) true in Faith, and he joined not gods with Allah: 121 He showed his gratitude for the favours of Allah, who chose him,

and guided him to a Straight Way. 122 And We gave him Good in this world, and he will be, in the Hereafter, in the ranks of the Righteous. 123 So We have taught you the inspired (Message), "Follow the ways of Abraham the True in Faith, and he joined not gods with Allah."

124 The Sabbath was only made (strict) for those who disagreed (as to its observance); but Allah will judge between them on the Day of Judgment, as to their differences.

125 Invite (all) to the Way of your Lord with wisdom and beautiful preaching; and argue with them in ways that are best and most gracious: for your Lord knows best, who have strayed from His Path, and who receive guidance.

126 And if you do catch them out, catch them out no worse than they catch you out: but if you show patience, that is indeed the best (course) for those who are patient. 127 And do you be patient, for your patience is but from Allah; nor grieve over them: and distress not yourself because of their plots. 128 For Allah is with those who restrain themselves, and those who do good.

17. THE NIGHT JOURNEY

In the name of Allah, Most Gracious, Most Merciful.

1 Glory to (Allah) who did take His Servant for a Journey by night from the Sacred Mosque to the Farthest Mosque, whose precincts We did bless—in order that We might show him some of Our Signs: for He is the One Who hears and sees (all things).

2 We gave Moses the Book, and made it a Guide to the Children of Israel—(Commanding): "Take not other than Me as Disposer of (your) affairs." 3 O you that are sprung from those whom We carried (in the Ark) with Noah! Certainly he was a devotee Most grateful.

4 And We gave (clear) warning to the Children of Israel in the Book, that twice would they do mischief on the earth and be elated

with mighty arrogance (and twice would they be punished)! 5 When the first of the warnings came to pass, We sent against you Our servants given to terrible warfare: they entered the very inmost parts of your homes; and it was a warning (completely) fulfilled. 6 Then did We grant you the Return as against them: We gave you increase in resources and sons, and made you the more numerous in man-power.

7 If you did well, you did well for yourselves; if you did evil, (you did it) against yourselves. So when the second of the warnings came to pass, (We permitted your enemies) to disfigure your faces, and to enter your Temple as they had entered it before, and to visit with destruction all that fell into their power. 8 It may be that your Lord may (yet) show Mercy unto you; but if you revert (to your sins), We shall revert (to Our punishments): and we have made Hell a prison for those who reject (all Faith).

9 Surely this Qur'ān does guide to that which is most right (or stable), and gives the glad tidings to the believers who work deeds of righteousness, that they shall have a magnificent reward; 10 And to those who believe not in the Hereafter, (it announces) that We have prepared for them a Chastisement grievous (indeed).

11 The prayer that man should make for good, he makes for evil; for man is given to hasty (deeds). 12 We have made the Night and the Day as two (of Our) Signs: the Sign of the Night have We obscured, while the Sign of the Day We have made to enlighten you; that you may seek bounty from your Lord, and that you may know the number and count of the years: all things have We explained in detail.

13 Every man's fate We have fastened on his own neck: on the Day of Judgment We shall bring out for him a scroll, which he will see spread open. 14 (It will be said to him:) "Read your (own) record: sufficient is your soul this day to make out an account against you." 15 Who receives guidance, receives it for his own benefit: who goes astray does so to his own loss: no bearer of burdens can bear the burden of another: nor would We visit with Our Wrath until We had sent a Messenger (to give warning).

16 When We decide to destroy a population, We (first) send a

definite order to those among them who are given the good things of this life and yet transgress; so that the word is proved true against them: then (it is) we destroy them utterly. 17 How many generations have We destroyed after Noah? And enough is your Lord to note and see the sins of His servants.

18 If any do wish for the transitory things (of this life), We readily grant them—such things as We will, to such persons as We will: in the end have We provided Hell for them: they will burn therein, disgraced and rejected. 19 Those who do wish for the (things of) the Hereafter, and strive therefor with all due striving, and have Faith—they are the ones whose striving is acceptable (to Allah).

20 Of the bounties of your Lord We bestow freely on all—these as well as those: the bounties of your Lord are not closed (to anyone). 21 See how We have bestowed more on some than on others; but surely the Hereafter is more in rank and gradation and more in excellence.

22 Take not with Allah another object of worship; or you (O man!) will sit in disgrace and destitution. 23 Your Lord has decreed that you worship none but Him, and that you be kind to parents. Whether one or both of them attain old age in your life, say not to them a word of contempt, nor repel them, but address them in terms of honour. 24 And, out of kindness, lower to them the wing of humility, and say: "My Lord! bestow on them your Mercy even as they cherished me in childhood." 25 Your Lord knows best what is in your hearts: if you do deeds of righteousness, surely He is Most Forgiving to those who turn to Him again and again (in true penitence).

26 And render to the kindred their due rights, as (also) to those in want, and to the wayfarer: but squander not (your wealth) in the manner of a spendthrift. 27 Surely spendthrifts are brothers of the Satans; and the Satan is to his Lord (Himself) ungrateful. 28 And even if you have to turn away from them in pursuit of the Mercy from your Lord which you do expect, yet speak to them a word of easy kindness.

29 Make not your hand tied (like a niggard's) to your neck, nor

stretch it forth to its utmost reach, so that you become blameworthy and destitute. 30 Surely your Lord does provide sustenance in abundance for whom He pleases, and He provides in a just measure. For He does know and regard all His servants.

31 Kill not your children for fear of want: We shall provide sustenance for them as well as for you. Surely the killing of them is a great sin. 32 Nor come near to unlawful sex: for it is a shameful (deed) and an evil, opening the road (to other evils).

33 Nor take life — which Allah has made sacred — except for just cause. And if anyone is slain wrongfully, We have given his heir authority (to demand qiṣāṣ or to forgive): but let him nor exceed bounds in the matter of taking life; for he is helped (by the Law).

34 Come not near to the orphan's property except to improve it, until he attains the age of full strength; and fulfil (every) engagement, for (every) engagement will be enquired into (on the Day of Reckoning). 35 Give full measure when you measure, and weigh with a balance that is straight: that is the most fitting and the most advantageous in the final determination.

36 And pursue not that of which you have no knowledge; for every act of hearing, or of seeing or of (feeling in) the heart will be enquired into (on the Day of Reckoning). 37 Nor walk on the earth with insolence: for you can not rend the earth asunder, nor reach the mountains in height. 38 Of all such things the evil is hateful in the sight of your Lord.

39 These are among the (precepts of) wisdom, which your Lord has revealed to you. Take not, with Allah, another object of worship, lest you should be thrown into Hell, blameworthy and rejected.

40 Has then your Lord! (O Pagans!) preferred for you sons, and taken for Himself daughters among the angels? Truly you utter a most dreadful saying! 41 We have explained (things) in various (ways) in this Qur'ān, in order that they may receive admonition, but it only increases their flight (from the Truth)! 42 Say: If there had been (other) gods with Him — as they say — behold, they would certainly have sought out a way to the Lord of the Throne! 43 Glory to Him! He is high above all that they say! — Exalted and

Great (beyond measure)! 44 The seven heavens and the earth, and all beings therein, declare His glory: there is not a thing but celebrates His praise; and yet you understand not how they declare His glory! Surely He is Oft-Forbearing, most Forgiving!

45 When you recite the Qur'ān, We put, between you and those who believe not in the Hereafter, a veil invisible: 46 And We put coverings over their hearts (and minds) lest they should understand the Qur'ān, and deafness into their ears: when you commemorate your Lord — and Him alone — in the Qur'ān, they turn on their backs, fleeing (from the Truth).

47 We know best why it is they listen, when they listen to you; and when they meet in private conference, behold, the wicked say, "You follow none other than a man bewitched!" 48 See what similes they strike for you: but they have gone astray, and never can they find a way.

49 They say: "What! when we are reduced to bones and dust, should we really be raised up (to be) a new creation?" 50 Say: "(No!) be you stones or iron, 51 "Or created matter which, in your minds, is hardest (to be raised up) — (yet shall you be raised up)!" Then will they say: "Who will cause us to return?" Say: "He who created you first!" then will they wag their heads towards you, and say, "When will that be?" Say, "May be it will be quite soon! 52 "It will be on a Day when He will call you, and you will answer (His call) with (words of) His praise, and you will think that you tarried but a little while!"

53 Say to My servants that they should (only) say those things that are best: for Satan does sow dissensions among them: for Satan is to man an avowed enemy.

54 It is your Lord that knows you best: if He please, He grants you mercy, or if He please, punishment: We have not sent you to be a disposer of their affairs for them. 55 And it is your Lord that knows best all beings that are in the heavens and on earth: We did bestow on some Prophets more (and other) gifts than on others: and We gave to David (the gift Of) the Psalms.

56 Say: "Call on those — besides Him — whom you fancy: they have neither the power to remove your troubles from you nor to

change them." 57 Those whom they call upon do desire (for themselves) means of access to their Lord—even those who are nearest: they hope for His Mercy and fear His Wrath: for the Wrath of your Lord is a thing to take heed of.

58 There is not a population but We shall destroy it before the Day of Judgment or punish it with a dreadful Punishment! That is written in the (eternal) Record.

59 And We refrain from sending the Signs, only because the men of former generations treated them as false: We sent the She-camel to the Thamūd to open their eyes, but they treated her wrongfully: We only send the Signs by way of terror (and warning from evil).

60 Behold! We told you that your Lord does encompass mankind round about: We granted the Vision which We showed you, but as a trial for men—as also the Cursed Tree (mentioned) in the Qur'ān: We put terror (and warning) into them, but it only increases their inordinate transgression!

61 Behold! We said to the angels: "Bow down unto Adam": they bowed down except Iblīs: He said, "Shall I bow down to one whom You did create from clay?" 62 He said: "Do you see? This is the one whom You have honoured above me! If You will but respite me to the Day of Judgment, I will surely bring his descendants under my sway—all but a few!"

63 (Allah) said: "Go your way; if any of them follow you, surely Hell will be the recompense of you (all)—an ample recompense. 64 "Lead to destruction those whom you can among them, with your (seductive) voice; make assaults on them with your cavalry and your infantry; mutually share with them wealth and children; and make promises to them." But Satan promises them nothing but deceit. 65 "As for My servants, no authority shall you have over them:" enough is your Lord for a Disposer of affairs.

66 Your Lord is He that makes the Ship go smoothly for you through the sea, in order that you may seek of his Bounty. For He is to you most Merciful. 67 When distress seizes you at sea, those that you call upon—besides Himself—leave you in the lurch! But when He brings you back safe to land, you turn away (from Him). Most ungrateful is man!

68 Do you then feel secure that He will not cause you to be swallowed up beneath the earth when you are on land, or that He will not send against you a violent tornado (with showers of stones) so that you shall find no one to carry out your affairs for you? 69 Or do you feel secure that He will not send you back a second time to sea and send against you a heavy gale to drown you because of your ingratitude, so that you find no helper therein against Us?

70 We have honoured the sons of Adam; provided them with transport on land and sea; given them for sustenance things good and pure; and conferred on them special favours, above a great part of Our Creation.

71 One day We shall call together all human beings with their (respective) Imāms: those who are given their record in their right hand will read it (with pleasure), and they will not be dealt with unjustly in the least. 72 But those who were blind in this world, will be blind in the Hereafter, and most astray from the Path.

73 And their purpose was to tempt you away from that which We had revealed unto you, to substitute in our name something quite different; (in that case), behold! They would certainly have made you (their) friend! 74 And had We not given you strength, you would nearly have inclined to them a little. 75 In that case We should have made you taste an equal portion (of punishment) in this life, and an equal portion in death: and moreover you would have found none to help you against Us!

76 Their purpose was to scare you off the land, in order to expel you; but in that case they would not have stayed (therein) after you, except for a little while. 77 (This was Our) way with the Messengers We sent before you: you will find no change in Our ways.

78 Establish regular prayers—at the sun's decline till the darkness of the night, and the recital of the Qur'ān for, the recital of the Qur'ān at dawn is witnessed.

79 And keep awake a part of the night; (an additional prayer of spiritual benefit) for you: soon will your Lord raise you to a Station of Praise and Glory!

80 Say: "O my Lord! Let my entry be by the Gate of Truth and Honour, and likewise my exit by the Gate of Truth and Honour; and grant me from Your Presence an authority to aid (me)." 81 And say: "Truth has (now) arrived, and Falsehood perished: for Falsehood is (by its nature) bound to perish."

82 We send down (stage by stage) in the Qur'ān that which is a healing and a mercy to those who believe: to the unjust it causes nothing but loss after loss.

83 Yet when We bestow our favours on man, he turns away and becomes remote on his side (instead of coming to Us), and when evil seizes him he gives himself up to despair! 84 Say: "Everyone acts according to his own disposition: but your Lord knows best who it is that is best guided on the Way."

85 They ask you concerning the Spirit (of inspiration). Say: "The Spirit (comes) by command of my Lord: of knowledge it is only a little that is communicated to you, (O men!)"

86 If it were Our Will, We could take away that which We have sent you by inspiration: then would you find none to plead your affair in that matter as against Us— 87 Except for Mercy from your Lord: for His Bounty is to you (indeed) great. 88 Say: "If the whole of mankind and Jinns were to gather together to produce the like of this Qur'ān, they could not produce the like thereof, even if they backed up each other with help and support.

89 And We have explained to man, in this Qur'ān, every kind of similitude: yet the greater part of men refuse (to receive it) except with ingratitude! 90 They say: "We shall not believe in you, until you cause a spring to gush forth for us from the earth, 91 "Or (until) you have a garden of date trees and vines, and cause rivers to gush forth in their midst, carrying abundant water; 92 "Or you cause the sky to fall in pieces, as you say (will happen), against us; or you bring Allah and the angels before (us) face to face: 93 "Or you have a house adorned with gold, or you mount a ladder right into the skies. No, we shall not even believe in your mounting until you send down to us a book that we could read." Say: "Glory to my Lord! Am I any but a man—a Messenger?"

94 What kept men back from Belief when Guidance came to

them, was nothing but this: they said, "Has Allah sent a man (like us) to be (His) Messenger?" 95 Say, "If there were settled, on earth, angels walking about in peace and quiet, We should certainly have sent them down from the heavens an angel for a Messenger." 96 Say: "Enough is Allah for a witness between me and you: for He is well acquainted with His servants, and He sees (all things).

97 It is he whom Allah guides, that is on true guidance; but he whom He leaves astray—for such will you find no protector besides Him. On the Day of Judgment We shall gather them together, prone on their faces, blind, dumb, and deaf: their abode will be Hell: every time it shows abatement, We shall increase for them the fierceness of the Fire. 98 That is their recompense, because they rejected Our Signs, and said, "When we are reduced to bones and broken dust, should we really be raised up (to be) a new Creation?"

99 See they not that Allah, who created the heavens and the earth, has power to create the like of them (anew)? Only He has decreed a term appointed, of which there is no doubt. But the unjust refuse (to receive it) except with ingratitude.

100 Say: "If you had control of the Treasures of the Mercy of my Lord, behold, you would keep them back, for fear of spending them: for man is (ever) niggardly!"

101 To Moses We did give nine Clear Signs: ask the Children of Israel: when he came to them, Pharaoh said to him: "O Moses! I consider you, indeed, to have been worked upon by sorcery! 102 Moses said, "You know well that these things have been sent down by none but the Lord of the heavens and the earth as eye-opening evidence: and I consider you indeed, O Pharaoh, to be one doomed to destruction!" 103 So he resolved to remove them from the face of the earth: but We did drown him and all who were with him. 104 And We said thereafter to the Children of Israel, "Dwell securely in the land (of promise)": but when the second of the warnings came to pass, We gathered you together in a mingled crowd.

105 We sent down the (Qur'ān) in Truth, and in Truth has it descended: and We sent you but to give Glad Tidings and to warn

(sinners). 106 (It is) a Qur'ān which We have divided (into parts from time to time), in order that you might recite it to men at intervals: We have revealed it by stages.

107 Say: "Whether you believe in it or not, it is true that those who were given knowledge beforehand, when it is recited to them, fall down on their faces in humble prostration, 108 "And they say: 'Glory to our Lord! Truly has the promise of our Lord been fulfilled!'" 109 They fall down on their faces in tears, and it increases their (earnest) humility.

110 Say: "Call upon Allah, or call upon Raḥmān: by whatever name you call upon Him, (it is well): for to Him belong the Most Beautiful Names. Neither speak your Prayer aloud, nor speak it in a low tone, but seek a middle course between." 111 Say: "Praise be to Allah, who begets no son, and has no partner in (His) dominion: nor (needs) He any to protect Him from humiliation: yes, glorify Him for His greatness and glory!"

18. THE CAVE

In the name of Allah, Most Gracious, Most Merciful.

1 Praise be to Allah, who has sent to His Servant the Book, and has allowed therein no Crookedness: 2 (He has made it) Straight (and Clear) in order that He may warn (the godless) of a terrible Punishment from Him, and that He may give Glad Tidings to the Believers who work righteous deeds, that they shall have a goodly Reward, 3 Wherein they shall remain for ever: 4 Further, that He may warn those (also) who say, "Allah has begotten a son": 5 No knowledge have they of such a thing, nor had their fathers. It is a grievous thing that issues from their mouths as a saying. What they say is nothing but falsehood!

6 You would only, perchance, fret yourself to death, following after them, in grief, if they believe not in this Message. 7 That which is on earth We have made but as a glittering show for the

earth, in order that We may test them—as to which of them are best in conduct. 8 Surely what is on earth We shall make but as dust and dry soil (without growth or herbage).

9 Or do you reflect that the Companions of the Cave and of the Inscription were wonders among Our Signs? 10 Behold, the youths betook themselves to the Cave: they said, "Our Lord! bestow on us mercy from Yourself, and dispose of our affair for us in the right way!" 11 Then We drew (a veil) over their ears, for a number of years, in the Cave, (so that they heard not): 12 Then We roused them in order to test which of the two parties was best at calculating the term of years they had tarried!

13 We relate to you their story in truth: they were youths who believed in their Lord, and We advanced them in guidance: 14 We gave strength to their hearts: behold, they stood up and said: "Our Lord is the Lord of the heavens and of the earth: never shall we call upon any god other than Him: if we did, we should indeed have uttered an enormity!" 15 "These our people have taken for worship gods other than Him: why do they not bring forward an authority clear (and convincing) for what they do? Who does more wrong than such as invent a falsehood against Allah?

16 "When you turn away from them and the things they worship other than Allah, betake yourselves to the Cave: your Lord will shower His mercies on you and dispose of your affair towards comfort and ease."

17 You would have seen the sun, when it rose, declining to the right from their Cave, and when it set, turning away from them to the left, while they lay in the open space in the midst of the Cave. Such are among the Signs of Allah: he whom Allah guides is rightly guided; but he whom Allah leaves to stray— for him will you find no protector to lead him to the Right Way.

18 You would have deemed them awake, while they were asleep, and We turned them on their right and on their left sides: their dog stretching forth his two forelegs on the threshold: if you had come up on to them, you would have certainly turned back from them in flight, and would certainly have been filled with terror of them.

19 Such (being their state), We raised them up (from sleep), that they might question each other. Said one of them, "How long have you stayed (here)?" They said, "We have stayed (perhaps) a day, or part of a day." (At length) they (all) said, "Allah (alone) knows best how long you have stayed here… now, send one of you with this money of yours to the town: let him find out which is the best food (to be had) and bring some to you, that (you may) satisfy your hunger therewith: and let him behave with care and courtesy, and let him not inform any one about you. 20 "For if they should come upon you, they would stone you or force you to return to their cult, and in that case you would never attain success."

21 Thus did We make their case known to the people, that they might know that the promise of Allah is true, and that there can be no doubt about the Hour of Judgment. Behold, they dispute among themselves as to their affair. (Some) said, "Construct a building over them": Their Lord knows best about them: those who prevailed over their affair said, "Let us surely build a place of worship over them."

22 (Some) say they were three, the dog being the fourth among them; (others) say they were five, the dog being the sixth— doubtfully guessing at the unknown; (yet others) say they were seven, the dog being the eighth. Say you: "My Lord knows best their number; it is but few that know their (real case)." Enter not, therefore, into controversies concerning them, except on a matter that is clear, nor consult any of them about (the affair of) the Sleepers.

23 Nor say of anything, "I shall be sure to do so and so tomorrow"— 24 Without adding, "So please Allah!" and call your Lord to mind when you forget, and say, "I hope that my Lord will guide me ever closer (even) than this to the right road."

25 So they stayed in their Cave three hundred years, and (some) add nine (more). 26 Say: "Allah knows best how long they stayed: with Him is (the knowledge of) the secrets of the heavens and the earth: how clearly He sees, how finely He hears (everything)! They have no protector other than Him; nor does He share His Command with any person whatsoever.

27 And recite (and teach) what has been revealed to you of the Book of your Lord: none can change His Words, and none will you find as a refuge other than Him. 28 And keep your soul content with those who call on their Lord morning and evening, seeking His Face; and let not your eyes pass beyond them, seeking the pomp and glitter of this Life; nor obey any whose heart We have permitted to neglect the remembrance of Us, one who follows his own desires, whose case has gone beyond all bounds.

29 Say, "The Truth is from your Lord": let him who will, believe, and let him who will, reject (it): for the wrongdoers We have prepared a Fire whose (smoke and flames), like the walls and roof of a tent, will hem them in: if they implore relief they will be granted water like melted brass, that will scald their faces. How dreadful the drink! How uncomfortable a couch to recline on!

30 As to those who believe and work righteousness, surely We shall not suffer to perish the reward of any who do a (single) righteous deed. 31 For them will be Gardens of Eternity; beneath them rivers will flow; they will be adorned therein with bracelets of gold, and they will wear green garments of fine silk and heavy brocade: they will recline therein on raised thrones. How good the recompense! How beautiful a couch to recline on!

32 Set forth to them the parable of two men: for one of them We provided two gardens of grape-vines and surrounded them with date palms; in between the two We placed cornfields. 33 Each of those gardens brought forth its produce, and failed not in the least therein: in the midst of them We caused a river to flow. 34 (Abundant) was the produce this man had: he said to his companion, in the course of a mutual argument: "More wealth have I than you, and more honour and power in (my following of) men." 35 He went into his garden in a state (of mind) unjust to his soul: he said, "I deem not that this will ever perish. 36 "Nor do I deem that the Hour (of Judgment) will (ever) come: even if I am brought back to my Lord, I shall surely find (there) something better in exchange."

37 His companion said to him, in the course of the argument

with him: "Do you deny Him Who created you out of dust, then out of a sperm-drop, then fashioned you into a man? 38 "But (I think) for my part that He is Allah, my Lord, and none shall I associate with my Lord. 39 "Why did you not, as you went into your garden, say: 'Allah's will (be done)! There is no power but with Allah!' If you do see me less than you in wealth and sons, 40 "It may be that my Lord will give me something better than your garden, and that He will send on your garden thunderbolts (by way of reckoning) from heaven, making it (but) slippery sand!— 41 "Or the water of the garden will run off underground so that you will never be able to find it."

42 So his fruits (and enjoyment) were encompassed (with ruin), and he remained twisting and turning his hands over what he had spent on his property, which had (now) tumbled to pieces to its very foundations, and he could only say, "Woe is me! Would I had never ascribed partners to my Lord and Cherisher!" 43 Nor had he numbers to help him against Allah, nor was he able to deliver himself. 44 There, the (only) protection comes from Allah, the True One. He is the Best to reward, and the Best to give success.

45 Set forth to them the similitude of the life of this world: it is like the rain which We send down from the skies: the earth's vegetation absorbs it. But soon it becomes dry stubble, which the winds do scatter: it is (only) Allah who prevails over all things. 46 Wealth and sons are allurements of the life of this world: but the things that endure, Good Deeds, are best in the sight of your Lord, as rewards, and best as (the foundation for) hopes.

47 One Day We shall remove the mountains, and you will see the earth as a level stretch, and We shall gather them, all together, nor shall We leave out any one of them. 48 And they will be marshalled before your Lord in ranks, (with the announcement), "Now have you come to Us (bare) as We created you first: yes, you thought We shall not fulfil the appointment made to you to meet (Us)!"

49 And the Book (of Deeds) will be placed (before you); and you will see the sinful in great terror because of what is (recorded) therein; they will say, "Ah! woe to us! What a book is this! It

leaves out nothing small or great, but takes account thereof!" They will find all that they did, placed before them: and not one will your Lord treat with injustice.

50 Behold! We said to the angels, "Bow down to Adam": they bowed down except Iblīs. He was one of the Jinns, and he broke the Command of his Lord. Will you then take him and his progeny as protectors rather than Me? And they are enemies to you! Evil would be the exchange for the wrongdoers!

51 I called them not to witness the creation of the heavens and the earth, nor (even) their own creation: nor is it for Me to take as helpers such as lead (men) astray!

52 One Day He will say, "Call on those whom you thought to be My partners," And they will call on them, but they will not listen to them; and We shall make for them a place of common perdition. 53 And the Sinful shall see the Fire and apprehend that they have to fall therein: no means will they find to turn away therefrom.

54 We have explained in detail in this Qur'ān, for the benefit of mankind, every kind of similitude: but man is, in most things, Contentious. 55 And what is there to keep back men from believing, now that guidance has come to them, nor from praying for forgiveness from their Lord, but that (they ask that) the ways of the ancients be repeated with them, or the Wrath be brought to them face to face?

56 We only send the Messengers to give glad tidings and to give warnings: but the Unbelievers dispute with vain argument, in order therewith to weaken the truth, and they treat My Signs as a jest, as also the fact that they are warned! 57 And who does more wrong than one who is reminded of the Signs of his Lord, but turns away from them, forgetting the (deeds) which his hands have sent forth? Surely We have set veils over their hearts lest they should understand this, and over their ears, deafness, if you call them to guidance, even then will they never accept guidance.

58 But your Lord is Most Forgiving, full of Mercy. If He were to call them (at once) to account for what they have earned, then

surely He would have hastened their Punishment: but they have their appointed time, beyond which they will find no refuge. 59 Such were the populations We destroyed when they committed iniquities; but We fixed an appointed time for their destruction.

60 Behold, Moses said to his attendant, "I will not give up until I reach the junction of the two seas or (until) I spend years and years in travel." 61 But when they reached the Junction, they forgot (about) their Fish, which took its course through the sea (straight) as in a tunnel. 62 When they had passed on (some distance), Moses said to his attendant: "Bring us our early meal; truly we have suffered much fatigue at this (stage of) our journey."

63 He replied: "Did you see (what happened) when we betook ourselves to the rock? I did indeed forget (about) the Fish: none but Satan made me forget to tell (you) about it: it took its course through the sea in a marvellous way!" 64 Moses said: "That was what we were seeking after:" So they went back on their footsteps, following (the path they had come). 65 So they found one of Our servants, on whom We had bestowed mercy from Ourselves and whom We had taught knowledge from Our own presence.

66 Moses said to him: "May I follow you, on the footing that you teach me something of the (Higher) Truth which you have been taught?" 67 (The other) said: "Surely you will not be able to have patience with me!" 68 "And how can you have patience about things about which your understanding is not complete?" 69 Moses said: "You will find me, if Allah so will, (truly) patient: nor shall I disobey you in anything." 70 The other said: "If then you would follow me, ask me no questions about anything until I myself speak to you concerning it."

71 So they both proceeded: until, when they were in the boat, he scuttled it. Said Moses: "Have you scuttled it in order to drown those in it? Truly a strange thing have you done!" 72 He answered: "Did I not tell you that you can have no patience with me?" 73 Moses said: "Rebuke me not for forgetting, nor grieve me by raising difficulties in my case." 74 Then they proceeded: until, when they met a young boy, he slew him. Moses said: "Have you

slain an innocent person who had slain none? Truly a foul (unheard-of) thing have you done!"

75 He answered: "Did I not tell you that you can have no patience with me?" 76 (Moses) said: "If ever I ask you about anything after this, keep me not in your company: then would you have received (full) excuse from my side." 77 Then they proceeded: until, when they came to the inhabitants of a town, they asked them for food, but they refused them hospitality. They found there a wall on the point of falling down, but he set it up straight. (Moses) said: "If you had wished, surely you could have exacted some recompense for it!" 78 He answered: "This is the parting between me and you: now will I tell you the interpretation of (those things) over which you were unable to hold patience.

79 "As for the boat, it belonged to certain men in dire want: they plied on the water: I but wished to render it unserviceable, for there was after them a certain king who seized on every boat by force.

80 "As for the youth, his parents were people of Faith, and we feared that he would grieve them by obstinate rebellion and ingratitude (to Allah and man). 81 "So we desired that their Lord would give them in exchange (a son) better in purity (of conduct) and closer in affection.

82 "As for the wall, it belonged to two youths, orphans, in the Town; there was, beneath it, a buried treasure, to which they were entitled: their father had been a righteous man: so your Lord desired that they should attain their age of full strength and get out their treasure—a mercy (and favour) from your Lord. I did it not of my own accord. Such is the interpretation of (those things) over which you were unable to hold patience."

83 They ask you concerning Dhu'l-Qarnayn. Say, "I will rehearse to you something of his story." 84 Surely We established his power on earth, and We gave him the ways and the means to all ends.

85 One (such) way he followed, 86 Until, when he reached the setting of the sun, he found it set in a spring of murky water:

near it he found a People: We said: "O Dhu'l-Qarnayn! (You have authority) either to punish them, or to treat them with kindness." 87 He said: "Whoever does wrong, him shall we punish; then shall he be sent back to his Lord; and He will punish him with a punishment unheard-of (before). 88 "But whoever believes, and works righteousness—he shall have a goodly reward, and easy will be his task as we order it by our command."

89 Then followed he (another) way, 90 Until, when he came to the rising of the sun, he found it rising on a people for whom We had provided no covering protection against the sun. 91 (He left them) as they were: We completely understood what was before him.

92 Then followed he (another) way, 93 Until, when he reached (a tract) between two mountains, he found, beneath them, a people who scarcely understood a word. 94 They said: "O Dhu'l-Qarnayn! The Gog and Magog (people) do great mischief on earth: shall we then render you tribute in order that you might erect a barrier between us and them?

95 He said: "(The power) in which my Lord has established me is better (than tribute): help me therefore with strength (and labour): I will erect a strong barrier between you and them: 96 "Bring me blocks of iron." At length, when he had filled up the space between the two steep mountain-sides, he said, "Blow (with your bellows)" then, when he had made it (red) as fire, he said: "Bring me, that I may pour over it, molten lead." 97 Thus were they made powerless to scale it or to dig through it. 98 He said: "This is a mercy from my Lord: but when the promise of my Lord comes to pass, He will make it into dust; and the promise of my Lord is true."

99 On that day We shall leave them to surge like waves on one another: the trumpet will be blown, and We shall collect them all together. 100 And We shall present hell that day for Unbelievers to see, all spread out— 101 (Unbelievers) whose eyes had been under a veil from Remembrance of Me, and who had been unable even to hear.

102 Do the Unbelievers think that they can take my servants as

protectors besides Me? Surely We have prepared Hell for the Unbelievers for (their) entertainment.

103 Say: "Shall we tell you of those who lose most in respect of their deeds?— 104 "Those whose efforts have been wasted in this life, while they thought that they were acquiring good by their works?" 105 They are those who deny the Signs of their Lord and the fact of their having to meet Him (in the Hereafter): vain will be their works, nor shall We, on the Day of Judgment, give them any weight. 106 That is their reward, hell, because they rejected faith, and took My Signs and My Messengers by way of jest.

107 As to those who believe and work righteous deeds, they have, for their entertainment, the Gardens of Paradise, 108 Wherein they shall dwell (for ever): no change will they wish for from them.

109 Say: "If the ocean were ink (wherewith to write out) the words of my Lord, sooner would the ocean be exhausted than would the words of my Lord, even if we added another ocean like it, for its aid."

110 Say: "I am but a man like yourselves, (but) the inspiration has come to me, that your God is one God: whoever expects to meet his Lord, let him work righteousness, and, in the worship of his Lord, admit no one as partner.

19. MARY

In the name of Allah, Most Gracious, Most Merciful.

1 *Kāf, Hā', Yā', 'Ayn, Sād.* 2 (This is) a recital of the Mercy of your Lord to His servant Zakariyyā. 3 Behold! he cried to his Lord in secret, 4 Praying: "O my Lord! Infirm indeed are my bones, and the hair of my head does glisten with grey: but never am I unblessed o my Lord, in my prayer to You! 5 "Now I fear (what) my relatives (and colleagues) (will do) after me: but my wife is barren: so give me an heir as from Yourself— 6 "(One

that) will (truly) represent me, and represent the posterity of Jacob; and make him, O my Lord! one with whom You are well-pleased!"

7 (His prayer was answered): "O Zakariyyā! We give you good news of a son: his name shall be Yahyā: on none by that name have We conferred distinction before." 8 He said: "O my Lord! How shall I have a son, when my wife is barren and I have grown quite decrepit from old age?"

9 He said: "So (it will be): your Lord says, 'That is easy for Me: I did indeed create you before, when you had been nothing!'" 10 (Zakariyyā) said: "O my Lord! Give me a Sign." "Your Sign," was the answer, "Shall be that you shall speak to no man for three nights, although you are not dumb." 11 So Zakariyyā came out to his people from his chamber: he told them by signs to celebrate Allah's praises in the morning and in the evening.

12 (To his son came the command): "O Yahya! take hold of the Book with might": and We gave him Wisdom even as a youth, 13 And pity (for all creatures) as from Us, and purity: he was devout, 14 And kind to his parents, and he was not overbearing or rebellious. 15 So Peace on him the day he was born, the day that he dies, and the day that he will be raised up to life (again)!

16 Relate in the Book (the story of) Mary, when she withdrew from her family to a place in the East. 17 She placed a screen (to screen herself) from them; then We sent to her Our angel, and he appeared before her as a man in all respects. 18 She said: "I seek refuge from you to (Allah) most gracious: (come not near) if you do fear Allah." 19 He said: "No, I am only a Messenger from your Lord, (to announce) to you the gift of a holy son." 20 She said: "How shall I have a son, seeing that no man has touched me, and I am not unchaste?" 21 He said: "So (it will be): your Lord says, 'That is easy for Me: and (We wish) to appoint him as a Sign unto men and a Mercy from Us: it is a matter (so) decreed."

22 So she conceived him, and she retired with him to a remote place. 23 And the pains of childbirth drove her to the trunk of

a palm-tree: she cried (in her anguish): "Ah! would that I had died before this! would that I had been a thing forgotten and out of sight!"

24 But (a voice) said to her from beneath the (palm-tree): "Grieve not! for your Lord has provided a rivulet beneath you; 25 "And shake towards thyself the trunk of the palm-tree: it will let fall fresh ripe dates upon you. 26 "So eat and drink and cool (your) eye. And if you see any human, say, 'I have vowed a fast to (Allah) most Gracious, and this day will I enter into no talk with any human being'"

27 At length she brought the (babe) to her people, carrying him (in her arms). They said: "O Mary! truly a strange thing have you brought! 28 "O sister of Aaron! your father was not a man of evil, nor your mother a woman unchaste!"

29 But she pointed to the babe. They said: "How can we talk to one who is a child in the cradle?" 30 He said: "I am indeed a servant of Allah: He has given me revelation and made me a Prophet; 31 "And He has made me blessed wheresoever I be, and has enjoined on me Prayer and Charity as long as I live; 32 "(He) has made me kind to my mother, and not overbearing or miserable; 33 "So Peace is on me the day I was born, the day that I die, and the day that I shall be raised up to life (again)"!

34 Such (was) Jesus the son of Mary: (it is) a statement of truth, about which they (vainly) dispute. 35 It is not befitting to (the majesty of) Allah that He should beget a son. Glory be to Him! when He determines a matter, He only says to it, "Be," and it is.

36 Surely Allah is my Lord and your Lord: Him therefore you serve: this is a way that is straight. 37 But the sects differ among themselves: and woe to the Unbelievers because of the (coming) Judgment of a momentous Day! 38 How plainly will they see and hear, the Day that they will appear before Us! but the unjust today are in error manifest!

39 But warn them of the Day of Distress, when the matter will be determined: for (behold,) they are negligent and they do not

believe! 40 It is We Who will inherit the earth, and all beings thereon: to Us will they all be returned.

41 (Also) mention in the Book (the story of) Abraham: He was a man of Truth, a Prophet. 42 Behold, he said to his father: "O my father! why worship that which hears not and sees not, and can profit you nothing? 43 "O my father! to me has come knowledge which has not reached you: so follow me: I will guide you to a way that is even and straight. 44 "O my father! serve not Satan: for Satan is a rebel against (Allah) Most Gracious. 45 "O my father! I fear lest a penalty afflict you from (Allah) Most Gracious, so that you become to Satan a friend."

46 (The father) replied: "Do you hate my gods, O Abraham? If you forbear not, I will indeed stone you: now get away from me for a good long while!" 47 Abraham said: "Peace be on you: I will pray to my Lord for your forgiveness: for He is to me Most Gracious. 48 "And I will turn away from you (all) and from those whom you invoke besides Allah: I will call on my Lord: perhaps, by my prayer to my Lord, I shall be not unblessed."

49 When he had turned away from them and from those whom they worshipped besides Allah, We bestowed on him Isaac and Jacob, and each one of them We made a Prophet. 50 And We bestowed of Our Mercy on them, and We granted them lofty honour on the tongue of truth.

51 Also mention in the Book (the story of) Moses: for he was specially chosen, and he was a messenger (and) a prophet. 52 And We called him from the right side of Mount (Sinai), and made him draw near to Us, for mystic (converse). 53 And, out of Our Mercy, We gave him his brother Aaron, (also) a Prophet.

54 Also mention in the Book (the story of) Ishmael: he was (strictly) true to what he promised, and he was a messenger (and) a Prophet. 55 He used to enjoin on his people prayer and charity, and he was most acceptable in the sight of his Lord. 56 Also mention in the Book the case of Idrīs: he was a man of truth (and sincerity), (and) a Prophet: 57 And We raised him to a lofty station.

58 Those were some of the Prophets on whom Allah did bestow

His Grace— of the posterity of Adam, and of those whom We carried (in the Ark) with Noah, and of the posterity of Abraham and Israel—of those whom We guided and chose. Whenever the signs of (Allah) Most Gracious were rehearsed to them, they would fall down in prostrate adoration and in tears.

59 But after them there followed a posterity who missed prayers and followed after lusts soon, then, will they face Destruction— 60 Except those who repent and believe, and work righteousness: for these will enter the garden and will not be wronged in the least—

61 Gardens of Eternity, those which (Allah) Most Gracious has promised to His servants in the Unseen: for His promise must (necessarily) come to pass. 62 They will not there hear any vain discourse, but only salutations of Peace: and they will have therein their sustenance, morning and evening. 63 Such is the Garden which We give as an inheritance to those of Our servants who guard against evil.

64 (The angels say:) "We descend not but by command of your Lord: to Him belongs what is before us and what is behind us, and what is between: and your Lord never does forget— 65 "Lord of the heavens and of the earth, and of all that is between them; so worship Him, and be constant and patient in His worship: know you of any who is worthy of the same Name as He?"

66 Man says: "What! when I am dead, shall I then be raised up alive?" 67 But does not man call to mind that We created him before out of nothing? 68 So, by your Lord, without doubt, We shall gather them together, and (also) the Satans (with them); then shall We bring them forth on their knees round about Hell.

69 Then shall We certainly drag out from every sect all those who were worst in obstinate rebellion against (Allah) Most Gracious. 70 And certainly We know best those who are most worthy of being burned therein. 71 Not one of you but will pass over it: this is, with your Lord, a Decree which must be accomplished. 72 But We shall save those who guarded against evil, and We shall leave the wrongdoers therein, (humbled) to their knees.

73 When Our Clear Signs are rehearsed to them, the Unbelievers say to those who believe, "Which of the two sides is best in point of position? Which makes the best show in Council?" 74 But how many (countless) generations before them have We destroyed, who were even better in equipment and in glitter to the eye?

75 Say: "If any men go astray, (Allah) Most Gracious extends (the rope) to them, until, when they see the warning of Allah (being fulfilled)—either in punishment or in (the approach of) the Hour—they will at length realise who is worst in position, and (who) weakest in forces!

76 "And Allah does advance in guidance those who seek guidance: and the things that endure, Good Deeds, are best in the sight of your Lord, as rewards, and best in respect of (their) eventual returns."

77 Have you then seen the (sort of) man who rejects Our Signs, yet says: "I shall certainly be given wealth and children?" 78 Has he penetrated to the Unseen, or has he taken a contract with (Allah) Most Gracious? 79 No! We shall record what he says, and We shall add and add to his punishment. 80 To Us shall return all that he talks of and he shall appear before Us bare and alone.

81 And they have taken (for worship) gods other than Allah, to give them power and glory! 82 Instead, they shall reject their worship, and become adversaries against them.

83 Do not you see that We have set the Satans on against the unbelievers, to incite them with fury? 84 So make no haste against them, for We but count out to them a (limited) number (of days). 85 The day We shall gather the righteous to (Allah) Most Gracious, like a band presented before a king for honours, 86 And We shall drive the sinners to hell, like thirsty cattle driven down to water— 87 None shall have the power of intercession, but such a one as has received permission (or promise) from (Allah) Most Gracious.

88 They say: "(Allah) Most Gracious has begotten a son!" 89 Indeed you have put forth a thing most monstrous! 90 As if the skies are ready to burst, the earth to split asunder, and the mountains to fall down in utter ruin. 91 That they should invoke

a son for (Allah) Most Gracious. 92 For it is not consonant with the majesty of (Allah) Most Gracious that He should beget a son.

93 Not one of the beings in the heavens and the earth but must come to (Allah) Most Gracious, as a servant. 94 He does take an account of them (all), and has numbered them (all) exactly. 95 And everyone of them will come to Him singly on the Day of Judgment. 96 On those who believe and work deeds of righteousness, will (Allah) Most Gracious bestow Love.

97 So have We made the (Qur'ān) easy in your own tongue, that with it you may give glad tidings to the righteous, and warnings to people given to contention. 98 But how many (countless) generations before them have We destroyed? Can you find a single one of them (now) or hear (so much as) a whisper of them?

20. ȚĀ HĀ

In the name of Allah, Most Gracious, Most Merciful.

1 *Tā Hā*. 2 We have not sent down the Qur'ān to you to be (an occasion) for your distress, 3 But only as an admonition to those who fear (Allah)— 4 A revelation from Him Who created the earth and the heavens on high. 5 (Allah) Most Gracious is firmly established on the throne (of authority). 6 To Him belongs what is in the heavens and on earth, and all between them, and all beneath the soil.

7 If you pronounce the word aloud, (it is no matter): for surely He knows what is secret and what is yet more hidden. 8 Allah! there is no god but He! To Him belong the Most Beautiful Names.

9 Has the story of Moses reached you? 10 Behold, he saw a fire: so he said to his family, "Tarry you; I perceive a fire; perhaps I can bring you some burning brand therefrom, or find some guidance at the fire."

11 But when he came to the fire, a voice was heard: "O Moses! 12 "Surely I am your Lord! therefore (in My presence) put off your shoes: you are in the sacred valley Țuwā. 13 "I have chosen you: listen, then, to the inspiration (sent to you). 14 "Surely, I

am Allah: there is no god but I: so serve Me (only), and establish regular prayer for celebrating My praise. 15 "Surely the Hour is coming— My design is to keep it hidden—for every soul to receive its reward by the measure of its Endeavour. 16 "Therefore let not such as believe not therein but follow their own lusts, divert you therefrom, lest you perish!"

17 "And what is that in your right hand, O Moses?" 18 He said, "It is my staff: on it I lean; with it I beat down fodder for my flocks; and in it I find other uses." 19 (Allah) said, "Throw it, O Moses!" 20 He threw it, and behold! it was a snake, active in motion. 21 (Allah) said, "Seize it, and fear not: We shall return it at once to its former condition"...

22 "Now draw your hand close to your side: it shall come forth white (and shining), without harm (or stain)—as another Sign— 23 "In order that We may show you (two) of our Greater Signs. 24 "Go you to Pharaoh, for he has indeed transgressed all bounds."

25 (Moses) said: "O my Lord! expand me my breast;" 26 "Ease my task for me; 27 "And remove the impediment from my speech. 28 "So they may understand what I say: 29 "And give me a Minister from my family, 30 "Aaron, my brother; 31 "Add to my strength through him, 32 "And make him share my task: 33 "That we may celebrate your praise without stint, 34 "And remember You without stint: 35 "For You are He that (ever) regards us." 36 (Allah) said: "Granted is your prayer, O Moses!"

37 "And indeed We conferred a favour on you another time (before). 38 "Behold! We sent to your mother, by inspiration, the message: 39 "'Throw (the child) into the chest, and throw (the chest) into the river: the river will cast him up on the bank, and he will be taken up by one who is an enemy to Me and an enemy to him': but I cast (the garment of) love over you from Me: and (this) in order that you may be reared under mine eye." 40 "Behold! your sister goes forth and says, 'Shall I show you one who will nurse and rear the (child)?' So We brought you back to your mother, that her eye might be cooled and she should not grieve. Then you did slay a man, but We saved you from trouble, and We tried you in various ways. Then did you tarry a number

of years with the people of Midian. Then did you come hither as ordained, O Moses!

41 "And I have prepared you for Myself (for service)"... 42 "Go, you and your brother with My Signs, and slacken not, either of you, in keeping Me in remembrance. 43 "Go, both of you, to Pharaoh, for he has indeed transgressed all bounds; 44 "But speak to him mildly; perchance he may take warning or fear (Allah)."

45 They (Moses and Aaron) said: "Our Lord! We fear lest he hasten with insolence against us, or lest he transgress all bounds." 46 He said: "Fear not: for I am with you: I hear and see (everything). 47 "So go you both to him, and say, 'Surely we are messengers sent by your Lord: send forth, therefore, the Children of Israel with us, and afflict them not: with a Sign, indeed, have we come from your Lord! and peace to all who follow guidance! 48 "'Surely it has been revealed to us that the Penalty (awaits) those who reject and turn away.'"

49 (When this message was delivered), (Pharaoh) said: "Who, then, O Moses, is the Lord of you two?" 50 He said: "Our Lord is He Who gave to each (created) thing its form and nature, and further, gave (it) guidance." 51 (Pharaoh) said: "What then is the condition of previous generations?" 52 He replied: "The knowledge of that is with my Lord, duly recorded: my Lord never errs, nor forgets—

53 "He Who has, made for you the earth like a carpet spread out; has enabled you to go about therein by roads (and channels); and has sent down water from the sky." With it have We produced diverse pairs of plants each separate from the others. 54 Eat (for yourselves) and pasture your cattle: surely, in this are Signs for men endued with understanding. 55 From the (earth) did We create you, and into it shall We return you, and from it shall We bring you out once again.

56 And We showed Pharaoh all Our Signs, but he did reject and refuse. 57 He said: "Have you come to drive us out of our land with your magic, O Moses? 58 "But we can surely produce magic to match yours! so make a tryst between us and you, which we

shall not fail to keep—neither we nor you—in a place where both shall have even chances."

59 Moses said: "Your tryst is the Day of the Festival, and let the people be assembled when the sun is well up." 60 So Pharaoh withdrew: he concerted his plan, and then came (back). 61 Moses said to them: Woe to you! Forge not a lie against Allah, lest He destroy you (at once) utterly by chastisement: the forger must suffer frustration!"

62 So they disputed, one with another, over their affair, but they kept their talk secret. 63 They said: "These two are certainly (expert) magicians: their object is to drive you out from your land with their magic, and to do away with your most cherished institutions. 64 "Therefore concert your plan, and then assemble in (serried) ranks: he wins (all along) today who gains the upper hand."

65 They said: "O Moses! whether you will that you throw (first) or that we be the first to throw?" 66 He said, "No, throw you first!" Then behold their ropes and their rods-so it seemed to him on account of their magic— began to be in lively motion! 67 So Moses conceived in his mind a (sort of) fear. 68 We said: "Fear not! for you have indeed the upper hand: 69 "Throw that which is in your right hand: quickly will it swallow up that which they have faked: what they have faked is but a magician's trick: and the magician thrives not, (no matter) where he goes." 70 So the magicians were thrown down to prostration: they said, "We believe in the Lord of Aaron and Moses."

71 (Pharaoh) said: "Believe you in Him before I give you permission? surely this must be your leader, who has taught you magic! Be sure I will cut off your hands and feet on opposite sides, and I will have you crucified on trunks of palm-trees: so shall you know for certain which of us can give the more severe and the more lasting punishment!"

72 They said: "Never shall we regard you as more than the clear signs that have come to us, or than him who created us! So decree whatever you desire to decree: for you can only decree (touching) the life of this world. 73 "For us, we have believed in our Lord:

may He forgive us our faults, and the magic to which you did compel us: for Allah is best and most abiding."

74 Surely he who comes to his Lord as a sinner (at judgment)— for him is hell: therein shall he neither die nor live. 75 But such as come to Him as Believers who have worked righteous deeds— for them are ranks exalted— 76 Gardens of Eternity, beneath which flow rivers: they will dwell therein for aye: such is the reward of those who purify themselves (from evil).

77 We sent an inspiration to Moses: "Travel by night with My servants, and strike a dry path for them through the sea, without fear of being overtaken (by Pharaoh) and without (any other) fear." 78 Then Pharaoh pursued them with his forces, but the waters completely overwhelmed them and covered them up. 79 Pharaoh led his people astray instead of leading them aright.

80 O you Children of Israel! We delivered you from your enemy, and We made a Covenant with you on the right side of Mount (Sinai), and We sent down to you manna and quails: 81 (Saying): "Eat of the good things We have provided for your sustenance, but commit no excess therein, lest My Wrath should justly descend on you: and those on whom descends My Wrath do perish indeed! 82 "But, without doubt, I am (also) He that forgives again and again, to those who repent, believe, and do right—who, in fine, are ready to receive true guidance."

83 (When Moses was up on the Mount, Allah said:) "What made you hasten in advance of your people, O Moses?" 84 He replied: "Behold, they are close on my footsteps: I hastened to You, O my Lord, to please you." 85 (Allah) said: "We have tested your people in your absence: the Sāmirī has led them astray."

86 So Moses returned to his people in a state of indignation and sorrow. He said: "O my people! did not your Lord make a handsome promise to you? Did then the promise seem to you long (in coming)? Or did you desire that Wrath should descend from your Lord on you, and so you broke your promise to me?"

87 They said: "We broke not the promise to you, as far as lay in our power: but we were made to carry the weight of the

ornaments of the (whole) people, and we threw them (into the fire), and that was what the Sāmirī suggested. 88 "Then he brought out (of the fire) before the (people) the image of a calf: it seemed to low: so they said: 'This is your god, and the god of Moses, but (Moses) has forgotten!'" 89 Could they not see that it could not return them a word (for answer), and that it had no power either to harm them or to do them good?

90 Aaron had already, before this said to them: "O my people! you are being tested in this: for surely your Lord is (Allah) Most Gracious; so follow me and obey my command." 91 They had said: "We will not abandon this cult, but we will devote ourselves to it until Moses returns to us."

92 (Moses) said: "O Aaron! what kept you back, when you saw them going wrong, 93 "From following me? Did you then disobey my order?" 94 (Aaron) replied: "O son of my mother! Seize (me) not by my beard nor by (the hair of) my head! Truly I feared lest you should say, 'You caused a division among the children of Israel, and you did not respect my word!'"

95 (Moses) said: "What then is your case, O Sāmirī?" 96 He replied: "I saw what they saw not: so I took a handful (of dust) from the footprint of the Messenger, and threw it (into the calf): thus did my soul suggest to me." 97 (Moses) said: "Get you gone! But your (punishment) in this life will be that you will say, 'Touch me not'; and moreover (for a future penalty) you have a promise that will not fail: now look at your god, of whom you have become a devoted worshipper: we will certainly (melt) it in a blazing fire and scatter it broadcast in the sea!" 98 But the God of you all is Allah: there is no god but He: all things He comprehends in His knowledge.

99 Thus do We relate to you some stories of what happened before: for We have sent you a Message from Our own Presence. 100 If any do turn away therefrom, surely they will bear a burden on the Day of Judgment; 101 They will abide in this (state): and grievous will the burden be to them on that Day— 102 The Day when the Trumpet will be sounded: that Day, We shall gather the sinful, blear-eyed (with terror). 103 In whispers will they consult

each other: "You tarried not longer than ten (Days);" 104 We know best what they will say, when their leader most eminent in Conduct will say: "You tarried not longer than a day!"

105 They ask you concerning the Mountains: say, "My Lord will uproot them and scatter them as dust;" 106 "He will leave them as plains smooth and level;" 107 "Nothing crooked or curved will you see in their place." 108 On that Day will they follow the Caller (straight): no crookedness (can they show) him: all sounds shall humble themselves in the Presence of (Allah) Most Gracious: nothing shall you hear but the tramp of their feet (as they march).

109 On that Day shall no intercession avail except for those for whom permission has been granted by (Allah) Most Gracious and whose word is acceptable to Him. 110 He knows what (appears to His creatures as) before or after or behind them: but they shall not compass it with their knowledge. 111 (All) faces shall be humbled before (Him) — the Living, the Self-Subsisting, Eternal: hopeless indeed will be the man that carries iniquity (on his back). 112 But he who works deeds of righteousness, and has faith, will have no fear of harm nor of any curtailment (of what is his due).

113 Thus have We sent this down — an Arabic Qur'ān — and explained therein in detail some of the warnings, in order that they may fear Allah, or that it may cause their remembrance (of Him). 114 High above all is Allah, the King, the Truth! Be not in haste with the Qur'ān before its revelation to you is completed, but say, "O my Lord! advance me in knowledge."

115 We had already, beforehand, taken the Covenant of Adam, but he forgot: and We found on his part no firm resolve. 116 When We said to the angels, "Prostrate yourselves to Adam," they prostrated themselves, but not Iblīs: he refused. 117 Then We said: "O Adam! surely, this is an enemy to you and your wife: so let him not get you both out of the Garden, so that you are landed in misery.

118 "There is therein (enough provision) for you not to go hungry nor to go naked," 119 "Nor to suffer from thirst, nor from the sun's heat." 120 But Satan whispered evil to him: he said, "O Adam! shall I lead you to the tree of eternity and to a kingdom

that never decays?" 121 In the result, they both ate of the tree, and so their nakedness appeared to them: they began to sew together, for their covering, leaves from the Garden: thus did Adam disobey his Lord, and allow himself to be seduced. 122 But his Lord chose him (for his grace): He turned to him, and gave him Guidance.

123 He said: "Get you down, both of you—all together, from the Garden, with enmity one to another: but if, as is sure, there comes to you guidance from me, whosoever follows My Guidance, will not lose his way, nor fall into misery. 124 "But whosoever turns away from my message, surely for him is a life narrowed down, and We shall raise him up blind on the day of judgment." 125 He will say: "O my Lord! why have you raised me up blind, while I had sight (before)?" 126 (Allah) will say: "Thus did you, when Our signs come to you, disregard them: so will you, this day, be disregarded." 127 And thus do We recompense him who transgresses beyond bounds and believes not in the Signs of his lord: and the penalty of the Hereafter is far more grievous and more enduring.

128 Is it not a warning to such men (to call to mind) how many generations before them We destroyed, in whose haunts they (now) move? Surely, in this are Signs for men endued with understanding. 129 Had it not been for a Word that went forth before from your Lord, (their punishment) must necessarily have come; but there is a term appointed (for respite). 130 Therefore be patient with what they say, and celebrate (constantly) the praises of your lord before the rising of the sun, and before its setting; yes, celebrate them for part of the hours of the night, and at the sides of the day: that you may have (spiritual) joy.

131 Nor strain your eyes in longing for the things We have given for enjoyment to parties of them, the splendour of the life of this world, through which We test them: but the provision of your Lord is better and more enduring. 132 Enjoin prayer on your people, and be constant therein. We ask you not to provide sustenance: We provide it for you. But the (fruit of) the Hereafter is for Righteousness.

133 They say: "Why does he not bring us a Sign from his Lord?" Has not a Clear Sign come to them of all that was in the former books of Revelation? 134 And if We had inflicted on them a penalty before this, they would have said: "Our Lord! If only You had sent us a messenger, we should certainly have followed your Signs before we were humbled and put to shame." 135 Say: "Each one (of us) is waiting: wait you, therefore, and soon shall you know who it is that is on the straight and even way, and who it is that has received Guidance."

21. THE PROPHETS

In the name of Allah, Most Gracious, Most Merciful.

1 Closer and closer to mankind comes their Reckoning: yet they heed not and they turn away. 2 Never comes (aught) to them of a renewed message from their Lord, but they listen to it as in jest— 3 Their hearts toying as with trifles. The wrongdoers conceal their private counsels, (saying), "Is this (one) more than a man like yourselves? Will you go to witchcraft with your eyes open?" 4 Say: "My Lord knows (every) word (spoken) in the heavens and on earth: He is the One that hears and knows (all things)."

5 "No," they say, "(these are) medleys of dreams!—No, he forged it!—No, he is (but) a poet! let him then bring us a Sign like the ones that were sent to (Prophets) of old!" 6 (As to those) before them, not one of the populations which We destroyed believed: will these believe?

7 Before you, also, the Messengers We sent were but men, to whom We granted inspiration: if you realise this not, ask of those who possess the Message. 8 Nor did We give them bodies that ate no food, nor were they exempt from death. 9 In the end We fulfilled to them Our promise, and We saved them and those whom We pleased, but We destroyed those who transgressed beyond bounds.

10 We have revealed for you (O men!) a book in which is a Message for you: will you not then understand? 11 How many were the populations We utterly destroyed because of their iniquities, setting up in their places other peoples? 12 Yet, when they felt our Punishment (coming), behold, they (tried to) flee from it. 13 Flee not, but return to the good things of this life which were given you, and to your homes, in order that you may be called to account. 14 They said: "Ah! woe to us! we were indeed wrongdoers!" 15 And that cry of theirs ceased not, till We made them as a field that is mown, as ashes silent and quenched.

16 Not for (idle) sport did We create the heavens and the earth and all that is between! 17 If it had been Our wish to take (just) a pastime, We should surely have taken it from the things nearest to Us, if We would do (such a thing)! 18 No, We hurl the Truth against falsehood, and it knocks out its brain, and behold, falsehood does perish! Ah! woe be to you for the (false) things you ascribe (to Us).

19 To Him belong all (creatures) in the heavens and on earth: even those who are in His (very) Presence are not too proud to serve Him, nor are they (ever) weary (of His service): 20 They celebrate His praises night and day, nor do they ever flag or intermit.

21 Or have they taken (for worship) gods from the earth who can raise (the dead)? 22 If there were, in the heavens and the earth, other gods besides Allah, there would have been confusion in both! But glory to Allah, the Lord of the Throne: (high is He) above what they attribute to Him! 23 He cannot be questioned for His acts, but they will be questioned (for theirs).

24 Or have they taken for worship (other) gods besides him? Say, "Bring Your convincing proof: this is the Message of those with me and the Message of those before me." But most of them know not the truth, and so turn away. 25 Not a Messenger did We send before you without this inspiration sent by Us to him: that there is no god but I; therefore, worship and serve Me.

26 And they say: "(Allah) Most Gracious has begotten offspring." Glory to Him! They are (but) servants raised to honour. 27 They

speak not before He speaks, and they act (in all things) by His command. 28 He knows what is before them, and what is behind them, and they offer no intercession except for those who are acceptable, and they stand in awe and reverence of his (glory). 29 If any of them should say, "I am a god besides Him," such a one We should reward with Hell: thus do We reward those who do wrong.

30 Do not the Unbelievers see that the heavens and the earth were joined together (as one unit of Creation), before We clove them asunder? We made from water every living thing. Will they not then believe?

31 And We have set on the earth mountains standing firm, lest it should shake with them, and We have made therein broad highways (between mountains) for them to pass through: that they may receive guidance. 32 And We have made the heavens as a canopy well guarded: yet do they turn away from the Signs which these things (point to)! 33 It is He Who created the Night and the Day, and the sun and the moon: all (the celestial bodies) swim along, each in its rounded course.

34 We granted not to any man before you permanent life (here): if then you should die, would they live permanently? 35 Every soul shall have a taste of death: and We test you by evil and by good by way of trial. To Us must you return.

36 When the Unbelievers see you, they treat you not except with ridicule. "Is this," (they say), "the one who talks of your gods?" And they blaspheme at the mention of (Allah) Most Gracious!

37 Man is a creature of haste: soon (enough) will I show you My Signs; then you will not ask Me to hasten them! 38 They say: "When will this promise come to pass, if you are telling the truth?" 39 If only the Unbelievers knew (the time) when they will not be able to ward off the fire from their faces, nor yet from their backs, and (when) no help can reach them! 40 No, it may come to them all of a sudden and confound them: no power will they have then to avert it, nor will they (then) get respite. 41 Mocked were (many) Messengers before you; but their scoffers were hemmed in by the thing that they mocked.

42 Say: "Who can keep you safe by night and by day from (the Wrath of) (Allah) Most Gracious?" Yet they turn away from the mention of their Lord. 43 Or have they gods that can guard them from Us? They have no power to aid themselves, nor can they be defended from Us.

44 No, We gave the good things of this life to these men and their fathers until the period grew long for them; see they not that We gradually reduce the land (in their control) from its outlying borders? Is it then they who will win?

45 Say, "I do but warn you according to revelation:" but the deaf will not hear the call, (even) when they are warned! 46 If but a breath of the Wrath of your Lord do touch them, they will then say, "Woe to us! we did wrong indeed!"

47 We shall set up scales of justice for the day of Judgment, so that not a soul will be dealt with unjustly in the least. And if there be (no more than) the weight of a mustard seed, We will bring it (to account): and enough are We to take account.

48 In the past We granted to Moses and Aaron the Criterion (for judgment), and a Light and a Message for those who would do right— 49 Those who fear their Lord in their most secret thoughts, and who hold the Hour (of Judgment) in awe. 50 And this is a blessed message which We have sent down: will you then reject it?

51 We bestowed aforetime on Abraham his rectitude of conduct, and well were We acquainted with him. 52 Behold! he said to his father and his people, "What are these images, to which you are (so assiduously) devoted?" 53 They said, "We found our fathers worshipping them." 54 He said, "Indeed you have been in manifest error—you and your fathers."

55 They said, "Have you brought us the Truth, or are you one of those who jest?" 56 He said, "No, your Lord is the Lord of the heavens and the earth, He Who created them (from nothing): and I am a witness to this (truth). 57 "And by Allah, I have a plan for your idols—after you go away and turn your backs"... 58 So he broke them to pieces, (all) but the biggest of them, that they might turn (and address themselves) to it.

59 They said, "Who has done this to our gods? He must indeed be some man of impiety!" 60 They said, "We heard a youth talk of them: he is called Abraham." 61 They said, "Then bring him before the eyes of the people, that they may bear witness." 62 They said, "Are you the one that did this with our gods, O Abraham?" 63 He said: "No, this was done by — this is their biggest one! Ask them, if they can speak intelligently!"

64 So they turned to themselves and said, "Surely you are the ones in the wrong!" 65 Then were they confounded with shame: (they said), "You know full well that these (idols) do not speak!" 66 (Abraham) said, "Do you then worship, besides Allah, things that can neither be of any good to you nor do you harm? 67 "Fie upon you, and upon the things that you worship besides Allah! have you no sense?"...

68 They said, "Burn him and protect your gods, if you do (anything at all)!" 69 We said, "O Fire! be you cool, and (a means of) safety for Abraham!" 70 Then they sought a stratagem against him: but We made them the ones that lost most!

71 But We delivered him and (his nephew) Lūṭ (and directed them) to the land which We have blessed for the nations. 72 And We bestowed on him Isaac and, as an additional gift, (a grandson), Jacob, and We made righteous men of every one (of them). 73 And We made them leaders, guiding (men) by our Command, and We sent them inspiration to do good deeds, to establish regular prayers, and to give zakat (poor-due); and they constantly served Us (and Us only).

74 And to Lūṭ, too, We gave Judgment and Knowledge, and We saved him from the town which practised abominations: truly they were a people given to Evil, a rebellious people. 75 And We admitted him to Our Mercy: for he was one of the Righteous.

76 (Remember) Noah, when he cried (to Us) aforetime: We listened to his (prayer) and delivered him and his family from great distress. 77 We helped him against people who rejected Our Signs: truly they were a people given to evil: so We drowned them (in the Flood) all together.

78 And remember David and Solomon, when they gave

judgment in the matter of the field into which the sheep of certain people had strayed by night: We did witness their judgment. 79 To Solomon We inspired the (right) understanding of the matter: to each (of them) We gave Judgment and Knowledge; it was Our power that made the hills and the birds celebrate Our praises, with David: it was We who did (all these things). 80 It was We Who taught him the making of coats of mail for your benefit, to guard you from each other's violence: will you then be grateful?

81 (It was Our power that made) the violent (unruly) wind flow (tamely) for Solomon, to his order, to the land which We had blessed: for We do know all things. 82 And of the Satans, were some who dived for him, and did other work besides; and it was We who guarded them.

83 And (remember) Job, when he cried to his Lord, "Truly distress has seized me, but You are the Most Merciful of those that are merciful." 84 So We listened to him: We removed the distress that was on him, and We restored his people to him, and doubled their number—as a Grace from Ourselves, and a thing for commemoration, for all who serve Us.

85 And (remember) Ishmael, Idrīs, and Dhu'l-Kifl, all (men) of constancy and patience; 86 We admitted them to Our Mercy: for they were of the Righteous ones.

87 And remember Dhu'n-Nūn, when he departed in wrath: he imagined that We had no power over him! But he cried through the depths of darkness, "There is no god but You: Glory to You: I was indeed wrong!" 88 So We listened to him: and delivered him from distress: and thus do We deliver those who have faith.

89 And (remember) Zakariyyā, when he cried to his Lord: "O my Lord! leave me not without offspring, though You are the best of inheritors." 90 So We listened to him: and We granted him Yaḥyā: We cured his wife's (barrenness) for him. These (three) were ever quick in emulation in good works: they used to call on Us with love and reverence, and humble themselves before Us.

91 And (remember) her who guarded her chastity: We breathed

into her of Our Spirit, and We made her and her son a Sign for all peoples.

92 Surely, this Brotherhood of yours is a single Brot   nood, and I am your Lord and Cherisher: therefore, serve Me (and no other). 93 But (later generations) cut off their affair (of unity), one from another: (yet) will they all return to Us. 94 Whoever works any act of Righteousness and has Faith— his endeavour will not be rejected: We shall record it in his favour.

95 But there is a ban on any population which We have destroyed: that they shall not return, 96 Until the Gog and Magog (people) are let through (their barrier), and they swiftly swarm from every hill. 97 Then will the True Promise draw near (of fulfilment): then behold! the eyes of the Unbelievers will fixedly stare in horror: "Ah! Woe to us! we were indeed heedless of this; no, we truly did wrong!"

98 Surely you, (Unbelievers), and the (false) gods that you worship besides Allah, are (but) fuel for Hell! To it will you (surely) come! 99 If these had been gods, they would not have got there! But each one will abide therein. 100 There, sobbing will be their lot, nor there will they hear (anything else). 101 Those for whom the good (record) from Us has gone before, will be removed far therefrom. 102 Not the slightest sound will they hear of Hell: what their souls desired, in that will they dwell. 103 The Great Terror will bring them no grief: but the angels will meet them (with mutual greetings): "This is your Day—(the day) that you were promised."

104 The Day that We roll up the heavens like a scroll rolled up for books (completed)—even as We produced the first Creation, so shall We produce a new one: a promise We have undertaken: truly shall We fulfil it. 105 Before this We wrote in the Psalms, after the Message (given to Moses): "My servants, the righteous, shall inherit the earth." 106 Surely in this (Qur'ān) is a Message for people who would (truly) worship Allah.

107 We sent you not, but as a Mercy for all creatures. 108 Say: "What has come to me by inspiration is that your God is One God: will you therefore bow to His Will (in Islam)?" 109 But if they

turn back, say: "I have proclaimed the Message to you all alike and in truth; but I know not whether that which you are promised is near or far. 110 "It is He Who knows what is open in speech and what you hide (in your hearts). 111 "I know not but that it may be a trial for you, and a grant of (worldly) livelihood (to you) for a time." 112 Say: "O my Lord! Judge You in truth!" "Our Lord Most Gracious is the One Whose assistance should be sought against the blasphemies you utter!"

22. THE PILGRIMAGE

In the name of Allah, Most Gracious, Most Merciful.

1 O mankind! fear your Lord! for the convulsion of the Hour (of Judgment) will be a thing terrible! 2 The Day you shall see it, every mother giving suck shall forget her suckling babe, and every pregnant female shall drop her load (unformed): you shall see mankind as in a drunken riot, yet not drunk: but dreadful will be the Wrath of Allah. 3 And yet among men there are such as dispute about Allah, without knowledge, and follow every Satan obstinate in rebellion! 4 About (Satan) it is decreed that whoever turns to him for friendship, him will he lead astray, and he will guide him to the penalty of the fire.

5 O mankind! if you have a doubt about the resurrection, (consider) that We created you out of dust, then out of sperm, then out of a leech-like clot, then out of a morsel of flesh, partly formed and partly unformed, in order that We might manifest (Our power) to you; and We cause whom We will to rest in the wombs for an appointed term, then do We bring you out as babes, then (foster you) that you may reach your age of full strength; and some of you are called to die, and some are sent back to the feeblest old age, so that they know nothing after having known (much), and (further), you see the earth barren and lifeless, but when We pour down rain on it, it is stirred (to life), it swells, and it puts forth every kind of beautiful growth in pairs. 6 This is so, because Allah is the Reality: it is He Who gives life to the

dead, and it is He Who has power over all things. 7 And, surely, the Hour will come: there can be no doubt about it, or about (the fact) that Allah will raise up all who are in the graves.

8 Yet there is among men such a one as disputes about Allah, without knowledge, without guidance, and without a Book of Enlightenment— 9 (Disdainfully) bending his side, in order to lead (men) astray from the path of Allah: for him there is disgrace in this life, and on the day of Judgment We shall make him taste the torment of burning (Fire). 10 (It will be said): "This is because of the deeds which your hands sent forth, for surely Allah is not unjust to His servants."

11 There are among men some who serve Allah, as it were, on the verge: if good befalls them, they are, therewith, well content; but if a trial comes to them, they turn on their faces: they lose both this world and the hereafter: that is loss for all to see!

12 They call on such deities, besides Allah, as can neither hurt nor profit them: that is straying far indeed (from the Way)! 13 (Perhaps) they call on one whose hurt is nearer than his profit: evil, indeed, is the patron, and evil the companion (for help)! 14 Surely, Allah will admit those who believe and work righteous deeds, to Gardens, beneath which rivers flow: for Allah carries out all that He plans.

15 If any think that Allah will not help him (his Messenger) in this world and the Hereafter, let him stretch out a rope to the ceiling and cut (himself) off: then let him see whether his plan will remove that which enrages (him)! 16 Thus have We sent down clear Signs; and, surely, Allah does guide whom He will!

17 Those who believe (in the Qur'ān), those who follow the Jewish (scriptures), and the Sabians, Christians, Magians, and Polytheists—Allah will judge between them on the Day of Judgment: for Allah is witness of all things.

18 See you not that to Allah bow down in worship all things that are in the heavens and on earth—the sun, the moon, the stars; the hills, the trees, the animals; and a great number among mankind? But a great number are (also) such as are fit for

Punishment: and such as Allah shall disgrace— none can raise to honour: for Allah carries out all that He wills.

19 These two antagonists dispute with each other about their Lord: but those who deny (their Lord)— for them will be cut out a garment of Fire: over their heads will be poured out boiling water. 20 With it will be scalded what is within their bodies, as well as (their) skins. 21 In addition there will be maces of iron (to punish) them. 22 Every time they wish to get away therefrom, from anguish, they will be forced back therein, and (it will be said), "Taste you the Penalty of Burning!"

23 Allah will admit those who believe and work righteous deeds, to Gardens beneath which rivers flow: they shall be adorned therein with bracelets of gold and pearls; and their garments there will be of silk. 24 For they have been guided (in this life) to the purest of speeches; they have been guided to the Path of Him Who is Worthy of (all) Praise.

25 As to those who have rejected (Allah), and would keep back (men) from the Way of Allah, and from the Sacred Mosque, which We have made (open) to (all) men—equal is the dweller there and the visitor from the country—and any whose purpose therein is profanity or wrong-doing—them will We cause to taste of a most Grievous Penalty.

26 Behold! We gave the site, to Abraham, of the (Sacred) House, (saying): "Associate not anything (in worship) with Me; and sanctify My House for those who compass it round, or stand up, or bow, or prostrate themselves (therein in prayer).

27 "And proclaim the Pilgrimage among men: they will come to you on foot and (mounted) on every kind of camel, lean on account of journeys through deep and distant mountain highways; 28 "That they may witness the benefits (provided) for them, and celebrate the name of Allah, through the Days appointed, over the cattle which He has provided for them (for sacrifice): then eat you thereof and feed the distressed ones in want. 29 "Then let them complete the rites prescribed for them, perform their vows, and (again) circumambulate the Ancient House."

30 Such (is the Pilgrimage): whoever honours the sacred rites of Allah, for him it is good in the sight of his Lord. Lawful to you (for food in Pilgrimage) are cattle, except those mentioned to you (as exceptions): but shun the abomination of idols, and shun the word that is false —

31 Being true in faith to Allah, and never assigning partners to Him: if anyone assigns partners to Allah, he is as if he had fallen from heaven and been snatched up by birds, or the wind had swooped (like a bird on its prey) and thrown him into a far-distant place.

32 Such (is his state): and whoever holds in honour the symbols of Allah, (in the sacrifice of animals), such (honour) should come truly from piety of heart. 33 In them you have benefits for a term appointed: in the end their place of sacrifice is near the Ancient House.

34 To every people did We appoint rites (of sacrifice), that they might celebrate the name of Allah over the sustenance He gave them from animals (fit for food). But your God is One God: submit then your wills to Him (in Islam): and give you the good news to those who humble themselves — 35 To those whose hearts, when Allah is mentioned, are filled with fear, who show patient perseverance over their afflictions, keep up regular prayer, and spend (in charity) out of what We have bestowed upon them.

36 The sacrificial camels We have made for you as among the Symbols from Allah: in them is (much) good for you: then pronounce the name of Allah over them as they line up (for sacrifice): when they are down on their sides (after slaughter), eat you thereof and feed such as (beg not but) live in contentment, and such as beg with due humility: thus have We made animals subject to you, that you may be grateful. 37 It is not their meat nor their blood, that reaches Allah: it is your piety that reaches Him: He has thus made them subject to you, that you may glorify Allah for His Guidance to you and proclaim the Good News to all who do right.

38 Surely, Allah will defend (from ill) those who believe: surely, Allah loves not any that is a traitor to faith, or shows ingratitude.

39 To those against whom war is made, permission is given (to fight), because they are wronged—and surely, Allah is Most Powerful for their aid— 40 (They are) those who have been expelled from their homes in defiance of right— (for no cause) except that they say, "Our Lord is Allah." Did not Allah check one set of people by means of another, there would surely have been pulled down monasteries, churches, synagogues, and mosques, in which the name of Allah is commemorated in abundant measure. Allah will certainly aid those who aid His (cause)—for, surely, Allah is Full of Strength, Exalted in Might, (Able to enforce His Will).

41 (They are) those who, if We establish them in the land, establish regular prayer and give Zakat (poor-due), enjoin the right and forbid wrong: with Allah rests the end (and decision) of (all) affairs.

42 If they treat your (mission) as false, so did the Peoples before them (with their Prophets)— the People of Noah, the 'Ād and Thamūd; 43 Those of Abraham and Lūṭ; 44 And the Companions of the Madyan People; and Moses was rejected (in the same way). But I granted respite to the Unbelievers, and (only) after that did I punish them: but how (terrible) was My rejection (of them)!

45 How many populations have We destroyed, which were given to wrongdoing? They tumbled down on their roofs. And how many wells are lying idle and neglected, and castles lofty and well-built? 46 Do they not travel through the land, so that their hearts (and minds) may thus learn wisdom and their ears may thus learn to hear? Truly it is not their eyes that are blind, but their hearts which are in their breasts.

47 Yet they ask you to hasten on the Punishment! But Allah will not fail in His Promise. Surely, a Day in the sight of your Lord is like a thousand years of your reckoning. 48 And to how many populations did I give respite, which were given to wrong-doing? In the end I punished them. To Me is the destination (of all).

49 Say: "O men! I am (sent) to you only to give a Clear Warning: 50 "Those who believe and work righteousness, for them is forgiveness and a sustenance most generous. 51 "But those who

strive against Our Signs, to frustrate them—they will be companions of the Fire."

52 Never did We send a Messenger or a Prophet before you, but, when he framed a desire, Satan threw some (vanity) into his desire: but Allah will cancel anything (vain)that Satan throws in, and Allah will confirm (and establish) His Signs: for Allah is full of knowledge and wisdom: 53 That He may make the suggestions thrown in by Satan, but a trial for those in whose hearts is a disease and who are hardened of heart: surely, the wrongdoers are in a schism far (from the Truth): 54 And that those on whom knowledge has been bestowed may learn that the (Qur'ān) is the Truth from your Lord, and that they may believe therein, and their hearts may be made humbly (open) to it: for, surely, Allah is the Guide of those who believe, to the Straight Way.

55 Those who reject Faith will not cease to be in doubt concerning (Revelation) until the Hour (of Judgment) comes suddenly upon them, or there comes to them the Penalty of a Day of Disaster. 56 On that Day the Dominion will be that of Allah: He will judge between them: so those who believe and work righteous deeds will be in Gardens of Delight. 57 And for those who reject Faith and deny Our Signs, there will be a humiliating punishment.

58 Those who leave their homes in the cause of Allah, and are then slain or die— on them will Allah bestow, surely, a goodly Provision: truly Allah is He Who bestows the best Provision. 59 Surely, He will admit them to a place with which they shall be well pleased: for Allah is All-Knowing, Most Forbearing.

60 That (is so). And if one has retaliated to no greater extent than the injury he received, and is again set upon inordinately, Allah will help him: for Allah is One that blots out (sins) and forgives (again and again).

61 That is because Allah merges Night into Day, and He merges Day into Night, and, surely, it is Allah Who hears and sees (all things). 62 That is because Allah—He is the Reality; and those besides Him whom they invoke— they are but vain Falsehood: surely, Allah is He, Most High, Most Great.

63 See you not that Allah sends down rain from the sky, and forthwith the earth becomes clothed with green? for Allah is He Who understands the finest mysteries, and is well-acquainted (with them). 64 To Him belongs all that is in the heavens and on earth: for, surely, Allah—He is free of all wants, Worthy of all Praise.

65 See you not that Allah has made subject to you (men) all that is on the earth, and the ships that sail across the sea by His command? He withholds the sky (rain) from failing on the earth except by His leave: for Allah is Most Kind and Most Merciful to man. 66 It is He Who gave you life, will cause you to die, and will again give you life: truly man is a most ungrateful creature!

67 To every People have We appointed rites and ceremonies which they must follow: let them not then dispute with you on the matter, but do you invite (them) to your Lord: for you are assuredly on the Right Way. 68 If they do wrangle with you, say, "Allah knows best what it is you are doing. 69 "Allah will judge between you on the Day of Judgment concerning the matters in which you differ." 70 Do not you know that Allah knows all that is in heaven and on earth? indeed, it is all in a Record, and that is easy for Allah.

71 Yet they worship, besides Allah, things for which no authority has been sent down to them, and of which they have (really) no knowledge: for those that do wrong there is no helper. 72 When Our Clear Signs are rehearsed to them, you will notice a denial on the faces of the Unbelievers! They nearly attack with violence those who rehearse Our Signs to them. Say, "Shall I tell you of something (far) worse than these Signs? It is the Fire (of Hell)! Allah has promised it to the Unbelievers! And evil is that destination!"

73 O men! Here is a parable set forth! Listen to it! Those on whom, besides Allah, you call, cannot create (even) a fly, if they all met together for the purpose! And if the fly should snatch away anything from them, they would have no power to release it from the fly. Feeble are those who petition and those whom they petition! 74 No just estimate have they made of Allah: for Allah is He Who is strong and able to carry out His Will.

75 Allah chooses Messengers from angels and from men for Allah is He Who hears and sees (all things). 76 He knows what is before them and what is behind them: and to Allah go back all questions (for decision).

77 O you who believe! Bow down, prostrate yourselves, and adore your Lord; and do good; that you may prosper. 78 And strive in His cause as you ought to strive, (with sincerity and under discipline). He has chosen you, and has imposed no difficulties on you in religion; it is the cult of your father Abraham. It is He Who has named you Muslims, both before and in this (Revelation); that the Messenger may be a witness for you, and you be witnesses for mankind! so establish regular Prayer, give Zakat (poor-due), and hold fast to Allah! He is your Protector— the Best to protect and the Best to help!

23. THE BELIEVERS

In the name of Allah, Most Gracious, Most Merciful.

1 The believers must (Eventually) win through— 2 Those who humble themselves in their prayers; 3 Who avoid vain talk; 4 Who are active in giving zakat (poor-due); 5 Who abstain from sex, 6 Except with those joined to them in the marriage bond, or (the captives) whom their right hands possess— for (in their case) they are free from blame, 7 But those whose desires exceed those limits are transgressors— 8 Those who faithfully observe their trusts and their covenants; 9 And who (strictly) guard their prayers— 10 These will be the heirs, 11 Who will inherit Paradise: they will dwell therein (forever).

12 Man We did create from a quintessence (of clay); 13 Then We placed him as (a drop of) sperm in a place of rest, firmly fixed; 14 Then We made the sperm into a clot of congealed blood; then of that clot We made a (foetus) lump; then We made out of that lump bones and clothed the bones with flesh; then We

developed out of it another creature. So blessed be Allah, the best to create! 15 After that, at length you will die. 16 Again, on the Day of Judgment, will you be raised up.

17 And We have made, above you, seven tracts; and We are never unmindful of (Our) Creation. 18 And We send down water from the sky according to (due) measure, and We cause it to soak into the soil; and We certainly are able to drain it off (with ease). 19 With it We grow for you gardens of date-palms and vines: in them have you abundant fruits: and of them you eat (and have enjoyment)— 20 Also a tree springing out of Mount Sinai, which produces oil, and relish for those who use it for food. 21 And in cattle (too) you have an instructive example: from within their bodies we produce (milk) for you to drink; there are, in them, (besides), numerous (other) benefits for you; and of their (meat) you eat; 22 And on them, as well as in ships, you ride.

23 (Further, We sent a long line of Prophets for your instruction). We sent Noah to his people: he said, "O my people! Worship Allah! You have no god other than Him. Will you not fear (Him)?" 24 The chiefs of the Unbelievers among his people said: "He is no more than a man like yourselves: his wish is to assert his superiority over you: if Allah had wished (to send Messengers), He could have sent down angels; never did we hear such a thing (as he says), among our ancestors of old." 25 (And some said): "He is only a man possessed: wait (and have patience) with him for a time."

26 (Noah) said: "O my Lord! Help me: for that they accuse me of falsehood!" 27 So We inspired him (with this message): "Construct the Ark within Our sight and under Our guidance: then when comes Our command, and the fountains of the earth gush forth, take you on board pairs of every species, male and female, and your family—except those of them against whom the Word has already gone forth: and address Me not in favour of the wrongdoers; for they shall be drowned (in the Flood).

28 "And when you have embarked on the Ark—you and those with you—say: 'Praise be to Allah, Who has saved us from the people who do wrong.' 29 "And say: 'O my Lord! enable me to

disembark with Your blessing: for You are the Best to enable (us) to disembark.'" 30 Surely, in this there are signs (for men to understand); (thus) do We try (men).

31 Then We raised after them another generation. 32 And We sent to them a Messenger from among themselves, (saying), "Worship Allah! You have no other god but Him. Will you not fear (Him)?" 33 And the chiefs of his people, who disbelieved and denied the Meeting in the Hereafter, and on whom We had bestowed the good things of this life, said: "He is no more than a man like yourselves: he eats of that of which you eat, and drinks of what you drink. 34 "If you obey a man like yourselves, behold, it is certain you will be lost.

35 "Does he promise that when you die and become dust and bones, you shall be brought forth (again)? 36 "Far, very far is that which you are promised! 37 "There is nothing but our life in this world! We shall die and we live! But we shall never be raised up again! 38 "He is only a man who invents a lie against Allah, but we are not the ones to believe in him!"

39 (The Prophet) said: "O my Lord! help me: for that they accuse me of falsehood." 40 (Allah) said: "In but a little while, they are sure to be sorry!" 41 Then the Blast overtook them with justice, and We made them as rubbish of dead leaves (floating on the stream of Time)! So away with the people who do wrong!

42 Then We raised after them other generations. 43 No people can hasten their term, nor can they delay (it).

44 Then sent We Our Messengers in succession: every time there came to a people their Messenger, they accused him of falsehood: so We made them follow each other (in punishment): We made them as a tale (that is told): so away with a people that will not believe! 45 Then We sent Moses and his brother Aaron, with Our Signs and authority manifest, 46 To Pharaoh and his Chiefs: but these behaved insolently: they were an arrogant people. 47 They said: "Shall we believe in two men like ourselves? And their people are subject to us!" 48 So they accused them of falsehood, and they became of those who were destroyed. 49 And We gave Moses the Book, in order that they might receive guidance.

50 And We made the son of Mary and his mother as a Sign: We gave them both shelter on high ground, affording rest and security and furnished with springs.

51 O you Messengers! enjoy (All) things good and pure, and work righteousness: for I am well-acquainted with (all) that you do.   52 And, surely, this Brotherhood of yours is a single Brotherhood, and I am your Lord and Cherisher: therefore fear Me (and no other).

53 But people have cut off their affair (of unity), between them, into sects: each party rejoices in that which is with itself.   54 But leave them in their confused ignorance for a time.   55 Do they think that because we have granted them abundance of wealth and sons, 56 We would hasten them on in every good? No, they do not understand.

57 Surely, those who live in awe for fear of their Lord; 58 Those who believe in the Signs of their Lord; 59 Those who join not (in worship) partners with their Lord; 60 And those who dispense their charity with their hearts full of fear, because they will return to their Lord— 61 It is these who hasten in every good work, and these who are foremost in them. 62 On no soul do We place a burden greater than it can bear: before Us is a record which clearly shows the truth: they will never be wronged.

63 But their hearts are in confused ignorance of this; and there are, besides that, deeds of theirs, which they will (continue) to do— 64 Until, when We seize in Punishment those of them who received the good things of this world, behold, they will groan in supplication!   65 (It will be said): "Groan not in supplication this day: for you shall certainly not be helped by Us. 66 "My Signs used to be rehearsed to you, but you used to turn back on your heels— 67 "In arrogance: talking nonsense about the (Qur'ān), like one telling fables by night."

68 Do they not ponder over the Word (of Allah), or has anything (new) come to them that did not come to their fathers of old? 69 Or do they not recognise their Messenger, that they deny him? 70 Or do they say, "He is possessed"? No, he has brought them the Truth, but most of them hate the Truth. 71 If the Truth had

been in accord with their desires, truly the heavens and the earth, and all beings therein would have been in confusion and corruption! No, We have sent them their admonition, but they turn away from their admonition.

72 Or is it that you ask them for some recompense? But the recompense of your Lord is best: He is the Best of those who give sustenance. 73 But, surely, you call them to the Straight Way; 74 And, surely, those who believe not in the hereafter are deviating from that Way.

75 If We had mercy on them and removed the distress which is on them, they would obstinately persist in their transgression, wandering in distraction hither and thither. 76 We inflicted Punishment on them, but they humbled not themselves to their Lord, nor do they submissively entreat (Him)! 77 Until We open on them a gate leading to a severe Punishment: then Lo! they will be plunged in despair therein!

78 It is He Who has created for you (the faculties of) hearing, sight, feeling and understanding: little thanks it is you give! 79 And He has multiplied you through the earth, and to Him shall you be gathered back. 80 It is He Who gives life and death, and to Him (is due) the alternation of Night and Day: will you not then understand?

81 On the contrary, they say things similar to what the ancients said. 82 They say: "What! when we die and become dust and bones, could we really be raised up again? 83 "Such things have been promised to us and to our fathers before! they are nothing but tales of the ancients!"

84 Say: "To whom belong the earth and all beings therein? (say) if you know!" 85 They will say, "To Allah!" say: "Yet will you not receive admonition?" 86 Say: "Who is the Lord of the seven heavens, and the Lord of the Throne (of Glory) Supreme?" 87 They will say, "(They belong) to Allah." Say: "Will you not then be filled with awe?" 88 Say: "Who is it in whose hands is the governance of all things — who protects (all), but is not protected (of any)? (Say) if you know." 89 They will say, "(It belongs) to Allah." Say: "Then how are you deluded?"

90 We have sent them the Truth: but they indeed practise falsehood! 91 No son did Allah beget, nor is there any god along with Him: (if there were many gods), behold, each god would have taken away what he had created, and some would have lorded it over others! Glory to Allah! (He is free) from the (sort of) things they attribute to Him! 92 He knows what is hidden and what is open: too high is He for the partners they attribute to Him!

93 Say: "O my Lord! If You will show me (in my lifetime) that which they are warned against— 94 "Then, O my Lord! put me not amongst the people who do wrong!" 95 And We are certainly able to show you (in fulfilment) that against which they are warned.

96 Repel evil with that which is best: We are well acquainted with the things they say. 97 And say "O my Lord! I seek refuge with You from the suggestions of the Satans. 98 "And I seek refuge with You o my Lord! lest they should come near me."

99 (In Falsehood will they be) until, when death comes to one of them, he says: "O my Lord! send me back (to life)— 100 "In order that I may work righteousness in the things I neglected."— By no means! It is but a word he says."— Before them is a Partition till the day they are raised up. 101 Then when the Trumpet is blown, there will be no more relationships between them that day nor will one ask after another! 102 Then those whose balance (of good deeds) is heavy— They will attain salvation: 103 But those whose balance is light, will be those who have lost their souls; in Hell will they abide. 104 The Fire will burn their faces, and they will therein grin, with their lips displaced.

105 "Were not My Signs rehearsed to you, and you did but treat them as falsehoods?" 106 They will say: "Our Lord! Our misfortune overwhelmed us, and we became a people astray! 107 "Our Lord! bring us out of this: if ever we return (to evil), then shall we be wrongdoers indeed!" 108 He will say: "Be you driven into it (with ignominy)! and speak you not to Me!

109 "A part of My servants there was, who used to pray 'Our Lord! we believe; then do You forgive us, and have mercy upon

us: for You are the Best of those who show mercy!' 110 "But you treated them with ridicule, so much so that (ridicule of) them made you forget My Message while you were laughing at them! 111 "I have rewarded them this Day for their patience and constancy: they are indeed the ones that have achieved Bliss..."

112 He will say: "What number of years did you stay on earth?" 113 They will say: "We stayed a day or part of a day: but ask those who keep account." 114 He will say: "You stayed not but a little — if you had only known!

115 "Did you then think that We had created you in jest, and that you would not be brought back to Us (for account)?" 116 Therefore exalted be Allah, the King, the Reality: there is no god but He, the Lord of the Throne of Honour! 117 If anyone invokes, besides Allah, any other god, he has no authority therefor; and his reckoning will be only with his Lord! And, surely, the Unbelievers will fail to win through! 118 So say: "O my Lord! Grant you forgiveness and mercy for You are the Best of those who show mercy!"

24. LIGHT

In the name of Allah, Most Gracious, Most Merciful.

1 A sūrah which We have sent down and which We have ordained: in it have We sent down Clear Signs, in order that you may receive admonition. 2 The woman and the man guilty of fornication — flog each of them with a hundred stripes: let not compassion move you in their case, in a matter prescribed by Allah, if you believe in Allah and the Last Day: and let a party of the Believers witness their punishment. 3 Let no man guilty of adultery or fornication marry any but a woman similarly guilty, or an Unbeliever: nor let any but such a man or an Unbeliever marry such a woman: to the Believers such a thing is forbidden.

4 And those who launch a charge against chaste women, and

produce not four witnesses (to support their allegations)— flog them with eighty stripes; and reject their evidence ever after: for such men are wicked transgressors— 5 Unless they repent thereafter and mend (their conduct); for Allah is Oft-forgiving, Most Merciful.

6 And for those who launch a charge against their spouses, and have (in support) no evidence but their own—their solitary evidence (can be received) if they bear witness four times (with an oath) by Allah that they are solemnly telling the truth; 7 And the fifth (oath) (should be) that they solemnly invoke the curse of Allah on themselves if they tell a lie. 8 But it would avert the punishment from the wife, if she bears witness four times (with an oath) by Allah, that (her husband) is telling a lie; 9 And the fifth (oath) should be that she solemnly invokes the wrath of Allah on herself if (her accuser) is telling the truth. 10 If it were not for Allah's grace and mercy on you, and that Allah is Oft-Returning, full of Wisdom— (you would be ruined indeed).

11 Those who brought forward the lie are a body among yourselves: think it not to be an evil to you; on the contrary it is good for you: to every man among them (will come the punishment) of the sin that he earned, and to him who took on himself the lead among them, will be a Penalty grievous.

12 Why did not the Believers—men and women—when you heard of the affair—put the best construction on it in their own minds and say, "This (charge) is an obvious lie"? 13 Why did they not bring four witnesses to prove it? When they have not brought the witnesses, such men, in the sight of Allah, (stand forth) themselves as liars!

14 Were it not for the grace and mercy of Allah on you, in this world and the Hereafter, a grievous torment would have seized you in that you rushed glibly into this affair. 15 Behold, you received it on your tongues. And said out of your mouths things of which you had no knowledge; and you thought it to be a light matter, while it was most serious in the sight of Allah. 16 And why did you not, when you heard it, say?—"It is not right of us to speak of this: glory to Allah! this is a most serious slander!"

17 Allah does admonish you, that you may never repeat such (conduct), if you are (true) Believers. 18 And Allah makes the Signs plain to you: for Allah is full of knowledge and wisdom.

19 Those who love (to see) scandal circulate among the Believers, will have a grievous Chastisement in this life and in the Hereafter: Allah knows, and you know not. 20 Were it not for the grace and mercy of Allah on you, and that Allah is full of kindness and mercy, (you would be ruined indeed).

21 O you who believe! Follow not Satan's footsteps: if any will follow the footsteps of Satan, he will (but) command what is shameful and wrong: and were it not for the grace and mercy of Allah on you, not one of you would ever have been pure: but Allah does purify whom He pleases: and Allah is One Who hears and knows (all things).

22 Let not those among you who are endued with grace and amplitude of means resolve by oath against helping their kinsmen, those in want, and those who have left their homes in Allah's cause: let them forgive and overlook, do you not wish that Allah should forgive you? For Allah is Oft-Forgiving, Most Merciful.

23 Those who slander chaste women, simple and believing, are cursed in this life and in the Hereafter: for them is a horrible Chastisement— 24 On the Day when their tongues, their hands, and their feet will bear witness against them as to their actions. 25 On that Day Allah will pay them back (all) their just dues, and they will realise that Allah is the (very) Truth, that makes all things manifest.

26 Women impure are for men impure, and men impure for women impure and women of purity are for men of purity, and men of purity are for women of purity: these are innocent of all what people say: for them there is forgiveness, and a provision honourable.

27 O you who believe! Enter not houses other than your own, until you have asked permission and saluted those in them: that is best for you, in order that you may heed (what is seemly). 28 If you find no one in the house, enter not until permission is

given to you: if you are asked to go back, go back: that makes for greater purity for yourselves: and Allah knows well all that you do. 29 It is no fault on your part to enter houses not used for living in, which serve some (other) use for you: and Allah has knowledge of what you reveal and what you conceal.

30 Say to the believing men that they should lower their gaze and guard their chastity: that will make for greater purity for them: and Allah is well acquainted with all that they do.

31 And say to the believing women that they should lower their gaze and guard their chastity; that they should not display their beauty and ornaments except what (must ordinarily) appear thereof; that they should draw their veils over their bosoms and not display their beauty except to their husbands, their fathers, their husbands' fathers, their sons, their husbands' sons, their brothers or their brothers' sons, or their sisters' sons, or their womenfolk, or those whom their right hands possess, or male servants free of carnal desires, or small children who have no carnal knowledge of women; and that they should not strike their feet in order to draw attention to their hidden ornaments. And O you Believers! turn you all together towards Allah, that you may achieve success.

32 Marry those among you who are single, and the virtuous ones among your slaves, male or female: if they are in poverty, Allah will give them means out of His grace: for Allah is ample-giving, and He knows all things. 33 Let those who find not the wherewithal for marriage keep themselves chaste, until Allah gives them means out of His grace. And if any of your slaves ask for a deed in writing (to enable them to earn their freedom for a certain sum), give them such a deed if you know any good in them: yes, give them something yourselves out of the means which Allah has given to you. But force not your maids to prostitution when they desire chastity, in order that you may make a gain in the goods of this life. But if anyone compels them, yet, after such compulsion, is Allah Oft-forgiving, Most Merciful (to them). 34 We have already sent down to you verses making things clear, an illustration from

(the story of) people who passed away before you, and an admonition for those who fear (Allah).

35 Allah is the Light of the heavens and the earth. The parable of His Light is as if there were a Niche and within it a Lamp: the Lamp enclosed in Glass: the glass as it were a brilliant star: lit from a blessed Tree, an Olive, neither of the East nor of the West, whose oil is of itself luminous, though fire scarce touched it: light upon light! Allah does guide whom He will to His Light: Allah does set forth Parables for men: and Allah does know all things.

36 (Lit is such a Light) in houses, which Allah has permitted to be raised to honour; for the celebration, in them, of His name: in them is He glorified in the mornings and in the evenings, (again and again)— 37 By men whom neither traffic nor merchandise can divert from the Remembrance of Allah, nor from regular Prayer, nor from paying zakat (poor-due): their (only) fear is for the Day when hearts and eyes will be transformed (in a world wholly new)— 38 That Allah may reward them according to the best of their deeds, and add even more for them out of His Grace: for Allah does provide for those whom He will, without measure.

39 But the Unbelievers—their deeds are like a mirage in sandy deserts, which the man parched with thirst mistakes for water; until when he comes up to it, he finds it to be nothing: but he finds Allah (ever) with him, and Allah will pay him his account: and Allah is swift in taking account. 40 Or (the Unbelievers' state) is like the depths of darkness in a vast deep ocean, overwhelmed with billow topped by billow, topped by (dark) clouds: depths of darkness, one above another: if a man stretches out his hands, he can hardly see it! For any to whom Allah gives not light, there is no light!

41 Do you not see that it is Allah Whose praises all beings in the heavens and on earth do celebrate, and the birds (of the air) with wings outspread? Each one knows its own (mode of) prayer and praise. And Allah knows well all that they do. 42 Yes, to Allah belongs the dominion of the heavens and the earth; and to Allah is the final return (of all).

43 Do you not see that Allah makes the clouds move gently, then joins them together, then makes them into a heap? — then will you see rain issue forth from their midst. And He sends down from the sky mountain masses (of clouds) wherein is hail: He strikes therewith whom He pleases and He turns it away from whom He pleases, the vivid flash of His lightning almost blinds the sight. 44 It is Allah Who alternates the Night and the Day: surely, in these things is an instructive example for those who have vision!

45 And Allah has created every animal from water: of them there are some that creep on their bellies; some that walk on two legs; and some that walk on four. Allah creates what He wills for, surely, Allah has power over all things. 46 We have indeed sent down signs that make things manifest: and Allah guides whom He wills to a Way that is straight.

47 They say, "We believe in Allah and in the Messenger, and we obey": but even after that, some of them turn away: they are not (really) Believers. 48 When they are summoned to Allah and His Messenger, in order that He may judge between them, behold some of them decline (to come). 49 But if the right is on their side, they come to him with all submission. 50 Is it that there is a disease in their hearts? Or do they doubt, or are they in fear, that Allah and His Messenger will deal unjustly with them? No, it is they themselves who do wrong.

51 The answer of the Believers, when summoned to Allah and His Messenger, in order that He may judge between them, is no other than this: they say, "We hear and we obey." It is such as these that will attain felicity. 52 It is such as obey Allah and His Messenger, and fear Allah and do right, that will win (in the end).

53 They swear their strongest oaths by Allah that, if only you would command them, they would leave (their homes). Say: "Swear you not; obedience is the real thing; surely, Allah is well acquainted with all that you do." 54 Say: "Obey Allah, and obey the Messenger: but if you turn away, he is only responsible for the duty placed on him and you for that placed on you. If you

obey him, you shall be on right guidance. The Messenger's duty is only to preach the clear (Message)."

55 Allah has promised, to those among you who believe and work righteous deeds, that He will, of a surety, grant them in the land, inheritance (of power), as He granted it to those before them; that He will establish in authority their religion—the one which He has chosen for them; and that He will change (their state), after the fear in which they (lived), to one of security and peace: 'They will worship Me (alone) and not associate any with Me.' If any do reject Faith after this, they are rebellious and wicked.

56 So establish regular Prayer and give zakat (poor-due); and obey the Messenger, that you may receive mercy. 57 Never do think you that the Unbelievers are going to frustrate (Allah's Plan) on earth: their abode is the Fire— and it is indeed an evil refuge!

58 O you who believe! Let those whom your right hands possess, and the (children) among you who have not come of age ask your permission (before they come to your presence), on three occasions: before morning prayer; the while you doff your clothes for the noonday heat; and after the late-night prayer: these are your three times of undress: outside those times it is not wrong for you or for them to move about attending to each other: thus does Allah make clear the Signs to you: for Allah is full of knowledge and wisdom. 59 But when the children among you come of age, let them (also) ask for permission, as do those senior to them (in age): thus does Allah make clear his Signs to you: for Allah is full of knowledge and wisdom. 60 Such elderly women as are past the prospect of marriage—there is no blame on them if they lay aside their (outer) garments, provided they make not a wanton display of their beauty: but it is best for them to be modest: and Allah is One Who sees and knows all things.

61 It is no fault in the blind nor in one born lame, nor in one afflicted with illness, nor in yourselves, that you should eat in your own houses, or those of your fathers, or your mothers, or your brothers, or your sisters, or your father's brothers or your father's sisters, or your mother's brothers, or your mother's sisters, or in houses of which the keys are in your possession, or

in the house of a sincere friend of yours: there is no blame on you, whether you eat in company or separately. But if you enter houses, salute each other — a greeting of blessing and purity as from Allah. Thus does Allah make clear the Signs to you: that you may understand.

62 Only those are Believers, who believe in Allah and His Messenger: when they are with him on a matter requiring collective action, they do not depart until they have asked for his leave; those who ask for the leave are those who believe in Allah and His Messenger; so when they ask for your leave, for some business of theirs, give leave to those of them whom you will, and ask Allah for their forgiveness: for Allah is Oft-Forgiving, Most Merciful.

63 Deem not the summons of the Messenger among yourselves like the summons of one of you to another: Allah does know those of you who slip away under shelter of some excuse: then let those beware who withstand the Messenger's order, lest some trial befall them, or a grievous chastisement be inflicted on them. 64 Be quite sure that to Allah does belong whatever is in the heavens and on earth. Well does He know what you are intent upon: and one day they will be brought back to Him, and He will tell them the truth of what they did: for Allah does know all things.

25. THE CRITERION

In the name of Allah, Most Gracious, Most Merciful.

1 Blessed is He Who sent down the Criterion to His servant, that it may be an admonition to all creatures — 2 He to Whom belongs the dominion of the heavens and the earth: no son has He begotten, nor has He a partner in His dominion: it is He Who created all things, and ordered them in due proportions. 3 Yet have they taken, besides Him, gods that can create nothing but are themselves created; that have no control of hurt or good to themselves; nor can they control Death nor Life nor Resurrection.

4 But the Disbelievers say: "This is nothing but a lie which he has forged, and others have helped him at it." In truth it is they who have put forward an iniquity and a falsehood. 5 And they say: "Tales of the ancients, which he has caused to be written: and they are dictated before him morning and evening." 6 Say: "The (Qur'ān) was sent down by Him Who knows the Secret (that is) in the heavens and the earth: surely, He is Oft-Forgiving, Most Merciful."

7 And they say: "What sort of a Messenger is this, who eats food, and walks through the streets? Why has not an angel been sent down with him to give admonition with him? 8 "Or (why) has not a treasure been bestowed on him, or why has he (not) a garden for enjoyment?" The wicked say: "You follow none other than a man bewitched." 9 See what kinds of companions they make for you! but they have gone astray, and never a way will they be able to find!

10 Blessed is He who, if that were His Will, could give you better (things) than those — Gardens beneath which rivers flow; and He could give you Palaces (secure to dwell in). 11 No they deny the Hour (of the Judgment to come): but We have prepared a Blazing Fire for such as deny the Hour: 12 When it sees them from a place far off, they will hear its fury and its raging sigh. 13 And when they are cast, bound together, into a constricted place therein, they will plead for destruction there and then! 14 "This day plead not for a single destruction: plead for destruction oft-repeated!" 15 Say: "Is that best, or the eternal Garden, promised to the righteous? For them, that is a reward as well as a goal (of attainment). 16 "For them there will be therein all that they wish for: they will dwell (there) for ever: a promise binding your Lord."

17 The Day He will gather them together as well as those whom they worship besides Allah, He will ask: "Was it you who led these My servants astray, or did they stray from the Path themselves?" 18 They will say: "Glory to You! not meet was it for us that we should take for protectors others besides You: but You did bestow, on them and their fathers, good things (in life), until they forgot the Message: for they were a people (worthless and) lost."

19 (Allah will say): "Now have they proved you liars in what you say: so you cannot avert (your penalty) nor (get) help." And whoever among you does wrong, him shall We cause to taste of a grievous chastisement.

20 And the Messengers whom We sent before you were all (men) who ate food and walked through the streets: We have made some of you as a trial for others: will you have patience? For Allah is One Who sees (all things).

21 Such as believe not the meeting with Us (for Judgment) say: "Why are not the angels sent down to us, or (why) do we not see our Lord?" indeed they have an arrogant conceit of themselves, and mighty is the insolence of their impiety! 22 The Day they see the angels—no joy will there be to the sinners that Day: the (angels) will say: "There is a barrier forbidden (to you) altogether!" 23 And We shall turn to whatever deeds they did (in this life), and We shall make such deeds as floating dust scattered about. 24 The Companions of the Garden will be well, that Day, in their abode, and have the fairest of places for repose.

25 The Day the heaven shall be rent asunder with clouds, and angels shall be sent down, descending (in ranks)— 26 That Day, the dominion as of right and truth, shall be (wholly) for (Allah) Most Merciful: it will be a Day of dire difficulty for the Disbelievers. 27 The Day that the wrongdoer will bite at his hands, he will say, "Oh! would that I had taken a (straight) path with the Messenger! 28 "Ah! woe is me! would that I had never taken such a one for a friend! 29 "He did lead me astray from the Message (of Allah) after it had come to me! Ah! the Satan is but a traitor to man!" 30 Then the Messenger will say: "O my Lord! Truly my people treated this Qur'ān with neglect." 31 Thus have We made for every Prophet an enemy among the sinners: but enough is your Lord to guide and to help.

32 Those who reject Faith say: "Why is not the Qur'ān revealed to him all at once?" Thus (is it revealed), that We may strengthen your heart thereby, and We have rehearsed it to you in slow, well-arranged stages, gradually. 33 And no question do they bring to you but We reveal to you the truth and the best explanation

(thereof). 34 Those who will be gathered to Hell (prone) on their faces— they will be in an evil plight, and, as to Path, most astray.

35 (Before this,) We sent Moses the Book, and appointed his brother Aaron with him as Minister; 36 And We commanded: "Go you both, to the people who have rejected Our Signs." And those (people) We destroyed with utter destruction. 37 And the people of Noah— when they rejected the Messengers, We drowned them, and We made them as a Sign for mankind; and We have prepared for (all) wrongdoers a grievous chastisement— 38 As also 'Ād and Thamūd, and the People of the Rass, and many a generation between them. 39 To each one We set forth Parables and examples; and each one We broke to utter annihilation (for their sins). 40 And the (Unbelievers) must indeed have passed by the town on which was rained a shower of evil: did they not then see it (with their own eyes)? But they fear not the Resurrection.

41 When they see you, they treat you no otherwise than in mockery: "Is this the one whom Allah has sent as a Messenger?" 42 "He indeed would well have misled us from our gods, had it not been that we were constant to them!"— Soon will they know, when they see the Chastisement, who it is that is most misled in Path!

43 Do you see such a one as takes for his god his own passion (or impulse)? Could you be a disposer of affairs for him? 44 Or do you think that most of them listen or understand? They are only like cattle—no, they are worse astray in Path.

45 Have you not turned your vision to your Lord?— how He does prolong the Shadow! If He willed, He could make it stationary! Then do We wake the sun its guide; 46 Then We draw it in towards Ourselves— a contraction by easy stages. 47 And He it is Who makes the Night as a Robe for you, and Sleep as Repose, and makes the Day (as it were) a Resurrection. 48 And He it is Who sends the Winds as heralds of glad tidings, going before His Mercy, and We send down pure water from the sky— 49 That with it, We may give life to a dead land, and slake the thirst of things We have created— cattle and men in great numbers.

50 And We have distributed the (water) amongst them, in order that they may celebrate (Our) praises, but most men are averse (to aught) but (rank) ingratitude. 51 Had it been Our Will, We could have sent a warner to every centre of population. 52 Therefore listen not to the Unbelievers, but strive against them with the utmost strenuousness, with the (Qur'ān).

53 It is He Who has let free the two bodies of flowing water: one palatable and sweet, and the other saltish and bitter; yet has He made a barrier between them, a partition that is forbidden to be passed. 54 It is He Who has created man from water: then has He established relationships of lineage and marriage: for your Lord has power (over all things).

55 Yet do they worship, besides Allah, things that can neither profit them nor harm them: and the Disbeliever is a helper (of Evil), against his own Lord! 56 But you We only sent to give glad tidings and warnings. 57 Say: "No reward do I ask of you for it but this: that each one who will may take a (straight) Path to his Lord."

58 And put your trust in Him Who lives and dies not; and celebrate His praise; and enough is He to be acquainted with the faults of His servants— 59 He Who created the heavens and the earth and all that is between, in six days, then He established Himself on the Throne (of Authority): Allah, Most Gracious: ask you, then, about Him of any acquainted (with such things). 60 When it is said to them, "Adore you (Allah) Most Gracious!," they say, "And what is (Allah) Most Gracious? Shall we adore that which you command us?" And it increases them in aversion (for Truth).

61 Blessed is He Who made constellations in the skies, and placed therein a Lamp and a Moon giving light; 62 And it is He who made the Night and the Day to follow each other: for such as have the will to celebrate His praises or to show their gratitude.

63 And the servants of (Allah) Most Gracious are those who walk on the earth in humility, and when the ignorant address them, they say, "Peace!" 64 Those who spend the night in adoration of their Lord prostrate and standing; 65 Those who say, "Our Lord!

Avert from us the Wrath of hell, for its Wrath is indeed an affliction grievous— 66 "Evil indeed is it as an abode, and as a place to rest in;" 67 Those who, when they spend, are not extravagant and not niggardly, but hold a just (balance) between those (extremes);

68 Those who invoke not, with Allah, any other god, nor slay such life as Allah has made sacred except for just cause, nor commit fornication—and any that does this (not only) meets punishment 69 (But) the chastisement on the Day of Judgment will be doubled to him, and he will dwell therein in ignominy— 70 Unless he repents, believes, and works righteous deeds, for Allah will change the evil of such persons into good, and Allah is oft-Forgiving, Most Merciful, 71 And whoever repents and does good has truly turned to Allah with an (acceptable) conversion— in repentance: 72 Those who witness no falsehood, and, if they pass by futility, they pass by it with honourable (avoidance); 73 Those who, when they are admonished with the Signs of their Lord, droop not down at them as if they were deaf or blind; 74 And those who pray, "Our Lord! Grant unto us wives and offspring who will be the comfort of our eyes, and give us (the grace) to lead the righteous."

75 Those are the ones who will be rewarded with the highest place in heaven, because of their patient constancy: therein shall they be met with salutations and peace, 76 Dwelling therein— how beautiful an abode and place of rest! 77 Say (to the Rejecters): "My Lord would not concern Himself with you but for your call on Him: but you have indeed rejected (Him), and soon will come the inevitable (punishment)!"

26. THE POETS

In the name of Allah, Most Gracious, Most Merciful.

1 *Tā' Sīn Mīm*. 2 These are Verses of the Book that makes (things) clear. 3 It may be you frettest your soul with grief, that they do not become believers. 4 If (such) were Our Will, We could

send down to them from the sky a Sign, to which they would bend their necks in humility. 5 But there comes not to them a newly-revealed message from (Allah) Most Gracious, but they turn away therefrom. 6 They have indeed rejected (the Message): so they will know soon (enough) the truth of what they mocked at!

7 Do they not look at the earth—how many noble things of all kinds we have produced therein? 8 Surely, in this is a Sign: but most of them do not believe. 9 And, surely, your Lord is He, the Exalted in Might, Most Merciful.

10 Behold, your Lord called Moses: "Go to the people of iniquity— 11 "The people of the Pharaoh: will they not fear Allah?" 12 He said: "O my Lord! I do fear that they will charge me with falsehood: 13 "My breast will be straitened. And my speech may not go (smoothly): so send Aaron. 14 "And (further), they have a charge of crime against me; and I fear they may slay me."

15 Allah said: "By no means! proceed then, both of you, with Our Signs; We are with you, and will listen (to your call). 16 "So go forth, both of you, to Pharaoh, and say: 'We have been sent by the Lord and Cherisher of the worlds; 17 "'Send you with us the Children of Israel.'" 18 (Pharaoh) said: "Did we not cherish you as a child among us, and did you not stay in our midst many years of your life? 19 "And you did a deed of yours which (you know) you did, and you are an ungrateful (wretch)!"

20 Moses said: "I did it then, when I was in error. 21 "So I fled from you (all) when I feared you; but my Lord has (since) invested me with judgment (and wisdom) and appointed me as one of the Messengers. 22 "And this is the favour with which you reproach me—that you have enslaved the Children of Israel!"

23 Pharaoh said: "And what is the 'Lord and Cherisher of the Worlds?'" 24 (Moses) said: "The Lord and Cherisher of the heavens and the earth, and all between— if you had but sure belief." 25 (Pharaoh) said to those around: "Do you not listen (to what he says)?" 26 (Moses) said: "Your Lord and the Lord of your fathers from the beginning!" 27 (Pharaoh) said: "Truly your

Messenger who has been sent to you is a veritable madman!"
28 (Moses) said: "Lord of the East and the West, and all between!
If you only had sense!" 29 (Pharaoh) said: "If you dare put forward
any god other than me, I will certainly put you in prison!"
30 (Moses) said: "Even if I showed you something clear (and)
convincing?" 31 (Pharaoh) said: "Show it then, if you tell the
truth!" 32 So (Moses) threw his staff, and behold, it was a serpent,
plain (for all to see)! 33 And he drew out his hand, and behold,
it was white to all beholders! 34 (Pharaoh) said to the Chiefs
around him: "This is indeed a sorcerer well-versed: 35 "His plan
is to get you out of your land by his sorcery; then what is it you
counsel?"

36 They said: "Keep him and his brother in suspense (for a
while), and dispatch to the Cities heralds to collect— 37 "And
bring up to you all (our) sorcerers well-versed." 38 So the
sorcerers were got together for the appointment of a day well-
known, 39 And the people were told: "Are you (now)
assembled?— 40 "That we may follow the sorcerers (in religion)
if they win?" 41 So when the sorcerers arrived, they said to
Pharaoh: "Of course—shall we have a (suitable) reward if we
win? 42 He said: "Yes, (and more)—for you shall in that case
be (raised to posts) nearest (to my person)."

43 Moses said to them: "Throw you—that which you are about
to throw!" 44 So they threw their ropes and their rods, and said:
"By the might of Pharaoh, it is we who will certainly win!"
45 Then Moses threw his staff, when, behold, it straightway
swallows up all the falsehoods which they fake! 46 Then did the
sorcerers fall down, prostrate in adoration, 47 Saying: "We
believe in the Lord of the Worlds, 48 "The Lord of Moses and
Aaron."

49 Said (Pharaoh): "Do you believe in Him before I give you
permission? Surely he is your leader, who has taught you sorcery!
But soon shall you know! "Be sure I will cut off your hands and
your feet on opposite sides, and I will cause you all to die on the
cross!" 50 They said: "No matter! for us, we shall but return to
our Lord!

51 "Only, our desire is that our Lord will forgive us our faults, that we may become foremost among the believers!" 52 By inspiration We told Moses: "Travel by night with my servants; for surely you shall be pursued." 53 Then Pharaoh sent heralds to (all) the Cities, 54 (Saying): "These (Israelites) are but a small band, 55 "And they have surely enraged us; 56 "And we are a multitude amply forewarned." 57 So We expelled them from gardens, springs, 58 Treasures, and every kind of honourable position.

59 Thus it was, but We made the Children of Israel inheritors of such things. 60 So they pursued them at sunrise. 61 And when the two bodies saw each other, the people of Moses said: "We are sure to be overtaken." 62 (Moses) said: "By no means! My Lord is with me! Soon will He guide me!" 63 Then We told Moses by inspiration: "Strike the sea with your staff." so it divided, and each separate part became like the huge, firm mass of a mountain. 64 And We made the other party approach there. 65 We delivered Moses and all who were with him; 66 But We drowned the others. 67 Surely, in this is a Sign: but most of them do not believe.

68 And, surely, your Lord is He, the Exalted in Might, Most Merciful. 69 And rehearse to them (something of) Abraham's story. 70 Behold, he said to his father and his people: "Whom do you worship?" 71 They said: "We worship idols, and we remain constantly in attendance on them." 72 He said: "Do they listen to you when you call (on them), 73 Or do you good or harm?" 74 They said: "No, but we found our fathers doing thus (what we do)."

75 He said: "Do you then see whom you have been worshipping— 76 "You and your fathers before you?— 77 "For they are enemies to me; not so the Lord and Cherisher of the Worlds; 78 "Who created me, and it is He Who guides me; 79 "Who gives me food and drink, 80 "And when I am ill, it is He Who cures me; 81 "Who will cause me to die, and then to live (again); 82 "And who, I hope, will forgive me my faults on the Day of Judgment.

83 "O my Lord! bestow wisdom on me, and join me with the righteous; 84 "Grant me honourable mention on the tongue of truth

among the latest (generations); 85 "Make me one of the inheritors of the Garden of Bliss; 86 "Forgive my father, for that he is among those astray; 87 "And let me not be in disgrace on the Day when (men) will be raised up— 88 "The Day whereon neither wealth nor sons will avail, 89 "But only he (will prosper) that brings to Allah a sound heart.

90 "To the righteous, the Garden will be brought near, 91 "And to those straying in Evil, the Fire will be placed in full view; 92 "And it shall be said to them: 'Where are the (gods) you worshipped— 93 "'Besides Allah? Can they help you or help themselves?' 94 "Then they will be thrown headlong into the (Fire)— they and those straying in Evil, 95 "And the whole hosts of Iblīs together. 96 "They will say there in their mutual bickerings: 97 "'By Allah, we were truly in an error manifest, 98 "'When we held you as equals with the Lord of the Worlds; 99 "'And our seducers were only those who were steeped in guilt. 100 "'Now, then, we have none to intercede (for us), 101 "'Nor a single friend to feel (for us). 102 "'Now if we only had a chance of return we shall truly be of those who believe!'" 103 Surely, in this is a Sign, but most of them do not believe. 104 And, surely, your Lord is He, the Exalted in Might, Most Merciful.

105 The people of Noah rejected the Messengers. 106 Behold, their brother Noah said to them: "Will you not fear (Allah)? 107 "I am to you a Messenger worthy of all trust: 108 "So fear Allah, and obey me. 109 "No reward do I ask of you for it: my reward is only from the Lord of the Worlds: 110 "So fear Allah, and obey me." 111 They said: "Shall we believe in you when it is the meanest that follow you?" 112 He said: "And what do I know as to what they do? 113 "Their account is only with my Lord, if you could (but) understand. 114 "I am not one to drive away those who believe. 115 "I am sent only to warn plainly in public."

116 They said: "If you desist not, O Noah! you shall be stoned (to death)." 117 He said: "O my Lord! truly my people have rejected me. 118 "Judge You, then, between me and them openly,

and deliver me and those of the Believers who are with me."
119 So We delivered him and those with him, in the Ark filled
(with all creatures). 120 Thereafter, We drowned those who
remained behind. 121 Surely, in this is a Sign: but most of them
do not believe. 122 And, surely, your Lord is He, the Exalted in
Might, Most Merciful.

123 The 'Ād (people) rejected the Messengers. 124 Behold, their
brother Hūd said to them: "Will you not fear (Allah)? 125 "I am
to you a Messenger worthy of all trust: 126 "So fear Allah and
obey me. 127 "No reward do I ask of you for it: my reward is
only from the Lord of the Worlds. 128 "Do you build a landmark
on every high place to amuse yourselves? 129 "And do you get
for yourselves fine buildings in the hope of living therein
(forever)? 130 "And when you exert your strong hand, do you
do it like men of absolute power? 131 "Now fear Allah, and obey
me. 132 "Yes, fear Him Who has bestowed on you freely all that
you know. 133 "Freely has He bestowed on you cattle and sons —
134 "And Gardens and Springs. 135 "Truly, I fear for you the
Chastisement of a Great Day."

136 They said: "It is the same to us whether you admonish us
or be not among (our) admonishers! 137 "This is no other than
a customary device of the ancients, 138 "And we are not the ones
to receive Pains and Penalties!" 139 So they rejected him, and We
destroyed them. Surely, in this is a Sign: but most of them do
not believe. 140 And, surely, your Lord is He, the Exalted in
Might, Most Merciful.

141 The Thamūd (people) rejected the Messengers. 142 Behold,
their brother Ṣāliḥ said to them: "Will you not fear (Allah)?
143 "I am to you a Messenger worthy of all trust. 144 "So fear Allah,
and obey me. 145 "No reward do I ask of you for it: my reward
is only from the Lord of the Worlds. 146 "Will you be left secure,
in (the enjoyment of) all that you have here? — 147 "Gardens and
Springs, 148 "And corn-fields and date-palms with spathes near
breaking (with the weight of fruit)? 149 "And you carve houses
out of (rocky) mountains with great skill. 150 "But fear Allah and
obey me; 151 "And follow not the bidding of those who are

extravagant— 152 "Who make mischief in the land, and mend not (their ways)."

153 They said: "You are only one of those bewitched! 154 "You are no more than a mortal like us: then bring us a Sign, if you tell the truth!" 155 He said: "Here is a she-camel: she has a right of watering, and you have a right of watering, (severally) on a day appointed. 156 "Touch her not with ˙harm, lest the chastisement of a Great Day seize you." 157 But they hamstrung her: then did they become full of regrets. 158 But the Penalty seized them. Surely, in this is a Sign: but most of them do not believe. 159 And, surely, your Lord is He, the Exalted in Might, Most Merciful.

160 The people of Lūṭ rejected the Messengers. 161 Behold, their brother Lūṭ said to them: "Will you not fear (Allah)? 162 "I am to you a Messenger worthy of all trust. 163 "So fear Allah and obey me. 164 "No reward do I ask of you for it: my reward is only from the Lord of the Worlds. 165 "Of all the creatures in the world, will you approach males, 166 "And leave those whom Allah has created for you to be your mates? No, you are a people transgressing (all limits)!"

167 They said: "If you desist not, O Lūṭ! you will assuredly be cast out!" 168 He said: "I do detest your doings." 169 "O my Lord! deliver me and my family from such things as they do!" 170 So We delivered him and his family—all 171 Except an old woman who lingered behind. 172 But the rest We destroyed utterly. 173 We rained down on them a shower (of brimstone): and evil was the shower on those who were admonished (but heeded not)! 174 Surely, in this is a Sign: but most of them do not believe. 175 And, surely, your Lord is He, the Exalted in Might Most Merciful.

176 The People of the Wood rejected the Messengers. 177 Behold, Shu'ayb said to them: "Will you not fear (Allah)? 178 "I am to you a Messenger worthy of all trust. 179 "So fear Allah and obey me. 180 "No reward do I ask of you for it: my reward is only from the Lord of the Worlds. 181 "Give just measure, and cause no loss (to others by fraud). 182 "And weigh with scales true and upright. 183 "And withhold not things justly

due to men, nor do evil in the land, working mischief. 184 "And fear Him Who created you and (Who created) the generations before (you)."

185 They said: "You are only one of those bewitched! 186 "You are no more than a mortal like us, and indeed we think you are a liar! 187 "Now cause a piece of the sky to fall on us, if you are truthful!" 188 He said: "My Lord knows best what you do." 189 But they rejected him. Then the punishment of a day of overshadowing gloom seized them, and that was the chastisement of a Great Day. 190 Surely, in that is a Sign: but most of them do not believe. 191 And, surely, your Lord is He, the Exalted in Might, Most Merciful.

192 Surely, this is a Revelation from the Lord of the Worlds: 193 With it came down the Spirit of Faith and Truth— 194 To your heart and mind, that you may admonish 195 In the perspicuous Arabic tongue. 196 Without doubt it is (announced) in the revealed Books of former peoples. 197 Is it not a Sign to them that the Learned of the Children of Israel knew it (as true)?

198 Had We revealed it to any of the non-Arabs, 199 And had he recited it to them, they would not have believed in it. 200 Thus have We caused it to enter the hearts of the Sinners. 201 They will not believe in it until they see the grievous chastisement; 202 But it will come to them of a sudden, while they perceive it not; 203 Then they will say: "Shall we be respited?"

204 Do they then ask for Our chastisement to be hastened on? 205 Do you see? If We do let them enjoy (this life) for a few years, 206 Yet there comes to them at length the (Punishment) which they were promised! 207 It will profit them not that they enjoyed (this life)! 208 Never did We destroy a population, but had its warners— 209 By way of reminder; and We never are unjust. 210 No Satan has brought down this (Revelation): 211 It would neither suit them nor would they be able (to produce it). 212 Indeed they have been removed far from even (a chance of) hearing it.

213 So call not on any other deity with Allah, or you will be among those under the Penalty. 214 And admonish your nearest kinsmen, 215 And lower your wing to the Believers who follow

you. 216 Then, if they disobey you, say: "I am free (of responsibility) for what you do!" 217 And put your trust in the Exalted in Might, the Merciful— 218 Who sees you standing forth (in prayer), 219 And your movements among those who prostrate themselves, 220 For it is He who hears and knows all things.

221 Shall I inform you, (O people!), on whom it is that the Satans descend? 222 They descend on every lying, wicked person, 223 (Into whose ears) they pour hearsay vanities, and most of them are liars. 224 And the Poets— It is those straying in Evil, who follow them: 225 See you not that they wander distracted in every valley?— 226 And that they say what they practise not?— 227 Except those who believe, work righteousness, engage much in the remembrance of Allah, and defend themselves only after they are unjustly attacked. And soon will the unjust assailants know what vicissitudes their affairs will take!

27. THE ANTS

In the name of Allah, Most Gracious, Most Merciful.

1 *Tā' Sīn*. These are verses of the Qur'ān—a Book that makes (things) clear; 2 A Guide: and Glad Tidings for the Believers— 3 Those who establish regular prayers and give zakat (poor-due), and also have (full) assurance of the Hereafter. 4 As to those who believe not in the Hereafter, We have made their deeds pleasing in their eyes; and so they wander about in distraction. 5 Such are they for whom a grievous chastisement awaits; and in the Hereafter theirs will be the greatest loss. 6 As to you, the Qur'ān is bestowed upon you from the presence of One who is Wise and All-Knowing.

7 Behold! Moses said to his family: "I perceive a fire; soon will I bring you from there some information, or I will bring you a burning brand to light our fuel, that you may warm yourselves." 8 But when he came to the (Fire), a voice was heard: "Blessed are those in the Fire and those around: and Glory to Allah, the Lord of the Worlds.

9 "O Moses! Surely, I am Allah, the Exalted in Might, the Wise!
10 "Now do you throw your staff!" But when he saw it moving
(of its own accord) as if it had been a snake, he turned back in
retreat, and retraced not his steps: "O Moses!" (it was said), "Fear
not: truly, in My presence, those called as Messengers have no
fear— 11 "But if any have done wrong and have thereafter
substituted good to take the place of evil, truly, I am Oft-
Forgiving, Most Merciful. 12 "Now put your hand into your
bosom, and it will come forth white without stain (or harm): (these
are) among the nine Signs (you will take) to Pharaoh and his
people: for they are a people rebellious in transgression." 13 But
when Our Signs came to them, that should have opened their
eyes, they said: "This is sorcery manifest!" 14 And they rejected
those Signs in iniquity and arrogance, though their souls were
convinced thereof: so see what was the end of those who acted
corruptly!

15 We gave (in the past) knowledge to David and Solomon: and
they both said: "Praise be to Allah, Who has favoured us above
many of His servants who believe!" 16 And Solomon was David's
heir. He said: "O you people! We have been taught the speech
of Birds, and on us has been bestowed (a little) of all things: this
is indeed Grace manifest (from Allah.)"

17 And before Solomon were marshalled his hosts —of Jinns
and men and birds, and they were all kept in order and ranks.
18 At length, when they came to a (lowly) valley of ants, one of
the ants said: "O you ants, get into your habitations, lest Solomon
and his hosts crush you (under foot) without knowing it." 19 So
he smiled, amused at her speech; and he said: "O my Lord! so
order me that I may be grateful for Your favours, which You have
bestowed on me and on my parents, and that I may work the
righteousness that will please You: and admit me, by Your Grace,
to the ranks of Your righteous Servants."

20 And he took a muster of the Birds; and he said: "Why is it
I see not the Hoopoe? Or is he among the absentees? 21 "I will
certainly punish him with a severe punishment, or execute him,
unless he brings me a clear reason (for absence)." 22 But the
Hoopoe tarried not far: he (came up and) said: "I have compassed

(territory) which you have not compassed, and I have come to you from Sabā' with tidings true. 23 "I found (there) a woman ruling over them and provided with every requisite; and she has a magnificent throne. 24 "I found her and her people worshipping the sun besides Allah: Satan has made their deeds seem pleasing in their eyes, and has kept them away from the Path—so they receive no guidance— 25 "(Kept them away from the Path), that they should not worship Allah, Who brings to light what is hidden in the heavens and the earth, and knows what you hide and what you reveal. 26 "Allah!—there is no god but He!—Lord of the Throne Supreme!"

27 (Solomon) said: "Soon shall we see whether you have told the truth or lied! 28 "Go you, with this letter of mine, and deliver it to them: then draw back from them, and (wait to) see what answer they return"… 29 (The Queen) said: "You chiefs! Here is—delivered to me— a letter worthy of respect. 30 "It is from Solomon, and is (as follows): 'In the name of Allah, Most Gracious, Most Merciful: 31 "'Be you not arrogant against me, but come to me in submission (to the true Religion).'" 32 She said: "O chiefs! advise me in (this) my affair: no affair have I decided except in your presence." 33 They said: "We are endued with strength, and given to vehement war: but the command is with you; so consider what you will command." 34 She said: "Kings, when they enter a country, despoil it, and make the noblest of its people its meanest. Thus do they behave. 35 "But I am going to send him a present, and (wait) to see with what (answer) return (my) ambassadors."

36 Now when (the embassy) came to Solomon, he said: "Will you give me abundance in wealth? But that which Allah has given me is better than that which He has given you! No it is you who rejoice in your gift! 37 "Go back to them, and be sure we shall come to them with such hosts as they will never be able to meet: we shall expel them from there in disgrace, and they will feel humbled (indeed)."

38 He said (to his own men): "Chiefs! which of you can bring me her throne before they come to me in submission?" 39 Said an 'Ifrīt, of the Jinns: "I will bring it to you before you rise from

your council: indeed I have full strength for the purpose, and may be trusted." 40 Said one who had knowledge of the Book: "I will bring it to you within the twinkling of an eye!" then when (Solomon) saw it placed firmly before him, he said: "This is by the Grace of my Lord!—To test me whether I am grateful or ungrateful! And if any is grateful, truly his gratitude is (a gain) for his own soul; but if any is ungrateful, truly my Lord is Free of all Needs, Supreme in Honour!"

41 He said: "Transform her throne out of all recognition by her: let us see whether she is guided (to the truth) or is one of those who receive no guidance." 42 So when she arrived, she was asked, "Is this your throne?" She said, "It was just like this." (and Solomon said:) "We were given the knowledge before this and we had surrendered (to Allah)." 43 And (all) that she was wont to worship instead of Allah hindered her, for she came of disbelieving folk. 44 She was asked to enter the lofty Palace: but when she saw it, she thought it was a lake of water, and she (tucked up her skirts), uncovering her legs. He said: "This is but a palace paved smooth with slabs of glass." She said: "O my Lord! I have indeed wronged my soul: I do (now) submit (in Islam), with Solomon, to the Lord of the Worlds."

45 We sent (aforetime), to the Thamūd, their brother Ṣāliḥ, saying, "Serve Allah:" But behold, they became two factions quarrelling with each other. 46 He said: "O my people! Why do you ask to hasten on the evil in preference to the good? If only you ask Allah for forgiveness, you may hope to receive mercy. 47 They said: "Ill omen do we augur from you and those that are with you." He said: "Your ill omen is with Allah; yes, you are a people under trial."

48 There were in the City nine men of a family, who made mischief in the land, and would not reform. 49 They said: "Swear a mutual oath by Allah that we shall make a secret night attack on him and his people, and that we shall then say to his heir (when he seeks vengeance): 'We were not present at the slaughter of his people, and we are positively telling the truth.'" 50 They plotted and planned, but We too planned, even while they perceived it not. 51 Then see what was the end of their plot!—this, that We

destroyed them and their people, all (of them). 52 Now such were their houses — in utter ruin — because they practised wrongdoing. Surely, in this is a Sign for people of knowledge. 53 And We saved those who believed and practiced righteousness.

54 (We also sent) Lūṭ (as a Messenger): behold, he said to his people, "Do you do what is shameful though you see (its iniquity)? 55 Would you really approach men in your lusts rather than women? No, you are a people (grossly) ignorant!" 56 But his people gave no other answer but this: they said, "Drive out the followers of Lūṭ from your city: these are indeed men who want to be clean and pure!" 57 But We saved him and his family, except his wife; her We destined to be of those who lagged behind. 58 And We rained down on them a shower (of brimstone): and evil was the shower on those who were admonished (but heeded not)! 59 Say: Praise be to Allah, and Peace on His servants whom He has chosen (for His Message). (Who) is better? — Allah or the false gods they associate (with Him)?

60 Or, Who has created the heavens and the earth, and who sends you down rain from the sky? Yes, with it We cause to grow well-planted orchards full of beauty and delight: it is not in your power to cause the growth of the trees in them. (Can there be another) god besides Allah? No, they are a people who swerve from justice. 61 Or, who has made the earth firm to live in; made rivers in its midst; set thereon mountains immovable; and made a separating bar between the two bodies of flowing water? (Can there be another) god besides Allah? No, most of them know not.

62 Or, Who listens to the (soul) distressed when it calls on Him, and Who relieves its suffering, and makes you (mankind) inheritors of the earth? (Can there be another) god besides Allah? Little it is that you heed! 63 Or, Who guides you through the depths of darkness on land and sea, and Who sends the winds as heralds of glad tidings, going before His mercy? (Can there be another) god besides Allah? — High is Allah above what they associate with Him! 64 Or, Who originates Creation, then repeats it, and Who gives you sustenance from heaven and earth? (Can there be another) god besides Allah? Say, "Bring forth your argument, if you are telling the truth!"

65 Say: None in the heavens or on earth, except Allah, knows what is hidden: nor can they perceive when they shall be raised up (for Judgment). 66 Still less can their knowledge comprehend the Hereafter: no, they are in doubt and uncertainty thereanent; no, they are blind thereunto! 67 The Unbelievers say: "What! when we become dust— we and our fathers—shall we really be raised (from the dead)? 68 "It is true we were promised this— we and our fathers before (us): these are nothing but tales of the ancients." 69 Say: "Go you through the earth and see what has been the end of those guilty (of sin)."

70 But grieve not over them, nor distress yourself because of their plots. 71 They also say: "When will this promise (come to pass)? (say) if you are truthful." 72 Say: "It may be that some of the events which you wish to hasten on may be (close) in your pursuit!" 73 But, surely, your Lord is full of grace to mankind: yet most of them are ungrateful. 74 And, surely, your Lord knows all that their hearts do hide, as well as all that they reveal. 75 Nor is there anything of the Unseen, in heaven or earth, but is (recorded) in a clear record.

76 Surely, this Qur'ān does explain to the Children of Israel most of the matters in which they disagree. 77 And it certainly is a Guide and a Mercy to those who believe. 78 Surely, your Lord will decide between them by His Decree: and He is Exalted in Might, All-Knowing. 79 So put your trust in Allah: for you are on (the path of) manifest Truth. 80 Truly, you can not cause the Dead to listen, nor can you cause the Deaf to hear the call, (especially) when they turn back in retreat. 81 Nor can you be a guide to the blind, (to prevent them) from straying: only those will you get to listen who believe in Our Signs, and they will bow in Islam.

82 And when the Word is fulfilled against them (the unjust), We shall produce from the earth a Beast to (face) them: he will speak to them, for that mankind did not believe with assurance in Our Signs. 83 One Day We shall gather together from every people a troop of those who reject Our Signs, and they shall be kept in ranks— 84 Until, when they come (before the Judgement Seat), (Allah) will say: "Did you reject My Signs, though you comprehended them not in knowledge, or what was it you did?"

85 And the Word will be fulfilled against them, because of their wrongdoing, and they will be unable to speak (in plea). 86 See they not that We have made the Night for them to rest in and the Day to give them light? Surely, in this are Signs for any people that believe!

87 And the Day that the Trumpet will be sounded—then will be smitten with terror those who are in the heavens, and those who are on earth, except such as Allah will please (to exempt): and all shall come to His (Presence) as beings conscious of their lowliness. 88 You see the mountains and think them firmly fixed: but they shall pass away as the clouds pass away: (such is) the artistry of Allah, who disposes of all things in perfect order: for He is well acquainted with all that you do. 89 If any do good, even better will (accrue) to them therefrom; and they will be secure from terror that Day. 90 And if any do evil, their faces will be thrown headlong into the Fire: "Do you receive a reward other than that which you have earned by your deeds?"

91 For me, I have been commanded to serve the Lord of this City, Him Who has sanctified it and to Whom (belong) all things: and I am commanded to be of those who bow in Islam to Allah's Will— 92 And to rehearse the Qur'ān: and if any accept guidance, they do it for the good of their own souls, and if any stray, say: "I am only a Warner." 93 And say: "Praise be to Allah, who will soon show you His Signs, so that you shall know them;" and your Lord is not unmindful of all that you do.

28. THE NARRATIONS

In the name of Allah, Most Gracious, Most Merciful.

1 Tā' Sīn Mīm. 2 These are Verses of the Book that makes (things) clear. 3 We rehearse to you some of the story of Moses and Pharaoh in Truth, for people who believe. 4 Truly Pharaoh elated himself in the land and broke up its people into sections, depressing a small group among them: their sons he slew, but he kept alive their females: for he was indeed a maker of mischief.

5 And We wished to be gracious to those who were being depressed in the land, to make them leaders (in Faith) and make them heirs, 6 To establish a firm place for them in the land, and to show Pharaoh, Hāmān, and their hosts, at their hands, the very things against which they were taking precautions.

7 So We sent this inspiration to the mother of Moses: "Suckle (your child), but when you have fears about him, cast him into the river, but fear not nor grieve: for We shall restore him to you, and We shall make him one of Our Messengers." 8 Then the people of Pharaoh picked him up (from the river): (it was intended) that (Moses) should be to them an adversary and a cause of sorrow: for Pharaoh and Hāmān and (all) their hosts were men of sin. 9 The wife of Pharaoh said: "(Here is) joy of the eye, for me and for you: slay him not. It may be that he will be of use to us, or we may adopt him as a son." And they perceived not (what they were doing)!

10 But there came to be a void in the heart of the mother of Moses: she was going almost to disclose his (case), had We not strengthened her heart (with faith), so that she might remain a (firm) believer. 11 And she said to the sister of (Moses), "Follow him." So she (the sister) watched him in the character of a stranger. And they knew not. 12 And We ordained that he refused suck at first, until (His sister came up and) said: "Shall I point out to you the people of a house that will nourish and bring him up for you and be sincerely attached to him?"... 13 Thus did We restore him to his mother, that her eye might be comforted, that she might not grieve, and that she might know that the promise of Allah is true: but most of them do not understand. 14 When he reached full age, and was firmly established (in life), We bestowed on him wisdom and knowledge: for thus do We reward those who do good.

15 And he entered the City at a time when its people were not watching: and he found there two men fighting— one of his own people, and the other, of his foes. Now the man of his own people appealed to him against his foe, and Moses struck him with his fist and made an end of him. He said: "This is a work of Evil

(Satan): for he is an enemy that manifestly misleads!" 16 He prayed: "O my Lord! I have indeed wronged my soul! Do You then forgive me!" So (Allah) forgave him: for He is the Oft-Forgiving, Most Merciful. 17 He said: "O my Lord! for that You have bestowed Your Grace on me, never shall I be a help to those who sin!"

18 So he saw the morning in the City, looking about, in a state of fear, when behold, the man who had, the day before, sought his help called aloud for his help (again). Moses said to him: "You are truly, it is clear, a quarrelsome fellow!" 19 Then, when he decided to lay hold of the man who was an enemy to both of them, the man said: "O Moses! Is it your intention to slay me as you slew a man yesterday? Your intention is none other than to become a powerful tyrant in the land, and not to be one who sets things right!" 20 And there came a man, running, from the furthest end of the City. He said: "O Moses! the Chiefs are taking counsel together about you, to slay you: so get you away, for I do give you sincere advice." 21 He therefore got away therefrom, looking about, in a state of fear. He prayed: "O my Lord! save me from people given to wrongdoing."

22 Then, when he turned his face towards (the land of) Madyan, he said: "I do hope that my Lord will show me the smooth and straight Path." 23 And when he arrived at the watering (place) in Madyan, he found there a group of men watering (their flocks), and besides them he found two women who were keeping back (their flocks). He said: "What is the matter with you?" they said: "We cannot water (our flocks) until the shepherds take back (their flocks): and our father is a very old man." 24 So he watered (their flocks) for them; then he turned back to the shade, and said: "O my Lord! truly am I in (desperate) need of any good that You send me!"...

25 Afterwards one of the (damsels) came (back) to him, walking bashfully. She said: "My father invites you that he may reward you for having watered (our flocks) for us." So when he came to him and narrated the story, he said: "Fear you not: (well) have you escaped from unjust people." 26 Said one of the (damsels):

"O my (dear) father! Engage him on wages: truly the best of men for you to employ is the (man) who is strong and trustworthy." 27 He said: "I intend to wed one of these my daughters to you, on condition that you serve me for eight years; but if you complete ten years, it will be (grace) from you. But I intend not to place you under a difficulty: you will find me, indeed, if Allah wills, one of the righteous." 28 He said: "Be that (the agreement) between me and you: whichever of the two terms I fulfil, let there be no ill-will to me. Be Allah a witness to what we say."

29 Now when Moses had fulfilled the term, and was travelling with his family, he perceived a fire in the direction of Mount Ṭūr. He said to his family: "Tarry you; I perceive a fire; I hope to bring you from there some information, or a burning firebrand, that you may warm yourselves." 30 But when he came to the (fire), a Voice was heard from the right bank of the valley, from a tree in hallowed ground: "O Moses! Surely, I am Allah, the Lord of the Worlds... 31 "Now you throw your staff!" but when he saw it moving (of its own accord) as if it had been a snake, he turned back in retreat, and retraced not his steps: "O Moses!" (It was said), "Draw near, and fear not: for you are of those who are secure. 32 "Thrust your hand into your bosom, and it will come forth white without stain (or harm), and draw your hand close to your side (to guard) against fear. Those are the two credentials from your Lord to Pharaoh and his Chiefs: for truly they are a people rebellious and wicked."

33 He said: "O my Lord! I have slain a man among them, and I fear lest they slay me. 34 "And my brother Aaron— He is more eloquent in speech than I: so send him with me as a helper, to confirm (and strengthen) me: for I fear that they may accuse me of falsehood." 35 He said: "We will certainly strengthen your arm through your brother, and invest you both with authority, so they shall not be able to touch you: with Our Signs shall you triumph— you two as well as those who follow you."

36 When Moses came to them with Our Clear Signs, they said: "This is nothing but sorcery faked up: never did we hear the like among our fathers of old!" 37 Moses said: "My Lord knows best

who it is that comes with guidance from Him and whose End will be best in the Hereafter: certain it is that the wrongdoers will not prosper." 38 Pharaoh said: "O Chiefs! No god do I know for you but myself: therefore, O Hāmān! light me a (kiln to bake bricks) out of clay, and build me a lofty palace, that I may mount up to the god of Moses: but as far as I am concerned, I think (Moses) is a liar!"

39 And he was arrogant and insolent in the land, beyond reason— he and his hosts: they thought that they would not have to return to Us! 40 So We seized him and his hosts, and We flung them into the sea: now behold what was the end of those who did wrong! 41 And We made them (but) leaders inviting to the Fire; and on the Day of Judgment no help shall they find. 42 In this world We made a Curse to follow them and on the Day of Judgment they will be among the loathed (and despised). 43 We did reveal to Moses the Book after We had destroyed the earlier generations, (to give) Insight to men, and Guidance and Mercy, that they might receive admonition.

44 You were not on the Western side when We decreed the Commission to Moses, nor were you a witness (of those events). 45 But We raised up (new) generations, and long were the ages that passed over them; but you were not a dweller among the people of Madyan, rehearsing Our Signs to them; but it is We Who send messengers (with inspiration). 46 Nor were you at the side of (the Mountain of) Ṭūr when We called (to Moses). Yet (are you sent) as a Mercy from your Lord, to give warning to a people to whom no warner had come before you: in order that they may receive admonition.

47 If (We had) not (sent you to the Quraysh)—in case a calamity should seize them for (the deeds) that their hands have sent forth, they might say: "Our Lord! why did You not send us a Messenger? We should then have followed Your Signs and been amongst those who believe!" 48 But (now), when the Truth has come to them from Ourselves, they say, "Why are not (Signs) sent to him, like those which were sent to Moses?" Do they not then reject (the Signs) which were formerly sent to Moses? They say: "Two

kinds of sorcery, each assisting the other!" and they say: "For us, we reject all (such things)!"

49 Say: "Then bring you a Book from Allah, which is a better Guide than either of them, that I may follow it! (Do), if you are truthful!" 50 But if they hearken not to you, know that they only follow their own lusts: and who is more astray than one who follows his own lusts, devoid of guidance from Allah? For Allah guides not people given to wrongdoing. 51 Now have We caused the Word to reach them themselves, in order that they may receive admonition.

52 Those to whom We sent the Book before this—they do believe in this (Revelation): 53 And when it is recited to them, they say: "We believe therein, for it is the Truth from our Lord: indeed we have been Muslims (bowing to Allah's Will) from before this." 54 Twice will they be given their reward, for that they have persevered, that they avert evil with Good, and that they spend (in charity) out of what We have given them. 55 And when they hear vain talk, they turn away therefrom and say: "To us our deeds, and to you yours; peace be to you: we seek not the ignorant." 56 It is true you will not be able to guide every one, whom you love; but Allah guides those whom He wills. And He knows best those who receive guidance.

57 They say: "If we were to follow the guidance with you, we should be snatched away from our land." Have We not established for them a secure sanctuary, to which are brought as tribute fruits of all kinds— a provision from Ourselves? But most of them understand not.

58 And how many townships we destroyed, which exulted in their life (of ease and plenty)! Now those habitations of theirs, after them, are deserted— all but a (miserable) few! And We are their heirs! 59 Nor was your Lord the one to destroy a township until he had sent to its Centre a Messenger, rehearsing to them Our Signs; nor are We going to destroy a population except when its members practise iniquity.

60 The (material) things which you are given are but the

conveniences of this life and the glitter thereof; but that which is with Allah is better and more enduring: will you not then be wise? 61 Are (these two) alike?— one to whom We have made a goodly promise, and who is going to reach its (fulfilment), and one to whom We have given the good things of this life, but who, on the Day of Judgment, is to be among those brought up (for punishment)?

62 That Day (Allah) will call to them, and say: "Where are My 'partners'?—whom you imagined (to be such)?" 63 Those against whom the charge will be proved, will say: "Our Lord! These are the ones whom we led astray: we led them astray, as we were astray ourselves: we free ourselves (from them) to You, it was not us they worshipped."

64 It will be said (to them): "Call upon your 'partners' (for help):" they will call upon them, but they will not listen to them; and they will see the torment (before them); (how they will wish) 'if only they had been open to guidance!' 65 That Day (Allah) will call to them, and say: "What was the answer you gave to the Messengers?" 66 Then the (whole) story that day will seem obscure to them (like light to the blind) and they will not be able (even) to question each other. 67 But any that (in this life) had repented, believed, and worked righteousness, will have hopes to be among those who achieve salvation.

68 Your Lord does create and choose as He pleases: no choice have they (in the matter): glory to Allah! and far is He above the partners they ascribe (to Him)! 69 And your Lord knows all that their hearts conceal and all that they reveal. 70 And He is Allah: there is no god but He. To Him be praise, at the first and at the last: for Him is the Command, and to Him shall you (all) be brought back.

71 Say: "Do you see? If Allah were to make the Night perpetual over you to the Day of Judgment, what god is there other than Allah, who can give you enlightenment? Will you not then hearken?" 72 Say: "Do you see? If Allah were to make the Day perpetual over you to the Day of Judgment, what god is there other than Allah, who can give you a Night in which you can

rest? Will you not then see?" 73 It is out of His Mercy that He has made for you Night and Day— that you may rest therein, and that you may seek of His Grace— and in order that you may be grateful.

74 The Day that He will call on them, He will say: "Where are My 'partners'?— whom you imagined (to be such)?" 75 And from each people shall We draw a witness, and We shall say: "Produce your Proof:" then shall they know that the Truth is with Allah (alone), and the (lies) which they invented will leave them in lurch.

76 Qārūn was doubtless, of the people of Moses; but he acted insolently towards them: such were the treasures We had bestowed on him that their very keys would have been a burden to a body of strong men. Behold, his people said to him: "Exult not, for Allah loves not those who exult (in riches). 77 "But seek, with the (wealth) which Allah has bestowed on you, the Home of the Hereafter, nor forget your portion in this world: but do and be good, as Allah has been good to you, and seek not (occasions for) mischief in the land: for Allah loves not those who do mischief."

78 He said: "This has been given to me because of a certain knowledge which I have." Did he not know that Allah had destroyed, before him, (whole) generations— which were superior to him in strength and greater in the amount (of riches) they had collected? But the wicked are not called (immediately) to account for their sins.

79 So he went forth among his people in the (pride of his worldly) glitter. Said those whose aim is the Life of this World: "Oh! that we had the like of what Qārūn has got! For he is truly a lord of mighty good fortune!" 80 But those who had been granted (true) knowledge said: "Alas for you! The reward of Allah (in the Hereafter) is best for those who believe and work righteousness: but this none shall attain, save those who steadfastly persevere (in good)."

81 Then We caused the earth to swallow him up and his house; and he had not (the least little) party to help him against Allah, nor could he defend himself. 82 And those who had envied his

position the day before began to say on the morrow: "Ah! It is indeed Allah who enlarges the provision or restricts it, to any of His servants He pleases! Had it not been that Allah was gracious to us, He could have caused the earth to swallow us up! Ah! Those who reject Allah will assuredly never prosper."

83 That Home of the Hereafter We shall give to those who intend not high-handedness or mischief on earth: and the End is (best) for the righteous. 84 If any does good, the reward to him is better than his deed; but if any does evil, the doers of evil are only punished (to the extent) of their deeds.

85 Surely, He Who ordained the Qur'ān for you, will bring you back to the Place of Return. Say: "My Lord knows best who it is that brings true guidance. And who is in manifest error." 86 And you have not expected that the Book would be sent to you except as a Mercy from your Lord: therefore, lend not you support in any way to those who reject (Allah's Message). 87 And let nothing keep you back from the Signs of Allah after they have been revealed to you: and invite (men) to your Lord, and be not of the company of those who join gods with Allah. 88 And call not, besides Allah, on another god. There is no god but He. Everything (that exists) will perish except His Own Face. To Him belongs the Command, and to Him will you (all) be brought back.

29. THE SPIDER

In the name of Allah, Most Gracious, Most Merciful.

1 *Alif Lām Mīm.* 2 Do men think that they will be left alone on saying, "We believe," and that they will not be tested? 3 We did test those before them, and Allah will certainly know those who are true from those who are false.

4 Do those who practise evil think that they will get the better of Us? Evil is their judgment! 5 For those whose hopes are in the meeting with Allah (in the Hereafter, let them strive); for the

Term (appointed) by Allah is surely coming: and He hears and knows (all things). 6 And if any strive (with might and main), they do so for their own souls: for Allah is free of all needs from all creation. 7 Those who believe and work righteous deeds — from them shall We blot out all evil (that may be) in them, and We shall reward them according to the best of their deeds.

8 We have enjoined on man kindness to parents: but if they (either of them) strive (to force) you to join with Me (in worship) anything of which you have no knowledge, obey them not. You have (all) to return to Me, and I will tell you (the truth) of all that you did. 9 And those who believe and work righteous deeds — them shall We admit to the company of the Righteous.

10 Then there are among men such as say, "We believe in Allah"; but when they suffer affliction in (the cause of) Allah, they treat men's oppression as if it were the Wrath of Allah! And if help comes (to you) from your Lord, they are sure to say, "We have (always) been with you!" Does not Allah know best all that is in the hearts of all Creation? 11 And Allah most certainly knows those who believe, and as certainly those who are Hypocrites.

12 And the Unbelievers say to those who believe: "Follow our path, and we will bear (the consequences) of your faults." Never in the least will they bear their faults: in fact they are liars! 13 They will bear their own burdens, and (other) burdens along with their own, and on the Day of Judgment they will be called to account for their falsehoods.

14 We (once) sent Noah to his people, and he tarried among them a thousand years less fifty: but the Deluge overwhelmed them while they (persisted in) sin. 15 But We saved him and the Companions of the Ark, and We made the (Ark) a Sign for all Peoples!

16 And (We also saved) Abraham: behold, he said to his people, "Serve Allah and fear Him: that will be best for you — if you understand! 17 "For you do worship idols besides Allah, and you invent falsehood. The things that you worship besides Allah have no power to give you sustenance: then seek you sustenance from Allah, serve Him, and be grateful to Him: to Him will be your

return.　18 "And if you reject (the Message), so did generations before you: and the duty of the Messenger is only to preach publicly (and clearly)."

19 See they not how Allah originates creation, then repeats it: truly that is easy for Allah. 20 Say: "Travel through the earth and see how Allah did originate creation; so will Allah produce a later creation: for Allah has power over all things. 21 "He punishes whom He pleases, and He grants Mercy to whom he pleases, and towards Him are you turned. 22 "Not on earth nor in heaven will you be able (fleeing) to frustrate (His Plan), nor have you, besides Allah, any protector or helper." 23 Those who reject the Signs of Allah and the Meeting with Him (in the Hereafter)— It is they who shall despair of My Mercy: it is they who will (suffer) a most grievous chastisement.

24 Not else was the answer of (Abraham's) people except that they said: "Slay him or burn him." But Allah did save him from the Fire. Surely, in this are Signs for people who believe. 25 And he said: "For you, you have taken (for worship) idols besides Allah, out of mutual love and regard between yourselves in this life; but on the Day of Judgment you shall disown each other and curse each other: and your abode will be the Fire, and you shall have none to help." 26 But Lūṭ had faith in Him: he said: "I will leave home for the sake of my Lord: for He is Exalted in Might, and Wise." 27 And We gave (Abraham) Isaac and Jacob, and ordained among his progeny Prophethood and Revelation, and We granted him his reward in this life; and he was in the Hereafter (of the company) of the Righteous.

28 And (remember) Lūṭ: behold, he said to his people: "You do commit lewdness, such as no people in Creation (ever) committed before you. 29 "Do you indeed approach men, and cut off the highway?— and practise wickedness (even) in your councils?" But his people gave no answer but this: they said: "Bring us the Wrath of Allah if you tell the truth." 30 He said: "O my Lord! help me against people who do mischief!"

31 When Our Messengers came to Abraham with the good news, they said: "We are indeed going to destroy the people of this

township: for truly they are (addicted to) crime." 32 He said: "But there is Lūṭ there." They said: "Well do we know who is there: we will certainly save him and his following— except his wife: she is of those who lag behind!" 33 And when Our Messengers came to Lūṭ, he was grieved on their account, and felt himself powerless (to protect) them: but they said: "Do not fear, nor grieve: we are (here) to save you and your following, except your wife: she is of those who lag behind. 34 "For we are going to bring down on the people of this township a Punishment from heaven, because they have been wickedly rebellious." 35 And We have left thereof an evident Sign, for any people who (care to) understand.

36 To the Madyan (people) (we sent) their brother Shu'ayb. Then he said: "O my people! Serve Allah, and fear the Last day: nor commit evil on the earth, with intent to do mischief." 37 But they rejected him: then the mighty Blast seized them, and they lay prostrate in their homes by the morning.

38 (Remember also) the 'Ād and the Thamud (people): clearly will appear to you from (the traces) of their buildings (their fate): Satan made their deeds alluring to them, and kept them back from the Path though they were gifted with Intelligence and Skill.

39 (Remember also) Qārūn, Pharaoh, and Hāmān: there came to them Moses with Clear Signs, but they behaved with insolence on the earth; yet they could not overreach (Us). 40 Each one of them We seized for his crime: of them, against some We sent a violent tornado (with showers of stones); some were caught by a (mighty) Blast; some We caused the earth to swallow up; and some We drowned (in the waters): it was not Allah Who injured (or oppressed) them: they injured (and oppressed) their own souls.

41 The parable of those who take protectors other than Allah is that of the Spider, who builds (to itself) a house; but truly the flimsiest of houses is the Spider's house— if they but knew. 42 Surely, Allah does know of (every thing) whatever that they call upon besides Him: and He is Exalted (in power), Wise. 43 And such are the Parables We set forth for mankind, but only

those understand them who have knowledge. 44 Allah created the heavens and the earth in truth: surely, in that is a Sign for those who believe.

45 Recite what is sent of the Book by inspiration to you, and establish regular Prayer: for Prayer restrains from shameful and unjust deeds; and remembrance of Allah is the greatest (thing in life) without doubt. And Allah knows the (deeds) that you do.

46 And dispute not with the People of the Book, except with means better (than mere disputation), unless it be with those of them who inflict wrong (and injury); but say, "We believe in the revelation which has come down to us and in that which came down to you; our God and your God is One; and it is to Him We bow (in Islam)."

47 And thus (it is) that We have sent down the Book to you. So the People of the Book believe therein, as also do some of these (pagan Arabs): and none but Unbelievers reject Our Signs. 48 And you were not (able) to recite a Book before this (Book came), nor are you (able) to transcribe it with your right hand: in that case, indeed, would the talkers of vanities have doubted. 49 No, here are Signs self-evident in the hearts of those endowed with knowledge: and none but the unjust reject Our Signs.

50 Yet they say: "Why are not Signs sent down to him from his Lord?" Say: "The Signs are indeed with Allah: and I am indeed a clear Warner." 51 And is it not enough for them that We have sent down to you the Book which is rehearsed to them? Surely, in it is Mercy and a Reminder to those who believe. 52 Say: "Enough is Allah for a witness between me and you: He knows what is in the heavens and on earth. And it is those who believe in vanities and reject Allah, that will perish (in the end).

53 They ask you to hasten on the Punishment (for them): had it not been for a term (of respite) appointed, the Punishment would certainly have come to them: and it will certainly reach them— of a sudden, while they perceive not! 54 They ask you to hasten on the Punishment: but, of a surety, Hell will encompass the Rejecters of Faith!— 55 On the Day that the Punishment shall cover them from above them and from below them, and (a Voice) shall say: "Taste you (the fruits) of your deeds!"

56 O My servants who believe! Truly, spacious is My Earth: therefore serve you Me— (and Me alone)! 57 Every soul shall have a taste of death: in the end to Us shall you be brought back. 58 But those who believe and work deeds of righteousness— to them shall We give a Home in Heaven— lofty mansions beneath which flow rivers—to dwell therein for ever—an excellent reward for those who do (good)!— 59 Those who persevere in patience, and put their trust, in their Lord and Cherisher. 60 How many are the creatures that carry not their own sustenance? It is Allah who feeds (both) them and you, for He hears and knows (all things).

61 If indeed you ask them who has created the heavens and the earth and subjected the sun and the moon (to His Law), they will certainly reply, "Allah." How are they then deluded away (from the truth)? 62 Allah enlarges the sustenance (which He gives) to whichever of His servants He pleases: and He (similarly) grants by (strict) measure, (as He pleases): for Allah has full knowledge of all things. 63 And if indeed you ask them who it is that sends down rain from the sky, and gives life therewith to the earth after its death, they will certainly reply, "Allah!" Say, "Praise be to Allah!" But most of them understand not.

64 What is the life of this world but amusement and play? But, surely, the Home in the Hereafter—that is life indeed, if they but knew. 65 Now, if they embark on a boat, they call on Allah, making, their devotion sincerely (and exclusively) to Him; but when He has delivered them safely to (dry) land, behold, they give a share (of their worship to others)!— 66 Disdaining ungratefully Our gifts, and giving themselves up to (worldly) enjoyment! But soon will they know.

67 Do they not then see that We have made a sanctuary secure, and that men are being snatched away from all around them? Then, do they believe in that which is vain, and reject the Grace of Allah? 68 And who does more wrong than he who invents a lie against Allah or rejects the Truth when it reaches him? Is there not a home in Hell for those who reject Faith? 69 And those who strive in Our (Cause)—We will certainly guide them to Our Paths: for, surely, Allah is with those who do right.

30. THE ROMANS

In the name of Allah, Most Gracious, Most Merciful.

1 *Alif Lām Mīm.* 2 The Roman Empire has been defeated—
3 In a land close by; but they, (even) after (this) defeat of theirs,
will soon be victorious— 4 Within a few years, with Allah is the
Decision, in the Past and in the Future: on that Day shall the
Believers rejoice— 5 With the help of Allah. He helps whom He
wills, and He is Exalted in Might, Most Merciful. 6 (It is) the
promise of Allah. Never does Allah depart from His promise: but
most men understand not. 7 They know but the outer (things)
in the life of this world: but of the End of things they are heedless.

8 Do they not reflect in their own minds? Not but for just ends
and for a term appointed, did Allah create the heavens and the
earth, and all between them: yet are there truly many among men
who deny the meeting with their Lord (at the Resurrection)!
9 Do they not travel through the earth, and see what was the End
of those before them? They were superior to them in strength:
they tilled the soil and populated it in greater numbers than these
have done: there came to them their Messengers with Clear
(Signs) (which they rejected, to their own destruction): it was not
Allah Who wronged them, but they wronged their own souls. 10
In the long run evil in the extreme will be the End of those who
do evil; for that they rejected the Signs of Allah, and held them
up to ridicule.

11 It is Allah Who begins (the process of) creation; then repeats
it; then shall you be brought back to Him. 12 On the Day that
the Hour will be established, the guilty will be struck dumb with
despair. 13 No intercessor will they have among their "Partners,"
and they will (themselves) reject their "Partners." 14 On the Day
that the Hour will be established— that Day shall (all men) be
sorted out. 15 Then those who have believed and worked righteous
deeds, shall be made happy in a Mead of Delight. 16 And those
who have rejected faith and falsely denied Our Signs and the
meeting of the Hereafter— such shall be brought forth to

Punishment.   17 So glory be to Allah, when you reach eventide and when you rise in the morning;   18 Yes, to Him be praise, in the heavens and on earth; and in the late afternoon and when the day begins to decline.

19 It is He Who brings out the living from the dead, and brings out the dead from the living, and Who gives life to the earth after it is dead: and thus shall you be brought out (from the dead). 20 Among His Signs is this, that He created you from dust; and then— behold, you are men scattered (far and wide)!   21 And among His Signs is this, that He created for you mates from among yourselves, that you may dwell in tranquillity with them, and He has put love and mercy between your (hearts): surely, in that are Signs for those who reflect.

22 And among His Signs is the creation of the heavens and the earth, and the variations in your languages and your colours: surely, in that are Signs for those who know.   23 And among His Signs is the sleep that you take by night and by day, and the quest that you (make for livelihood) out of His Bounty: surely, in that are Signs for those who hearken.   24 And among His Signs, He shows you the lightning, by way both of fear and of hope, and He sends down rain from the sky and with it gives life to the earth after it is dead: surely, in that are Signs for those who are wise.

25 And among His Signs is this, that heaven and earth stand by His command: then when He calls you, by a single call, from the earth, behold, you (straightway) come forth.   26 To Him belongs every being that is in the heavens and on earth: all are devoutly obedient to Him.   27 It is He Who begins (the process of) creation; then repeats it; and for Him it is most easy. To Him belongs the loftiest similitude (we can think of) in the heavens and the earth: for He is Exalted in Might, full of wisdom.

28 He does propound to you a similitude from your own (experience): do you have partners among those whom your right hands possess, to share as equals in the wealth We have bestowed on you? Do you fear them as you fear each other? Thus do We explain the Signs in detail to a people that understand.   29 No, the wrongdoers (merely) follow their own lusts, being devoid of

knowledge. But who will guide those whom Allah leaves astray? To them there will be no helpers.

30 So set you your face steadily and truly to the Faith: (Establish) Allah's handiwork according to the pattern on which He has made mankind: no change (let there be) in the work (wrought) by Allah: that is the true Religion: but most among mankind understand not. 31 Turn you back in repentance to Him, and fear Him: establish regular prayers, and be not you among those who join gods with Allah— 32 Those who split up their Religion, and become (mere) Sects— each party rejoicing in that which is with itself!

33 When trouble touches men, they cry to their Lord, turning back to Him in repentance: but when He gives them a taste of Mercy from Himself, behold, some of them pay part-worship to other gods besides their Lord— 34 (As if) to show their ingratitude for the (favours) We have bestowed on them! Then enjoy (your brief day); but soon will you know (your folly). 35 Or have We sent down authority to them, which points out to them the things to which they pay part-worship?

36 When We give men a taste of Mercy, they exult thereat: and when some evil afflicts them because of what their (own) hands have sent forth, behold, they are in despair! 37 See they not that Allah enlarges the provision and restricts it, to whomsoever He pleases? Surely, in that are Signs for those who believe. 38 So give what is due to kindred, the needy, and the wayfarer. That is best for those who seek the Countenance, of Allah, and it is they who will prosper. 39 That which you lend on interest for increase through the property of (other) people, will have no increase with Allah: but that which you give out for charity, seeking the Countenance of Allah, (will increase): it is these who will get a recompense multiplied.

40 It is Allah Who has created you: further, He has provided for your sustenance; then He will cause you to die; and again He will give you life. Are there any of your (false) "Partners" who can do any single one of these things? Glory to Him! and High is He above the partners they attribute (to Him)! 41 Mischief has

appeared on land and sea because of (the meed) that the hands of men have earned, that (Allah) may give them a taste of some of their deeds: in order that they may turn back (from Evil). 42 Say: "Travel through the earth and see what was the End of those before (you): most of them worshipped others besides Allah."

43 But set you your face to the right Religion before there comes from Allah the Day which there is no chance of averting: on that Day shall men be divided (in two). 44 Those who reject Faith will suffer from that rejection: and those who work righteousness will spread their couch (of repose) for themselves (in heaven): 45 That He may reward those who believe and work righteous deeds, out of His Bounty. For He loves not those who reject Faith.

46 Among His Signs is this, that He sends the Winds, as heralds of Glad Tidings, giving you a taste of His (Grace and) Mercy— that the ships may sail (majestically) by His Command and that you may seek of His Bounty: in order that you may be grateful. 47 We did indeed send, before you, Messengers to their (respective) peoples, and they came to them with Clear Signs: then, to those who transgressed, we meted out Retribution: and it was due from Us to aid those who believed.

48 It is Allah Who sends the Winds, and they raise the Clouds: then does He spread them in the sky as He wills, and break them into fragments, until you see raindrops issue from the midst thereof: then when He has made them reach such of His servants as He wills behold, they do rejoice!— 49 Even though, before they received (the rain)—just before this— they were dumb with despair! 50 Then contemplate (O man!) the Tokens of Allah's Mercy!—How He gives life to the earth after its death: surely, the Same will give life to the men who are dead: for He has power over all things. 51 And if We (but) send a Wind from which they see (their tilth) turn yellow—behold, they become, thereafter, ungrateful (Unbelievers)! 52 So, surely, you can not make the dead to hear, nor can you make the deaf to hear the call, when they show their backs and turn away. 53 Nor can you lead back the blind from their straying: only those will you make to hear, who believe in Our Signs and submit (their wills in Islam).

54 It is Allah Who created you in a state of (helpless) weakness, then gave (you) strength after weakness, then, after strength, gave (you) weakness and a hoary head: He creates as He wills, and it is He Who has all knowledge and power. 55 On the Day that the Hour (of reckoning) will be established, the transgressors will swear that they tarried not but an hour: thus were they used to being deluded! 56 But those endued with knowledge and faith will say: "Indeed you did tarry, within Allah's Decree, to the Day of Resurrection, and this is the Day of Resurrection: but you— you were not aware!" 57 So on that Day no excuse of theirs will avail the Transgressors, nor will they be allowed (then) to seek grace (by repentance).

58 Surely, We have propounded for men, in this Qur'ān every kind of Parable: but if you bring to them any Sign, the Unbelievers are sure to say, "You do nothing but talk vanities." 59 Thus does Allah seal up the hearts of those who understand not. 60 So patiently persevere: for surely, the promise of Allah is true: nor let those shake your firmness, who have (themselves) no certainty of faith.

31. LUQMĀN

In the name of Allah, Most Gracious, Most Merciful.

1 *Alif Lām Mīm.* 2 These are Verses of the Wise Book— 3 A Guide and a Mercy to the Doers of Good— 4 Those who establish regular Prayer, and give zakat, and have (in their hearts) sure faith in the Hereafter. 5 These are on (true) guidance from their Lord: and these are the ones who will prosper.

6 But there are, among men, those who purchase idle tales, without knowledge (or meaning), to mislead (men) from the Path of Allah and throw ridicule (on the Path): for such there will be a humiliating chastisement. 7 When Our Signs are rehearsed to such a one, he turns away in arrogance, as if he heard them not, as if there were deafness in both his ears: announce to him a grievous chastisement. 8 For those who believe and work righteous deeds, there will be Gardens of Bliss— 9 To dwell

therein. The promise of Allah is true: and He is Exalted in Power, Wise.

10 He created the heavens without any pillars that you can see; He set on the earth mountains standing firm, lest it should shake with you; and He scattered through it beasts of all kinds. We send down rain from the sky, and produce on the earth every kind of noble creature, in pairs. 11 Such is the Creation of Allah: now show Me what is there that others besides Him have created: no, but the Transgressors are in manifest error.

12 We bestowed (in the past) wisdom on Luqmān: "Show (your) gratitude to Allah." Any who is (so) grateful does so to the benefit of his own soul: but if any is ungrateful, surely, Allah is free of all wants, worthy of all praise. 13 Behold, Luqmān said to his son by way of instruction: "O my son! Join not in worship (others) with Allah: for false worship is indeed the highest wrongdoing."

14 And We have enjoined on man (to be good) to his parents: in travail upon travail did his mother bear him, and in years twain was his weaning: (hear the command), "Show gratitude to Me and to your parents: to Me is (your final) Goal. 15 "But if they strive to make you join in worship with Me things of which you have no knowledge, obey them not; yet bear them company in this life with justice (and consideration), and, follow the way of those who turn to me (in love): in the End the return of you all is to Me, and I will tell you the truth (and meaning) of all that you did."

16 "O my son!" (said Luqmān), "If there be (but) the weight of a mustard-seed and it were (hidden) in a rock, or (anywhere) in the heavens or on earth, Allah will bring it forth: for Allah understands the finest mysteries, (and) is well-acquainted (with them). 17 "O my son! establish regular prayer, enjoin what is just, and forbid what is wrong: and bear with patient constancy whatever betide you; for this is firmness (of purpose) in (the conduct of) affairs. 18 "And swell not your cheek (for pride) at men, nor walk in insolence through the earth; for Allah loves not any arrogant boaster. 19 "And be moderate in your pace, and lower your voice; for the harshest of sounds without doubt is the braying of the ass."

20 Do you not see that Allah has subjected to your (use) all things in the heavens and on earth, and has made His bounties flow to you in exceeding measure, (both) seen and unseen? Yet there are among men those who dispute about Allah, without knowledge and without guidance, and without a Book to enlighten them! 21 When they are told to follow the (Revelation) that Allah has sent down, they say: "No, we shall follow the ways that we found our fathers (following)." What! even if it is Satan beckoning them to the chastisement of the (blazing) Fire?

22 Whoever submits his whole self to Allah, and is a doer of good, has grasped indeed the most trustworthy hand-hold: and with Allah rests the End and Decision of (all) affairs. 23 But if any reject Faith, let not his rejection grieve you: to Us is their return, and We shall tell them the truth of their deeds: for Allah knows well all that is in (men's) hearts. 24 We grant them their pleasure for a little while: in the end shall We drive them to a chastisement unrelenting.

25 If you ask them, who it is that created the heavens and the earth, they will certainly say, "Allah." Say: "Praise be to Allah!" But most of them understand not. 26 To Allah belong all things in heaven and earth: surely, Allah is He (that is) free of all wants, Worthy of all Praise. 27 And if all the trees on earth were pens and the Ocean (were ink), with seven Oceans behind it to add to its (supply), yet would not the Words of Allah be exhausted (in the writing): for Allah is Exalted in Power, full of Wisdom.

28 And your creation or your resurrection is in no wise but as an individual soul: for Allah is He Who hears and sees (all things). 29 Do you not see that Allah merges Night into Day and He merges Day into Night; that He has subjected the sun, and the moon (to His Law), each running its course for a term appointed; and that Allah is well-acquainted with all that you do? 30 That is because Allah is the Truth, and because whatever else they invoke besides Him is Falsehood; and because Allah — He is the Most High, Most Great.

31 Do not you see that the ships sail through the Ocean by the Grace of Allah? — that He may show you of His Signs? Surely,

in this are Signs for all who constantly persevere and give thanks. 32 When a wave covers them like the canopy (of clouds), they call to Allah, offering Him sincere devotion. But when He has delivered them safely to land, there are among them those that halt between (right and wrong). But none reject Our Signs except only a perfidious ungrateful (wretch)!

33 O mankind! do your duty to your Lord, and fear (the coming of) a Day when no father can avail at all for his son, nor a son avail at all for his father. Surely, the promise of Allah is true: let not then this present life deceive you, nor let the Chief Deceiver deceive you about Allah. 34 Surely, the knowledge of the Hour is with Allah (alone). It is He Who sends down rain, and He Who knows what is in the wombs. Nor does anyone know what it is that he will earn on the morrow; nor does anyone know in what land he is to die. Surely, with Allah is full knowledge and He is acquainted (with all things).

32. THE PROSTRATION

In the name of Allah, Most Gracious, Most Merciful.

1 *Alif Lām Mīm.* 2 (This is) the revelation of the Book in which there is no doubt— from the Lord of the Worlds. 3 Or do they say, "He has forged it?" No, it is the Truth from your Lord, that you may admonish a people to whom no warner has come before you: in order that they may receive guidance.

4 It is Allah Who has created the heavens and the earth, and all between them, in six Days, then He established Himself on the Throne (of authority): you have none, besides Him, to protect or intercede (for you): will you not then receive admonition? 5 He directs (all) affairs from the heavens to the earth: then it ascends to Him, on a Day, the space whereof will be (as) a thousand years of your reckoning. 6 Such is He, the Knower of all things, hidden and open, the Exalted (in power), the

Merciful— 7 He Who has made everything which He has created Most Good: He began the creation of man with (nothing more than) clay, 8 And made his progeny from a quintessence of the nature of a fluid despised: 9 But He fashioned him in due proportion, and breathed into him of His spirit. And He gave you (the faculties of) hearing and sight and feeling (and understanding): little thanks do you give!

10 And they say: "What! When we lie, hidden and lost, in the earth, shall we indeed be in a Creation renewed?" No, they deny the Meeting with their Lord! 11 Say: "The Angel of Death, put in charge of you, will (duly) take your souls: then shall you be brought back to your Lord." 12 If only you could see when the guilty ones will bend low their heads before their Lord, (saying:) "Our Lord! We have seen and we have heard: now then send us back (to the world): we will work righteousness: for we do indeed (now) believe." 13 If We had so willed, We could certainly have brought every soul its true guidance: but the Word from Me will come true, "I will fill Hell with Jinns and men all together. 14 "Taste you then—for you forgot the Meeting of this Day of yours. And We too will forget you—taste you the Chastisement of Eternity for your (evil) deeds!"

15 Only those believe in Our Signs, who, when they are recited to them, fall down in adoration, and celebrate the praises of their Lord, nor are they (ever) puffed up with pride. 16 They forsake their beds of sleep, the while they call on their Lord, in Fear and Hope: and they spend (in charity) out of the sustenance which We have bestowed on them. 17 Now no person knows what delights of the eye are kept hidden (in reserve) for them—as a reward for their (good) Deeds.

18 Is then the man who believes no better than the man who is rebellious and wicked? Not equal are they. 19 For those who believe and do righteous deeds are Gardens as hospitable homes, for their (good) deeds. 20 As to those who are rebellious and wicked, their abode will be the Fire: every time they wish to get away therefrom, they will be forced back thereinto, and it will be said to them: "Taste you the chastisement of the Fire, the which

you were wont to reject as false." 21 And indeed We will make them taste of the Torment in this (life) prior to the supreme Chastisement, in order that they may (repent and) return. 22 And who does more wrong than one to whom are recited the Signs of his Lord, and who then turns away therefrom? Surely, from those who transgress We shall exact (due) Retribution.

23 We did indeed aforetime give the Book to Moses: be not then in doubt of its reaching (you): and We made it a guide to the Children of Israel. 24 And We appointed, from among them, leaders, giving guidance under Our command, so long as they persevered with patience and continued to have faith in Our Signs. 25 Surely, your Lord will judge between them on the Day of Judgment, in the matters wherein they differ (among themselves). 26 Does it not teach them a lesson, how many generations We destroyed before them, in whose dwellings they (now) walk through? Surely, in that are Signs: do they not then listen?

27 And do they not see that We do drive Rain to parched soil (bare of herbage), and produce therewith crops, providing food for their cattle and themselves? Have they not the vision? 28 They say: "When will this Decision be, if you are telling the truth?" 29 Say: "On the Day of Decision, of no benefit will it be to Unbelievers if they (then) believe! Nor will they be granted a respite." 30 So turn away from them, and wait: they too are waiting.

33. THE CONFEDERATES

In the name of Allah, Most Gracious, Most Merciful.

1 O Prophet! Fear Allah, and hearken not to the Unbelievers and the Hypocrites: surely, Allah is full of knowledge and wisdom. 2 But follow that which comes to you by inspiration from your Lord: for Allah is well acquainted with (all) that you do. 3 And put your trust in Allah, and enough is Allah as a disposer of affairs.

4 Allah has not made for any man two hearts in his (one) body:

nor has He made your wives whom you divorce by ẓihār[a] your mothers: nor has He made your adopted sons your sons. Such is (only) your (manner of) speech by your mouths. But Allah tells (you) the Truth, and He shows the (right) Way. 5 Call them after (the names of) their fathers: that is more just in the sight of Allah. But if you know not their father's (names, call them) your Brothers in faith, or your mawlās (freed men). But there is no blame on you if you make a mistake therein: (what counts is) the intention of your hearts: and Allah is Oft-Forgiving, Most Merciful.

6 The Prophet is closer to the Believers than their own selves, and his wives are their mothers. Blood-relations among each other have closer personal ties, in the Decree of Allah. Than (the Brotherhood of) believers and Muhājirs: nevertheless, you do what is just to your closest friends: such is the writing in the Decree (of Allah).

7 And remember We took from the Prophets their Covenant: as (We did) from you: from Noah, Abraham, Moses, and Jesus the son of Mary: We took from them a solemn Covenant: 8 That (Allah) may question the (custodians) of Truth concerning the Truth they (were charged with): and He has prepared for the Unbelievers a grievous chastisement.

9 O you who believe! Remember the Grace of Allah, (bestowed) on you, when there came down on you hosts (to overwhelm you): but We sent against them a hurricane and forces that you saw not: but Allah sees (clearly) all that you do. 10 Behold! they came on you from above you and from below you, and behold, the eyes became dim and the hearts gaped up to the throats, and you imagined various (vain) thoughts about Allah! 11 In that situation were the Believers tried: they were shaken as by a tremendous shaking.

12 And behold! The Hypocrites and those in whose hearts is a disease (even) say: "Allah and His Messenger promised us nothing but delusions!" 13 Behold! A party among them said: "You men

---

a. *Zihar:* an ancient Arab custom. A husband would pronounce words implying that his wife was like his mother. After that she could not demand her rights as wife, nor could she contract another marriage.

of Yathrib! You cannot stand (the attack)! Therefore go back!"
·and a band of them ask for leave of the Prophet, saying, "Truly
our houses are bare and exposed," though they were not exposed
they intended nothing but to run away. 14 And if an entry had
been effected to them from the sides of the (City), and they had
been incited to sedition, they would certainly have brought it to
pass, with none but a brief delay! 15 And yet they had already
covenanted with Allah not to turn their backs, and a covenant with
Allah must (surely) be answered for. 16 Say: "Running away will
not profit you, if you are running away from death or slaughter;
and even if (you do escape), no more than a brief (respite) will
you be allowed to enjoy!" 17 Say: "Who is it that can screen you
from Allah if it be His wish to give you Punishment or to give
you Mercy?" nor will they find for themselves, besides Allah, any
protector or helper.

18 Surely, Allah knows those among you who keep back (men)
and those who say to their brethren, "Come along to us," but come
not to the fight except for just a little while, 19 Covetous over
you. Then when fear comes, you will see them looking to you,
their eyes revolving, like (those of) one over whom hovers death:
but when the fear is past, they will smite you with sharp tongues,
covetous of goods. Such men have no faith, and so Allah has made
their deeds of none effect: and that is easy for Allah. 20 They
think that the Confederates have not withdrawn; and if the
Confederates should come (again), they would wish they were
in the deserts (wandering) among the Bedouins, and seeking news
about you (from a safe distance); and if they were in your midst,
they would fight but little.

21 You have indeed in the Messenger of Allah a beautiful pattern
(of conduct) for anyone whose hope is in Allah and the Final Day,
and who engages much in the Praise of Allah. 22 When the
Believers saw the Confederate forces, they said: "This is what
Allah and His Messenger had promised us, and Allah and His
Messenger told us what was true." And it only added to their faith
and their zeal in obedience. 23 Among the Believers are men who
have been true to their Covenant with Allah: of them some have
completed their vow (to the extreme), and some (still) wait: but

they have never changed (their determination) in the least: 24 That Allah may reward the men of Truth for their Truth, and punish the Hypocrites if that be His Will, or turn to them in Mercy: for Allah is Oft-Forgiving, Most Merciful.

25 And Allah turned back the Unbelievers for (all) their fury: no advantage did they gain; and enough is Allah for the Believers in their fight. And Allah is full of Strength, able to enforce His Will. 26 And those of the People of the Book who aided them— Allah did take them down from their strongholds and cast terror into their hearts. (So that) some you slew, and some you made captives. 27 And He made you heirs of their lands, their houses, and their goods, and of a land which you had not frequented (before). And Allah has power over all things.

28 O Prophet! say to your Consorts: "If it be that you desire the life of this World, and its glitter—then come! I will provide for your enjoyment and set you free in a handsome manner." 29 But if you seek Allah and His Messenger, and the Home of the Hereafter, surely, Allah has prepared for the well-doers amongst you a great reward. 30 O Consorts of the Prophet! If any of you were guilty of evident unseemly conduct, the Punishment would be doubled to her, and that is easy for Allah.

31 But any of you that is devout in the service of Allah and His Messenger, and works righteousness— to her shall We grant her reward twice: and We have prepared for her a generous Sustenance. 32 O Consorts of the Prophet! You are not like any of the (other) women: if you do fear (Allah), be not too complaisant of speech, lest one in whose heart is a disease should be moved with desire: but speak you a speech (that is) just.

33 And stay quietly in your houses, and make not a dazzling display, like that of the former Times of Ignorance; and establish regular Prayer, and give Zakat; and obey Allah and His Messenger. And Allah only wishes to remove all abomination from you, you Members of the Family, and to make you pure and spotless. 34 And recite what is rehearsed to you in your homes, of the Signs of Allah and His Wisdom: for Allah understands the finest mysteries and is well-acquainted (with them).

35 For Muslim men and women—for believing men and women, for devout men and women, for true men and women, for men and women who are patient and constant, for men and women who humble themselves, for men and women who give in Charity, for men and women who fast, for men and women who guard their chastity, and for men and women who engage much in Allah's praise— for them has Allah prepared forgiveness and great reward.

36 It is not fitting for a Believer, man or woman, when a matter has been decided by Allah and His Messenger to have any option about their decision: if anyone disobeys Allah and His Messenger, he is indeed on a clearly wrong Path.

37 Behold! You did say to one who had received the grace of Allah and your favour: "Retain you (in wedlock) your wife, and fear Allah." But you did hide in your heart that which Allah was about to make manifest: you did fear the people, but it is more fitting that you should fear Allah. Then when Zayd had dissolved (his marriage) with her, (with the necessary formality), We joined her in marriage to you: in order that (in future) there may be no difficulty to the Believers in (the matter of) marriage with the wives of their adopted sons, when the latter have dissolved with the necessary (formality) (their marriage) with them. And Allah's command must be fulfilled.

38 There can be no difficulty to the Prophet in what Allah has indicated to him as a duty. It was the practice (approved) by Allah amongst those of old that have passed away, and the command of Allah is a decree determined. 39 (It is the practice of those) who preach the Messages of Allah, and fear Him, and fear none but Allah. And enough is Allah to call (men) to account. 40 Muḥammad is not the father of any of your men, but (he is) the Messenger of Allah, and the Seal of the Prophets: and Allah has full knowledge of all things.

41 O you who believe! Celebrate the praises of Allah, and do this often; 42 And glorify Him morning and evening. 43 He it is Who sends blessings on you, as do His angels, that He may bring you out from the depths of Darkness into Light: and He

is Full of Mercy to the Believers. 44 Their salutation on the Day they meet Him will be "Peace!"; and He has prepared for them a generous Reward.

45 O Prophet! Truly We have sent you as a Witness, a Bearer of Glad Tidings, and a Warner— 46 And as one who invites to Allah's (Grace) by His leave, and as a lamp spreading light. 47 Then give the Glad Tidings to the Believers, that they shall have from Allah a very great Bounty. 48 And obey not (the behests) of the Unbelievers and the Hypocrites, and disregard their insolence, but put your Trust in Allah. For enough is Allah as a Disposer of affairs.

49 O you who believe! when you marry believing women, and then divorce them before you have touched them, no period of 'iddah have you to count in respect of them: so give them a present. And release them in a handsome manner.

50 O Prophet! We have made lawful to you your wives to whom you have paid their dowers; and those whom your right hand possesses out of the captives of war whom Allah has assigned to you; and daughters of your paternal uncles and aunts, and daughters of your maternal uncles and aunts, who migrated (from Makkah) with you; and any believing woman who dedicates herself to the Prophet if the Prophet wishes to wed her—this only for you, and not for the Believers (at large); We know what We have appointed for them as to their wives and those whom their right hands possess—in order that there should be no difficulty for you. And Allah is Oft-Forgiving, Most Merciful.

51 You may defer (the turn of) any of them that you please, and you may receive any you please: and there is no blame on you if you invite one whose (turn) you have set aside. This were nearer to the cooling of their eyes, the prevention of their grief, and their satisfaction—that of all of them—with that which you have to give them: and Allah knows (all) that is in your hearts: and Allah is All-Knowing, Most Forbearing. 52 It is not lawful for you (to marry more) women after this, nor to change them for (other) wives, even though their beauty attract you, except any your right hand should possess (as handmaidens): and Allah does watch over all things.

53 O you who believe! Enter not the Prophet's houses—until leave is given you— for a meal, (and then) nor (so early as) to wait for its preparation: but when you are invited, enter; and when you have taken your meal, disperse, without seeking familiar talk. Such (behaviour) annoys the Prophet: he is shy to ask you to go, but Allah is not shy (to tell you) the truth. And when you ask (his ladies) for anything you want, ask them from the front of a screen: that makes for greater purity for your hearts and for theirs. Nor is it right for you that you should annoy Allah's Messenger, or that you should marry his widows after him at any time. Truly such a thing is in Allah's sight an enormity. 54 Whether you reveal anything or conceal it, surely, Allah has full knowledge of all things.

55 There is no blame (on these ladies if they appear) before their fathers or their sons, their brothers, or their brothers' sons, or their sisters' sons, or their women, or the (slaves) whom their right hands possess. And, (O women!), fear Allah; for Allah is Witness to all things.

56 Allah and His Angels send blessings on the Prophet: O you that believe! send you blessings on him, and salute him with all respect. 57 Those who annoy Allah and His Messenger—Allah has cursed them in this world and in the Hereafter, and has prepared for them a humiliating Punishment. 58 And those who annoy believing men and women undeservedly, bear (on themselves) a calumny and a glaring sin.

59 O Prophet! Tell your wives and daughters, and the believing women, that they should cast their outer garments over their persons (when go out): that is most convenient, that they should be known (as such) and not molested. And Allah is Oft-Forgiving, Most Merciful. 60 Truly, if the Hypocrites, and those in whose hearts is a disease, and those who spread slanderous rumours in the City, desist not, We shall certainly stir you up against them: then will they not be able to stay in it as your neighbours for any length of time. 61 They shall have a curse on them: wherever they are found, they shall be seized and slain (without mercy). 62 (Such was) the practice (approved) by Allah among those who lived

aforetime: no change will you find in the practice (approved) by Allah.

63 Men ask you concerning the Hour: say, "The knowledge thereof is with Allah (alone):" and what will make you understand?—perchance the Hour is near! 64 Surely, Allah has cursed the Unbelievers and prepared for them a Blazing Fire— 65 To dwell therein forever: no protector will they find, nor helper. 66 The Day that their faces will be turned upside down in the Fire, they will say: "Woe to us! Would that we had obeyed Allah and obeyed the Messenger!" 67 And they would say: "Our Lord! We obeyed our chiefs and our great ones, and they misled us as to the (right) Path. 68 "Our Lord! Give them double Chastisement and curse them with a very great Curse!"

69 O you who believe! Be you not like those who vexed and pained Moses, but Allah cleared him of the (calumnies) they had uttered: and he was honourable in Allah's sight. 70 O you who believe! Fear Allah, and (always) say a word directed to the Right: 71 That He may make your conduct whole and sound and forgive you your sins: he that obeys Allah and His Messenger, has already attained the highest achievement.

72 We did indeed offer the Trust to the Heavens and the Earth and the Mountains; but they refused to undertake it, being afraid thereof: but man undertook it— he was indeed unjust and foolish— 73 (With the result) that Allah has to punish the Hypocrites, men and women, and the Unbelievers, men and women, and Allah turns in Mercy to the Believers, men and women: for Allah is Oft-Forgiving, Most Merciful.

34. SHEBA

In the name of Allah, Most Gracious, Most Merciful.

1 Praise be to Allah, to Whom belong all things in the heavens and on earth: to Him be Praise in the Hereafter: and He is Full of Wisdom, acquainted with all things. 2 He knows all that goes into the earth, and all that comes out thereof; all that comes down

from the sky and all that ascends thereto and He is the Most Merciful, the Oft-Forgiving.

3 The Unbelievers say, "Never to us will come the Hour:" say, "No! but most surely, by my Lord, it will come upon you—by Him Who knows the unseen—from Whom is not hidden the least little atom in the heavens or on earth: nor is there anything less than that, or greater, but is in the Record Perspicuous: 4 That He may reward those who believe and work deeds of righteousness: for such is Forgiveness and a Sustenance most Generous." 5 But those who strive against Our Signs, to frustrate them—for such will be a Penalty—a Punishment most humiliating. 6 And those to whom knowledge has come see that the (Revelation) sent down to you from your Lord—that is the Truth, and that it guides to the Path of the Exalted (in Might), Worthy of all praise.

7 The Unbelievers say (in ridicule): "Shall we point out to you a man that will tell you, when you are all scattered to pieces in disintegration, that you shall (then be raised) in a New Creation? 8 "Has he invented a falsehood against Allah, or has an evil spirit (seized) him?"—No, it is those who believe not in the Hereafter, that are in for chastisement, and in farthest Error. 9 See they not what is before them and behind them, of the sky and the earth? If We wished, We could cause the earth to swallow them up, or cause a piece of the sky to fall upon them. Surely in this is a Sign for every devotee that turns to Allah (in repentance).

10 We bestowed Grace aforetime on David from Ourselves: "O you Mountains! Echo you back the Praises of Allah with him! and you birds (also)! And We made the iron soft for him— 11 (Commanding), "Make you coats of mail, balancing well the rings of chain armour, and work righteousness; for be sure I see (clearly) all that you do."

12 And to Solomon (We made) the Wind (obedient): its early morning (stride) was a month's (journey), and its evening (stride) was a month's (journey); and We made a Font of molten brass to flow for him; and there were Jinns that worked in front of him, by the leave of his Lord, and if any of them turned aside from Our Command, We made him taste of the Chastisement of the

Blazing Fire. 13 They worked for him as he desired, (making) Arches, Images, Basons as large as Reservoirs, and (cooking) Cauldrons fixed (in their places): "Work you, sons of David, with thanks! But few of My servants are grateful!"

14 Then, when We decreed (Solomon's) death, nothing showed them his death except a little worm of the earth, which kept (slowly) gnawing away at his staff: so when he fell down, the Jinns saw plainly that if they had known the Unseen, they would not have tarried in the humiliating punishment (of their Task).

15 There was, for Sabā', aforetime, a Sign in their homeland— two Gardens to the right and to the left. "Eat of the Sustenance (provided) by your Lord, and be grateful to Him: a territory fair and happy, and a Lord Oft-Forgiving!" 16 But they turned away (from Allah), and We sent against them the Flood (released) from the Dams, and We converted their two garden (rows) into "gardens" producing bitter fruit, and tamarisks, and some few (stunted) Lote-trees. 17 That was the Requital We gave them because they ungratefully rejected Faith: and never do We give (such) requital except to such as are ungrateful rejecters.

18 Between them and the Cities on which We had poured our blessings, We had placed cities in prominent positions, and between them We had appointed stages of journey in due proportion: "Travel therein, secure, by night and by day." 19 But they said: "Our Lord! Place longer distances between our journey-stages:" But they wronged themselves (therein). At length We made them as a tale (that is told), and We dispersed them all in scattered fragments. Surely in this are Signs for every (soul that is) patiently constant and grateful.

20 And on them did Satan prove true his idea, and they followed him, all but a party that believed. 21 But he had no authority over them—except that We might test the man who believes in the Hereafter from him who is in doubt concerning it: and your Lord does watch over all things.

22 Say: "Call upon other (gods) whom you fancy, besides Allah: they have no power—not the weight of an atom—in the heavens or on earth: no (sort of) share have they therein, nor is any of

them a helper to Allah. 23 "No intercession can avail in His Presence, except for those for whom He has granted permission. So far (is this the case) that, when terror is removed from their hearts (at the Day of Judgment, then) will they say, 'What is it that your Lord commanded?' They will say, 'That which is true and just; and He is the Most High, Most Great.'"

24 Say: "Who gives you sustenance, from the heavens and the earth?" Say: "It is Allah; and certain it is that either we or you are on right guidance or in manifest error!" 25 Say: "You shall not be questioned as to our sins, nor shall we be questioned as to what you do." 26 Say: "Our Lord will gather us together and will in the end decide the matter between us (and you) in truth and justice: and He is the One to decide, the One Who knows all." 27 Say: "Show me those whom you have joined with Him as partners: by no means (can you). No, He is Allah, The Exalted in Power, The Wise."

28 We have not sent you but as a universal (Messenger) to men, giving them glad tidings, and warning them (against sin), but most men understand not. 29 They say: "When will this promise (come to pass) if you are telling the truth?" 30 Say: "The appointment to you is for a Day, which you cannot put back for an hour nor put forward."

31 The Unbelievers say: "We shall neither believe in this scripture nor in (any) that (came) before it." Could you but see when the wrong-doers will be made to stand before their Lord, throwing back the word (of blame) on one another! Those who had been weak will say to the arrogant ones: "Had it not been for you, we should certainly have been believers!" 32 The arrogant ones will say to those who had been weak: "Was it we who kept you back from Guidance after it reached you? No, rather, it was you who transgressed." 33 Those who had been weak will say to the arrogant ones:" No! it was a plot (of yours) by day and by night: behold! You (constantly) ordered us to be ungrateful to Allah and to attribute equals to Him!" They will filled with remorse when they see the Chastisement: We shall put yokes on the necks of the unbelievers: it would only be a requital for their (ill) Deeds.

34 Never did We send a warner to a population, but the wealthy ones among them said: "We believe not in the (Message) with which you have been sent."　35 They said: "We have more in wealth and in sons, and we cannot be chastised."　36 Say: "Surely my Lord enlarges and restricts the Provision to whom He pleases, but most men understand not."　37 It is not your wealth nor your sons, that will bring you nearer to Us in degree: but only those who believe and work righteousness—these are the ones for whom there is a multiplied Reward for their deeds, while secure they (reside) in the dwellings on high!　38 Those who strive against Our Signs, to frustrate them, will be given over into Chastisement. 39 Say: "Surely my Lord enlarges and restricts the Sustenance to such of His servants as He pleases: and nothing do you spend in the least (in His Cause) but He replaces it: for He is the Best of those who grant Sustenance.

40 One Day He will gather them all together, and say to the angels, "Was it you that these men used to worship?"　41 They will say, "Glory to You! our (tie) is with You—as Protector—not with them. No, but they worshipped the Jinns: most of them believed in them."　42 So on that Day no power shall they have over each other, for profit or harm: and We shall say to the wrong-doers, "Taste you the Chastisement of the Fire—the which you were wont to deny!"

43 When Our Clear Signs are rehearsed to them, they say, "This is only a man who wishes to hinder you from the (worship) which your fathers practised." And they say, "This is only a falsehood invented!" And the Unbelievers say of the Truth when it comes to them, "This is nothing but evident magic!"　44 But We had not given them Books which they could study, nor sent Messengers to them before you as Warners.　45 And their predecessors rejected (the Truth); these have not received a tenth of what We had granted to those: yet when they rejected my Messengers, how (terrible) was My rejection (of them)!

46 Say: "I do admonish you on one point: that you do stand up before Allah—(it may be) in pairs, or (it may be) singly—and reflect (within yourselves): your Companion is not possessed: he

is no less than a warner to you, in face of a terrible chastisement."
47 Say: "No reward do I ask of you: it is (all) in your interest: my reward is only due from Allah: and He is witness to all things."

48 Say: "Surely my Lord does cast the (mantle of) Truth (over His servants)— He that has full knowledge of (all) that is hidden."
49 Say: "The Truth has arrived, and Falsehood neither begins anything new, nor repeats anything." 50 Say: "If I am astray, I only stray to the loss of my own soul: but if I receive guidance, it is because of the inspiration of my Lord to me: it is He Who hears all things, and is (ever) near."

51 If you could but see when they will quake with terror; but then there will be no escape (for them), and they will be seized from a position (quite) near. 52 And they will say, "We do believe (now) in the (Truth);" but how could they receive (Faith) from a position (so) far off— 53 Seeing that they did reject faith (entirely) before, and that they (continually) cast (slanders) on the Unseen from a position far off? 54 And between them and their desires, is placed a barrier, as was done in the past with their partisans: for they were indeed in suspicious (disquieting) doubt.

35. THE ORIGINATOR

In the name of Allah, Most Gracious, Most Merciful.

1 Praise be to Allah, who created (out of nothing) the heavens and the earth, who made the angels, messengers with wings— two, or three, or four (pairs): He adds to Creation as He pleases: for Allah has power over all things. 2 What Allah out of His Mercy does bestow on mankind there is none can withhold: what He does withhold, there is none can grant, apart from Him: and He is the Exalted in Power, Full of Wisdom.

3 O men! Call to mind the grace of Allah unto you! Is there a Creator, other than Allah, to give you sustenance from heaven or earth? There is no god but He: how then are you deluded away

from the Truth? 4 And if they reject you, so were Messengers rejected before you: to Allah go back for decision all affairs.

5 O men! Certainly the promise of Allah is true. Let not then this present life deceive you, nor let the Chief Deceiver deceive you about Allah. 6 Surely Satan is an enemy to you: so treat him as an enemy. He only invites his adherents, that they may become companions of the Blazing Fire. 7 For those who reject Allah, is a terrible Chastisement: but for those who believe and work righteous deeds, is Forgiveness, and a magnificent Reward.

8 Is he, then, to whom the evil of his conduct is made alluring, so that he looks upon it as good, (equal to one who is rightly guided)? For Allah leaves to stray whom He wills, and guides whom He wills. So let not your soul go out in (vainly) sighing after them: for Allah knows well all that they do!

9 It is Allah Who sends forth the Winds, so that they raise up the Clouds, and We drive them to a land that is dead, and revive the earth therewith after its death: even so (will be) the Resurrection! 10 If any do seek for glory and power— to Allah belong all glory and power. To Him mount up (all) words of Purity: it is He Who exalts each Deed of Righteousness. Those that lay Plots of Evil—for them is a Chastisement terrible; and the plotting of such will be void (of result).

11 And Allah did create you from dust; then from a sperm-drop; then He made you in pairs. And no female conceives, or lays down (her load), but with His knowledge. Nor is a man long-lived granted length of days, nor is a part cut off from his life, but is in a Book (ordained). All this is easy to Allah.

12 Nor are the two bodies of flowing water alike—the one palatable, sweet, and pleasant to drink, and the other, salty and bitter. Yet from each (kind of water) do you eat flesh fresh and tender, and you extract ornaments to wear; and you see the ships therein that plough the waves, that you may seek (thus) of the Bounty of Allah that you may be grateful. 13 He merges Night into Day, and He merges Day into Night, and He has subjected the sun and the moon (to His Law). each one runs its course for

a term appointed. Such is Allah your Lord: to Him belongs all Dominion. And those whom you invoke besides Him own not even a straw. 14 If you invoke them, they will not listen to your call, and if they were to listen, they cannot answer your (prayer). On the Day of Judgment they will reject your "Partnership." And none, (O man!) can tell you (the Truth) like the One who is acquainted with all things.

15 O you men! It is you that have need of Allah: but Allah is the One Free of all wants, worthy of all praise. 16 If He so pleased, He could blot you out and bring in a New Creation. 17 Nor is that (at all) difficult for Allah. 18 Nor can a bearer of burdens bear another's burden. If one heavily laden should call another to (bear) his load. Not the least portion of it can be carried (by the other). Even though he be nearly related. You can but warn such as fear their Lord Unseen and establish regular Prayer. And whoever purifies himself does so for the benefit of his own soul; and the destination (of all) is to Allah.

19 The blind and the seeing are not alike; 20 Nor are the depths of Darkness and the Light; 21 Nor are the (chilly) shade and the (genial) heat of the sun: 22 Nor are alike those that are living and those that are dead. Allah can make any that He wills to hear; but you can not make those to hear who are (buried) in graves. 23 You are no other than a warner. 24 Surely We have sent you in truth, as a bearer of Glad Tidings, and as a warner: and there never was a people, without a warner having lived among them (in the past). 25 And if they reject you, so did their predecessors, to whom came their Messengers with Clear Signs, Scriptures, and the Book of Enlightenment. 26 In the end did I punish those who rejected faith: and how (terrible) was My rejection (of them)!

27 See you not that Allah sends down rain from the sky? With it We then bring out produce of various colours. And in the mountains are tracts white and red, of various shades of colour, and black intense in hue. 28 And so amongst men and crawling creatures and cattle, are they of various colours. Those truly fear Allah, among His Servants, who have knowledge: for Allah is Exalted in Might, Oft-Forgiving.

29 Those who rehearse the Book of Allah, establish regular Prayer, and spend (in Charity) out of what We have provided for them, secretly and openly, hope for a Commerce that will never fail: 30 For He will pay them their meed, no, He will give them (even) more out of His Bounty: for He is Oft-Forgiving, Most Ready to appreciate (service). 31 That which We have revealed to you of the Book is the Truth—confirming what was (revealed) before it: for Allah is assuredly—with respect to His Servants—well acquainted and fully Observant.

32 Then We have given the Book for inheritance to such of Our Servants as We have chosen: but there are among them some who wrong their own souls; some who follow a middle course; and some who are, by Allah's leave, foremost in good deeds; that is the highest Grace. 33 Gardens of Eternity will they enter: therein will they be adorned with bracelets of gold and pearls; and their garments there will be of silk. 34 And they will say: "Praise be to Allah, who has removed from us (all) sorrow: for our Lord is indeed Oft-Forgiving ready to appreciate (service): 35 "Who has, out of His Bounty, settled us in a Home that will last: no toil nor sense of weariness shall touch us therein."

36 But those who reject (Allah)—for them will be the Fire of Hell: no term shall be determined for them, so they should die, nor shall its Chastisement be lightened for them. Thus do We reward every ungrateful one! 37 Therein will they cry aloud (for assistance): "Our Lord! Bring us out: we shall work righteousness, not the (deeds) we used to do!"—"Did We not give you long enough life so that he that would should receive admonition? And (moreover) the warner came to you. So taste you (the fruits of your deeds): for the wrong-doers their is no helper."

38 Surely Allah knows (all) the hidden things of the heavens and the earth: surely He has full knowledge of all that is in (men's) hearts. 39 He it is That has made you inheritors in the earth: if, then, any do reject (Allah), their rejection (works) against themselves: their rejection but adds to the odium for the Unbelievers in the sight of their Lord: their rejection but adds to (their own) undoing.

40 Say: "Have you seen (these) 'Partners' of yours whom you call upon besides Allah? Show me what it is they have created in the (wide) earth. Or have they a share in the heavens? Or have We given them a Book from which they (can derive) clear (evidence)?—No, the wrongdoers promise each other nothing but delusions. 41 It is Allah Who sustains the heavens and the earth, lest they cease (to function): and if they should fail, there is none— not one—can sustain them thereafter: surely He is Most Forbearing, Oft-Forgiving.

42 They swore their strongest oaths by Allah that if a warner came to them, they would follow his guidance better than any (other) of the Peoples: but when a warner came to them, it only increased their flight (from righteousness)— 43 On account of their arrogance in the land and their plotting of Evil, but the plotting of Evil will hem in only the authors thereof. Now are they but looking for the way the ancients were dealt with? But no change will you find in Allah's way (of dealing): no turning off will you find in Allah's way (of dealing). 44 Do they not travel through the earth, and see what was the End of those before them—though they were superior to them in strength? Nor is Allah to be frustrated by anything whatever in the heavens or on earth: for He is All-Knowing. All-Powerful.

45 If Allah were to punish men according to what they deserve, He would not leave on the back of the (earth) a single living creature: but He gives them respite for a stated Term: when their Term expires, surely Allah has in His sight all His servants.

36. YĀ SĪN

In the name of Allah, Most Gracious, Most Merciful.

1 *Yā Sīn*. 2 By the Qur'ān, full of Wisdom— 3 You are indeed one of the Messengers, 4 On a Straight Way. 5 It is a Revelation sent down by (Him), the Exalted in Might, Most Merciful, 6 In order that you may warn a people, whose forefathers had received no warning, and who therefore remain heedless (of the Signs of Allah).

7 The Word is proved true against the greater part of them: for they do not believe. 8 We have put yokes round their necks right up to their chins, so that their heads are forced up (and they cannot bow). 9 And We have put a bar in front of them and a bar behind them, and further, We have covered them up; so that they cannot see. 10 The same is it to them whether you warn them or you do not warn them: they will not believe. 11 You can but warn such a one as follows the Message and fears the (Lord) Most Gracious, unseen: give such a one, therefore, good tidings, of Forgiveness and a Reward most generous.

12 Surely We shall give life to the dead, and We record that which they send before and that which they leave behind, and of all things have We taken account in a clear Book (of evidence).

13 Set forth to them, by way of a parable, the (story of) the Companions of the City. Behold!, there came Messengers to it. 14 When We (first) sent to them two Messengers, they rejected them: but We strengthened them with a third: they said, "Truly, we have been sent on a mission to you." 15 The (people) said: "You are only men like ourselves; and (Allah) Most Gracious sends no sort of revelation: you do nothing but lie." 16 They said: "Our Lord does know that we have been sent on a mission to you: 17 "And our duty is only to convey the clear Message." 18 The (people) said: "For us, We augur an evil omen from you: if you desist not, we will certainly stone you. And a grievous punishment indeed will be inflicted on you by us." 19 They said: "Your evil omens are with yourselves: (deem you this an evil omen). If you are warned? No, but you are a people transgressing all bounds!"

20 Then there came running, from the farthest part of the City, a man, saying, "O my people! Obey the Messengers: 21 "Obey those who ask no reward of you (for themselves), and who have themselves received Guidance.

22 "It would not be reasonable of me if I did not serve Him Who created me, and to Whom you shall (all) be brought back. 23 "Shall I take (other) gods besides Him? If (Allah) the Most Gracious should intend some adversity for me, of no use whatever will be their intercession for me, nor can they deliver me. 24 "I

would indeed, if I were to do so, be in manifest Error. 25 "For me, I have faith in the Lord of you (all): listen, then, to me!" 26 It was said: "Enter you the Garden." He said: "Ah me! Would that my People knew (what I know)! — 27 "For that my Lord has granted me Forgiveness and has enrolled me among those held in honour!"

28 And We sent not down against his People, after him, any hosts from heaven, nor was it needful for Us so to do. 29 It was no more than a single mighty Blast, and behold! they were (like ashes) quenched and silent. 30 Ah! alas for (My) servants! There comes not a Messenger to them but they mock him! 31 See they not how many generations before them We destroyed? Not to them will they return: 32 But each one of them all—will be brought before Us (for Judgment).

33 A Sign for them is the earth that is dead: We do give it life, and produce grain therefrom, of which you do eat. 34 And We produce therein orchards with date-palms and vines, and We cause springs to gush forth therein: 35 That they may enjoy the fruits of this (artistry): it was not their hands that made this: will they not then give thanks? 36 Glory to Allah, Who created in pairs all things that the earth produces, as well as their own (human) kind and (other) things of which they have no knowledge.

37 And a Sign for them is the Night: We withdraw therefrom the Day, and behold they are plunged in darkness; 38 And the sun runs his course into a resting place for him: that is the decree of (Him), the Exalted in Might, the All-Knowing. 39 And the Moon— We have measured for it stations (to traverse) till she returns like the old (and withered) lower part of a date-stalk. 40 It is not permitted to the Sun to catch up the Moon, nor can the Night outstrip the Day: each (just) swims along in (its own) orbit (according to Law).

41 And a Sign for them is that We bore their race (through the Flood) in the loaded Ark; 42 And We have created for them similar (vessels) on which they ride. 43 If it were Our Will, We could drown· them: then would there be no helper (to hear their cry), nor could they be delivered 44 Except by way of Mercy from Us, and by way of (worldly) convenience (to serve them) for a time.

45 When they are told, "Fear that which is before you and that which will be after you, in order that you may receive Mercy," (they turn back). 46 Not a Sign comes to them from among the Signs of their Lord, but they turn away therefrom. 47 And when they are told, "Spend of (the bounties) with which Allah has provided you," the Unbelievers say to those who believe: "Shall we then feed those whom, if Allah had so willed, He would have fed, (Himself)?— "You are in nothing but manifest error."

48 Further, they say, "When will this promise (come to pass), if what you say is true?" 49 They will not (have to) wait for nothing but a single Blast: it will seize them while they are yet disputing among themselves! 50 No (chance) will they then have, by will, to dispose (of their affairs), nor to return to their own people! 51 The trumpet shall be sounded, when behold! from the sepulchres (men) will rush forth to their Lord! 52 They will say: "Ah! woe unto us! Who has raised us up from our beds of repose?"... (A voice will say:) "This is what (Allah) Most Gracious had promised. And true was the word of the Messengers!" 53 It will be no more than a single Blast, when lo! they will all be brought up before Us!

54 Then, on that Day, not a soul will be wronged in the least, and you shall but be repaid the meeds of your past Deeds. 55 Surely the Companions of the Garden shall that Day have joy in all that they do; 56 They and their spouses will be in groves of (cool) shade, reclining on raised couches; 57 (Every) fruit (enjoyment) will be there for them; they shall have whatever they call for; 58 "Peace!"—a Word (of salutation) from a Lord Most Merciful!

59 "And O you in sin! get you apart this Day! 60 "Did I not enjoin on you, O you children of Adam, that you should not worship Satan; for that he was to you an enemy avowed?— 61 "And that you should worship Me, (for that) this was the Straight Way? 62 "But he did lead astray a great multitude of you. Did you not, then, understand? 63 "This is the Hell of which you were (repeatedly) warned! 64 "Embrace you the (Fire) this Day, for that you (persistently) rejected (Truth)." 65 That Day shall We set a seal on their mouths. But their hands will speak to Us, and their feet bear witness, to all that they did.

66 If it had been Our Will, We could surely have blotted out their eyes; then should they have run about groping for the Path, but how could they have seen? 67 And if it had been Our Will, We could have transformed them in their places; then should they have been unable to move about, nor could they have returned (after error). 68 If We grant long life to any, We cause him to be reversed in nature: will they not then understand?

69 We have not instructed the (Prophet) in Poetry, nor is it meet for him: this is no less than a Message and a Qur'ān making things clear: 70 That it may give admonition to any (who are) alive, and that the word may be proved against those who reject (Truth).

71 See they not that it is We Who have created for them—among the things which Our hands have fashioned—cattle, which are under their dominion?— 72 And that We have subjected them to their (use)? Of them some do carry them and some they eat: 73 And they have (other) benefits from them (besides), and they get (milk) to drink. Will they not then be grateful? 74 Yet they take (for worship) gods other than Allah, (hoping) that they might be helped! 75 They have not the power to help them: but they will be brought up (before Our Judgment Seat) as a troop (to be condemned). 76 Let not their speech, then, grieve you. Surely We know what they hide as well as what they disclose.

77 Does not man see that it is We Who created him from sperm? Yet behold! he (stands forth) as an open adversary! 78 And he makes comparisons for Us, and forgets his own (Origin and) Creation: he says, "Who can give life to (dry) bones and decomposed ones (at that)?" 79 Say, "He will give them life Who created them in the first instance! For He is well-versed in every kind of creation!— 80 "The same Who produces for you fire out of the green tree, when behold! You kindle therewith (your own fires)! 81 "Is not He Who created the heavens and the earth able to create the like thereof?"—Yes, indeed! For He is the Creator Supreme, of skill and knowledge (infinite)! 82 Surely, when He intends a thing, His Command is, "Be," and it is! 83 So glory to Him in Whose hands is the dominion of all things: and to Him will you be all brought back.

37. THOSE RANGED IN RANKS

In the name of Allah, Most Gracious, Most Merciful.

1 By those who range themselves in ranks, 2 And so are strong in repelling (evil), 3 And thus proclaim the Message (of Allah)! 4 Surely, surely, your God is One! — 5 Lord of the heavens and of the earth, and all between them, and Lord of every point at the rising of the sun!

6 We have indeed decked the lower heaven with beauty (in) the stars — 7 (For beauty) and for guard against all obstinate rebellious Satans. 8 (So) they should not strain their ears in the direction of the Exalted Assembly but be cast away from every side, 9 Repulsed, for they are under a perpetual torment, 10 Except such as snatch away something by stealth, and they are pursued by a flaming fire, of piercing brightness.

11 Just ask their opinion: are they the more difficult to create, or the (other) beings We have created? Them have We created out of a sticky clay! 12 Truly you marvel, while they ridicule, 13 And, when they are admonished, pay no heed — 14 And, when they see a Sign, turn it to mockery, 15 And say, "This is nothing but evident sorcery! 16 "What! when we die, and become dust and bones, shall we (then) be raised up (again) 17 "And also our fathers of old?" 18 Say you: "Yes, and you shall then be humiliated (on account of your evil)."

19 Then it will be a single (compelling) cry; and behold, they will begin to see! 20 They will say, "Ah! woe to us! This is the Day of Judgment!" 21 (A voice will say,) "This is the Day of Sorting Out, whose truth you (once) denied!" 22 "Bring you up," it shall be said, "The wrongdoers and their wives, and the things they worshipped — 23 "Besides Allah, and lead them to the Way to the (Fierce) Fire! 24 "But stop them, for they must be asked: 25 'What is the matter with you that you help not each other?'" 26 No, but that day they shall submit (to Judgement).

27 And they will turn to one another, and question one another. 28 They will say: "It was you who used to come to us from the

right hand (of power and authority)!" 29 They will reply: "No, you yourselves had no Faith! 30 "Nor had we any authority over you. No, it was you who were a people in obstinate rebellion! 31 "So now has been proved true, against us, the Word of our Lord that we shall indeed (have to) taste (the punishment of our sins). 32 "We led you astray: for truly We were ourselves astray." 33 Truly, that Day, they will (all) share the Chastisement.

34 Surely that is how We shall deal with Sinners. 35 For they, when they were told that there is no god except Allah, would puff themselves up with Pride, 36 And say: "What! Shall we give up our gods for the sake of a Poet possessed?" 37 No! he has come with the (very) Truth, and he confirms (the Message of) the Messengers (before him). 38 You shall indeed taste of the Grievous Chastisement— 39 But it will be no more than the retribution of (the Evil) that you have wrought—

40 But the sincere (and devoted) servants of Allah— 41 For them is a Sustenance determined, 42 Fruits (Delights); and they (shall enjoy) honour and dignity, 43 In Gardens of Felicity, 44 Facing each other on raised couches: 45 Round will be passed to them a Cup from a clear-flowing fountain, 46 Crystal-white, of a taste delicious to those who drink (thereof), 47 Free from headiness; nor will they suffer intoxication therefrom. 48 And besides them will be chaste women, restraining their glances, with big eyes (of wonder and beauty). 49 As if they were (delicate) eggs closely guarded.

50 Then they will turn to one another and question one another. 51 One of them will start the talk and say: "I had an intimate companion (on the earth), 52 "Who used to say, 'What! are you amongst those who bear witness to the Truth (of the Message)? 53 "'When we die and become dust and bones, shall we indeed receive rewards and punishments?'" 54 (A voice) said: "Would you like to look down?" 55 He looked down and saw him in the midst of the Fire. 56 He said: "By Allah! You were little short of bringing me to perdition! 57 "Had it not been for the Grace of my Lord, I should certainly have been among those brought (there)! 58 "Is it (the case) that we shall not die, 59 "Except our

first death, and that we shall not be punished?" 60 Surely this is the supreme achievement! 61 For the like of this let all strive, who wish to strive.

62 Is that the better entertainment or the Tree of Zaqqūm? 63 For We have truly made it (as) a trial for the wrongdoers. 64 For it is a tree that springs out of the bottom of Hell-fire: 65 The shoots of its fruit-stalks are like the heads of devils: 66 Truly they will eat thereof and fill their bellies therewith. 67 Then on top of that they will be given a mixture made of boiling water. 68 Then shall their return be to the (Blazing) Fire. 69 Truly they found their fathers on the wrong Path; 70 So they (too) were rushed down on their footsteps! 71 And truly before them, many of the ancients went astray — 72 But We sent aforetime, among them, (Messengers) to warn them — 73 Then see what was the end of those who were warned (but heeded not) — 74 Except the sincere (and devoted) servants of Allah.

75 (In the days of old), Noah cried to Us, and We are the Best to hear prayer. 76 And We delivered him and his people from the Great Calamity, 77 And made his progeny to endure (on this earth); 78 And We left (this blessing) for him among generations to come in later times: 79 "Peace and salutation to Noah among the nations!" 80 Thus indeed do We reward those who do right. 81 For he was one of Our believing Servants. 82 Then the rest We overwhelmed in the Flood.

83 Surely among those who followed his Way was Abraham. 84 Behold! he approached his Lord with a sound heart. 85 Behold! he said to his father and to his people, "What is that which you worship? 86 "Is it a Falsehood — gods other than Allah — that you desire? 87 "Then what is your idea about the Lord of the Worlds?"

88 Then did he cast a glance at the Stars. 89 And he said, "I am indeed sick (at heart)!" 90 So they turned away from him, and departed. 91 Then did he turn to their gods and said, "Will you not eat (of the offerings before you)?... 92 "What is the matter with you that you speak not?" 93 Then did he turn upon them, striking (them) with the right hand. 94 Then came (the

worshippers) with hurried steps, and faced (him). 95 He said: "Worship you that which you have (yourselves) carved? 96 "But Allah has created you and your handiwork!" 97 They said, "Build him a furnace, and throw him into the blazing fire!" 98 (This failing), they then sought a stratagem against him, but We made them the ones most humiliated! 99 He said: "I will go to my Lord! He will surely guide me! 100 "O my Lord! grant me a righteous (son)!" 101 So We gave him the good news of a boy ready to suffer and forbear.

102 Then, when (the son) reached (the age of) (serious) work with him, he said: "O my son! I see in vision that I offer you in sacrifice: now see what is your view!" (The son) said: "O my father! Do as you are commanded: you will find me, if Allah so wills, one of the steadfast!" 103 So when they had both submitted their wills (to Allah), and he had laid him prostrate on his forehead (for sacrifice), 104 We called out to him "O Abraham!" 105 "You have already fulfilled the vision!"—thus indeed do We reward those who do right. 106 For this was obviously a trial— 107 And We ransomed him with a momentous sacrifice: 108 And We left (this blessing) for him among generations (to come) in later times: 109 "Peace and salutation to Abraham!" 110 Thus indeed do We reward those who do right. 111 For he was one of Our believing Servants. 112 And We gave him the good news of Isaac—a prophet— one of the Righteous. 113 We blessed him and Isaac: but of their progeny are (some) that do right, and (some) that obviously do wrong, to their own souls.

114 Again (of old) We bestowed Our favour on Moses and Aaron. 115 And We delivered them and their people from (their) Great distress; 116 And We helped them, so they were victorious; 117 And We gave them the Book which helps to make things clear; 118 And We guided them to the Straight Way. 119 And We left (this blessing) for them among generations (to come) in later times: 120 "Peace and salutation to Moses and Aaron!" 121 Thus indeed do We reward those who do right. 122 For they were two of Our believing Servants.

123 So also was Elias among those sent (by Us). 124 Behold,

he said to his people, "Will you not fear (Allah)? 125 "Will you call upon Ba'l[1] and forsake the Best of Creators— 126 "Allah, your Lord and Cherisher and the Lord and Cherisher of your fathers of old?" 127 But they rejected him, and they will certainly be called up (for punishment)— 128 Except the sincere and devoted servants of Allah (among them). 129 And We left (this blessing) for him among generations (to come) in later times: 130 "Peace and salutation to such as Elias!" 131 Thus indeed do We reward those who do right. 132 For he was one of Our believing Servants.

133 So also was Lūt among those sent (by Us). 134 Behold, We delivered him and his adherents, all 135 Except an old woman who was among those who lagged behind: 136 Then We destroyed the rest. 137 Surely, you pass by their (sites), by day— 138 And by night: will you not understand?

139 So also was Jonah among those sent (by Us). 140 When he ran away (like a slave from captivity) to the ship (fully) laden, 141 He (agreed to) cast lots, and he was of the doomed. 142 Then the big Fish did swallow him, and he had done acts worthy of blame. 143 Had it not been that he (repented and) glorified Allah, 144 He would certainly have remained inside the Fish till the Day of Resurrection. 145 But We cast him forth on the naked shore in a state of sickness, 146 And We caused to grow, over him, a spreading plant of the Gourd kind. 147 And We sent him (on a mission) to a hundred thousand (men) or more. 148 And they believed; so We permitted them to enjoy (their life) for a while.

149 Now ask them their opinion: is it that your Lord has (only) daughters, and they have sons?— 150 Or that We created the angels female, and they are witnesses (thereto)? 151 Is it not that they say, from their own invention, 152 "Allah has begotten children"? But they are liars! 153 Did He (then) choose daughters rather than sons? 154 What is the matter with you? How judge you? 155 Will you not then receive admonition? 156 Or have you an authority manifest? 157 Then bring you your Book (of authority) if you be Truthful!

158 And they have invented a kinship between Him and the Jinns:

---

1. The sun god worshipped in ancient Syria.

but the Jinns know (quite well) that they have indeed to appear (before His Judgment Seat)! 159 Glory to Allah! (He is free) from the things they ascribe (to Him)! 160 Not (so do) the Servants of Allah, sincere and devoted. 161 For, surely, neither you nor those you worship— 162 Can lead (any) into temptation concerning Allah, 163 Except such as are (themselves) going to the blazing Fire! 164 (Those ranged in ranks say): "Not one of us but has a place appointed; 165 "And we are surely ranged in ranks (for service); 166 "And we are surely those who declare (Allah's) glory!"

167 And there were those who said, 168 "If only we had had before us a Message from those of old, 169 "We should certainly have been Servants of Allah, sincere (and devoted)!" 170 But (now that the Qur'ān has come), they reject it: but soon will they know! 171 Already has Our Word been passed before (this) to Our Servants sent (by Us), 172 That they would certainly be assisted, 173 And that Our forces— they surely must conquer 174 So turn away from them for a little while, 175 And watch them (how they fare), and they soon shall see (how you fare)!

176 Do they wish (indeed) to hurry on Our Punishment? 177 But when it descends into the open space before them, evil will be the morning for those who were warned (and heeded not)! 178 So turn away from them for a little while, 179 And watch (how they fare) and they soon shall see (how you fare)! 180 Glory to your Lord, the Lord of Honour and Power! (He is free) from what they ascribe (to Him)! 181 And Peace on the Messengers! 182 And Praise to Allah, the Lord and Cherisher of the Worlds.

38. ṢĀD

In the name of Allah, Most Gracious, Most Merciful.

1 Ṣād: By the Qur'ān, full of Admonition: (this is the Truth). 2 But the Unbelievers (are steeped) in Self-glory and Opposition. 3 How many generations before them did We destroy? In the end they cried (for mercy)— when there was no longer time for being saved!

4 So they wonder that a Warner has come to them from among themselves! and the Unbelievers say, "This is a sorcerer telling lies! 5 "Has he made the gods (all) into one God? Truly this is an astonishing thing!" 6 And the leader among them go away (impatiently), (saying), "Walk away, and remain constant to your gods! for this is truly a thing designed (against you)! 7 "We never heard (the like) of this among the people of these latter days: this is nothing but a made-up tale!" 8 "What! Has the Message been sent to him— (of all persons) among us?"...But they are in doubt concerning My (own) Message! No, they have not yet tasted My Punishment!

9 Or have they the Treasures of the mercy of your Lord— the Exalted in Power, the Grantor of Bounties without measure? 10 Or have they the dominion of the heavens and the earth and all between? If so, let them mount up with the ropes and means (to reach that end)! 11 But there—will be put to flight even a host of confederates. 12 Before them (were many who) rejected Messengers— the people of Noah, and 'Ād, and Pharaoh, the lord of stakes, 13 And Thamūd, and the People of Lūṭ, and the People of the Wood—such were the Confederates. 14 Not one (of them) but rejected the Messengers, but My punishment came justly and inevitably (on them). 15 These (today) only wait for a single mighty Blast, which (when it comes) will brook no delay. 16 They say: "Our Lord! Hasten to us our sentence (even) before the Day of Account!"

17 Have patience at what they say, and remember Our Servant David, the man of strength: for he ever turned (to Allah). 18 It was We that made the hills declare, in unison with him, Our Praises, at eventide and at break of day, 19 And the birds gathered (in assemblies): all with him did turn (to Allah). 20 We strengthened his kingdom, and gave him wisdom and sound judgment in speech and decision.

21 Has the Story of the Disputants reached you? Behold, they climbed over the wall of the private chamber; 22 When they entered the presence of David, and he was afraid of them, they said: "Fear not: we are two disputants, one of whom has wronged

the other: decide now between us with truth, and treat us not with injustice, but guide us to the even Path.

23 "This man is my brother: he has nine and ninety ewes, and I have (but) one: yet he says, 'Commit her to my care,' and he overwhelmed me in the argument." 24 (David) said: "He has undoubtedly wronged you in demanding your (single) ewe to be added to his (flock of) ewes: truly many are the Partners (in business) who wrong each other: not so do those who believe and work deeds of righteousness, and how few are they?"... and David gathered that We had tested him: he asked forgiveness of his Lord, fell down, bowing (in prostration), and turned (to Allah in repentance). 25 So We forgave him this (lapse): he enjoyed, indeed, a Near Approach to Us, and a beautiful place of (final) Return.

26 O David! We did indeed make you a vicegerent on earth: so judge you between men in truth (and justice): nor follow you the lusts (of your heart), for they will mislead you from the Path of Allah: for those who wander astray from the Path of Allah, is a Penalty Grievous, for that they forget the Day of Account.

27 Not without purpose did We create heaven and earth and all between! That were the thought of unbelievers! But woe to the Unbelievers because of the Fire (of Hell)! 28 Shall We treat those who believe and work deeds of righteousness, the same as those who do mischief on earth? Shall We treat those who guard against evil, the same as those who turn aside from the right? 29 (Here is) a Book which we have sent down unto you, full of blessings, that they may meditate on its Signs, and that men of understanding may receive admonition.

30 To David We gave Solomon (for a son)— How excellent in Our service! Ever did he turn (to Us)! 31 Behold, there were brought before him, at eventide, coursers of the highest breeding, and swift of foot; 32 And he said, "Truly do I love the love of good, with a view to the glory of my Lord"— until (the sun) was hidden in the veil (of night): 33 "Bring them back to me." Then began he to pass his hand over (their) legs and their necks.

34 And We did test Solomon: We placed on his throne a body

(without life); but he did turn (to Us in true devotion): 35 He said, "O my Lord! Forgive me, and grant me a kingdom like which, may not have another after me: for You are the Grantor of Bounties (without measure). 36 Then We subjected the Wind to his power, to flow gently to his order, whithersoever he willed— 37 As also the Satans, (including) every kind of builder and diver— 38 As also others bound together in fetters. 39 "Such are Our Bounties: whether you bestow them (on others) or withhold them, no account will be asked." 40 And he enjoyed, indeed, a Near Approach to Us, and a beautiful Place of (final) Return.

41 Commemorate Our Servant Job. "Behold", he cried to his Lord: "Satan has afflicted me with distress and suffering!" 42 (The command was given:) "Strike with your foot: here is (water) wherein to wash, cool and refreshing, and (water) to drink." 43 And We gave him (back) his people, and doubled their number—as a Grace from Ourselves, and a thing for commemoration for all who have Understanding. 44 "And take in your hand a little grass, and strike therewith: and break not (your oath)." Truly We found him full of patience and constancy. How excellent in Our service! Ever did he turn (to Us)!

45 And commemorate Our Servants Abraham, Isaac, and Jacob, possessors of Power and Vision. 46 Surely, We did choose them for a special (purpose)—proclaiming the Message of the Hereafter. 47 They were, in Our Sight, truly, of the company of the Elect and the Good. 48 And commemorate Ishmael, Elisha, and Dhu'l-Kifl: each of them was of the Company of the Good.

49 This is a Message (of admonition): and surely, for the righteous, is a beautiful Place of (Final) Return— 50 Gardens of Eternity, whose doors will (ever) be open to them; 51 Therein will they recline (at ease): therein can they call (at pleasure) for fruit in abundance, and (delicious) drink; 52 And beside them will be chaste women restraining their glances, (companions) of equal age. 53 Such is the Promise made, to you for the Day of Account! 54 Truly such will be our Bounty (to you); it will never fail—

55 Yes, such! But— for the wrongdoers will be an evil place

of (final) Return!— 56 Hell!— they will burn therein—an evil bed (indeed, to lie on)!— 57 Yes, such!—Then shall they taste it— a boiling fluid, and a fluid dark, murky, intensely cold!— 58 And other Penalties of a similar kind, to match them! 59 Here is a troop rushing headlong with you! No welcome for them! Truly, they shall burn in the Fire! 60 (The followers shall cry to the misleaders:) "No, you (too)! No welcome for you! It is you who have brought this upon us! Now evil is (this) place to stay in!" 61 They will say: "Our Lord! Whoever brought this upon us— add to him a double chastisement in the Fire!" 62 And they will say: "What has happened to us that we see not men whom we used to number among the bad ones? 63 "Did we treat them (as such) in ridicule, or have (our) eyes failed to perceive them?" 64 Truly that is just and fitting— the mutual recriminations of the People of the Fire!

65 Say: "Truly am I a Warner: no god is there but the One God, Supreme and Irresistible— 66 "The Lord of the heavens and the earth, and all between—Exalted in Might, able to enforce His Will, forgiving again and again." 67 Say: "That is a Message supreme (above all)— 68 "From which you do turn away! 69 "No knowledge have I of the Chiefs on high, when they discuss (matters) among themselves. 70 "Only this has been revealed to me: that I am to give warning plainly and publicly."

71 Behold, your Lord said to the angels: "I am about to create man from clay: 72 "When I have fashioned him (in due proportion) and breathed into him of My spirit, fall you down in obeisance unto him." 73 So the angels prostrated themselves, all of them together: 74 Not so Iblīs: he was haughty, and became one of those who reject Faith. 75 (Allah) said: "O Iblīs! What prevents you from prostrating yourself to one whom I have created with My hands? Are you haughty? Or are you one of the high (and mighty) ones?" 76 (Iblīs) said: "I am better than he: You created me from fire, and him You created from clay." 77 (Allah) said: "Then get you out from here: for you are rejected, accursed. 78 "And My curse shall be on you till the Day of Judgment."

79 (Iblīs) said: "O my Lord! Give me then respite till the Day the (dead) are raised." 80 (Allah) said: "Respite then is granted you— 81 "Till the Day of the Time Appointed." 82 (Iblīs) said: "Then, by Your power, I will put them all in the wrong— 83 "Except Your Servants amongst them, sincere and purified (by Your Grace)." 84 (Allah) said: "Then it is just and fitting— and I say what is just and fitting— 85 "That I will certainly fill Hell with you and those that follow you— every one."

86 Say: "No reward do I ask of you for this (Qur'ān), nor am I a pretender. 87 "This is no less than a Message to (all) the Worlds. 88 "And you shall certainly know the truth of it (all) after a while."

39. THE CROWDS

In the name of Allah, Most Gracious, Most Merciful.

1 The revelation of this Book is from Allah, the Exalted in Power, full of Wisdom. 2 Surely it is We Who have revealed the Book to you in Truth: so serve Allah, offering Him sincere devotion. 3 Is it not to Allah that sincere devotion is due? But those who take for protectors others than Allah (say): "We only serve them in order that they may bring us nearer to Allah." Truly Allah will judge between them in that wherein they differ. But Allah guides not such as are false and ungrateful.

4 Had Allah wished to take to Himself a son, He could have chosen whom He pleased out of those whom He does create: but Glory be to Him! (He is above such things.) He is Allah, the One, the Overpowering. 5 He created the heavens and the earth in true (proportions): He makes the Night overlap the Day, and the Day overlap the Night: He has subjected the sun and the moon (to His law): each one follows a course for a time appointed. Is not He the Exalted in Power—He Who forgives again and again?

6 He created you (all) from a single Person: then created, of like nature, his mate; and He sent down for you eight head of

cattle in pairs: He shapes you, in the wombs of your mothers, in stages, one after another, in three veils of darkness. Such is Allah, your Lord and Cherisher: to Him belongs (all) dominion. There is no god but He: then how are you turned away (from your true Lord)?

7 If you reject (Allah), truly Allah has no need of you; but He likes not ingratitude from His servants: if you are grateful, He is pleased with you. No bearer of burdens can bear the burden of another. In the end, to your Lord is your Return, when He will tell you the truth of all that you did (in this life). For He knows well all that is in (men's) hearts.

8 When some trouble touches man, he cries unto his Lord, turning to Him in repentance: but when He bestowes a favour upon him as from Himself, (man) does forget what he cried and prayed for before, and he does set up rivals unto Allah, thus misleading others from Allah's Path. Say, "Enjoy your blasphemy for a little while: surely you are (one) of the Companions of the Fire!" 9 Is one who worships devoutly during the hours of the night prostrating himself or standing (in adoration), who takes heed of the Hereafter, and who places his hope in the Mercy of his Lord — (like one who does not)? Say: "Are those equal, those who know and those who do not know? It is those who are endued with understanding that receive admonition.

10 Say: "O you my servants who believe! Fear your Lord, good is (the reward) for those who do good in this world. Spacious is Allah's earth! Those who patiently persevere will truly receive a reward without measure!"

11 Say: "Surely, I am commanded to serve Allah with sincere devotion; 12 "And I am commanded to be the first of those who submit to Allah in Islam." 13 Say: "I would, if I disobeyed my Lord, indeed have fear of the chastisement of a Mighty Day." 14 Say: "It is Allah I serve, with my sincere (and exclusive) devotion: 15 "Serve you what you will besides him." Say: "Truly, in loss are those who lose their own souls and their People on the Day of Judgment: Ah! that is indeed the (real and) evident

Loss! 16 They shall have Layers of Fire above them, and Layers (of Fire) below them: with this does Allah warn off his Servants: "O My Servants! Then fear you Me!"

17 Those who eschew Taghut— and fall not into its worship— and turn to Allah (in repentance)— for them is Good News: so announce the Good News to My Servants— 18 Those who listen to the Word, and follow the best (meaning) in it: those are the ones whom Allah has guided, and those are the ones endued with understanding.

19 Is, then, one against whom the decree of Punishment is justly due (equal to one who eschews evil)? Would you, then, deliver one (who is) in the Fire? 20 But it is for those who fear their Lord. That lofty mansions, one above another, have been built: beneath them flow rivers (of delight): (such is) the Promise of Allah: never does Allah fail in (His) promise.

21 Do you not see that Allah sends down rain from the sky, and leads it through springs in the earth? Then He causes to grow, therewith, produce of various colours: then it withers; you will see it grow yellow; then He makes it dry up and crumble away. Truly, in this, is a Message of remembrance to men of understanding. 22 Is one whose heart Allah has opened to Islam, so that he has received enlightenment from Allah, (no better than one hard-hearted)? Woe to those whose hearts are hardened against celebrating the praises of Allah! They are manifestly wandering (in error)!

23 Allah has revealed (from time to time) the most beautiful Message in the form of a Book, consistent with itself, (yet) repeating (its teaching in various aspects): the skins of those who fear their Lord tremble thereat; then their skins and their hearts do soften to the celebration of Allah's praises. Such is the guidance of Allah: He guides therewith whom He pleases, but such as Allah leaves to stray, can have none to guide.

24 Is, then, one who has to fear the brunt of the Chastisement on the Day of Judgment (and receive it) on his face, (like one guarded therefrom)? It will be said to the wrongdoers: "Taste you

(the fruits of) what you earned!" 25 Those before them (also) rejected (revelation), and so the Punishment came to them from directions they did not perceive. 26 So Allah gave them a taste of humiliation in the present life, but greater is the Punishment of the Hereafter, if they only knew!

27 We have put forth for men, in this Qur'ān every kind of Parable, in order that they may receive admonition. 28 (It is) a Qur'ān in Arabic, without any crookedness (therein): in order that they may guard against Evil. 29 Allah puts forth a Parable — a man belonging to many partners at variance with each other, and a man belonging entirely to one master: are those two equal in comparison? Praise be to Allah! But most of them have no knowledge. 30 Truly you will die (one day), and truly they (too) will die (one day). 31 In the End will you (all), on the Day of Judgment, settle your disputes in the presence of your Lord.

32 Who, then, does more wrong than one who utters a lie concerning Allah, and rejects the Truth when it comes to him; is there not in Hell an abode for the unbelievers? 33 And he who brings the Truth and he who confirms (and supports) it — such are the men who do right. 34 They shall have all that they wish for from their Lord: such is the reward of those who do good: 35 So that Allah will remit from them (even) the worst in their deeds and give them their reward according to the best of what they have done.

36 Is not Allah enough for His servant? But they try to frighten you with other (gods) besides Him! For such as Allah leaves to stray, there can be no guide. 37 And such as Allah does guide there can be none to lead astray. Is not Allah Exalted in Power, (Able to enforce his Will), Lord of Retribution?

38 If indeed you ask them who it is that created the heavens and the earth, they would be sure to say, "Allah." Say: "Do you see then? The things that you invoke besides Allah — can they, if Allah wills some affliction for me, remove that affliction? — or if He wills some Grace for me, can they keep back His Grace?" Say: "Sufficient is Allah for me! In Him trust those who put their trust."

39 Say: "O my people! Do whatever you can: I will do (my part): but soon will you know— 40 "Who it is to whom comes a Chastisement of ignominy, and on whom descends a Chastisement that abides." 41 Certainly We have revealed the Book to you in Truth, for (instructing) mankind. He, then, that receives guidance benefits his own soul: but he that strays injures his own soul. Nor are you set a Custodian over them.

42 It is Allah that takes the souls (of men) at death; and those that die not (He takes) during their sleep: those on whom He has passed the decree of death, He keeps back (from returning to life), but the rest He sends (to their bodies) for a term appointed. Certainly in this are Signs for those who reflect.

43 What! Do they take for intercessors others besides Allah? Say: "Even if they have no power whatever and no intelligence?" 44 Say: "To Allah belongs exclusively (the right to grant) intercession: to Him belongs the dominion of the heavens and the earth: in the End, it is to Him that you shall be brought back." 45 When Allah, the One and Only, is mentioned, the hearts of those who believe not in the Hereafter are filled with disgust and horror; but when (gods) other than He are mentioned, behold, they are filled with joy! 46 Say: "O Allah! Creator of the heavens and the earth! Knower of all that is hidden and open! It is You that will judge between Your Servants in those matters about which they have differed." 47 Even if the wrongdoers had all that there is on earth, and as much more, (in vain) would they offer it for ransom from the pain of the Chastisement on the Day of Judgment: but something will confront them from Allah, which they could never have counted upon! 48 For the evils of their Deeds will confront them, and they will be (completely) encircled by that which they used to mock at!

49 Now, when trouble touches man, he cries to Us: but when We bestow a favour upon him as from Ourselves, he says, "This has been given to me because of a certain knowledge (I have)!" No, but this is but a trial, but most of them understand not! 50 Thus did the (generations) before them say! But all that they

did was of no benefit to them. 51 No, the evil results of their deeds overtook them. And the wrongdoers of this (generation)— the evil results of their deeds will soon overtake them (too), and they will never be able to frustrate (Our Plan)! 52 Know they not that Allah enlarges the provision or restricts it, for any He pleases? Surely, in this are Signs for those who believe!

53 Say: "O my Servants who have transgressed against their souls! Despair not of the Mercy of Allah: for Allah forgives all sins: for He is Oft-Forgiving, Most Merciful. 54 "Turn you to our Lord (in repentance) and submit to His (Will), before the chastisement comes on you: after that you shall not be helped.

55 "And follow the Best of (the courses) revealed to you from your Lord, before the chastisement comes on you—of a sudden, while you perceive not!— 56 "Lest the soul should (then) say: 'Ah! woe is me!— in that I neglected (my Duty) towards Allah, and was but among those who mocked!'— 57 "Or (lest) it should say: 'If only Allah had guided me, I should certainly have been among the righteous!'— 58 "Or (lest) it should say when it (actually) sees the Chastisement: 'If only I had another chance, I should certainly be among those who do good!' 59 "(The reply will be:) 'No, but there came to you My Signs, and you did reject them: you were haughty, and became one of those who reject faith!'" 60 On the Day of Judgment will you see those who told lies against Allah— Their faces will be turned black; is there not in Hell an abode for the Haughty? 61 But Allah will deliver the righteous to their place of salvation: no evil shall touch them, nor shall they grieve.

62 Allah is the Creator of all things, and He is the Guardian and Disposer of all affairs. 63 To Him belong the keys of the heavens and the earth: and those who reject the Signs of Allah— it is they who will be in loss. 64 Say: "Is it some one other than Allah that you call upon me to worship, O you ignorant ones?" 65 But it has already been revealed to you— as it was to those before you— "If you were to join (gods with Allah), truly fruitless will be your work (in life), and you will surely be in the ranks of those who

are the losers." 66 No, but worship Allah, and be of those who give thanks.

67 No just estimate have they made of Allah, such as is due to Him: on the Day of Judgment the whole of the earth will be but His handful, and the heavens will be rolled up in His right hand: glory to Him! High is He above the Partners they attribute to Him! 68 The Trumpet will (just) be sounded, when all that are in the heavens and on earth will swoon, except such as it will please Allah (to exempt). Then will a second one be sounded, when, behold, they will be standing and looking on! 69 And the Earth will shine with the Light of its Lord: the Record (of Deeds) will be placed (open); the prophets and the witnesses will be brought forward; and a just decision pronounced between them; and they will not be wronged (in the least). 70 And to every soul will be paid in full (the fruit) of its Deeds; and (Allah) knows best all that they do.

71 The Unbelievers will be led to Hell in crowds: until, when they arrive, there, its gates will be opened. And its keepers will say, "Did not Messengers come to you from among yourselves, rehearsing to you the Signs of your Lord, and warning you of the Meeting of this Day of yours?" The answer will be: "True: but the Decree of Chastisement has been proved true against the Unbelievers!" 72 (To them) will be said: "Enter the gates of Hell, to dwell therein: and evil is (this) abode of the arrogant!"

73 And those who feared their Lord will be led to the Garden in crowds: until, behold, they arrive there; its gates will be opened; and its Keepers will say: "Peace be upon you! Well have you done! Enter you here, to dwell therein." 74 They will say: "Praise be to Allah, Who has truly fulfilled His Promise to us, and has given us (this) land in heritage: we can dwell in the Garden as we will: how excellent a reward for those who work (righteousness)!" 75 And you will see the angels surrounding the Throne (Divine) on all sides, singing Glory and Praise to their Lord. The Decision between them (at Judgment) will be in (perfect) justice, and the cry (on all sides) will be, "Praise be to Allah, the Lord of the Worlds!"

40. THE BELIEVER

In the name of Allah, Most Gracious, Most Merciful.

1 *Hā Mīm* 2 The revelation of this Book is from Allah, Exalted in Power, full of Knowledge— 3 Who forgives Sin, accepts Repentance, is Strict in Punishment, and has a Long Reach (in all things). There is no god but He: to Him is the Final Goal.

4 None can dispute about the Signs of Allah but the Unbelievers. Let not, then, their strutting about through the land deceive you! 5 But (there were people) before them, who denied (the Signs)— the People of Noah, and the Confederates (of Evil) after them; and every People plotted against their Prophet, to seize him, and disputed by means of vanities, therewith to repulse the Truth; but it was I that seized them! And how (terrible) was My Requital! 6 Thus was the Decree of your Lord proved true against the Unbelievers; that truly they are companions of the Fire!

7 Those who sustain the Throne (of Allah) and those around it sing Glory and Praise to their Lord; believe in Him; and implore Forgiveness for those who believe: "Our Lord! Your Reach is over all things, in Mercy and Knowledge. Forgive, then, those who turn in Repentance, and follow your Path; and save them from the Chastisement of the Blazing Fire! 8 "And grant, our Lord! That they enter the Gardens of Eternity, which You have promised to them, and to the righteous among their fathers, their wives, and their posterity! For You are (He), the Exalted in Might, full of Wisdom. 9 "And preserve them from (all) ills; and any whom You do preserve from ills that Day—on them will You have bestowed mercy indeed: and that will be truly (for them) the highest Achievement."

10 The Unbelievers will be addressed: "Greater was the aversion of Allah to you than (is) your aversion to yourselves, seeing that you were called to the Faith and you used to refuse." 11 They will say: "Our Lord! Twice⋅have You made us to die, and twice have You given us Life! Now have we recognised our sins: is there

any way out (of this)?" 12 (The answer will be:) "This is because, when Allah was invoked as the Only (object of worship), you did reject Faith, but when partners were joined to Him, you believed! The Command is with Allah, Most High, Most Great!"

13 He it is Who shows you His Signs, and sends down Sustenance for you from the sky: but only those receive admonition who turn (to Allah). 14 Call you, then, upon Allah with sincere devotion to Him, even though the Unbelievers may detest it. 15 Exalted is He. in His attributes (He is) the Lord of the Throne (of Authority): by His Command does He send the spirit (of inspiration) to any of His servants He pleases, that it may warn (men) of the Day of Mutual Meeting— 16 The Day whereon they will (all) come forth: not a single thing concerning them is hidden from Allah. Whose will be the Dominion that Day?" that of Allah, the One, the Irresistible! 17 That Day will every soul be requited for what it earned; no injustice will there be that Day, for Allah is Swift in taking account.

18 Warn them of the Day that is (ever) drawing near, when the hearts will (come) right up to the Throats to choke (them); no intimate friend nor intercessor will the wrongdoers have, who could be listened to. 19 (Allah) knows the treachery of the eyes, and all that the hearts (of men) conceal. 20 And Allah will judge with (justice and) Truth: but those whom (men) invoke besides Him, will not (be in a position) to judge at all. Surely it is Allah (alone) who hears and sees (all things).

21 Do they not travel through the earth and see what was the End of those before them? They were even superior to them in strength, and in the traces (they have left) in the land: but Allah did call them to account for their sins, and none had they to defend them against Allah. 22 That was because there came to them their Messengers with Clear (Signs), but they rejected them: so Allah called them to account: for He is full of Strength, Strict in Punishment.

23 Of old We sent Moses, with Our Signs and an Authority manifest, 24 To Pharaoh, Hāmān, and Qārūn; but they called

(him) "a sorcerer telling lies!"... 25 Now, when he came to them in Truth, from Us, they said, "Slay the sons of those who believe with him, and keep alive their females," but the plots of Unbelievers (end) in nothing but errors (and delusions)!...

26 Said Pharaoh: "Leave me to slay Moses; and let him call on his Lord! What I fear is lest he should change your religion, or lest he should cause mischief to appear in the land!" 27 Moses said: "I have indeed called upon my Lord and your Lord (for protection) from every arrogant one who believes not in the Day of Account!"

28 A Believer, a man from among the people of Pharaoh, who had concealed his faith, said: "Will you slay a man because he says, 'My Lord is Allah'?—When he has indeed come to you with Clear (Signs) from your Lord? And if he be a liar, on him is (the sin of) his lie: but, if he is telling the Truth, then will fall on you something of the (calamity) of which he warns you: truly Allah guides not one who transgresses and lies! 29 "O my People! yours is the dominion this day: you have the upper hand in the land: but who will help us from the Punishment of Allah, should it befall us?" Pharaoh said: "I but point out to you that which I see (myself); nor do I guide you but to the Path of Right!"

30 Then said the man who believed: "O my people! Truly I do fear for you something like the Day (of disaster) of the Confederates (in sin)!— 31 "Something like the fate of the People of Noah, the 'Ād, and the Thamūd, and those who came after them: but Allah never wishes injustice to His Servants. 32 "And O my People! I fear for you a Day when there will be mutual calling (and wailing)— 33 "A Day when you shall turn your backs and flee: no defender shall you have from Allah: any whom Allah leaves to stray, there is none to guide...

34 "And to you there came Joseph in times gone by, with Clear Signs, but you ceased not to doubt of the (mission) for which he had come: at length, when he died, you said: 'No Messenger will Allah send after him.' Thus does Allah leave to stray such as transgress and live in doubt— 35 "(Such) as dispute about the

Signs of Allah, without any authority that has reached them. Grievous and odious (is such conduct) in the sight of Allah and of the Believers. Thus does Allah seal up every heart — of arrogant and tyrannical."

36 Pharaoh said: "O Hāmān! build me a lofty palace, that I may attain the ways and means— 37 "The ways and means of (reaching) the heavens, and that I may mount up to the God of Moses: but as far as I am concerned, I think (Moses) is a liar!" thus was made alluring, in Pharaoh's eyes, the evil of his deeds, and he was hindered from the Path; and the plot of Pharaoh led to nothing but perdition (for him).

38 The man who believed said further: "O my People! Follow me: I will lead you to the Path of Right. 39 "O my People! This life of the present is nothing but (temporary) enjoyment: it is the Hereafter that is the Home that will last. 40 "He that works evil will not be requited but by the like thereof: and he that works a righteous deed — whether man or woman — and is a Believer — such will enter the Garden (of Bliss): therein will they have abundance without measure. 41 "And O my People! How (strange) it is for me to call you to Salvation while you call me to the Fire! 42 "You do call upon me to blaspheme against Allah, and to join with Him partners of whom I have no knowledge; and I call you to the Exalted in Power, Who forgives again and again!" 43 "Without doubt you do call me to one who is not fit to be called to, whether in this world, or in the Hereafter; our Return will be to Allah; and the Transgressors will be Companions of the Fire! 44 "Soon will you remember what I say to you (now), my (own) affair I commit to Allah: for Allah (ever) watches over His Servants."

45 Then Allah saved him from (every) ill that they plotted (against him), but the brunt of the Chastisement encompassed on all sides the People of Pharaoh. 46 In front of the Fire will they be brought, morning and evening: and (the Sentence will be) on the Day that judgment will be established: "Cast you the People of Pharaoh into the severest Penalty!"

47 Behold, they will dispute with each other in the Fire! The weak ones (who followed) will say to those who had been arrogant, "We but followed you: can you then take (on yourselves) from us some share of the Fire? 48 Those who had been arrogant will say: "We are all in this (Fire)! Truly, Allah has judged between (His) Servants!" 49 Those in the Fire will say to the Keepers of Hell: "Pray to your Lord to lighten the Chastisement for a Day (at least)!" 50 They will say: "Did there not come to you your Messengers with Clear Signs?" They will say, "Yes." They will reply, "Then pray (as you like)! But the prayer of those without Faith is nothing but (futile wandering) in (mazes of) error!"

51 We will, without doubt, help our Messengers and those who believe, (both) in this world's life and on the Day when the Witnesses will stand forth— 52 The Day when of no profit will it be to Wrongdoers to present their excuses, but they will (only) have the Curse and the Home of Misery. 53 We did aforetime give Moses the (Book of) Guidance, and We gave the Book in inheritance to the Children of Israel— 54 A Guide and a Reminder to men of Understanding. 55 Patiently, then, persevere: for the Promise of Allah is true: and ask forgiveness for your fault, and celebrate the Praises of your Lord in the evening and in the morning.

56 Those who dispute about the Signs of Allah without any authority bestowed on them—there is nothing in their breasts but (the quest of) greatness, which they shall never attain: seek refuge, then, in Allah: it is He who hears and sees (all things).

57 Assuredly the creation of the heavens and the earth is a greater (matter) than the creation of men: yet most men understand not. 58 Not equal are the blind and those who (clearly) see: nor are (equal) those who believe and work deeds of righteousness, and those who do evil. Little do you learn by admonition! 59 The Hour will certainly come: therein is no doubt: yet most men believe not.

60 And your Lord says: "Call on Me; I will answer your (Prayer):

but those who are too arrogant to serve Me will surely find themselves in Hell—in humiliation!" 61 It is Allah Who has made the Night for you, that you may rest therein, and the Day, as that which helps (you) to see. Surely Allah is full of Grace and Bounty to men: yet most men give no thanks. 62 Such is Allah, your Lord, the Creator of all things. There is no god but He: then how you are deluded away from the Truth! 63 Thus are deluded those who are wont to reject the Signs of Allah.

64 It is Allah Who has made for you the earth as a resting place, and the sky as a canopy, and has given you shape— and made your shapes beautiful—and has provided for you Sustenance, of things pure and good—such is Allah your Lord. So Glory to Allah, the Lord of the Worlds! 65 He is the Living (One): there is no deity save Him: call upon Him, giving Him sincere devotion. Praise be to Allah, Lord of the Worlds!

66 Say: "I have been forbidden to invoke those whom you invoke besides Allah—seeing that the Clear Signs have come to me from my Lord; and I have been commanded to submit (in Islam) to the Lord of the Worlds." 67 It is He Who has created you from dust, then from a sperm-drop, then from a leech-like clot; then does He get you out (into the light) as a child: then lets you (grow and) reach your age of full strength; then lets you become old— Though of you there are some who die before—and lets you reach a Term appointed; in order that you may learn wisdom. 68 It is He Who gives Life and Death; and when He decides upon an affair, He says to it, "Be," and it is.

69 Do you not see those that dispute concerning the Signs of Allah? How are they turned away (from Reality)?— 70 Those who reject the Book and the (revelations) with which We sent Our Messengers: but soon shall they know— 71 When the yokes (shall be) round their necks, and the chains; they shall be dragged along— 72 In the boiling fetid fluid; then in the Fire shall they be burned; 73 Then shall it be said to them: "Where are the (deities) to which you gave part-worship— 74 "Besides Allah?" They will reply: "They have left us in the lurch: no, we invoked

not, of old, anything (that had real existence)." Thus does Allah leave the Unbelievers to stray. 75 "That was because you were wont to rejoice on the earth in things other than the Truth, and that you were wont to be insolent. 76 "Enter you the gates of Hell, to dwell therein: and evil is (this) abode of the arrogant!"

77 So persevere in patience; for the Promise of Allah is true: and whether We show you (in this life) some part of what We promise them—or We take your soul (to Our Mercy) (before that)—(in any case) it is to Us that they shall (all) return.

78 We did aforetime send messengers before you: of them there are some whose story We have related to you, and some whose story We have not related to you. It was not (possible) for any Messenger to bring a Sign except by the leave of Allah: but when the Command of Allah issued, the matter was decided in truth and justice, and there perished, there and then, those who stood on Falsehoods.

79 It is Allah Who made cattle for you, that you may use some for riding and some for food; 80 And there are (other) advantages in them for you (besides); that you may through them attain to any need (there may be) in your hearts; and on them and on ships you are carried. 81 And He shows you (always) His Signs: then which of the Signs of Allah will you deny?

82 Do they not travel through the earth and see what was the End of those before them? They were more numerous than these and superior in strength and in the traces (they have left) in the land: yet all that they accomplished was of no good to them. 83 For when their Messengers came to them with Clear Signs, they exulted in such knowledge (and skill) as they had; but that very (Wrath) at which they were wont to scoff hemmed them in. 84 But when they saw Our Punishment, they said: "We believe in Allah—the One God—and we reject the partners we used to join with Him." 85 But their professing the Faith when they (actually) saw Our Punishment was not going to profit them. (such has been) Allah's way of dealing with His servants (from the most ancient times). And even thus did the rejecters of Allah perish (utterly)!

41. EXPOUNDED

In the name of Allah, Most Gracious, Most Merciful.

1 *Hā Mīm:* 2 A Revelation from (Allah), Most Gracious, Most Merciful— 3 A Book, whereof the verses are explained in detail— a Qur'ān in Arabic, for people who understand— 4 Giving Good News and Admonition: yet most of them turn away, and so they hear not. 5 They say: "Our hearts are under veils, (concealed) from that to which you invite us, and in our ears in a deafness, and between us and you is a screen: so do you (what you will); for us, we shall do (what we will!)"

6 Say you: "I am but a man like you: it is revealed to me by inspiration, that your God is One God: so stand true to Him, and ask for His Forgiveness." And woe to those who join gods with Allah— 7 Those who pay not Zakat, and who even deny the Hereafter. 8 For those who believe and work deeds of righteousness is a reward that will never fail.

9 Say: Is it that you deny Him Who created the earth in two Days? And do you join equals with Him? He is the Lord of (all) the Worlds. 10 He set on the (earth), mountains standing firm, high above it, and bestowed blessings on the earth, and measure therein all things to give them nourishment in due proportion, in four Days, in accordance with (the needs of) those who seek (Sustenance). 11 Moreover He comprehended in His design the sky, and it had been (as) smoke: He said to it and to the earth: "Come you together, willingly or unwillingly." They said: "We do come (together), in willing obedience." 12 So He completed them as seven firmaments in two Days, and He assigned to each heaven its duty and command. And We adorned the lower heaven with lights, and (provided it) with guard. Such is the Decree of (Him) the Exalted in Might, full of Knowledge.

13 But if they turn away, say you: "I have warned you of a stunning Punishment (as of thunder and lightning) like that which (overtook) the 'Ād and the Thamūd!" 14 Behold, the Messengers came to them, from before them and behind them, (preaching):

"Serve none but Allah." They said, "If our Lord had so pleased, He would certainly have sent down angels (to preach). Now we reject your mission (altogether)."

15 Now the 'Ād behaved arrogantly through the land, against (all) truth and reason, and said: "Who is superior to us in strength?" What! Did they not see that Allah, Who created them, was superior to them in strength? But they continued to reject Our Signs! 16 So We sent against them a furious Wind through days of disaster, that We might give them a taste of a Torment of humiliation in this Life; but the Penalty of the Hereafter will be more humiliating still: and they will find no help. 17 As to the Thamūd, We gave them Guidance, but they preferred blindness (of heart) to Guidance: so the humiliating Punishment of thunderbolt seized them, because of what they had earned. 18 But We delivered those who believed and practised righteousness.

19 On the Day that the enemies of Allah will be gathered together to the Fire, they will be marched in ranks. 20 At length, when they reach the (Fire), their hearing, their sight, and their skins will bear witness against them, as to (all) their deeds. 21 They will say to their skins: "Why do you bear witness against us?" They will say: "Allah has given us speech—(He) Who gives speech to everything: He created you in the first instance, and unto Him were you to return. 22 "You did not seek to hide yourselves, lest your hearing, your sight, and your skins should bear witness against you! But you did think that Allah knew not many of the things that you used to do! 23 "But this thought of yours which you did entertain concerning your Lord, has brought you to destruction, and (now) have you become of those utterly lost!" 24 If, then, they have patience, the Fire will even then be a Home for them! And if they beg to be received into favour, into favour will they not (then) be received.

25 And We have destined for them intimate companions (of like nature), who made alluring to them what was before them and behind them; and the sentence against the previous generations of Jinns and men, who have passed away, is set against them too; for they are utterly lost.

26 The Unbelievers say: "Listen not to this Qur'ān, but make noise in the midst of its (reading), that you may gain the upper hand!" 27 But We will certainly give the Unbelievers a taste of a severe Chastisement, and We will requite them for the worst of their deeds. 28 Such is the requital of the enemies of Allah— the Fire: therein will be for them the Eternal Home: a (fit) requital, for that they were wont to reject Our Signs.

29 And the Unbelievers will say: "Our Lord! Show us those, among Jinns and men, who misled us: we shall crush them beneath our feet, so that they become the vilest (before all)." 30 In the case of those who say, "Our Lord is Allah," and, further, stand straight and steadfast, the angels descend on them (from time to time): "Do not fear!" (they suggest), "Nor grieve! But receive the Glad Tidings of the Garden (of Bliss), that which you were promised! 31 "We are your protectors in this life and in the Hereafter: therein shall you have all that your souls shall desire; therein shall you have all that you ask for!— 32 "A hospitable gift from One Oft-Forgiving, Most Merciful!"

33 Who is better in speech than one who calls (men) to Allah, works righteousness, and says, "I am of those who submit in Islam"? 34 Nor can Goodness and Evil be equal. Repel (Evil) with what is better: then will he between whom and you was hatred become as it were your friend and intimate! 35 And no one will be granted such goodness except those who exercise patience and self-restraint— none but persons of the greatest good fortune. 36 And if (at any time) an incitement to discord is made to you by the Satan, seek refuge in Allah. He is the One who hears and knows all things.

37 Among His Signs are the Night and the Day, and the Sun and the Moon. Prostrate not before the sun and the moon, but worship Allah, Who created them, if it is Him you wish to serve. 38 But if the (Unbelievers) are arrogant, (no matter): for in the presence of your Lord are those who celebrate His praises by night and by day. And they never flag (nor feel themselves above it).

39 And among His Signs is this: you see the earth barren and desolate; but when We send down rain to it, it is stirred to life

and yields increase. Truly, He Who gives life to the (dead) earth can surely give life to (men) who are dead. For He has power over all things. 40 Those who pervert the Truth in Our Signs are not hidden from Us. Which is better?—he that is cast into the Fire, or he that comes safe through, on the Day of Judgment? Do what you will: surely He sees (clearly) all that you do.

41 Those who reject the Message when it comes to them (are not hidden from Us). And indeed it is a Book of exalted power. 42 No falsehood can approach it from the front or rear: it is sent down by One Full of Wisdom, Worthy of all Praise. 43 Nothing is said to you that was not said to the Messengers before you: that your Lord has at His command (all) Forgiveness as well as a most grievous Chastisement.

44 Had We sent this as a Qur'ān (in a language) other than Arabic, they would have said: "Why are not its verses explained in detail? What! (a Book) not in Arabic and (a Messenger) an Arab?" Say: "It is a guide and a healing to those who believe; and for those who believe not, there is a deafness in their ears, and it is blindness in their (eyes): they are (as it were) being called from a place far distant!"

45 We certainly gave Moses the Book aforetime: but disputes arose therein. Had it not been for a Word that went forth before from your Lord, (their differences) would have been settled between them: but they remained in suspicious disquieting doubt thereon. 46 Whoever works righteousness benefits his own soul; whoever works evil, it is against his own soul: nor is your Lord ever unjust (in the least) to His servants.

47 To Him is referred the Knowledge of the Hour (of Judgment: He knows all): no fruit comes out of its sheath, nor does a female conceive (within her womb) nor bring forth (young), but by His knowledge. The Day that (Allah) will propound to them the (question), "Where are the Partners (you attributed) to Me?" They will say, "We do assure You not one of us can bear witness!" 48 The (deities) they used to invoke aforetime will leave them in the lurch, and they will perceive that they have no way of escape.

49 Man does not weary of asking for good (things), but if ill touches him, he gives up all hope (and) is lost in despair. 50 When We give him a taste of some mercy from Ourselves, after some adversity has touched him, he is sure to say, "This is due to my (merit): I think not that the Hour (of Judgment) will (ever) be established; but if I am brought back to my Lord, I have (much) good (stored) in His sight!" But We will show the Unbelievers the truth of all that they did, and We shall give them the taste of a severe Chastisement.

51 When We bestow favours on man, he turns away, and makes himself remote on his side (instead of coming to Us); and when evil seizes him, (he comes) full of prolonged prayer! 52 Say: "Do you see if the (Revelation) is (really) from Allah, and yet do you reject it? Who is more astray than one who is in a schism far (from any purpose)?"

53 Soon will We show them our Signs in the (furthest) regions (of the earth), and in their own souls, until it becomes manifest to them that this is the Truth. Is it not enough that your Lord does witness all things? 54 Ah indeed! Are they in doubt concerning the Meeting with their Lord? Ah indeed! It is He that does encompass all things!

42. CONSULTATION

In the name of Allah, Most Gracious, Most Merciful.

1 Hā Mīm; 2 'Ayn. Sīn. Qāf. 3 Thus does (He) send inspiration to you as (He did) to those before you — Allah, Exalted in Power, full of Wisdom. 4 To Him belongs all that is in the heavens and on earth: and He is Most High, Most Great. 5 The heavens are almost rent asunder from above them (by His Glory): and the angels celebrate the Praises of their Lord, and pray for forgiveness for (all) beings on earth: Behold! Surely Allah is He, the Oft-Forgiving, Most Merciful. 6 And those who take as protectors

others besides Him—Allah does watch over them; and you are not the disposer of their affairs.

7 Thus have We sent by inspiration to you an Arabic Qur'ān: that you may warn the Mother of Cities and all around her—and warn (them) of the Day of Assembly, of which there is no doubt: (when) some will be in the Garden, and some in the Blazing Fire.

8 If Allah had so willed, He could have made them a single people; but He admits whom He will to His Mercy; and the wrongdoers will have no protector nor helper. 9 What! Have they taken (for worship) protectors besides Him? But it is Allah—He is the Protector, and it is He Who gives life to the dead: it is He Who has power over all things, 10 Whatever it be wherein you differ, the decision thereof is with Allah: such is Allah my Lord: in Him I trust, and to Him I turn.

11 (He is) the Creator of the heavens and the earth: He has made for you pairs from among yourselves, and pairs among cattle: by this means does He multiply you: there is nothing whatever like unto Him, and He is the One that hears and sees (all things). 12 To Him belong the keys of the heavens and the earth: He enlarges and restricts the Sustenance to whom He will: for He knows full well all things.

13 The same religion has He established for you as that which He enjoined on Noah— That which We have sent by inspiration to you—and that which We enjoined on Abraham, Moses, and Jesus: namely, that you should remain steadfast in Religion, and make no divisions therein: to those who worship other things than Allah, hard is the (way) to which you call them. Allah chooses to Himself those whom He pleases, and guides to Himself those who turn (to Him).

14 And they became divided only after knowledge reached them—through selfish envy as between themselves. Had it not been for a Word that went forth before from your Lord, (tending) to a Term appointed, the matter would have been settled between them: but truly those who have inherited the Book after them are in suspicious (disquieting) doubt concerning it.

15 Now then, for that (reason), call (them to the Faith), and stand steadfast as you are commanded, nor follow you their vain desires; but say: "I believe in the Book which Allah has sent down; and I am commanded to judge justly between you. Allah is our Lord and your Lord: on us (is the responsibility for) our deeds, and on you for your deeds. There is no contention between us and you. Allah will bring us together, and to Him is (our) final goal. 16 But those who dispute concerning Allah after He has been accepted—futile is their dispute in the Sight of their Lord: on them is Wrath, and for them will be a Chastisement terrible.

17 It is Allah Who has sent down the Book in Truth, and the Balance (by which to weigh conduct). And what will make you realise that perhaps the Hour is close at hand? 18 Only those wish to hasten it who believe not in it: those who believe hold it in awe, and know that it is the Truth. Behold, surely those that dispute concerning the Hour are far astray.

19 Gracious is Allah to His servants: He gives Sustenance to whom He pleases: and He has Power and can carry out His Will. 20 To any that desires the tilth of the Hereafter, We give increase in his tilth, and to any that desires the tilth of this world, We grant somewhat thereof, but he has no share or lot in the Hereafter.

21 What! Have they partners (in godhead), who have established for them some religion without the permission of Allah? Had it not been for the Decree of Judgment, the matter would have been decided between them (at once). But surely the wrongdoers will have a grievous Chastisement. 22 You will see the wrongdoers in fear on account of what they have earned, and (the burden of) that must (necessarily) fall on them. But those who believe and perform righteous deeds will be in the luxuriant meads of the Gardens: they shall have, from their Lord, all that they wish for. That will indeed be the magnificent Bounty (of Allah). 23 That is (the Bounty) whereof Allah gives Glad Tidings to His Servants who believe and do righteous deeds. Say: "No reward do I ask of you for this except the love of those near of kin." And if anyone earns any good, We shall give him an increase of good in respect thereof: for Allah is Oft-Forgiving, Most Ready to appreciate (service).

24 What! Do they say, "He has forged a falsehood against Allah"? But if Allah willed, He could seal up your heart. And Allah blots out Vanity, and proves the Truth by His Words. For He knows well the secrets of all hearts. 25 He is the One that accepts repentance from His Servants and forgives sins: and He knows all that you do. 26 And He listens to those who believe and do deeds of righteousness, and gives them increase of His Bounty: but for the Unbelievers there is a terrible Chastisement.

27 If Allah were to enlarge the provision for His Servants, they would indeed transgress beyond all bounds through the earth; but He sends (it) down in due measure as He pleases. For He is with His Servants well-acquainted, Watchful. 28 He is the One that sends down rain (even) after (men) have given up all hope, and scatters His Mercy (far and wide). And He is the Protector, Worthy of all Praise. 29 And among His Signs is the creation of the heavens and the earth, and the living creatures that He has scattered through them: and He has power to gather them together when He wills.

30 Whatever misfortune happens to you, is because of the things your hands have wrought, and for many (of them) He grants forgiveness. 31 Nor can you escape, through the earth; nor have you, besides Allah, any one to protect or to help.

32 And among His Signs are the ships, smooth-running through the ocean, (tall) as mountains. 33 If it be His Will He can still the Wind: then would they become motionless on the back of the (ocean). Certainly in this are Signs for everyone who patiently perseveres and is grateful. 34 Or He can cause them to perish because of the (evil) which (the men) have earned; but much does He forgive. 35 But let those know, who dispute about Our Signs, that there is for them no way of escape.

36 Whatever you are given (here) is (but) the enjoyment of this life: but that which is with Allah is better and more lasting: (it is) for those who believe and put their trust in their Lord: 37 Those who avoid the greater sins and shameful deeds, and, when they are angry even then forgive; 38 Those who respond to their Lord, and establish regular Prayer; who (conduct) their affairs

by mutual Consultation; who spend out of what We bestow on them for Sustenance; 39 And those who, when an oppressive wrong is inflicted on them, (are not cowed but) help and defend themselves. 40 The recompense for an injury is an injury equal thereto (in degree): but if a person forgives and makes reconciliation, his reward is due from Allah: for (Allah) loves not those who do wrong. 41 But indeed if any do help and defend themselves after a wrong (done) to them, against such there is no cause of blame. 42 The blame is only upon those who oppress men with wrongdoing and insolently transgress beyond bounds through the land, defying right and justice: for such there will be a Chastisement grievous. 43 But indeed if any show patience and forgive, that would truly be an exercise of courageous will and resolution in the conduct of affairs.

44 For any whom Allah leaves astray, there is no protector thereafter. And you will see the wrongdoers, when in sight of the Chastisement, say: "Is there any way (to effect) a return?" 45 And you will see them brought forward to the (Penalty), in a humble frame of mind because of (their) disgrace, (and) looking with a stealthy glance. And the Believers will say: "Those are indeed in loss, who have given to perdition their own selves and those belonging to them on the Day of Judgment. Behold! Truly the wrongdoers are in a lasting Chastisement!" 46 And no protectors have they to help them, other than Allah. And for any whom Allah leaves to stray, there is no way (to the Goal).

47 Hearken you to your Lord, before there come a Day which there will be no putting back, because of (the ordainment of) Allah! That Day there will be for you no place of refuge nor will there be for you any room for denial (of your sins)! 48 If then they turn away, We have not sent you as a guard over them. Your duty is but to convey (the Message). And truly, when We give man a taste of a Mercy from Ourselves, he does exult thereat, but when some ill happens to him, on account of the deeds which his hands have sent forth, truly then is man ungrateful!

49 To Allah belongs the dominion of the heavens and the earth. He creates what He wills (and plans). He bestows (children) male

or female according to His Will (and Plan), 50 Or He bestows
both males and females, and He leaves barren whom He will:
for He is full of knowledge and power.

51 It is not fitting for a man that Allah should speak to him except
by inspiration, or from behind a veil, or by the sending of a
Messenger to reveal, with Allah's permission, what Allah wills:
for He is Most High, Most Wise. 52 And thus have We, by Our
command, sent inspiration to you: you knew not (before) what
was Revelation, and what was Faith; but We have made the
(Qur'ān) a Light, wherewith We guide such of Our servants as
We will; and assuredly you do guide (men) to the Straight Way —
53 The Way of Allah, to Whom belongs whatever is in the heavens
and whatever is on earth. Behold (how) all affairs tend towards
Allah!

43. THE GOLD ADORNMENTS

In the name of Allah, Most Gracious, Most Merciful.

1 Hā Mīm 2 By the Book that makes things clear— 3 We have
made it a Qur'ān in Arabic, that you may be able to understand
(and learn wisdom). 4 And surely, it is in the Mother of the Book,
in Our Presence, high (in dignity), full of wisdom.

5 Shall We then take away the Message from you and repel
(you), for that you are a people transgressing beyond bounds?
6 But how many were the Prophets We sent amongst the peoples
of old? 7 And never came there a Prophet to them but they mocked
him. 8 So We destroyed (them)— stronger in power than these —
and (thus) has passed on the Parable of the peoples of old.

9 If you were to question them, 'Who created the heavens and
the earth?' They would be sure to reply, 'They were created by
(Him), the Exalted in Power, full of Knowledge'— 10 (Yes, the
same that) has made for you the earth (like a carpet) spread out,
and has made for you roads (and channels) therein, in order that

you may find guidance (on the way); 11 That sends down (from time to time) rain from the sky in due measure—and We raise to life therewith a land that is dead; even so will you be raised (from the dead)— 12 That has created pairs in all things, and has made for you ships and cattle on which you ride, 13 In order that you may sit firm and square on their backs, and when so seated, you may celebrate the (kind) favour of your Lord, and say, "Glory to Him Who has subjected these to our (use), for we could never have accomplished this (by ourselves), 14 "And to our Lord, surely, must we turn back!"

15 Yet they attribute to some of His servants a share with Him (in his godhead)! Truly is man a blasphemous ingrate avowed! 16 What! Has He taken daughters out of what He himself creates, and granted to you sons for choice? 17 When news is brought to one of them of (the birth of) what he sets up as a likeness to (Allah) Most Gracious, his face darkens, and he is filled with inward grief! 18 Is then one brought up among trinkets, and unable to give a clear account in a dispute (to be associated with Allah)? 19 And they make into females angels who themselves serve Allah. Did they witness their creation? Their evidence will be recorded, and they will be called to account!

20 ("Ah!") they say, "If it had been the will of (Allah) Most Gracious, we should not have worshipped such (deities)!" Of that they have no knowledge! They do nothing but lie! 21 What! have We given them a Book before this, to which they are holding fast? 22 No! they say: "We found our fathers following a certain religion, and we do guide ourselves by their footsteps." 23 Just in the same way, whenever We sent a Warner before you to any people, the wealthy ones among them said: "We found our fathers following a certain religion, and we will certainly follow in their footsteps." 24 He said: "What! even if I brought you better guidance than that which you found your fathers following?" They said: "For us, we deny all that which you (Prophets) are sent with." 25 So We exacted retribution from them: now see what was the end of those who rejected (Truth)!

26 Behold! Abraham said to his father and his people: "I do

indeed clear myself of what you worship: 27 "(I worship) only Him who created me, and He will certainly guide me." 28 And he left it as a Word to endure among those who came after him, that they may turn back (to Allah). 29 Yes, I have given the good things of this life to these (men) and their fathers, until the Truth has come to them, and a Messenger making things clear. 30 But when the Truth came to them, they said: "This is sorcery, and we do reject it."

31 Also, they say: "Why is not this Qur'ān sent down to some leading man in either of the two (chief) cities?" 32 Is it they who would portion out the Mercy of your Lord? It is We Who portion out between them their livelihood in the life of this world: and We raise some of them above others in ranks, so that some may command work from others. But the Mercy of your Lord is better than the (wealth) which they amass. 33 And were it not that (all) men might become of one (evil) way of life, We would provide, for everyone that blasphemes against (Allah) Most Gracious, silver roofs for their houses and (silver) stairways on which to go up, 34 And (silver) doors to their houses, and couches (of silver) on which they could recline, 35 And also adornments of gold. But all this were nothing but enjoyment of the present life: the Hereafter, in the sight of your Lord is for the Righteous.

36 If anyone withdraws himself from remembrance of (Allah) Most Gracious, We appoint for him a Satan, to be an intimate companion to him. 37 Such (Satans) really hinder them from the Path, but they think that they are being guided aright! 38 At length, when (such a one) comes to Us, he says (to his evil companion): "Would that between me and you were the distance of East and West!" Ah! evil is the companion (indeed)! 39 When you have done wrong, it will avail you nothing, that day, that you shall be partners in punishment!

40 Can you then make the deaf to hear, or give direction to the blind or to such as (wander) in manifest error? 41 Even if We take you away, We shall be sure to exact retribution from them, 42 Or We shall show you that (accomplished) which We have promised them: for certainly We can prevail over them. 43 So

hold you fast to the Revelation sent down to you; certainly you are on a Straight Way. 44 The (Qur'ān) is indeed a reminder, for you and for your people; and soon shall you (all) be brought to account. 45 And question you Our Messengers whom We sent before you; did We appoint any deities other than (Allah) Most Gracious, to be worshipped?

46 We did send Moses aforetime, with Our Signs, to Pharaoh and his Chiefs: he said, "I am a Messenger of the Lord of the Worlds." 47 But when he came to them with Our Signs, behold they ridiculed them. 48 We showed them Sign after Sign, each greater than its fellow, and We seized them with Punishment, in order that they might turn (to Us). 49 And they said, "O you sorcerer! Invoke your Lord for us according to His Covenant with you; for we shall truly accept guidance." 50 But when We removed the Chastisement from them, behold, they broke their word.

51 And Pharaoh proclaimed among his people, saying: "O my people! Does not the dominion of Egypt belong to me, (witness) these streams flowing underneath my (palace)? What! Do you not see then? 52 "Am I not better than this (Moses), who is a contemptible wretch and can scarcely express himself clearly? 53 "Then why are not gold bracelets bestowed on him, or (why) come (not) with him angels accompanying him in procession?" 54 Thus did he make fools of his people, and they obeyed him: truly they were a people rebellious (against Allah). 55 When at length they enraged Us, We exacted retribution from them, and we drowned them all. 56 And We made them (A people) of the Past and an Example to later ages.

57 When (Jesus) the son of Mary is held up as an example, behold, your people raise a clamour thereat (in ridicule)! 58 And they say, "Are our gods best, or he?" This they set forth to you, only by way of disputation: yes, they are a contentious people. 59 He was no more than a servant: We granted our favour to him, and We made him an example to the Children of Israel. 60 And if it were Our Will, We could make angels from amongst you, succeeding each other on the earth. 61 And (Jesus) shall be a Sign

(for the coming of) the Hour (of Judgment): therefore have no doubt about the (Hour), but follow you Me: this is a Straight Way. 62 Let not Satan hinder you: for he is to you an enemy avowed.

63 When Jesus came with Clear Signs, he said: "Now have I come to you with Wisdom, and in-order to make clear to you some of the (points) on which you dispute: therefore fear Allah and obey me. 64 "For Allah, He is my Lord and your Lord: so worship him: this is a Straight Way." 65 But sects from among themselves fell into disagreement: then woe to the wrongdoers, from the Chastisement of a Grievous Day!

66 Do they only wait for the Hour—that it should come on them all of a sudden, while they perceive not? 67 Friends on that Day will be foes, one to another—except the Righteous. 68 My devotees! No fear shall be on you that Day, nor shall you grieve— 69 (Being) those who have believed in Our Signs and submitted (their wills to Ours) in Islam. 70 Enter the Garden, you and your wives, in (beauty and) rejoicing. 71 To them will be passed round, dishes and goblets of gold: there will be there all that the souls could desire, all that the eyes could delight in: and you shall abide therein (for ever). 72 Such will be the Garden of which you are made heirs for your (good) deeds (in life). 73 You shall have therein abundance of fruit, from which you shall have satisfaction.

74 The sinners will be in the Punishment of Hell, to dwell therein (for ever): 75 Nowise will the (Punishment) be lightened for them, and in despair will they be there overwhelmed. 76 Nowise shall We be unjust to them: but it is they who have been unjust themselves. 77 They will cry: "O Mālik! would that your Lord put an end to us!" He will say, "No, but you shall abide!" 78 Surely We have brought the Truth to you: but most of you have an aversion for Truth. 79 What! have they settled some plan (among themselves)? But it is We Who settle things. 80 Or do they think that We hear not their secrets and their private counsels? Indeed ('We do), and Our messengers are by them, to record.

81 Say: "If (Allah) Most Gracious had a son, I would be the first to worship." 82 Glory to the Lord of the heavens and the earth, the Lord of the Throne (of Authority)! (He is free) from the things they attribute (to Him)! 83 So leave them to babble and play (with vanities) until they meet that Day of theirs, which they have been promised.

84 It is He Who is God in heaven and God on earth; and He is full of Wisdom and Knowledge. 85 And blessed is He to Whom belongs the dominion of the heavens and the earth, and all between them: with Him is the Knowledge of the Hour (of Judgment): and to Him shall you be brought back.

86 And those whom they invoke besides Allah have no power of intercession—only he who bears witness to the Truth, and they know (him). 87 If you ask them, "Who created them, they will certainly say, Allah: how then are they deluded away (from the Truth)? 88 (Allah has knowledge) of the (Prophet's) cry, "O my Lord! Truly these are a people who do not believe!" 89 But turn away from them, and say "Peace!" but soon shall they know!

44. THE SMOKE

In the name of Allah, Most Gracious, Most Merciful.

1 *Hā Mīm*. 2 By the Book that makes things clear— 3 We sent it down during a blessed night: for We (ever) wish to warn (against Evil). 4 In that (night) is made distinct every affair of wisdom, 5 By command, from Our presence. For We (ever) send (revelations), 6 As a Mercy from your Lord: for He hears and knows (all things); 7 The Lord of the heavens and the earth and all between them, if you (but) have an assured faith. 8 There is no deity save Him: it is He Who gives life and gives death—The Lord and Cherisher to you and your earliest ancestors.

9 Yet they play about in doubt. 10 Then watch you for the Day that the sky will bring forth a kind of smoke (or mist) plainly visible, 11 Enveloping the people: this will be a Chastisement

grievous. 12 (They will say:) "Our Lord! Remove the Chastisement from us, for we do really believe!" 13 How shall the Message be (effectual) for them, seeing that a Messenger explaining things clearly has (already) come to them — 14 Yet they turn away from him and say: "Tutored (by others), a man possessed!" 15 We shall indeed remove the Chastisement for a while, (but) truly you will revert (to your ways). 16 One day We shall seize you with a mighty onslaught: We will indeed (then) exact Retribution!

17 We did, before them, try the people of Pharaoh: there came to them a Messenger most honourable, 18 Saying: "Restore to me the Servants of Allah: I am to you a Messenger worthy of all trust; 19 "And be not arrogant as against Allah: for I come to you with authority manifest. 20 "For me, I have sought safety with my Lord and your Lord, against your injuring me. 21 "If you believe me not, at least keep yourselves away from me."

22 (But they were aggressive:) then he cried to his Lord: "These are indeed a people given to sin." 23 (The reply came:) "March forth with My servants by night: for you are sure to be pursued. 24 "And leave the sea as a furrow (divided): for they are a host (destined) to be drowned." 25 How many were the gardens and springs they left behind, 26 And corn-fields and noble buildings, 27 And wealth (and conveniences of life), wherein they had taken such delight! 28 Thus (was their end)! and We made other people inherit (those things)! 29 And neither heaven nor earth shed a tear over them: nor were they given a respite (again).

30 We did deliver aforetime the Children of Israel from humiliating Punishment, 31 Inflicted by Pharaoh, for he was arrogant (even) among inordinate transgressors. 32 And We chose them aforetime above the nations, knowingly, 33 And granted them Signs in which there was a manifest trial.

34 As to these (Quraysh), they say forsooth: 35 "There is nothing beyond our first death, and we shall not be raised again. 36 "Then bring (back) our forefathers, if what you say is true!" 37 What! Are they better than the people of Tubba‘ and those who were before them? We destroyed them because they were guilty of sin.

38 We created not the heavens, the earth, and all between them,

merely in (idle) sport: 39 We created them not except for just ends: but most of them do not understand. 40 Surely the Day of sorting out is the time appointed for all of them— 41 The Day when no protector can avail his client in aught, and no help can they receive, 42 Except such as receive Allah's Mercy: for He is Exalted in Might, Most Merciful.

43 Surely the tree of Zaqqūm 44 Will be the food of the Sinful— 45 Like molten brass; it will boil in their insides, 46 Like the boiling of scalding water. 47 (A voice will cry:) "Seize him and drag him into the midst of the Blazing Fire! 48 "Then pour over his head the Chastisement of Boiling Water 49 "Taste you (this)! Truly were you mighty, full of honour! 50 "Truly this is what you used to doubt!"

51 As to the Righteous (they will be) in a position of Security, 52 Among Gardens and Springs; 53 Dressed in fine silk and in rich brocade, they will face each other; 54 So; and We shall join them to Companions with beautiful, big, and lustrous eyes. 55 There can they call for every kind of fruit in peace and security; 56 Nor will they there taste Death, except the first death; and He will preserve them from the Chastisement of the Blazing Fire— 57 As a Bounty from your Lord! That will be the supreme achievement!

58 Surely, We have made this (Qur'ān) easy, in your tongue, in order that they may give heed. 59 So wait and watch; for they (too) are waiting.

45. THE KNEELING DOWN

In the name of Allah, Most Gracious, Most Merciful.

1 Hā Mīm. 2 The revelation of the Book is from Allah the Exalted in Power, full of Wisdom. 3 Surely in the heavens and the earth, are Signs for those who believe. 4 And in the creation of yourselves and the fact that animals are scattered (through the earth), are Signs for those of assured Faith. 5 And in the alternation of Night and Day, and the fact that Allah sends down

Sustenance from the sky, and revives therewith the earth after its death, and in the change of the winds—are Signs for those that are wise. 6 Such are the Signs of Allah, which We rehearse to you in truth; then in what exposition will they believe after (rejecting) Allah and His Signs?

7 Woe to each sinful dealer in Falsehoods: 8 He hears the Signs of Allah rehearsed to him, yet is obstinate and lofty, as if he had not heard them: then announce to him a Chastisement Grievous! 9 And when he learns something of Our Signs, he takes them in jest: for such there will be a humiliating Chastisement. 10 In front of them is hell: and of no profit to them is anything they may have earned, nor any protectors they may have taken to themselves besides Allah: for them is a tremendous Chastisement. 11 This is (true) Guidance: and for those who reject the Signs of their Lord, is a Grievous Chastisement of abomination.

12 It is Allah Who has subjected the sea to you, that ships may sail upon it by His command, that you may seek of His Bounty, and that you may be grateful. 13 And He has subjected to you, as from Him, all that is in the heavens and on earth: behold, in that are Signs indeed for those who reflect.

14 Tell those who believe, to forgive those who do not look forward to the Days of Allah: it is for Him to recompense (for good or ill) each People according to what they have earned. 15 If anyone does a righteous deed, it ensures to the benefit of his own soul; if he does evil, it works against (His own soul). In the end will you (all) be brought back to your Lord.

16 We did aforetime grant to the Children of Israel the Book, the Power of Command, and Prophethood; We gave them, for Sustenance, things good and pure; and We favoured them above the nations. 17 And We granted them clear Signs in affairs (of Religion): it was only after knowledge had been granted to them that they fell into schisms, through insolent envy among themselves. Surely your Lord will judge between them on the Day of Judgment as to those matters in which they set up differences. 18 Then We put you on the (right) Way of Religion: so follow that (Way), and follow not the desires of those who

know not. 19 They will be of no use to you in the sight of Allah: it is only wrongdoers (that stand as) protectors, one to another: but Allah is the Protector of the Righteous. 20 These are clear evidences to men and a Guidance and Mercy to those of assured Faith.

21 What! Do those who seek after evil ways think that We shall hold them equal with those who believe and do righteous deeds — that equal will be their life and their death? Ill is the judgment that they make. 22 Allah created the heavens and the earth for just ends, and in order that each soul may find the recompense of what it has earned, and none of them be wronged.

23 Then do you see such a one as takes as his god his own vain desire? Allah has, knowing (him as such), left him astray, and sealed his hearing and his heart (and understanding), and put a cover on his sight. who, then, will guide him after Allah (has withdrawn guidance)? Will you not then receive admonition?

24 And they say: "What is there but our life in this world? We shall die and we live, and nothing but time can destroy us." But of that they have no knowledge: they merely conjecture: 25 And when Our Clear Signs are rehearsed to them their argument is nothing but this: they say, "Bring (back) our forefathers, if what you say is true!" 26 Say: "It is Allah Who gives you life, then gives you death; then He will gather you together for the Day of Judgment about which there is no doubt": but most men do not understand.

27 To Allah belongs the dominion of the heavens and the earth, and the Day that the Hour of Judgment is established — that Day will the dealers in Falsehood perish! 28 And you will see every sect bowing the knee: every sect will be called to its Record: "This Day shall you be recompensed for all that you did! 29 "This Our Record speaks about you with truth: for We were wont to put on record all that you did."

30 Then, as to those who believed and did righteous deeds, their Lord will admit them to His Mercy that will be the Achievement Manifest. 31 But as to those who rejected Allah, (to them will be said): "Were not our Signs rehearsed to you? But you were

arrogant, and were a people given to sin! 32 "And when it was said that the promise of Allah was true, and that the Hour— there was no doubt about its (coming), you used to say, 'We know not what is the Hour: we only think it is a conjecture, and we have no firm assurance."

33 Then will appear to them the evil (fruits) of what they did, and they will be completely encircled by that which they used to mock at! 34 It will also be said: "This Day We will forget you as you forgot the meeting of this Day of yours! And your abode is the Fire, and no helpers have you! 35 "This, because you used to take the Signs of Allah in jest, and the life of the world deceived you:" (from) that Day, therefore, they shall not be taken out thence, nor shall they be able to avert Allah's Wrath.

36 Then Praise be to Allah, Lord of the heavens and Lord of the earth— Lord and Cherisher of all the Worlds! 37 To Him be Glory throughout the heavens and the earth: and He is Exalted in Power, full of Wisdom!

46. WINDING SAND-TRACTS

In the name of Allah, Most Gracious, Most Merciful.

1 *Hā Mīm.* 2 The Revelation of the Book is from Allah the Exalted in Power, full of Wisdom. 3 We created not the heavens and the earth and all between them but for just ends, and for a term appointed : but those who reject Faith turn away from that whereof they are warned.

4 Say: "Do you see what it is you invoke besides Allah? Show me what it is they have created on earth, or have they a share in the heavens? Bring me a Book (revealed) before this, or any remnant of knowledge (you may have), if you are telling the truth! 5 And who is more astray than one who invokes besides Allah, such as will not answer him to the Day of Judgment, and who (in fact) are unconscious of their call (to them)? 6 And when

mankind are gathered together (at the Resurrection), they will be hostile to them and reject their worship (altogether)!

7 When Our Clear Signs are rehearsed to them, the Unbelievers say, of the Truth when it comes to them: "This is evident sorcery!" 8 Or do they say, "He has forged it"? Say: "Had I forged it, then you have no power to help me against Allah. He knows best of that whereof you talk (so glibly)! Enough is He for a witness between me and you! And He is Oft-Forgiving, Most Merciful."

9 Say: "I am no bringer of new-fangled doctrine among the Messengers, nor do I know what will be done with me or with you. I follow but that which is revealed to me by inspiration; I am but a Warner open and clear." 10 Say: "Do you see? If (this teaching) be from Allah, and you reject it, and a witness from among the Children of Israel testifies to its similarity (with earlier scripture), and has believed while you are arrogant, (how unjust you are!) Truly, Allah guides not a people unjust."

11 The Unbelievers say of those who believe: "If (this Message) were a good thing, (such men) would not have gone to it first, before us!" and seeing that they guide not themselves thereby, they will say, "This is an (old) falsehood!"

12 And before this, was the Book of Moses as a guide and a mercy: and this Book confirms (it) in the Arabic tongue; to admonish the unjust, and as Glad Tidings to those who do right. 13 Surely those who say, "Our Lord is Allah," and remain firm (on that Path)— on them shall be no fear, nor shall they grieve. 14 Such shall be Companions of the Garden, dwelling therein (for ever): a recompense for their (good) deeds.

15 We have enjoined on man kindness to his parents: in pain did his mother bear him, and in pain did she give him birth. The carrying of the (child) to his weaning is (a period of) thirty months. At length, when he reaches the age of full strength and attains forty years, he says, "O my Lord! Grant me that I may be grateful for Your favour which You have bestowed upon me, and upon both my parents, and that I may work righteousness such as You may approve; and be gracious to me in my issue. Truly have I turned to You and truly do I bow (to You) in Islam."

16 Such are they from whom we shall accept the best of their deeds and pass by their ill deeds: (they shall be) among the Companions of the Garden: a promise! Of truth, which was made to them (in this life).

17 But (there is one) who says to his parents, "Fie on you! Do you hold out the promise to me that I shall be raised up, even though generations have passed before me (without rising again)?" And they two seek Allah's aid, (and rebuke the son): "Woe to you! Have Faith! For the promise of Allah is true." But he says, "This is nothing but tales of the ancients!" 18 Such are they against whom is proved the Sentence among the previous generations of Jinns and men, that have passed away; for they will be (utterly) lost.

19 And to all are (assigned) degrees according to the deeds which they (have done), and in order that (Allah) may recompense their deeds, and no injustice be done to them. 20 And on the Day that the Unbelievers will be placed before the Fire, (It will be said to them): "You squandered your good things in the life of the world, and you took your pleasure out of them: but today shall you be recompensed with a Penalty of humiliation: for that you were arrogant on earth without just cause, and that you (ever) transgressed."

21 Mention (Hūd) one of 'Ād's (own) brethren: Behold, he warned his people about the winding Sand-tracts: but there have been Warners before him and after him: "Worship you none other than Allah: truly I fear for you the Chastisement of a Mighty Day." 22 They said: "Have you come in order to turn us aside from our gods? Then bring upon us the (calamity) with which you threaten us, if you are telling the truth?" 23 He said: "The Knowledge (of when it will come) is only with Allah: I proclaim to you the mission on which I have been sent: but I see that you are a people in ignorance!"...

24 Then, when they saw the (Penalty in the shape of) a cloud traversing the sky, coming to meet their valleys, they said, "This cloud will give us rain!" "No, it is the (calamity) you were asking to be hastened! — a wind wherein is a Grievous Chastisement! 25 "Everything will it destroy by the command of its Lord!" Then

by the morning nothing was to be seen but (the ruins of) their houses! Thus do We recompense those given to sin!

26 And We had firmly established them in a (prosperity and) power which We have not given to you (you Quraysh!) and We had endowed them with (faculties of) hearing, seeing, heart and intellect: but of no benefit to them were their (faculties of) hearing, sight, and heart and intellect, when they went on rejecting the Signs of Allah; and they were (completely) encircled by that which they used to mock at! 27 We destroyed aforetime populations round about you; and We have shown the Signs in various ways, that they may turn (to Us). 28 Why then was no help forthcoming to them from those whom they worshipped as gods, besides Allah, as a means of access (to Allah)? No, they left them in the lurch: but that was their falsehood and their invention.

29 Behold, We turned towards you a company of Jinns (quietly) listening to the Qur'ān: when they stood in the presence thereof, they said, "Listen in silence!" When the (reading) was finished, they returned to their people, to warn (them of their sins). 30 They said, "O our people! We have heard a Book revealed after Moses, confirming what came before it: it guides (men) to the Truth and to a Straight Path. 31 "O our people, hearken to the one who invites (you) to Allah, and believe in Him: He will forgive you your faults, and deliver you from a Chastisement Grievous. 32 "If any does not listen to the one who invites (us) to Allah, he cannot escape in the earth, and no protectors can he have besides Allah: such men (wander) in manifest error."

33 See they not that Allah, Who created the heavens and the earth, and never wearied with their creation, is able to give life to the dead? Yes, surely He has power over all things. 34 And on the Day that the Unbelievers will be placed before the Fire, (they will be asked,) "Is this not the Truth?" They will say, "Yes, by our Lord!" (one will say:) "Then taste you the Chastisement, for that you were wont to deny (Truth)!"

35 Therefore patiently persevere, as did (all) Messengers of inflexible purpose; and be in no haste about the (Unbelievers). On the Day that they see the (Punishment) promised them, (it will be) as if they had not tarried more than an hour in a single

day. (Yours is but) to deliver the Message: but shall any be destroyed except those who transgress?

47. MUHAMMAD

In the name of Allah, Most Gracious, Most Merciful.

1 Those who reject Allah and hinder (men) from the Path of Allah— Their deeds will Allah make futile and fruitless. 2 But those who believe and work deeds of righteousness, and believe in the (Revelation) sent down to Muhammad—for it is the Truth from their Lord— He will remove from them their ills and improve their condition. 3 This because those who reject Allah follow vanities, while those who believe follow the Truth from their Lord: thus does Allah set forth for men their lessons by similitudes.

4 Therefore, when you meet the Unbelievers (in fight), smite at their necks; at length, when you have thoroughly subdued them, bind (the captives) firmly: thereafter (is the time for) either generosity or ransom: until the war lays down its burdens. Thus (are you commanded): but if it had been Allah's Will, He could certainly have exacted retribution from them (Himself); but (He lets you fight) in order to test you, some with others. But those who are slain in the Way of Allah— He will never let their deeds be lost. 5 Soon will He guide them and improve their condition, 6 And admit them to the Garden which He has announced for them.

7 O you who believe! If you will aid (the cause of) Allah, He will aid you, and plant your feet firmly. 8 But those who reject (Allah)— for them is destruction, and (Allah) will make their deeds go waste. 9 That is because they hate the Revelation of Allah; so He has made their deeds fruitless. 10 Do they not travel through the earth, and see what was the End of those before them (who did evil)? Allah brought utter destruction on them, and similar (fates await) those who reject Allah. 11 That is because Allah is the Protector of those who believe, but those who reject Allah have no protector.

12 Surely Allah will admit those who believe and do righteous deeds, to Gardens beneath which rivers flow; while those who reject Allah will enjoy (this world) and eat as cattle eat; and the Fire will be their abode. 13 And how many cities, with more power than your city which has driven you out, have We destroyed (For their sins)? and there was none to help them.

14 Is then one who is on a clear (Path) from his Lord, no better than one to whom the evil of his conduct seems pleasing, and such as follow their own lusts? 15 (Here is) a description of the Garden which the righteous are promised: in it are rivers of water incorruptible; rivers of milk of which the taste never changes; rivers of wine, a joy to those who drink; and rivers of honey pure and clear. In it there are for them all kinds of fruits; and Grace from their Lord. (Can those in such Bliss) be compared to such as shall dwell forever in the Fire, and be given, to drink, boiling water, so that it cuts up their bowels (into pieces)?

16 And among them are men who listen to you, but in the end, when they go away from you, they say to those who have received Knowledge, "What is it he said just then?" Such are men whose hearts Allah has sealed, and who follow their own lusts. 17 But to those who receive guidance, He increases the (light of) Guidance, and bestows on them their Piety and Restraint (from evil).

18 Do they then only wait for the Hour—that it should come on them of a sudden? But already have come some tokens thereof, and when it (actually) is on them, how can they benefit then by their admonition? 19 Know, therefore, that there is no god but Allah, and ask forgiveness for your fault, and for the men and women who believe: for Allah knows how you move about and how you dwell in your homes.

20 Those who believe say, "Why is not a sūrah sent down (for us)?" But when a sūrah of basic or categorical meaning is revealed, and fighting is mentioned therein, you will see those in whose hearts is a disease looking at you with a look of one in swoon at the approach of death. But more fitting for them— 21 Were it to obey and say what is just, and when a matter is resolved on,

it were best for them if they were true to Allah. 22 Then, is it to be expected of you, if you were put in authority, that you will do mischief in the land, and break your ties of kith and kin? 23 Such are the men whom Allah has cursed, for He has made them deaf and blinded their sight.

24 Do they not then earnestly seek to understand the Qur'ān, or are their hearts locked up by them? 25 Those who turn back as apostates after Guidance was clearly shown to them— Satan has instigated them and buoyed them up with false hopes. 26 This, because they said to those who hate what Allah has revealed, "We will obey you in part of (this) matter." But Allah knows their (inner) secrets. 27 But how (will it be) when the angels take their souls at death, and smite their faces and their backs? 28 This because they followed that which called forth the Wrath of Allah, and they hated Allah's good pleasure; so He made their deeds of no effect.

29 Or do those in whose hearts is a disease, think that Allah will not bring to light all their rancour? 30 Had We so willed, We could have shown them up to you, and you should have known them by their marks: but surely you will know them by the tone of their speech! And Allah knows all that you do.

31 And We shall try you until We test those among you who strive their utmost and persevere in patience; and We shall try your reported (mettle). 32 Those who reject Allah, hinder (men) from the Path of Allah, and resist the Messenger, after Guidance has been clearly shown to them, will not injure Allah in the least, but He will make their deeds of no effect.

33 O you who believe! Obey Allah, and obey the Messenger, and make not vain your deeds! 34 Those who reject Allah, and hinder (men) from the Path of Allah, then die rejecting Allah— Allah will not forgive them. 35 Be not weary and fainthearted, crying for peace, when you are the uppermost: for Allah is with you, and will never put you in loss for your (good) deeds.

36 The life of this world is but play and amusement: and if you believe and guard against evil, He will grant you your recompense, and will not ask you (to give up) your possessions.

37 If He were to ask you for all of them, and press you, you would covetously withhold, and He would bring out all your ill-feeling. 38 Behold, you are those invited to spend (of your substance) in the Way of Allah: but among you are some that are niggardly. But any who are niggardly are so at the expense of their own souls. But Allah is free of all wants, and it is you that are needy. If you turn back (from the Path), He will substitute in your stead another people; then they would not be like you!

48. THE VICTORY

In the name of Allah, Most Gracious, Most Merciful.

1 Surely We have granted you a manifest Victory: 2 That Allah may forgive you your faults of the past and those to follow; fulfil His favour to you; and guide you on the Straight Way; 3 And that Allah may help you with powerful help.

4 It is He Who sent down Tranquillity into the hearts of the Believers, that they might add faith to their faith — for to Allah belong the Forces of the heavens and the earth; and Allah is full of Knowledge and Wisdom — 5 That He may admit the men and women who believe, to Gardens beneath which rivers flow, to dwell therein for ever, and remove their wrong-doings from them — and that is, in the sight of Allah, the highest achievement (for man) — 6 And that He may punish the Hypocrites, men and women, and the Polytheists men and women, who harbour an evil opinion of Allah. On them is a round of Evil: the Wrath of Allah is on them: He has cursed them and got Hell ready for them: and evil is it for a destination. 7 For to Allah belong the Forces of the heavens and the earth; and Allah is exalted in Power, full of Wisdom.

8 We have truly sent you as a witness, as a bringer of Glad Tidings, and as a Warner: 9 In order that you (O men) may believe in Allah and His Messenger, that you may assist and honour Him, and celebrate His praises morning and evening. 10 Surely those

who plight their fealty to you do no less than plight their fealty to Allah: the Hand of Allah is over their hands: then anyone who violates his oath, does so to the harm of his own soul, and anyone who fulfils what he has covenanted with Allah— Allah will soon grant him a great Reward.

11 The desert Arabs who lagged behind will say to you: "We were engaged in (looking after) our flocks and herds, and our families: do you then ask forgiveness for us." They say with their tongues what is not in their hearts. Say: "Who then has any power at all (to intervene) on your behalf with Allah, if His Will is to give you some loss or to give you some profit? But Allah is well acquainted with all that you do. 12 "No, you thought that the Messenger and the Believers would never return to their families; this seemed pleasing in your hearts, and you conceived an evil thought, for you are a people doomed to perish." 13 And if any believe not in Allah and His Messenger, We have prepared, for those who reject Allah, a Blazing Fire! 14 To Allah belongs the dominion of the heavens and the earth: He forgives whom He wills, and He punishes whom He wills: but Allah is Oft-Forgiving, Most Merciful.

15 Those who lagged behind (will say), when you set forth to acquire booty (in war): "Permit us to follow you." They wish to change Allah's decree: say: "Not thus will you follow us: Allah has already declared (this) beforehand": then they will say, "But you are jealous of us." No, but little do they understand (such things).

16 Say to the desert Arabs who lagged behind: "You shall be summoned (to fight) against a people given to vehement war: then shall you fight, or they shall submit. Then if you show obedience, Allah will grant you a goodly reward, but if you turn back as you did before, He will punish you with a Grievous Chastisement." 17 No blame is there on the blind, nor is there blame on the lame, nor on one ill (if he joins not the war): but he that obeys Allah and His Messenger —(Allah) will admit him to Gardens beneath which rivers flow: and he who turns back, (Allah) will punish him with a Grievous Chastisement.

18 Allah's Good Pleasure was on the Believers when they swore Fealty to you under the Tree: He knew what was in their hearts, and He sent down Tranquillity to them; and He rewarded them with a speedy Victory; 19 And many gains will they acquire (besides): and Allah is Exalted in Power, Full of Wisdom. 20 Allah has promised you many gains that you shall acquire, and He has given you these beforehand; and He has restrained the hands of men from you; that it may be a Sign for the Believers, and that He may guide you to a Straight Path; 21 And other gains (there are), which are not within your power, but which Allah has compassed: and Allah has power over all things.

22 If the Unbelievers were to fight you, they would certainly have turned their backs; then would they have found neither protector nor helper. 23 (Such has been) the practice of Allah already in the past: no change will you find in the practice (approved) of Allah. 24 And it is He Who has restrained their hands from you and your hands from them in the midst of Makkah; after that He gave you the victory over them. And Allah sees well all that you do.

25 They are the ones who denied Revelation and hindered you from the Sacred Mosque and the sacrificial animals, detained from reaching their place of sacrifice. Had there not been believing men and believing women whom you did not know that you were trampling down and on whose account a crime would have accrued to you without (your) knowledge, (Allah would have allowed you to force your way, but he held back your hands) that He may admit to His Mercy whom He will. If they had been apart, We should certainly have punished the Unbelievers among them with a grievous Punishment.

26 While the Unbelievers got up in their hearts heat and cant — the heat and cant of ignorance — Allah sent down His Tranquillity to His Messenger and to the Believers, and made them stick close to the command of self-restraint; and well were they entitled to it and 'worthy of it. And Allah has full knowledge of all things.

27 Truly did Allah fulfil the vision for His Messenger: you shall enter the Sacred mosque, if Allah wills, with minds secure, heads

shaved, hair cut short, and without fear. For He knew what you knew not, and He granted, besides, a victory soon to come.

28 It is He Who has sent His Messenger with Guidance and the Religion of Truth, to proclaim it over all religion: and enough is Allah for a Witness.

29 Muhammad is the Messenger of Allah; and those who are with him are strong against Unbelievers, (but) compassionate amongst each other. You will see them bow and prostrate themselves (in prayer), seeking Grace from Allah and (His) Good Pleasure. On their faces are their marks, (being) the traces of their prostration. This is their similitude in the Torah; and their similitude in the Gospel is: like a seed which sends forth its blade, then makes it strong; it then becomes thick, and it stands on its own stem, (filling) the sowers with wonder and delight. As a result, it fills the Unbelievers with rage at them. Allah has promised those among them who believe and do righteous deeds forgiveness, and a great Reward.

49. THE INNER APARTMENTS

In the name of Allah, Most Gracious, Most Merciful.

1 O you who believe! Put not yourselves forward before Allah and His Messenger; but fear Allah: for Allah is He Who hears and knows all things.

2 O you who believe! Raise not your voices above the voice of the Prophet, nor speak aloud to him in talk, as you may speak aloud to one another, lest your deeds become vain and you perceive not. 3 Those that lower their voices in the presence of Allah's Messenger—their hearts has Allah tested for piety: for them is Forgiveness and a great Reward. 4 Those who shout out to you from without the Inner Apartments— most of them lack understanding. 5 If only they had patience until you could come out to them, it would be best for them: but Allah is Oft-Forgiving, Most Merciful.

6 O you who believe! If a wicked person comes to you with any news, ascertain the truth, lest you harm people unwittingly, and afterwards become full of repentance for what you have done. 7 And know that among you is Allah's Messenger: were he, in many matters, to follow your (wishes), you would certainly fall into misfortune: but Allah has endeared the Faith to you, and has made it beautiful in your hearts, and He has made hateful to you unbelief, wickedness, and rebellion: such indeed are those who walk in righteousness;— 8 A Grace and Favour from Allah; and Allah is full of Knowledge and Wisdom.

9 If two parties among the Believers fall into a quarrel, make you peace between them: but if one of them transgresses beyond bounds against the other, then fight you (all) against the one that transgresses until it complies with the command of Allah; but if it complies, then make peace between them with justice, and be fair: for Allah loves those who are fair (and just). 10 The Believers are but a single Brotherhood: so make peace and reconciliation between your two (contending) brothers; and fear Allah, that you may receive Mercy.

11 O you who believe! Let not some men among you laugh at others: it may be that the (latter) are better than the (former): nor let some women laugh at others: it may be that the (latter) are better than the (former): nor defame nor be sarcastic to each other, nor call each other by (offensive) nicknames: ill-seeming is a name connoting wickedness, (to be used of one) after he has believed: and those who do not desist are (indeed) doing wrong.

12 O you who believe! Avoid suspicion as much (as possible): for suspicion in some cases is a sin: and spy not on each other behind their backs. Would any of you like to eat the flesh of his dead brother? No, you would abhor it...But fear Allah: for Allah is Oft-Returning, Most Merciful.

13 O mankind! We created you from a single (pair) of a male and a female, and made you into nations and tribes, that you may know each other (not that you may despise each other). Surely the most honoured of you in the sight of Allah is (he who is) the most righteous of you. And Allah has full knowledge and is well acquainted (with all things).

14 The desert Arabs say, "We believe." Say, "You have no faith; but you (only) say, 'We have submitted our wills to Allah,' for not yet has Faith entered your hearts. But if you obey Allah and His Messenger, He will not belittle any of your deeds: for Allah is Oft-Forgiving, Most Merciful." 15 Only those are Believers who have believed in Allah and His Messenger, and have never since doubted, but have striven with their belongings and their persons in the Cause of Allah: such are the sincere ones.

16 Say: "What! Will you inform Allah about your religion? But Allah knows all that is in the heavens and on earth: He has full knowledge of all things. 17 They impress on you as a favour that they have embraced Islam. Say, "Count not your Islam as a favour upon me: No, Allah has conferred a favour upon you that He has guided you to the Faith, if you be true and sincere. 18 "Surely Allah knows the Unseen of the heavens and the earth: and Allah sees well all that you do."

50. QĀF

In the name of Allah, Most Gracious, Most Merciful.

1 Qāf: By the Glorious Qur'ān (you are Allah's Messenger). 2 But they wonder that there has come to them a Warner from among themselves. So the Unbelievers say: "A strange thing is this! 3 "What! When we die and become dust, (shall we live again?) That is a (sort of) return far (from our understanding)." 4 We already know how much of them the earth takes away: with Us is a record guarding (the full account). 5 But they deny the Truth when it comes to them: so they are in a confused state.

6 Do they not look at the sky above them?— How We have made it and adorned it, and there are no flaws in it? 7 And the earth— We have spread it out, and set thereon mountains standing firm, and produced therein every kind of beautiful growth (in pairs)— 8 To be observed and commemorated by every devotee turning (to Allah). 9 And We send down from the sky rain charged with blessing, and We produce therewith gardens and Grain for harvests; 10 And tall (and stately) palm-trees, with shoots of fruit-

stalks, piled one over another— 11 As sustenance for (Allah's)
Servants— and We give (new) life therewith to land that is dead:
thus will be the Resurrection.

12 Before them was denied (the Hereafter) by the People of
Noah, the People of the Rass, the Thamūd, 13 The 'Ād, Pharaoh,
the brethren of Lūt, 14 The People of the Wood, and the People
of Tubba'; each one (of them) rejected the Messengers, and My
warning was duly fulfilled (in them). 15 Were We then weary
with the first Creation, that they should be in confused doubt about
a new Creation?

16 It was We Who created man, and We know what dark
suggestions his soul makes to him: for We are nearer to him
than (his) jugular vein. 17 Behold, two (guardian angels)
appointed to learn (his doings) learn (and note them), one sitting
on the right and one on the left. 18 Not a word does he utter but
there is a sentinel by him, ready (to note it).

19 And the stupor of death will bring Truth (before his eyes):
"This was the thing which you were trying to escape!" 20 And
the Trumpet shall be blown: that will be the Day whereof
Warning (had been given). 21 And there will come forth every
soul: with each will be an (angel) to drive, and an (angel) to bear
witness. 22 (It will be said:) "You were heedless of this; now have
We removed your veil, and sharp is your sight this Day!"
23 And his Companion will say: "Here is (his Record) ready with
me!" 24 (The sentence will be:) "Throw, throw into Hell every
contumacious Rejecter (of Allah)!— 25 "Who forbade what was
good, transgressed all bounds, cast doubts and suspicions;
26 "Who set up another god beside Allah: throw him into a severe
Chastisement." 27 His Companion will say: "Our Lord! I did not
make him transgress, but he was (himself) far astray." 28 He will
say: "Dispute not with each other in My Presence: I had already
in advance sent you Warning. 29 "The Word changes not with
Me, and I do not the least injustice to My Servants."

30 One Day We will ask Hell, "Are you filled to the full?" It
will say, "Are there any more (to come)?" 31 And the Garden
will be brought near to the Righteous— no more a thing distant.
32 (A voice will say:) "This is what was promised for you— for

everyone who turned (to Allah) in sincere repentance, who kept
(His Law), 33 "Who feared (Allah) most Gracious Unseen, and
brought a heart turned in devotion (to Him): 34 "Enter you therein
in Peace and Security; this is a Day of Eternal Life!" 35 There
will be for them therein all that they wish— and more besides
in Our Presence.

36 But how many generations before them did We destroy (for
their sins)—stronger in power than they? Then did they wander
through the land: was there any place of escape (for them)?
37 Certainly in this is a Message for any that has a heart and
understanding or who gives ear and earnestly witnesses (the
truth).

38 We created the heavens and the earth and all between them
in Six Days, nor did any sense of weariness touch Us. 39 Bear,
then, with patience, all that they say, and celebrate the praises
of your Lord, before the rising of the sun and before (its) setting.
40 And during part of the night, (also,) celebrate His praises, and
(so likewise) after the Prostration.

41 And listen for the Day when the Caller will call out from
a place quite near— 42 The Day when they will hear a (mighty)
Blast in (very) truth: that will be the Day of Resurrection.
43 Surely it is We Who give Life and Death; and to Us is the Final
Return— 44 The Day when the Earth will be rent asunder, letting
(men) hurrying out: that will be a gathering together— quite easy
for Us.

45 We know best what they say; and you are not one to compel
them by force. So admonish with the Qur'ān such as fear My
Warning!

51. THE WINDS THAT SCATTER

In the name of Allah, Most Gracious, Most Merciful.

1 By the (Winds) that scatter broadcast; 2 And those that lift and
bear away heavy weights; 3 And those that flow with ease and
gentleness; 4 And those that distribute and apportion by
Command— 5 Surely that which you are promised is true; 6 And

surely Judgment and Justice must indeed come to pass. 7 By the Sky with (its) numerous Paths, 8 Truly you are in a doctrine discordant, 9 Through which are deluded (away from the Truth) such as would be deluded.

10 Woe to the conjecturers— 11 Those who (flounder) heedless in a flood of confusion: 12 They ask, "When will be the Day of Judgment and Justice?" 13 (It will be) a Day when they will be tried (and tested) over the Fire! 14 "Taste you your trial! This is what you used to ask to be hastened!" 15 As to the Righteous, they will be in the midst of Gardens and Springs, 16 Taking joy in the things which their Lord gives them, because, before then, they lived a good life. 17 They were in the habit of sleeping but little by night, 18 And in the hours of early dawn, they (were found) praying for Forgiveness; 19 And in their wealth and possessions (was remembered) the right of the (needy,) him who asked, and him who (for some reason) was prevented (from asking).

20 On the earth are signs for those of assured Faith, 21 As also in your own selves: will you not then see? 22 And in heaven is your Sustenance, as (also) that which you are promised. 23 Then, by the Lord of heaven and earth, this is the very Truth, as much as the fact that you can speak intelligently to each other.

24 Has the story reached you, of the honoured guests of Abraham?   25 Behold, they entered his presence, and said: "Peace!" He said, "Peace!" (and thought, "These seem) unusual people." 26 Then he turned quickly to his household, brought out a fatted calf, 27 And placed it before them.. he said, "Will you not eat?" 28 (When they did not eat), he conceived a fear of them. They said, "Fear not," and they gave him glad tidings of a son endowed with knowledge. 29 But his wife came clamouring (in surprise): she smote her forehead and said: "A barren old woman!" 30 They said, "Even so has your Lord spoken: and He is full of Wisdom and Knowledge."

31 (Abraham) said: "And what, O you Messengers, is your errand (now)?" 32 They said, "We have been sent to a people (deep) in sin— 33 "To bring on, on them, (a shower of) stones

of clay (brimstone), 34 "Marked as from your Lord for those who trespass beyond bounds." 35 Then We evacuated those of the Believers who were there, 36 But We found not there any just (Muslim) persons except in one house: 37 And We left there a Sign for such as fear the Grievous Chastisement.

38 And in Moses (was another Sign): behold, We sent him to Pharaoh, with authority manifest. 39 But (Pharaoh) turned back with his Chiefs, and said, "A sorcerer, or one possessed!" 40 So We took him and his forces, and threw them into the sea; and his was the blame. 41 And in the 'Ad (people) (was another Sign): Behold, We sent against them the devastating Wind: 42 It left nothing whatever that it came up against, but reduced it to ruin and rottenness. 43 And in the Thamūd (was another Sign): Behold, they were told, "Enjoy (your brief day) for a little while!" 44 But they insolently defied the Command of their Lord: so the stunning noise of a thunderbolt seized them, even while they were looking on. 45 Then they could not even stand (on their feet), nor could they help themselves. 46 So were the People of Noah before them: for they wickedly transgressed.

47 With power and skill did We construct the Firmament: for it is We who create the vastness of Space. 48 And We have spread out the (spacious) earth: how excellently We do spread out! 49 And of every thing We have created pairs: that you may reflect. 50 Hasten you then (at once) to God: I am from Him a Warner to you, clear and open! 51 And make not another an object of worship with Allah: I am from Him a Warner to you, clear and open!

52 Similarly, no Messenger came to the Peoples before them, but they said (of him) in like manner, "A sorcerer, or one possessed"! 53 Is this the legacy they have transmitted, one to another? No, they are themselves a people transgressing beyond bounds! 54 So turn away from them: not yours is the blame. 55 But Remind them for Reminding benefits the Believers.

56 I have only created Jinns and men, that they may serve Me. 57 No Sustenance do I require of them, nor do I require that they should feed Me. 58 For Allah is He Who gives (all) Sustenance —

Lord of Power—steadfast (forever). 59 For the wrongdoers, their portion is like unto the portion of their fellows (of earlier generations): then let them not ask Me to hasten (that portion)! 60 Woe, then, to the Unbelievers, on account of that Day of theirs which they have been promised!

52. THE MOUNT

In the name of Allah, Most Gracious, Most Merciful.

1 By the Mount (of Revelation); 2 By a Book Inscribed 3 In a Scroll unfolded; 4 By the much-frequented House (of worship); 5 By the Canopy Raised High; 6 And by the Ocean filled with Swell— 7 Surely, the Chastisement from your Lord will indeed come— 8 There is none can avert it— 9 On the Day when the firmament will be in dreadful commotion. 10 And the mountains will fly hither and thither. 11 Then woe that Day to those that treat (truth) as Falsehood— 12 That play (and paddle) in shallow trifles. 13 That Day shall they be thrust down to the Fire of Hell, irresistibly. 14 "This," it will be said, "Is the Fire—which you were wont to deny! 15 "Is this then a fake, or is it you that do not see? 16 "Burn you therein: the same is it to you whether you bear it with patience, or not: you but receive the recompense of your (own) deeds."

17 As to the Righteous, they will be in Gardens, and in Happiness— 18 Enjoying the (Bliss) which their Lord has bestowed on them, and their Lord shall deliver them from the Chastisement of the Fire. 19 (To them will be said:) "Eat and drink, with profit and health, because of your (good) deeds." 20 They will recline (with ease) on couches (of dignity) arranged in ranks; and We shall join them to maidens, with beautiful big and lustrous eyes.

21 And those who believe and whose families follow them in Faith—to them shall We join their families: nor shall We deprive

them (of the fruit) of any of their works: (yet) is each individual in pledge for his deeds. 22 And We shall bestow on them, of fruit and meat, anything they shall desire. 23 They shall there exchange, one with another, a (loving) cup free of frivolity, free of all taint of ill. 24 Round about them will serve, (devoted) to them, youths (handsome) as Pearls well-guarded. 25 They will advance to each other, engaging in mutual enquiry. 26 They will say: "Aforetime, we were not without fear for the sake of our people. 27 "But Allah has been good to us, and has delivered us from the Chastisement of the Scorching Wind. 28 "Truly, we did call unto Him from of old: truly it is He, the Beneficent, the Merciful!"

29 Therefore proclaim you the praises (of your Lord): for by the Grace of your Lord, you are no (vulgar) soothsayer, nor are you one possessed. 30 Or do they say— "A Poet! we await for him some calamity (hatched) by Time!" 31 You say: "Await!— I too will wait along with you!" 32 Is it that their faculties of understanding urge them to this, or are they but a people transgressing beyond bounds? 33 Or do they say, "He fabricated the (Message)"? No, they have no faith! 34 Let them then produce a recital like unto it— if (it be) they speak the truth!

35 Were they created of nothing, or were they themselves the creators? 36 Or did they create the heavens and the earth? No, they have no firm belief. 37 Or are the Treasures of your Lord with them, or have they control over them? 38 Or have they a ladder, by which they can (climb up to heaven and) listen (to its secrets)? Then let (such a) listener of theirs produce a manifest proof. 39 Or has He only daughters and you have sons?

40 Or is it that you do ask for a reward, so that they are burdened with a load of debt?— 41 Or that the Unseen is in their hands, and they write it down? 42 Or do they intend a plot (against you)? But those who defy God are themselves ensnared in a Plot! 43 Or have they a god other than Allah? Exalted is Allah far above the things they associate with Him!

44 Were they to see a piece of the sky falling (on them), they would (only) say: "Clouds gathered in heaps!" 45 So leave them alone until they encounter that Day of theirs, wherein they shall

(perforce) swoon (with terror)— 46 The Day when their plotting will avail them nothing and no help shall be given them. 47 And surely, for those who do wrong, there is another punishment besides this: but most of them understand not.

48 Now await in patience the command of your Lord: for surely you are in Our eyes: And celebrate the praises of your Lord the while you stand forth, 49 And for part of the night also praise Him— and at the retreat of the stars!

53. THE STAR

In the name of Allah, Most Gracious, Most Merciful.

1 By the Star when it goes down— 2 Your Companion is neither astray nor being misled. 3 Nor does he say anything of (his own) Desire. 4 It is no less than inspiration sent down to him: 5 He was taught by one Mighty in Power, 6 Endued with Wisdom: for he appeared (in stately form) 7 While he was in the highest part of the horizon: 8 Then he approached and came closer, 9 And was at a distance of but two bow-lengths or (even) nearer; 10 So did (Allah) convey the inspiration to His Servant— (conveyed) what He (meant) to convey. 11 The (Prophet's) (mind and) heart in no way falsified that which he saw. 12 Will you then dispute with him concerning what he saw? 13 For indeed he saw him at a second descent, 14 Near the Lote-tree of the farthest boundary. 15 Near it is the Garden of Abode. 16 Behold, the Lote-tree was shrouded (in mystery unspeakable!) 17 (His) sight never swerved, nor did it go wrong! 18 For truly did he see, of the Signs of his Lord, the Greatest!

19 Have you seen Al-Lāt and al-'Uzzā, 20 And another, the third (goddess), Manāt? 21 What! for you the male sex, and for Him, the female? 22 Behold, such would be indeed a division most unfair! 23 These are nothing but names which you have devised— you and your fathers— for which Allah has sent down no authority (whatever). They follow nothing but conjecture and what their

own souls desire! — even though there has already come to them Guidance from their Lord! 24 No, shall man have (just) anything he hankers after? 25 But it is to Allah that the End and the Beginning (of all things) belong.

26 However many be the angels in the heavens, their intercession will avail nothing except after Allah has given leave for whom He pleases and that he is acceptable to Him. 27 Those who believe not in the Hereafter, name the angels with female names. 28 But they have no knowledge therein. They follow nothing but conjecture; and conjecture avails nothing against Truth. 29 Therefore shun those who turn away from Our Message and desire nothing but the life of this world. 30 That is as far as knowledge will reach them. Surely, your Lord knows best those who stray from his Path, and He knows best those who receive guidance.

31 Yes, to Allah belongs all that is in the heavens and on earth: so that He rewards those who do evil, according to their deeds, and He rewards those who do good, with what is best. 32 Those who avoid great sins and indecent deeds, only (falling into) small faults — certainly, your Lord is ample in forgiveness. He knows you well when He brings you out of the earth, and when you are hidden in your mothers' wombs. Therefore make not claims of piety: He knows best who it is that guards against evil.

33 Do you see one who turns back, 34 Gives a little, then hardens (his heart)? 35 What! Has he knowledge of the Unseen so that he can see? 36 No, is he not acquainted with what is in the books of Moses — 37 And of Abraham who was true to his pledges: 38 Namely, that no bearer of burdens can bear the burden of another; 39 That man can have nothing but what he strives for; 40 That (the fruit of) his striving will soon come in sight: 41 Then will he be rewarded with a reward complete; 42 That to your Lord is the final Goal; 43 That it is He Who grants Laughter and Tears; 44 That it is He Who grants Death and Life; 45 That He did create in pairs — male and female, 46 From a seed when lodged (in its place); 47 That He has promised a

Second Creation (raising of the Dead); 48 That it is He Who gives wealth and satisfaction; 49 That He is the Lord of Sirius (the Mighty Star).

50 And that it is He who destroyed the (powerful) ancient 'Ād (people), 51 And the Thamūd, nor He spared any other (Rebellious) people. 52 And before them, the people of Noah, for that they were (all) most unjust and most insolent transgressors, 53 And He destroyed the Overthrown Cities (of Sodom and Gomorrah). 54 So that (ruins unknown) have covered them up. 55 Then which of the gifts of your Lord, (O man,) will you dispute about?

56 This is a Warner, of the (series of) Warners of old! 57 The (Judgment) ever approaching draws near: 58 No (soul) but Allah can avert it. 59 Do you then wonder at this recital? 60 And will you laugh and not weep— 61 Wasting your time in vanities? 62 But fall you down in prostration to Allah, and adore (Him)!

54. THE MOON

In the name of Allah, Most Gracious, Most Merciful.

1 The Hour (of Judgment) is near, and the moon is cleft asunder. 2 But if they see a Sign, they turn away, and say, "This is (but) continuing magic." 3 They reject (the warning) and follow their (own) lusts but every matter has its appointed time. 4 There have already come to them news of the past enough as eye-opener, 5 Full of wisdom—but (the preaching of) Warners profits them not. 6 Therefore, (O Prophet) turn away from them. (and wait for) the Day that the Caller will call (them) to a terrible affair, 7 They will come forth— their eyes humbled— from (their) graves, (torpid) like locusts scattered abroad, 8 Hastening, with eyes transfixed, towards the Caller!—"Hard is this Day!" the Unbelievers will say.

9 Before them the People of Noah rejected (their Messenger):

they rejected Our servant, and said, "Here is one possessed!" and he was driven out. 10 Then he called on his Lord: "I am one overcome: do You then help (me)!" 11 So We opened the gates of heaven, with water pouring forth. 12 And We caused the earth to gush forth with springs, so the waters met (and rose) to the extent decreed. 13 But We bore him on an (Ark) made of broad planks and caulked with palm-fibre: 14 She floats under Our eyes (and care): a recompense to one who had been rejected (with scorn)! 15 And We have left this as a Sign (for all time): then is there any that will receive admonition? 16 But how (terrible) was My Chastisement and My Warning? 17 And We have indeed made the Qur'ān easy to understand and remember: then is there any that will receive admonition?

18 The 'Ād (people) (too) rejected (Truth): then how terrible was My Chastisement and My Warning? 19 For We sent against them a furious wind, on a Day of violent Disaster, 20 Plucking out men as if they were roots of palm-trees torn up (from the ground). 21 Yes, how (terrible) was My Chastisement and My Warning! 22 But We have indeed made the Qur'ān easy to understand and remember: then is there any that will receive admonition?

23 The Thamūd (also) rejected (their) Warners. 24 For they said: "What! A man! a solitary one from among ourselves! Shall we follow such a one? Truly should we then be straying in mind, and mad! 25 "Is it that the Message is sent to him, of all people amongst us? No, he is a liar, an insolent one!" 26 Ah! they will know on the morrow, which is the liar, the insolent one! 27 For We will send the she-camel by way of trial for them. So watch them, (O Ṣāliḥ), and possess yourself in patience! 28 And tell them that the water is to be divided between them: each one's right to drink being brought forward (by suitable turns). 29 But they called to their companion, and he took a sword in hand, and hamstrung (her). 30 Ah! how (terrible) was My Chastisement and My Warning! 31 For We sent against them a single Mighty Blast, and they became like the dry stubble used by one who pens cattle.

32 And We have indeed made the Qur'ān easy to understand and remember: then is there any that will receive admonition?

33 The people of Lūṭ rejected (His) Warning. 34 We sent against them a violent tornado with showers of stones, (which destroyed them), except lūṭ's household: them We delivered by early Dawn— 35 As a Grace from Us: thus do We reward those who give thanks. 36 And (Lūṭ) did warn them of Our Punishment, but they disputed about the Warning. 37 And they even sought to snatch away his guests from him, but We blinded their eyes. (They heard:) "Now taste you My Wrath and My Warning." 38 Early on the morrow an abiding Chastisement seized them: 39 "So taste you My Wrath and My Warning." 40 And We have indeed made the Qur'ān easy to understand and remember: then is there any that will receive admonition?

41 To the People of Pharaoh, too, aforetime, came Warners (from Allah). 42 The (people) rejected all our Signs; but We seized them with the seizure (as comes) from One exalted in Power, able to carry out His Will.

43 Are your Unbelievers, (O Quraysh), better than they? Or have you an immunity in the Sacred Books? 44 Or do they say: "We acting together can defend ourselves"? 45 Soon will their multitude be put to flight, and they will show their backs. 46 No, the Hour (of Judgment) is the time promised them (for their full recompense): and that Hour will be most grievous and most bitter. 47 Truly those in sin are the ones straying in mind, and mad. 48 The Day they will be dragged through the Fire on their faces, (they will hear:) "Taste you the touch of Hell!"

49 Surely, all things have We created in proportion and measure. 50 And Our Command is but a single (Word)— like the twinkling of an eye. 51 And (oft) in the past, have We destroyed gangs like you: then is there any that will receive admonition? 52 All that they do is noted in (their) books (of Deeds): 53 Every matter, small and great, is on record. 54 As to the Righteous, they will be in the midst of Gardens and Rivers, 55 In an abode of honour, in the Presence of a Sovereign Omnipotent.

55. THE MOST GRACIOUS

In the name of Allah, Most Gracious, Most Merciful.

1 (Allah) Most Gracious! 2 It is He Who has taught the Qur'ān. 3 He has created man. 4 He has taught him speech (and Intelligence). 5 The sun and the moon follow courses (exactly) computed 6 And the herbs and the trees— both (alike) bow in adoration. 7 And the Firmament has He raised high, and He has set up the Balance (of Justice), 8 In order that you may not transgress (due) balance. 9 So establish weight with justice and fall not short in the balance.

10 It is He Who has spread out the earth for (His) creatures: 11 Therein is fruit and date-palms, producing spathes (enclosing dates); 12 Also corn, with (its) leaves and stalk for fodder, and sweet-smelling plants. 13 Then which of the favours of your Lord will you deny? 14 He created man from ringing clay like unto pottery, 15 And He created Jinns from fire free of smoke: 16 Then which of the favours of your Lord will you deny? 17 (He is) Lord of the two Easts and Lord of the two Wests: 18 Then which of the favours of your Lord will you deny? 19 He has let free the two seas meeting together (by His Command): 20 Between them is a Barrier which they do not transgress: 21 Then which of the favours of your Lord will you deny? 22 Out of them come pearls and Coral: 23 Then which of the favours of your Lord will you deny? 24 And His are the Ships sailing smoothly across the seas, lofty as mountains: 25 Then which of the favours of your Lord will you deny?

26 All that is on earth will perish: 27 But will abide (for ever) the Face of your Lord— full of Majesty, bounty and Honour. 28 Then which of the favours of your Lord will you deny? 29 Of Him seeks (its need) every creature in the heavens and on earth: every day in (new) Splendour does He (shine)! 30 Then which of the favours of your Lord will you deny?

31 Soon shall We settle your affairs, O both you worlds! 32 Then which of the favours of your Lord will you deny? 33 O you

assembly of Jinns and men! If it be you can pass beyond the zones of the heavens and the earth, pass you! Not without authority shall you be able to pass! 34 Then which of the favours of your Lord will you deny? 35 On you will be sent (O you evil ones twain!) A flame of fire (to burn) and a smoke (to choke): no escape will you have: 36 Then which of the favours of your Lord will you deny?

37 When the sky is rent asunder, and it becomes red like ointment: 38 Then which of the favours of your Lord will you deny? 39 On that Day no question will be asked of man or Jinn as to his sin, 40 Then which of the favours of your Lord will you deny? 41 (For) the sinners will be known by their Marks: and they will be seized by their forelocks and their feet. 42 Then which of the favours of your Lord will you deny? 43 This is the Hell which the Sinners deny: 44 In its midst and in the midst of boiling hot water will they wander round! 45 Then which of the favours of your Lord will you deny?

46 But for such as fear the time when they will stand before (the Judgment Seat of) their Lord, there will be two Gardens— 47 Then which of the favours of your Lord will you deny? 48 Abounding in branches— 49 Then which of the favours of your Lord will you deny? 50 In them (each) will be two Springs flowing (free); 51 Then which of the favours of your Lord will you deny? 52 In them will be Fruits of every kind, two and two. 53 Then which of the favours of your Lord will you deny? 54 They will recline on Carpets, whose inner linings will be of rich brocade: the Fruit of the Gardens will be near (and easy of reach). 55 Then which of the favours of your Lord will you deny? 56 In them will be (Maidens), chaste, restraining their glances, whom no man or Jinn before them has touched— 57 Then which of the favours of your Lord will you deny? 58 Like unto rubies and coral. 59 Then which of the favours of your Lord will you deny? 60 Is there any Reward for Good—other than Good? 61 Then which of the favours of your Lord will you deny?

62 And besides these two, there are two other Gardens— 63 Then which of the favours of your Lord will you deny? 64 Dark-green

in colour (from plentiful watering). 65 Then which of the favours of your Lord will you deny? 66 In them (each) will be two Springs pouring forth water in continuous abundance: 67 Then which of the favours of your Lord will you deny? 68 In them will be Fruits, and dates and pomegranates: 69 Then which of the favours of your Lord will you deny? 70 In them will be fair (Damsels), good, beautiful— 71 Then which of the favours of your Lord will you deny? 72 Damsels restrained (as to their glances), in (goodly) pavilions— 73 Then which of the favours of your Lord will you deny? 74 Whom no man or Jinn before them has touched— 75 Then which of the favours of your Lord will you deny? 76 Reclining on green Cushions and rich Carpets of beauty. 77 Then which of the favours of your Lord will you deny? 78 Blessed be the name of your Lord, full of Majesty, Bounty and Honour.

56. THE INEVITABLE

In the name of Allah, Most Gracious, Most Merciful.

1 When the Event inevitable comes to pass, 2 Then will no (soul) entertain doubt concerning its coming. 3 (Many) will it bring low; (many) will it exalt; 4 When the earth shall be shaken to its depths, 5 And the mountains shall be crumbled to atoms, 6 Becoming dust scattered abroad, 7 And you shall be sorted out into three classes.

8 Then (there will be) the Companions of the Right Hand— what will be the Companions of the Right Hand? 9 And the Companions of the Left Hand— what will be the Companions of the Left Hand? 10 And those Foremost (in Faith) will be foremost (in the Hereafter). 11 These will be those Nearest to Allah: 12 In Gardens of Bliss: 13 A number of people from those of old, 14 And a few from those of later times. 15 (They will be) on couches encrusted (with gold and precious stones), 16 Reclining on them, facing each other. 17 Round about them will (serve) youths of perpetual (freshness), 18 With goblets, (shining) beakers, and cups (filled) out of clear-flowing fountains: 19 No after-ache will they receive therefrom, nor will they suffer intoxication: 20 And with fruits,

any that they may select: 21 And the flesh of fowls, any that they may desire. 22 And (there will be) Companions with beautiful, big, and lustrous eyes— 23 Like unto Pearls well-guarded. 24 A Reward for the Deeds of their past (Life). 25 Not frivolity will they hear therein, nor any sinful talk— 26 Only the saying, "Peace! Peace."

27 The Companions of the Right Hand— what will be the Companions of the Right Hand? 28 (They will be) among lote-trees without thorns, 29 Among Ṭalḥ trees with flowers (or fruits) piled one above another— 30 In shade long-extended, 31 By water flowing constantly, 32 And fruit in abundance. 33 Whose season is not limited, nor (supply) forbidden, 34 And on couches (of Dignity), raised high. 35 We have created (their Companions) of special creation. 36 And made them virgin-pure (and undefiled)— 37 Loving (by nature), equal in age— 38 For the Companions of the Right Hand. 39 A (goodly) number from those of old, 40 And a (goodly) number from those of later times.

41 The Companions of the Left Hand— what will be the Companions of the Left Hand? 42 (They will be) in the midst of a fierce Blast of Fire and in Boiling Water, 43 And in the shades of Black Smoke: 44 Neither cool nor refreshing! 45 For that they were wont to be indulged, before that, in wealth (and luxury), 46 And persisted obstinately in wickedness supreme! 47 And they used to say, "What! when we die and become dust and bones, shall we then indeed be raised up again?— 48 "(We) and our fathers of old?" 49 Say: "Yes, those of old and those of later times, 50 "All will certainly be gathered together for the meeting appointed for a Day well-known. 51 "Then will you truly— O you that go wrong, and treat (Truth) as Falsehood!— 52 "You will surely taste of the Tree of Zaqqūm. 53 "Then will you fill your insides therewith, 54 "And drink Boiling Water on top of it: 55 "Indeed you shall drink like diseased camels raging with thirst!" 56 Such will be their entertainment on the Day of Requital!

57 It is We Who have created you: why will you not, then, admit the Truth? 58 Do you then see?— the (human Seed) that you emit— 59 Is it you who create it, or are We the Creators? 60 We have decreed Death to be your common lot, and We are not to

be frustrated 61 From changing your Forms and creating you (again) in (forms) that you know not. 62 And you certainly know already the first form of creation: why then do you not take heed? 63 Do you see the seed that you sow in the ground? 64 Is it you that cause it to grow, or are We the Cause? 65 Were it Our Will, We could crumble it to dry powder, and you would be left in wonderment, 66 (Saying), "We are indeed left with debts (for nothing): 67 "Indeed are we shut out (of the fruits of our labour)." 68 Do you see the water which you drink? 69 Do you bring it Down (in rain) from the Cloud or do We? 70 Were it Our Will, We could make it salty (and unpalatable): then why do you not give thanks? 71 Do you see the Fire which you kindle? 72 Is it you who grow the tree which feeds the fire, or do We grow it? 73 We have made it a memorial (of Our handiwork), and an article of comfort and convenience for the denizens of deserts. 74 Then glorify the name of your Lord, the Supreme!

75 Furthermore I call to witness the setting of the Stars— 76 And that is indeed a mighty adjuration if you but knew— 77 That this is indeed a Qur'ān Most Honourable, 78 In a Book well-guarded, 79 Which none shall touch but those who are clean: 80 A Revelation from the Lord of the Worlds. 81 Is it such a Message that you would hold in light esteem? 82 And have you made it your livelihood that you should declare it false?

83 Then why do you not (intervene) when (the soul of the dying man) reaches the throat— 84 And you the while (sit) looking on— 85 But We are nearer to him than you, and yet see not— 86 Then why do you not— if you are exempt from (future) account— 87 Call back the soul, if you are true (in your claim of Independence)? 88 Thus, then, if he be of those Nearest to Allah, 89 (There is for him) Rest and Satisfaction, and a Garden of Delights. 90 And if he be of the Companions of the Right Hand, 91 (For him is the salutation), "Peace be unto you," from the Companions of the Right Hand. 92 And if he be of those who deny (the Truth) who go wrong, 93 For him is Entertainment with Boiling Water. 94 And burning in Hell-Fire. 95 Surely, this is the Very Truth of assured Certainty. 96 So celebrate with praises the name of your Lord, The Supreme.

57. THE IRON

In the name of Allah, Most Gracious, Most Merciful.

1 Whatever is in the heavens and on earth— let it declare the Praises and Glory of Allah: for He is the Exalted in Might, the Wise. 2 To Him belongs the dominion of the heavens and the earth: it is He Who gives life and Death; and He has Power over all things. 3 He is the First and the Last, the Evident and the Hidden: and He has full knowledge of all things. 4 He it is Who created the heavens and the earth in Six Days, and then firmly established Himself on the Throne (of authority). He knows what enters within the earth and what comes forth out of it, what comes down from heaven and what mounts up to it. And He is with you wheresoever you may be. And Allah sees well all that you do. 5 To Him belongs the dominion of the heavens and the earth: and all affairs go back to Allah. 6 He merges Night into Day, and He merges Day into Night; and He has full knowledge of the secrets of (all) hearts.

7 Believe in Allah and His Messenger, and spend (in charity) out of the (substance) whereof He has made you heirs. For those of you who believe and spend (in charity)—for them is a great Reward. 8 How is it then that you do not believe in Allah?—And the Messenger invites you to believe in your Lord, and has indeed taken your Covenant, if you are men of Faith. 9 He is the One Who sends to His Servant manifest Signs, that He may lead you from the depths of Darkness into the Light. And surely, Allah is to you Most Kind and Merciful. 10 And why is it that you do not spend in the cause of Allah?— for to Allah belongs the heritage of the heavens and the earth. Not equal among you are those who spent (freely) and fought, before the Victory, (with those who did so later). Those are higher in rank than those who spent (freely) and fought afterwards. But to all has Allah promised a goodly (reward). And Allah is well acquainted with all that you do.

11 Who is he that will loan to Allah a beautiful loan? For (Allah) will increase it manifold to his credit, and he will have (besides)

a liberal reward. 12 One Day shall you see the believing men and the believing women— how their Light runs forward before them and by their right hands: (their greeting will be): "Good News for you this Day! Gardens beneath which flow rivers! To dwell therein for ever! This is indeed the highest Triumph!" 13 The Day the Hypocrites— men and women—will say to the Believers: "Wait for us! Let us borrow (a light) from your Light!" It will be said: "Turn you back to your rear! Then seek a light (where you can)!" So a wall will be put up between them, with a gate therein. Within it will be Mercy throughout, and outside it, all alongside, will be (wrath and) Punishment! 14 (Those outside) will call out, "Were we not with you?" (the others) will reply, "True! But you led yourselves into temptation; you looked forward (to our ruin); you doubted (Allah's Promise); and (your false) desires deceived you; until there issued the Command of Allah. And the Deceiver deceived you in respect of Allah. 15 "This Day shall no ransom be accepted of you, nor of those who rejected Allah." Your abode is the Fire: that is the proper place to claim you: and an evil refuge it is!"

16 Has not the time arrived for the Believers that their hearts in all humility should engage in the remembrance of Allah and of the Truth which has been revealed (to them), and that they should not become like those to whom was given The Book aforetime, but long ages passed over them and their hearts grew hard? For many among them are rebellious transgressors. 17 Know you (all) that Allah gives life to the earth after its death! Already have We shown the Signs plainly to you, that you may understand.

18 For those who give in Charity, men and women, and loan to Allah a Beautiful Loan, it shall be increased manifold (to their credit), and they shall have (besides) a liberal reward. 19 And those who believe in Allah and His Messengers— they are the Sincere (lovers of Truth), and the witnesses (who testify), in the eyes of their Lord: they shall have their Reward and their Light. But those who reject Allah and deny Our Signs— they are the Companions of Hell-Fire.

20 Know you (all), that the life of this world is but play and amusement, pomp and mutual boasting and multiplying, (in rivalry) among yourselves, riches and children. Here is a similitude: how rain and the growth which it brings forth, delight (the hearts of) the tillers; soon it withers; you will see it grow yellow; then it becomes dry and crumbles away. But in the Hereafter is a Chastisement severe (for the devotees of wrong) And Forgiveness from Allah and (His) Good Pleasure (for the devotees of Allah). And what is the life of this world, but goods and chattels of deception? 21 Be you foremost (in seeking) forgiveness from your Lord, and a Garden (of Bliss), the width whereof is as the width of heaven and earth, prepared for those who believe in Allah and His Messengers: that is the Grace of Allah, which He bestows on whom He pleases: and Allah is The Lord of Grace bounding.

22 No misfortune can happen on earth or in your souls but is recorded in a decree before We bring it into existence: that is truly easy for Allah: 23 In order that you may not despair over matters that pass you by, nor exult over favours bestowed upon you. For Allah loves not any vainglorious boaster— 24 Such persons as are covetous and commend covetousness to men. And if any turn back (from Allah's Way), surely Allah is free of all needs, worthy of all praise.

25 We sent aforetime our Messengers with Clear Signs and sent down with them the Book and the Balance (of Right and Wrong), that men may stand forth in justice; and We sent down Iron, in which there is awesome power, as well as many benefits for mankind, that Allah may test who it is that will help, unseen, Him and His Messengers: for Allah is Full of Strength, Exalted in Might (and able to enforce His Will).

26 And We sent Noah and Abraham, and established in their line Prophethood and Revelation: and some of them were on right guidance, but many of them became rebellious transgressors. 27 Then, in their wake, We followed them up with (others of) Our Messengers: We sent after them Jesus, the son of Mary, and bestowed on him the Gospel; and We ordained in the hearts of

those who followed him Compassion and Mercy. But the Monasticism which they invented for themselves, We did not prescribe for them: (We commanded) only the seeking for the Good Pleasure of Allah; but that they did not foster as they should have done. Yet We bestowed, on those among them who believed, their (due) reward, but many of them are rebellious transgressors.

28 O you that believe! Fear Allah, and believe in His Messenger, and He will bestow on you a double portion of His Mercy: He will provide for you a Light by which you shall walk (straight in your path), and He will forgive you (your past): for Allah is Oft-Forgiving, Most Merciful: 29 That the People of the Book may know that they have no power whatever over the Grace of Allah, that (His) Grace is (entirely) in His Hand, to bestow it on whomsoever He wills. For Allah is the Lord of Grace abounding.

58. THE PLEADING

In the name of Allah, Most Gracious, Most Merciful.

1 Allah has indeed heard (and accepted) the statement of the woman who pleads with you concerning her husband and carries her complaint (in prayer) to Allah: and Allah (always) hears the arguments between both sides among you: for Allah hears and sees (all things).

2 If any men among you divorce their wives by ẓihār (calling them mothers), they cannot be their mothers: none can be their mothers except those who gave birth to them. And in fact they use words (both) iniquitous and false: but truly Allah is one that blots out (sins), and forgives (again and again). 3 But those who divorce their wives by ẓihār, then wish to go back on the words they uttered— (It is ordained that such a one) should free a slave before they touch each other: thus are you admonished to perform: and Allah is well-acquainted with (all) that you do. 4 And if any has not (the wherewithal), he should fast for two

months consecutively before they touch each other. But if any is unable to do so, he should feed sixty indigent ones, this, that you may show your faith in Allah and His Messenger. Those are limits (set by) Allah. For those who reject (Him), there is a grievous Chastisement.

5 Those who oppose Allah and His Messenger will be humbled to dust, as were those before them: for We have already sent down clear Signs. And the Unbelievers (will have) a humiliating Chastisement. 6 On the Day that Allah will raise them all up (again) and show them the Truth (and meaning) of their conduct. Allah has reckoned its (value), though they may have forgotten it, for Allah is Witness to all things.

7 Do you not see that Allah does know (all) that is in the heavens and on earth? There is not a secret consultation between three, but He makes the fourth among them— nor between five but He makes the sixth— nor between fewer nor more, but He is in their midst, wheresoever they be: in the end will He tell them the truth of their conduct, on the Day of Judgment. For Allah has full knowledge of all things. 8 Do you not see those who were forbidden secret counsels yet revert to that which they were forbidden (to do)? And they hold secret counsels among themselves for iniquity and hostility, and disobedience to the Messenger. And when they come to you, they salute you, not as Allah salutes you, (but in crooked ways): and they say to themselves, "Why does not Allah punish us for our words?" Enough for them is Hell: in it will they burn, and evil is that destination!

9 O you who believe! When you hold secret counsel, do it not for iniquity and hostility, and disobedience to the Messenger; but do it for righteousness and self-restraint; and fear Allah, to Whom you shall be brought back. 10 Secret counsels are only (inspired) by Satan, in order that he may cause grief to the Believers; but he cannot harm them in the least, except as Allah permits; and on Allah let the Believers put their trust.

11 O you who believe! When you are told to make room in the assemblies, (spread out and) make room: (ample) room will Allah

provide for you. And when you are told to rise up, rise up: Allah will raise up, to (suitable) ranks (and degrees), those of you who believe and who have been granted knowledge. And Allah is well-acquainted with all you do.

12 O you who believe! When you consult the Messenger in private, spend something in charity before your private consultation. That will be best for you, and most conducive to purity (of conduct). But if you find not (the wherewithal), Allah is Oft-Forgiving, Most Merciful. 13 Is it that you are afraid of spending sums in charity before your private consultation (with him)? If, then, you do not so, and Allah forgives you, then (at least) establish regular prayer; practise Zakat; and obey Allah and His Messenger. And Allah is well-acquainted with all that you do.

14 Do you not see those who turn (in friendship) to such as have the Wrath of Allah upon them? They are neither of you nor of them, and they swear to falsehood knowingly. 15 Allah has prepared for them a severe Chastisement: evil indeed are their deeds. 16 They have made their oaths a screen (for their misdeeds): Thus they obstruct (men) from the Path of Allah: therefore shall they have a humiliating Chastisement.

17 Of no profit whatever to them, against Allah, will be their riches nor their sons: they will be Companions of the Fire, to dwell therein (for ever)! 18 One Day will Allah raise them all up (for Judgment): then will they swear to Him as they swear to you: and they think that they have something (to stand upon). No, indeed! they are but liars! 19 Satan has got the better of them: so he has made them lose the remembrance of Allah. They are the Party of the Satan. Truly, it is the Party of the Satan that will perish! 20 Those who resist Allah and His Messenger will be among those most humiliated. 21 Allah has decreed: "It is I and My Messengers who must prevail": for Allah is One full of strength, able to enforce His Will.

22 You will not find any people who believe in Allah and the Last Day, loving those who resist Allah and His Messenger, even though they were their fathers or their sons, or their brothers, or

their kindred. For such he has written Faith in their hearts, and strengthened them with a spirit from Himself. And He will admit them to Gardens beneath which Rivers flow, to dwell therein (forever). Allah will be well pleased with them, and they with Him. They are the Party of Allah. Truly it is the Party of Allah that will achieve Felicity.

59. THE MUSTERING

In the name of Allah, Most Gracious, Most Merciful.

1 Whatever is in the heavens and on earth, let it declare the Praises and Glory of Allah: for He is the Exalted in Might, the Wise. 2 It is He Who got out the Unbelievers among the People of the Book from their homes at the first gathering (of the forces). Little did you think that they would get out: and they thought that their fortresses would defend them from Allah! But the (Wrath of) Allah came to them from quarters from which they little expected (it), and cast terror into their hearts, so that they destroyed their dwellings by their own hands and the hands of the Believers, take warning, then, O you with eyes (to see)!

3 And had it not been that Allah had decreed banishment for them, He would certainly have punished them in this world: and in the Hereafter they shall (certainly) have the Punishment of the Fire. 4 That is because they resisted Allah and His Messenger: and if anyone resists Allah, surely, Allah is severe in Punishment. 5 Whether you cut down (O you Muslims!) the tender palm-trees, or you left them standing on their roots, it was by leave of Allah, and in order that He might cover with shame the rebellious transgressors.

6 What Allah has bestowed on His Messenger (and taken away) from them — for this you made no expedition with either cavalry or camelry: but Allah gives power to His Messengers over any He pleases: and Allah has power over all things. 7 What Allah has bestowed on His Messenger (and taken away) from the people of the townships — belongs to Allah — to His Messenger and to

kindred and orphans, the needy and the wayfarer; in order that it may not (merely) make a circuit between the wealthy among you. So take what the Messenger assigns to you, and deny yourselves that which he withholds from you. And fear Allah; for Allah is strict in Punishment. 8 (Some part is due) to the indigent Muhājirs, those who were expelled from their homes and their property, while seeking Grace from Allah and (His) Good Pleasure, and aiding Allah and His Messenger: such are indeed the sincere ones —

9 But those who before them, had homes (in Madīnah) and had adopted the Faith — show their affection to such as came to them for refuge, and entertain no desire in their hearts for things given to the (latter), but give them preference over themselves, even though poverty was their (own lot). And those saved from the covetousness of their own souls — they are the ones that achieve prosperity. 10 And those who came after them say: "Our Lord! Forgive us, and our brethren who came before us into the Faith, and leave not, in our hearts, rancour (or sense of injury) against those who have believed. Our Lord! You are indeed Full of Kindness, Most Merciful."

11 Have you not observed the Hypocrites say to their misbelieving brethren among the People of the Book? — "If you are expelled, we too will go out with you, and we will never listen to anyone in your affair; and if you are attacked (in fight) we will help you." But Allah is witness that they are indeed liars. 12 If they are expelled, never will they go out with them; and if they are attacked (in fight), they will never help them; and if they do help them, they will turn their backs; so they will receive no help.

13 Of a truth you are stronger (than they) because of the terror in their hearts, (sent) by Allah. This is because they are men devoid of understanding. 14 They will not fight you (even) together, except in fortified townships, or from behind walls. Strong is their fighting (spirit) amongst themselves: you would think they were united, but their hearts are divided: that is because they are a people devoid of wisdom.

15 Like those who lately preceded them, they have tasted the evil result of their conduct; and (in the Hereafter there is) for them

a grievous Chastisement. 16 (Their allies deceived them), like Satan, when he says to man, "Deny Allah": but when (Man) denies Allah, (Satan) says, "I am free of you: I do fear Allah, the Lord of the Worlds!" 17 The end of both will be that they will go into the Fire, dwelling therein forever. Such is the reward of the wrongdoers.

18 O you who believe! Fear Allah, and let every soul look to what (provision) he has sent forth for the morrow. Yes, fear Allah: for Allah is well-acquainted with (all) that you do. 19 And be you not like those who forgot Allah; and He made them forget their own souls! Such are the rebellious transgressors! 20 Not equal are the Companions of the Fire and the Companions of the Garden: it is the Companions of the Garden, that will achieve Felicity.

21 Had We sent down this Qur'ān on a mountain, surely, you would have seen it humble itself and cleave asunder for fear of Allah. Such are the similitudes which We propound to men, that they may reflect. 22 Allah is He, than Whom there is no other god— who knows (all things) both secret and open; He, Most Gracious, Most Merciful. 23 Allah is He, than Whom there is no other god— The Sovereign, the Holy One, the Source of Peace (and Perfection), the Guardian of Faith, the Preserver of Safety, the Exalted in Might, the Irresistible, the Supreme: glory to Allah! (High is He) above the partners they attribute to Him. 24 He is Allah, the Creator, the Evolver, the Bestower of Forms (or Colours). To Him belong the Most Beautiful Names: whatever is in the heavens and on earth, does declare His Praises and Glory: and He is the Exalted in Might, the Wise.

60. THE EXAMINED ONE

In the name of Allah, Most Gracious, Most Merciful.

1 O you who believe! Take not My enemies and yours as friends (or protectors)—offering them (your) love, even though they have rejected the Truth that has come to you, and have (on the

contrary) driven out the Prophet and yourselves (from your homes), (simply) because you believe in Allah your Lord! If you have come out to strive in My Way and to seek My Good Pleasure, (take them not as friends), holding secret converse of love (and friendship) with them: for I know full well all that you conceal and all that you reveal. And any of you that does this has strayed from the Straight Path. 2 If they were to get the better of you, they would behave to you as enemies, and stretch forth their hands and their tongues against you for evil: and they desire that you should reject the Truth. 3 Of no profit to you will be your relatives and your children on the Day of Judgment: He will judge between you: for Allah sees well all that you do.

4 There is for you an excellent example (to follow) in Abraham and those with him, when they said to their people: "We are clear of you and of whatever you worship besides Allah: we have rejected you, and there has arisen, between us and you, enmity and hatred for ever—unless you believe in Allah and Him alone:" But not when Abraham said to his father: "I will pray for forgiveness for you, though I have no power (to get) anything on your behalf from Allah." (They prayed): "Our Lord! In You do we trust, and to You do we turn in repentance: to You is (our) Final Goal. 5 "Our Lord! Make us not a (test and) trial for the Unbelievers, but forgive us, our Lord! For You are the Exalted in Might, the Wise." 6 There was indeed in them an excellent example for you to follow—for those whose hope is in Allah and in the Last Day. But if any turn away, truly Allah is Free of all wants, Worthy of all Praise. 7 It may be that Allah will grant love (and friendship) between you and those whom you (now) hold as enemies. For Allah has power (over all things); and Allah is Oft-Forgiving, Most Merciful.

8 Allah forbids you not, with regard to those who fight you not for (your) Faith nor drive you out of your homes, from dealing kindly and justly with them: for Allah loves those who are just. 9 Allah only forbids you, with regard to those who fight you for (your) Faith, and drive you out of your homes, and support

(others) in driving you out, from turning to them (for friendship and protection). It is such as turn to them (in these circumstances), that do wrong.

10 O you who believe! When there come to you believing women refugees, examine (and test) them: Allah knows best as to their Faith: if you ascertain that they are Believers, then send them not back to the Unbelievers. They are not lawful (wives) for the Unbelievers, nor are the (Unbelievers) lawful (husbands) for them. But pay the Unbelievers what they have spent (on their dower). And there will be no blame on you if you marry them on payment of their dower to them. But hold not to the custody of unbelieving women: ask for what you have spent on their dowers, and let the (Unbelievers) ask for what they have spent (on the dowers of women who come over to you). Such is the command of Allah: He judges (with justice) between you. And Allah is Full of knowledge and wisdom. 11 And if any of your wives deserts you to the Unbelievers, and you have your turn (by the coming over of a woman from the other side), then pay to those whose wives have deserted the equivalent of what they had spent (on their dower). And fear Allah, in Whom you believe.

12 O Prophet! When believing women come to you to take the oath of fealty to you, that they will not associate in worship any other thing whatever with Allah, that they will not steal, that they will not commit adultery (or fornication), that they will not kill their children, that they will not utter slander, intentionally forging falsehood, and that they will not disobey you in any just matter— then you accept their fealty, and pray to Allah for the forgiveness (of their sins): for Allah is Oft-Forgiving, Most Merciful.

13 O you who believe! Turn not (for friendship) to people on whom is the Wrath of Allah. Of the Hereafter they are already in despair, just as the Unbelievers are in despair about those (buried) in graves.

61. THE RANKS

In the name of Allah, Most Gracious, Most Merciful.

1 Whatever is in the heavens and on earth, let it declare the Praises and Glory of Allah: for He is the Exalted in Might, the Wise. 2 O you who believe! Why do you say that which you do not? 3 Grievously odious is it in the sight of Allah that you say that which you do not. 4 Truly Allah loves those who fight in His Cause in battle array, as if they were a solid cemented structure.

5 And remember, Moses said to his people: "O my people! Why do you vex and insult me, though you know that I am the Messenger of Allah (sent) to you?" Then when they went wrong, Allah let their hearts go wrong. For Allah guides not those who are rebellious transgressors.

6 And remember, Jesus, the son of Mary, said: "O Children of Israel! I am the Messenger of Allah (sent) to you, confirming the Law (which came) before me, and giving Glad Tidings of a Messenger to come after me, whose name shall be Ahmad." But when he came to them with Clear Signs, they said, "This is evident sorcery!" 7 Who does greater wrong than one who invents falsehood against Allah, even as he is being invited to Islam? And Allah guides not those who do wrong. 8 Their intention is to extinguish Allah's Light (by blowing) with their mouths: but Allah will complete (the revelation of) His Light, even though the Unbelievers may detest (it). 9 It is He Who has sent his Messenger with Guidance and the Religion of Truth, that He may proclaim it over all religion, even though the Pagans may detest (it).

10 O you who believe! Shall I lead you to a bargain that will save you from a grievous Chastisement?— 11 That you believe in Allah and His Messenger, and that you strive (your utmost) in the Cause of Allah, with your property and your persons: that will be best for you, if you but knew! 12 He will forgive you your sins, and admit you to Gardens beneath which rivers flow, and to beautiful mansions in Gardens of Eternity: that is indeed

the Supreme Achievement. 13 And another (favour will He bestow), which you do love—help from Allah and a speedy victory. So give the Glad Tidings to the Believers.

14 O you who believe! Be you helpers of Allah: as said Jesus the son of Mary to the Disciples, "Who will be My helpers to (the work of) Allah?" Said the Disciples, "We are Allah's helpers!" Then a portion of the Children of Israel believed, and a portion disbelieved: but We gave power to those who believed, against their enemies, and they became the ones that prevailed.

62. FRIDAY

In the name of Allah, Most Gracious, Most Merciful.

1 Whatever is in the heavens and on earth, does declare the Praises and Glory of Allah,—the Sovereign, the Holy One, the Exalted in Might, the Wise. 2 It is He Who has sent amongst the Unlettered a Messenger from among themselves, to rehearse to them His Signs, to purify them, and to instruct them in Scripture and Wisdom—although they had been, before, in manifest error— 3 As well as (to confer all these benefits upon) others of them, who have not already joined them: and He is Exalted in Might, Wise. 4 Such is the Bounty of Allah, which He bestows on whom He will: and Allah is the Lord of the highest bounty.

5 The similitude of those who were charged with the (obligations of the) Mosaic Law, but who subsequently failed in those (obligations), is that of a donkey which carries huge tomes (but understands them not). Evil is the similitude of people who falsify the Signs of Allah: and Allah guides not people who do wrong. 6 Say: "O you that stand on Judaism! If you think that you are friends to Allah, to the exclusion of (other) men, then express your desire for Death, if you are truthful!" 7 But never will they express their desire (for Death), because of the (deeds) their hands have sent on before them! And Allah knows well those that do

wrong! 8 Say: "The Death from which you flee will truly overtake you: then will you be sent back to the Knower of things secret and open: and He will tell you (the truth of) the things that you did!"

9 O you who believe! When the call is made to prayer on Friday (the Day of Assembly), hasten earnestly to the Remembrance of Allah, and leave off business (and traffic): that is best for you if you but knew! 10 And when the Prayer is finished, then may you disperse through the land, and seek of the Bounty of Allah: and celebrate the Praises of Allah often (and without stint): that you may prosper. 11 But when they see some bargain or some amusement, they disperse headlong to it, and leave you standing. Say: "The (blessing) from the Presence of Allah is better than any amusement or bargain! And Allah is the Best to provide (for all needs)."

63. THE HYPOCRITES

In the name of Allah, Most Gracious, Most Merciful.

1 When the Hypocrites come to you, they say, "We bear witness that you are indeed the Messenger of Allah." Yes, Allah knows that you are indeed His Messenger, and Allah bears witness that the Hypocrites are indeed liars. 2 They have made their oaths a screen (for their misdeeds): thus they obstruct (men) from the Path of Allah: truly evil are their deeds. 3 That is because they believed, then they rejected Faith: so a seal was set on their hearts: therefore they understand not.

4 When you look at them, their exteriors please you; and when they speak, you listen to their words. They are as (worthless as hollow) pieces of timber propped up, (unable to stand on their own). They think that every cry is against them. They are the enemies; so beware of them. The curse of Allah be on them! How are they deluded (away from the Truth)! 5 And when it is said to them, "Come, the Messenger of Allah will pray for your

forgiveness," they turn aside their heads, and you would see them turning away their faces in arrogance. 6 It is equal to them whether you pray for their forgiveness or not. Allah will not forgive them. Truly Allah guides not rebellious transgressors.

7 They are the ones who say, "Spend nothing on those who are with Allah's Messenger, to the end that they may disperse (and quit Madīnah)." But to Allah belong the treasures of the heavens and the earth; but the Hypocrites understand not. 8 They say, "If we return to Madīnah, surely the more honourable (element) will expel therefrom the meaner." But honour belongs to Allah and His Messenger, and to the Believers; but the Hypocrites know not.

9 O you who believe! Let not your riches or your children divert you from the remembrance of Allah. If any act thus, the loss is their own. 10 And spend something (in charity) out of the substance which We have bestowed on you, before Death should come to any of you and he should say, "O my Lord! why did you not give me respite for a little while? I should then have given (largely) in charity, and I should have been one of the doers of good." 11 But to no soul will Allah grant respite when the time appointed (for it) has come; and Allah is well acquainted with (all) that you do.

64. THE MUTUAL LOSS AND GAIN

In the name of Allah, Most Gracious, Most Merciful.

1 Whatever is in the heavens and on earth, does declare the Praises and Glory of Allah: to Him belongs dominion, and to Him belongs praise: and He has power over all things. 2 It is He Who has created you; and of you are some that are unbelievers, and some that are Believers: and Allah sees well all that you do. 3 He has created the heavens and the earth in just proportions, and has given you shape, and made your shapes beautiful: and to Him is the final Goal. 4 He knows what is in the heavens and on earth;

and He knows what you conceal and what you reveal: yes, Allah knows well the (secrets) of (all) hearts.

5 Has not the story reached you, of those who rejected Faith aforetime? So they tasted the evil result of their conduct; and they had a grievous Chastisement. 6 That was because there came to them Messengers with Clear Signs, but they said: "Shall (mere) human beings direct us?" So they rejected (the Message) and turned away. But Allah can do without (them): and Allah is free of all needs, worthy of all praise.

7 The Unbelievers think that they will not be raised up (for Judgment). Say: "Yes, By my Lord, you shall surely be raised up: then shall you be told (the truth) of all that you did. And that is easy for Allah." 8 Believe, therefore, in Allah and His Messenger, and in the Light which We have sent down. And Allah is well acquainted with all that you do. 9 The Day that He assembles you (all) for a Day of Assembly — that will be a Day of mutual loss and gain (among you), and those who believe in Allah and work righteousness — He will remove from them their ills, and He will admit them to Gardens beneath which rivers flow, to dwell therein for ever: that will be the Supreme Achievement. 10 But those who reject Faith and treat Our Signs as falsehoods, they will be companions of the Fire, to dwell therein for ever: and evil is that Goal.

11 No kind of calamity can occur, except by the leave of Allah: and if any one believes in Allah, (Allah) guides his heart (aright): for Allah knows all things. 12 So obey Allah, and obey His Messenger: but if you turn back, the duty of Our Messenger is but to proclaim (the Message) clearly and openly. 13 Allah! There is no god but He: and on Allah, therefore, let the Believers put their trust.

14 O you who believe! Truly, among your wives and your children are (some that are) enemies to yourselves: so beware of them! But if you forgive and overlook, and cover up (their faults), surely, Allah is Oft-Forgiving, Most Merciful. 15 Your riches and your children may be but a trial: but in the Presence of Allah, are the highest Reward. 16 So fear Allah as much as you can; listen

and obey; and spend in charity for the benefit of your own souls. And those saved from the covetousness of their own souls—they are the ones that achieve prosperity. 17 If you loan to Allah, a beautiful loan, He will double it to your (credit), and He will grant you forgiveness: for Allah is Most Ready to appreciate (service), Most Forbearing— 18 Knower of what is hidden and what is open, Exalted in Might, full of Wisdom.

65. DIVORCE

In the name of Allah, Most Gracious, Most Merciful.

1 O Prophet! When you do divorce women, divorce them at their prescribed periods, and count (accurately), their prescribed periods: and fear Allah your Lord: and turn them not out of their houses, nor shall they (themselves) leave, except in case they are guilty of some open lewdness, those are limits set by Allah: and any who transgresses the limits of Allah, does surely wrong his (own) soul: you know not if perchance Allah will bring about thereafter some new situation. 2 Thus when they approach their term appointed, either take them back on equitable terms or part with them on equitable terms; and take for witness two persons from among you, endued with justice, and establish the evidence (as) before Allah. Such is the admonition given to him who believes in Allah and the Last Day. And for those who fear Allah, He (ever) prepares a way out, 3 And He provides for him from (sources) he never could imagine. And if any one puts his trust in Allah, Sufficient is (Allah) for him. For Allah will surely accomplish his purpose: surely, for all things has Allah appointed a due proportion.

4 Such of your women as have passed the age of monthly courses, for them the prescribed period, if you have any doubts, is three months, and for those who have no courses (it is the same): for those who carry (life within their wombs), their period is until

they deliver their burdens: and for those who fear Allah, He will make things easy for them. 5 That is the Command of Allah, which He has sent down to you: and if any one fears Allah, He will remove his ills, from him, and will enlarge his reward.

6 Let the women live (in 'iddah) in the same style as you live, according to your means: harm them not, so as to tease them. And if they carry (life in their wombs), then spend (your substance) on them until they deliver their burden: and if they suckle your (offspring), give them their recompense: and take mutual counsel together, according to what is just and reasonable. And if you find yourselves in difficulties, let another woman suckle (the child) on the (father's) behalf. 7 Let the man of means spend according to his means: and the man whose resources are restricted, let him spend according to what Allah has given him. Allah puts no burden on any person beyond what He has given him. After a difficulty, Allah will soon grant relief.

8 How many populations that insolently opposed the Command of their Lord and of His Messengers, did We not then call to account—to severe account?— and We imposed on them an exemplary punishment. 9 Then did they taste the evil result of their conduct, and the End of their conduct was Perdition. 10 Allah has prepared for them a severe Punishment (in the Hereafter). Therefore fear Allah, O you men of understanding—who have believed!—for Allah has indeed sent down to you a Message— 11 A Messenger, who rehearses to you the Signs of Allah containing clear explanations, that he may lead forth those who believe and do righteous deeds from the depths of Darkness into Light. And those who believe in Allah and work righteousness, He will admit to Gardens beneath which rivers flow, to dwell therein for ever: Allah has indeed granted for them a most excellent Provision.

12 Allah is He Who created seven Firmaments and of the earth a similar number. Through the midst of them (all) descends His Command: that you may know that Allah has power over all things, and that Allah comprehends, all things in (His) Knowledge.

66. PROHIBITION

In the name of Allah, Most Gracious, Most Merciful.

1 O Prophet! Why hold you to be forbidden that which Allah has made lawful to you? You seek to please your consorts. But Allah is Oft-Forgiving, Most Merciful. 2 Allah has already ordained for you, (O men), the expiation of your oaths (in some cases): and Allah is your Protector, and He is Full of Knowledge and Wisdom.

3 When the Prophet disclosed a matter in confidence to one of his consorts, and she then divulged it (to another), and Allah made it known to him, he confirmed part thereof and passed over a part. Then when he told her thereof, she said, "Who told you this?" He said, "He told me who knows and is well-acquainted (with all things)." 4 If you two turn in repentance to Him, your hearts are indeed so inclined; but if you back up each other against him, truly Allah is his Protector, and Gabriel, and (every) righteous one among those who believe — and furthermore, the angels — will back (him) up. 5 It may be, if he divorced you (all), that Allah will give him in exchange Consorts better than you — who submit (their wills), who believe, who are devout, who turn to Allah in repentance, who worship (in humility), who travel (for Faith) and fast — previously married or virgins.

6 O you who believe! Save yourselves and your families from a Fire whose fuel is Men and Stones, over which are (appointed) angels stern (and) severe, who flinch not (from executing) the Commands they receive from Allah, but do (precisely) what they are commanded. 7 (They will say), "O you Unbelievers! Make no excuses this Day! You are being but requited for all that you did!"

8 O you who believe! Turn to Allah with sincere repentance: in the hope that your Lord will remove from you your ills and admit you to Gardens beneath which rivers flow — the Day that Allah will not permit to be humiliated the Prophet and those who believe with him. Their Light will run forward before them and

by their right hands, while they say, "Our Lord! Perfect our Light for us, and grant us Forgiveness: for You have power over all things."

9 O Prophet! Strive hard against the Unbelievers and the Hypocrites, and be firm against them. Their abode is Hell— an evil refuge (indeed). 10 Allah sets forth, for an example to the Unbelievers, the wife of Noah and the wife of Lūt: they were (respectively) under two of our righteous servants, but they were false to their (husbands), and they profited nothing before Allah on their account, but were told: "Enter the Fire along with (others) that enter!"

11 And Allah sets forth, as an example to those who believe the wife of Pharaoh: behold she said: "O my Lord! build for me, in nearness to You, a mansion in the Garden, and save me from Pharaoh and his doings, and save me from those that do wrong;" 12 And Mary the daughter of 'Imrān, who guarded her chastity; and We breathed into (her body) of Our spirit; and she testified to the truth of the words of her Lord and of His Revelations, and was one of the devout (servants).

67. THE DOMINION

In the name of Allah, Most Gracious, Most Merciful.

1 Blessed be He in Whose hands is Dominion; and He over all things has Power— 2 He Who created Death and Life, that He may test which of you is best in deed: and He is the Exalted in Might, Oft-Forgiving— 3 He Who created the seven heavens one above another: no want of proportion will you see in the Creation of (Allah) Most Gracious. So turn your vision again: do you see any flaw? 4 Again turn your vision a second time: (your) vision will come back to you dull and discomfited, in a state worn out.

5 And we have, (from of old), adorned the lowest heaven with Lamps, and We have made such (Lamps) (as) missiles to drive away Satans, and have prepared for them the Chastisement of the

Blazing Fire. 6 For those who reject their Lord (and Cherisher) is the Chastisement of Hell: and evil is (such) destination. 7 When they are cast therein, they will hear the (terrible) drawing in of its breath even as it blazes forth, 8 Almost bursting with fury: every time a Group is cast therein, its Keepers will ask, "Did no Warner come to you?" 9 They will say: "Yes indeed; a Warner did come to us, but we rejected him and said, 'Allah never sent down any (Message): you are in nothing but an egregious delusion!" 10 They will further say: "Had we but listened or used our intelligence, we should not (now) be among the Companions of the Blazing Fire!" 11 They will then confess their sins: but far will be (Forgiveness) from the Companions of the Blazing Fire!

12 As for those who fear their Lord unseen, for them is Forgiveness and a great Reward. 13 And whether you hide your word or publish it, He certainly has (full) knowledge, of the secrets of (all) hearts. 14 Should He not know — He that created? And He is the One that understands the finest mysteries (and) is well-acquainted (with them).

15 It is He Who has made the earth manageable for you, so traverse through its tracts and enjoy of the Sustenance which He furnishes: but unto Him is the Resurrection. 16 Do you feel secure that He Who is in heaven will not cause you to be swallowed up by the earth when it shakes (as in an earthquake)? 17 Or do you feel secure that He Who is in Heaven will not send against you a violent tornado (with showers of stones), so that you shall know how (terrible) was My warning? 18 But indeed men before them rejected (My warning): then how (terrible) was my rejection (of them)?

19 Do they not observe the birds above them, spreading their wings and folding them in? None can uphold them except (Allah) Most Gracious: truly it is He that watches over all things. 20 No, who is there that can help you, (even as) an army, besides (Allah) Most Merciful? In nothing but delusion are the Unbelievers. 21 Or who is there that can provide you with Sustenance if He were to withhold His provision? No, they obstinately persist in insolent impiety and flight (from the Truth).

22 Is then one who walks headlong, with his face grovelling, better guided— Or one who walks evenly on a Straight Way? 23 Say: "It is He Who has created you (and made you grow), and made for you the faculties of hearing, seeing, feeling and understanding: little thanks it is you give. 24 Say: "It is He Who has multiplied you through the earth, and to Him shall you be gathered together."

25 They ask: When will this promise be (fulfilled)?— If you are telling the truth. 26 Say: "As to the knowledge of the time, it is with Allah alone: I am (sent) only to warn plainly in public." 27 At length, when they see it close at hand, grieved will be the faces of the Unbelievers, and it will be said (to them): "This is (the promise fulfilled), which you were calling for!" 28 Say: "Do you see?— If Allah were to destroy me, and those with me, or if He bestows His Mercy on us— Yet who can deliver the Unbelievers from a grievous Chastisement?" 29 Say: "He is (Allah) Most Gracious: we have believed in Him, and on Him have we put our trust: so, soon will you know which (of us) it is that is in manifest error." 30 Say: "Do you see?— If your stream be some morning lost (in the underground earth), who then can supply you with clear-flowing water?"

68. THE PEN

In the name of Allah, Most Gracious, Most Merciful.

1 *Nūn*. By the Pen and by the (Record) which (men) write— 2 You are not, by the Grace of your Lord, mad or possessed. 3 No, certainly for you is a Reward unfailing: 4 And you (stand) on an exalted standard of character. 5 Soon will you see, and they will see, 6 Which of you is afflicted with madness. 7 Certainly, it is your Lord that knows best, which (among men) has strayed from His Path: and He knows best those who receive (true) Guidance.

8 So listen not to those who deny (the Truth). 9 Their desire

is that you should be pliant: so would they be pliant. 10 Heed not the type of despicable men— ready with oaths, 11 A slanderer, going about with calumnies, 12 (Habitually) hindering (all) good, transgressing beyond bounds, deep in sin, 13 Violent (and cruel)— with all that, base-born— 14 Because he possesses wealth and (numerous) sons. 15 When to him are rehearsed our Signs, "Tales of the Ancients," he cries! 16 Soon shall We brand (the beast) on the snout!

17 Surely, We have tried them as We tried the People of the Garden, when they resolved to gather the fruits of the (garden) in the morning, 18 But made no reservation, ("If it be Allah's Will"). 19 Then there came on the (garden) a visitation from your Lord, (which swept away) all around, while they were asleep. 20 So the (garden) became, by the morning, like a dark and desolate spot, (whose fruit had been gathered). 21 As the morning broke, they called out, one to another— 22 "Go you to your tilth (betimes) in the morning, if you would gather the fruits." 23 So they departed, conversing in secret low tones, (saying)— 24 "Let not a single indigent person break in upon you into the (garden) this day." 25 And they opened the morning, strong in an (unjust) resolve. 26 But when they saw the (garden), they said: "We have surely lost our way: 27 "Indeed we are shut out (of the fruits of our labour)!" 28 Said one of them, more just (than the rest): "Did I not say to you, 'Why not glorify (Allah)?'" 29 They said: "Glory to our Lord! Surely, we have been doing wrong!" 30 Then they turned, one against another, in reproach. 31 They said: "Alas for us! We have indeed transgressed! 32 "It may be that our Lord will give us in exchange a better (garden) than this: for we do turn to Him (in repentance)!" 33 Such is the Punishment (in this life); but greater is the Punishment in the Hereafter— if only they knew!

34 Surely, for the Righteous, are Gardens of Delight, in the Presence of their Lord. 35 Shall We then treat the People of Faith like the People of Sin? 36 What is the matter with you? How do you judge? 37 Or have you a Book through which you learn— 38 That you shall have, through it whatever you choose? 39 Or have you Covenants with Us on oath, reaching to the Day of

Judgment, (providing) that you shall have whatever you shall demand? 40 Ask of them, which of them will stand surety for that! 41 Or have they some "Partners" (in Godhead)? Then let them produce their "partners," if they are truthful!

42 The Day that the Shin shall be laid bare, and they shall be summoned to prostrate in adoration, but they shall not be able— 43 Their eyes will be cast down—ignominy will cover them; seeing that they had been summoned aforetime to prostrate, while they were hale and healthy, (and had refused). 44 Then leave Me alone with such as reject this Message: by degrees shall We punish them from directions they perceive not. 45 A (long) respite will I grant them: truly powerful is My Plan.

46 Or is it that you ask them for a reward, so that they are burdened with a load of debt?— 47 Or that the Unseen is in their hands, so that they can write it down? 48 So wait with patience for the Command of your Lord, and be not like the Companion of the Fish—when he cried out in agony. 49 Had not Grace from his Lord reached him, he would indeed have been cast off on the naked shore, in disgrace. 50 Thus did his Lord choose him and make him of the company of the Righteous. 51 And the Unbelievers would almost trip you up with their eyes when they hear the Message; and they say: "Surely he is possessed!" 52 But it is nothing less than a Message to all the worlds.

69. THE SURE REALITY

In the name of Allah, Most Gracious, Most Merciful.

1 The Sure Reality! 2 What is the Sure Reality? 3 And what will make you realise what the Sure Reality is? 4 The Thamūd and the 'Ād People (branded) as false the Stunning Calamity! 5 But the Thamūd— they were destroyed by a terrible Storm of thunder and lightning! 6 And the 'Ād— they were destroyed by a furious Wind, exceedingly violent; 7 He made it rage against them seven

nights and eight days in succession: so that you could see the (whole) people lying prostrate in its (path), as if they had been roots of hollow palm-trees tumbled down! 8 Then do you see any of them left surviving? 9 And Pharaoh, and those before him, and the Cities Overthrown, committed habitual Sin, 10 And disobeyed (each) the Messenger of their Lord; so He punished them with an abundant Penalty. 11 We, when the water (of Noah's Flood) overflowed beyond its limits, carried you (mankind), in the floating (Ark), 12 That We might make it a Reminder for you, and that ears (that should hear the tale and) retain its memory should bear its (lessons) in remembrance.

13 Then, when one blast is sounded on the Trumpet, 14 And the earth is moved, and its mountains, and they are crushed to powder at one stroke— 15 On that Day shall the (Great) Event come to pass. 16 And the sky will be rent asunder, for it will that Day be flimsy, 17 And the angels will be on its sides, and eight will, that Day, bear the Throne of your Lord above them. 18 That Day shall you be brought to Judgment: not an act of yours that you hide will be hidden.

19 Then he that will be given his Record in his right hand will say: "Ah here! Read you my Record! 20 "I did really understand that my Account would (one Day) reach me!" 21 And he will be in a life of Bliss, 22 In a Garden on high, 23 The Fruits whereof (will hang in bunches) low and near. 24 "Eat and drink, with full satisfaction; because of the (good) that you sent before you, in the days that are gone!" 25 And he that will be given his Record in his left hand, will say: "Ah! would that my Record had not been given to me! 26 "And that I had never realised how my account (stood)! 27 "Ah! Would that (Death) had made an end of me! 28 "Of no profit to me has been my wealth! 29 "My power has perished from me!"... 30 (The stern command will say): "Seize him, and bind him, 31 "And burn him in the Blazing Fire. 32 "Further, make him march in a chain, whereof the length is seventy cubits! 33 "This was he that would not believe in Allah Most High, 34 "And would not encourage the feeding of the indigent! 35 "So no friend has he here this Day. 36 "Nor has he

any food except the corruption from the washing of wounds,.
37 "Which none do eat but those in sin."

38 So I do call to witness what you see, 39 And what you see
not, 40 That this is surely the word of an honoured Messenger;
41 It is not the word of a poet: little it is you believe! 42 Nor is
it the word of a soothsayer: little admonition it is you receive.
43 (This is) a Message sent down from the Lord of the Worlds.
44 And if the Messenger were to invent any sayings in Our name,
45 We should certainly seize him by his right hand, 46 And We
should certainly then cut off the artery of his heart: 47 Nor could
any of you withhold him (from Our wrath). 48 But, surely, this
is a Message for the God-fearing. 49 And We certainly know that
there are amongst you those that reject (it). 50 But truly
(Revelation) is a cause of sorrow for the Unbelievers. 51 But,
surely, it is Truth of assured certainty. 52 So glorify the name
of your Lord Most High.

70. THE WAYS OF ASCENT

In the name of Allah, Most Gracious, Most Merciful.

1 A questioner asked about a Chastisement to befall— 2 The
Unbelievers, the which there is none to ward off— 3 (A Penalty)
from Allah, lord of the Ways of Ascent. 4 The angels and the
Spirit ascend unto Him in a Day the measure whereof is (as) fifty
thousand years: 5 Therefore do you hold patience—a Patience
of beautiful (contentment). 6 They see the (Day) indeed as a far-
off (event): 7 But We see it (quite) near. 8 The Day that the
sky will be like molten brass, 9 And the mountains will be like
wool, 10 And no friend will ask after a friend, 11 Though they
will be put in sight of each other— The sinner's desire will be:
would that he could redeem himself from the Chastisement of
that Day by giving in ransom his children, 12 His wife and his
brother, 13 His kindred who sheltered him, 14 And all, all that
is on earth—so it could deliver him.

15 By no means! For it would be the Fire of Hell!— 16 Plucking out (his being) right to the skull!— 17 Inviting (all) such as turn their backs and turn away their faces (from the Right). 18 And collect (wealth) and hide it (from use)! 19 Truly man was created very impatient— 20 Fretful when evil touches him; 21 And niggardly when good reaches him— 22 Not so those devoted to Prayer— 23 Those who remain steadfast to their prayer; 24 And those in whose wealth is a recognised right. 25 For the (needy) who asks and him who is prevented (for some reason from asking); 26 And those who hold to the truth of the Day of Judgment; 27 And those who fear the displeasure of their Lord— 28 For their Lord's displeasure is the opposite of Peace and Tranquillity— 29 And those who guard their chastity, 30 Except with their wives and the (captives) whom their right hands possess— for (then) they are not to be blamed, 31 But those who trespass beyond this are transgressors— 32 And those who respect their trusts and covenants; 33 And those who stand firm in their testimonies; 34 And those who guard (the sacredness) of their worship— 35 Such will be the honoured ones in the Gardens (of Bliss).

36 Now what is the matter with the Unbelievers that they rush madly before you— 37 From the right and from the left, in crowds? 38 Does every man of them long to enter the Garden of Bliss? 39 By no means! For We have created them out of the (base matter) they know!

40 Now I do call to witness the Lord of all points in the East and the West that We can certainly— 41 Substitute for them better (men) than they; and We are not to be defeated (in Our Plan). 42 So leave them to plunge in vain talk and amuse themselves, until they encounter that Day of theirs which they have been promised!— 43 The Day whereon they will issue from their sepulchres in sudden haste as if they were men rushing to a standard (fixed for them)— 44 Their eyes lowered in dejection— Ignominy covering them (all over)! Such is the Day the which they are promised!

71. NOAH

In the name of Allah, Most Gracious, Most Merciful.

1 We sent Noah to his People (with the Command): "You warn your People before there comes to them a grievous Chastisement."
2 He said: "O my People! I am to you a Warner, clear and open:
3 "That you should worship Allah, fear Him and obey me: 4 "So He may forgive you your sins and give you respite for a stated Term: for when the Term given by Allah is accomplished, it cannot be put forward: if you only knew."

5 He said: "O my Lord! I have called to my People night and day 6 "But my call only increases (their) flight (from the Right).
7 "And every time I have called to them, that You might forgive them, they have (only) thrust their fingers into their ears, covered themselves up with their garments, grown obstinate, and given themselves up to arrogance. 8 "So I have called to them Aloud;
9 "Further I have spoken to them in public and secretly in private,
10 "Saying, 'Ask forgiveness from your Lord; for He is Oft-Forgiving; 11 "'He will send rain to you in abundance; 12 "'Give you increase in wealth and sons; and bestow on you gardens and bestow on you rivers (of flowing water). 13 "'What is the matter with you, that you are not conscious of Allah's Majesty and Glory— 14 "'Seeing that it is He that has created you in diverse stages? 15 "'Do you not see how Allah has created the seven heavens one above another, 16 "'And made the moon a light in their midst, and made the sun as a (Glorious) Lamp? 17 "'And Allah has produced you from the earth growing (gradually), 18 "'And in the End He will return you into the (earth), and raise you forth (again at the Resurrection)? 19 "'And Allah has made the earth for you as a carpet (spread out), 20 "'That you may go about therein, in spacious roads.'"

21 Noah said: "O my Lord! They have disobeyed me, but they follow (men) whose wealth and children give them no increase but only Loss. 22 "And they have devised a tremendous Plot.

23 "And they have said (to each other), 'Abandon not your gods: abandon neither Wadd nor Suwā', neither Yaghūth nor Ya'ūq, nor Nasr'— 24 "They have already misled many; and grant You no increase to the wrongdoers but in straying (from their mark)." 25 Because of their sins they were drowned (in the flood), and were made to enter the Fire (of Punishment): and they found— in lieu of Allah— none to help them.

26 And Noah, said: "O my Lord! Leave not of the Unbelievers, a single one on earth! 27 "For, if You leave (any of) them, they will but mislead Your devotees, and they will breed none but wicked ungrateful ones. 28 "O my Lord! Forgive me, my parents, all who enter my house in Faith, and (all) believing men and believing women: and to the wrongdoers grant You no increase but in perdition!"

72. THE SPIRITS

In the name of Allah, Most Gracious, Most Merciful.

1 Say: It has been revealed to me that a company of Jinns listened (to the Qur'ān). They said, 'We have really heard a wonderful Recital! 2 'It gives guidance to the Right, and we have believed therein: we shall not join (in worship) any (gods) with our Lord. 3 'And Exalted is the Majesty of our Lord: He has taken neither a wife nor a son. 4 'There were some foolish ones among us, who used to utter extravagant lies against Allah; 5 'But we do think that no man or jinn should say anything that is untrue against Allah. 6 'True, there were persons among mankind who took shelter with persons among the Jinns, but they increased them into further error. 7 'And they (came to) think as you thought, that Allah would not raise up any one (to Judgment).

8 'And we pried into the secrets of heaven; but we found it filled with stern guards and flaming fires. 9 'We used, indeed, to sit there in (hidden) stations, to (steal) a hearing; but any who listens

now will find a flaming fire watching him in ambush. 10 'And we understand not whether ill is intended to those on earth, or whether their Lord (really) intends to guide them to right conduct. 11 'There are among us some that are righteous, and some the contrary: we follow divergent paths. 12 'But we think that we can by no means frustrate Allah throughout the earth, nor can we frustrate Him by flight. 13 'And as for us, since we have listened to the Guidance, we have accepted it: and any who believes in his Lord has no fear, either of a short (account) or of any injustice. 14 'Amongst us are some that submit their wills (to Allah), and some that swerve from justice. Now those who submit their wills—they have sought out (the path) of right conduct: 15 'But those who swerve—they are (but) fuel for Hell-fire'—

16 (And Allah's Message is): "If they (the Pagans) had (only) remained on the (right) Way, We should certainly have bestowed on them Rain in abundance. 17 "That We might try them by that (means). But if any turns away from the remembrance of his Lord, He will cause him to undergo a severe Chastisement. 18 "And the places of worship are for Allah (alone): so invoke not any one along with Allah; 19 "Yet when the Devotee of Allah stands forth to invoke Him, they just make round him a dense crowd." 20 Say: "I do no more than invoke my Lord, and I join not with Him any (false god)." 21 Say: "It is not in my power to cause you harm, or to bring you to right conduct." 22 Say: "No one can deliver me from Allah (if I were to disobey Him), nor should I find refuge except in Him, 23 "Unless I proclaim what I receive from Allah and His Messages: for any that disobey Allah and His Messenger—for them is Hell: they shall dwell therein for ever."

24 At length, when they see (with their own eyes) that which they are promised— then will they know who it is that is weakest in (his) helper and least important in point of numbers. 25 Say: "I know not whether the (Punishment) which you are promised is near, or whether my Lord will appoint for it a distant term. 26 "He (alone) knows the Unseen, nor does He make any one acquainted with His Mysteries— 27 "Except a Messenger whom

He has chosen: and then He makes a band of watchers march in front of him and behind him, 28 "That He may know that they have (truly) brought and delivered the Messages of their Lord: and He encompasses all that is with them, and takes account of every single thing."

73. THE ENFOLDED ONE

In the name of Allah, Most Gracious, Most Merciful.

1 O you folded in garments! 2 Stand (to prayer) by night, but not all night— 3 Half of it— or a little less, 4 Or a little more; and recite the Qur'ān in slow, measured rhythmic tones. 5 Soon shall We send down to you a weighty Message.

6 Truly the rising by night is most potent for governing (the soul), and most suitable for (framing) the Word (of Prayer and Praise). 7 True, there is for you by day prolonged occupation with manifold duties: 8 But keep in remembrance the name of your Lord and devote yourself to Him wholeheartedly. 9 (He is) Lord of the East and the West: there is no god but He: take Him therefore for (your) Disposer of Affairs. 10 And have patience with what they say, and leave them with noble (dignity). 11 And leave Me (alone to deal with) those in possession of the good things of life, who (yet) deny the Truth; and bear with them for a little while. 12 With Us are Fetters (to bind them), and a Fire (to burn them), 13 And a Food that chokes, and a Chastisement Grievous. 14 One Day the earth and the mountains will be in violent commotion. And the mountains will be as a heap of sand poured out and flowing down.

15 We have sent to you, (O men!) a Messenger, to be a witness concerning you, even as We sent a Messenger to Pharaoh. 16 But Pharaoh disobeyed the Messenger; so We seized him with a heavy Punishment. 17 Then how shall you, if you deny (Allah), guard yourselves against a Day that will make children hoary-headed?— 18 Whereon the sky will be cleft asunder? His Promise needs must

be accomplished. 19 Surely, this is an Admonition: therefore, whoso will, let him take a (straight) path to his Lord!

20 Your Lord does know that you stand forth (to prayer) near two-thirds of the night, or half the night, or a third of the night, and so does a party of those with you. But Allah does appoint night and day in due measure. He knows that you are unable to keep count thereof. So He has turned to you (in mercy): read, therefore, of the Qur'ān as much as may be easy for you. He knows that there may be (some) among you in ill-health; others travelling through the land, seeking of Allah's bounty; yet others fighting in Allah's Cause. Read, therefore, as much of the Qur'ān as may be easy (for you); and establish regular Prayer and give Zakat; and loan to Allah a Beautiful Loan. And whatever good you send forth for your souls you shall find it in Allah's Presence— Yes, better and greater, in Reward. And seek the Grace of Allah: for Allah is Oft-Forgiving, Most Merciful.

74. THE ONE WRAPPED UP

In the name of Allah, Most Gracious, Most Merciful.

1 O you wrapped up (in a mantle)! 2 Arise and deliver your warning! 3 And your Lord do you magnify! 4 And your garments keep free from stain! 5 And all abomination shun! 6 Nor expect, in giving, any increase (for yourself)! 7 But, for your Lord's (Cause), be patient and constant!

8 Finally, when the Trumpet is sounded, 9 That will be — that Day — a Day of Distress — 10 Far from easy for those without Faith. 11 Leave Me alone, (to deal) with the (creature) whom I created (bare and) alone! — 12 To whom I granted resources in abundance, 13 And sons to be by his side! — 14 To whom I made (life) smooth and comfortable! 15 Yet is he greedy — That I should add (yet more) — 16 By no means! For to Our Signs he has been refractory! 17 Soon will I visit him with a mount of calamities!

18 For he thought and he plotted— 19 And woe to him! How he plotted!— 20 Yes, woe to him: how he plotted!— 21 Then he looked round; 22 Then he frowned and he scowled; 23 Then he turned back and was haughty; 24 Then said he: "This is nothing but magic, derived from of old; 25 "This is nothing but the word of a mortal!"

26 Soon will I cast him into Hell-Fire! 27 And what will explain to you what Hell-Fire is? 28 Nothing does it permit to endure, and nothing does it leave alone!— 29, Darkening and changing the colour of man! 30 Over it are Nineteen. 31 And We have set none but angels as guardians of the Fire; and We have fixed their number only as a trial for Unbelievers—in order that the People of the Book may arrive at certainty, and the Believers may increase in Faith—and that no doubts may be left for the People of the Book and the Believers, and that those in whose hearts is a disease and the unbelievers may say, "What does Allah intend by this?" Thus does Allah leave to stray whom He pleases, and guide whom He pleases: and none can know the forces of your Lord, except He. And this is no other than a Reminder to mankind.

32 No, surely: by the Moon, 33 And by the Night as it retreat, 34 And by the Dawn as it shines forth— 35 This is but one of the mighty (portents), 36 A warning to mankind— 37 To any of you that chooses to press forward, or to follow behind;— 38 Every soul will be (held) in pledge for its deeds. 39 Except the Companions of the Right Hand. 40 (They will be) in Gardens (of Delight): they will question each other, 41 And (ask) of the Sinners: 42 "What led you into Hell-Fire?" 43 They will say: "We were not of those who prayed; 44 "Nor were we of those who fed the indigent; 45 "But we used to talk vanities with vain talkers; 46 "And we used to deny the Day of Judgment, 47 "Until there came to us (the Hour) that is certain." 48 Then will no intercession of (any) intercessors profit them.

49 Then what is the matter with them that they turn away from admonition?— 50 As if they were frightened asses, 51 Fleeing from a lion! 52 Forsooth, each one of them wants to be given scrolls (of revelation) spread out! 53 By no means! But they fear

not the Hereafter. 54 No, this surely is an admonition: 55 Let any who will, keep it in remembrance! 56 But none will keep it in remembrance except as Allah wills: He is the Lord of Righteousness, and the Lord of Forgiveness.

75. THE RESURRECTION

In the name of Allah, Most Gracious, Most Merciful.

1 I do swear by the Resurrection Day; 2 And I do swear by the self-reproaching soul; 3 Does man think that We cannot assemble his bones? 4 No, We are able to put together in perfect order the very tips of his fingers. 5 But man wishes to do wrong (even) in the time in front of him. 6 He questions: "When is the Day of Resurrection?" 7 At length, when the sight is dazed, 8 And the moon is buried in darkness, 9 And the sun and moon are joined together— 10 That Day will Man say: "Where is the refuge?" 11 By no means! No place of safety! 12 Before your Lord (alone), that Day will be the place of rest. 13 That Day will Man be told (all) that he put forward, and all that he put back. 14 No, man will be witness against himself, 15 Even though he were to put up his excuses.

16 Move not your tongue concerning the (Qur'ān) to make haste therewith. 17 It is for Us to collect it and to recite it: 18 But when We have recited it, follow you its recital (as promulgated): 19 No more, it is for us to explain it (and make it clear).

20 No, (you men!) but you love the fleeting life, 21 And give up the Hereafter. 22 Some faces, that Day, will beam (in brightness and beauty)— 23 Looking towards their Lord; 24 And some faces, that Day, will be sad and dismal, 25 In the thought that some back-breaking calamity was about to be inflicted on them; 26 Yes, when (the soul) reaches to the collar-bone (in its exit), 27 And there will be a cry, "Who is an enchanter (to restore him)?" 28 And he will conclude that it was (the Time) of Parting;

29 And one shin will be joined with another: 30 That Day the Drive will be (all) to your Lord!

31 So he gave nothing in charity, nor did he pray! — 32 But on the contrary, he rejected Truth and turned away! 33 Then did he stalk to his family in full conceit! 34 Woe to you, (O man!), yes, woe! 35 Again, woe to you, (O man!), yes, woe! 36 Does Man think that he will be left uncontrolled, (without purpose)? 37 Was he not a drop of sperm emitted (in lowly form)? 38 Then did he become a leech-like clot; then did (Allah) make and fashion (him) in due proportion. 39 And of him He made two sexes, male and female. 40 Has not He, (the same), the power to give life to the dead?

76. MAN

In the name of Allah, Most Gracious, Most Merciful.

1 Has there not been over Man a long period of Time, when he was nothing — (not even) mentioned? 2 Surely, We created man from a drop of mingled sperm, in order to try him: so We gave him (the gifts) of Hearing and Sight. 3 We showed him the Way: whether he be grateful or ungrateful (rests on his will).

4 For the Rejecters We have prepared chains, yokes, and a blazing Fire. 5 As to the Righteous, they shall drink of a Cup (of Wine) mixed with *kāfūr* (Camphor) 6 A Fountain where the Devotees of Allah do drink, making it flow in unstinted abundance. 7 They perform (their) vows, and they fear a Day whose evil flies far and wide. 8 And they feed, for the love of Allah, the indigent, the orphan, and the captive — 9 (Saying), "We feed you for the sake of Allah alone: no reward do we desire from you, nor thanks. 10 "We only fear a Day of distressful Wrath from the side of our Lord." 11 But Allah will deliver them from the evil of that Day, and will shed over them a Light of Beauty and (blissful) Joy. 12 And because they were patient and constant,

He will reward them with a Garden and (garments of) silk.
13 Reclining in the (Garden) on raised couches, they will see there
neither the sun's (excessive heat) nor (the moon's) excessive cold.
14 And the shades of the (Garden) will come low over them, and
the bunches (of fruit), there, will hang low, within easy reach.
15 And amongst them will be passed round vessels of silver and
goblets of crystal— 16 Crystal-clear, made of silver: they will
determine the measure thereof (according to their wishes).

17 And they will be given to drink there of a Cup (of Wine)
mixed with Zanjabīl — 18 A fountain there, called Salsabīl.
19 And round about them will (serve) youths of perpetual
(freshness): if you see them, you would think them scattered
Pearls. 20 And when you look, it is there you will see a Bliss and
a Realm Magnificent. 21 Upon them will be green Garments of
fine silk and heavy brocade, and they will be adorned with
Bracelets of silver; and their Lord will give to them to drink of
a Wine Pure and Holy. 22 "Surely this is a Reward for you, and
your Endeavour is accepted and recognised."

23 It is We Who have sent down the Qur'ān to you by stages.
24 Therefore be patient with constancy to the Command of your
Lord, and follow not the sinner or the ingrate among them.
25 And celebrate the name of your Lord morning and evening,
26 And part of the night, prostrate yourself to Him; and glorify
Him a long night through. 27 As to these, they love the fleeting
life, and put away behind them a Day (that will be) hard. 28 It
is We Who created them, and We have made their joints strong;
but, when We will, We shall exchange their likes. By a complete
change. 29 This is an admonition: whosoever will, let him take
a (straight) Path to his Lord. 30 But you will not, except as Allah
wills; for Allah is full of Knowledge and Wisdom. 31 He will
admit to His Mercy whom He will; but the wrongdoers — for them
has He prepared a grievous Chastisement.

77. THOSE SENT FORTH

In the name of Allah, Most Gracious, Most Merciful.

1 By the (Winds) sent forth one after another (to man's benefit); 2 Which then blow violently in tempestuous Gusts, 3 And scatter (things) far and wide; 4 Then separate them, one from another, 5 Then spread abroad a Message, 6 Whether of Justification or of Warning— 7 Assuredly, what you are promised must come to pass.

8 Then when the stars become dim; 9 When the heaven is cleft asunder; 10 When the mountains are scattered (to the winds) as dust; 11 And when the Apostles are (all) appointed a time (to collect)— 12 For what Day are these (portents) deferred? 13 For the Day of Sorting out. 14 And what will explain to you what is the Day of Sorting out? 15 Ah woe, that Day, to the Rejecters of Truth! 16 Did We not destroy the men of old (for their evil)? 17 So shall We make later (generations) follow them. 18 Thus do We deal with men of sin. 19 Ah woe, that Day, to the Rejecters of Truth!

20 Have We not created you from a fluid (held) despicable?— 21 The which We placed in a place of rest, firmly fixed, 22 For a period (of gestation), determined? 23 For We do determine for We are the best to determine (things). 24 Ah woe, that Day! To the Rejecters of Truth! 25 Have We not made the earth (as a place) to draw together. 26 The living and the dead, 27 And made therein mountains standing firm, lofty (in stature); and provided for you water sweet (and wholesome)? 28 Ah woe, that Day, to the Rejecters of Truth!

29 (It will be said:) "Depart to that which you used to reject as false! 30 "Depart to a Shadow (of smoke ascending) in three columns, 31 "(Which yields) no shade of coolness, and is of no use against the fierce Blaze. 32 "Indeed it throws about sparks (huge) as Forts, 33 "As if there were (a string of) yellow camels (marching swiftly)." 34 Ah woe, that Day, to the Rejecters of Truth! 35 That will be a Day when they shall not be able to speak.

36 Nor will it be open to them to put forth pleas. 37 Ah woe, that Day, to the Rejecters of Truth! 38 That will be a Day of Sorting out! We shall gather you together and those before (you)! 39 Now, if you have a trick (or plot), use it against Me! 40 Ah woe, that Day, to the Rejecters of Truth!

41 As to the Righteous, they shall be amidst (cool) shades and springs (of water). 42 And (they shall have) fruits—all they desire. 43 "Eat and drink to your heart's content: for that you worked (righteousness). 44 Thus do We certainly reward the Doers of Good. 45 Ah woe, that Day, to the Rejecters of Truth! 46 (O you Unjust!) eat and enjoy yourselves (but) a little while, for that you are Sinners. 47 Ah woe, that Day, to the Rejecters of Truth! 48 And when it is said to them, "Prostrate yourselves!" they do not so. 49 Ah woe, that Day, to the Rejecters of Truth! 50 Then what Message, after that, will they believe in?

78. THE GREAT NEWS

In the name of Allah, Most Gracious, Most Merciful.

1 Concerning what are they disputing? 2 Concerning the Great News, 3 About which they cannot agree. 4 Surely, they shall soon (come to) know! 5 Surely, surely, they shall soon (come to) know! 6 Have We not made the earth as a wide expanse, 7 And the mountains as pegs? 8 And (have We not) created you in pairs, 9 And made your sleep for rest, 10 And made the night as a covering, 11 And made the day as a means of subsistence? 12 And (have We not) built over you the seven firmaments, 13 And placed (therein) a blazing lamp? 14 And do We not send down from the clouds water in abundance, 15 That We may produce therewith corn and vegetables, 16 And gardens of luxurious growth? 17 Surely, the Day of Sorting Out is a thing appointed—

18 The Day that the Trumpet shall be sounded, and you shall come forth in crowds; 19 And the heavens shall be opened as if

there were doors, 20 And the mountains shall vanish, as if they were a mirage. 21 Truly Hell is as a place of ambush— 22 For the transgressors a place of destination: 23 They will dwell therein for ages. 24 Nothing cool shall they taste therein, nor any drink, 25 Save a boiling fluid and a fluid, dark, murky, intensely cold— 26 A fitting recompense (for them). 27 For that they used not to fear any account (for their deeds), 28 But they (impudently) treated our Signs as false. 29 And all things have We preserved on record. 30 "So taste you (the fruits of your deeds); for no increase shall We grant you, except in Chastisement."

31 Surely, for the Righteous there will be a fulfilment of (the Heart's) desires; 32 Gardens enclosed, and Grapevines; 33 Maidens of Equal Age; 34 And a Cup full (to the Brim). 35 No Vanity shall they hear therein, nor Untruth, 36 Recompense from your Lord, a Gift, (amply) sufficient— 37 (From) the Lord of the heavens and the earth, and all between—(Allah) Most Gracious: none shall have power to argue with Him. 38 The Day that the Spirit and the angels will stand forth in ranks, none shall speak except any who is permitted by (Allah) Most Gracious, and He will say what is right. 39 That Day will be the sure Reality: therefore, whosoever will, let him take a (straight) Return to his Lord! 40 Surely, We have warned you of a Chastisement near— the Day when man will see (the Deeds) which his hands have sent forth, and the Unbeliever will say, "Woe unto me! Would that I were (mere) dust!"

79. THOSE WHO TEAR OUT

In the name of Allah, Most Gracious, Most Merciful.

1 By the (angels) who tear out (the souls of the wicked) with violence; 2 By those who gently draw out (the souls of the blessed); 3 And by those who glide along (on errands of mercy), 4 Then press forward as in a race, 5 Then arrange to do (the Commands of their Lord)— 6 One Day everything that can be in commotion will be in violent commotion, 7 Followed by oft-

repeated (commotions): 8 Hearts that Day will be in agitation; 9 Cast down will be (their owners') eyes. 10 They say (now): "What! Shall we indeed be returned to (our) former state?— 11 "What!—When we shall have become rotten bones?" 12 They say: "It would, in that case, be a return with loss!" 13 But surely, it will be but a single (compelling) Cry, 14 When, behold, they will be brought out in the open.

15 Has the story of Moses reached you? 16 Behold, your Lord did call to him in the sacred valley of Tuwā:— 17 "Go you to Pharaoh, for he has indeed transgressed all bounds: 18 "And say to him, 'Would you that you should be purified (from sin)?— 19 "'And that I guide you to your Lord, so you should fear Him?'" 20 Then did (Moses) show him the Great Sign. 21 But (Pharaoh) rejected it and disobeyed (guidance); 22 Further, he turned his back, striving hard (against Allah). 23 Then he collected (his men) and made a proclamation, 24 Saying, "I am your Lord, Most High." 25 But Allah did punish him, (and made an) example of him—in the Hereafter, as in this life. 26 Surely, in this is an instructive warning for whosoever fears (Allah).

27 What! Are you the more difficult to create or the heaven (above)? (Allah) has constructed it: 28 On high has He raised its canopy, and He has given it order and perfection. 29 Its night does He endow with darkness, and its splendour does He bring out (with light). 30 And the earth, moreover, has He extended (to a wide expanse); 31 He draws out therefrom its moisture and its pasture; 32 And the mountains has He firmly fixed; 33 For use and convenience to you and your cattle.

34 Therefore, when there comes the great, overwhelming (Event)— 35 The Day when Man shall remember (all) that he strove for, 36 And Hell-Fire shall be placed in full view for (all) to see— 37 Then, for such as had transgressed all bounds, 38 And had preferred the life of this world, 39 The Abode will be hell-Fire; 40 And for such as had entertained the fear of standing before their Lord's (tribunal) and had restrained (their) soul from lower Desires, 41 Their abode will be the Garden. 42 They ask you about the Hour—'When will be its appointed time?' 43 Wherein are

you (concerned) with the declaration thereof? 44 With your Lord is the Limit fixed therefor. 45 You are but a Warner for such as fear it. 46 The Day they see it, (it will be) as if they had tarried but a single evening, or (at most till) the following morn!

80. HE FROWNED

In the name of Allah, Most Gracious, Most Merciful.

1 (The Prophet) frowned and turned away, 2 Because there came to him the blind man (interrupting). 3 But what could tell you but that perchance he might grow in purity?— 4 Or that he might receive admonition, and the teaching might profit him? 5 As to one who regards himself as self-sufficient, 6 To him you attend; 7 Though it is no blame to you if he grow not in purity. 8 But as to him who came to you striving earnestly, 9 And with fear (in his heart), 10 Of him were you unmindful. 11 By no means (should it be so)! For it is indeed a Message of remembrance: 12 Therefore, let whoso will, keep it in remembrance. 13 (It is) in Books held (greatly) in honour, 14 Exalted (in dignity), kept pure and holy, 15 (Written) by the hands of scribes— 16 Honourable and Pious and Just.

17 Woe to man! What has made him reject Allah? 18 From what stuff has He created him? 19 From a sperm-drop: He has created him, and then moulds him in due proportions; 20 Then does He make his path smooth for him; 21 Then He causes him to die, and puts him in his Grave; 22 Then, when it is His Will, He will raise him up (again). 23 By no means has he fulfilled what Allah has commanded him. 24 Then let man look at his Food, (and how We provide it): 25 For that We pour forth water in abundance, 26 And We split the earth in fragments, 27 And produce therein Corn, 28 And Grapes and nutritious Plants, 29 And Olives and Dates, 30 And enclosed Gardens, dense with lofty trees, 31 And fruits and Fodder— 32 For use and convenience to you and your cattle.

33 At length, when there comes the Deafening Noise— 34 That Day shall a man flee from his own brother, 35 And from his mother and his father, 36 And from his wife and his children 37 Each one of them, that Day, will have enough concern (of his own) to make him indifferent to the others. 38 Some Faces that Day will be beaming, 39 Laughing, rejoicing. 40 And other faces that Day will be dust-stained; 41 Blackness will cover them: 42 Such will be the Rejecters of Allah, the Doers of Iniquity.

81. THE FOLDING UP

In the name of Allah, Most Gracious, Most Merciful.

1 When the sun (with its spacious light) is folded up; 2 When the stars fall, losing their lustre; 3 When the mountains vanish (like a mirage); 4 When the she-camels, ten months with young, are left untended; 5 When the wild beasts are herded together (in the human habitations); 6 When the oceans boil over with a swell; 7 When the souls are sorted out, (being joined, like with like); 8 When the female (infant), buried alive, is questioned— 9 For what crime she was killed; 10 When the Scrolls are laid open; 11 When the World on High is unveiled; 12 When the Blazing Fire is kindled to fierce heat; 13 And when the Garden is brought near— 14 (Then) shall each soul know what it has put forward.

15 So surely I call to witness the planets— that recede, 16 Go straight, or hide; 17 And the Night as it dissipates; 18 And the Dawn as it breathes away the darkness— 19 Surely, this is the word of a most honourable Messenger, 20 Endued with Power, held in honour by the Lord of the Throne, 21 With authority there, (and) faithful to his trust. 22 And (O people!) your Companion is not one possessed; 23 And without doubt he saw him in the clear horizon. 24 Neither does he withhold grudgingly a knowledge of the Unseen. 25 Nor is it the word of a Satan accursed. 26 Then whither do you go? 27 Surely, this is no less than a Message to (all) the Worlds: 28 (With profit) to whoever among you wills to go straight: 29 But you shall not will except as Allah wills— the Cherisher of the Worlds.

82. THE CLEAVING ASUNDER

In the name of Allah, Most Gracious, Most Merciful.

1 When the Sky is cleft asunder; 2 When the Stars are scattered; 3 When the Oceans are suffered to burst forth; 4 And when the Graves are turned upside down— 5 (Then) shall each soul know what it has sent forward and (what it has) kept back. 6 O man! What has seduced you from your Lord Most Beneficent?— 7 Him Who created you, fashioned you in due proportion, and gave you a just bias; 8 In whatever Form He wills, does He put you together. 9 No! but you do reject Right and Judgment! 10 But, surely, over you (are appointed angels) to protect you— 11 Kind and honourable— writing down (your deeds): 12 They know (and understand) all that you do. 13 As for the Righteous, they will be in Bliss; 14 And the Wicked— they will be in the Fire, 15 Which they will enter on the Day of Judgment, 16 And they will not be able to keep away therefrom. 17 And what will explain to you what the Day of Judgment is? 18 Again, what will explain to you what the Day of Judgment is? 19 (It will be) the Day when no soul shall have power (to do) aught for another: for the command, that Day, will be (wholly) with Allah.

83. THE DEALERS IN FRAUD

In the name of Allah, Most Gracious, Most Merciful.

1 Woe to those that deal in fraud— 2 Those who. when they have to receive by measure from men, exact full measure, 3 But when they have to give by measure or weight to men, give less than due. 4 Do they not think that they will be raised up (to account)?— 5 On a Mighty Day, 6 A Day when (all) mankind will stand before the Lord of the Worlds? 7 No! Surely the Record of the Wicked is (preserved) in *Sijjīn*. 8 And what will explain to you what sijjīn is? 9 (There is) a Register (fully) inscribed. 10 Woe, that Day, to those that deny— 11 Those that deny the Day of Judgment.

12 And none can deny it but the Transgressor beyond bounds the Sinner! 13 When Our Signs are rehearsed to him, he says, "Tales of the ancients!" 14 By no means! But on their hearts is the stain of the (ill) which they do! 15 Surely, from (the Light of) their Lord, that Day, will they be veiled. 16 Further, they will enter the Fire of Hell. 17 Further, it will be said to them: "This is the (reality) which you rejected as false!

18 No, surely, the Record of the Righteous is (preserved) in 'illīyīn. 19 And what will explain to you what 'illīyūn is? 20 (There is) a Register (fully) inscribed, 21 To which bear witness those Nearest (to Allah). 22 Truly the Righteous will be in Bliss: 23 On raised couches will they command a sight (of all things): 24 You will recognise in their Faces the beaming brightness of Bliss. 25 Their thirst will be slaked with Pure Wine sealed: 26 The seal thereof will be Musk: and for this let those aspire, who have aspirations: 27 With it will be (given) a mixture of Tasnīm: 28 A spring, from (the waters) whereof drink those Nearest to Allah. 29 Those in sin used to laugh at those who believed, 30 And whenever they passed by them, used to wink at each other (in mockery); 31 And when they returned to their own people, they would return jesting; 32 And whenever they saw them, they would say, "Behold! These are the people truly astray!" 33 But they had not been sent as Keepers over them! 34 But on this Day the Believers will laugh at the Unbelievers: 35 On raised couches they will command (a sight) (of all things). 36 Will not the Unbelievers have been paid back for what they did?

84. THE RENDING ASUNDER

In the name of Allah, Most Gracious, Most Merciful.

1 When the Sky is rent asunder, 2 And hearkens to (the Command of) its Lord—and it must needs (do so)— 3 And when the Earth is flattened out, 4 And casts forth what is within it and becomes (clean) empty, 5 And hearkens to (the Command of) its Lord— and it must needs (do so)—(then will come home the full Reality).

6 O you man! Surely, you are ever toiling on towards your Lord — painfully toiling — but you shall meet Him. 7 Then he who is given his Record in his right hand, 8 Soon will his account be taken by an easy reckoning, 9 And he will turn to his people, rejoicing! 10 But he who is given his Record behind his back — 11 Soon will he cry for Perdition, 12 And he will enter a Blazing Fire. 13 Truly, did he go about among his people, rejoicing! 14 Truly, did he think that he would not have to return (to Us)! 15 No, no! for his Lord was (ever) watchful of him! 16 So I do call to witness the ruddy glow of Sunset; 17 The Night and its Homing; 18 And the Moon in her Fulness: 19 You shall surely travel from stage to stage. 20 What then is the matter with them, that they believe not? — 21 And when the Qur'ān is read to them, they fall not prostrate, 22 But, on the contrary, the Unbelievers reject (it). 23 But Allah has full Knowledge of what they conceal (in their hearts). 24 So announce to them a Chastisement Grievous, 25 Except to those who believe and work righteous deeds: for them is a Reward that will never fail.

85. THE CONSTELLATIONS

In the name of Allah, Most Gracious, Most Merciful.

1 By the sky, (displaying) the Zodiacal Signs; 2 By the promised Day (of Judgment); 3 By one that witnesses, and the subject of the witness — 4 Woe to the makers of the pit (of fire), 5 Fire supplied (abundantly) with Fuel: 6 Behold! they sat over against the (fire), 7 And they witnessed (all) that they were doing against the Believers. 8 And they ill-treated them for no other reason than that they believed in Allah, Exalted in Power, Worthy of all Praise! — 9 Him to Whom belongs the dominion of the heavens and the earth! and Allah is Witness to all things. 10 Those who persecute (or draw into temptation) the Believers, men and women, and do not turn in repentance, will have the Chastisement of Hell: they will have the Chastisement of the Burning Fire.

11 For those who believe and do righteous deeds, will be Gardens, beneath which Rivers flow: that is the great Salvation, (the fulfilment of all desires), 12 Truly strong is the Grip (and Power) of your Lord. 13 It is He Who creates from the very beginning, and He can restore (life). 14 And He is the Oft-Forgiving, Full of loving-kindness, 15 Lord of the Throne of Glory, 16 Doer (without let) of all that He intends. 17 Has the story reached you, of the Forces— 18 Of Pharaoh and the Thamūd? 19 And yet the Unbelievers (persist) in rejecting (the Truth)! 20 But Allah does encompass them from behind! 21 No, this is a Glorious Qur'ān, 22 (Inscribed) in a Tablet Preserved!

86. THE NIGHT-VISITANT

In the name of Allah, Most Gracious, Most Merciful.

1 By the Sky and the Night-Visitant (therein)— 2 And what will explain to you what the Night-Visitant is?— 3 (It is) the Star of piercing brightness— 4 There is no soul but has a protector over it. 5 Now let man but think from what he is created! 6 He is created from a drop emitted— 7 Proceeding from between the backbone and the ribs: 8 Surely (Allah) is able to bring him back (to life)! 9 The Day that (all) things secret will be tested, 10 (Man) will have no power, and no helper. 11 By the Firmament which gives the returning rain, 12 And by the Earth which opens out (for the gushing of springs or the sprouting of vegetation)— 13 Behold this is the Word that distinguishes (Good from Evil): 14 It is not a thing for amusement. 15 As for them, they are but plotting a scheme, 16 And I am planning a scheme. 17 Therefore grant a delay to the Unbelievers: give respite to them gently (for a while).

87. THE MOST HIGH

In the name of Allah, Most Gracious, Most Merciful.

1 Glorify the name of your Guardian-Lord Most High, 2 Who has created, and further, given order and proportion; 3 Who has measured, and granted guidance; 4 And Who brings out the (green and luscious) pasture, 5 And then does make it (but) swarthy stubble. 6 By degrees shall We teach you to declare (the Message), so you shall not forget, 7 Except as Allah wills: for He knows what is manifest and what is hidden. 8 And We will make it easy for you (to follow) the simple (Path). 9 Therefore, give admonition in case the admonition profits (the hearer). 10 The admonition will be received by him who fears (Allah): 11 But it will be avoided by the most unfortunate one, 12 Who will enter the Great Fire, 13 In which he will then neither die nor live. 14 But he will prosper who purified himself, 15 And glorified the name of his Guardian-Lord, and (lifts his heart) in prayer. 16 No (behold), you prefer the life of this world; 17 But the Hereafter is better and more enduring. 18 And this is in the Books of the earliest (Revelation)— 19 The Books of Abraham and Moses.

88. THE OVERWHELMING EVENT

In the name of Allah, Most Gracious, Most Merciful.

1 Has the story reached you, of the Overwhelming (Event)? 2 Some faces, that Day, will be humiliated, 3 Labouring (hard), weary— 4 The while they enter the Blazing Fire— 5 The while they are given, to drink, of a boiling hot spring, 6 No food will there be for them but a bitter *Dharī*ʿ(A bitter and thorny plant) 7 Which will neither nourish nor satisfy hunger. 8 (Other) faces that Day will be joyful, 9 Pleased with their Striving— 10 In a Garden on high, 11 Where they shall hear no (word) of vanity: 12 Therein will be a bubbling spring: 13 Therein will be couches

(of dignity), raised on high, 14 Goblets placed (ready), 15 And cushions set in rows, 16 And rich carpets (all) spread out. 17 Do they not look at the Camels, how they are made?— 18 And at the Sky, how it is raised high?— 19 And at the Mountains, how they are fixed firm?— 20 And at the Earth, how it is spread out? 21 Therefore you give admonition, for you are one to admonish. 22 You are not one to manage (men's) affairs. 23 But if any turn away and reject Allah— 24 Allah will punish him with a mighty Punishment, 25 For to Us will be their Return; 26 Then it will be for Us to call them to account.

89. THE BREAK OF DAY

In the name of Allah, Most Gracious, Most Merciful.

1 By the break of Day; 2 By the Nights twice five; 3 By the even and odd (contrasted); 4 And by the Night when it passes away— 5 Is there (not) in these an adjuration (or evidence) for those who understand? 6 Do you not see how your Lord dealt with the 'Ād (people)— 7 Of the (city of) Iram, with lofty pillars, 8 The like of which were not produced in (all) the land? 9 And with the Thamūd (people), who cut out (huge) rocks in the valley?— 10 And with Pharaoh, lord of Stakes? 11 (All) these transgressed beyond bounds in the lands, 12 And heaped therein mischief (on mischief). 13 Therefore did your Lord pour on them a scourge of diverse chastisements: 14 For your Lord is (as a Guardian) is ever watchful. 15 Now, as for man, when his Lord tries him, giving him honour and gifts, then says he, (puffed up), "My Lord has honoured me." 16 But when He tries him, restricting his subsistence for him, then says he (in despair), "My Lord has humiliated me!" 17 No, no! but you honour not the orphans! 18 Nor do you encourage one another to feed the poor!— 19 And you devour inheritance— all with greed, 20 And you love wealth with inordinate love! 21 No! When the earth is pounded to

powder, 22 And your Lord comes, and His angels, rank upon rank, 23 And Hell, that Day, is brought (face to face)— on that Day will man remember, but how will that remembrance profit him? 24 He will say: "Ah! Would that I had sent forth (Good Deeds) for (this) my (Future) Life!" 25 For, that Day, His Chastisement will be such as none (else) can inflict, 26 And His bonds will be such as none (other) can bind. 27 (To the righteous soul will be said:) "O (you) soul, in (complete) rest and satisfaction! 28 "Come back you to your Lord— well pleased (yourself), and well-pleasing unto Him! 29 "Enter, then, among My devotees! 30 "Yes, enter My Heaven!"

90. THE CITY

In the name of Allah, Most Gracious, Most Merciful.

1 No I do swear by this City— 2 And you are an inhabitant of this City— 3 And by the begetter and that he begot-- 4 Surely, We have created man into toil and struggle. 5 Does he think, that none has power over him? 6 He may say (boastfully): wealth have I squandered in abundance! 7 Does he think that none beholds him? 8 Have We not made for him a pair of eyes?— 9 And a tongue, and a pair of lips?— 10 And shown him the two highways? 11 But he has made no haste on the path that is steep. 12 And what will explain to you the path that is steep?— 13 (It is:) freeing the bondman; 14 Or the giving of food in a day of privation 15 To the orphan with claims of relationship, 16 Or to the indigent (down) in the dust. 17 Then will he be of those who believe, and enjoin patience, (constancy, and self-restraint), and enjoin deeds of kindness and compassion. 18 Such are the Companions of the Right Hand. 19 But those who reject Our Signs, they are the (unhappy) Companions of the Left Hand. 20 On them will be Fire vaulted over (all round).

91. THE SUN

In the name of Allah, Most Gracious, Most Merciful.

1 By the Sun and his (glorious) splendour; 2 By the Moon as she follows him; 3 By the Day as it shows up (the Sun's) glory; 4 By the Night as it conceals it; 5 By the Firmament and its (wonderful) structure; 6 By the Earth and its (wide) expanse: 7 By the Soul, and the proportion and order given to it; 8 And its enlightenment as to its wrong and its right— 9 Truly he succeeds that purifies it, 10 And he fails that corrupts it! 11 The Thamūd (people) rejected (their prophet) through their inordinate wrongdoing, 12 Behold, the most wicked man among them was deputed (for impiety). 13 But the Messenger of Allah said to them: "It is a She-camel of Allah! And (bar her not from) having her drink!" 14 Then they rejected him (as a false prophet), and they hamstrung her. So their Lord, on account of their crime, obliterated their traces and made them equal (in destruction, high and low)! 15 And for Him is no fear of its consequences.

92. THE NIGHT

In the name of Allah, Most Gracious, Most Merciful.

1 By the Night as it conceals (the light); 2 By the Day as it appears in glory; 3 By (the mystery of) the creation of male and female— 4 Surely, (the ends) you strive for are diverse. 5 So he who gives (in charity) and fears (Allah), 6 And (in all sincerity) testifies to the Best— 7 We will indeed make smooth for him the path to Bliss. 8 But he who is a greedy miser and thinks himself self-sufficient, 9 And gives the lie to the Best— 10 We will indeed make smooth for him the Path to Misery; 11 Nor will his wealth profit him when he falls headlong (into the Pit). 12 Surely, We take upon Ourselves to guide, 13 And, surely, unto Us (belong) the End and the Beginning. 14 Therefore, do I warn you of a Fire blazing fiercely; 15 None shall burn therein but those most

unfortunate ones 16 Who give the lie to Truth and turn their backs. 17 But those most devoted to Allah shall be removed far from it— 18 Those who spend their wealth for increase in self-purification, 19 And have in their minds no favour from anyone for which a reward is expected in return, 20 But only the desire to seek for the Countenance of their Lord Most High; 21 And soon will they attain (complete) satisfaction.

93. THE GLORIOUS MORNING LIGHT

In the name of Allah, Most Gracious, Most Merciful.

1 By the Glorious morning Light, 2 And by the Night when it is still— 3 Your Guardian-Lord has not forsaken you, nor is He displeased. 4 And, surely, the hereafter will be better for you than the present. 5 And soon will your Guardian-Lord give you (that wherewith) you shall be well-pleased. 6 Did He not find you an orphan and give you shelter (and care)? 7 And He found you wandering, and He gave you guidance. 8 And He found you in need, and made you independent. 9 Therefore, treat not the orphan with harshness, 10 Nor repulse him who asks; 11 But the Bounty of the Lord— rehearse and proclaim!

94. THE EXPANSION OF THE BREAST

In the name of Allah, Most Gracious, Most Merciful.

1 Have We not expanded you your breast?— 2 And removed from you your burden 3 The which did gall your back?— 4 And raised high the esteem (in which) you (are held)? 5 So, surely, with every difficulty, there is relief: 6 Surely, with every difficulty there is relief. 7 Therefore, when you are free (from yours immediate task), still labour hard, 8 And to your Lord turn (all) your attention.

95. THE FIG

In the name of Allah, Most Gracious, Most Merciful.

1 By the Fig and the Olive, 2 And the Mount of Sinai, 3 And this City of security — 4 We have indeed created man in the best of moulds, 5 Then do We abase him (to be) the lowest of the low — 6 Except such as believe and do righteous deeds: for they shall have a reward unfailing. 7 Then what can, after this, make you deny the Last Judgment? 8 Is not Allah the Wisest of Judges?

96. THE CLINGING CLOT

In the name of Allah, Most Gracious, Most Merciful.

1 Proclaim! (or Read!) in the name of your Lord and Cherisher, who created — 2 Created man, out of a (mere) clot of congealed blood: 3 Proclaim! And your Lord is Most Bountiful — 4 He Who taught (the use of) the Pen — 5 Taught man that which he knew not. 6 No, but man does transgress all bounds, 7 In that he looks upon himself as self-sufficient. 8 Surely, to your Lord is the return (of all). 9 Do you see one who forbids — 10 A votary when he (turns) to pray? 11 Do you see if he is on (the road of) Guidance? — 12 Or enjoins Righteousness? 13 See you if he denies (Truth) and turns away? 14 Knows he not that God does see? 15 Let him beware! If he desist not, We will drag him by the forelock — 16 A lying, sinful forelock! 17 Then, let him call (for help) to his council (of comrades): 18 We will call on the angels of punishment (to deal with him)! 19 No, heed him not: but bow down in ador ion, and bring yourself the closer (to Allah)!

97. THE NIGHT OF POWER OR HONOUR

In the name of Allah, Most Gracious, Most Merciful.

1 We have indeed revealed this (Message) in the Night of Power:
2 And what will explain to you what the Night of Power is?
3 The Night of Power is better than a thousand Months. 4 Therein
come down the angels and the Spirit by Allah's permission, on
every errand: 5 Peace!...This until the rise of morn!

98. THE CLEAR EVIDENCE

In the name of Allah, Most Gracious, Most Merciful.

1 Those who reject (Truth), among the People of the Book and
among the Polytheists, were not going to depart (from their ways)
until there should come to them clear Evidence— 2 A Messenger
from Allah, rehearsing scriptures kept pure and holy: 3 Wherein
are laws (or decrees) right and straight. 4 Nor did the People of
the Book make schisms, until after there came to them Clear
Evidence. 5 And they have been commanded no more than this:
to worship Allah, offering Him sincere devotion, being True (in
faith); to establish regular Prayer; and to give Zakat; and that is
the Religion right and Straight. 6 Those who reject (Truth),
among the People of the Book and among the Polytheists, will
be in hell-fire, to dwell therein (for ever). They are the worst
of creatures. 7 Those who have faith and do righteous deeds—
they are the best of creatures. 8 Their reward is with Allah:
gardens of Eternity, beneath which rivers flow; they will dwell
therein for ever; Allah well pleased with them, and they with Him:
all this for such as fear their Lord and Cherisher.

99. THE EARTHQUAKE

In the name of Allah, Most Gracious, Most Merciful.

1 When the Earth is shaken to her (utmost) convulsion, 2 And the earth throws up her burdens (from within), 3 And man cries (distressed): 'What is the matter with her?'— 4 On that Day will she declare her tidings: 5 For that your Lord will have given her inspiration. 6 On that Day will men proceed in groups sorted out, to be shown the Deeds that they (had done). 7 Then shall anyone who has done an atom's weight of good, see it! 8 And anyone who has done an atom's weight of evil, shall see it.

100. THE CHARGERS

In the name of Allah, Most Gracious, Most Merciful.

1 By the (Steeds) that run, with panting (breath), 2 And strike sparks of fire, 3 And push home the charge in the morning, 4 And raise the dust in clouds the while, 5 And penetrate forthwith into the midst (of the foe) En masse— 6 Truly Man is, to his Lord, ungrateful; 7 And to that (fact) he bears witness (by his deeds); 8 And violent is he in his love of wealth. 9 Does he not know—when that which is in the graves is scattered abroad 10 And that which is (locked up) in (human) breasts is made manifest— 11 That their Lord had been well-acquainted with them, (even to) that Day?

101. THE GREAT CALAMITY

In the name of Allah, Most Gracious, Most Merciful.

1 The (Day) of Noise and Clamour: 2 What is the (Day) of Noise and Clamour? 3 And what will explain to you what the (Day) of Noise and Clamour is? 4 (It is) a Day whereon men will be

like moths scattered about, 5 And the mountains will be like carded wool. 6 Then, he whose balance (of good deeds) will be (found) heavy, 7 Will be in a Life of good pleasure and satisfaction. 8 But he whose balance (of good deeds) will be (found) light— 9 Will have his home in a (bottomless) Pit. 10 And what will explain to you what this is? 11 (It is) a Fire blazing fiercely!

102. THE PILING UP

In the name of Allah, Most Gracious, Most Merciful.

1 The mutual rivalry for piling up (the good things of this world) diverts you (from the more serious things), 2 Until you visit the graves. 3 But no, you soon shall know (the reality). 4 Again, you soon shall know! 5 No, were you to know with certainty of mind, (you would beware!) 6 You shall certainly see hell-fire! 7 Again, you shall see it with certainty of sight! 8 Then, shall you be questioned that Day about the joy (you indulged in!).

103. THE TIME

In the name of Allah, Most Gracious, Most Merciful.

1 By (the Token of) time (through the Ages), 2 Surely, Man is in loss, 3 Except such as have Faith, and do righteous deeds, and (join together) in the mutual teaching of Truth, and of Patience and Constancy.

104. THE SCANDALMONGER

In the name of Allah, Most Gracious, Most Merciful.

1 Woe to every (kind of) scandal-monger and backbiter, 2 Who piles up wealth and lays it by, 3 Thinking that his wealth would

make him last for ever! 4 By no means! He will be sure to be thrown into that which Breaks to Pieces. 5 And what will explain to you That which Breaks to Pieces? 6 (It is) the Fire of (the Wrath of) Allah kindled (to a blaze), 7 The which does mount (right) to the Hearts: 8 It shall be made into a vault over them, 9 In columns outstretched.

105. THE ELEPHANT

In the name of Allah, Most Gracious, Most Merciful.

1 Do you not see how your Lord dealt with the Companions of the Elephant? 2 Did He not make their treacherous plan go astray? 3 And He sent against them flights of Birds, 4 Striking them with stones of baked clay. 5 Then did He make them like an empty field of stalks and straw, (of which the corn) has been eaten up.

106. THE QURAYSH

In the name of Allah, Most Gracious, Most Merciful.

1 For the familiarity of the Quraysh, 2 Their familiarity with the journeys by winter and summer— 3 So they should worship the Lord of this House, 4 Who provides them with food against hunger, and with security against fear (of danger).

107. THE NEIGHBOURLY ASSISTANCE

In the name of Allah, Most Gracious, Most Merciful.

1 See you one who denies the Judgment (to come)? 2 Then such is the one who repulses the orphan (with harshness), 3 And

encourages not the feeding of the indigent. 4 So woe to the worshippers 5 Who are neglectful of their Prayers, 6 Those who (want but) to be seen (of men), 7 But refuse (to supply) (even) neighbourly needs.

108. ABUNDANCE

In the name of Allah, Most Gracious, Most Merciful.

1 To you have We granted the Fount (of Abundance). 2 Therefore to your Lord turn in Prayer and Sacrifice. 3 For he who hates you—he will be cut off (from Future Hope).

109. THOSE WHO REJECT FAITH

In the name of Allah, Most Gracious, Most Merciful.

1 Say: O you that reject Faith! 2 I worship not that which you worship, 3 Nor will you worship that which I worship. 4 And I will not worship that which you have been wont to worship, 5 Nor will you worship that which I worship. 6 To you then be your way, and to me mine.

110. THE HELP

In the name of Allah, Most Gracious, Most Merciful.

1 When comes the Help of Allah, and Victory, 2 And you do see The people enter Allah's Religion in crowds, 3 Celebrate the Praises of your Lord, and pray for His Forgiveness: for He is Oft-Returning (in Grace and Mercy)

111. THE PLAITED ROPE

In the name of Allah, Most Gracious, Most Merciful.

1 Perish the hands of the Father of Flame! Perish he! 2 No profit to him from all his wealth, and all his gains! 3 Burnt soon will he be in a Fire of blazing Flame! 4 His wife shall carry the (crackling) wood—as fuel!— 5 A twisted rope of palm-leaf fibre round her (own) neck!

112. PURITY OF FAITH

In the name of Allah, Most Gracious, Most Merciful.

1 Say: He is Allah, the One; 2 Allah, the Eternal, Absolute; 3 He begets not, nor is He begotten; 4 And there is none like unto Him.

113. THE DAYBREAK

In the name of Allah, Most Gracious, Most Merciful.

1 Say: I seek refuge with the Lord of the Dawn 2 From the mischief of created things; 3 From the mischief of Darkness as it overspreads; 4 From the mischief of those who blow on Knots; 5 And from the mischief of the envious one as he practises envy.

114. THE MANKIND

In the name of Allah, Most Gracious, Most Merciful.

1 Say: I seek refuge with the Lord and Cherisher of Mankind, 2 The King (or Ruler) of Mankind, 3 The God (or Judge) of Mankind— 4 From the mischief of the Whisperer (of Evil), who withdraws (after his whisper) — 5 (The same) who whispers into the hearts of Mankind— 6 Among Jinns and among Men.

INDEX

Aaron, 6:84; 20:29-36, 90-94.

'Abasa, S.80.

Ablutions, 4:43; 5:6.

Abraham, fulfilled God's Commands, 2:124; and Ka'bah, 2:125-127; 3:96,97; religion of, 2:130, 135; not Jew nor Christian, 3:67; nor Pagan, 3:95; rejects worship of heavenly bodies, 4:75-79; argues with sceptic, 2:258; argues with his father against idolatry, 4:74; 19:41-50; argues with his people against idols, 21:51-71; 26:70-82; 29:16-18, 24-25; 37:83-98; on life to the dead, 2:260; preaches to his people, 6:80-83; prays for father, 9:113-114; 26:86; sacrifice of son, 37:99-111; Angels visit him to announce son, 11:69-73; 15:51-56; 2:24-30; pleads for Lut's people, 11:74-76; his prayer, 14:35-41; 26:83-87; a model, 16:120-123; safe in fire, 21:69; Book of, 53:37; 87:19; his example in dealing with Unbelievers, 60:4-6,

Abū Lahab (Father of Flame), 111:1-5;

'Ād people, 7:65-72; 11:50-60;25:38; 26:123-140; 29:38; 41:15-16; 46:21-26; 2:41-42; 54:18-21;69:4-8; 89:6-14.

Adam, creation, 2:30-34; fall, 2:35-39; 7:19-25; two sons (Abel and Cain), 5:27-31; tempted by Satan, 20:120-121.

'Ādiyat, S.100.

Admonition, 87:9-13; 88:21 26.

Adultery, 17:32; 26:2-3, 4-10.

Ahmad, coming prophesied, 61:6.

Ahqāf, S.46.

Ahzāb, S.33.

Akala, 13:35.

A'lā, S.87.

'Alaq, S.96.

Āli 'Imran, S.3.

Allah, see God.

An'ām, S.6.

Anbiyā, S.21.

Anfāl, S.8.

Angels, plea to God 2:30-34; Gabriel and Michael, 2:97-98; not sent except for just cause, 15:7-8; sent for warning to men, 16:2; the impious and the angels, 25:21-22; on the Day of Judgement, 25:25; as messengers with wings, 35:1; pray for forgiveness for all on earth, 42:5; unbelievers give female names to, 53:27; and the Spirit ascend to God, 70:4; on errands of justice and mercy, 79:1-5; to protect men, 82:10-12; recording angels, 50:17-18,

Animals, form communities, 6:38; serve man, 16:5-8.

'Ankabūt, S.29.

Apes, transgressors become as, 2:65; 7:166.

Apostates, 47:25.

A'rāf, S.7.

'Asr, S.103.

Āyāt, see Signs of God.

Badr (battle of), 3:13; lessons of, 8:5-19, 42-48.

Bakkah (Makkah), 3:96.

Balad, S.90.

Balance, 43:17; 55:7-9; 57:25; 101:6-9.

Banī Isra'īl, see Isrā', S.17.

Banū Nadīr, 59:2-6.

Baptism of God, 2:138.

Baqarah, S.2.

Barā'ah, see Tawbah, S.9.

Barzakh, 23:100; 15:53; 55:20.

Bayyinah, S.98.

Beast (of the Last Days), 27:82.

Believers, fear God, 3:102; to fear nothing else, 10:62; hold together, 3:103; enjoin right and forbid wrong, 3:104,110; protected from harm, 3:111;

5:105; protected by angels, 41:30-31; warned against Unbelievers, 3:118-120,196; 9:23-24; 60:13; their lives sacred, 4:92-93; not to slight those who salute, 4:94; those who strive and fight, 4:95; 9:20-21,88-89; if weak and oppressed, 4:97-100; not sit where God's Signs are ridiculed, 4:140; 6:68; to prefer Believers for friends, 4:144; 5:57-58; witnesses to fair dealing, 5:8; duties to God. 5:35; 66:8; not to ask inquisitive questions, 5:101-102; grades of dignity, 8:4; described, 8:2-4; 9:71; 111-112; 10:104-106; 13:20-24,28-29; 23:1-11; 57-61; 28:53-55; 32:15-17; 42:36-39; 49:7,15; to be firm, 7:45; to obey and not lose heart, 8:46; not to be weary and fainthearted, 47:35; affection between their hearts, 8:63; to conquer against odds, 8:65-66; adopt exile, fight for God (Muhājir), 8:72, 74-75; help and give asylum (Ansār), 8:72; ask for no exemption from danger, 9:43-45; protect each other, 9:71; rejoice in their (spiritual) bargain, 9:111; 61:10-11; to be with those true in word and deed, 9:119; to study and teach, 9:122; will be established in strength, 14:27; to practice prayer and charity, 14:31; to say what is best, 17:53-55; to be heirs, to inherit Paradise, 23:10-11; promise to, 29:55-57; manners, 29:62-63; evil will be blotted out from, 29:7; their ills removed, 47:2; conduct, 33:69-71; 48:29; prayer for them by those around Throne of God, 40:7-9; not to despair or exult, 57:23; to make peace, 49:9; to avoid suspicion and spying, 49:12; to remember God in humility, 57:16; sincere

lovers of truth and witnesses, 57:19; receive special Mercy, Light, and Forgiveness, 57:28; do what they say, 61:2-3; helpers to God's work, 61:14; trust in God, 44:13; persecuted, but will reach Salvation, 85:6-11.

Bequests, 2:180.

Birds, 67:19.

Blasphemy, monstrous, to attribute begotten son to God, 19:88-92.

Book, (Revelation), is guidance sure, 2:2; to be studied, 2:121; Qur'an, verses fundamental and allegorical, 3:7; Qur'an, light and guide, 5:15-16; People of the, 3:64-80, 98-99, 113-115, 187, 199:4-47, 153-161; appeal to People of the, 5:59-60, 68; their hypocrisy, 5:61-63; forgiven if they had stood fast to their light, 5:66; know but refuse to believe, 6:20; mother or foundation of the, 3:7; 13:39; 43:4; for each period, 13:38; on a blessed Night, 44:3-4: from God, 46:2; See also Qur'an, Revelation.

Booty, 48:15; see also Spoils of War.

Brotherhood, one, of the Righteous, 21:92; of the Prophets, 23:52-54.

Burdens of others, none can bear, 6:164; 17:15; 29:12-13: 35:18; 39:7; 53:38; unbelievers will bear double, 16:25, no soul has burdens greater than it can bear, 2:286; 7:42; 23:62

Burūj, S.85.

Cave of Thawr, 9:40.

Cave, Companions of the, 18:9-22; 25-26.

Certainty, 56:95.

Charity, 2:110, 177, 195, 215, 219, 254, 261-274; 3:134; 30:39; 57:18; 63:10; 64:16-17, objects of, 2:273; 9:60;

Children, 2:233; 42:49-50.
Christ, *see* Jesus
Christians, 2:138-140; 5:14;
     nearest in love to Islam, 5:82-
     85.
Cities overthrown, 69:9.
Cleanliness, 4:43; 5:6.
Commerce that will never fail,
     35:29.
Confederates, 33:9-20, 22:27.
Consultation, mutual, 42:38.
Courtesy, 4:86.
Covetousness, 3:180; 4:32; 57:24.
Cowardice, 3:122.
Creation begins and repeated,
     10:4, 27:64; 29:19-20; a new,
     8:5: 14:48; 17:49, 98; 21:104,
     35:16; for just ends, 15:85;
     16:3; 44:39; 45:22; 46:3; doth
     obeisance to God, 16:48-50;
     not for sport, 21:16-17; of
     man, 23:12-14; in six Days,
     7:54, 32:4, 57:4; variety in,
     35:27-28; God commands 'Be'
     and it is, 2:117; 16:40, 36:82;
     40:68; in true proportions,
     39:5; of heaven and earth
     greater than creation of man,
     40:57, 79:27; purpose of,
     51:56-58.
Criterion, 2:53; 8:29; 21:48-50;
     25:1.

Dahr, see Insān, S.76; Time, 76:1
Dari', 88:6.
David, 6:84; 21:78-80; 34:10-11;
     38:17-26; fights Goliath,
     2:251.
Day, 7:54; 22:47; 32:4-5; 41:12,
     70:4.
Dead will be raised to life, 6:36.
Death, by God's leave, 3:145;
     inevitable, 3:185; 4:78,
     confusion of the wicked, 6:93-
     94, angels reproach
     Unbelievers, 8:50-54; in death
     the transgressor will not die,
     14:17; 20:74; 87:13; for
     wrongdoers, 16:28-29; for
     righteous, 16:30-32; taste of,
     3:185, 21:35, 29:57; first,
     37:59; not the end of all

things, 14:24-26; and changed
     form thereafter, 56:60-61;
     scene at, 56:83-87; 75:26-29;
     sincere men flee not from
     death, 62:6-8.
Degrees, according to good and
     evil done, 6:132.
Despair, deprecated, 3:139, 146;
     not of the Mercy of God,
     39:53.
Desert Arabs, 9:90-99; 101-106;
     48:11-12, 16; 49:14.
Desertion in fight, 4:89-91.
Dhariyāt, S.51.
Dhū al Kifl, 21:85; 38:48.
Dhū al Nun, 21:87-88; 68:48-50;
     see also Jonah.
Dhū al Qarnayn, 18:83-98.
Differences, decision with God,
     42:10.
Difficulty, there is relief with
     every, 94:5-8.
Discipline, 3:152; 61:4.
Discord, incited by Evil, 41:36.
Disease in the hearts of Hypocrites
     and Unbelievers, 2:10; 5:52;
     8:49; 9:125; 22:53; 24:50;
     33:12; 32, 60; 47:20, 29;
     74.31.
Disputations deprecated, 29:46
Distribution of Charity, 2:177.
Distribution of property taken
     form the enemy, anfāl, if after
     fighting, 8:41; fay, if without
     lighting, 59:7-8.
Divorce, 2:228-232, 236-237,
     241; 65:1-7. See also Zihār.
Dower, 2:229, 236-237; 4:4, 19-
     21, 25.
Duhā, S.93.
Dukhān, S.44.

Earth, will be change to a
     different Earth, 14:48.
     prepared for God's creatures,
     15:19-20; 26:7; 77:25-28;
     spacious is God's Earth, 29:56;
     manageable for man, 67:15;
     convulsion of, a symbol, 99:1-
     6.
Eating (akala) or enjoyment, 5:66;
     77:43, 46.

Elephant, Companions of the, 105:1-5.

Elias (Elijah), 6:85; 37:123-132.

Elisha, 6:86; 38:48.

Evidence, *re* transactions, 2:282-283; *re* bequests, 5:106-108; *re* charges against chaste women, 24:4-10.

Evil, 4:51-55, 123; 10:27-30; 26:221-226; 42:36-39; comes from ourselves, but good from God, 4:79; makes fools of men, 6:71; recompensed justly, 6:160; will destroy Evil, 19:83; will come to evil end, 30:10, deceives evil, 59:15-17; repel evil with good, 13:22; 23:96; 41:34.

Evil Spirit, rejected, accursed, 3:36; 15:17; 16:98.

Excess forbidden, in food, 5:87; in religion, 4:171; 5:77-81.

Eyes, ears, and skins will bear witness against sinners, 41:20-23,

'Face' of God, 2:112, 272; 6:52; 13:22; 18:28; 28:88; 30:39; 60:27.

Faith, rejectors of, 2:6-7, 165-167; 3:4, 10, 12, 21-22, 90-91, 116, 181-184; 4:136, 137, 167-168; ransom not accepted, 5:36-37; follow ancestral ways, 5:104; destroyed, 6:6; ask for angel to be sent down, 6:8-9; lie against their own souls, 6:24; will see Truth in Hereafter, 6:28-30; will be in confusion, 6:110; hearts inclined to deceit, 6:113; taste evil result of conduct, 64:5-6; their way and worship repudiated, 109:1-6; signs of, 2:165, 285; sellers of, 3:77, 177, strengthened in danger, and disaster, 3:173; and righteousness, 5:69; followed by unbelief, 16:106-109; and charity, 57:7-11.

Fajr, S.89.

Falaq, S.113.

*False gods, 7:194-198, 16; 20-21; 21:22, 24; 34:22-27; 41:47-48; 46:5-6; 53:19-24; 71:23-24.

Falsehood perishes, 21:18; deludes, 51:8-11.

Famines in Makkah, 23:75, 44:10.

Fasting, 2:184-185, 187.

Fate, man's fate on his own neck, 17:13.

Fath, S.48.

Fātiḥah, S.1.

Faṭir, S.35.

Fear of God, what is, 2:2; as He should be feared, 3:102; command to People of the Book and Muslims, 4:131; piety and restraint *(Taqwā)*, 47:17; unseen, 67:12; of His displeasure, 70:27; righteousness, 74:56.

Fear as motive for reclamation, 2:74; in signs of God, 17:59;

Fear no evil, 3:175.

Fear, none for the Righteous, 2:38; or for Believers, 2:62; or those who submit to God, 2:112; or who spend for God, 2:262, 274; or who believe and do good, 2:277; 5:69; or who believe and amend, 6:48, 7:35; or for friends of God, 10:62; or for God's devotees, 43:68, or for those who remain firm in God, 46:13.

Fear of men, 4:77.

Fig, as a symbol, 95:1.

Fighting, in cause of God, 2:190-193; 4:84; prescribed, 2:216; 2:244; in Prohibited month, 2:217; by Children of Israel, 2:246-251, in cause of God and oppressed men and women, 4:74-76; till no more, 8:39; against odds, 8:65; in case of, 9:5-6, 12, 13-16; those who believe not, and reject Truth, 9:29; with firmness, 9:123; permitted to those who are wronged, 22:39-41; when, and till when, 47:4; and the fainthearted, 47:20; exemptions from,

48:17.

Fīl, S.105.

Fire, parable, 2:17-18; mystic Fire of Moses, 20:10; God's gift, 56:72-73.

Fire, *see* Hell.

Food, lawful and unlawful, 2:168, 172-173; 5:1,3,5, 87-88; 6:118-119, 121, 145-146; 16:114-118; less important than righteousness, 5:93.

Forbidden, conduct, 6:151-152; 7:33; not things clean and pure, 7:32.

Forgiveness, 2:109; 4:48, 110, 116; 7:199; 39:53; 42:5; 45:14; 53:32; 57:21; duty of Believers, 42:37, 40; 45:14; Forgiveness, by Believers, for people of the Book, 2:109; by God, for sins other than joining gods with God, 4:48, 110, 116; hold to, and command the right, 7:199; God forgives all sins, 39:53; angels pray for forgiveness of all beings on earth, 42:5; forgive, even when angry, 42:37; and reconciliation, 42:40; Believers to forgive those who do not look forward to the days of God, 45:14; God forgives those who avoid great sins and shameful deeds, 53:32; be foremost in seeking, 57:21.

Fraud, 83:1-6.

Free will; no compulsion to believe, 10:99; Truth offered, to be accepted or rejected, 18:29; limited by God's Will, 74:56; 76:29-31, 81:28-29; just bias, 82:7

Friday Prayers, 62:9-11.

Friends, 3:28

Fruits and eating; metaphorical meaning of, 43:73; 47:15; 77:42-43.

Furqān, S.25.

Gabriel, 2:97, 98, 66:4.

Gambling, 2:219; 5:90.

Game, not to be killed in Sacred Precincts, 5:94-96.

Ghāshiyah, S.88.

Glad Tidings to men, 2:25; 5:19; 16:89; 48:8.

God, Cherisher, 1:2; 6:164; Guardian Lord, 2:21-22; as a Guardian on a Watchtower, 89:14; protector, 2:257; 3:150; 22:78; sets guardians over man, 6:61; Helper, 3:150; 4:45; 11:51; help of, how to be celebrated, 110:1-3; refuge to Him from all ills and mischief, 93:1-5; 94:1-6; Creator of all, 2:29, 117; 6:73; creates and sustains all, 7:54; 11:6-7; 13:16-17; 21:30-33;66:2-3; created all nature, 25:61-62; to Him belongs the heritage of the heavens and the earth, 3:180; 15:23;19:40; gives Sustenance 29:60-62, 51:58, Lord of Bounties, 3:174; His Bounties open to all, 17:20-21; Most Bountiful, 96:3, Merciful, 6:26; 5:74; 6:12, 54, 133; Most Kind, 9:117-118; Full of loving-kindness, 85:14; Beneficent, 52:28; His love bestowed on the Righteous, 19:96; Forgiving, 4:25, 26; 5:74; 15:49; 16:119; 39:53; 85:14; guides, 6:71, 88; 92:12; ordains laws and grants guidance, 87:3; calls to Home of Peace, 10:25;

God, His favours: Gardens and Fruits, 6:141; cattle, 6:142; mercy after adversity, 10:21; traverse through land and sea, 10:22, in life and death, 10:31, 56; 22:6; Cherisher and Sustainer, 10:32, direction, healing, guidance, mercy, 10:57; gifts from heaven and earth. 14:32-33; numberless, 14:34; 16:18; cattle and things ye know not, 16:5-8; rain, corn, and fruit, 16:10-11; night and day, sun, moon, and stars, gifts from heaven and earth, 16:12-13; sea and ships, 16:14; 17:66; mountains, rivers, roads, 16:15-16; cattle and fruits, 16:66-67; the Bee, 16:68-69; bestowed variously; be grateful, 16:71-73; in our birth, our faculties and affections, 16:77-78; in our homes and in the service of animals, 16:80-81; subjection of earth and sea, 22:65; blessings form heaven and earth, 23:17-22; long line of prophets, 23:23; faculties, and progeny, 23:78-79; shadows and the sun, 25:45-46; night and day, sleep, 25:47; wind and rain, 25:48-50; bodies of water, 25:53; man's creation, lineage and marriage, 25:54; creation of heavens and earth and man's benefits, 27:60-61;

God listens to the soul and makes man inherit the earth, 27:62; guides through darkness, winds as heralds, 27:63; originates and repeats creation, gives sustenance, 27:64; feeds creation, 29:60-62; sends rain and revives the earth, 29:63; made heaven and earth with all its produce, 31:10; subjected all things to your use, 31:20; 36:71-73; 45:12-13; His Mercy, gifts none can withhold, 35:2-3; life, grain, fruits, and springs, 36:33-35; earth and the heavens, 41:10-12; 51:47-48; accepts repentance and forgives, 42:25; listens and gives increase, 42:26-28; heavens and earth, rain and life, 43:9-11; creation in pairs, ships and cattle, 43:12-13; 51:49; created man and taught him speech, 55:3-4; set up justice, 55:7-9; spread out earth, with fruit, corn and plants, 55:10-12; two bodies of water, 55:19-20;

pearls and coral, 55:22; ships, 55:24; grants the need of every creature, 55:29, settles their affairs, 55:31; stream and flowing water, 67:30; given heaven's canopy its order and perfection, 79:27-28; night, its darkness and splendour, 79:29; expanse of the earth, its moisture pasture, and mountains, 79:30-33; orphan's shelter, 93:6; wanderer's guide, 93:7; satisfies need, 93:8; expanded thy breast, 94:1; removed thy burden, 94:2; raised high thy esteem, 94:4; present everywhere, 2:115; 7:7; gave you life, 2:28; 6:122; gives life and death, 3:156; 4:95; 15:23; takes the souls of men, 39:42;

God, to Him go back all questions for decision, 3:109, 128; to Him tend all affairs, 42:53; to Him is the Goal, 53:42; to Him is the return of all, 96:8;

God, His Unity, 2:163; 6:19; 16:22; 23:91-92; 37:1-5; 38:65-68; 92:1-4; One, not one in a Trinity, 5:72; nor one of two, 16:51; no begotten son, 2:116; 6:100; 10:68; 19:35; 23:91; nor consort nor daughters, 6:100-101; 16:57; 37:149-157; 43:16-19; no partners, 6:22-23, 136-137, 163;

God, Wise, 4:26; 6:18; best Disposer of Affairs, 3:173; 73:9; Most High, Great, 4:34; 87:1; Irresistible, 6:18, 61; Doer of all He intends, 85:16; power, 2:284; 3:29,6:12-13,65; 10:55; 16:77-81; 53:42-54; 85:12-16; Self-Sufficient, 6:133; Ready to appreciate service, 14:5; 35:30; 64:7, Most Forbearing, 2:225, 235, 263; 3:155; 5:101; 22:59; 64:17; Wisest of Judges, 95:8; Justice, 21:47; never unjust, 4:40; Best of

Planners, 3:54, 13:42; will separate evil from good, 3:179; His Wrath, 1:7; 7:97-99; quick in retribution, but forgiving and merciful, 7:167; 13:6; Swift in taking account, 24:39; Best to decide, 10:109; Best of those who show mercy, 13:109, 118; Most Merciful of those who show mercy, 7:151; 12:64, 92; 21:83; decision with Him, 42:10; Exalted in power, Wise, 31:9; 39:1; Free of all wants, 31:26; 35:15; Worthy of all praise, 31:26; Ample in forgiveness, 63:32; Living, 2:255; 40:65; Eternal, 2:255; 20:111; His Artistry, 27:88; His Face will abide forever, 55:27; all will perish except His own Self, 28:38; His knowledge, 2:284; 3:5, 29; 6:3, 117; 13:8-10, 16:23; 21:4; 31:34; 34:2, 64:4; His dominion, 3:189; 4:126; 5:120; 67:1; Command rests with Him, 6:57; 13:41;

God, Lord of the Throne of Glory Supreme, 9:129; 23:86; 40:15; 85:15; Lord of the Throne of Honour, 23:16; Lord of the mystery of heaven and earth, 16:77; Lord of Power, 51:58; Lord of the two East's and the two West's, 55:17; 70:40; 73:9, Lord of the Dawn, 93:1; Lord of the Ways of Ascent, 70:3; in heaven and on earth, 43:84; to Him belong the End and the Beginning, 92:13; listens to prayer, 2:186; sends calm or tranquility, 3:154; 9:26; 43:4, 18, 26; purges, 3:141, 154; tests, 3:142, 154, 166; 6:53; 29:2-5; 67:2; sees all, 3:163; sufficeth, 3:173; 8:64; 39:36; 65:3; will lighten difficulties, 4:28; sanctifies, 4:49; recognises all good, 4:147; wilt accept from the Good the best of their deeds, and pass by their ill deeds,

29:7; 46.16; removes affliction, 6:17; delivers from dangers, 6:63-64; sends revelations, 6:91; orders all things, 6:95-99; gives Light to men, 6:122; His Light wilt be perfected, 9:32-33; 61:8; is the Light of heavens and earth, 24:35-36;

God, changes not His Grace unless people change themselves, 7:53; 13:11; will not mislead, 9:115; suffers not reward to be lost, 9:120-121; 11:115; sufferers in His Cause to be rewarded, 16:41-42; doth provide without measure, 24:38; witnesses all things, 10:61; understands the finest mysteries, 67:14; nature of, 2:255; 3:2-3, 6, 18; 6:95-103; 25:2-3, 6; 32:2-9; 40:2-3; 43:84-85; 57:1-6; 59:22-24; 92:1-4; 94:1-3; close to man, 2:186; ever near, 34:50; near to man, 50:16; 56:85; compasses mankind round about, 17:60; with you wherever ye may be, 57:4; only Reality, 6:62; 31:30; The Truth, 20:114; to Him belong the Forces of heavens and earth, 47:7; decrees unalterable, 6:34; 18:27; His word finds fulfillment, 6:115; no vision can grasp Him, 6:103; most beautiful names, 7:180. 17:110; 20:8; 59:24;

God, worship of, 2:114, 152; to be worshipped and trusted, 11:123; sincere devotion due to Him, 39:3-11; 40:14; we trust in Him, 67:29: His promise is true, 4:122; 14:47; seek his Face, 6:52; 18:28; dedicate life to Him, 6:162; call on Him humbly, with fear and longing, 7:55-56; forget Him not, 59:19; to God, turn thy attention, 94:8; all Creation speaks of Him, 13:12-13; 17:44; 24:41-46; 57:1; praise

and glory to Him, 1:1; 17:111;
30:17-19; 34:1; 37:180-182,
45:36-37; 55:78; 56:74,96;
59:1; 61:1; 62:1; 64:1; 87:1;
and His Signs, 10:3-6; 13:2-4;
see Signs of God; His
Command must come to pass,
16:1; His command is but a
single Act, 54:50; all good
from Him, 16:53; what He
commands, 16:90-91; what is
with Him will endure, 16:96;
His words inexhaustible,
18:109; 31:27; rejecters of,
will not injure God, 47:32;
rejecter of, described, 50:24-
26; who are His servants,
25:63-76; those most devoted
to God, 92:17-21; claim to
exclusive friendship of,
condemned, 62:6; "so please
God", 18:23-24.

Goliath, 2:249-251.

Good, rewarded double, 4:40;
rewarded ten times, 6:160;
increased progressively, 42:23.

Good and Evil, 4:79, 85.

Good for evil, 23:96; 28:54,
41:34.

Gospel, 5:47.

Hadīd, S.57.

Hajj, *see* Pilgrimage.

Hajj, S.22.

Hāmān, 28:6, 38; 29:39; 40:36-37.

Hā Mīm, S.41.

Hands and feet will bear witness
against sinners, 36:65.

Hāqqah, S.69.

Harūt, 2:102.

Hashr, S.59.

Heaven, as gardens, in nearness to
God, rivers flowing, eternal
home, 3:15, 198; Companions
pure and holy, cool shades,
4:57 for righteous deeds,
4:124; truthful to profit from
truth; gardens with flowing
rivers; eternal home; God well
pleased with them, and they
with God; the great Salvation.
5; 119; no lurking sense of

injury in hearts, 7:43; mercy
from God, Good Pleasure,
Gardens, eternity, 9:21-22;
Gardens, mansions, Good
Pleasure of God, 9:72;
Gardens, fountains, peace and
security, no lurking sense of
injury, nor fatigue, 15:45-48;
Gardens of eternity, rivers,
adornments, thrones, 18:31;
22:23; Gardens of Eternity, no
vain discourse, peace,
sustenance, 19:61-63; Gardens
as hospitable homes, 32:19;
Gardens of eternity;
adornments; sorrow removed;
no toil or weariness, 35:33-35;
joy; associates; cool shade;
thrones; all they call for;
Peace, 36:55-58; fruits; honour
and dignity; gardens; thrones;
cup; chaste women, 37:41-49;
final return, gardens of
eternity, ease, fruit and drink,
chaste women; 38:49-52; lofty
mansions, rivers, 39:20,
garden, peace, eternity, angels
singing, 39:73-75; meads of
gardens; all they wish for;
Bounty, 42:22; no fear nor
grief; Gardens; rejoicing;
dishes and goblets of gold;
eternity; satisfaction, 43:68-73;
security, gardens and springs,
adornments, companions, fruit,
no further death; supreme
achievement, 44:51-57,
parable of garden, rivers,
Grace from God, 47:15;
Garden; peace and security;
more than all They wish; in
Our Presence, 50:31-35;
Garden, happiness, food and
drink; Thrones of dignity;
companions; families; service,
52:17-24; Gardens and Rivers;
Assembly of Truth; Presence
of Sovereign Omnipotent,
54:54-55; Gardens, Springs,
Fruits, Carpets, Chaste
Companions, 55:46-77; nearest
to God; Gardens; Thrones;

Service; Fruits and Meat; Companions; no frivolity nor taint of Ill; Peace, 56:11-38; nearest to God; Rest and Satisfaction, Garden of Delights, Companions, Salutation of Peace. 56:88-91; Light runs before Them; Gardens, Eternity; Highest Achievement, 57:12; Bliss; Garden; Fruits, 69:21-24; Cup, Fountain of Abundance, 76:5-6; Garden, Adornments; Thrones; No Excess of heat or Cold; Shades, Cup; Fountain; Service; Realm Magnificent, 76:5-22; Fulfilment of heart's desires; Gardens; Companions; Cup; No vanity or Untruth, 78:31-35; Garden, 79:41; Thrones; In their faces the beaming Brightness of Bliss, Pure Wine; Spring, 88:22-28, Joy; Striving; Garden; no Vanity; Spring; Throne; Cushions; Carpets, 88:8, 16; Rest and Satisfaction, coming back to God; well-pleased and well-pleasing to Him; among God's Devotees; God's Heaven, 89:27-30; Gardens of Eternity; Rivers; God well pleased with them, and they with Him, 98:8; salutation in, 10:10; 15:46; 56:91; "Yea, enter thou My Heaven!" 89:30

Heavens in poetic imagery, 37:5-6, 39:67; 41:12; 67:3.

Hell, skins roasted and renewed, 4:56; of no profit are hoards and arrogant ways, 7:48; for such as took religion to be amusement, and were deceived by the life of the world, 7:51; filled with jinn's and men, 11:119; drink, boiling fetid water, 14:16-17; Death will come, but will not die, 14:17; fetters, liquid pitch, faces covered with Fire, 14:49-50; garment of Fire, boiling water, maces of iron, 22:19-22;

Blazing fire, furious, 25:11-12; Sinners bound together; will plead for destruction, but the destruction will be oft-repeated 25:13-14; Punishment to cover them from above and below, 25:55; Fire, wicked forced into it every time they wish to get away, 32:20; men repeatedly warned; 36:63; Tree of *Zaqqum*, and boiling water, 3:62-67; 44:43-48; 55:52-55, to burn in Hell and taste of boiling fluid; and other Penalties, 38:55-58; Unbelievers led in crowds, previously warned; abode of the arrogant; 39:71-72; dispute and self-recrimination, 40:47-50; to dwell for aye; punishment not lightened; overwhelming despair. 43:74; God not unjust; sinners unjust themselves; 43:76; capacity unlimited, 50:30, Sinners known by their marks, 55:41; Hell, which they denied; boiling water, 55:43-44; Blast of Fire, Boiling Water, Shades of Black Smoke, 56:42-44; drawing in its breath, bursting with fury, 67:6-8; record in left hand; vain regrets, 69:25-29; seize him, bind him, burn him, make him march in a chain, 69:30-37; naught doth it permit to endure, and naught doth it leave alone, 74:26-29; Over it are Nineteen, 74:30-31; a place of ambush; destination for transgressors; to dwell therein for ages; taste there nothing cool nor drink, save boiling fluid, or intensely cold, 78:21-25; Day when hellfire shall be placed in full view, 79:35-39; stain on sinners' hearts; Light of God veiled from them; enter the Fire, 83:14-16; faces humiliated, enter the Fire; drink boiling water; food bitter

Dari, 88:2-7; brought face to face; will then remember; chastisement and bonds, 89:23-26; bottomless Pit; fire blazing fiercely, 2:9-11; That which Breaks to Pieces; wrath of God, 104:4-9; they will neither die nor live, 20:74; 87:13; to it are seven Gates, 15:44, is it enternal? 11:107; who will pass over it? 19:71; 102:6.

Hereafter, not a falsehood, 6:31; man must meet God, 6·31; Home in the, 6:32; Wrath of God, 6:40-41; 12:107; Home of Peace, 6:127; wrongdoers will not prosper, 6:135; prophets and those to whom Message was sent will be questioned, 7:6; deeds will be balanced, 7:8-9; no intercession for those who disregarded Hereafter, 7:53; Fire and Garden endure, except as God wills, 11:107-108, the arrogant and the weak in the, 14:21; wrongdoers will ask for respite, 14:44-46; Home of the, 28:83; 29:64, better than silver and gold, 43:33-35; denied by men, 50:12-14; better than the present, 93:4.

Hijr, see Rocky Tract.

Hijr, S.15.

Houses, manners about entering, 24:27-29.

Hūd, 7:65-72; 11:50-60; 26:123-140; 46:21-26.

Hūd, S.11.

Hujurāt, S.49,

Humazah, S.104.

Humility, 4:42-43; 7:161; 57:16; shadows show humility to. God, 13:15; 74:14.

Hunayn, 9:25,

Hūr, companions in heaven, 44:54; 52:20,

Hypocrites, do not believe in God and the Last Day. 2:8; deceive themselves, 2:9; disease in their hearts, 2:10; make mischief, 2:11-12, fools and mockers, 2:13-15; barter guidance for error, 2:16; deaf, dumb, and blind, 2:17-18; in terror and darkness, 2:19-20; dazzling speech; led by arrogance, 2:204-206; refuse to fight, 3:167-168; resort to evil; turn away from Revelation; come when seized by misfortune; to be kept clear of and admonised, 4:60-63; tarry behind in misfortune; wish to share good fortune, 4:70-73; thrown out of the way; reject Faith; renegades; to be seized and slain, 4:88-89; wait events; think of overreaching God; distracted in mind, 4:41-143; in lowest depths of Fire; no helper, 4:145; afraid of. being found out, 9:64-65, understanding with each other; perverse; curse of God, 9:67-69; not to be taken as friends, 58:14-19; liars and deceivers, 59:11-14; liars; screen misdeeds with oaths, 63:1-4.

Iblīs, *(see also* Satan), 2:34; 7:11-18, 15:31-44; 17:61-65; 18:50, 20:116-123; 38:71-85.

Ibrāhīm, *see* Abraham.

Ibrāhīm, S.14.

'Iddah, 2:228, 231-232, 234-235; 33:49; 65:4, 6-7.

Idrīs, 19:56-57; 21:85.

Ikhlās S.112.

'Illīyūn, 83:18-21,

Immorality, 4·15-18.

'Imrān, family of; 3:35.

Infitār, S.82.

Inheritance, 2:180, 240; 4:7-9, 11-12, 19,33, 176; 5:105-108.

Injury, forgiveness or self-defence, 42:39-43

Insān, see Dahr, S.76.

Inshiqāq, S.84.

Inshirāh, see Sharh, S.94.

Inspiration, 17:85-87; 40:15, 42:3, 7, 51-53.

Intercession, 6:51, 70, 10.3, 19:87; 39:44; 43:86; 53:26.

Intoxicants see Wine.

Iqra', see 'Alaq, S.96.

Iram, 89:7.

Isaac, 6:84; 21:72; 37:112-113.

Islam, to be first to bow in, 6:14, 163; 39:12; vanguard of, 9:100; heart opened to, 39:22; a favour and privilege, 49:17.

Isma'il, 2:125-129; 6:86; 19:54-55; 21:85.

Isrā', S.17.

Israel, Children of, 2:40-86; favours, 2:47-53; 2:60, 122; 45:16-17; contumacy, 2:54-59, 61, 63-74; 5:71; 7:138-141; their relations with Muslims, 2:75-79; their arrogance, 2:80, 88, 91; their Covenants, 2:83-86, 93, 100; 5:12, 13, 70; their love of this life, 2:96; ask for a king, 2:246-251; divided and rebellious, 7:161-171; twice warned, 17:4-8; delivered from enemy, 20:80-82; given Book and Leaders, 32:23-25; 40:53-54; the learned among them knew the Qur'an to be true, 26:197.

Jacob, 2:132-133, 6:84; 19:49; 21:72.

Jāthiyah, S.45.

Jesus, a righteous prophet, 6:85; birth, 3:45-47; 19:22-23; messenger to Israel, 3:49-51; disciples, 3:52-53; 5:111-115; taken up, 3:55-58; 4:157-159; like Adam, 3:59; not crucified, 4:157; no more than messenger, 4:171; 5:75; 43:59, 63-64; not God, 5:17,72; sent with Gospel, 5:46; not son of God, 9:30; Message and miracles, 5:19:30-33; prays for Table of viands, 5:114; taught no false worship, 5:116-118; disciples declare themselves Muslims, 5:111; followers have compassion and mercy, 57:27; disciples as God's helpers,

61:14; as a Sign, 23:50; 43:61; prophesied Ahmad. 61:6.

Jews, will listen to falsehood, 5:41-42; utter blasphemy, 5:64; enmity lo Islam, 5:82; and Christians, 2:140; 4:153-161, 171; 5:18; *See also* Israel, Children of.

Jihād, *see* fighting; striving.

Jinn, S.72.

Jinns, 6:100; 15:27; 34:41; 46:29-32; 55:15; 72:1-15.

Job, 6:84; 21:83-84; 38:41-44

John (the Baptist), *see* Yahyā.

Jonah (or Jonas, or Yunus), 4:163; 6:86; 10:98; 37:139-148; (Dhū al Nun) 21:87; 68:48-50; (Companion of the Fish).

Joseph, 6:84; his story, 12:4-101; his vision, 12:4-6; jealousy of his brothers, 12:7-10; their plot, 12:11-18; sold by his brethren, 12:19-20; bought by 'Azīz of Egypt, 12:21; tempted by 'Azīz's wife, 12:22-29, her ruse, 12:30-34; in prison, 12:35-42; interprets King's vision, 12:43-54; established in power, 12:55-57; his dealings with his brethren, 12:58-93; reunion of whole family, 12:94-101.

Judgment, must come, 6:51; 6:128; 34:3-5; 40:59; 51:5-6, 12-14; 52:7-10; 56:1-7; 64:7-10; 95:7; will come suddenly, 7:187; 36:48-50; as the twinkling of an eye, 16:77; 54:50; Hour known to God alone, 33:63, 67:26; 79:42-46; is near, 54:1-5; men will be sorted out into three classes, 56:7-56; Foremost in Faith, nearest to God, 56:11-26; Companions of Right Hand, 56:27-40; Companions of Left Hand, 56:41-56; Lesser Judgment, 75:22-30; the Great News, 78:1-5; deniers of, 107:1-7.

Judgment Day, full recompense only then, 3:185; earth

changed, and men fathered; Book of Deeds, 18:47-49; men surge like waves; trumpet blown; Unbelievers will see and hear, 18:99-101; sectarian differences to be solved; Distress for lack of Faith, 19:37-39; rejecters of the message will bear a grievous burden, 20:100-101; trumpet will sound; sinful in terror; interval will seem short, 20:102-104; they will follow the Caller; tramp of their feet; all sounds humbled; 20:108; no Intercession except by permission, 20:109; no fear for the righteous, 20:112; rejecters will be raised up blind, 20:124-127; scales of Justice, 21:47; True Promise will approach fulfillment; sobs of Unbelievers; the Good will suffer no grief, 21:97-103; heavens will be rolled up like a scroll; new creation, 21:104; terrible convulsion; men in drunken riot; Wrath of God, 22:1-2; Trumpet is blown; Balance of Good Deeds, heavy or light, 23:101-104; Voice of Judgement, 23:105-111; Time will seem short, 23:112-115; false worship will be exposed, 25:17-19; heavens rent as under; angels sent down; Dominion wholly for God, 25:25-26; wrongdoer's regrets, 25:27-30; terror for evildoers, not for doer of good, 27:83-90; guilty in despair, no Intercessor, 30:12-13; justice done, 36:51-54; joy and peace for the Good, 36:55-58; Day of Sorting Out, 30:14-16; 37:20-21; Wrongdoers questioned; recriminations, 37:22-23; contrast between the righteous, with sound hearts and those straying in evil, 37:88-102; Wrongdoers' arrogances, 37:33-36;

retribution for evil, 37:37-39; felicity for servants of God, 37:40-61; Tree of *Zaqqum*, 37:62-68; wrongdoers rushed on their fathers' footsteps, 37:69-74; trumpet; all in heaven and earth will swoon; second trumpet, renewed Earth will shine with God's Glory; recompense, 39:67-70; no intercession, justice and truth, 40:18-20; sudden; friends will be foes, except the righteous, 43:66-67; no fear on God's devotees, 43:68-69; dealers in falsehood to perish; righteous to obtain Mercy, 45:27-35; not to be averted; Fire for the false and the triflers, 52:7-16; wrongdoers swoon in terror, 52:45-47; Caller to a terrible affair, 54:6-8; no defence for the evil; known by their Marks, 55:35-44; mutual gain and loss, 64:9-10; Shin to be laid bare, 68:42-43; trumpet; Great Event; Angels will bear the Throne; nothing hidden; Good and Evil recompensed, 69:13-37; sky like molten brass; no friend will ask after friend; no deliverance for evil, 70:8, 18; wicked will issue from sepulchers in haste, 70:43-44; Will know reality, not known whether near or far, 72:24-25; children hoary-headed; sky cleft asunder, 73:17-18; trumpet; Day of Distress for those without Faith, 74:8-10; stars become dim; messengers collect; sorting out, 77:7-15; woe to Rejecters of Truth, 77:29-50; sorting out; Trumpet; heavens opened; mountains vanish; 78:17-20; Spirit and Angels stand forth; Day of Reality, 78:38-40; commotion and agitation, 79:6-9; single Cry, 79:13-14; Deafening Noise; no one for another; some Faces

beaming; some dust stained,
80:33-42; sun, stars,
mountains, outer nature
change; souls sorted out;
World on High unveiled,
81:1-14; sky cleft asunder;
stars and Oceans scattered;
Graves turned upside down;
each soul will know its deeds,
82:1-5; no soul can do aught
for another, 82:17-19; sky and
earth changed; man ever
toiling on towards his Lord;
Record of Good or Ill, 84:1-
15; things secret tested, 86:9-
10; Overwhelming Event;
Faces humiliated and Faces
joyful, 88:1-16; Earth pounded
to powder; Lord cometh; hell
and heaven shown, 89:21-30;
Earth in convulsion; man in
distress; sorted out, 99:1-8;
Contents of graves scattered
abroad; of human breasts made
manifest; Lord well acquainted,
100:9-11; Noise and Clamour;
Good and Evil rewarded,
101:1-11.

Jūdī, Mount, 11:44.

Jumu'ah, S.62.

Justice, 4:58, 65, and 105, 135,
7:29; 16:90; 57:25;

Ka'bah, built by Abraham, 2:125-
127; no killing of game, 5:94-
96; asylum of security for
men, 5:97.

Kāfirūn, S.109.

Kāfūr, Cup mixed with, 76:5.

Kahf, S.18.

Kawthar (Fount of Abundance),
108:1-2;

Kawthar, S.108.

Keys of heavens and earth, 39:63;
42:12.

Khandaq, battle, 33:9-20

Kindred, rights of, 2:83, 177 4:7-
9, 36; 8:41; 16:90; 17:26;
24:22; 42:23.

Knowledge (Certainty), 102:5-7;
of five things, with God alone,
31:34.

Lahab. see Masad, S.111.

Languages, variations in man's
and colours, 30:22.

Lāt, 53:19.

Layl, S.92. "Leaves to stray",
14:4; 16:93; 39:23.

Life of this world, 6:32; 57:20.

Life sacred, 17:33.

Light, manifest, 4:174; and
Darkness, 6:1; parable of,
24:35-36; goes before and
with Believers, 57:12-15; 66:8;
provided by God, that
Believers may walk straight,
57:28; of God, veiled from
unbelievers, 88:15.

Loan, beautiful, to God, 2:245,
and 57:11, 18; 64:17; 78:20.

Loss (spiritual), 39:15.

Lote tree, 34:16; 53:14-18; 56:28.

Luqmān, 31:12; his teaching,
31:12-19.

Luqmān, S.31.

Lūṭ (Lot), 6:86, 7:80-84; 11:77-
83; 15:57-77; 21:74-75;
26:160-175; 27:54-58; 29:26;
28-35; 37:133-138; 51:31-37;
54:33-39; his wife disobedient,
11:81; 15:60; 66:10.

Ma'ārij, S.70.

Madīnah, 33:9-27.

Madyan, 7:85-93; 11:84-95;
29:36-37.

Magians *(Majūs),* 12:17.

Mā'idah, S.5.

Makkah, Bakkah, 3:96; mystic
relation to Prophet, 90:1-4;
city of security, 95:3.

Man, vicegerent on earth, 2:30;
6:165; tested by God, 2:155;
3:186; 47:31; 57:25; things
men covet, 3:14; duty, 4:1-36;
17:23-39; 29:8-9; 30:38; 3:33;
46:14; 70:22-35; created from
clay, for a term, 6:2; 15:26;
called to account, 6:44; will
return to God, 6:60, 72;
10:45-46; confusion of the
wicked at death, 6:93-94, plots
against own soul, 6:123;
10:44; personal responsibility,

6:164; ungrateful, 7:10; 36:45-47; 74:15-25; 100:1-8; warned against Satan, 7:27; knows of God, but misled by Evil, 7:172-175; and family life, 7:189-190; limited Free Will, 10:99; behaviour in and out of trouble, 10:12; 11:9-11; 16:53-55; 17:67-70; 29:10, 65-66, 30:33-34; 31:32, 39:8, 49; 41:49-51; 42:48; 89:15-16; God's spirit breathed into him, 15:29; lowly in origin, but blessed with favours, 16:4-8, 32:7-9; 35:11; 36:77-78; 76:1-3: 77:20-24; 80:17-32; 86:5-8; 96:2-5; prays for evil, 17:11; is given to hasty deeds, 17:11; 16:37; his fate fastened round his neck, 17:13; to be judged by his record, 17:71; his physical growth, 22:5, 23:12-14; 40:67; death and resurrection, 23:15-16; tongues, hands, and feet will bear witness against men, 24:24; made from water, 25:54; relationships of lineage and marriage, 25:54; should submit Self to God, 31:22; not two hearts in one breast, 33:4; to worship God, 39:64-66; misfortunes, due to his deeds, 42:30, angels note his doings, 50:17-18, 23; his growth and activity depend on God, 56:57-74; to be created again after death in new forms, 56:60-61; riches and family may be a trial, 64:14-15; created and provided for by God, 67:23-24; 74:12-15; is impatient, 70:19-21; who will be honoured ones among men, 70:22-35; evidence against himself, 75:14-15; his arrogance, 75:31-40; 90:5-7; loves the fleeting world, 76:27; seduced from God, 82:6-12; painfully toiling on to God, 84:6; travels from stage to stage, 84:16-19, guilty of sins,

89:17-20; created into toil and struggle, 90:4; gifted with faculties, 90:8-10; strives for diverse ends, 92:4-11; created in best of moulds, 95:4; abased unless he believes and does righteousness, 95:5-6; transgresses all bounds, 96:6-14.

Manāt, 53:20.

Mankind, one nation, 2:213; 10:19; created from single pair, 4:1; 39:6; 49:13; transgress insolently, 10:23; heed not, though Reckoning near, 21:1-3; pattern according to which God has made mankind, 30:30; honour depends on righteousness, 49:13.

Manners, about entering houses, 24:27-29; in the home, 24:58-61;in the Prophet's presence, 29:62-63; 49:1-5; in the Prophet's houses, 33:53; to bless and salute the Prophet, 33:56; not to annoy Prophet or believing men or women, 33:57-58; require verification of news before belief, 49:6; among the community, 49:11; in assemblies, 58:11.

Marriage, to unbelievers or slaves, 2:221, to how many, lawful, 4:3; dower not to be taken back (in case of divorce), 4:20-21; prohibited degrees, 4:22-24; it' no means to wed free believing women, 4:25; if breach feared, two arbiters to be appointed, 4:35; if wife fears cruelty or desertion, amicable settlement, 4:128: turn not away from a woman, 4:129; with chaste ones among People of the Book, 5:6; of adulterers, 24:3; to those who are poor, 24:32; those who cannot afford marriage, to keep themselves chaste until God gives them means, 24:33; Prophet's Consorts, 33:28-29,

50 52; without cohabitation, no 'Iddah on divorce, 33:49; conditions for the Prophet, 33:50-52;

Martyrs, not dead, 2:154; 3:169; rejoice in glory, 3:170-171; receive forgiveness and mercy, 3:157-158; will receive best Provision, 22:58-59.

Mārūt, 2:102.

Mary (mother of Jesus], birth, 3:35-37; annunciation of Jesus, 3:42-51, 4:156; 19:16-21; in child birth, 19:23-26; brought the babe to her people, 19:27-33; guarded her chastity, 21:91; 66:12.

Maryam. S.19.

Masad, S.111.

Mā'ūn, S.107.

Measure and weight, give full, 17:35; 83:1-3.

Miracles, see Signs of God.

Mi'rāj, 17:1.

Mischief on land and sea, 30:41; of created things, 93:1-5; 94:4-6.

Monasticism disapproved, 57:27.

Months, number of, 9:35-37.

Moses, and his people, 2:51-61; advises Israelites, 5:23-29; guided by God, 6:84; and Pharaoh, 7:103-137; 10:75-92; 11:96-99; 17:101-103; 20:42-53; 56-79; 23:45-49; 25:35-36; 26:10-69; 28:4-21,31-42; 11:23-46; 43:45-56; 51:38-40; 79:15-26; resists idol worship, 7:138-141; sees the Glory on the Mount, 7:142-145; reproves his people for calf-worship, and prays for them, 7:148-156; his people, 7:159-162; his Book, doubts and differences, 11:110; to teach his people gratitude, 14:5-8; nine clear Signs, 7:133; 17:101; to the junction of the two Seas, 18:60-82; his call, 19:51-53; 20:9-56; 28:29-35; his childhood, mother, and sister, 20:38-40; 28:7-13;

converts Egyptian magicians, 20:70-73; 26:46-52; indignant at calf-worship, 20:86-98; and the mystic Fire, 27:7-14; 28:29-35; his mishap in the City, 28:14-21; in Madyan, 28:22-28; guided to straight way, 37:114-122; Books of, 53:36; 87:19; vexed by his people, 61:5.

Mosque (of Quba, 9:107-108.

Mosques, 9:17-19, 28.

Mountains, 20:105-107; 21:31; 31:10, 59:21; 73:14; 101:5.

Muddathlhir, S.74.

Muhājirs, 59:8-9.

Muhammad, the Holy Prophet, his mission, 7:158; 48:8-9, respect due to messenger, 2:104; 4:46; no more than a messenger, 3:144; gentle, 3:159; sent as favour to Believers, 3:164; 4:170; and to People of the Book, 5:21; a mercy to Believers, 9:61; mercy to all creatures, 21:107; as a mercy from God, 28:46-47; 33:45-48; 36:6; 42:48; 72:20-23, 27-28; 76:24-26; his work, 3:164; 4:70-71; 6:107; 7:156-157; 10:2; 52:29-34; 74:1-7; not mad or possessed, 7:184; 68:2; 81:22; warner, 7:184, 188; 15:89; 53:56-62; anxious for the Believers, 11:128; brings Message as revealed, 10:15-16; his teaching, 11:2-4; 12:108; 34:46-50; to deliver revelation entirely as it comes to him, 11:12-14; 46:9; God is witness to his mission, 13:43; 29:52; 46:8; heart distressed for men, 15:97; 16:127; 18:6; 25:30; to invite and argue, in ways most gracious, 16:125-128; inspired, 18:110; 63:2-18; mocked, 25:41-42; 34:7-8; asks no reward, 25:57; 34:47; 38:86; 42:23; his duty, 27:91-93; 30:30; his household (consorts), 33:28-34, 50-53, 55, 59; 64:1, 3-6; close to

Believers, 33:6; beautiful pattern of conduct, 33:21; seal of the Prophets, 33:40; universal Messenger to men, 34:28; fealty to him is fealty to God, 48:10, 18; Messenger of God, 48:29; resist him not, 58:20-22; foretold by Jesus, 61:6, foretold by Moses, 46:10, his Religion to prevail over all religion, 61:9; unlettered, 7:157; 62:2; leads from darkness to light, 65:11; to strive hard, 66:9; exalted standard of character, 68:4: not a poet or soothsayer, 69:40-43; devoted to prayer, 73:1-8, 20; 74:3; witness, 73:15-16; and the blind man, 80:1-10; saw the Angel of Revelation, 53:4-18; 81:22-25; to adore God and bring himself closer to him, 96:19; rehearsing scriptures, 98:2.

Muhammad, S.47.

Mujādilah, S.58.

Mulk, S.67.

Mu'min, see Ghāfir, S.40.

Mu'minūn, S.23.

Mumtahinah, S.60.

Munāfiqūn, S.63.

Murder, 2:178-179; 5:35.

Mursalāt, S.77.

Muslim men and women, befitting conduct, 33:35-36.

Muzzammil, S.73.

Naba', S.78.

Nahl, S.16.

Najm, S.53.

Names, most beautiful, of God, 7:180, 17:110; 20:8; 59:24.

Naml, S.27.

Nās, S.114.

Nasr, S.110.

Nature declares God's praises, 24:41-44; 50:6-11; shows God's goodness, and that His Promise is true, 78:6-16

Nāzi-āt, S.79.

"Neither die nor live", 20:74; 87:13.

New Moon, 2:189

News, to be tested, 4:83

Niggards condemned, 17:29; 47:38

Night as a symbol, 79:29, 92:1; 93:2.

Night of Power, 97:1-5.

Nisā, S.4

Noah, 6:84; 7:59-64; 10:71-73; 11:25-49; 21:76-77; 23:23-30; 25:37; 26:105-122; 229:14-15; 37:75-82, 51:46; 54:9-15; 69:11-12; 71:1-28; unrighteous son not saved, 11:45-47; Wife unrighteous, 66:10.

Nūh, S.71.

Nūr, S.24.

Oaths, 2:224-227; 5:92; 16:94; 24:22, 53; 66:2; 68:10.

Obedience, 3:132; 4:59, 64, 66, 80-81; 5:95; 14:12; 8:20-25, 46; 24:51-52, 54; 47:33; 64-11-12.

Obligations to be fulfilled, 5:1.

Olive, as a symbol, 23:20; 24:35; 95:1;

Orphans, 2:220; 4:2, 6, 10, 127; 17:34; guardians of, 4:6.

Pairs, in all creatures, 13:3; 31:10; 36:36; 42:11; 43:12; 51:49; 53:45.

Parables, man who kindled a lire, 2:17-18; rain-laden cloud 2:19-20; goatherd, 2:171; hamlet in ruins, 2:259; grain of corn, 2:261; hard, barren rock, 2:264; fertile garden, 2:265-266; rope, 3:103, frosty wind, 3:117; dog who lolls out his tongue, 7:176; undermined sandcliff, 9:109-110; rain and storm, 10:24; blind and deaf, 11:24; garden of joy, 13:35; ashes blown about by wind, 14:18; goodly trees, with roots, branches, and fruit, 14:24-25; evil tree, 14:26; slave versus man liberally favoured, 16:75; dumb man versus one who commands justice, 16:76; women who untwists her yarn, 16:92, City favoured but ungrateful, 16:112-113; two men, one proud of his possessions and the other absorbed in God, 18:32-44; this life like rain, pleasant but transitory, 18:45-46; fall from Unity, like being snatched up by birds or carried off by winds, 22:31; a fly, 22:73; Light, 24:35-36; mirage, 24:39; depths of darkness, 24:40; spider, 29:41; partners, 30:28; Companions of the City, 36:13-32; one master and several masters, 39:29; Garden promised to the Righteous with four kinds of rivers, 47:15; seed growing, 48:29; rain and physical growth, 57:20; mountain that humbles itself; 59:21; donkey, 62:51; if stream of water be lost, 67:30; People of the Garden, 68:17-33.

Parents, kindness to, 17:23; 29:8; 31:14; 46:15-18.

'Partners' of God, a falsehood, 10:34-35, 66: 16:86; 28:62-64; 71-75; 30:40; 42:21.

Passion or Impulse, worship of, 25:43.

Path, see Way.

Patience and perseverance, 2:45, 153; 3:186, 200; 10:109; 11:115; 16:126-127; 20:130-132; 40:55, 77; 46:35; 50:39; 70:5; 73:10-11

"Peace," the greeting of the Righteous, 7:46; 10:10; 14:23:36:58.

Peace, incline towards, 8:61.

Peace, Salām, meaning, 19:62.

Peace, Sakīnah, Tranquility, 11:26, 40; 48:4, 18, 26.

Pearls well guarded, 52:24; 56:23.

Pen, 68:1; 96:4-5.

Penalty for sin, 3:188; 6:15-16; 10:50-53; 11:101-104; 13:34; 16-88; 46:20; 70:1-3.

Persecution with Fire, 85:1-11.

Personal responsibility, 4:164; 10:30; 14:51:53:38-41.

Pharaoh, cruelty, 2:49; drowned, 2:50, people of, 14:41-42; dealings with Moses, 7:103-137; 10:75-92; see Moses; body saved, on account of repentance, 10:90-92; denies God, 28:38; 79:24; a man from his People confesses Faith, 40-28-44; arrogant to the Israelites, 44:17-33; wife righteous, 66:11; sin and disobedience, 69:9; 73:16; 85:17-20; 89:10-14

Pilgrimage, 2:158, 196-203; 3:97; 5:2; 22:26-33.

Piling up (the good things of this world), 102:1-4.

Pledge, everyone in pledge for his deeds, 52:21; 74:38.

Plotters, 16:45-47.

Poet, 26:224-227, 36:69; 69:41.

Prayer, 1:1-7; 2:238-239; 3:8, 26-27, 147, 191-194; 4:43; 5:6; 11:114; 17:78-81; 23:118; 50:39-40, 52:48-49; 73:1-8, 20; be steadfast in, 2:110, during travel, or in danger, 4:101-104; for Unbelievers, 9:113-114; due to God alone, 13:14-15.

Prayers, the five canonical, 11:144; 17:78-79; 20:130; 30:17-18; why all prayers not answered, 42:27.

Precautions in danger, 4:71.

Priests and anchorites, 9:31, 34.

Prisoners of War, 8:67-71.

Prohibited Degrees in marriage, 4:22-24.

Property, 2:188; 4:5, 29; to be distributed equitably, 59:7-9.

Prophets, 2:253; continuous line, 3:33-34; 4:163-165; 5:19; 6:84-90; 23:23-50, 57:26-27; covenants from, 3:81; 33:7-8; never false to their trusts, 3:161; rejected, 3:184; 6:34; 25:37, 34:45; 51:52-55; slain, 3:183; all to be believed in,

4:150-152, to give account,
5:109; mocked, 6:10; 13:32;
15:11; 21:41; why sent, 6:48,
131; 14:4-6; had enemies,
6:112; 25:31; rehearse God's
Signs, 7:35-36; sent to every
people, 10:47; 16:36; had
families, 13:38; human, but
guided, 14:10-12; 16:43-44;
17:94-95; 21:7-8; 25:7-8, 20;
persecuted and threatened,
14:13; witnesses against their
people, 16:89; and Messengers,
meaning, 19:51; one
brotherhood, 23:52-54; some
named, some not, 40:78.

Prophet's Consorts, extra
responsibilities and duties,
33:28-34; who are to be,
33:50-52, respect due to them,
33:53-55; respect due to
Prophet's Consorts and
believing men and women,
33:56-58; Prophet's wives and
daughters and all believing
women to be modest. 33:59-
62; Prosperity (spiritual) 87:4-
15; success, 91:9-10.

Publicity versus secrecy, 4:148.

Punishment, for man's arrogance
and rebellion, 96:15-18,
abiding - for wilful rebellion,
but not after repentance, nor
for minor sins, 79:37.

Qadr, S.97.
Qāf, S.50.
Qalam, S.68.
Qamar, S.54.
Qāri'ah, S.101.
Qārūn, 28:76-82; 29:39.
QaHaH, S.28.
Qiblah, 2:142-145, 149-150.
Qiyāmah, S.75.
Qubā' (Mosque), 11:107-108.
Qur'ān, Message, 4:82, 6:19;
cannot be produced by other
than divine agency, 2:23;
10:38; 11:13; 17:89; verses,
fundamental and allegorical,
3:7; 11:1;God is witness, 6:19;
God's revelation, 6:92; 7:105-
107; 27:6; 45:2; follow it and
do right, 6:155; respect and
attention due to, 7:204-206;
Book of Wisdom, 10:1; 31:2;
36:2; in Arabic, 12:2; 13:37;
41:44, 42:7; 43:30, described,
13:31, 36-37; 14:1; 56:77-80,
makes things clear, 15:1;
25:33; 26:2; 27:1; 28:2;
36:69-70, 43:2; not to be
made into shreds, 15:91;
purpose of revelation, 16:64-
65; language pure Arabic,
16:103; good news and
warning, 17:9-10; and the
Unbelievers, 17:45-47; healing
and mercy, 17:82; explains
similitude's, 17:89; 18:54;
39:27; no crookedness therein,
18:1-2; teaching, 18:2-4;
19:97; 20:2-7; 26:210-220;
easy, 19:97; 44:58, 54:17, 22,
32, 40; revealed in stages,
17:106; 25:32; 76:23; 87:6-7;
"my people took it for
nonsense", 25:30; solves
Israel's controversies, 27:76;
recite Qur'an, 73:4; and pray,
29:45; carries own evidence,
29:47-49, 51; guide and
mercy, 31:3; Truth from God,
32:3; 35:31; beautiful Message
consistent with itself, 39:23;
instructs mankind, 39:41,
80:11-12; no falsehood can
approach it, 41:42; same
Message to earlier prophets,
41:43; 43:44-45; not sent to
worldly leaders; 43:31-32;
seek earnestly to understand,
47:24, admonish with, 50:45;
taught by God, 55:1-2; to be
received with humility, 59:21;
how to be read and studied,
2:121; 75:16-18; in books of
honour and dignity; 80:13-16;
Message to all the Worlds,
81:26-29, Unbelievers reject it,
84:20-25; Tablet Preserved,
85:21-22; See also Book, and
Revelation.

Quraysh, S.106.

Quraysh, unbelieving, 54:43-46,
    51; appeal to, 106:1-4

Ra'd, S.13.
Rahmān, S.55.
Raiment of righteousness is best,
    7:26.
Rain, God's gift, 56:68-70
Ramadān, 2:185.
Ransom, sought in vain by sinners,
    3:91; 10-54; 13:18.
Rass, Companions of the, 25:38;
    50:12.
Reality, the sure, 69:1-3.
Record, 50:4; 69:19, 25; 83:7-9,
    18-21; 84:7-15
Religion, no compulsion in, 2:256;
    of Islam, 3:19-20, 83-84; no
    excesses in, 4:171; 5:77-81;
    perfected, 5:3; not play and
    amusement, 6:70; do not
    divide and make sects, 6:159;
    30:32; no difficulties imposed
    in, 22:78; standard religion is
    to establish pattern according
    to which God has made man,
    30:30; same for all prophets,
    42:13-15; ancestral, 43:22-24;
    right way of, 45:18.
Repentance, with amendment,
    accepted, 6:54,42:25.
Respite for Evil, 3:178; 10:11;
    12:110; 14:42-43, 44; 29:53-
    55; 86:15-17.
Resurrection, 16:38-40; 17:49-52;
    19:66-72; 22:5; 46:33-34;
    50:3, 20-29, 41-44; 75:1-15;
    79:10-12; 86:5-8.
Retaliation disapproved, 5:45.
Revelation, doubts solved, 2:23; of
    Moses and Jesus, 2:87;
    abrogated or forgotten, 2:106;
    guidance, 3:73; to Prophet and
    those before him, 5:48; Word
    that distinguishes Good from
    Evil, 86:11-14; do not
    entertain doubt about, 6:114;
    11:17; purpose of, 7:2, 203; in
    stages, 16:101; through the
    Holy Spirit, 16:102-103;
    26:192-199; to be proclaimed,
    96:1; nature of, 41:2-4, 6-8;

69:50-51; 81:15-21; *See also*
    Book, and Qur'an.
Revile not false gods, 6:108
Reward, without measure, 3:27;
    39:10; better than deed
    deserves, 27:84; 30:39;
    according to best of deeds,
    and more, 24:38; 29:7; 39:35;
    for good, no reward other
    than good, 55:60.
Righteous, company of the, 4:69;
    shall inherit the earth,
    21:105;described, 51:15-19;
    76:5-12.
Righteousness, 2:177, 207-208,
    212; 3:16-17,92, 133-135;
    191-195; 4:36, 125; 5:93;
    7:42-43; 16:97; steep path of,
    90:11-18.
Rocky Tract, Companions of,
    15:80-83.
Roman Empire, 30:2-5.
Rūm, S.30.

Sabā', S.34.
Sabā', 27:22; 34:15-21.
Sabbath, transgressors of, 7:163-
    166; made strict, 16:124.
Sabians, 2:26, 5:69; 22:17.
Sacrifice, 22:34-37.
Ṣād, S.38.
Ṣafā and Marwah, 2:158.
Ṣaff, S.61.
Ṣāffāt, S.37.
Sajdah, S.32.
Ṣāliḥ, 7:73-79; 11:61-68; 26:141-
    159; 27:45-53.
Salsabīl, 76:18.
Samīriy, 20:85, 20:95-97.
Satan *(see* also Iblis), 2:36; 4:117-
    120; 24:21; excites enmity and
    hatred, 5:91; resist his
    suggestions, 7:200-201;
    deceives, 8:48; reproaches own
    followers, 14:22;evil spirit,
    rejected, accursed, 3:36; 15:17;
    15:34; 16:98;has no authority
    over Believers, 16:99-100;
    suggests vanity, 22:52-53; is
    an enemy, 35:6; 36:60.
Scandal, 24:19; 104:1.
Scriptures, people of the, 2:62;

kept pure and holy, 98:2.

Secrecy, when permissible, 4:114; in counsels, disapproved, 58:7-10, 12-13.

Sects and divisions disapproved, 30:32, 42:13-14; 43:64-65, 45:17, 28.

Seed, grows by God's providence, 56:63-67.

Seven Tracts or Firmaments, 2:29; 23:17, 65:12, 67:3, 71:15.

Shadow, allegory, 25:45.

Shameful things to be shunned, 7:28.

Shams, S.91.

She-camel as a Symbol to Thamūd 7:75; 17:59; 26:155-158.

Ship, sailing of, as a Sign, 2:164; 14:32; 16:14, 17:66, 22:65 31:31; 5:12; 42:32-33; 45:12; 55:24.

Shu'arā', S.26.

Shu'ayb, 7:85-93; 11:84-95; 29:36-37.

Shūrā, S.42.

Siege of Madīnah, 33:9-27.

Signs of God, demanded by those without knowledge, clear to those with Faith, 2:118; in the creation of the heavens and the earth, 2:164; 3:190; made clear, that men may consider, 2:219-220; sign of authority to the prophet Samuel, 2:248; denial of, 3:11, 108; rejecters, deaf and dumb, in darkness, 6:39; in all things, 6:95-99; wicked demand special Signs, 6:124; rejecters make excuse, 6:156-158; consequences of rejection, 7:36-41, 146-147; rejecters wrong their own souls, 7:177; rejecters get respite, 7:182; rejecters lose guidance. 6:186; day and night as Signs, 17:12; in nature and all creation, 10:5-6; 30:20-27; 45:3-6; self evident Signs, the Book, 29: 49-51; winds and ships, 30:46; 42:32-35; ships, 31:31; the Night, sun and moon, 36:37-40; the Ark

through the Flood, and similar ships, 36:41-44; in this life, 39:59; rejecters are deluded, 40:63; rain and revived Earth, 41:39-40; in the farthest regions of the earth, and in their own souls, 41:59; rejected or taken in jest, 45:8-9; on earth, in your own selves, and in heaven, 51:20-23; creation of man from Seed, 56:: ·9; death. 56:60-62; seed in the ground, 56:63-67; water, 56:68-70; fire, 56:71-73; mocked, 68:15; camels, sky, mountains, earth, 88:17-20; forces of nature, 89:1-5; no special Sign (miracle) given, 6:109; 10:20; 8:7; 17:59, 21:5-6.

Sijjīn, 88:7-9.

Sin, 4:30-32, 36-39, 107-112, 116; 7:100-102; 10:54; 74:43-48; wrongdoers will be cut off, 6:45; to be eschewed, 6:120; causes destruction, 7:4-5; 77:16-19; will not prosper, 10:17; and faith have different goals, 68:35-41; God forgives all sins, 39:53.

Sinai, 19:52; 95:2.

Sinners, 23:63-77; 26:200-209; 83:29-36; their hearing, sight, and skins will bear witness, 41:20-23.

Slander, 11:79; 24:23; 68:11-12.

Solomon, 2:102; 6:84; 21:79, 81-82; 27; 15-44; 34:12-14; 38:30-40; and the ants, 27:18-19; and the Hoopoe, 27:22-26; and the Queen of Saba', 27:22-44.

Son, adopted, 33:4-5.

Soul, burden not greater than it can bear, 2:286; 7:42; 23:62; responsibility, 3:30; 74:38; justly dealt with, 16:111; taste of death, 21:35; enters heaven, not body, 89:27-30.

Spendthrifts condemned, 17:26-29; 25:67.

Spirit, the, 70:4, n. 5677; 78:38;

97:4. the Holy, God strengthened Jesus with, 2:87, 253; God's, breathed into man, 15:29; of inspiration, 17:85-86; God strengthens Believers with, 58:22.

Spoils of war, 8:1,41.

Star, adjuration by, 53:1; 86:1-4.

Stars, 7:54; 16:12, 16; 22:18; 37:6-10, 67:5, 77:8,81:2-82:2.

Straight Way, 1:6; 6:153; etc.

Striving, 9:20, 81; 22:78; 25:52; 29:69, 61:11.

Suffering, adversity, and prosperity, 7:94-96.

Sun, 91:1.

Superstitions, 5:103; 6:138-140, 143-144.

Surah, revelation increases faith, 9:124-127.

Sustenance, literal and figurative, 10:59, 16:73, 19:62,42:12; 51:57-58,67:21.

Suwā', 71:23.

Tabūk. 9:40-42, 43-59, 81-99, 120-122.

Taghābūn, S.64.

Tā Hā. S.20.

Tahrīm, S.66.

Takāthur, S.102.

Takwīr, S.81.

Talāq, S.65.

Talh (tree), 56:29.

Tālūt 2:247-249.

Taqwā, meaning, 2:2, 59:18-19.

Tāriq, S.86.

Tasnīm, 83:27-28.

Tatfīf, see Mutaffifin, S.83.

Tawbah, S.9.

Term appointed, for every people, 7:34; 10:49; 15:4-5; 16:61; 20:129.

Testing, by God, 3:154, and 34:21.

Thamud, 7:73-79; 11:61-68; 25:38; 26:141-159; 27:45-53; 29:38, 41:17; 51:43-45; 54:23-31; 69:4-8; 85:17-20; 89:9-14; 91:11-15

Theft, punishment, 5:38-39.

Time, 103:1-3;

Tīn, S.95.

Traffic and Trade, 4:29.

Travel through the earth, 6:11; 22:46; 27:69; 29:20-22; 30:9,42, 35:44; 40:21, 82; 47:10.

Treasures of God, 6:50; 6:59; 11:31; 15:21.

Treaties, 11:1-4; 11:7-10.

Trials, 2:214-218.

Trumpet, on Day of Judgement, 6:73; 23:101; 39:68; 69:13.

Trust offered to Heavens, earth, and Mountains, undertaken by Man, 33:72-73; Trusts, 4:58; 8:27.

Truth, 23:70-71, 90; Rejecters of, 77:1-50; 98:1-6.

Tubba', 44:37.

Tūr, 5; 52.

Uhud, lessons of, 3:121-128, 140-180.

Ummah, 2:143-144.

'Umrah, 2:196.

Unbelievers, plot in vain, 8:30; despise revelation, 8:31; challenge a Penalty, 8:32-35; prayers empty, 8:35; spend for wrong purposes, 8:36; past forgiven; if they repent, 8:38; 9:11; break covenants, 8:56; will not frustrate the godly, 8:60-61; protect each other, 8:73, described, 9:73-78; 14:3, will wish they had believed, 15:2; will bear double burdens, 16:25; to be covered with shame, 16:27; dispute vainly, 18:56-57; their efforts wasted, 18:102-106; their arrogance, 19:73-82; 35:43, deeds like mirage, 24:39; as in depths of darkness, 24:40; mutual recriminations at Judgement, 34:31-33; self-glory and separatism, 38:2-14; dispute about the Signs of God, 40:4-6, hate truth, 43:78; will turn back from fight. 48:22-23; their high-handedness, 48:25-26; vain fancies, 52:35-44; give them not friendship but kind and just dealing, 60:1-9; rush madly, 70:36-39.

Unity, 2:163; 6:19; 92:1-4.

Usury, 2:275-276; 2:278-280; 3:130.

'Uzayr, 9:30.

'Uzzā, 53:19.

Vain discourse to be avoided, 6:68.

Vicegerent, God's, on earth, 2:30.

Victory, uses of, 48:1-3; through help of God, 61:13.

Virtues *see* Righteousness, *and* Believers.

Wadd, 71:23.

"Wait ye, we too shall wait," 9:52; 10:102; 11:122; 20:135; 44:59; 52:31.

Wāqi'ah, S.56.

War against God, 5:33-34.

Warning before destruction, 17:16.

Waste not, 6:141; 7:31.

Water, animals created from, 21:30; 24:45; 25:54; two bodies of flowing water, 25:53; 18:60, 35:12; 55:19-20, God's Throne over the waters, 11:7; circulation of, 23:1.

Way, the, 1:6; 42:52-53; 90:10-18; etc.

Wealth, hoarding condemned, 104:2-3.

"We" and "Me": transition between the first person plural and singular in reference to God: 2:38, 2:150-151; 31:10, 11; 68:44; 70:40,

Wicked, their faces headlong in the fire, 27:90, 67:22.

Widows, 2:234-235, 240.

Will of God, 10:99-100; 81:29; 82:8.

Winds, like heralds of glad tidings, 7:57-58; 15:22, 30:46, 48, 51; mystic symbolism, 77:1-6.

Wine, 2:219, 5:90, heavenly wine, 47:15; 76:21; 83:25.

Witnesses, among men, 2:143; 22:78.

Woman, wronged, plea accepted, 58:1-2.

Women, 2:222-223; 4:15, 19-22, 34, 127; to be reverenced, 4:1; false charges against, 24:4-5, 11-20; 24:23-26; modesty, 24:30-31; believing, refugees, 60:10-12.

Wood, Companions of the, 15:78; 26:176-191.

World, this, but play and amusement, 6:32; 29:64; 47:36; 57:20; deceives men, 6:130; not to be preferred, 9:38-39; 13:26; 28:60-61; gets its reward, but not in Hereafter, 11:15-17; 17:18; 42:20, man loves, 75:20-21; 76:27;

Worship, true worship and charity, 107:2-7.

Writing, for contracts, 2.282.

Wrongdoers, 11:18-22, 101-104, 116-117; 39:47, *See also* Unbelievers.

Yaghūth, 71:23.

Yahya (John the Baptist), birth, 3:39; 6:85; his character and position, 19:12-15; reverenced God, 21:90.

Yā Sīn, S.36.

Ya'ūq, 71:23.

Yūnus, S.10; *see also* Jonah.

Yūsuf S.12; *see also* Joseph.

Zayd the freed man, 33:37-38.

Zakarīya, 3:37-11; 6:85; 19:2-11; 21:90.

Zakah (Regular Charity), 2:43, 110, 177, 277; 4:162; 5:55.

Zanjabil, 76:17.

Zaqqūm, 37:62-66; 44:43-46; 56:52.

Zaynab, daughter of Jahsh, 33:37-38.

Zihār, 33:4; 58:2-4.

Zalzalah, S.99.

Zodiacal Signs, 15:16.

Zakhruf, S.43.

Zumar, S.39.

Prophet's Last Sermon

All praise is due to Allah, so we praise Him, and seek His pardon and we turn to Him. We seek refuge with Allah from the evils of ourselves and from the evil consequences of our deeds. Whom Allah guideth aright, there is none to lead him astray; and there is none to guide him aright whom Allah leads astray. I bear witness that there is no God but Allah, the One, having no partner with Him. His is the Sovereignty and to Him is due all praise. He grants life and causes death and is Powerful over everything. There is no God but Allah, the One; He fulfilled His promise and helped His servant and He alone routed the confederates.

O people, listen to my words! for I do not know whether we shall meet again and perform Hajj after this year.

O ye people! Allah says: "O people we created you from one male and one female and made you into tribes and nations, so that you are known to one another. Verily in the sight of Allah, the most honoured amongst you is the one who is the most God-fearing." There is no superiority for an Arab over a non-Arab and for a non-Arab over an Arab, nor for the white over the black nor for the black over the white except in piety. All mankind is the progeny of Adam and was fashioned out of clay.

Behold! every claim of privilege whether that of blood or property, is under my feet except that of the custody of Allah's House (Ka'aba) and supplying of waters to the pilgrimage.

Then he said:

O people of Quraysh! Do not appear with the burden of this world around your necks, whereas other people may appear (before their Lord) with the rewards of the Hereafter. In that case I shall avail you naught against Allah.

Behold! all practices of the days of Ignorance are now under my feet. The blood revenges of the days of

Ignorance are remitted. And the first claim on blood I abolish is that of Ibne Rabi'ah bin Al-Harith who was nursed (brought up) in Beni Sa'd and who was killed by the Hudhayls. All interest and usurious dues accruing from the age of Ignorance stand wiped out. And the first amount of interest that I remit is that which Abbas bin Abdul Mutallib had to receive. Verily, it is being remitted entirely.

O people! Verily your blood, your property and your honour are sacred and inviolable until you appear before your Lord, as the sacred inviolability of this day of yours, this month of yours, and this very town (of yours). Verily, you will soon meet your Loard and you will be held accountable for your deeds.

O people! Verily, you have got certain rights over your women - and your women have certain rights over you. It is your right upon them that they must not allow anybody save you to come to your bed and admit none to enter your homes whom you do not like but with your permission. And it is for them not to commit acts of impropriety, which if they do, you are authorised by Allah to separate them from your beds and chastise them, but not severely, and if they refrain, then clothe and feed them properly.

Behold! It is not permissible for a woman to give anything from the wealth of her husband to anyone but with his consent.

Treat the women kindly, since they are your helpers and are not in a position to manage their affairs themselves. Fear Allah concerning them, for verily you have taken them on the security of Allah and have made their persons lawful unto you by words of Allah.

O people! Allah, the Mighty and Exalted, has ordained to everyone his due share (of inheritance). Hence there is no need (of special) testament for a heir (departing from the rules laid down by the Shari'ah).

The child belongs to the marriage-bed and the violator of wedlock shall be stoned. And reckoning of their deeds rests with Allah.

He, who attributes his ancestary to other than his father or claims his clientship to other than his master, the curse of Allah is upon him.

All debts must be repaid, all borrowed property must be returned, gifts should be reciprocated and a surety must make good the loss to the assured.

Beware! No one committing a crime is responsible for it but himself, Neither the child is responsible for the crime of his father, nor the father is responsible for the crime of his child.

Nothing of his brother is lawful for a Muslim except what he himself gives willingly. So do not wrong yourselves.

O people! Every Muslim is the brother of other Muslim, and all the Muslims form one brotherhood.

And your slaves! see that you feed them with such food as you eat yourselves, and clothe them with the clothes as you yourselves wear.

Beware that you go not astray after me and strike one another's necks. He who (amongst you) has any trust with him, he must return it to its owner.

If a mangled black slave is appointed you Amir, listen to him, and obey him provided he executes the Ordinance of the Book of Allah amongst you.

O people! There is no Prophet to come after me and there would be no Ummah to form after you.

Verily I have left amongst you that which would never lead you astray, the Book of Allah, and the Sunnah of His Messenger, which, if you hold fast, you shall never be misled. And beware of transgressing the limits set in the matters of Deen, for it is transgression of (the proper bounds of) Deen, that brought destruction to many people before you.

Verily the Satan is disappointed at ever being worshipped in this land of yours, but if obedience in anything (short of worship is expected that is): he will be pleased in matters you may be disposed to think unsignificant, so beware of him in the matters of your Deen.

Behold! worship your Lord; offer prayers five times a day; observe fast in the month of Ramazan ; Pay readily the Zakat (poor-due) on your property; and perform pilgrimage to the House of God and obey your rulers and you will be admitted to the Paradise of your Lord.

O people! Postponement (of a sacred month)[1] is only an excess of disbelief whereby those who disbelieve are misled, they allow it one year and forbid it (another year) that they may make up the number of the months which Allah hath hallowed, so that they allow that which Allah hath forbidden.

And verily the time hath adopted the shape of the day when Allah hath created the heavens and the earth. And Lo! the number of months with Allah is twelve months. Four of them are sacred. Three are consecutive months (Sha'aban, Zeeqadh and Zil-Hijja) and the Rajab, in between the months of Jumadah I and Sha'aban.

Let him that is present, convey it unto him who is absent. For many people to whom the message is conveyed may be more mindful of it than the audience.

And if you were asked about me, what would you say?

They answered: we bear witness that you have conveyed the trust (of Deen) and discharged your ministry of apostlehood and looked to our welfare.

Thereupon Allah's Messenger (may Allah's peace be upon him) lifted his fore-finger towards the sky and then pointing towards people said:

- O Lord: Bear Thou witness unto it.
- O Lord: Bear Thou witness unto it.
- O Lord: Bear Thou witness unto it.

---

[1] 1. The Idolaters used to postopone a sacred month in which war was forbidden, when they wanted to wage war and make it for up by hallowing another month.